LETTERS OF DELEGATES
1774 ☆ 1789
TO CONGRESS

Letters of delegates to Congress

May 16–August 15, 1776

Paul H. Smith, Editor

Gerard W. Gawalt, Rosemary Fry Plakas, Eugene R. Sheridan
Assistant Editors

LIBRARY OF CONGRESS   WASHINGTON   1979

This volume is printed on permanent/durable paper.

Library of Congress Cataloging in Publication Data (Revised)
Main entry under title:

Letters of delegates to Congress, 1774–1789.

Includes bibliographical references and indexes.
CONTENTS: v. 1. August 1774–August 1775.–
v. 2 September–December 1775.– v. 3 Jan. 1–May 15, 1776.–
v. 4. May 16–Aug. 15, 1776.

1. United States. Continental Congress—History—
Sources—Collected works. I. Smith, Paul Hubert, 1931–
II. United States. Library of Congress.
JK1033.L47   328.73'09   76–2592
ISBN 0–8444–0177–3 (set)

ISBN for this volume: 0–8444–0260–5

For sale by the Superintendent of Documents, U.S. Government Printing Office
Washington, D.C. 20402

Stock No. 030–000–00103–6

Foreword

Well before the signing on July 4, 1966, of Public Law 89–491, establishing a national American Revolution Bicentennial Commission, the Library of Congress began considering how it could contribute to the Bicentennial celebration. In 1968 Congress approved the Library's general plan and later authorized the addition to the Library's staff of several American historians. The Library took as the theme for its program "Liberty and Learning" from James Madison, who asked: "What spectacle can be more edifying or more seasonable, than that of Liberty & Learning, each leaning on the other for their mutual and surest support." Reflecting the Library's rich resources for the study of the revolutionary era, its Bicentennial program ranges widely—from the compilation of bibliographies and guides to the recording of folk music and the presentation of symposia.

In preparing the guide *Manuscript Sources in the Library of Congress for Research on the American Revolution,* the Bicentennial Office staff discovered large numbers of letters written by members of the Continental Congresses not published in Edmund C. Burnett's magisterial 8-volume edition of *Letters of Members of the Continental Congress.* As additional unpublished delegate letters turned up and as a cursory survey of other repositories suggested that even more existed, the Library decided that an expanded edition of letters would be a valuable Bicentennial project.

This edition has benefited immensely from Burnett's pathfinding work and from the generous cooperation of the editors of several other documentary publications with a common focus on the revolutionary era. From them the Library has borrowed heavily and to them it owes a debt it can never adequately acknowledge. It is a pleasure to give special thanks to the editors of the papers of John Adams, Benjamin Franklin, Thomas Jefferson, Henry Laurens, James Madison, and George Washington.

Thanks are also due the Advisory Committee on the Library's Bicentennial Program for support and encouragement. To the Ford Foundation, which supplied a generous grant to help underwrite the project, we are grateful. And, finally, we are beholden to the Congress of the United States for appropriations of funds for the publication of these volumes and understanding support of the Library's Bicentennial program.

Elizabeth Hamer Kegan
Assistant Librarian of Congress
for American and Library Studies

iii

Editorial Method and Apparatus

In its treatment of documents this edition of delegate letters strives to achieve a middle ground between facsimile reproduction and thorough modernization. The original spelling and grammar are allowed to stand except in cases where editorial changes or insertions are required to make the text intelligible. For example, when a badly misspelled word is misleading, the correct spelling is inserted in roman type in brackets after the word. Moreover, words omitted through oversight have been supplied at appropriate places in italic type in brackets. Obvious slips of the pen and inadvertent repetitions are usually silently corrected. Capitalization and punctuation have been standardized according to certain conventions. Each sentence begins with a capital letter, as do all proper and geographic names as well as days of the week and months of the year. Doubtful cases have been resolved in favor of modern usage; otherwise the usage of the original texts has been followed. Generally, abbreviations, contractions, and monetary signs are preserved as they appear in manuscript except when they are ambiguous or misleading. On the other hand, the thorn and the tilde are consistently expanded. "Ye" always appears as "The," for instance, and "recvd" as "received." Likewise, "pr." and "℈" are always expanded to "per," "pre," or "pro," as the case demands. Finally, superscript letters are always lowered to the line.

Gaps in the text are indicated by ellipses in brackets for missing words and by blank spaces in brackets for missing numbers. Conjectural readings are supplied in roman type in brackets, and editorial insertions in italic type in brackets. Material canceled in manuscript but restored to the printed text is included in italic type in angle brackets ("square parentheses"). Marginalia in letters are treated as postscripts, and postscripts which appear without explicit designation are supplied with a *P.S.* in brackets. Documents are arranged chronologically, with more than one document of the same date being arranged alphabetically according to writer. Documents dated only by the month or by the year are placed at the end of the respective month or year. Place-and-date lines always appear on the same line with the salutation regardless of their position in the manuscript.

A descriptive note at the foot of each entry provides abbreviations indicating the nature and location of the document when it was copied for this project, except for privately owned manuscripts whose ownership is fully explained. The descriptive note also contains information on the document's authorship if explanation is necessary, and endorsements or addresses are quoted when they contain more

iv

than routine information. Other editorial practices employed in this work are explained in the sections on editorial apparatus which follow.

TEXTUAL DEVICES

The following devices will be used in this work to clarify the text.

[. . .], [. . . .]	One or two words missing and not conjecturable.
[. . .]¹, [. . . .]¹	More than two words missing; subjoined footnote estimates amount of material missing.
[ ]	Number or part of a number missing or illegible.
[ ]¹	Blank space in manuscript; explanation in subjoined footnote.
[roman]	Conjectural reading for missing or illegible matter; question mark inserted if reading is doubtful.
[*italic*]	Editorial insertion in the text.
⟨*italic*⟩	Matter crossed out in manuscript but restored.

DESCRIPTIVE SYMBOLS

The following symbols are used in this work to describe the kinds of documents drawn upon. When more than one symbol is used in the descriptive note, the first to appear is that from which the main text is taken.

RC	recipient's copy
FC	file copy
LB	letterbook copy
MS	manuscript
Tr	transcript (used to designate not only contemporary and later handwritten copies of manuscripts, but also printed documents)

LOCATION SYMBOLS

The following symbols, denoting institutions holding the manuscripts printed in the present volume, are taken from *Symbols of American Libraries,* 11th ed. (Washington: Library of Congress, 1976).

CCamarSJ	Saint John's Seminary, Camarillo, Calif.
CSmH	Henry E. Huntington Library, San Marino, Calif.
Ct	Connecticut State Library, Hartford
CtHi	Connecticut Historical Society, Hartford
CtNhHi	New Haven Colony Historical Society, New Haven, Conn.

CtNlHi	New London Historical Society, New London, Conn.
CtW	Wesleyan University, Middletown, Conn.
CtY	Yale University, New Haven, Conn.
DLC	Library of Congress
DNA	National Archives and Records Service
DeHi	Historical Society of Delaware, Wilmington
ICHi	Chicago Historical Society
InU	Indiana University, Bloomington
M-Ar	Massachusetts Archives, Boston
MB	Boston Public Library, Boston, Mass.
MBNEH	New England Historic Genealogical Society, Boston, Mass.
MH	Harvard University, Cambridge, Mass.
MHi	Massachusetts Historical Society, Boston
MWA	American Antiquarian Society, Worcester, Mass.
MdAA	Maryland Hall of Records, Annapolis
MdHi	Maryland Historical Society, Baltimore
MeHi	Maine Historical Society, Portland
MnHi	Minnesota Historical Society, St. Paul
N	New York State Library, Albany
NHi	New-York Historical Society, New York
NN	New York Public Library, New York
NNC	Columbia University, New York
NNPM	Pierpont Morgan Library, New York
Nc-Ar	North Carolina State Department of Archives and History, Raleigh
NcD	Duke University, Durham, N.C.
Nh	New Hampshire State Library, Concord
NhHi	New Hampshire Historical Society, Concord
NjHi	New Jersey Historical Society, Newark
NjP	Princeton University, Princeton, N.J.
NjR	Rutgers University, New Brunswick, N.J.
PCarlD	Dickinson College, Carlisle, Pa.
PHC	Haverford College, Haverford, Pa.
PHarH	Pennsylvania Historical and Museum Commission, Harrisburg, Pa.
PHi	Historical Society of Pennsylvania, Philadelphia
PP	Free Library of Philadelphia
PPAmP	American Philosophical Society, Philadelphia
PPL	Library Company of Philadelphia
PPRF	Rosenbach Foundation, Philadelphia
PWW	Washington and Jefferson College, Washington, Pa.
R-Ar	Rhode Island State Archives, Providence
RHi	Rhode Island Historical Society, Providence
RPJCB	John Carter Brown Library, Providence
ScU	University of South Carolina, Columbia

ViHi	Virginia Historical Society, Richmond
ViU	University of Virginia, Charlottesville
ViWC	Colonial Williamsburg, Inc., Williamsburg, Va.
WHi	State Historical Society of Wisconsin, Madison

ABBREVIATIONS AND SHORT TITLES

Abbreviations and short titles for works frequently cited in the present volume are identified below.

Adams, *Diary* (Butterfield)
Adams, John. *Diary and Autobiography of John Adams.* Edited by Lyman H. Butterfield et al. 4 vols. Cambridge: Harvard University Press, Belknap Press, 1961.

Adams, *Family Correspondence* (Butterfield)
Butterfield, Lyman H., et al., eds. *Adams Family Correspondence.* Cambridge: Harvard University Press, Belknap Press, 1963–.

Adams, *Writings* (Cushing)
Adams, Samuel. *The Writings of Samuel Adams.* Edited by Harry A. Cushing. 4 vols. Boston: G.P. Putnam's Sons, 1904–8.

Adams, *Works* (Adams)
Adams, John. *The Works of John Adams, Second President of the United States . . . .* Edited by Charles Francis Adams. 10 vols. Boston: Charles C. Little and James Brown, 1850–56.

Am. Archives
Force, Peter, ed. *American Archives: Consisting of a Collection of Authentick Records, State Papers, Debates, and Letters and Other Notices of Publick Affairs.* 4th series, 6 vols. 5th series, 3 vols. Washington: U.S. Government Printing Office, 1837–53.

Austin, *Life of Gerry*
Austin, James T. *The Life of Elbridge Gerry, with Contemporary Letters to the Close of the American Revolution.* 2 vols. Boston: Wells and Lilly, 1828–29.

Bio. Dir. Cong.
U. S. Congress. *Biographical Directory of the American Congress, 1774–1971.* Washington: U.S. Government Printing Office, 1971.

Burnett, *Letters*
Burnett, Edmund C., ed. *Letters of Members of the Continental Congress.* 8 vols. Washington: Carnegie Institution of Washington, 1921–36.

Clark, *Naval Documents*
Clark, William Bell, et al., eds. *Naval Documents of the American Revolution.* Washington: Department of the Navy, 1964–.

DAB
Dictionary of American Biography. Edited by Allen Johnson and Dumas Malone.

DNB
  Dictionary of National Biography . . . . Edited by Sir Leslie Stephen and Sir Sidney Lee.
Franklin, *Writings* (Smyth)
  Franklin, Benjamin. *The Writings of Benjamin Franklin*. Edited by Albert Smyth. 10 vols. New York: Macmillan Co., 1905–7.
Jay, *Papers* (Morris)
  Jay, John. *John Jay, the Making of a Revolutionary: Unpublished Papers, 1745–1780*. Edited by Richard B. Morris et al. New York: Harper & Row, 1975–.
JCC
  U.S. Continental Congress. *Journals of the Continental Congress, 1774–1789*. 34 vols. Edited by Worthington C. Ford et al. Washington: Library of Congress, 1904–37.
Jefferson, *Papers* (Boyd)
  Jefferson, Thomas. *The Papers of Thomas Jefferson*. Edited by Julian P. Boyd et al. Princeton: Princeton University Press, 1950–.
Journals of N.Y. Prov. Cong.
  New York. *Journals of the Provincial Congress, Provincial Convention, Committee of Safety and Council of Safety of the State of New York, 1775–1777*. 2 vols. Albany: T. Weed, 1842.
Md. Archives
  Archives of Maryland. Edited by William H. Browne et al. Baltimore: Maryland Historical Society, 1883–.
Md. Hist. Magazine
  Maryland Historical Magazine.
N.C. Colonial Records
  North Carolina. *The Colonial Records of North Carolina*. Edited by William L. Saunders. 10 vols. Raleigh and Goldsboro, N.C.: P.M. Hale et al., 1886–90.
N.C. State Records
  North Carolina. *The State Records of North Carolina*. Edited by Walter Clark. Vols. 11–26. Winston and Goldsboro, N.C.: M.I. and J.C. Stewart et al., 1895–1914.
N.H. Provincial Papers
  New Hampshire. *Provincial and State Papers*. 40 vols. Concord, 1867–1943.
N.H. State Papers
  New Hampshire. *Provincial and State Papers*. 40 vols. Concord, 1867–1943.
NYHS Collections
  Collections of the New-York Historical Society.
Pa. Archives
  Pennsylvania Archives. 9 series, 119 vols. in 120. Philadelphia: J. Severns & Co., 1852–56; Harrisburg: State printer, 1874–1935.

PCC

Papers of the Continental Congress. National Archives and Records Service. Washington, D.C.

PMHB

Pennsylvania Magazine of History and Biography.

Rodney, *Letters* (Ryden)

Rodney, Caesar. *Letters to and from Caesar Rodney, 1756–1784.* Edited by George H. Ryden. Philadelphia: University of Pennsylvania Press, 1933.

Shipton, *Harvard Graduates*

Shipton, Clifford K. *Biographical Sketches of Those Who Attended Harvard College.* Sibley's Harvard Graduates. Boston: Massachusetts Historical Society, 1873–.

Sullivan, *Letters* (Hammond)

Sullivan, John. *Letters and Papers of Major-General John Sullivan.* Edited by Otis G. Hammond. 3 vols. Collections of the New Hampshire Historical Society, vols. 13–15. Concord: New Hampshire Historical Society, 1930–39.

Warren-Adams Letters

Warren-Adams Letters, Being Chiefly a Correspondence among John Adams, Samuel Adams, and James Warren. 2 vols. Massachusetts Historical Society Collections, vols. 72–73. Boston: Massachusetts Historical Society, 1917–25.

Washington, *Writings* (Fitzpatrick)

Washington, George. *The Writings of George Washington.* Edited by John C. Fitzpatrick. 39 vols. Washington: U.S. Government Printing Office, 1931–44.

Wharton, *Diplomatic Correspondence*

Wharton, Francis, ed. *The Revolutionary Diplomatic Correspondence of the United States.* 6 vols. Washington: U.S. Government Printing Office, 1889.

Acknowledgments

To the Library of Congress, the Congress of the United States, and the Ford Foundation this edition owes its existence. It is fitting, therefore, that we take this opportunity to acknowledge the foresight of the Library's administration in planning a timely and comprehensive observation of the American Revolution Bicentennial, of the Congress in funding a Bicentennial Office in the Library, and of the Ford Foundation in making a generous grant in support of this project as a scholarly contribution to the celebration of the Bicentennial era. It is with the most profound gratitude that the editors acknowledge their appreciation to all those who bore responsibility for the decisions that made possible these contributions. Our appreciation is also extended to the innumerable persons who have contributed to enriching the holdings of the Library of Congress to make it the premier institution for conducting research on the American Revolution.

The photocopies of the more than 20,000 documents that have been collected for this project have been assembled through the cooperation of several hundred institutions and private persons devoted to preserving the documentary record upon which the history and traditions of the American people rest, and it is to their work that a documentary publication of this nature should ultimately be dedicated. Unfortunately, the many individual contributors to this collecting effort cannot be adequately recognized, but for permission to print documents appearing in the present volume, we are especially grateful to the following institutions: the American Antiquarian Society, American Philosophical Society, Boston Public Library, John Carter Brown Library, Chicago Historical Society, Colonial Williamsburg, Inc., Columbia University, Connecticut Historical Society, Connecticut State Library, Historical Society of Delaware, Dickinson College, Duke University, Harvard University, Haverford College, Henry E. Huntington Library, Indiana University, Maine Historical Society, Maryland Hall of Records, Maryland Historical Society, Massachusetts Archives, Massachusetts Historical Society, Pierpont Morgan Library, National Archives and Records Service, New England Historic Genealogical Society, New Hampshire Historical Society, New Hampshire State Library, New Haven Colony Historical Society, New Jersey Historical Society, New London Historical Society, New-York Historical Society, New York Public Library, New York State Library, North Carolina State Department of Archives and History, Pennsylvania Historical and Museum Commission, Historical Society of Pennsylvania, Free Library of Philadelphia, Library Company of Philadelphia, Princeton University, Rhode Island Historical Society, Rhode Island State Archives, Rosenbach Foundation, Rutgers University, Saint John's Seminary, University of South Carolina, University of Virginia, Virginia Historical Society, Washington and Jefferson College, Wesleyan University, State Historical Society of Wisconsin, and Yale University. In addition we express our thanks and appreciation to the following persons: Mr. Francis W. Bartlett, Mr. Sol Feinstone, Mr. Ronald von Klaussen, Mr. Kenneth W. Rendell, Mr. Paul C. Richards, Mrs. Elsie O. Sang and Mr. Philip D. Sang, Capt. J. G. M. Stone, and Mrs Rodney M. Wilson. Finally we owe thinks to the historians who have served on the Advisory Committee on the Library's American Revolution Bicentennial Program, and especially to Mr. Julian P. Boyd, Mr. Lyman H. Butterfield, and Mr. Merrill Jensen, who generously act as an advisory committee for the *Letters* project.

Chronology of Congress

MAY 16–AUGUST 15, 1776

May 16   Requests General Washington's presence in Philadelphia to consult on forthcoming campaign.

May 17   Adjourns to observe Fast Day.

May 21   Receives news of George III's negotiations for nearly 17,000 German mercenaries to be sent to America.

May 22   Adopts measures to bolster American forces in Canada; resolves to emit additional $5 million in bills of credit.

May 24   Begins consultations with Generals Washington, Gates, and Mifflin on forthcoming campaign.

May 25   Resolves "that it is highly expedient to engage the Indians in the service of the United Colonies."

May 27   Holds audience with deputies of the Six Nations; receives instructions directed to the North Carolina and Virginia delegates pertaining to independence.

June 1   Requests 6,000 militia reinforcements for Canada.

June 3   Requests nearly 24,000 militia reinforcements for General Washington at New York.

June 7   Receives Richard Henry Lee's resolution respecting independence, foreign alliances, and confederation.

June 10   Postpones debate on independence resolution; appoints committee to prepare a declaration of independence.

June 11   Receives Indian delegation; receives report from commissioners to Canada.

June 12   Appoints committees to prepare "the form of a confederation" and "a plan of treaties to be proposed to foreign powers"; creates Board of War and Ordnance.

June 14   Recommends "detecting, restraining, and punishing disaffected and dangerous persons" in New York; embargoes salt beef and pork.

June 17   Adopts general reform of the forces in Canada.

June 19   Recommends seizure and confinement of Gov. William Franklin.

June 21   Orders inquiry into the causes of miscarriages in Canada.

June 24   Adopts resolves on allegiance and treason and recommends legislation for punishing counterfeiters in the several colonies; suspends enlistment of Mohegan and Stockbridge Indians.

June 26   Adopts bounty for three-year enlistments.

June 28   Reads draft declaration of independence.

July 2   Declares independence.

July 4   Adopts Declaration of Independence; prepares mobilization for the defense of New York, New Jersey, and Pennsylvania.

July 8   Clarifies jurisdictions of northern commanders Gates and Schuyler; augments Washington's discretionary powers and commissary general's authority.

July 10   Denounces British treatment of prisoners captured at the Cedars in Canada.

July 12   Reads and orders printing of draft articles of confederation.

July 17   Adopts "rules and orders for the government of this house."

July 18   Reads draft "plan of treaties to be entered into with foreign states."

July 19   Orders publication of Lord Howe's commission and correspondence to expose false expectations for a negotiated peace.

July 20   Commends commanders of the American victory at Charleston.

July 22   Adopts procedures for negotiating prisoner exchange; authorizes emission of additional $5 million in bills of credit; opens debate on articles of confederation.

July 24   Broadens regulations for confiscating British goods on the high seas.

July 26   Orders publication of an account of a conference between General Washington and a representative of Lord Howe.

July 30   Recommends southern expedition against Cherokees; adopts sundry resolves in response to report on the miscarriages in Canada.

August 2   Delegates sign engrossed Declaration of Independence; Congress authorizes employment of the Stockbridge Indians.

August 6   Proposes general prisoner-of-war exchange.

August 8   Orders General Lee to return to Philadelphia from Charleston; concludes three-week debate on articles of confederation.

August 12   Holds inquiry into conduct of Commodore Esek Hopkins.

August 13   Opens debate on revision of articles of war.

August 14   Adopts plan for encouraging desertion of foreign mercenaries.

August 15   Rebukes Commodore Esek Hopkins.

List of Delegates to Congress

This section lists both the dates on which delegates were elected to terms falling within the period covered by this volume and the inclusive dates of their attendance. The former are generally ascertainable from contemporary state records, but the latter are often elusive bits of information derived from the journals of Congress or extrapolated from references contained in the delegates' correspondence, and in such cases the "facts" are inevitably conjectural. It is not possible to determine interruptions in the attendance of many delegates, and no attempt has been made to record interruptions in service caused by illness or brief trips home, especially of delegates from New Jersey, Delaware, Maryland, and Pennsylvania living within easy access of Philadelphia. For occasional references to such periods of intermittent service as survive in the correspondence and notes of various delegates, see the index under individual delegates. Until fuller information is provided in a consolidated summary of delegate attendance in the final volume of this series, the reader is advised to consult Burnett, *Letters*, 1:xli-lxvi, 2:xxxix-lxxiii, for additional information on conjectural dates of attendance. Brief biographical sketches of all the delegates are available in the *Biographical Directory of the American Congress, 1774–1971*, and fuller sketches of more than half of the delegates can be found in the *Dictionary of American Biography*.

CONNECTICUT

Titus Hosmer
  Elected: October 12, 1775
  Did not attend in 1776
Samuel Huntington
  Elected: October 12, 1775
  Attended: May 16–24?; June 26? to August 15, 1776
Roger Sherman
  Elected: October 12, 1775
  Attended: May 16 to August 15, 1776
William Williams
  Elected: October 12, 1775
  Attended: July 28? to August 15, 1776
Oliver Wolcott
  Elected: October 12, 1775
  Attended: May 16 to June 27? 1776

DELAWARE

Thomas McKean
    Elected: October 21, 1775
    Attended: May 16 to June 8?; June 16 to July 11? 1776
George Read
    Elected: October 21, 1775
    Attended: June 26? to August 15, 1776
Caesar Rodney
    Elected: October 21, 1775
    Attended: May 16 to June 8?; July 2 to August 15, 1776

GEORGIA

Archibald Bulloch
    Elected: February 2, 1776
    Did not attend in 1776
Button Gwinnett
    Elected: February 2, 1776
    Attended: May 20 to August 2? 1776
Lyman Hall
    Elected: February 2, 1776
    Attended: May 20 to August 15, 1776
John Houstoun
    Elected: February 2, 1776
    Did not attend in 1776
George Walton
    Elected: February 2, 1776
    Attended: June 29? to August 15, 1776

MARYLAND

Robert Alexander
    Elected: January 15; May 21; July 4, 1776
    Did not attend after May 15, 1776
Charles Carroll of Carrollton
    Elected: July 4, 1776
    Attended: July 17 to August 10? 1776
Samuel Chase
    Elected: January 15; May 21; July 4, 1776
    Attended: (on mission to Canada to June 11) June 11–14; July 17
    to August 9, 1776
Robert Goldsborough
    Elected: January 15; May 21, 1776
    Did not attend after May 15, 1776

Thomas Johnson
  Elected: January 15; May 21; July 4, 1776
  Did not attend May 16 to August 15, 1776
William Paca
  Elected: January 15; May 21; July 4, 1776
  Attended: June 15 to August 10? 1776
John Rogers
  Elected: January 15; May 21, 1776
  Attended: (temporarily withdrawn May 16–23) May 24 to July 14, 1776
Thomas Stone
  Elected: January 15; May 21; July 4, 1776
  Attended: (temporarily withdrawn May 16–23) May 24 to August 15, 1776
Matthew Tilghman
  Elected: January 15; May 21; July 4, 1776
  Attended: (temporarily withdrawn May 16–23) May 24 to June 14, 1776

MASSACHUSETTS

John Adams
  Elected: January 18, 1776
  Attended: May 16 to August 15, 1776
Samuel Adams
  Elected: January 18, 1776
  Attended: May 16 to August 12, 1776
Elbridge Gerry
  Elected: January 18, 1776
  Attended: May 16 to July 16, 1776
John Hancock
  Elected: January 18, 1776
  Attended: May 16 to August 15, 1776
Robert Treat Paine
  Elected: January 18, 1776
  Attended: May 16 to August 15, 1776

NEW HAMPSHIRE

Josiah Bartlett
  Elected: January 23, 1776
  Attended: May 18 to August 15, 1776
John Langdon
  Elected: January 23, 1776
  Did not attend after January 1776

William Whipple
  Elected: January 23, 1776
  Attended: May 16 to August 12, 1776

NEW JERSEY

Abraham Clark
  Elected: June 21, 1776
  Attended: July 1?–11; July 29? to August 15, 1776
John Cooper
  Elected: February 14, 1776
  Did not attend Congress
John DeHart
  Elected: February 14, 1776
  Attended: May 16 to ante June 13, 1776
John Hart
  Elected: June 21, 1776
  Attended: July ? to August ? 1776
Francis Hopkinson
  Elected: June 21, 1776
  Attended: June 28 to August 15, 1776
William Livingston
  Elected: February 14, 1776
  Attended: May 16 to June ? 1776
Jonathan Dickinson Sergeant
  Elected: February 14, 1776
  Attended: May 16 to June 6? 1776
Richard Smith
  Elected: February 14, 1776
  Did not attend after March 1776
Richard Stockton
  Elected: June 21, 1776
  Attended: July 1 to August 15, 1776
John Witherspoon
  Elected: June 21, 1776
  Attended: July 1? to August 15, 1776

NEW YORK

John Alsop
  Elected: April 21, 1775
  Attended: June 3? to July 15? 1776
George Clinton
  Elected: April 21, 1775
  Attended: June 24? to July 5? 1776

James Duane
  Elected: April 21, 1775
  Attended: May 16–31, 1776
William Floyd
  Elected: April 21, 1775
  Attended: May 16 to August 15, 1776
John Jay
  Elected: April 21, 1775
  Did not attend May 16 to August 15, 1776
Francis Lewis
  Elected: April 21, 1775
  Attended: June 3? to August 15, 1776
Philip Livingston
  Elected: April 21, 1775
  Attended: July 2? to August 15, 1776
Robert R. Livingston
  Elected: April 21, 1775
  Attended: May 16 to July 5? 1776
Lewis Morris
  Elected: April 21, 1775
  Attended: May 16 to June ? 1776
Henry Wisner
  Elected: April 21, 1775
  Attended: May 27? to July 19? 1776

NORTH CAROLINA

Joseph Hewes
  Elected: September 2, 1775
  Attended: May 16 to August 15, 1776
William Hooper
  Elected: September 2, 1775
  Attended: July 24 to August 15, 1776
John Penn
  Elected: September 8, 1775
  Attended: June 20? to August 15, 1776

PENNSYLVANIA

Andrew Allen
  Elected: November 4, 1775
  Attended: May 16–20? 1776
Edward Biddle
  Elected: November 4, 1775
  Did not attend in 1776

George Clymer
Elected: July 20, 1776
Attended: July 20?–30? 1776
John Dickinson
Elected: November 4, 1775
Attended: May 16 to July 4? 1776
Benjamin Franklin
Elected: November 4, 1775; July 20, 1776
Attended: (on mission to Canada to May 31) June 1 to August 15, 1776
Charles Humphreys
Elected: November 4, 1775
Attended: May 16 to July 20? 1776
Robert Morris
Elected: November 4, 1775; July 20, 1776
Attended: May 16 to August 15, 1776
John Morton
Elected: November 4, 1775; July 20, 1776
Attended: May 16–20; June 14 to August 15, 1776
George Ross
Elected: July 20, 1776
Did not return to Congress until September 1776
Benjamin Rush
Elected: July 20, 1776
Attended: July 22 to August 15, 1776
James Smith
Elected: July 20, 1776
Attended: August ?–15, 1776
George Taylor
Elected: July 20, 1776
Attended: July 20? to August ? 1776
Thomas Willing
Elected: November 4, 1775
Attended: May 16 to July 5? 1776
James Wilson
Elected: November 4, 1775; July 20, 1776
Attended: May 16 to August 15, 1776

RHODE ISLAND

William Ellery
Elected: May 4, 1776
Attended: May 16 to August 15, 1776
Stephen Hopkins
Elected: May 3, 1776
Attended: May 16 to August 15, 1776

SOUTH CAROLINA

Thomas Heyward
Elected: February 16, 1776
Attended: May 16 to August 15, 1776
Thomas Lynch, Sr.
Elected: February 16, 1776
Probably did not attend after suffering a stroke in February 1776
Thomas Lynch, Jr.
Elected: March 23, 1776
Attended: May 16 to August 15, 1776
Arthur Middleton
Elected: February 16, 1776
Attended: May 16 to August 15, 1776
Edward Rutledge
Elected: February 16, 1776
Attended: May 16 to August 15, 1776
John Rutledge
Elected: February 16, 1776
Did not attend in 1776

VIRGINIA

Carter Braxton
Elected: December 15, 1775
Attended: May 16 to August 2? 1776
Benjamin Harrison
Elected: August 11, 1775
Attended: May 16 to August 10, 1776
Thomas Jefferson
Elected: August 11, 1775; June 20, 1776
Attended: May 16 to August 15, 1776
Francis Lightfoot Lee
Elected: August 15, 1775; June 20, 1776
Attended: May 16 to August 15, 1776
Richard Henry Lee
Elected: August 11, 1775; June 20, 1776
Attended: May 16 to June 13, 1776
Thomas Nelson
Elected: August 11, 1775; June 20, 1776
Attended: June 9? to August 15, 1776
George Wythe
Elected: August 11, 1775; June 20, 1776
Attended: May 16 to June 13, 1776

Illustrations

"An East Prospect of the City of Philadelphia; taken by George Heap from the Jersey Shore, under the Direction of Nicholas Scull Surveyor General of the Province of Pennsylvania." This detail is from an engraving by Thomas Jefferys based on an etching of the city published in Thomas Jefferys, *A General Topography of North America and the West Indies. Being a Collection of All the Maps, Charts, Plans, and Particular Surveys, That Have Been Published of That Part of the World, Either in Europe or America* (London: R. Sayer, 1768).

Washington, who had been a delegate to Congress in September–October 1774 and May–June 1775, returned to Philadelphia at the end of May 1776 to confer with his former colleagues on the forthcoming campaign. Taking advantage of this rare opportunity, John Hancock personally commissioned Charles Willson Peale to do portraits of the general and his wife, and during the course of his visit Washington spent a few hours sitting for Peale.

"Rarely can a portrait be read so clearly as an historical document. Here is Washington at the end of his first campaign, and on the eve of that succession of humiliating defeats from which he and his army were to emerge in the next winter's cold, tempered, beaten into a new and steely strength. . . . There is a candid quality about this portrait, too. It was painted in two sittings, probably short ones, with no time for a studied, formal likeness. The smile, the eyes, the tilt of the head, are uncertain, unwilling, slightly embarrassed. Washington not only hated to sit for a painter, but he did not like Hancock very well. The shade of awkwardness is unfortunately accentuated by the awkwardness with which the figure is painted—a final work undoubtedly done after the subject's departure."

For both the citation to this appraisal of the painting by Charles Coleman Sellers and additional information on the circumstances pertaining to the commissioning of it, see note 3 to Hancock's letter to Washington of May 16, 1776.

Oil on canvas by Charles Willson Peale, 1776. Courtesy of the Brooklyn Museum, Dick S. Ramsay Fund.

Thomas Stone   48

A Maryland planter-lawyer and a conservative who was among the last of the delegates to abandon hope that the dispute with Britain might be accommodated through negotiation, Stone attended Congress in 1775–76 and again briefly in 1778 and 1784. He was a member of the Maryland delegation that temporarily withdrew from Congress in protest when the resolution of May 15, 1776, on the establishment of new governments was passed. His lengthy letter of May 20, which did not come to public attention until 1951, is the chief source of information on the delegation's position at that crucial stage in the movement for American independence. Elected to the Maryland Senate under the state's new constitution early in 1777, Stone declined reelection to Congress a few weeks later and played only a limited role on the national stage thereafter. He attended the Mount Vernon Conference in 1785 and was elected a delegate to the Philadelphia Convention in 1787, but he declined to attend because of his wife's failing health and died suddenly, at the age of 44, shortly after her death.

Oil on canvas by Robert Edge Pine. The Baltimore Museum of Art.

Richard Henry Lee's Draft Resolution on Independence   157

In the movement for American independence, Richard Henry Lee of Virginia occupies an honored place because it was he who offered the motion on June 7, 1776, proposing the momentous break with Great Britain. Indeed, Lee proposed not only that the colonies dissolve their ties with Britain but also that they negotiate foreign alliances and form a confederation. His famous tripartite resolution reads as follows: *"Resolved,* That these United Colonies are, and of right ought to be, free and independent States, that they are absolved from all allegiance to the British Crown, and that all political connection between them and the State of Great Britain is, and ought to be, totally dissolved.

"That it is expedient forthwith to take the most effectual measures for forming foreign Alliances.

"That a plan of confederation be prepared and transmitted to the respective Colonies for their consideration and approbation."

One of the earliest and most fiery revolutionary leaders to protest British policies in the 1760s, Lee was frequently seen as a political ally of New England radicals bidding for ever more forceful congressional action. He eventually served nine years as a delegate and in 1784 was elected president of Congress.

Papers of the Continental Congress, National Archives and Records Service.

According to the leading authority on Jefferson's writings, "Jefferson's extraordinary graphic account of the debates and proceedings in Congress during two critical months in the summer of 1776 is perhaps the best single source of information concerning the movement toward independence and the formation of the Articles of Confederation." They were composed for his friend James Madison, to whom they were sent in June 1783, and represent the only known attempt by a participant in the proceedings to recount systematically the steps by which Congress reached its momentous decisions on these subjects. Because the date of their composition is not known, controversy has long surrounded some specific statements contained in them, but the detection of errors in Jefferson's account has not detracted significantly from the value of his testimony. Analyzed afresh in this volume, the notes retain their unique luster despite the discovery of new evidence challenging a few previously unquestioned Jefferson assertions.

James Madison Papers, Library of Congress.

Jonathan Dickinson Sergeant, a New Jersey lawyer, served two terms in Congress in 1776–77. During his first term Sergeant aligned himself with the more advanced supporters of American independence like John Adams, and in June 1776 he returned to New Jersey in order to mobilize support for independence. As General Howe prepared to attack New York, Sergeant sent Adams a proposal to augment the New Jersey militia by raising a battalion of slaves, who would eventually be emancipated, but the "heretical" plan was never seriously considered. After the burning of his Princeton home by Hessians in December 1776, Sergeant moved to Philadelphia, where he joined the radical party and, after the end of his second term in Congress, served as attorney general of Pennsylvania from 1777 to 1780. Following his resignation from that office, Sergeant returned to the private practice of law, but he remained a proponent of change and later became a staunch advocate of the French Revolution. After Sergeant fell victim to the yellow fever epidemic that struck Philadelphia in 1793, John Adams, who abhorred Sergeant's enthusiasm for the revolution in France, declared that his death "saved the United States from a fatal revolution of Government"—a far cry from his assessment of Sergeant at the time of the First Congress as "a cordial Friend to American Liberty."

Oil on canvas by Charles Willson Peale. Princeton University.

A practicing physician of Kingston, N.H., and a delegate to Congress, 1775–76 and 1778, Bartlett played his most conspicuous role in Congress as a member of the committee appointed on June 12, 1776, "to prepare and digest the form of a confederation to be entered into between these colonies." His great interest in confederation is testified to by his references to the subject in his correspondence, by miscellaneous notes he made pertaining to representation, and by a surviving committee draft of the Articles of Confederation copied in his hand. As one student of Bartlett's work in Congress has stated: "Bartlett's whole career shows him to have been a stout nationalist." Although best remembered as a signer of the Declaration of Independence, he long remained a primary figure in New Hampshire after he withdrew from the national scene, serving as a judge from 1776 to 1790, a member of the New Hampshire ratifying convention in 1788, and as the state's chief executive from 1790 to 1794.

Pencil sketch by John Trumbull. New Hampshire Historical Society.

A native of Scotland, Wilson came to America at the time of the Stamp Act Crisis and a few years later won wide recognition for his brilliant essay on the legislative authority of Parliament over the colonies. Taking up the practice of law in Carlisle, Pa., he long represented that western community in the councils of his state and the nation but was often seen as at odds with his constituents. A consistent nationalist, he is remembered not only as a signer of the Declaration of Independence but also as a leader in the framing of the Constitution 11 years later. However, to counter reports circulating in June 1776 that he opposed independence, he secured the signatures of several delegates to a statement declaring that on the floor of Congress he had sought only a postponement of the vote on independence and had not actually spoken against taking that fateful step. Controversial during most of his adult life, he was generally unable to subordinate a strong drive for personal wealth to his public career and finally became involved in several speculative schemes that failed and led to bankruptcy. During his tenure on the United States Supreme Court he died in North Carolina in 1798 while fleeing from his creditors.

Engraving by J. B. Longacre. From John Sanderson, ed., *Biography of the Signers to the Declaration of Independence.* Prints and Photographs Division, Library of Congress.

This recently discovered July 4, 1776, letter calls into question the traditional view, resting upon a statement by Thomas Jefferson, that the Declaration of Independence was adopted at the end of the day's debates on this much-celebrated day. In Jefferson's words, "The debates having taken up the greater parts of the 2d. 3d. & 4th. days of July were, in the evening of the last closed." But this letter, written by a committee appointed *after* the Declaration was adopted, begins: "Gentlemen, The Congress this morning directed us to confer. . . ." This discovery not only enables historians to reinterpret other evidence bearing upon the day's activities in Congress but opens the way to a fresh examination of when Jefferson composed these notes and to a new assessment of the accuracy of several details contained in them.

Rare Book and Special Collections Division, Library of Congress.

John Hancock, a wealthy Boston merchant, served as president of Congress from May 1775 to October 1777, longer than any other delegate ever elected to that office. He apparently accepted the post anticipating that it would enhance his chances to become commander of the Continental Army, but much to his chagrin that position went instead to George Washington. As president, Hancock's meager formal powers were less extensive than his many pressing responsibilities, for in addition to presiding over Congress he maintained a voluminous official correspondence with a host of state and local officials, military officers, and private citizens. Hancock also served as chairman of the Marine Committee—a post for which his mercantile background well suited him, although his time-consuming presidential duties inevitably forced him to neglect the committee and led to criticism by delegates more concerned with naval affairs. His fame derives less from his election as president, however, than from the accident of his incumbency at the moment of American independence, which provided him the responsibility for placing his signature, the most celebrated in American annals, first on the Declaration of Independence.

Oil on canvas by John Singleton Copley. Collection of the James S. Copley Library, La Jolla, Calif. Photograph courtesy of the National Portrait Gallery, Smithsonian Institution.

Perhaps the most famous Fourth of July letter, this communication from Rodney to his brother documents the dramatic July 2 ride through "thunder and Rain" to Philadelphia that enabled him to break a tie in the Delaware delegation and permitted a unanimous vote on Richard Henry Lee's independence resolution. With George Read opposed to the resolution and Thomas McKean supporting it, Rodney's presence was necessary to ensure that every vote cast on the question was affirmative. The New York delegates, awaiting further instructions from their constituents, did not cast their state's vote on the issue, and it was not until July 15 that New York's concurrence —voted unanimously in the convention at White Plains on July 9— was recorded in the journals.

Rodney, a Kent County planter and lawyer, who had been attending Congress intermittently since September 1774, continued to serve until October. Although thrice later reelected a delegate he never returned to Congress after 1776. He was long active in Delaware politics and was the state's president from 1778 to 1781, during which time he played a crucial role in her war effort.

Property of the Estelle Doheny Collection of Rare Books and Art Objects of the Edward Laurence Doheny Memorial Library, St. John's Seminary, Camarillo, Calif.

John Alsop   467

John Alsop, a New York merchant and delegate to Congress since 1774, looked forward to a "reconcilliation" with Great Britain "free from Taxation." He was willing to support vigorous measures in order to oppose British tyranny, but not to the point of breaking up the British Empire. Accordingly, he resigned his seat in Congress after the New York Convention authorized the New York delegates to approve the Declaration of Independence. Unwilling to sever all ties with Great Britain, Alsop was equally reluctant to take an active part against his erstwhile colleagues in the revolutionary movement. Therefore he spent the remainder of the war living in comparative tranquillity in Middletown, Conn. In retrospect this was a wise decision, for it enabled him, upon the conclusion of peace, to return to his native state, where he eventually became president of the New York City Chamber of Commerce and an honored member of the Federalist party.

Prints and Photographs Division, Library of Congress.

Congress' July 19 Response to   488
    Lord Howe's Peace "Declaration"

For months before Congress declared independence, moderates both in and out of Congress had opposed taking this momentous step on the ground that it would be more prudent to await the arrival of British peace commissioners. When Lord Howe failed to reach America with authority to negotiate peace before Congress had approved the Declaration, some Americans thought the delay had

been fatal. But even had he arrived earlier it is doubtful that he
could have stemmed the tide of independence. As indicated in his
public declaration of June 20, 1776, prepared while still at sea,
Howe was not authorized to discuss terms of reconciliation until
after the colonies had submitted to royal authority—and even then
secret instructions permitted him to make no more than what most
Americans would have regarded as trifling concessions. So unappeal-
ing were the terms offered by Howe's declaration that Congress was
convinced that mere publication of the document would strengthen
support for independence, and accordingly on July 19, 1776, it took
steps to give it wide publicity. Although the American defeat at the
battle of Long Island subsequently led Congress to appoint a committee to confer with Lord Howe about peace terms, talks inevitably
foundered on the rock of Britain's insistence that submission must
precede negotiation.

From the *Pennsylvania Journal*, July 24, 1776.

Commodore Esek Hopkins   661

Esek Hopkins, the first commodore of the Continental Navy and
younger brother of Rhode Island delegate Stephen Hopkins, was
highly controversial during the early years of the war. He incurred
the ire of many delegates by failing to carry out orders from the
Naval Committee to engage vessels off the coasts of the southern
colonies, conducting instead a raid on the island of New Providence
in the Bahamas. He then compounded this fault by allowing the
British frigate *Glasgow* to escape despite the superior force at his
disposal during an engagement. Finally, he antagonized Congress
by giving cannon captured at New Providence to Rhode Island after
they had been ordered to be turned over to Connecticut. Accordingly, Congress censured Hopkins on August 16, 1776, although
allowing him to retain his command. Embittered by this vote, he
subsequently declared that Congress was "a pack of damn'd fools,
ignorant fellows, lawyers, clarks &c, a company of men wholly unacquainted with mankind, and perfectly unacquainted with their
business, and that if their measures were complied with the country
would be undone." Combined with continued congressional dissatisfaction with Hopkins' performance in office, disclosure of this out-
burst finally led to his suspension from command in March 1777 and
his dismissal from service in January 1778.

Mezzotint probably engraved by C. Corbutt. Published by Thomas
Hart, August 22, 1776.

LETTERS OF DELEGATES

4

May 16–August 15, 1776

TO CONGRESS

John Adams to Joseph Palmer

May 16. 1776

We have Spent a Number of Days in considering the State of Boston and the Massachusetts, and after all I dont know whether you will think We have done enough. The five Ba[tta]llions now there, were ordered to be recruited to their full Compliment, and three additional Battallions are ordered to be raised. You have raised one—that may be put upon continental Pay, as one of the three. The other two must be raised as you can. I am fearfull that drained as New England is, you will meet with Difficulty to raise more Men. Yet I should hope, that Stimulated by so urgent a Motive as that of defending Boston and its Harbour, two more Battallions might be raised. In What Proportions they are to be raised in Mass. Bay, Connecticutt & New Hampshire is not determined. Whether this Point will be determined here, or not, I cant Say. The Story of Such formidable Numbers of foreign Mercenaries, I conjecture to be chiefly Puff, but yet there may be Some Truth in it. If you should be invaded, the Militia will do their Duty. If an Impression should be made, and the Enemy make a Lodgment again with you, Congress will maintain a Standing Army, if it can be raised to oppose them, but the Continental Expences are so enormous as to raise the most alarming Apprehensions in the Minds of all, and Gentlemen are very reluctant to raising Forces where there is not an actual Enemy to oppose. A Major General and a Brigadier General are ordered to take the Command, in Boston.[1]

Can nothing be done to drive the Men of War from Nantaskett Road? A few Row Gallies here have attacked two formidable ships and driven them down to the Mouth of the River, where the Gallies cannot live. Would not a few of these, with some fire ships and Fire Rafts be very wholesome, to clear the Harbour of those Vermine. I never shall be happy untill I hear, they are driven out to sea.

Yesterday the Gordian Knot was cutt asunder. Congress passed a Resolve in these Words as nearly as I can recollect them by my Memory.[2]

"Whereas his Britanic Majesty, in Conjunction with his Lords and Commons, has, by a late Act of Parliament, excluded the Inhabitants of these united Colonies, from the Protection of his Crown, and Whereas no answer whatever, to the humble Petitions of the Colonies for Redress of their Grivances, and Reconciliation with Great Britain, has been, or is likely to be given: But the whole Force of that Kingdom, aided by foreign Mercenaries, is to be exerted for our Destruction,

"And Whereas it is irreconcileable to Reason and good Conscience for the People of these Colonies, to take the oaths and affirmations necessary for the Support of any Government, under the Said Crown and it is necessary, that the Exercise of every Kind of Authority under the Said Crown Should be totally Suppressed, and all the Powers of Government exerted under the Authority of the People of the Colonies, for the Preservation of internal Peace, Virtue and good order, as well as for the Defence of their Lives, Liberties, and Properties, against the hostile Invasions and cruel Depredations of their Enemies, therefore,

"Resolved that it be recommended, to the Several Assemblies and Conventions, to institute such Forms of Government as they shall judge necessary for the Happiness of the People."

If such a Resolution had been passed twelve Months ago, as it ought to have been, and it was not my fault that it was not, how different would have been our Situation? The Advantages of such a Measure were pointed out, very particularly Twelve Months ago, but then We must petition and negotiate, and the People were not ripe. I believe they were as ripe then, as they are now.

I have seen with great Pleasure in the News Papers and in private Letters, that the Citizens of Boston, the Inhabitants of Several Country Towns, as well as the Troops under General Ward, are exerting themselves to put the Country in a good Posture of Defence. I wish them all Health, and Wealth and May God almighty protect them from their Enemies. My best Respects to your good Family and to all Friends.

RC (MHi). In Adams' hand, though not signed. Recipient identified in *New York Review and Atheneum Magazine* 2 (May 1826): 446–47.

¹ See Samuel Adams to James Warren, May 12, 1776, note 2.

² *JCC*, 4:342, 357–58. See also John Adams to James Warren, May 15, 1776, note 1.

Commissioners to Canada to Philip Schuyler

Dear Sir,   16th May 1776. Montreal

We are favoured with yours of the 7th instant. The army here is suffering from want of Provisions particularly Pork. None, or next to none, is to be procured in Canada. For God sake send off Pork; or our troops will be greatly distressed for want of provisions, and may mutiny & desert to the enemy. The inclosed letters from G. Arnold ¹ will give you the latest intelligence we have recd. from below.

General Thompson & Colonel Sinclear [Arthur St. Clair] sailed from this place yesterday for the mouth of the Sorel, which place we hope he reached last night. They intended to proceed to Dechambault immediately. We hope we shall be able to maintain that port if Carleton has no more forces than mentioned in Arnolds letters from the intelligence given by Mr. Bondfield.

We have been alarmed this morning with the approach of some Indians & Soldiers from Detroit & the upper garrisons with a design to attack our post at the Cedars. We have detached 150 men commanded by Major Sherborne to reinforce that garrison already consisting of 300 effective men. We do not believe there is much to fear from that quarter.

For God sake send powder & Pork. You know we lost 20 barrels of the power which lately came over the lakes. We are with great esteem & sincere regard, Dr. Sir, yr. most hum. Sevts,

Ch. Carroll of Carrollton

Saml. Chase

RC (NN). Written by Carroll and signed by Carroll and Chase.
[1] Probably Gen. Benedict Arnold's two letters to the commissioners dated Sorel, May 15, in *Am. Archives*, 4th ser. 6:579–80.

James Duane to John Jay

Philad. 16 May 1776

Yesterday, my dear Friend, was an important day, productive of the Resolutions of which I enclose you a Copy. I shall not enter into particulars. The Resolution itself first passed and then a Committee was appointed to fit it with a preamble.[1] Compare them with each other and it will probably lead you into Reflections which I dare not point out. I hope you will relieve me soon as I am impatient to visit my Friends; & look upon Business here to be in such a Train that I can well be spared.

My Friend Robert is arrived here better in health than I expected. I like his & your plan for a Summer Residence very well as I take it for granted that you will both give your Attention here and leave me in Case I shou'd be reelected at large.

I beg you'l make my Complimt acceptable to Mrs Jay & the rest of our Friends, And am with the utmost Regard, My dear Sir, your affectionate & most obed Servant,   Jas. Duane

RC (NNC).
[1] See the resolution of May 10 urging the establishment of new provincial governments and the preamble thereto adopted by Congress on May 15. *JCC*, 4:342, 357–58. Duane's opposition to this preamble is set forth in John Adams' Notes of Debates, May 13–15, 1776.

John Hancock to the Connecticut and New Hampshire Assemblies

Gentlemen,   Philada. May 16th. 1776

You will perceive by the enclosed Resolve of Congress, which I am commanded to transmit you, that they have directed another Battalion to be raised in your Colony on Continental Pay.[1]

The Army under General Washington has been so extremely weakened by detaching ten Regiments into Canada on a most important Service, that it has become apparently necessary, for the Security of the Eastern Governments, to increase the Number of Troops in that Quarter. The Congress have accordingly resolved that two Regiments be raised in Massachusetts Bay, one in New Hampshire, and one in Connecticut for the Service of the United Colonies. They have also been pleased to appoint Horatio Gates Esqr. a Major General, and Tho. Mifflin Esqr. a Brigadier General in the Continental Army.

Your Zeal & Ardor in the American Cause will, I am persuaded, induce you to carry the enclosed Resolve into Effect, with all the Expedition which your own Situation, and the Public Good so evidently require.

I enclose you also blank Commissions for the Captains & Subalterns of the Regiment to be raised in your Colony to be filled up with the Names of the Persons you may please to appoint. With Respect to the Field Officers, I have it in Command to request you will please to recommend to Congress as early as possible the Names of Persons you judge proper for those offices, in order that they may be appointed & commissioned by the Congress. As soon as I have the Honour to receive your Recommendations, I will lay them before Congress, and immediately upon their Determination transmit you the Commissions filled up accordingly.[2]

I have the Honour to be, Gentlemen, your most obedt. & very hble Sevt.,   J. H. Pt.

LB (DNA: PCC, item 12A). Although Hancock's letterbook indicates that this letter was to be sent to the Connecticut Assembly and the New Hampshire Convention, the RC sent to New Hampshire was finally addressed to "The Assembly of New Hampshire." Signers Collection, MA.

[1] Congress ordered the raising of a new battalion in New Hampshire on May 14 and in Connecticut on May 16. *JCC*, 4:357, 360.

[2] For the New Hampshire Assembly's action on the appointment of field officers, see William Whipple to Meshech Weare, May 17, 1776, note 3. Connecticut governor Jonathan Trumbull submitted a list of officers for his province's battalion, which was approved by Congress on June 17. On the same day that Congress ratified Connecticut's choice of field officers it also changed the destination of the new Connecticut battalion from Boston, as stipulated in the congressional resolution of May 16, to Canada, as suggested by Trumbull. See Trumbull to Hancock, June 10, 1776, *Am. Archives*, 4th ser. 6:797; PCC, item 66, fol. 181; and *JCC*, 5:447–48.

John Hancock to the Massachusetts Assembly

Gentlemen,   Philadelphia May 16th. 1776

By the best Intelligence from Europe it appears, That the British Nation have proceeded to the last Extremity, and have actually taken into Pay a Number of foreign Troops; who, in all Probability, are on their Passage to America at this very Time. The Transactions of the Ministry are so much hid from View, that we are left to wander in the Field of Conjecture; and it is entirely to accident we are indebted, for any little Information we may receive with Regard to their Designs against us. This Uncertainty however, I hope, will have the proper Effect. It should stimulate the Colonies to greater Dilligence & Vigour in preparing to ward off the Blow, as our Enemies may, for any Thing we know, be at our very Door.

In this Situation of our Affairs, it is highly necessary, that the Town of Boston should receive a Reinforcement, to prevent it from falling again into the Hands of such Miscreants, as have just been driven out of it. The Congress therefore considering the small Number of Troops in that Place, and the Impossibility of detaching any from the Continental Army which has lately been much weakened by the two Brigades consisting of ten Regiments ordered into Canada, have come to the enclosed Resolutions, which I am commanded to transmit you, being fully assured, that you will do every Thing in your Power to carry the same into Effect as speedily as possible.[1]

I enclose to you also blank Commissions for the Captains and Subalterns of the two Regiments to be raised in Massachusetts Colony, to be filled up with the Names of the Persons you may please to appoint. With Respect to the Field Officers, I have it in Command to request, you will please to recommend to Congress as early as possible the Names of Persons you judge proper for those Offices, in Order that they may be appointed & commissioned by the Congress. As soon as I have the Honour to receive your Recommendations, I will lay them before Congress, and immediately upon their Determination transmit you the Commissions filled up accordingly.[2]

I have the Honour to be with every respectful sentiment, and much Esteem, Gentlemen, your most obed. hble Servt.

John Hancock Presidt.

[P.S.] The Congress have been pleased to appoint Horatio Gates Esqr to be a Major General and Thomas Mifflin Esqr to be a Brigadier General in the Continental Army. I have wrote to Genl. Washington to request him, if agreeable, that those Gentlemen may take the command at Boston.

I am prevented inclosing a Resolve by means of the Secy with the Journals being out of Town. It is a Resolution for the liberation

of Doctr. Church in his present infirm dangerous State, he is to
be sent by Govr. Trumball to the Assembly of Massachusetts & they
are requested to take Bail in £1000 L[awful] m[one]y for his appearance hereafter before a proper Court authorized to try him.[3]
I a few days ago deliver'd a Copy of the Resolve to the Drs Brother,
will transmit one to you by tomorrow's post.

Yours,   J. H. Pt.

I have advanc'd Mr. Jona. Park the Express Twelve dollars, which
I have charg'd to the province.

RC (M–Ar). In the hand of Jacob Rush and signed by Hancock.
    [1] See *JCC*, 4:355, 360.
    [2] The Massachusetts Assembly responded with a request for congressional ap-
proval of bounties for new troops and the assignment of Generals Gates and
Mifflin to Boston, promising to send the list of field officers at a later date. See the
assembly's letter of June 6 to the Massachusetts delegates, in *Am. Archives*, 4th
ser. 6:728.
    [3] See *JCC*, 4:352.

John Hancock to George Washington

Sir,   Philadelphia May 16th. 1776.
    I do myself the Honour to enclose you several Resolutions passed
by the Congress, to which I beg Leave to refer you.[1]
    The Congress being of Opinion, that it is necessary, as well for
your Health, as the public Service, that you should embrace the
earliest opportunity of coming to Philadelphia, have directed me to
write to you, and request, that you will repair to Philada. as soon
as you can conveniently, in order to consult with Congress, upon
such Measures as may be necessary for the carrying on the ensuing
Campaign.[2] I hope the Situation of the great Affairs with which
you are entrusted, will admit your making this Excursion, which I
apprehend may be serviceable to your Health. In which Case, I
request the Favour that you will please to honour me with your
and your Lady's Company at my House, where I have a Bed at
your Service during your Continuance here, and where every Endeavour of mine and Mrs. Hancock, shall be exerted to make your
Abode agreeable. I reside in an airy, open Part of the City in Arch
Street and Fourth Street. If this should be agreeable to you, it will
afford me much Pleasure.[3]
    I am to inform you, that the Congress have this Day appointed
Horatio Gates Esqr a Major General, and Thomas Mifflin Esqr a
Brigadier General in the Continental Army. A Commission for the
former Gentleman, I transmit by this Opportunity.[4] I have delivered one to Mr. Mifflin here.

I could wish, if consistent with the Service it might be agreeable to you to direct these two Gentlemen to repair to Boston. But I would not urge a Matter which entirely rests with you. I know however your Disposition will prompt you to make as agreeable an Arrangement as possible. I have the Honour to be, with respectful Sentiments & Esteem, Sir your most obedt. hble Sevt.

John Hancock Presidt

[*P.S.*] Since writing the foregoing I have been Told that your Lady, not having had the Small Pox, has intentions of taking it by Inoculation in this City, I Beg that that Circumstance may be no prevention to your making free use of my house, it is large & very Commodious, and every Accommodation about it is at your Service; and you may Depend Mrs. Hancock will give the greatest Attention to your Lady should she incline to Take the Disorder. I shall be peculiarly happy if my Scituation may be found agreeable to you.

RC (DLC). In the hand of Jacob Rush, with signature and postscript by Hancock.
[1] These resolutions, passed on May 14 and 16, concerned the procurement of arms and reinforcements for Washington's army and the promotions of Horatio Gates and Thomas Mifflin. *JCC*, 4:354–57, 359–60.
[2] In obedience to Congress' request, Washington came to Philadelphia and conferred with Congress about military affairs from May 24 to June 3, 1776. See *JCC*, 4:389, 391, 394–96, 399–401, 406, 408–11; and Washington, *Writings* (Fitzpatrick), 5:62, 87–88.
[3] Three days after extending this invitation to Washington, but before he had received a response from the general, Hancock visited Charles Willson Peale and "bespoke" a portrait "of Gen. Washington and Lady." Upon receiving a noncommittal reply from Washington on May 21, Hancock renewed his invitation, which the general ultimately declined. Despite the president's disappointment at this rebuff, there was no change in his arrangement with Peale, and Washington sat twice for his portrait at the end of May during his visit to Philadelphia (see illustration). Although Kenneth Silverman has recently asserted that Congress commissioned this as an official portrait "to honor Washington's expulsion of the British from Boston," it is clear that the initiative for it came solely from Hancock, who ultimately paid for and received the work in December. See Kenneth Silverman, *A Cultural History of the American Revolution* (New York: Thomas Y. Crowell Co., 1976), p. 317; and Charles Coleman Sellers, *Portraits and Miniatures by Charles Willson Peale, Transactions of the American Philosophical Society*, n.s., vol. 42 (Philadelphia, 1952), p. 220.
Hancock's efforts to ingratiate himself with the commander in chief at this time invite speculation about his motives and suggest that he had in mind more than simply engineering a social coup. Indeed, it seems likely that he still retained hopes for high military command and desired to have an important role in the forthcoming campaign. In this connection it is interesting to note his plea of the preceding July for an opportunity to serve under Washington and his more recent request to Thomas Cushing to have his commission as major general of the Massachusetts militia sent to Philadelphia "that I may Appear in Character." See Hancock to Washington, July 10, 1775, and to Thomas Cushing, March 7, 1776. See also Hancock's letters to Cushing of May 17 and June 12 and 16, 1776.
[4] Hancock sent Gates his commission as major general enclosed in a letter of this date commending him for the "very great Services you have performed for

George Washington

America by introducing Order & Discipline into the Army of the United Colonies, as well as your Zeal & Ardor in the American Cause." See Hancock to Horatio Gates, May 16, 1776, in *PCC*, item 12A, and *Am. Archives*, 4th ser. 6:473.

Joseph Hewes to Samuel Johnston

Dear Sir   Philadelphia 16th May 1776

I have had the honor to receive your several Favours of the 10th, 13th, 15th & 17th ultimo enclosing sundry resolutions of your Congress. I took the earliest oppertunity to lay those papers before Congress and have now the pleasure to inform you they have taken your Six Regiments into Continental Service, appointed Nicholas Long Esqr. deputy quarter master general with the rank of Colonel, ordered Twelve field pieces to be procured and sent to you, also Three Tons of Powder, Six Chests of Medicines and one hundred weight of bark.[1]

I urged the Necessity of taking your light Horse into their Service, but could not prevail on them to do it no Colonies having been yet allowed to raise any on Continental pay. It is said they are very expensive Troops and of little use in this Contest. I am informed a Company or two were raised in South Carolina but being found by experience to be too expensive the Horses were discharged and the men turned into the ranks of foot Regiments. I had it not in charge from you to make application for any Powder or Medicines, but apprehending they would be wanted I took the liberty to apply for them. The three Tons of Powder in Twenty five barrels went off yesterday in three Waggons for Halifax, the Medicines will be sent off next week. I hope these matters will meet the approbation of your Congress. Should you want drums, Colours, Shoes, Stockings and Blankets for your Soldiers I believe some might be procured here. Cannon fitt for field pieces cannot be purchased at any price. Before the resolution passed in Congress to procure and send Cannon or I had received your Orders, I had done my utmost to get them. I had Contracted with a person to Cast Twenty four double fortified four pounders which will do either for field pieces or Ship Guns. They are not yet done nor can I say when they will. I can only say that nothing on my part shall be wanting to get them soon, as possible.

I send you enclosed the Commissions for the field Officers of the Six Regiments and for Colonel Long, the Resolutions of Congress respecting the several matters before mentioned, also a resolution that passed yesterday together with sundry other papers.[2]

My endeavours to get a few Muskets for your Troops have hitherto been fruitless. It is impossible to procure any here at this time. Many of the Continental Troops in this City and in New York are without any. We are greatly distressed on that account. Some of our Vessels have returned without any, some have brought a few, a very few, and several that were expected with a Considerable quantity are missing, supposed to be taken by our Enemies. Every effort is exerted to get them made in these Colonies but this Source falls exceedingly short of our demands, however we have some Vessels out that may be expected about this time and we hope they will arrive safe with a seasonable Supply.

A few days ago Thirteen Row Gallies built at the expence of this Province each carrying one Eighteen pounder attacked the Roebuck & Liverpool Men of War in the River about Twenty Miles below and obliged them to return to the Capes in a Shattered condition. It is thought if they had been fully supplied with powder & Ball they would have destroyed those Ships. The Boats expended in the engagement about four Tons of powder. The report of this day is that the Ships are gone out to sea supposed either to Halifax or Virginia to repair the damage they received in this action.[3] For other News I beg leave to refer you to the papers inclosed.

I am with great respect & esteem, Dear Sir, your mo. Obedt. huml Sev,   Joseph Hewes

RC (Nc–Ar).
  [1] For these resolutions, which were passed by Congress on May 7, see *JCC*, 4:331–33. Letters of April 10 and 13 from Samuel Johnston, president of the North Carolina Provincial Congress, to the North Carolina delegates are in *N. C. Colonial Records*, 10:494–95. An extract of Johnston's April 15 letter to Hewes is in Clark, *Naval Documents*, 4:841–42.
  [2] The resolution "passed yesterday" included both the May 10 resolution on the establishment of new provincial governments and the preamble thereto adopted on May 15. *JCC*, 4:342, 357–58.
  [3] Although the *Liverpool* did return briefly to Cape May the following week, the departure of the *Roebuck* and *Liverpool* gave temporary relief to Pennsylvania shippers, and led immediately to preparations for getting out to sea vessels recently bottled up in the Delaware by the British men of war. This day, therefore, Robert Morris, writing as vice president of the Marine Committee, sent the following brief note to the Pennsylvania Committee of Safety: "The Marine Committee have ordered the Continental Armed Vessels to take under their convoy all Vessels which do not draw too much Water to go down the Cape May Channel." J. P. Morgan Collection, DLC.

Thomas Jefferson to Thomas Nelson

Dear Nelson   Philadelphia May. 16. 1776.
  I arrived here last Tuesday after being detained hence six weeks longer than I intended by a malady of which Gilmer can inform you. I have nothing new to inform you of as the last post carried you an account of the naval engagement in Delaware.[1] I inclose a

vote of yesterday on the subject of government [2] as the ensuing campaign is likely to require greater exertion than our unorganized powers may at present effect. Should our Convention propose to establish now a form of government perhaps it might be agreeable to recall for a short time their delegates. It is a work of the most interesting nature and such as every individual would wish to have his voice in.[3] In truth it is the whole object of the present controversy; for should a bad government be instituted for us in future it had been as well to have accepted at first the bad one offered to us from beyond the water without the risk and expence of contest. But this I mention to you in confidence, as in our situation, a hint to any other is too delicate however anxiously interesting the subject is to our feelings. In future you shall hear from me weekly while you stay, and I shall be glad to receive Conventional as well as publick intelligence from you. I am at present in our old lodgings tho' I think, as the excessive heats of the city are coming on fast, to endeavor to get lodgings in the skirts of the town where I may have the benefit of a freely circulating air.[4] Tell Page and Mc.lurgh [5] that I received their letters this morning and shall devote myself to their contents. I am here in the same uneasy anxious state in which I was the last fall without Mrs. Jefferson who could not come with me. I wish much to see you here, yet hope you will contrive to bring on as early as you can in convention the great questions of the session. I suppose they will tell us what to say on the subject of independence,[6] but hope respect will be expressed to the right of opinion in other colonies who may happen to differ from them. When at home I took great pains to enquire into the sentiments of the people on that head. In the upper counties I think I may safely say nine out of ten are for it. Adieu. My compliments to Mrs. Nelson.[7]

P.S. In the other colonies who have instituted government they recalled their delegates leaving only one or two to give information to Congress of matters which might relate to their country particularly, and giving them a vote during the interval of absence.[8]

RC (MWA). Jefferson, *Papers* (Boyd), 1:292.
  [1] See Marine Committee to John Barry, May 8, 1776, note 1.
  [2] See *JCC*, 4:342, 357–58. See also John Adams to James Warren, May 15, 1776.
  [3] This passage, written the day after Congress completed action on a resolution calling for the colonies to adopt new governments, reveals the great importance Jefferson attached to the process of constitution building. Indeed Virginia itself was in the forefront of this movement, and before Nelson received this letter the Virginia Convention had appointed a committee to begin drafting a new constitution for the commonwealth. Although Jefferson was not a member of the convention and remained in Philadelphia during the entire period the committee conducted its deliberations, he nevertheless contributed importantly to its work

by submitting to the committee a draft Virginia constitution he composed while
in Philadelphia.

The use made of this draft cannot be precisely determined, but the editor of
Jefferson's papers has examined the issue in great detail and assessed Jefferson's
influence on the committee and its chairman, George Mason. Two of Jefferson's
colleagues in Congress, George Wythe and Richard Henry Lee, did return to
Virginia in June, and Wythe carried with him to the convention a draft constitution used by Mason. Indeed, Jefferson is known to have made three drafts of the
document before Wythe left Philadelphia on June 13. He was probably at work
on the first of them at the time he was writing this letter to Nelson, since it is
apparent from internal evidence that this initial draft was completed sometime
before May 27, when he received resolutions from the Virginia Convention containing provisions subsequently incorporated into his second and third drafts.

Although these drafts only indirectly relate to Jefferson's work in Congress, they
are products of the pen of one of the principal participants in its deliberations
during a highly significant period in its history and clearly reflect his most fundamental political and constitutional views. Furthermore, it is now known that
Jefferson incorporated passages from them into the Declaration of Independence
when he drafted it during the last weeks of June. For a critical analysis and the
printed texts of these drafts, see Jefferson, *Papers* (Boyd), 1:329–65. See also the
letters written to Jefferson during this period by the president of the Virginia
Convention, Edmund Pendleton, in response to several letters from Jefferson that
do not survive, ibid., pp. 296–98, 471–72, 479–80, 484–85, 488–91, 507–8.

⁴ "Our old lodgings," which Jefferson and Nelson shared when they had been in
Philadelphia simultaneously during the autumn of 1775, is a reference to the
house of Benjamin Randolph on Chestnut Street between Third and Fourth. A
few days after writing this letter, Jefferson took lodging in the house of Jacob
Graff, which subsequently became celebrated as the house in which he wrote the
Declaration of Independence. See Jefferson, *Papers* (Boyd), 1:293.

Documentation on the residences of the delegates while they were in Philadelphia attending Congress is generally meager, but John Adams compiled an
interesting, fragmentary list of most of those in attendance in late April 1776
containing notations on the residences of approximately half of them. See Adams,
Diary (Butterfield), 2:237–38.

⁵ That is, James McClurg. See Jefferson to John Page, May 17, 1776, note 2.

⁶ For the Virginia Convention's instructions, see Richard Henry Lee to Edmund
Pendleton, May 12, 1776, note 3.

⁷ A draft of another letter written at about this time, dealing chiefly with the
affairs of Jefferson's mother's relatives and apparently intended for his uncle
William Randolph in Bristol, England, is in Jefferson, *Papers* (Boyd), 1:408–10.

⁸ For the continuation of this letter, see Jefferson to Nelson, May 19, 1776.

Massachusetts Delegates to George Washington

Sir   Philadelphia May 16. 1776

Congress yesterday appointed General Gates a Major General and
Mr Mifflin a Brigadier General, in the Continental Army, and ordered the Five Battallions in the Massachusetts Bay to be compleated to their full Compliments and those Additional Battallions
to be raised forthwith, in the Eastern Department, and further have
requested your Excellency to send a Major General and Brigadier
General to take the Command, in that Department.

We presume not to judge of the Exigencies of the public service, so far as to suggest any Plan of ours, for your Consideration, any further than to assure your Excellency that no officers in the service would be more agreable to Us, and We have Reason to believe to our Constituents, to take the Command in that Department, than the Generals Gates and Mifflin.[1]

We are, sir, with great Esteem and Respect, your Excellencies Friends and most obedient humble servants,

John Hancock   John Adams

Samuel Adams   R. T. Paine

Elbridge Gerry

RC (PHi). Written by John Adams and signed by John Adams, Samuel Adams, Gerry, Hancock, and Paine.

[1] See also Samuel Adams to George Washington, May 15, 1776. Artemas Ward continued in command at Boston, while Gates was given the Canadian command by Congress on June 17, 1776. JCC, 5:448; and John Hancock to Artemas Ward, April 26, 1776, note 1.

Secret Committee to George Washington

Sir   Philada. May 16th. 1776

The enclosed letters will discover to your Excellency that the Congress have ordered Two hundred & Forty four Muskets to be forwarded from Rhode Island to New York for the Continental Service and as it is probable you may think proper to give some directions about the mode of getting them safe down we trouble you with these open letters that you may have an opportunity of forwarding them & of adding thereto what you may think Necessary.[1]

We have the honor to be, Your Excellencys Obedt hble servts.

By order of the Secret Committee,

Robt Morris, ChairMan

RC (DLC). Written and signed by Morris.

[1] See JCC, 4:357. For Washington's May 20 response, see Washington, Writings (Fitzpatrick), 5:63–64. One of the enclosed letters, written by Morris on the 16th on behalf of the committee to Nicholas Brown and John Brown, directed "fourteen Muskets in your hands belonging to the Continent to be forwarded immediately to his Excellency Genl. Washington at New York." Brown Papers, RPJCB. Nicholas Brown's May 27 letter to Washington, explaining why only four muskets were sent, is in Am. Archives, 4th ser. 6:768.

William Whipple to Meshech Weare

Sir,   Philadelphia 16th May 1776

I have the pleasure to inclose you a Resolution of Congress for raising a Battn in New Hampshire. The design is that they are to be station'd at Portsmth, subject, however, to the Officer commanding in the Eastern department.[1] Its the wish of Congress that the men may be inlisted for three Years, but if they cannot be prevailed on to engage for a longer time they may be inlisted for one Year, the Battalion to consist of 728 men including officers. Please to observe they are not to be in pay 'till arm'd & accoutred. The five Battalions that are at Boston are to be recruited to their full Compliment & three new ones rais'd, two Battalions are also station'd for the Present at Road Island, in all Eleven Battalions in the Eastern department [and] two Genl Officers will be sent there.[2]

Britain will no doubt use Her utmost efforts this summer to effect the Infernal designs of the King & his Ministry. It is therefore necessary that we shod exert ourselves to frustrate their plans which with divine assistance no doubt we shall be able to accomplish. If any men can be spar'd besides the Battalion before mention'd, I hope all proper incouragement will be given to the recruiting officers for filling up those in Boston. Inclosed is recommendation to the Colonies to assume all the powers of Government which I hope will meet your approbation.[3]

I am with great Respect, Your Most Obt Sevt,

Wm Whipple

RC (DLC).
[1] *JCC*, 4:357. For further information on the original New Hampshire request for a Continental battalion, see Whipple to Weare, March 2, 1776.
[2] See Samuel Adams to James Warren, May 12, 1776, note 2.
[3] *JCC*, 4:342, 357–58. See also John Adams to James Warren, May 15, 1776.

Oliver Wolcott to Samuel Lyman

Sir,   Philidelpa. 16 May 1776

Your Letter of the 4t instant came safe, there was not the least Occasion of an Excuse on Acco. of the length of your Letters, you may be assured that I read them with great Pleasure. I suppose this tho't might occur to you, as I sometimes Write you Letters the whole of which is on the outside. This you might charitably suppose was owing to the Want of Time, and that you would learn the News from the Letter inclosed if any. I hope you will not fail of Writing and Write as long as you please. You Acco. of the Cherokee is what might have been expected from a Man of his extreme ill nature.

The News is inclosed. A Revolution in Government, you will perceive is about to take Effect. May God grant a happy establishment of it, and security to the Rights of the People. If this Recommendation takes Effect, which undouptedly it will, There will be an instance Real not implyed or Ideal, of a Government founded in

Compact, Express and Clear Made in its Principles by the People at large.[1]

A strange Infatuation has possessed the British Councills to drive Matters to the length they have gone. Every Thing convinces Me that the Abilities of a Child might have governed this Country, so strong has been their Attachment to Britain. May the supreme Ruler of the Universe carry us thro the hardy Conflict to Liberty, safety and Peace. My Compliments to Mr. Morrice and Friends. I am sir with Esteem, your Most obedient and humble Servant,

Oliver Wolcott

RC (PHi).

[1] See *JCC*, 4:342, 357–58; and John Adams to James Warren, May 15, 1776. Wolcott also wrote a brief letter to his wife this day enclosing news of the May 10 and 15 resolves on establishing new governments and speculating on his possible return home. "By the Enclosed you will perceive that a Revolution in Government is recommended—to swear Allegiance to and Act under an Authority which had not only cast us out of it's Protection but for so long a Time has been carrying on the Most cruel War against us, was tho't not only Absurd but impious. . . . When I shall Return is Very uncertain. But yet I hope to make my Family a Visit the latter End of July or the beginning of August." Wolcott to Laura Wolcott, May 16, 1776. Wolcott Papers, CtHi.

John Adams to Abigail Adams

May 17. 1776

I have this Morning heard Mr. Duffil upon the Signs of the Times. He run a Parrallell between the Case of Israel and that of America, and between the Conduct of Pharaoh and that of George.

Jealousy that the Israelites would throw off the Government of Egypt made him issue his Edict that the Midwives should cast the Children into the River, and the other Edict that the Men should make a large Revenue of Brick without Straw. He concluded that the Course of Events, indicated strongly the Design of Providence that We should be seperated from G. Britain, &c.

Is it not a Saying of Moses, who am I, that I should go in and out before this great People? When I consider the great Events which are passed, and those greater which are rapidly advancing, and that I may have been instrumental of touching some Springs, and turning some small Wheels, which have had and will have such Effects, I feel an Awe upon my Mind, which is not easily described.

G B has at last driven America, to the last Step, a compleat Seperation from her, a total absolute Independence, not only of her Parliament but of her Crown, for such is the Amount of the Resolve of the 15th.[1]

Confederation among ourselves, or Alliances with foreign Nations are not necessary, to a perfect Seperation from Britain. That is effected by extinguishing all Authority, under the Crown, Parliament and Nation as the Resolution for instituting Governments, has done, to all Intents and Purposes. Confederation will be necessary for our internal Concord, and Alliances may be so for our external Defence.

I have Reasons to believe that no Colony, which shall assume a Government under the People, will give it up. There is something very unnatural and odious in a Government 1000 Leagues off. An whole Government of our own Choice, managed by Persons whom We love, revere, and can confide in, has charms in it for which Men will fight. Two young Gentlemen from South Carolina, now in this City, who were in Charlestown when their new Constitution was promulgated, and when their new Governor and Council and Assembly walked out in Procession, attended by the Guards, Company of Cadetts, Light Horse &c., told me, that they were beheld by the People with Transports and Tears of Joy. The People gazed at them, with a Kind of Rapture. They both told me, that the Reflection that these were Gentlemen whom they all loved, esteemed and revered, Gentlemen of their own Choice, whom they could trust, and whom they could displace if any of them should behave amiss, affected them so that they could not help crying.

They say their People will never give up this Government.

One of these Gentlemen is a Relation of yours, a Mr. Smith, son of Mr. Thomas Smith. I shall give him this Letter or another to you.

A Privateer fitted out here by Coll. Roberdeau and Major Bayard, since our Resolves for Privateering, I am this Moment informed, has taken a valuable Prize. This is Encouragement, at the Beginning.

In one or two of your Letters you remind me to think of you as I ought. Be assured there is not an Hour in the Day, in which I do not think of you as I ought, that is with every Sentiment of Tenderness, Esteem, and Admiration.

RC (MHi). Adams, *Family Correspondence* (Butterfield), 1:410–11.
[1] See John Adams to James Warren, May 15, 1776.

Carter Braxton to Landon Carter

Philaa May 17 1776.

Dr Sir.

I did myself the Honor to write to you & my friend Bob about six weeks since in answer to your two friendly Letters & directed them Via Hobs Hole; but from a hint sent me by Coll Frank you had not recd them.[1] For this accident I am truly sorry because I had written with freedom for your private Inspection upon some facts not intended or proper for the publick Eye, and as that Letter would serve as a Key to my future ones. Unwilling farther to trust your host I have postponed writing again untill Mr Glascock should return from hence, where by the bye he has staid much longer than was expected. However he has waited to convey you a very important declaration & recommendation from the Congress, which you will say falls little short of Independence.[2] It was not so understood by Congress but I find those out of doors on both sides the question construe it in that manner. The Assumption of Governt. was necessary & to that resolution little Objection was made, but when the Preamble was reported much heat and debate did ensue for two or three Days. At length I think by 6 to 4 it was determined to be accepted & accordingly published.[3] Maryland withdrew after having desired in vain a Copy of the proceedings & their dissent; and gave us to understand they should not return nor deem our farther Resolutions obligatory, untill they had transmitted an Acct. of their Proceedings to their Convention & had their Instructions how to act or conduct themselves upon this alarming Occasion.[4] This Event is waited for with Impatience and while it is in agitation the Assembly of this Province will meet and it is not impossible but they may join in this extraordinary proceeding. What then will be the Consequence God only knows.

It will surely have this effect if *some Men* were capable of Conviction, to convince them of the great danger of Rashness & precipitancy.

It was seen & known that these & other Colonies could not consistent with their Instructions come into this measure and all knew that they would be recalled if Commissioners did not soon arrive or if when arrived their terms were not free & honourable. In this Case America with one united Voice would have joined hand in hand to repell the haughty Invaders & to have rejected with disdain their future Superiority. But the wise Men of the East & some from the *South* thought it a reprehensible delay which might give a turn to their favourite plan & defeat those pursuits they had so nearly compleated and the plan for which they had so wisely & so long laid down in their own Minds. It may and I presume will be objected to the Preamble that it is not altogether candid nor true. For it is well known & has even been in print, that the same Captain who brought an Acct. of the twelve thousand Hessians going to Boston with the other Armaments for different parts of America also said that twenty seven Commissioners were coming over at the same time and that the People of England had expressed great Uneasiness at the Number of Forces coming over agt. us which nothing could satisfy but an Assurance that the Persons appointed would undoubtedly make Peace. To suppress this & insert the other in my Judgmt. was not candid. Nor was it right to insert the worst part of an act without giving the substance of the whole, which I own is bad enough but not so bad as the part handed out to the People.

Deception is what at all events we should avoid, as we are about to determine the fate & fortunes of Millions who have placed the most implicit Confidence in us. That a Seperation will take place seems almost evident.

But in my Judgment there are a number of Precautions which should precede it. A Naval Alliance to protect our trade must be requisite, yet this is not obtained, nor do we know what friends we can procure. Our own Fleet is trifling as yet & before it will increase I fear some of them will fall into the Enemys Hands, as they are every where sought after & if seen will be taken. A Continental League was surely indespensable, & so was a Union of the Colonies. Justice has long since called forth for equal Representation here that the Wealth of the great Colonies might not be disposed of by Men who represent scarcely any Colony at all & who with all the pedantic Impudence will harangue us for Hours upon their Importance.

These with a variety of other things seemed absolutely necessary to me.

As I had long foreseen the Necessity of taking up Governt. in our Colony particularly, I had thrown my thoughts together on that Subject for yr Convention a Pamphlett containing which I send you & beg your opinion of it.[5] As it is the first Essay of a poor Genius unassisted by a good Education you will shew it all the Indulgence in yr Power & allow much for the Zeal of the Author, who wishes nothing so ardently as to see his Country happy & flourishing. We have no certain Accts. from Canada nor any of the arrival of Troops to the Northward tho daily expected. I fear you will say that tho you meant to get a Letter now & then from me you did not expect to have your patience tryed by such long Letters. Therefore I will appologize for this & be done when I have asured you of my regard for yr Family & my desire that you will make it known to them & that with all respect I am Sir, your affece Nephew,

Carter Braxton

[*P.S.*] Mrs. Braxton begs me to add her Respects to you & Family.

RC (MeHi).
    [1] See Braxton to Landon Carter, April 14, 1776. Braxton's letter to Robert Wormeley Carter has not been found.
    [2] See *JCC*, 4:342, 357–58; and John Adams to James Warren, May 15, 1776.
    [3] The only other surviving contemporary testimony on this vote is contained in the May 15, 1776, diary entry of James Allen, a Philadelphia lawyer who was not a delegate, in which he reported that the preamble carried by a vote of 7 to 4. If Braxton's recollection is correct, the alignment of the colonies on the motion was probably: New Hampshire, Massachusetts, Rhode Island, Connecticut, Virginia, and South Carolina in favor; New York, New Jersey, Delaware, and North Carolina opposed; and Pennsylvania and Maryland abstaining. If, however, Allen can be relied upon, the motion was probably supported by the six colonies listed above plus North Carolina (Joseph Hewes), with Pennsylvania voting in opposition. Georgia delegates Button Gwinnett and Lyman Hall did not attend until May 20. See *JCC*, 4:367; and "Diary of James Allen, Esq., of Philadelphia,

Counsellor-at-Law, 1770–1778," *PMHB* 9 (July 1885): 187. For additional information on Hewes' position on this issue, suggesting that he supported men of
Richard Henry Lee's persuasion in behalf of more vigorous measures leading in
the direction of independence, see Richard Henry Lee to Thomas Ludwell Lee,
May 28, 1776, note 4.

⁴ For additional information on the reaction of the Maryland delegates to the
congressional resolutions of May 10 and 15 advising reorganization of provincial
governments, see Thomas Stone to James Hollyday?, May 20, 1776. See also the
Maryland Delegates to the Maryland Council of Safety, June 11, 1776, for their
response to Richard Henry Lee's proposed resolutions of June 7, which confronted
them with a similar dilemma and led them to call upon the council of safety to
reconvene the Maryland Convention at once.

⁵ Carter Braxton, *An Address to the Convention of the Colony and Ancient
Dominion of Virginia; on the Subject of Government in General, and Recommending a Particular Form to their Confederation* (Philadelphia: John Dunlap, 1776).

Samuel Chase to Richard Henry Lee

Dear Sir.   Montreal, May 17. 1776
   I thank You for your Letter of the 3rd of April which Mcfinie
delivered Me last Tuesday.¹ Our Letters to Congress will give You
all the Information in our Power relative to our Affairs in this
Colony.
   I am at a Loss to express my Astonishmt. at the Conduct of
Congress. Almost two Months ago they voted 4 Battalions, and since
6 more Battalions for this Country, without the least provisions for
their Support.
   We have now 4,000 Troops in Canada & not a Mouthful of food.
Pork is not to be procured. Wheat may be bought for Specie, but
we have none. Necessity has compelled Us to take provisions. Will
this contribute to regain the Affections of this people? I entirely
agree with You as to the Importance of fortifying the pass at De
Chambault. On the Day after We arrived, it was determined to
possess that post and Jacques Cartier—but how can it be done? On
Tuesday Colo. Maxwell was at Jacques Cartier with a small force,
and Genl. Thomas was at De Chambault with 900 Men. They have
none or very little provisions. They have no Cannon or a few pieces
without Carriages (the greater part of the Carriages fell into the
Enemies Hands) and they have but little powder. Eight Tons came
with Us, We lost one, but can get no certain account of the rest.
Nothing is wanting but a Wind for the Enemies frigates to pass the
falls of Richlieu, & then all Communication by water will be cut
off.
   General Arnolds Letter will give You all we know of our
affairs below. I beg You would seriously attend to our Letters to
Congress. Our affairs here are almost desperate. Unless immediate
attention is given to this Country it will not only be lost to Us, but

added to the Enemy. For the Love of your Country cease the keen Encounter of your Tongues, discard your Tongue Artillery and send Us some field or We are undone. My God, an Army of 10,00o without provisions or powder! Remember our Army are naked, I mean the fugitives from Quebec.

I hope I shall be excused in Saying the Congress are not a fit Body to act as a Council of War. They are too large, too slow and their Resolutions can never be kept secret. Pray divide your Business into different Departments, a War office, a Treasury Board, et et. Follow the British Regulation as to your Army. They have not one officer too many. There must be a regimental paymaster. I am not able to point out the Remedy, but I see our affairs in so miserable a Condition, that I think they are almost desperate.

Since the above Mr. McCord, of Credit, arrived here; he left Loretto on Monday, he was told by some French people, our friends, who came out of Quebec on Sunday, that only one frigate & one Transport with only two Companies of the 29th Regiment, had arrived there from Halifax; that they came to see if the City was taken; that it was reported in the City, that Genl. Howe & his Army would come there—that there was no account of more ships arrived below. He left Jacques Cartier on Tuesday afternoon; our Troops had left it the Sunday before, he got to De Chambault on Tuesday night; our Troops had left it on Monday. He arrived at Three Rivers Wesday at 4 oClock P.M. That Genl. Thomas was there, that the Canadians in general were friendly—he was told the frigate that came in, lies in the Bason of Quebec. That he saw two small vessells at anchor at Aux Ecurueil, abot. 3 Leagues below the Rapids.

Mr. Murdock Steward, a Gent. of veracity—he left Three Rivers yesday Morning, the 16th, That Genl. Thomas was there with about 1000 Men.

I have been called at least twenty Times since I began this Scrawl —to act as Commissary, Genl, Justice, et et—in short I act in as many Capacities as Moliers Cook. Farewell, tell Mr. J. Adams he is indebted to Me several Letters. Your affectionate & obedt. Servt.

Saml Chase

[*P.S.*] Mr Carroll desires his Compliments.

RC (ViU).
¹ Not found.

Commissioners to Canada to John Hancock

Sir   Montreal May 17th. 1776
    Doctor Franklin who left this place the 11th Instt. will give you

the fullest information of the state of our Affairs in this Province. We are sorry to say that they have not mended Since the Doctors departure. We want words to describe the confusion which prevails thro' every department relating to the Army, Several of your Officers appear to us unfit for the Stations they fill, your troops live from hand to Mouth, they have of late been put to half allowance in several places and in some they have been without pork for 3 or 4 days past. Altho' there is plenty of Wheat & flour in the Country it was with difficulty that either could be procured a few days ago even for ready Specie. But from Gen. Arnolds Letters dated the 15th instant from the Mouth of the Sorrell and which we forwarded yesterday to G. Schuyler we have reason to conclude that the Army will not want flour much longer. In our present critical situation few, very few will accept of the Continental paper money in payt. A prosperous turn in our Affairs would we think give it a currency in that part of the Country which we possess, the most valuable and plentiful in Canada.

We think it impossible to subsist your forces in Canada in any other manner than by contract; careful, active & trusty Commissaries should be appointed to receive from the Contractors, and to deliver out to the Army the provisions which they Supply. Your Generals are now obliged to be contractors & Commissaries and your Commissioners who have neither Abilities or Inclination, are constrained to act as Generals. Such is the confusion which now prevails and will prevail till a total new arrangement takes place, and a strict discipline is introduced into the Army; of the latter you must dispair unless Soldiers can be inlisted for a Term of Years or the Continueance of the War. The inlisting Men for a Year, or for a less time occasioned the Death of the brave Montgomery, the recent disgraceful flight, & is the principal Source of all the disorders in your Army. The sending Soldiers into Canada whose times expire in a Month or two after their arrival is only putting the Colonies to an amazing Expence, to corrupt & disorder the rest; no duty must be expected from Soldiers whose times are out, let their Country stand eversomuch in need of their Services; witness the unfeeling flight, & return at this critical juncture of all the Soldiers and greater part of the Officers who are intitled to be discharged. Warners Regiment was inlisted for a Month only, his Conduct as to the Bounty Money has been communicated to Congress by Genl Schuyler. Immediately on the arrival of the New England Troops at the Camp they innoculated themselves contrary to the Generals Orders, and we are informed have done little or no Duty.

We shall take the Liberty of mentioning two Circumstances which shew the present state of Discipline amongst your forces. Colo. Campbell brot us the first account of the pricipitate flight of our Army. Colo. Bedel who Commands at the Cedars a post of great consequence abt 36 miles from this City up the St. Laurence being informed by two Indians that a body of Savages about 100 headed by some English Soldiers number unknown, were come within 9 miles of his Post with an intention to attack it, brought this intelligence himself to town and left his garrison consistg. of 300 effective Men. It is true according to his Accot. they were badly provided to receive the enemy & had been 4 days without any other provisions than bread; this Intelligence we conceive might have been communicated to the Commanding Officer here, by any other person, as well as Colonel Bedel. Col. Paterson who now commands in Montreal, immediately ordered a detachment from his Regt. of 150 Men to reinforce the Cedars. A fresh Supply of provisions & Amunition was sent with the detachment. We apprehend the report to be altogether groundless or occasioned by some very triffling circumstance. The importance of this Colony will be made known to you by Docr. Franklin, it is a fine Wheat Country, it produced in 1771 for exportation 4 hundred & 60 thousand bushels of Wheat. The Indian Trade is an object already sufficient to engage the attention of the Colonies & growing yearly of more importance. The inclinations of the common people are sd to be in general with us, but they are timorous & unsteady, no assistance can be expected from them unless they find themselves supported by an army able to cope with the English Forces. Should we be driven out of the Country, we make no doubt considerable numbers of them, would be prevailed on thro' fear to join the British Troops. We refer you for intelligence relating to the State of our Army below to Genl. Arnolds letters above mentioned which we make no doubt Genl. Schuyler has forwarded to Congress.

Necessity has compelled Us to desire a Mr. Wm. McCarty to execute the Office of Deputy Quarter Master Genl. and we hope Congress will send that Gentleman a Commission of this Date.[1] Our Generals here exercise the power of Appointing Officers but we have not nor do we remember that they have any such powers. We flatter Ourselves Congress will excuse our Exceeding our Commission in such Instances where the public Good requires it.

In the present situation of our Affairs it will not be possible for us to carry into execution the great Object of our instructions, as the possession of this country must finally be decided by the Sword; we think our stay here no longer of service to the public. We are however willing to sacrifice our time, labour, and even our lives for the good of our Country and we wait with Impatience the further orders of Congress and are with great respect, for yourself & Congress, Sir, Your most Obedt., humble Servants,

Samuel Chase

Ch. Carroll of Carrollton

RC (DNA: PCC, item 166). In a clerical hand and signed by Carroll and Chase.

Received and read in Congress, June 10, 1776. *JCC*, 5:428.
  [1] There is no evidence in the journals that Congress ever confirmed this appointment.

Commissioners to Canada to Philip Schuyler

Dear Sir,   Montreal 17th May 1776
    The following intelligence was communicated to us about an hour ago & we think may be depended on.
    John McChord Left Loretto in sight of Quebeck on Monday last; He was told by French people who came out of Quebeck on Sunday, only two companies arrived of the 29th regiment, one frigate, and one Transport from Hallifax on that day week; no account of more below. McChord left Jacques Cartier on Tuesday afternoon, our troops had left it on Sunday, he got to Dechambault Tuesday night; our troops left Dechambault Monday. He arrived at three Rivers on Wednesday P.M. General Thomas then there with about 1000 Men: says he saw 2 small vessels at Ecurueils 3 leagues below the Rapids of Richelieu: he was told the frigate arrived lies in the bason of Quebeck; it was reported in town she was only sent to see if the city was taken, if not that Gen. Howe & his army was to come there.
    At present we procure a little fresh Provision. We intend to the mouth of the Sorel where our army is collected. We have no fixed abode being obliged to follow your example & become Generals, commissaries, justices of the peace, in short to act in twenty different capacities. Things are in great confusion, but out [of] confusion we hope order will rise. We have heard nothing to day from the Cedars, from whence we conclude that report brought by Colonel Bedel is groundless.
    Press Congress to send paper money as well as specie, let the bills be small. Do not forget to send Pork Sufficient for the support of the army here, ammunition, powder &c; but the Generals no doubt will write for Such articles in the military as are more immediately wanted. A gondola built to carry a 24 pounder, or two of them, would now be exceedingly Serviceable. By what time could you finish one? Pray fit out the Royal Savage & the other vessel as Speedily as possible for War to keep the mastery of lake Champlain. Pray send back the batteau which Docr. Franklin & Mr. Carroll returned & remember us most affectionately to them. We desire our respectful complts to your family and are with great Sincerity & regard, Dr. Sir, Yr. most obt. hum. Servts.
                                        Samuel Chase
                                        Ch. Carroll of Carrollton

RC (NN). Written by Carroll and signed by Carroll and Chase.

John Hancock to Thomas Cushing

My Dear Sir   Philada. 17th May 1776
    I wait with the greatest Impatience to hear from you on the Subject of my late Letters, surely they must have got to hand. The Bills I wrote you I was to pay as soon as you Advis'd me of their being honour'd, you have never wrote me the fate of, & I in honour have been oblig'd to pay them, if to my own Loss I can't help it. Pray let me regularly hear from you. I paid Mr Barrell as you Desir'd for the Flour, & have also paid your Bill for 700 Dolls. I shall Send you some more money next Week.
    For News Refer you to my Publick Letter to the Assembly.[1] I hope Gates & Mifflin will soon be in Boston to Command, the former is made Major Genl., the latter Brigr.
    Inclos'd is the paper which [will] afford you a Resolve, that will at least afford some Conversation, If it is not Independence, it looks a good deal like it, we must Come to it.
    Remember me to all friends. Dont forget my Military Department in the Province. I am exceeding fond of it, & will if honor'd with that Command exert myself to the utmost, pray let it be Settled soon, I long to be improv'd in that way. Let me know the particulars of the Elections when they take place.
    I have no receipt for the last Money.
    Adieu. I am greatly Distress'd on the Melancholy Event of the Death of my Dear Aunt, she died very suddenly at Fairfield. How shall I Conduct as to her will, I do not Chuse to Send it down for fear of Accidents, will it do to Send it hereafter, do Advise me about it.
    My & Mrs Hancocks best Respects to Mrs Cushing, Miss Peggy, Mr & Mrs Avery & yourself & Connections. I am truly, your Real Friend & very hum   John Hancock

[P.S.] I have Remov'd into a noble House in an Airy open place, in Arch Street corner of Fourth Street, where I shall be Glad to See you. I have a Bed for you. I have wrote by order of Congress to Genl Washington for him to Come to this City for a few days to Consult.[2]

RC (MHi: Society for the Preservation of New England Antiquities deposit).
    [1] See John Hancock to the Massachusetts Assembly, May 16, 1776.
    [2] For a discussion of Hancock's invitation to General Washington, see Hancock to Washington, May 16, 1776, note 3.

Joseph Hewes to James Iredell

Dear Sir   Philadelphia 17th May 1776
    This being a day of humiliation, fasting and prayer (or in Vulgar

language Congress Sunday)[1] I mean to steal as much time from my
private devotions as will serve to acknowledge the receipt of your
agreeable favour of the 29th ultimo [2] which has just reached me.
Complaints of distresses made to our friends it is said is some allevi-
ation of them. I cannot say the observation is true, however I must
complain a little, an obstinate ague & Fever or rather an intermitting
Fever persecutes me continually. I have no way to remove it unless
I retire from Congress and from public business, this I am determined
not to do till No. Carolina sends a further delegation provided I am
able to crawl to the Congress Chamber. So much for self, a little
politicks and I have done. Much of our time is employed in raising
Men, making Cannon, Muskets & money, finding out ways & means
of supplying our Troops with Cloaths, provisions & amunition. We
appear to have everything we want. We resolve to raise regiments,
resolve to make Cannon, resolve to make & import muskets, powder
and Cloathing, but it is a melancholly truth that near half of our
men, Cannon, muskets, powder, Clothe &c is to be found no where
but on paper. We are not discouraged at this, if our Situation was
ten times worse I would not agree to give up our cause. To the whole
force of Great Britain has been added near half of Germany, 25,000
Hessians, Waldeckers and others have been expected for some time
past, indeed the report of this day is, that a large detachment of them
with the Commissioners are arived at Halifax in Nova Scotia. The
latter, it is said are coming here to treat with Congress, in the
mean time the former are to wait the event of the Treaty; if it suc-
ceeds not, they are to spread the horror and devastations of War
from one end of the Continent to the other. Whither this be true
or only the lye of the day I know not. It is too true that a great
number of those Germans are taken into British pay. I have not
heard any thing from your Congress at Halifax since the 22d of April.
I am anxious to know how they go on in forming a Constitution,
and more Anxious to know how they defend their Country, for I
expect a formal attack has been made on it before this day. This you
will receive by Mr Louther to whom I must refer you, he is just from
head quarters and will be able to give you some acco. of our army.
My Compliments to Mrs. Iredell & Mrs Blair. You and they have
always the best wishes of, Dear Sir, your much obliged, & very
huml Servt,   Joseph Hewes

RC (InU).
[1] Friday, May 17, had been declared a fast day pursuant to a resolution adopted
on March 16, 1776. See *JCC*, 4:201, 208–9.
[2] This letter is in *N.C. Colonial Records*, 10:1035–37.

Thomas Jefferson to John Page

Dear Page   Philadelphia May. 17. 1776.
    Having arrived here but lately I have little to communicate. I

have been so long out of the political world that I am almost a new man in it. You will have heard before this reaches you of the naval engagement in the Delaware. There are letters in town it is said from General Sullivan which inform that the lower town of Quebec is taken and a breach made in the wall of the upper; but I do not know myself that there are such letters; and if there be, whether Sullivan mentions his intelligence as authentic, as he could not then have reached Quebec himself. As to the articles of salt, blankets &c. every colony I beleive will be to shift for itself, as I see nothing but the measure of a foreign alliance which can promise a prospect of importing either, and for that measure several colonies, and some of them weighty, are not yet quite ripe. I hope ours is and that they will tell us so. But as to salt it is a shame we should say a word about it; the means of supplying the world with it is so much in our power, that nothing but the indolence of Southern constitutions could suffer themselves to be in danger of want. Mr. Innis tells me Gwatkin's books are left with Molly Digges for sale. I should be much obliged to you if you could procure and send me here a catalogue of them; and in the mean time purchase two of them which I recollect he had and have long wished to get; Histoire des Celtes de Pelloutier. 2. vols. 12mo. and Observations on Gardening printed by Payne, London. 8vo. For their cost I will get you to apply to Colo. Nelson to whom I can refund it here. This office will perhaps remind you of a box of books you have of mine which I am in hope some of the military or commissary's waggons will furnish you with an opportunity of sending to Albemarle, to Richmond, or to Mr. Eppes's in Charles City. Adieu.

May. 19. 1776. For the melancholy reverse of the Quebec news received yesterday I must refer you to Nelson.[1] For our disappointment in the office of director to the hospital, to Innis who will be with you soon, and will give yourself and Mc.lurgh a full account in what manner we were surprised out of it.[2]

RC (NN). Jefferson, *Papers* (Boyd), 1:293–94.

[1] See Jefferson to Thomas Nelson, May 19, 1776.

[2] Letters of John Page and James McClurg to Jefferson, dated April 6, 1776, and asking Jefferson to use his influence to secure McClurg's appointment as "Physician to the Continental Forces in Virginia," are in Jefferson, *Papers* (Boyd), 1:286–87. Although William Rickman was appointed director and chief physician of the hospital in Virginia on May 18, McClurg did become surgeon general of Virginia state troops in 1777. See *JCC*, 4:364.

Robert R. Livingston to John Jay

Dear John   Philadelphia 17th May 1776.
I was so unfortunate as to miss the last post by which means I was

prevented from letting you hear what I had done about geting you lodgings at Bristol, & the important business that had been transacted here before I arrived. I could not find a tolerable house in Bristol, the rooms that were unoccupied were all too small & hot for invalids, & there was no house that could furnish more than two so that we could not have been together, tho' had the rooms been tolerable we might have made out by taking two adjoyning houses had not one of the landlady's nose placed such an obstruction in my way as my regard for Your future posterity rendered it impossible for me to get over. However I have provided three Bed rooms & a large parlour in a retired country house, about two miles from Bristol upon the banks of the Shamony where we shall have plentiful provision for our horses, good fishing before the door, a tavern about a $\frac{1}{4}$ of a mile from us to lodge our friends, & in short every thing that we can wish to render our situation agreeable. The lodgings are to be entered upon next Wednesday, by which time I hope to see you & Mrs. Jay there. It is absolutely necessary you shd. come to settle the arrangement of our family And (what is much more important) to settle another arrangement which I most heartily wish we could unite in making. Mr. Duane tells me he has enclosed you a copy of the resolution of the 15th.[1] I make no observations on it in this place for fear of accidents. It had occationed a great alarm here, & the anxtious folk are very fearful of its being attended with many ill consequences next week when the Assembly are to meet. Some points of the last importance are to be agitated (as we imagine) very early, I wish to God you could be here. If you do not get this length meet me at least at Bristol next week from whence you may return in a few days & send some of our delegates as the province will otherwise be often unrepresented, since I find it inconsistent with my health to be close in my attendance in Congress. You have by this time sounded our people, I hope they are satisfied of the necessity of assuming a new form of Government. Let me hear (if you dont come yourself) in what channel it will probably run. Let me know the mode in which new powers (for the old are insufficient) are to be obtained. If by a dissolution it will be necessary to go home. Let me also know in what sphere you yourself chuse to move. You are so necessary here, that I will consent to no law which will make the honours I wish you to possess inconsistent with your attendance on Congress.

I have a thought which if carried into execution might render ours the favourite colony, & dispute the absurd claims of our neighbours, which may hereafter be very troublesome, but it requires much consideration, & may perhaps be impracticable. I will reserve it (with other of my reveries) till one of those happy hours in which I permit myself to think aloud in your hearing.

If you should see Benson it would not be amiss to let him know that I am a little hurt at his conduct, it may induce him to alter it

without my coming to an explanation which might possibly occasion
a coolness which I wish to avoid.

Farewell, may heaven bless you, & put an end to these devils which
break in so cruelly upon our domestick enjoyments, & ever render
our reflection on past pleasures, the most agreeable part of our
present friendship. Your friend &c.,   R R Livingston

RC (NNC). Addressed: "To Coll. John Jay, New York."
   [1] See James Duane to John Jay, May 16, 1776, note.

Caesar Rodney to Thomas Rodney

Sir   Philadelphia May 17th 1776
   Inclosed I have Sent you the printed Copy of the Resolution of
Congress mentioned in my last.[1] Most of those here who are Termed
the Cool Considerate Men think it amounts to a declaration of In-
dependance. It Certainly Savour's of it, but you will See and Judge
for Your Self. In the Evening-Post of Yesterday there is the following
Paragraph under the New-York head, dated May the 15th 1776—
"An Express Arrived here on Munday Evening from the Nothern
Army, who brought Letters from Generals Schuyler & Sullivan Which
Mention that our people had possessed and destroyed part of the
Lower Town of Quebec, and made a breach in the Walls of the
Upper Town." [2] Yesterday, for the first time since I came to Town, I
Was Confined to my Room all day by fit of the Astma, but now
bravely again am Yours &c   Caesar Rodney

P.S. I have inclosed and directed to you one Copy of the Resolution
for your Self, one for Coll. Haslet, one for Doctr. Tilton and one
for Doctr. McCall.   C. R.

RC (NjR: Elsie O. and Philip D. Sang deposit, 1972).
   [1] *JCC*, 4:342, 357–58.
   [2] For the reception of contrary news, see Rodney to Thomas Rodney, May 18,
1776.

William Whipple to Meschech Weare

Sir,   Philadelphia 17th May 1776
   The inclos'd Resolution of Congress [1] shod. have gone yesterday,
but I had sent off my letter before I discoverd the Omission. Congress
have reservd to themselves the appointment of Field Officers, but they
are nominated by the Assembly, Convention, or Committee of the
Colony where the Regiments are rais'd, it will therefore be necessary

that the names of the field officers shod. be transmitted here in order that the Commissions may be fill'd up, the President will forward to you the Blank Commissions for the other officers.[2] When I think of the number of men & Arms gone from the Eastern Colonies, I cannot help feeling for their scituation if a powerful attack shod be made there, but doubt not proper steps are taken to furnish arms, I think every Person who can do any thing towards making Arms shod. be employed in that Business. Britain will no doubt exert her utmost efforts for our destruction, but if they are repulsed in the manner I expect this Campaign, I am very confident they never will atempt another. This Summer will in all probability be the warmest America ever saw. May the Supreme Governour of the Universe Protect, & Defend us, Guide our Councils & Prosper our Arms.

I am with Great Respect, Your Most Obt. Servt,

Wm Whipple

May 18. Coll Bartlett arrivd last Evening very much Fatigued.

RC (PPRF).
  [1] See JCC, 4:357.
  [2] On June 12 the New Hampshire Assembly nominated James Hackett, Thomas Tash, and David Copp as field officers for the battalion. N.H. State Papers, 8:141.

John Adams to James Warren

My dear sir   May 18. 1776

Yours of 8 May recd this Morning,[1] and am as I ever have been much of your opinion that the Enemy would return to the Massachusetts if possible. They will probably land at Hingham or Braintree, or somewhere to the Northward of Boston, not make a direct Attempt upon Boston it self, the next Time. I hope no Pains, no Labour or expence will be neglected to fortify the Harbour of Boston however. Your Militia you say is in a broken state, but dont explain what you mean. I was in hopes that the late Militia Law had put them in a Good Condition. You must depend upon them chiefly. We have been labouring here to procure you Some assistance, and have obtaind a Vote, that the 5 Battallions now with you be filled up, and three Additional ones raised, two in Mass., one in Connecticutt. A Major General and Brigadier are to go to Boston. You must not hesitate at any Thing for your own Defence. New York and Canada will take an infinite Expence. We did our best, but could procure no more at present. If an Impression should be made on you, the Continent will interpose, but they never will believe it untill it takes Place.

This Day has brought us the Dismals from Canada.[2] Defeated most ignominiously. Where shall We lay the blame? America duped and bubbled with the Phantom of Commissioners, has been fast asleep and left that important Post undefended, unsupported. The Ministry have caught the Colonies, as I have often caught a Horse, by holding out an empty Hat, as if it was full of Corn or as many a Sportsman has shot Wood cockes, by making an old Horse Stalk before him, and hide him from the sight of the Bird. Nothing has ever put my Patience to the Tryal so much as to see Knaves imposing upon Fools, by such artifices. I wash my Hands of this Guilt. I have reasoned, I have ridiculed, I have fretted, and declaimed, against this fatal Delusion, from the Beginning. But a Torrent is not to be impeded by Reasoning nor a Storm allayed by Ridicule. In my situation, altho I have not and will not be restrained from a Freedom of Speech yet a Decorum must be observed, and ever has been by me. But I have often wished that all America knew, as much as I do of the Springs of Action and the Motives of the Machine. I do not think it prudent, nor Safe to write freely upon those Subjects even to my most faithfull Friends.

Providence has hitherto preserved us, and I firmly believe will continue to do so. But it gives me inexpressible Grief that by our own Folly, and Wickedness, We should deserve it so very ill as we do.

What shall We Say of this Scandalous Flight from Quebec? It seems to be fated that New England officers should not support a Character. Wooster is the object now of Contempt, and Detestation, of those who ought to be the Contempt and Detestation of all America for their indefatigable Obstruction to every Measure which has been meditated, for the Support of our Power in Canada. Our Province must find Some way of making better officers, and of ingaging abler Men, in her Councils as well as her Arms or I know not what will be the Consequence, instead of which she Seems to me to be contriving Means to drive every Man of real Abilities out of her service.

I hope you will not decline the Appointment you mention however —nothing would make me so happy as your Acceptance of that Place.[3] I am extreamly unhappy to hear of your ill Health—Hope that will mend. There is certainly no Man in the Province who would be so agreable to me. I cant bear the Thought of your refusing.

Rejoice to hear that my Friends Crafts and Trott are in the service. Will it do to promote my Pupil Austin? His Genius is equal to any Thing—would not promotion mend him of his Faults. Can nothing be done for Ward, Aid de Camp and Secretary to General Ward? He is an honest, faithfull, daring Man, I think, and Sensible enough. He really deserves Promotion.

Is it possible to get in Boston silver and Gold for the service in Canada? Our Affairs have been ruined there for want of it, and can never be retrieved without it. Pray let me know if any sum can be had in our Province.

I shall inclose you a News Paper, which when you have read send along to Braintree.

I am and have been these twelve Months, fully of your opinion that We have nothing to depend upon for our Preservation from Destruction, but the kind Assistance of Heaven to our own Union and vigorous Exertions. I was ripe therefore for as explicit Declarations as Language could express Twelve Months ago. But the Colonies seperately have neglected their Duty, as much as the Congress, and We cannot march faster than our Constituents will follow us. We dont always go quick enough to keep out of their Way.

RC (MHi). In Adams' hand, though not signed.
[1] Warren's May 8 letter to Adams is in *Warren-Adams Letters,* 1:339–41.
[2] See Commissioners to Canada to John Hancock, May 10, 1776, which reached Congress this day; and *JCC,* 4:362. Adams' colleague Robert Treat Paine made the following entry in his diary this day: "Rainy. By Express heard a Reinforcement had arrived at Quebec of 2 Men of Warr & 2 Frigates, & that our Army had retired. Dined at Mr Hancocks." MHi.
[3] That is, as a justice of the Massachusetts Superior Court of Judicature.

Josiah Bartlett to Mary Bartlett

My Dear   Philadelphia May 18th 1776
Yesterday afternoon I arrived here in good health, after a very fatigueing Journey. The weather has been, this week, uncommonly hot and Coming so suddenly after the Cold weather made it very uncomfortable both to horse & man. I wrote you by Col Gale which no Doubt you have Recd. After I left him I went by Norwich & New London to New Haven; went to meeting Sunday afternoon at Brandford, and rode after meeting to New Haven; on Monday rode from New Haven to Horseneck Tuesday morning. I understood the Eastern post was to Call there that morning & Breakfast, which I thought was a good opportunity to write to you, but while I was in another room writing & sealing a Letter he Came, left his papers and was gone. So I was Disappointed of Sending it at last. When I got to New York on Tuesday I found that General Sullivan and all the New Hampshire Regiments were Marched off for Canada, the two last Regiments had been gone about a fortnight. The account of the Roebuck & Liverpool men of war Coming up Deleware within 30 miles of this City & the Engagement of the Philadelphia Gondalos with them you will no Doubt See in the news papers.[1] The Gondalos had much the advantage of the men of war & obliged them to Sheer off; when the men of war were Coming up the people here were much frighted & many of them Sent out their goods into the Country.

The Congress have Sent out a General Recommendation to all the Colonies to take up a new form of Government.

You Desired me to write you how much forwarder the Spring was this way than with us; the people all the way as I Came Complain of the Backwardness of the Spring till this week. At the South part of Connecticut last Monday the apple trees were in full Blossom, peach trees & Cherry trees out of the Blossom: from New York to this City the trees all out of the Blossom & Cherries of Some Bigness, the winter Rye Eared out to its full heighth. However the people all the way were planting Indian Corn. I want to hear from you & in particular from Lieut Pearson. Hope one or more of your letters are on the road here. I shall now Constantly write to you Every week and at present Direct them to be left at Newbury Port. Tell Mrs Burbank that the Regiment her son is in was Encamped at Some Distance from New York so that I could not See him, but I Saw a Captain that Belonged to the Same Encampment and I Gave him the letter & he promised me to find him out & give him the letter. The Company where Mr. Flagg's Son is was Stationed at Stratton [Staten] Island four or five miles from New York but I took the best Care to Convey it to him. I am, yours &c,   Josiah Bartlett

RC (NhHi).
[1] See Marine Committee to John Barry, May 8, 1776.

James Duane to John Jay

Philad 18 May 1776

I wrote you, my dear Sir, a hasty Scrawl by the post on a most important Subject.[1] You know the Maryland Instructions and those of Pennsylvania. I am greatly in doubt whether either of their Assemblies or Conventions will listen to a Recommendation the preamble of which so openly avows Independance & Seperation. The lower Counties will probably adhere to Pensylvania. New Jersey you can form a good Judgment of from the Reception this important Resolution has met with. The orators of Virginia with Col. Henry at their Head are against a Change of Government. The Body of the People, Col. Nelson, on whose Authority you Hint, thinks are for it. The late Election of Deputies for the Convention of New York sufficiently proves that those who assumed clandestine power & gave Laws even to the Convention & Committees were unsupported by the people. There seems therefore no Reason that our Colony shou'd be too precipitate in changing the present mode of Government. I woud wish first to be well assured of the Opinion of the Inhabitants at large. Let them be rather followed than driven on an Occasion of such momentuous Concern. But, above all, let us see the Conduct of the middle Colonies before we come to a Decision. It cannot injure us to wait a few weeks: the Advantage will be great, for this trying Question will clearly discover the true principles & the Extent of the Union of the Colonies. This, my dear Sir, is a delicate Subject on which I cannot enlarge at present. If I coud be relievd I woud immediately set out and give you a meeting. Pray hasten the Return of one of the Gentlemen: I know *you ought* to be at the Convention who are too uninform'd of the State and Temper of their Neighbours, & want, at least in this Respect, some Assistance.

I am pleasd with the Situation Mr Livingston has fixd for your Saturday's Retreat on the Banks of the Shammony. Nothing coud have been more convenient. Present my Compliments to Mrs Jay and believe me to be with great Regard, Dr Sir, Your Affectionate & most Obed Sevt,   Jas. Duane

RC (NNC).
[1] See Duane to John Jay, May 16, 1776.

Joseph Hewes to William Tokeley

Sir,   Philadelphia 18th May 1776.
I have received yours of the 2d and am very sorry you are in such a situation, as you describe. You must get men and proceed to sea soon as possible. Apply to the Committee of Safety, and to Mr Harrison for assistance. You must beg and entreat them to assist you, and if that will not do you must send an express to Mr Smith and desire him to come and assist you. At all events Men must be had. They need not be afraid if they are taken. I have not the least doubt but they will be well used. All those that I have seen who have been taken give this Account. Pray exert yourself, and get the Vessel to sea. If you return Safe you will have an allowance over and above your wages which Congress has Agreed to give as an encouragement to those who exert themselves in order to serve the common cause.[1]

I hope by the time this reaches you, that you will be again fully manned and ready to proceed to sea. Pray leave nothing unattempted till you get your full complement and then desire Mr Harrison to give you sailing Orders, with which I hope you will strictly Comply.

I am Sir, Your very hume Serv,   Joseph Hewes

MS not found; reprinted from Burnett, *Letters,* 1:457. Addressed: "Captain William Tokeley, of the Brigg Fanny, Cumberland New Kent, Virginia."
[1] In February 1776 the Secret Committee authorized Benjamin Harrison, Jr., who was appointed Continental paymaster in Virginia shortly thereafter, to load a cargo on board the *Fanny,* a brigantine owned by Hewes, for shipment to Europe. See Secret Committee Minutes of Proceedings, February 13, 1776; and Clark, *Naval Documents,* 3:1285–87. For the next several months, however, Tokeley was unable

to man the *Fanny* owing to the presence of a British squadron off the coast of
Virginia. Not until after July 15, when Congress, in response to repeated requests
from Harrison, ordered Gov. Patrick Henry to use his authority to help man the
Fanny, was Tokeley able to find a crew and set sail for Europe. Even then Toke-
ley's troubles were not over. Late in September 1776 the *Fanny* was stopped off the
Massachusetts coast by Capt. Elijah Freeman Payne, commander of a Rhode
Island privateer, and taken into Plymouth, Mass., on suspicion of being bound
for London. The Secret Committee, learning of this incident, informed John
Bradford, the Massachusetts prize agent, that Tokeley was sailing under its
authority. As a result, the *Fanny* was able to leave Plymouth at the end of
October and proceed to Nantes. *JCC*, 5:561; and Clark, *Naval Documents*, 5:138–39,
417, 552, 822, 956, 6:1001, 1360, 1469–70.

Richard Henry Lee to Charles Lee

My dear friend,   Philadelphia 18th May 1776
    My last letter to you was founded on conversation without doors,[1]
but you will see by the papers this Express brings you, that Congress
has complied with your desires as far as they can for the present,[2]
and I hope hereafter we may be enabled to do more. I have no doubt
but the Convention of Virginia will exert themselves to have the additional Rifle Batallion raised with all possible dispatch. You will
easily discover by the inclosed paper that old Wooster has abominably
misconducted himself in Canada.[3] Our affairs in that Country begin
to wear an unfavorable aspect; however, we expect the arrival of
better officers, and better Troops, will put things there on a more
respectable footing. Not to have got Quebec is some inconvenience,
but if we can secure the pass at Falls of Richlieu & Trois Riviere we
shall do well enough, and for this purpose, as well as securing the
affections of the Canadians, every proper step will be taken. The
impossibility of crossing the Lakes sooner with Troops and good
Officers has been the cause of our ill success thus far. The Committee
of Congress is arrived at Montreal. My best affections are allways
with you. Farewell,   Richard Henry Lee

[*P.S.*] Our Canada Committee are of opinion that if we could remit
them about £20,000 specie, our affairs in that Country might soon
be set right.[4] I wish we had the hard Cash you extracted from the
Tory Ship in Virginia, as we are so greatly pressed for this Article,
that it remains doubtful whether this alone will not compel our
Army to evacuate Canada.

RC (NNPM).
    [1] See Lee to Charles Lee, May 11, 1776.
    [2] See *JCC*, 4:363–65; and John Hancock to Charles Lee, May 20, 1776.
    [3] See Commissioners to Canada to John Hancock, May 10, 1776.
    [4] See Commissioners to Canada to John Hancock, May 8, 1776.

Caesar Rodney to Thomas Rodney

Sir,   Philada. Saturday May the 18th. 1776
This day's post brings us letters from our Commissioners at Montreal in Canada by which we are informed of the following disagreable intelligence.[1] That 2 men of war, 2 frigates & (I think) one sloop of war had arrived at Quebec—that the garrison under the command of Gen. Charlton a thousand in number sallied out against our troops who then happened to be dispersed in small parties, compelled them to retreat, with the loss of a few killed, all their artillery, 300 small arms & all their sick in the hospitals &c. Gen. Arnold upon hearing it, marched from Montreal with his forces to meet them & make a stand in case the enemy should be reinforced so as to pursue. Our last 10 Battalions had not crossed the lake.

I am yours &c,   Caesar Rodney

P.S. The letter from the Commissioners to Congress was dated the 10th of May at Montreal.

Tr (DLC).
[1] The May 6, 8, and 10 letters of the commissioners to Canada to John Hancock reached Congress this day. *JCC*, 4:362.

Virginia Delegates
to the Virginia Convention

Gentlemen   Philadelphia, 18 April, [*i.e.* May] [1] 1776.
The inclosed resolutions were reported by a committee appointed to consider of a letter from general Lee to the president. We have nothing to observe upon them unless it be, that the surgeons whom the director general of the hospital is empowered to appoint, and the regimental surgeons to be nominated by the convention, according to a resolution lately forwarded to you,[2] are different officers. Upon the arrival of two ships of war, two frigates and one tender at Quebeck, the 6th instant, the garrison, consisting, with the forces the vessels brought, of no more than about a thousand men, made a sally upon our army there, and routed it. The resolution of the 15th of May we send a printed copy of, lest the manuscript, which we desired the secretary to furnish us with, should not come time enough to go by this opportunity. We are, Gentlemen, Your most obedient servants.

FC (DLC). In the hand of George Wythe.
[1] The resolutions enclosed in this letter, dealing with a variety of measures for the defense of Virginia, were adopted on May 18. See *JCC*, 4:363–65.
[2] For the resolve of May 6, see *JCC*, 4:330.

William Whipple to John Langdon

My Dear Sir,   Philadelphia 18th May 1776
This only serves to tell you Col Bartlett arrived yesterday and to enclose a Resolution of Congress which I know will not displease you.[1] You see how we come on. A confederation permanent and lasting, ought in my opinion to be the next thing and I hope is not far off: if so then the establishment of foreign Agencies I hope will fill our ports with ships from all parts of the world. By the enclosed Evening's Post you'll see the effects of their resolution—may it operate in the same manner through America.[2]
Your sincere friend,   Wm Whipple

Tr (DLC).
[1] Presumably the resolution of May 10 with its May 15 preamble, advising the provinces to institute new governments. *JCC*, 4:343, 357-58.
[2] Although it is not known what issue of the *Pennsylvania Evening Post* Whipple enclosed, the May 18 issue carried the May 4 resolve of the Rhode Island Assembly repealing "an act for the more effectual securing to his Majesty the allegiance of his subjects in this his colony and dominion of Rhode Island and Providence Plantations."

Josiah Bartlett to John Langdon

Dear Sir,   Philadelphia May 19th 1776
Last Friday afternoon I arrived here all well, and on Saturday we rec'd a sad, but very imperfect account of affairs at Quebeck;[1] according to the account rec'd it seems there was a most shocking and unaccountable misconduct in the whole affair—however cannot help hoping that affairs are not so bad as has been reported and if they are that the Generals and Soldiers who had not joined the army will in a great measure retrieve matters, and that things there will soon be in a better situation.
Hard money is very much wanted in Canada, and unless considerable sums are forthwith sent there, our affairs will suffer very much on that account; you will receive directions from the Chairman of the Secret Committee relative to what you have in your hands.[2]
The order of Congress concerning taking up Govt under the people, which Col Whipple sent forward,[3] has made a great noise in this Province. Enclosed I send you an address to the people of Pennsylvania and an order for the meeting of the City and Liberties tomorrow.[4] What will be the consequence I know not, but think the Assembly will be dissolved and a Convention called. As to other affairs I have had no time to be informed myself and Col Whipple tells me he has wrote you from time to time fully; as to the Agency

affair I shall make one more trial when that matter comes on. The order of Congress for raising a regt for the defence of our Colony you will receive before this comes to hand.[5] I hope good officers will be recommended and every thing put in the best posture of defence and the courage and resolution of the people kept up, as I have great reason to think we shall have a severe trial this summer with Britons, Hessians, Hanoverians, Indians, negroes and every other butcher the gracious King of Britain can hire against us. If we can stand it out this year (and I have no doubt, we can, by divine assistance) I think there will be a final end of British Tyranny and this country soon enjoy peace, liberty and safety. Use your best endeavors to keep up the spirit of the people; for our all is at stake, life, liberty and fortune. We have nothing to hope for, if conquered; and our misfortunes in the war ought to animate us the more to diligence, firmness and resolution; to conquer is better than life, to be subdued infinitely worse than death.

I have resolved punctually to answer all letters wrote to me from any persons in our Colony, but never to write a second to any person who does not answer mine—except what I am obliged to write officially to the Colony or Committee of Safety.

By an express rec'd from General Lee [6] we are informed a number of transports had arrived at Cape Fear with troops from England but had not landed when the express came away.[7]

Tr (DLC).
[1] See Commissioners to Canada to John Hancock, May 10, 1776, which was read in Congress on May 18.
[2] For congressional resolutions on the raising of specie for Canada, see *JCC*, 4:365–66, 375–78. The New Hampshire Assembly later reported to Congress that Langdon had collected about £900 in specie, which could be forwarded to Canada. See Meshech Weare to John Hancock, June 17, 1776, in PCC, item 64, fols. 9–11, and *N.H. State Papers*, 8:151–52.
[3] See William Whipple to John Langdon, May 18, 1776.
[4] Probably the Address of the Committee of Inspection for the County of Philadelphia. *Am. Archives*, 4th ser. 6:498–99. See also John Adams to James Warren, May 20, 1776.
[5] See William Whipple to Meshech Weare, May 17, 1776.
[6] Undoubtedly Charles Lee's May 10 letter to John Hancock, which was read in Congress on May 20. *JCC*, 4:368; *Am. Archives*, 4th ser. 6:403.
[7] For the continuation of this letter, see Bartlett to Langdon, May 21, 1776.

Thomas Jefferson to Thomas Nelson

May 19. [1776]

Yesterday we received the disagreeable news of a second defeat at Quebec.[1] Two men of war, two frigates and a tender arrived there early on the 6th instant. About 11. o'clock the same day the enemy

sallied out to the number of a thousand. Our forces were so dispersed
at different posts that not more than 200 could be collected at Head-
quarter's. This small force could not resist the enemy. All our cannon, 500 muskets and 200 sick men fell into their hands. Besides
this one of their frigates got possession of a batteau with 30. barrels
of powder and an armed vessel which our crew was forced to abandon. Our army was to retreat to the mouth of the Sorel. Genl.
Arnold was to set off from Montreal to join them immediately, upon
whose rejoining them it was hoped they might return as far as
Dechambeau. General Wooster has the credit of this misadventure,
and if he cannot give a better account of it than has yet been heard
I hope he will be made an example of. Generals Thomas and Sullivan were on their way with reinforcements. Arnold had gone up to
Montreal on business, or as some say, disgusted by Wooster.

The congress having ordered a new battalion of riflemen to be
raised in Virginia [2] Innis wishes much to be translated to it from the
Eastern shore which was so disagreeable to him that he had determined to have resigned.

RC (MWA). A continuation of Jefferson to Nelson, May 16, 1776.
   [1] See Commissioners to Canada to John Hancock, May 10, 1776, which was read
in Congress on May 18.
   [2] See *JCC*, 4:365.

John Adams to James Warren

My dear Sir   May 20. 1776
   Every Post and every Day rolls in upon Us Independance like a
Torrent. The Delegates from Georgia made their Appearance, this
Day, in Congress, with unlimited Powers, and these Gentlemen them-
selves are very firm.[1] South Carolina has erected her Government and
given her Delegates ample Powers, and they are firm enough. North
Carolina have given theirs full Powers after repealing an Instruction
given last August against Confederation and Independence. This
Days Post has brought a Multitude of Letters from Virginia, all of
which breath the same Spirit.[2] They agree they shall institute a
Government—all are agreed in this they say. Here are four Colonies
to the Southward, who are perfectly agreed now with the four to the
Northward. Five in the Middle are not yet quite so ripe. But they are
very near it. I expect that New York will come to a fresh Election of
Delegates in the Course of this Week, give them full Powers, and
determine to institute a Government.[3]

   The Convention of New Jersey, is about Meeting, and will assume
a Government.

   Pensylvania Assembly meets this Day and it is Said will repeal their Instruction to their Delegates which has made them So exceeding obnoxious to America in general, and their own Constituents in particular.

We have had an entertaining Maneuvre, this Morning in the State House Yard.[4] The Committee of the City Summoned a Meeting at Nine O Clock in the State House Yard, to consider of the Resolve of Congress of the fifteenth instant. The Weather was very rainy, and the Meeting was in the open Air, like the Comitia of the Romans. A Stage was erected, extempore for the Moderator, and the few orators to ascend. Coll Roberdeau was the Moderator. Coll McKean, Coll Cadwallader and Coll Matlack the principal orators. It was the very first Town Meeting, I ever Saw in Philadelphia and it was conducted with great order, Decency and Propriety.

The first Step taken was this: the Moderator produced the Resolve of Congress of the 15th inst, and read it with a loud Stentorean Voice that might be heard a Quarter of a Mile "Whereas his Britannic Majesty &c." As soon as this was read, the Multitude, several Thousands, some say, tho so wett, rended the Welkin with three Cheers, Hatts flying as usual &c.

Then a Number of Resolutions were produced and moved & determined, with great Unanimity. These Resolutions I will send you, as soon as published. The Drift of the whole was that the assembly was not a Body properly constituted, authorized and qualified to carry the Resolve for instituting a new Government into Execution and therefore that a Convention should be called, and at last they voted to support and defend the Measure of a Convention, at the utmost Hazard, and at all Events &c.

The Delaware Government, generally is of the Same opinion with the best Americans, very orthodox in their Faith and very exemplary in their Practice.[5] Maryland remains to be mentioned. That is so excentric a Colony—some times so hot, sometimes so cold—now so high, then so low—that I know not what to say about it or to expect from it. I have often wished it could exchange Places with Hallifax. When they get agoing I expect some wild extravagant Flight or other from it. To be sure they must go beyond every body else, when they begin to go.

Thus I have rambled through the Continent, and you will perceive by this state of it, that We cant be very remote from the most decisive Measures and the most critical Event.

What do you think must be my sensations, when I see the Congress now daily passing Resolutions, which I most earnestly pressed for against Wind and Tide, Twelve Months ago? and which I have not omitted to labour for, a Month together from that Time to this? What do you think must be my Reflections when I see the Farmer himself, now confessing the Falshood of all his Prophecies and the Truth of mine, and confessing himself, now for instituting Governments, forming a Continental Constitution, making alliances with foreigners, opening Ports and all that—and confessing that the Defence of the Colonies, and Preparations for defence have been neglected, in Consequence of fond delusive hopes and deceitfull Expectations?

I assure you this is no Gratification of my Vanity. The gloomy Prospect of Carnage and Devastation that now presents itself in every Part of the Continent and which has been in the most express and decisive nay dogmatical Terms foretold by me a thousand Times is too affecting to give me Pleasure. It moves my keenest Indignation— yet I dare not hint at these Things for I hate to give Pain to Gentlemen whom I believe sufficiently punished by their own Reflections.

RC (MHi). In Adams' hand, though not signed.
   [1] Button Gwinnett and Lyman Hall. See *JCC*, 4:367.
   [2] Particularly Gen. Charles Lee's letters of May 10 to John Hancock and to Richard Henry Lee. The former was read in Congress this day. See *JCC*, 4:368; and *Am. Archives*, 4th ser. 6:403, 407–8.
   [3] See also James Duane to John Jay, May 18, 1776.
   [4] For the proceedings of this meeting, see *Am. Archives*, 4th ser. 6:517–23. See also Josiah Bartlett to John Langdon, May 21; and James Duane to John Jay, May 25, 1776. Despite this political pressure, the Pennsylvania Assembly did not change its instructions to its delegates in Congress until June 8. *Pa. Archives*, 8th ser. 8:7539.
   [5] See Caesar Rodney to John Haslet, May 14, 1776; and John Adams to Samuel Chase, June 14, 1776, note 5.

Elbridge Gerry to James Warren

[May 20, 1776]

I enclose you a Virginia paper just come in, by which you will see the spirit of another county in that colony, exhibited in their instructions for independency.[1]

In this colony (Pennsylvania) the spirit of the people is great, if a judgement is to be formed by appearances. They are well convinced of the injury their assembly has done to the continent by their instructions to their delegates. It was these instructions which induced the middle colonies and some of the southern to backward every measure which had the appearance of independency: to them is owing the delay of congress in agitating questions of the greatest importance, which long ere now must have terminated in a separation from Great Britain: to them is owing the disadvantages we now experience for want of a full supply of every necessary for carrying on the war. Alliances might have been formed, and a diversion been given to the enemy's arms in Europe or the West Indies, had these instructions never appeared. But they have had their effect; and while we endeavour to recover the continent from the ill consequences of such feeble politics, we ought to show the cause of such miserable policy. It appears to me that the eyes of every unbeliever are now open; that all are sensible of the perfidy of Great Britain, and are convinced there is no medium between unqualified submission and actual independency. The colonies are determined on the latter. A final declaration is approaching with great rapidity. May the all-wise Disposer of events so direct our affairs that they may terminate in the salvation of these afflicted colonies.

Amidst all our difficulties you would be highly diverted to see the situation of our "moderate gentlemen." They have been more apprehensive of evils than any others, as we have frequently observed, and they have now the mortification to find that their measures for avoiding have but served to increase them. I sometimes think that Providence permitted them to clog the affairs of the colonies, that they may become in some degree desperate, and thus introduce into the circle of determined men those timid beings, whose constitution never admits of their defending freedom on the noblest principles, and are afterwards obliged to meet danger by the same motives that induced them to shun it. They are coming over to us, but I am sorry their counter influence so long prevented us from adopting the only means by which we could supply ourselves with the necessaries for defence.

MS not found; extract reprinted from Austin, *Life of Gerry,* 1:178–80.

[1] Presumably Purdie's *Virginia Gazette,* May 10, 1776, containing the April 23 instructions to Charlotte County's delegates to the Virginia Convention, or the April 26 issue containing James City County's April 24 instructions to its delegates. See *Am. Archives,* 4th ser. 5:1034, 1046.

John Hancock to Charles Lee

Sir,   Philada. May 20th. 1776

By the enclosed Resolves of Congress, which I have the Honour of transmitting, you will perceive, that your several Letters have been received, and that the Congress have fully expressed their Sense with Regard to the Subject of them.[1]

Congress highly approve of your Vigilance, and Attention to the important Duties of your Department. You may rest assured, they will always co-operate with you in all your laudable Schemes to establish the Liberties of the United Colonies; an Event, which I trust, by the Blessing of God, we shall be able finally to accomplish, in Spite of all the Efforts of our Enemies agt. us. I shall only add that I am commanded by Congress to direct you to carry the enclosed

Resolves in Execution as speedily as possible. I have the Honour to be, Sir, your most Obedt. & very hble Sevt.   J. H. Prst.

LB (DNA: PCC, item 12A). Addressed: "Major Genl. Lee Virginia."

[1] These resolutions dealt with various matters relating to the defense of Virginia and were passed by Congress on May 18 in response to General Lee's letters to Hancock of April 19 and May 7, 1776. *JCC*, 4:363–65. Lee's letters are in PCC, item 158, 1:45–48, 53–57; and *Am. Archives*, 4th ser. 5:981–82, 1220–22.

Francis Lewis to Robert Treat Paine

Dr. Sir,   New York 20 May 1776

Your favor of the 9th Inst. I received the 17th, and in complyance with your request I transmit you an abstract of my proceedings relative to the Cannon & shot &c. I had contracted for to supply the Ships of War building in this Coloney.[1]

I have been lately informed that Mr. S. Patrick (a partner in the Orange Iron Works) has been at Phila., where he learn't that the Committee of Congress had contracted with others at a higher price than what was stipulated for with me, this occasion'd the letter of which you have inclosed a Copy, and must desire the Committees instructions on that head.[2]

From the tenor of my Contract with Griffiths, I am induced to believe the Committee has been imposed upon in their Contracts entered into at Phila, and to urge the Orange Company to a complyance with theirs will I fear be attended with difficulties & disappointments, therefore think it reasonable that they Should have the same prices given to others. Shall therefore *in the intrim* urge them to proceed in casting as many pieces of Cannon &c they possibly can, at the same time assureing them the Committee will not let them be sufferers by their contract, *until* I have the Committee's further instructions on this head. It will be necessary to furnish me with the dimentions & weight &c of the respective pieces of Cannon. This Company having enlarged their Hearth, can now cast Cannon of any Size up to a 24 pounder, and they have been as far as Boston in order to procure sufficient workmen.

The Superintendent to one of our ships was with me Yesterday, and informs that both ships are planked up to the Wales, and expects they will be in the Water by the last of June, but that they met with many delays by the badness of Roads in haleing their Timber to the Shipyard.

Our Mr. P. Livingston is gone up to the Ship yard, upon his return will give you further information.

Please to inform Mr. Robt. Morris I have both his letters of

11th & 15 Inst.[3] and that when the sulphur arives it shall be forwarded agreeable to his request.

I am, Dr. Sir, Your very Humble Servt,   Frans Lewis

[*P.S.*] The following is a Copy of a proposal made me by Jno Griffiths a Partner to Saml. Patrick to which I acquisced March 8, 1776.

"An Estimate of Ball and Ballast for the Ships of War building in New York Province vizt
Ballast at the lowest

Computation	150 Tons Pig Iron @	£ 8. per Ton
Grape Shott	10 Tons @	£20. per Ton
Ball from 4 lb to 32 lb	50 Tons @	£15. per Ton
20 Cannon of 9 lb by the end of May	@	£28. per Ton

finished, proved, & delivered any where on Hudsons River.

"The Ballast can be delivered in the Month of April, The Balls and shott in May, provided the order be given soon as Flasks & other utensils will be necessary to cast the Ball & shott. Wooden patterns turned must be procured and the Number of Tons to each Size specified."

In consequence thereof I gave the Following orders & agreed for

30 Tons of 12 pd Shott	@ £15 per Ton
20 Tons of 9 pd do	@ £15 per Ton
4 Tons of 4 pd do	@ £15 per Ton
6 Tons of Grape do	@ £20. per Ton
20 Cannon of 9 poundrs finish'd &c	@ £28 per Ton
150 Tons Pig Iron for Ballastg both ships	@ £ 8. per Ton

of which 50 Tons are delivd at the ships &
paid for by me.   F. Lewis

N.B. In a former letter I furnishd Mr Wm. Livingston with the purport of the foregoing.[4]   F. L.

RC (MHi). Endorsed by Paine: "May 21st. 1776. Answered."

[1] Paine's letter of May 9 has not been found. The "Ships of War" were the frigates *Congress* and *Montgomery*, whose construction Congress had authorized in a December 13, 1775, resolution. See Lewis to William Livingston, March 20, 1776, note 2.

[2] Samuel Patrick's May 12 letter to Lewis is in Clark, *Naval Documents*, 5:66. The "Committee of Congress" was the "Committee on the ways and means of procuring cannons," of which Paine was a member. Ibid; and *JCC*, 4:55. See also Robert Treat Paine to John Griffith and Samuel Patrick, June 8, 1776.

[3] Not found.

[4] See Lewis to William Livingston, March 20, 1776.

Jonathan Dickinson Sergeant to John Adams

Dear Sir   Princeton 20 May 1776.

I wrote You soon after I arrived here a Letter which I hope You received; [1] but which You have not yet acknowledged.

The many studied Embarrassments thrown in the Way of the Canada-Expedition have at last in a great Measure answered the Purpose for which I fear they were all along intended.

Ever since I have seen the Inside of the Congress I have trembled. Nothing short of a radical Change in the Councils of our Middle Colonies can I am persuaded, by any Means save us. I preach this Doctrine continually; but I cannot make so many Proselytes as Parson Whitefield. With us the old Demagogues I fear are against us. Next Week is our Election. I wish I may obtain a Seat in the Convention; but am not over sanguine in my Hopes: tho I believe I could easily accomplish it by going out of my present County into the one I came from. However am in Hopes they will chuse good Men there.

After the Election I expect to pay You a Visit for a short Time; but am determined that I will not continue to attend along with my present Colleagues any longer than I cannot avoid.[2] At present several little Circumstances will form an Excuse for my being absent.

This Campaign I suppose will be a most awful one. I could yet abide the prospect of it if we were possessed of more Unanimity & Vigour. I wish People knew their Men better & the Steps they are taking; but alas! I fear they are betrayed with out knowing it.

I should be highly pleased & think myself greatly honoured by a Line from You on the present Posture of Affairs. If they do not mend I will try to get a Commission in the Army that I may get knocked on the Head betimes. This I think would be more eligible than to live to be a Spectator of our Country reduced to Submission.

I intended when I begun only to ask the Favour of a Line from You; but when I am writing to a Person I can speak openly to I can hardly forbear the Reflections I have made. Have only to add that Doctor Witherspoon will be the Bearer of this & You may send an answer safely by him.

I am, Your sincere Friend, & humble Servant,

Jona D Sergeant

RC (MHi).

[1] Not found.

[2] Sergeant "declined being appointed" to the new congressional delegation chosen by the New Jersey Provincial Congress on June 22, 1776, because of his conviction that "it is better that I stay in the Colony for the present than in the Continental Congress." Sergeant to Samuel Adams, June 24, 1776, Samuel Adams Papers, NN. See also Abraham Clark to Elias Dayton, July 4, 1776, note.

Thomas Stone to James Hollyday?

Dr. Sir.[1]   Phila. May 20. 1776

I am very much obliged by the Intelligence communicated in yours of the 17th and am much pleased by the Temper shewn in the Convention—tho I fear it can now be of little Service in the general Scale of American Politicks.[2] The Dye is cast. The fatal Stab is given to any future Connection between this Country & Britain: except in the relation of Conqueror & vanquished, which I can't think of without Horror & Indignation. Never was a fairer Cause, with more promising appearances of final Success ruined by the rash and precipitate Councils of a few men. In a very short Time we should have been restored to our rights & have enjoyed Peace if the Ministry are in Earnest in promoting a Negotiation with a Design to do Justice to America, which however I very much doubt, or upon their deceitfull Shew of reconciliation being detected, laid open & exposed, the General & almost unanimous Voice of America would have been for seperation, but just at the Time when anxious Expectations are raised & not satisfied one way or the other, to strike a decisive Stroke & at once when the Minds of Men are not prepared for such an Event, to cut the only Bond which held the discordant Members of the Empire together, appears to me the most weak and ill judged Measure I ever met with in a State which had the least Pretention to wisdom or Knowledge in the Affairs of Men. I think it probable You will before this reaches you have taken some decisive Measures in Consequence of the joint Letter of your Deputies in Congress.[3] It gave me exceeding Pain, that the Convention should be necessitated to take one or other of the perplexing alternatives suggested by the Preamble & Resolve sent you & our Conduct in Consequence thereof, but it could not be avoided. We postponed the Question somedays, and did every thing to prevent that destructive Precipitancy which seems so agreable to the Genius of some. Further delay could not be obtain[ed] Altho there was the strongest reason for it. Two Colonies being unrepresented & a representation shortly expected, it was in vain to reason or expostulate. The Majority of Colonies attending was known to be for the Proposition & the opportunity not to be let slip. We conceived ourselves bound to withdraw from Congress immediately on the Vote upon the Preamble, & have not voted since.[4] Having once determined in our Judgments against the Propriety of the Measure and of its Tendency, it became us not to hesitate obeying the Instructions of our constituents which in all Cases with me (& I am persuaded with my Brother Delegates) are sacred. The Vox Populi must in great measure influence your Determination of the part to be taken by the Province upon this great change in the *declared* End of the war—and I am strongly inclined to wish it could be well known before any decisive Step is taken in Convention and for this End, a little Time & delay might be profitably used.[5] You must I presume either declare explicitly that you will go all Lengths with the majority of Congress or that you will not join in a War to be carried on for the purposes

Thomas Stone

of Independency & new Establishments, and will break the Union
or rather not enter into one for these Ends, either of which are
dangerous Extremes. But in whatever is determined it will be wise
and prudent to have the Concurrence of the People. I wish much
to be with you & to remain with you to share in all your perplexities,
Difficulties & Dangers be they what they may. But I am denied the
only Comfort I could have in the present Situation of affairs by
the particular Circumstances of my family. I am distressed beyond
the Bearing of a Man who has much more Philosophy than ever
I was blessed with, by contemplating probable Events in this Country. And this mortifying Speculation is not the greatest uneasiness
I suffer at present. The Illness of a wife I esteem most dearly preys
most severely on my Spirits, she is I thank God something better
this afternoon, and this Intermission of her Disorder affords me
Time to write to you. The Doctr. thinks she is in a fair way of
being well in a few days. I wish I thought so. The People of this
Province are thrown into the most violent Convulsions by the resolve
of Congress sent you, the result of which it is impossible to foresee.[6]
A considerable number of People met this morning in Consequence
of an hand Bill for that purpose, & determined that Government
ought to be assumed, the Assembly suppressed, the Instructions to
the Delegates rescinded & a Convention called for the purpose of
judging of the Propriety of forming a new Government, & to form
the same. This Meeting as I am informed consisted of the people
only who are of one side, & that all their Determinations were
very unanimous. The County Committee I hear met yesterday and
determined by a great majority only two dissenting, to support
the assembly under the present form of Government. We have not
heard from the out counties. The assembly was to have met this
day, but I believe there were not members enough to make an House.
We shall know in a few days whether they will maintain their
Ground. Our affairs in Canada are ruined as you will see by the
Papers. I wish we may make a tolerable stand on any Ground the
other side the Lake. I hear Chase has wrote to a friend of his in
this city, that he could not be of any further service in Canada and
was determined to sit out the day after he wrote, to leave the County,
should this resolution be taken by our Commissioners there, which
however I hope for their Credit & our Safety will not be the Case,
the Soldiers will probably follow & will not even hazard a Stay
at Saint Johns or the Isle au Noix to raise fortifications, should
this be the case & the Enemy take the advantage of this consternation and regain the Lakes, assemble the Canadians who are very
generally irritated against us & the Indians who will join the Party
to appearance victorious, a most bloody & distructive war upon the
Frontiers of N York & N England will ensue, and how far it's Consequences may extend, cannot be foretold. On the contrary should

a proper Stand be made at St. Johns, the Isle au Noix fortified & the Lake secured, which I have yet Hopes will be done, we may keep them at least this Campaign from penetrating the back Parts of the Country. How we are provided with Warlike Stores for these purposes I have not been able to learn. Our Soldiery have behaved as we are told most licentiously in Canada, unrestrained by Decipline or Principle, they have commanded every thing in their Power by the Bayonet, unprovided with sufficiency of Provisions & the Credit of their money not affording them a supply, they have committed all the Disorders, incident to an Army out of Temper & without Controul in a Country where Appearances were rather hostile than friendly. All the Evil consequences which were seen and pointed out by men averse to this Canada Expedition will I fear be felt, and even then those who were for it will not ascribe them to the true Cause, the fundamental Error of the undertaking, but it will be said and indeed has been said in Publication here that the ill Success has been owing to a Delay occasioned by those who opposed the Measure. We hear of a considerable British Force having arrived in N Carolina, & that Genl. Lee is gone to oppose their Landing. A person who was taken in Canada with Allen is I am told just arrived in Town Via Hallifax. He was carried to England and examined as he said before the Council & was discharged.[7] He said he was treated in a most friendly manner, was found every thing he wanted. The people of England talk much of Settlement with America. No foreign Troops arrived in England the 24 of March. He brings Papers as low as the 20th but I have not seen them. He also brings Letters, as I am told, to several Gent. in Town & to the congress—reports that it is said 30 or 40 thousands Troops will be sent to America, 10000 for the South, 10000 for Canada, the rest for the Northern Provinces. He left How & his Troops at Hallifax in bad Condition, no Troops arrived to the Eastward. The person who gave me this relation did not hear any thing mentioned of Commissioners or forgot what he heard as he is averse to beleiving any thing of their coming over. I shall probably hear more of this affair in the morning and will subjoin the Intelligence if worth communicating. I think it very probably Commissioners will be sent with the Troops, tho I very much doubt of the Sincerity of administration to offer just & reasonable Terms to us. I do not form this opinion upon the Circumstance of Troops being sent for I think they will naturally suppose if Commissioners are sent without support we must dictate the Terms of Accomodation & they may also readily conceive they will not be of the most moderate kind. But I fear the Ministry are strongly attached to their Sistem, perhaps from Principle, that they have discovered the strong Inclination to Peace in many Colonies & are in hopes, by offering something like reasonable Terms at a Time when the Distresses of war are painted strongly upon the minds of those who have not been irritated & enraged by feeling them in reality, to create Divisions & Dissentions through the Country. The last act of Parliament seems to have been produced under the influence of this Idea, & is calculated to ansr. the purpose.[8] I wish I may be mistaken; However should the most reasonable Terms be offered preserving the subordinate relation of this Country to Britain I much question if they would be accepted by the present haughty Temper of America. A report prevailed in Town this morning that 90 Ships, Transports etca. were arrived near N York, but this is again contradicted. Indeed all our Intelligence is so very doubtfull that little credit is due to any. R[obert] A[lexander] was to have set out for the convention on Saturday but was prevented by rain. I don't expect he will be very expiditious even after he quits the City & when that will happen I can't tell. I have been spurring him to depart as I know the Convention would wish to see him & he would be serviceable. The Difficulties respecting Governor Eden's removal from or stay in Maryland which you mention occurred to me, but upon the whole I was of opinion it would be best to get him out of the Province in a peaceable Manner, if it could be done, because I thought it wrong in our present Circumstances to suffer a Correspondence to be carried on between any persons here & Administration the contents of which we were not acquainted with, And because I was apprehensive the Governor's unguarded Conduct whatever his Intentions may be would frequently afford an handle for designing Men to imbroil and inflame the Province, and I did not see any Disadvantages flowing from his Departure of so much consequence of these, however if he pledges his Honour & Safety not to correspond & conduct himself peaceably, perhaps his Stay may be reconciled to every Body, unless you should assume Government & appoint a Governor of your own & in that case I suppose the Ground must be given up entirely to the Master elect. I wrote to the convention signifying my Inclination to be recalled from hence,[9] in which I was & am much in Earnest. My situation is truly disagreable—could I sit with the same happy Indifference I observe in others when matters of the last consequence are in agitation or could I bring my mind to view with Apathy the destructive Tendency of Measures or at least appearing to me so, which I can't prevent, or could I bring my Temper to bend to the Principles of those, who perhaps are wiser than myself, I should be less miserable. But my feelings are too keen, my Concern for those whose happiness I wish to secure too exquisite & my Constitution too stiff to allow of my Continuance with tolerable Ease to myself. These things however should not weigh with me if I had any Prospect of my being serviceable: But I should ill reward the confidence reposed in me by the Convention if I was not to be explicit in my Information to them, that I was totally useless & only served to give a fruitless Opposition to Measures which I can't approve but which however may be right, as they are adopted by wiser men—And that no Advantage derived from my Stay here was equal to the Expence of my support, and this is in sober Sadness my opinion, if they think proper to order Deputies from there again to take a Seat in Congress & under all these circumstances to appoint me one I will most certainly serve them to the best of my Judgment, as I am principled against quitting any Post where my Countrymen think I may usefull however disagreable it may be to myself or whatever my own Opinion may be on the Subject provided it be not against my Principles of Morality, in which I will ever retain the absolute Dominion. I had much rather be in the Province where perhaps I might be of some Service, tho even there I am not ambitious of elevated Station. I give you freely these facts & my Inclination.[10] You will exercise your own Judgment. Tell our Friend Scott I am very thankfull for his letter & Could I spare time from the necessary attendance on my family would with pleasure write to him particularly, but I have committed to this Paper every thing worth communicating & you will be pleased [to] shew it to him & he will be so generous to excuse a personal address, & so obliging to continue his correspondence. I expected all the Dissentients you mention but Prince Georges. Let me hear from you & be assured I am with most sincere Esteem, Yr constant friend & obt. Servt.,

T. Stone

Monday night

I have missed the Post by attending to hear the Intelligence above referred to. I must now send this by Mr Alexander who will give you a particular account thereof. It is bad enough, & will be published. There are Treaties for foreign Troops to the amount I think of near 20000. Several Letters say we have nothing to rely on but our own Strength. The People of England [are] uneasy, & the American Cause gains Ground—One Letter mentions Commissioners—no names to any. The whole Number of Troops intended for America, 34000—this number tho it may appear large will I am hopefull & indeed convinced will not be adequate to the diabolical Purpose of Conquest for which they are designed. The Spaniards it seems will not suffer us to trade with them. What Part France will take is not known but it is most probable she will be influenced by the same vile motives with the other European Powers. If our councils Could but be tempered with a proper Degree of moderation & attention to the Inclinations & even weaknesses of our people all would be well; but I think they will not drive & an Attempt to do such an injury to the feelings of freemen will have fatal Consequences. May God attend your Deliberations & Direct them to the right way. We are anxious to hear something from you & most of us think you will probably [. . .] down before you decide finally—my wife is something better this morning & I hope will do well: Adieu my friend, remember me to all who you know I think worth being remembered by. Yrs,　　TS

RC (DLC).
[1] For identification of the recipient of this letter and a letter of May 26 from Hollyday to Stone which may have been a response to Stone's, see Herbert E. Klingelhofer, "The Cautious Revolution: Maryland and the Movement toward Independence, 1774–1776," *Md. Hist. Magazine* 60 (September 1965): 285, 288–89. James Hollyday (1722–86), Talbot County, Md., lawyer and formerly both a Maryland assemblyman and councillor, was a member of the several provincial conventions, 1774–76, and of the council of safety, 1775–76. George T. Hollyday, "Biographical Memoir of James Hollyday," *PMHB* 7 (1883): 426–47.
[2] Hollyday had apparently reported that the Maryland Convention would endorse the council of safety's conduct in rebuking Samuel Purviance for transmitting to Congress Governor Eden's intercepted correspondence, a serious challenge to its authority in the eyes of the council. This the convention did on May 22 by condemning Purviance for "usurping the power to direct the operations of the military force of this Province" and permitting persons outside Maryland [i.e., Gen. Charles Lee] "to interfere in the direction of the internal affairs, civil or military, of said Province." *Am. Archives*, 4th ser. 5:1590. For the convention's final disposition of the case of Governor Eden, who was forced to return to England because "the publick quiet and safety, in the judgment of this Convention, require that he leave this Province," see Klingelhofer, "The Cautious Revolution," pp. 288–89.
[3] The Maryland delegates wrote to the Maryland Convention on May 15 enclosing the congressional resolves of May 10 and 15 urging provincial assemblies and conventions to establish governments adequate to secure "the happiness and safety of their constituents." *JCC*, 4:342, 357–58. The letter has not been found, but its receipt was acknowledged in the convention's minutes of proceedings for May 20, where the enclosed resolves are printed. See *Am. Archives*, 4th ser. 5:1587.
[4] For additional information on the conduct of the Maryland delegates on May 15, see Carter Braxton to Landon Carter, May 17, 1776. Stone, Robert Alexander, John Rogers, and Matthew Tilghman were the delegates attending at this time. Samuel Chase was in Canada, and Robert Goldsborough, Thomas Johnson, and William Paca were attending the convention in Annapolis.
[5] In contrast to Stone's expectation, the Maryland Convention reacted to Congress' resolution of May 15 in extreme haste, undoubtedly oversensitive to threats to its authority because of the recent controversy relating to the transmission of Governor Eden's intercepted correspondence to Congress. The convention received Congress' resolution on Monday morning, May 20, immediately referred it to a committee which submitted a report the same afternoon, and passed a series of resolutions recommended in the report the following day. See *Am. Archives*, 4th ser. 5:1588–89.
[6] For the response of the Pennsylvania "Independents" to Congress' resolutions of May 10 and 15, which included the popular demonstration in Philadelphia this day to which Stone here alludes, see David Hawke, *In the Midst of a Revolution* (Philadelphia: University of Pennsylvania Press, 1961), pp. 130–38.
[7] See Josiah Bartlett to John Langdon, May 21, 1776, note 2.
[8] Stone is apparently referring to that portion of the Prohibitory Act empowering the king to appoint peace commissioners and promising "protection to those who are disposed to return to their duty," who would thereafter be exempt from the restrictions imposed by the act. For a discussion of the conciliatory features contained in this act, see Weldon A. Brown, *Empire or Independence: A Study in the Failure of Reconciliation, 1774–1783* (Baton Rouge: Louisiana State University Press, 1941), pp. 76–77.
[9] Not found.

¹⁰ On May 21 the Maryland Convention renamed Stone, Robert Alexander, Samuel Chase, Robert Goldsborough, Thomas Johnson, William Paca, John Rogers, and Matthew Tilghman to represent Maryland in Congress "until the end of the next session of Convention." *Am. Archives*, 4th ser. 5:1589.

William Whipple to John Langdon

Dear Sir   20th May 1776

Your favor of the 6th inst. is now before me. I am glad the money has got safe to hand. The list of officers you mention I suppose has reach'd you before now.¹ I inclos'd one sometime ago. I also gave you my Reasons for disaproving the Person you mention for 1st Lieut. I have no objection to the Mr. Roche you mention but am apprehensive his being appointed wod make some uneasiness as there are many masters of vessels of good carecters out of imploy & who perhaps will think themselves neglected. I shall nominate Capt. Thompson the first opportunity,² & think it won't be amiss to appoint such of the Warrent or petty officers as you think necessary. As to the other officers I think you might sound such persons as you may think proper & know what places they will accept without engaging them absolutely. The Canvas I hope will soon be with you but I very much fear it will be some time before you'll get the Guns. If they are to go from here I see no prospect of them 'till July. The furnices are at work at Providence & by what I can learn have made a considerable number. I think it wod be well for you to take a ride there. You will then be able to judge of the probability of getting them from thence & on the first notice from you I'll get an order for the first guns that are made after the ships that are building there are supply'd. I shall lay your proposals for purchasing the Powder before the Committee this evening, shall also apply for Cash. You dont mention the sum you shall want, but my application shall be for the round sum 10,000;³ if that should not be sufficient let me know seasonably and I'll endeavor you shall be supplied.

21st. The foregoing was wrote last evening to save time. I've got the order for the sum above mention[ed] & shall send it forward in a few days. The Chairman of the secret committee desires you'll buy the Powder & your draught shall be duely paid or the money sent you on the earliest notice; no doubt you'll buy it as cheap as you can. The highest price that has been given here is 5s this Currency. It is expected Provisions will be orderd from the Camp where a large quantity was left by the Army. I shall let you know more of that shortly.⁴ Col. Bartlett arrived the 17th afternoon—he writes to you this post.⁵ By the inclosed alarm you'll see the effect the late Resolve of Congress has had in this City—no doubt it will have the same in other places. By the next post will endeavor to send you the forms you mention, at present can only send you one.

Yours Sincerely,   Wm. Whipple

FC (Capt. J. G. M. Stone, Annapolis, Md., 1973). Tr (DLC).
    [1] A list of officers for a 32-gun frigate, taken from the John Langdon Papers, PHi, is in Clark, *Naval Documents*, 5:250.
    [2] Thomas Thompson was appointed to command the frigate *Raleigh* on June 6. *JCC*, 5:422.
    [3] Remainder of this sentence and the first sentence of the postscript supplied from Tr.
    [4] Remainder of MS supplied from Tr.
    [5] See Josiah Bartlett to John Langdon, May 19, 1776.

Josiah Bartlett to John Langdon

May 21st. [1776]

Yesterday the City met agreeable to notification in the field before the State House, a stage being erected for the Moderator (Col Roberdeau) and the chief speakers (Mr McKean &c). I am told they unanimously voted that the present House of Assembly are not competent to changing the form of Govt and have given orders for calling a Convention. Pennsylvania Assembly was to meet yesterday. I fear some convulsions in the Colony. The *infamous* instructions given by the Assembly to their Delegates which they, at their last meeting refused to alter, is the cause of their losing their confidence of the people.[1]

One of the rifle men taken at Quebeck, last fall is arrived in this City last evening. I am told he has brought letters sewed up in his clothes for the Congress and that he left England the 24th of March last.[2] I saw him last evening, when he first came in the Coffee House. I expect to know more at Congress as the letters are sent to the President, but the post is now setting off, so must conclude by assuring you I am, Your steady and sincere friend,

Josiah Bartlett

P.S. Col Whipple has enclosed one of the Addresses.

Tr (DLC). A continuation of Bartlett to Langdon, May 19, 1776.
    [1] See John Adams to James Warren, May 20, 1776, note 4.
    [2] Apparently Langdon himself had sent this man, George Merchant, to George Washington and to Congress, after Merchant escaped from Halifax to New Hampshire. Among the letters brought by Merchant were three Arthur Lee letters of February 13 and 14, 1776, containing information on "the Ministerial intentions, and their force for the next campaign." See John Langdon to George Washington, May 10, 1776, in *Am. Archives*, 4th ser. 6:501; and *JCC*, 4:369, 405. Lee's letters, two of which were disguised so as to appear to have been written to Lt. Gov. Cadwallader Colden at New York, are printed in *Am. Archives*, 4th ser. 4:1125–28. See also Benjamin Franklin to George Washington, June 21, 1776, note 1.

Elbridge Gerry to Samuel R. Gerry

Philadelphia, May 21, 1776. Asks his brother [1] to find out "what is likely to become of the *Rockingham,* why she was seized,[2] whether Messrs Guardoquis are likely to be sufferers & what it was which these Gentlemen desired them to communicate to me relative to the Matter." Gives advice about a family matter and warns that "As We have a prospect of War on every Side I think it adviseable for yourself & Brother to send your Wives & Children into the Country & Yourselves to continue at Marblehead while the same can be defended."

RC (MHi).
  [1] Marblehead, Mass., merchant Samuel R. Gerry (1750–1807). *Columbian Centinel* (Boston), February 4, 1807.
  [2] See Clark, *Naval Documents,* 5:369–70.

John Hancock to George Washington

Sir,   Philada. May 21t. 1776
     As I imagine this will meet you on the Road to this Place, I wave making any Mention of public Matters, except that it is the Wish of Congress, you would if consistent with the Good of the Service order one Battalion from New York to be posted at Amboy in the Jerseys agreable to the enclosed Resolve.[1]
     Genl. Gates arrived this Morning, soon after which I was honored with your Favour by Post which I laid before Congress;[2] and as they expect you so soon here, I imagine they will defer consulting Genl. Gates & wait your Arrival.
     Your Favour of the 20th Inst I received this Morning,[3] & can not help expressing the very great Pleasure it would afford both Mrs. Hancock & myself to have the Happiness of accommodating you during your Stay in this City. As the House I live in is large and roomy, it will be entirely in your Power to live in that Manner you should wish. Mrs. Washington may be as retired as she pleases while under Inocculation, & Mrs. Hancock will esteem it an Honour to have Mrs. Washington inocculated in her House; and as I am informed Mr. Randolph has not any Lady about his House to take the necessary Care of Mrs. Washington, I flatter myself she will be as well attended in my Family. In short, Sir, I must take the Freedom to repeat my Wish that you would be pleased to condescend to dwell under my Roof. I assure you, Sir, I will do all in my Power to render your Stay agreeable, & my House shall be entirely at your Disposal. I must however submit this to your Determination, & only add that you will

peculiarly gratify Mrs. H. and myself in affording me an opportunity of convincing you of this Truth, That I am with every Sentiment of Regard for you & your Connections & with much Esteem, Dear Sir, your faithful and most obedt. hble Sevt.   John Hancock

[*P.S.*] Fessenden complaing for the Want of Money I have advanced him sixteen Dollars, which you will please to order him to account for.

LB (DNA: PCC, item 12A).
   [1] See *JCC*, 4:365.
   [2] See Washington's May 18 and 19 letters to Hancock in PCC, item 152, 1:697–704, and Washington, *Writings* (Fitzpatrick), 5:56–57, 58–59.
   [3] This letter is in PCC, item 152, 1:705–8, and Washington, *Writings* (Fitzpatrick), 5:62.

Francis Lightfoot Lee to Landon Carter

My dear Col.   Philadelphia May 21. 1776
   I have received your very acceptable Letter of the 30 Apl. I wish it was in my power to make better return, but my situation here will not admit of it. Perhaps it wou'd be well if Congress was allowed to form a Governmt. for the Colonies; but it does not pretend nor will ever be allowed, to interfere with their internal policy. All it can do is to recommend it to them to establish such governmts. as will best contribute to their happiness, & this is done. However as I find there are many good men in the Convention I hope they will make such an establishment, as will put a stop to the rising disorders with you, & secure internal quiet for the future. The violent struggle we have to go thro' this summer, the hardships we must suffer, make it necessary to cultivate the utmost harmony among ourselves.
   This & the adjoining Colonies are going fast into Independency & constituting new Governmts. convinced of the necessity of it, both for the security of internal peace & good order; and for the vigorous exertion of their whole force against the common Enemy. I agree with you that the arbitrary & cruel proceedings of the British Court And The slavish indolence of the people of England, has made more independants, than Common sense, for however plausible in theory, the prospect of wealth & grandeur, old habits & prejudices, and fears, of what we know not, will ever be great obstructions to changes of Governmt. Tyranny & oppression often effect it. Letters & intelligence from London recd. yesterday,[1] leave no room to doubt of the diabolical intentions of Administration against us & their people are so plunged in Curruption, & willing slavery that nothing is to be expected from them so that we must stand entirely upon our own legs for the future. Indeed if we had our choice, I think any further

connection with them, wou'd be infamy & pollution. We have the
treaties with Hesse, Brunswick & Waldeck. They are curious, if they
are printed here I will send you a copy. We have been unfortunate
at Quebec. Genl. Wooster, an old woman, suffer'd himself to be surprised by a reinforcemt. that arrived there [the 6th] inst. & lost his
Cannon, [500] stand of arms, a good deal of powder, & his sick men.[2]
Bad weather had prevented better officers from joining the Army. We
are 10,000 strong there now with good Genls. & can throw in aid at
pleasure, therefore we fear them not. Colo. Tayloe has the papers, I
beg my afft. compts. may be accepted at Sabine Hall. Mrs. Lee joins
in the request. Believe me Dear Col. ever Yours,

Francis Lightfoot Lee

RC (InU).
  [1] See *JCC*, 4:369; and Josiah Bartlett to John Langdon, May 21, 1776, note 2.
  [2] See Commissioners to Canada to John Hancock, May 10, 1776.

Richard Henry Lee to Charles Lee

My Dear Friend,   Philadelphia, 21st May, 1776
    As I wrote you yesterday by your Express,[1] I have now only to
thank you for your favor by last post.[2] If you discovered any languor
in my letters it must have been merely corporeal, the mental powers
having been just as vigorous as ever. Excessive writing and constant
attention to business afflicts me a good deal I own, but they are
far from depressing my spirits in the great cause of America, and if
you were to consult with our *moderate men* in and out of doors you
would think me possessed of something else than languor. The mis-
chievous instructions from some Colonies have indeed fettered
Congressional Councils, but many of these are done away, and the
rest will be so immediately. The Resolve of Congress respecting government hath wrought a great change hereabouts, and very soon the
Public affairs will wear a different aspect, and be directed with better
spirit. I expect an expedition to Detroit will be undertaken, Niagara
will probably be suspended, as the Indians thereabout wish it to continue a place of trade yet awhile.[3] A Gentleman just from N. York,
tells us that 70 sail of Transports with 10,000 troops were arrived off
the Hook; and that Gen. Washington was despatching an Express to
Congress, a confirmation is hourly expected. They have made the
works about N. York very strong, and tho' the detachment of 10
Battalions to Canada, has not left above 8,000 yet 10, or 12000 militia
may be thrown in, so that we apprehend no danger from that quarter.
    Farewell, my dear Sir,   Richard Henry Lee

Early in April I gave you an Account [4] of the affair of the Annapolis Council.

MS not found; reprinted from *NYHS Collections* 5 (1872): 31–32.
[1] Not found.
[2] General Lee's letter of May 10 is in *NYHS Collections* 5 (1872): 20.
[3] Richard Henry Lee was a member of the committee appointed to consider General Lee's May 10 letter to Congress urging preparations for expeditions against Niagara and Detroit. Ibid., p. 17. Consideration of the committee's May 21 report, which recommended that an expedition be immediately undertaken against Detroit, was postponed until General Washington, then en route to Philadelphia, could be consulted. The committee that subsequently conferred with Washington eventually recommended that Indians be offered bounties for prisoners to encourage them to attack Niagara and Detroit, but the resolution Congress finally adopted on June 17 was simply a broad authorization for Washington to employ Indians wherever they might prove most useful. See *JCC*, 4:368, 373, 394–95; 5:452.
[4] Not found.

Robert R. Livingston to John Jay

Dear John   21st May 1776 Philadelphia
I am much mortified at not hearing from you. I wrote to you last week & am now setting out for Bristol in order to meet Mrs. Livingston. I could wish to find Mrs. Jay there also. Pray send some of our Colleagues along, otherwise I must be more confined than either my health or inclination will allow.[1] You have doubtless seen the acct. brought by the Rifleman from London by which it appears that we shall at least have 34000 Com[mission]ers.
If your Congress have any spirit they will at least build 14 or 15 light boats capable of carrying a 12 pounder to secure Hudsons River which is to be the chief scene of action. The carpenters employed on the frigate would build 2 or three in a day if they were built in the manner of Batoes which is the true construction. ⟨*Mr. Rogers desired I would write to you to take up a Letter brought by the packet directed to Josiah A Beal in Maryland.*⟩ I wish you would direct Gaine to send me his paper. God bless you. Yours Most Sincerely,
                                                    Robt R. Livingston

RC (NNC). Addressed: "To Coll. John Jay, New York."
[1] In a May 29 letter written from New York, Jay regretfully informed Livingston that Mrs. Jay would be unable to go to Bristol on account of ill health and that he would "again take a solitary Ride to Philadelphia whenever the Convention who have directed me to abide here till their further Order, shall think fit to dismiss me." He also noted: "Messrs. Alsop and Lewis set out next Saturday for Philadelphia. Mr. Duane informs me that he is about to return home, and considering how long he has been absent from his Family I think him intitled to that Indulgence. I pray God that your Health may enable you to attend constantly, at least till it may be in my Power to relieve you. Is Mr. Clinton returned?" Jay, *Papers* (Morris), p. 271. See also James Duane to John Jay, May 25, 1776.

John Adams to Abigail Adams

May 22d. 1776

When a Man is seated, in the Midst of forty People some of whom are talking, and others whispering, it is not easy to think, what is proper to write. I shall send you the News-Papers, which will inform you, of public Affairs, and the particular Flickerings of Parties in this Colony.

I am happy to learn from your Letter, that a Flame is at last raised among the People, for the Fortification of the Harbour. Whether Nantaskett, or Point Alderton would be proper Posts to be taken I cant say. But I would fortify every Place, which is proper, and which Cannon could be obtained for.

Generals Gates and Mifflin are now here. Gen. Washington will be here tomorrow—when We shall consult and deliberate, concerning the Operations of the ensuing Campain.[1]

We have dismal Accounts from Europe, of the Preparations against Us. This Summer will be very important to Us. We shall have a severe Tryal of our Patience, Fortitude and Perseverance. But I hope we shall do valiantly and tread down our Enemies.

I have some Thoughts of petitioning the General Court for Leave to bring my Family, here. I am a lonely, forlorn, Creature here. It used to be some Comfort to me, that I had a servant, and some Horses—they composed a Sort of Family for me. But now, there is not one Creature here, that I seem to have any Kind of Relation to.

It is a cruel Reflection, which very often comes across me, that I should be seperated so far, from those Babes, whose Education And Welfare lies so near my Heart. But greater Misfortunes than these, must not divert Us from Superiour Duties.

Your Sentiments of the Duties We owe to our Country, are such as become the best of Women, and the best of Men. Among all the Disappointments, and Perplexities, which have fallen to my share in Life, nothing has contributed so much to support my Mind, as the choice Blessing of a Wife, whose Capacity enabled her to comprehend, and whose pure Virtue obliged her to approve the Views of her Husband. This has been the cheering Consolation of my Heart, in my most solitary, gloomy and disconsolate Hours. In this remote Situation, I am deprived in a great Measure of this Comfort. Yet I read, and read again your charming Letters, and they serve me, in some faint degree as a substitute for the Company and Conversation of the Writer.

I want to take a Walk with you in the Garden—to go over to the Common—the Plain—the Meadow. I want to take Charles in one Hand and Tom in the other, and Walk with you, Nabby on your Right Hand and John upon my left, to view the Corn Fields, the orchards, &c.

Alass poor Imagination! how faintly and imperfectly do you supply the Want of original and Reality!

But instead of these pleasing Scænes of domestic Life, I hope you will not be disturbed with the Alarms of War. I hope yet I fear.

RC (MHi). Adams, *Family Correspondence* (Butterfield), 1:412–13.

[1] John Adams was appointed on May 23 to a committee to confer with Generals Washington, Gates, and Mifflin "upon the most speedy and effectual means for supporting the American cause in Canada." Its report was submitted and acted upon on May 24, and on the following day Adams was named to the committee to confer with Generals Washington, Gates, and Mifflin to "concert a plan of military operations for the ensuing campaign." See *JCC*, 4:383–84, 387–89, 391. See also Adams, *Diary* (Butterfield), 3:390–91.

Caesar Rodney to Thomas Rodney

Sir,   Philadelphia May 22d 1776

I find by your letter of the 19th Instant,[1] my Last letters to you, with which I inclosed you the Resolution of Congress to which is a Long preamble leading you to the design of the Resolution, had not then Come to hand. I sent them by Mr. William Gray who I believe did not leave this town Till Sunday Morning last. You don't say whether you had seen Collo. Haslet's letter to which I had Refered you.[2] By the next post Shall be glad to hear your opinion on the *mode* best to be adopted for Effecting the Change.[3] The people in this City I think have Acted rather unwisely. They have Called a Town Meeting—by which they have determined to apply to the Committees of Inspection of the Several Counties throughout the province, to depute a Certain number of each of those Committees to meet together at Philadelphia, And there agree on, and order What number of Members Shall be Elected by the people in Each County within the province, to meet in Convention at Philadelphia, The Whole number for the Province to be One hundred.[4] This Convention is to be Chose for the Special purpose of Laying the plan of Government—and when that is Done, and an Assembly Chose and Returned agreable to Such plan the Convention is to be disolved. This mode for Establishing a Government appears to be, and really is verry fair. Yet I think they are unwise, Because we are Certain that a verry powerfull force is Expected from England against us, some are Come, the rest will undoubtedly Arrive before Midsummer. We shall be Oblidged to Exert every Nerve, at every point, and we well know how necessary Regular Government is to this End—and by their Mode it will be impossible for them to have any Government for three months to Come, and during that time much Confusion. If the present Assembly Should take Order in the Matter, the work would be done in one Quarter of the time. However many of the Citizens seem to have little or no Confidence in the Assembly.

With us below I hardly know what Step will be best. In our County a New Choice Could not mend the Ticket, but might make it worse. In the Other Counties there is verry little probability of an Alteration for the better. I want to have the opinion of your Set Concerning it, by next Post.

You say you sent by Mr. Parke fifty pounds to be paid to some person in Town and that Parke let you know he had left the Money with me. That you now mention it because I had not wrote to you about it. I Assure you it is the first time I ever heard of the fifty pounds. Parke never paid, or even ever talked of paying that, or any other Sum of money to me, nor did he ever tell me of your giving him any money for me on any one Else.

As my Wheat is like to lie in the Granary for want of Such a price as I Can afforde to take, It will be necessary to have it frequently Turned to prevent the Weavell getting in it. Therefore hope you will not Neglect to see it done.

One of our Riflemen that travelled across the Country with Arnold, and taken prisoner while on Centry at Quebec, Was Sent to England. A few days after he landed, he was sent to London and put in Bridewell in Irons. Sawbridge (the Lord Mayor) went to him, Examined him and had him immediately discharged & sent down to Bristol, Where a number [of] Gentn. procured him a passage to Hallifax. He left Bristol the 24th of March, Arrived in this City the day before Yesterday, And tho Searched at Hallifax two or three times, brought undiscovered a Number of Letters and Newspapers to the Congress, by which we are possessed of all their plans for the destruction of America.[5] *No Commissioners.* Captn. Craige who was appointed to make the Exchange of prisoners with the Roebuck, has returned to Chester with Captn. Budden, Lt. Ball and all the rest of them. They Say (for I have seen Budden & Craige) that the men of War are gone off to Sea, that they Stood after them 12 Leagues without the Capes, then lost sight of them and Returned. I am Yrs.

Caesar Rodney

RC (PHi).
  [1] Thomas Rodney to Caesar Rodney, May 19, 1776, which contained information on a conversation that he had recently had with John Dickinson in Dover. "I mentioned to him the Resolution of Congress [of May 10 and the preamble of May 15]; and he answer'd it was made before he Left there; upon which I observed to him many advantages that would follow our assuming Government to which he agreed & observed many others 'And that it would not prevent but perhaps promote a more speedy reconciliation, because the longer they let Government exist before they offer Terms the more firm that Government would be, & therefore the more difficult to effect a reconciliation.' I should apprehend from the above sentiments that Mr. D—— has some glimmering hopes of reconciliation yet, or that he ment thereby, to flater those who have such hopes, to acquiese in the

resolution of Congress—Peace, and reconciliation will henceforth be my ardent wish but never to mix our Government with Britains any more. It is known here that the resolution is published—but the news only arrived last night; Torism is dum, and many suspected persons give it there approbation, I believe it will meet with no opposition in this County." Rodney, *Letters* (Ryden), p. 82.

[2] Caesar Rodney to John Haslet, May 14, 1776.

[3] For Thomas Rodney's recommendation on the best means to change the government of Delaware, see his May 26 letter to Caesar in Rodney, *Letters* (Ryden), pp. 83–84.

[4] The proceedings of this meeting are printed in *Am. Archives,* 4th ser. 6:517–23.

[5] See Josiah Bartlet to John Langdon, May 21, 1776, note 2.

John Hancock to Susannah Connolly

Madam,   Philada. May 23d. 1776.

I laid before Congress your Application for a Passport to proceed to Pittsburgh; and am now to acquaint you, that under the present Situation of Affairs they could not comply with your Request, and further they have judged it necessary, that you should, for the present, remain in this City, and agreeably to their Order I am to inform you, that they expect that you do not depart this City without the Permission of Congress. You will therefore abide here, until you hear further from me.[1] I am, Madam, your very hble Sert.

                                                                             J. H. Prst.

LB (DNA: PCC, item 12A).

[1] See *JCC,* 4:366. Susannah Connolly was the wife of Dr. John Connolly, who had been under arrest in Philadelphia since December 1775 as a result of his efforts to stir up Indian and loyalist opposition to the American cause. Mrs. Connolly's "Application" may have been turned down because Congress was currently considering a plan for an expedition against Detroit. Also Congress was probably still uneasy over the May 7 escape from a Philadelphia jail of Moses Kirkland, an active British supporter who had been apprehended in December 1775. See *JCC,* 4:337, 346; *Md. Archives,* 11:424–25; *Pennsylvania Evening Post,* May 8; *Virginia Gazette* (Purdie), May 17, 1776; and Richard Henry Lee to Charles Lee, May 21, 1776, note 3. Not until September 1776 did a committee of Congress report that Mrs. Connolly "may be enlarged with Safety to these States, and suffered to go to her family in Cumberland County, in the State of Pennsylvania." *JCC,* 5:748n.1. For her fate in Philadelphia until then, see her letters of June 10 to Hancock and of July 8 and September 9 to Congress. *Am. Archives,* 4th ser. 6:784, 5th ser. 2:254; and *Pa. Archives,* 1st ser. 4:782–83. See also *JCC,* 5:429, 525–26, 545; and *Am. Archives,* 5th ser. 1:1296.

John Hancock to Abraham Livingston

Sir,   Philada. May 23d. 1776.

The Congress having been pleased to accept your Resignation of the Contract for supplying the Forces in the Colony of New York, I am extremely happy in conveying to you the Sense they entertain of your Conduct on the Occasion.[1]

In thus voluntarily resigning so profitable a Contract, it is their Opinion which I am commanded to signify to you, That you have exhibited an Example of Public Spirit.

The generous & disinterested Virtue you have shewn, will undoubtedly entitle you hereafter to the Notice of Congress. Should any Appointment worthy of your Acceptance come before them, I shall do all in my Power to have it bestowed on a Gentleman, who has reflected the highest Honour upon himself, by an unsolicited Sacrifice of private Interest, to public Order & Œconomy.

I have the Honour to be, with great Esteem, Sir, your most obedt. & very hble Servt.   J. H. Presidt.

LB (DNA: PCC, item 12A).

[1] For a detailed account of this incident, see James Duane to the New York Provincial Convention, March 21, 1776, note 2.

Robert Treat Paine's Diary

[May 23, 1776]

Fair. 8 o'Clock Sett out [1] with Mr. Clement Biddle,[2] rode to Hendersons Tavern, Sign 7 Starrs up Reading Road 12m., thence to Pawling Ferry over Schuylkill 10m, thence to the Continental Powder Mill on French Creek 5m,[3] din'd, view'd the Mill, thence to Warwick Furnace owned by Potts, 12m, rough Country, lodged. Genl. Washington arrived at Philada.

MS (MHi).

[1] Undoubtedly as an outgrowth of his work on several committees concerned with the production and purchase of powder and arms for the Continental Army, Paine set out this day on an inspection trip to various Pennsylvania powder mills, saltpetre works, iron furnaces, and cannon foundries that took him to more than a dozen such manufactories in seven days. See JCC, 2:86, 4:55, 169, 171. The outline of his trip—in the course of which he recorded stops at Reading, Miers Town, Lebanon, Manheim Town, Ledits, Lancaster, and White Horse before he arrived back in Philadelphia and returned to Congress on May 29—is preserved in his diary entries for May 23–29, 1776. MHi.

[2] Clement Biddle (1740–1814), Philadelphia merchant, was appointed on July 8 deputy quartermaster general for the forces "ordered to rendezvous at Trenton" and served as commissary general of forage, 1777–80. DAB.

[3] For further information on the "Continental Powder Mill on French Creek" and other gunpowder mills in Pennsylvania, see David L. Salay, "The Production of Gunpowder in Pennsylvania during the American Revolution," PMHB 94 (October 1975): 422–42.

Elbridge Gerry to Richard Devens

Dear Sir,[1]   Philadelphia May 24th 1776

I recd your Favour of the 7th Instant & in Consequence of your Desire have employed Mr. Wm. Barrel to procure the Cloth for 1000 Tents & have them made in this Place. As the making is @ 8/ lawf[ul] here & 10/ or 10/3 in Massachusetts, I should have preferred his sending the Cloth—that the Tradesmen in our own Colony might have had the advantage but Mr. Barrel thinks he can deliver the Tents nearly as soon as the Canvas & hopes to be able to deliver them by the latter End of next Month. If the Quantity is too great You are to signify it to him by the first oppertunity, & furnish the Money for purchasing what is wanted. Mr Barrel informs me that there remains abt. 15000 Dollars of the Money sent by the Committee of the Court for purchasing 10,000 bbs flour, which he will convert to this Use if an order is obtained on the President for this purpose. He has purchased but 6061 bbs not having had Vessels for shipping a larger Quantity, & as the Risque is so exceedingly increased it is probable the Comee. will not think it proper to order the Residue, but purchase it elsewhere.

Mr. Commissary Trumbul is here & informs me that he can deliver what is wanted at Cambridge for 20/ law[ful] P[ennsylvania] C[urrency] which you may mention to the Committee (if necessary) that this very necessary article may be procured in Time. Possibly it may be procured still more reasonably.

The Committee of this City are collecting all the Window Weights of Lead in the same & replacing them with Iron, I hope a Committee will be appointed upon your application, by the hona House to apply to the Inhabitants of Boston for their leadn. Weights & Spouts, & that the price for effective Fire Arms manufactured in the Colony will be enhanced as they are greatly needed. I wish you Success in procuring all Necessaries & remain sir your Friend & hum sev,

Elb Gerry

P.S. I shall be glad of further Information relative to your Success on the Salt petre manufactory. The price of Ticklinburg is enhanced to 4/ Phila Currency per Ell.

RC (M–Ar).

[1] Richard Devens (1721–1807), Charlestown, Mass., merchant, was appointed commissary general of the Massachusetts militia in 1776 and held that post until 1782. L. Kinvin Wroth et al., eds., *Province in Rebellion: A Documentary History of the Founding of the Commonwealth of Massachusetts, 1774–1775*, 4 vols. (Cambridge: Harvard University Press, 1975), 4:2847–48.

John Hancock
to the Commissioners to Canada

Gentlemen,   Philada. May 24th. 1776.

By the enclosed Resolves of Congress which I do myself the
Honour of transmitting, you will perceive that every Step has been
taken to procure hard Money that could be devised.[1]

I have forwarded to Genl. Schuyler by this Conveyance the Sum
of sixteen Hundred & sixty two Pounds one Shilling & three Pence
in hard Money, which was all that was in the Treasury. Genl
Washington arrived here yesterday Afternoon in good Health, the
Congress having requested his Attendance in order to consult him
on the Operation of the approaching Campaign, and such other
Matters as should be necessary.

I have the Honour to be, Gentlemen, your most obedt. and very
hble Sert.   J. H. Prst.

LB (DNA: PCC, item 12A).
  [1] These resolutions were passed by Congress on May 22, partly in response to the
commissioners' letters to Hancock of May 1, 6, and 8. See *JCC*, 4:358, 362, 375–78.

John Hancock to Philip Schuyler

Sir,   Philada. May 24th. 1776

In Obedience to a Resolve of Congress[1] I herewith transmit the
Sum of Sixteen Hundred and sixty two Pounds, one Shilling & three
pence in three Bags, which I have committed to the Charge of
Captn. Graydon of the Pennsylvania Forces in the Continental
Service. This is all the hard Money that was in the Treasury.

Enclosed you have the Resolves of Congress with regard to our
Affairs in Canada.[2] At present I am so extremely hurried, that I
have only Time to add that, the Money voted by Congress to be sent
to you shall be forwarded in a few Days.

Genl. Washington arrived here yesterday in good Health, the
Congress having requested his Attendance to consult him on the
operations of the approaching Campaign.

I have the Honour to be, Sir, your most obedt. & very hble Servt
                                                        J. H. Prst.

LB (DNA: PCC, item 12A).
  [1] Passed on May 18. *JCC*, 4:366.
  [2] These resolves, passed by Congress on May 22, were mainly directions to
Schuyler and the Canadian commissioners for arresting the collapse of the American position in Canada, prompted by the reception of alarming intelligence from
there on May 16 and 18. On the 16th Congress appointed John Adams, Thomas

Jefferson, and William Livingston as a committee to consider letters describing numerous difficulties facing the American invading forces, and on the 18th it added five more delegates to the committee upon the arrival that day of several more letters bearing dismal news. This committee submitted a report on May 21, on the basis of which Congress passed the resolves which Hancock forwarded to Schuyler with this letter. See *JCC*, 4:358–59, 362–63, 374–78; and Washington to Hancock, May 15 and 17, 1776, PCC, item 152, 1:685–88, 693–96; and Washington, *Writings* (Fitzpatrick), 5:44–46, 54. For a survey of the deterioration of American fortunes in Canada during the first half of 1776, see Gustave Lanctot, *Canada & the American Revolution, 1774–1783*, trans. Margaret M. Cameron (Toronto and Vancouver: Clarke, Irwin & Co., 1967), chaps. 8 and 9.

John Hancock to Philip Schuyler

Sir,   Philada. May 24th. 1776.

I did myself the Honour of writing to you this Morning, and at the same Time transmitted all the hard Money that was in the Treasury, amounting to sixteen Hundred & sixty two Pounds, one Shilling, & three pence, which I hope you will duely receive.

The Congress have this Day come to the enclosed Resolutions, which I am commanded to forward to you by Express, as containing Matters of the highest Importance to the Wellfare of these United Colonies.[1]

It must no Doubt have occurred to you, Sir, that should our Enemics get Possession of any one Province, which may not only supply them with Provisions &c, but from which they may harrass the adjacent Country, the Preservation of American Liberty would be rendered thereby much more difficult and precarious. It is this Circumstance which at present gives perhaps a greater Weight to the War in Canada, than in any other Part of America; as the Danger of our Enemies getting Footing there is much greater. The Consequences, too, in Case they succeed in that Province, would be much more fatal; as we must expect, if that Event takes Place, to have all the Canadians and Indians join against us.

It is not conceiveable in my Mind that there was ever a Time or Situation that called for more Vigorous & decisive Measures than the present in Canada. Our Enemies seemed determined to prosecute their Plans agt. us with the greatest Violence: while their Schemes are kept so enveloped in Darkness that there is no Possibility of finding them out.

This much only we may be sure of—that they will aim the most deadly Blows at our devoted Country. It is our Duty therefore to shield and protect her from all Evil, but especially in those Parts where she is the most vulnerable. Whether or not the Province of Canada, is this Part, I shall leave to you to determine.

I have the Honour to be, Sir, your most obedt. & very hble Servt.

J. H. Prt.

LB (DNA: PCC, item 12A).

[1] These resolves, the most important of which declared that "the commanding officer in Canada, be informed, that the Congress are fully convinced of the absolute necessity of keeping possession of that country," were based upon the report of a committee appointed by Congress on May 23 to confer with Generals Washington, Gates, and Mifflin "upon the most speedy and effectual means for supporting the American cause in Canada." *JCC*, 4:383–84, 388.

John Hancock to John Thomas

Sir,   Philada. May 24th 1776.

You will perceive by the enclosed Resolutions of Congress which I do myself the Honour of transmitting, and to which I beg Leave to refer your attention that Canada, in their opinion is an object of the last Importance to the Welfare of the United Colonies.[1]

Should our Troops retire before the Enemy and entirely evacuate that Province, it is not in Human Wisdom to foretel the Consequences. In this Case, the Loss of Canada will not be all. The whole Frontiers of the New England & New York Governments will be exposed not only to the Ravages of the Indians, but also of the British Forces, not less savage & barbarous in the Prosecution of the present War.

In this View of the Matter it is needless to employ Arguments to excite you to the greatest Vigour & Dilligence on this Occasion.

The Congress having tried every Method to collect hard Money for the Army in Canada, without Success, are determined not to relinquish the Expedition or give it up. They have therefore resolved to supply our Troops there with Provisions & Cloathing from the other Colonies if they cannot be had in that Country; of which Resolution, I sent this Morning an Account to Genl. Schuyler accompanied with several other Resolutions, with regard to the Situation of Affairs in that Quarter.

Upon the whole, it seems from the latest Intelligence that Nothing but the greatest Exertions of Capacity and Vigour will ever retrieve our Misfortunes in Canada. The Eyes of the Continent are upon you. Display therefore, I entreat you for your own Honour, and the Good of your Country, those military Qualities, which you certainly possess. There are still Laurels to be acquired in Canada, which I have the most pleasing Hopes are reserved for you, as the Command of the Expedition is now given to you.

I have Nothing further to add, but that I am commanded by Congress to direct you will carry the enclosed Resolves into Execution as speedily as possible.

I have the Honour to be, Sir, your most obedt. & very hble Serv.

J. H. Prst.

LB (DNA: PCC, item 12A).

[1] See *JCC*, 4:388.

Commissioners to Canada
to David Wooster

Sir,   Montreal 25th May 1776

The inclosed [1] We desire You to forward by the Express to Saint Johns, which We presume You will send off in Consequence of our Letter of this Date.[2] Unless immediate Steps are taken to procure provisions for the Army, the Soldiers must starve or plunder the Inhabitants.

It is a Duty incumbent on our Generals to prevent such a dreadful Scene by every Means in their power.

We are, Sir, Your Most Obedt. Servants,

                                                             Saml. Chase

                                                     Ch. Carroll of Carrollton

RC (PHi). Written by Chase and signed by Chase and Carroll.

[1] Not found. Apparently a letter to James Price and William McCarty pertaining to the procurement of flour. See Commissioners to Canada to John Thomas, May 26, 1776.

[2] The commissioners wrote another brief letter to Wooster this day. "We think it would be proper for you to issue an order to the town Major to wait on the Merchants or others having provisions or merchandize for Sale and request a delivery of what our troops are in immediate want of, offering to give a receipt expressing the quantity delivered and engaging the faith of the United Colonies for payment, and on refusal we think our necessity requires that force should be used to compel a delivery." Burr MSS, MWA.

James Duane to John Jay

                                                        Philad 25 May 1776

I conclude, my dear Sir, that the late Resolution of Congress recommending the Assumption of Government will induce you to give your Attendance for a few days at our own Convention.[1] If this shoud be the Case it will [be] of advantage to you to be informed of the Temper and proceedings of the neighbouring Colonies on this great Revolution.

You recollect the Maryland Instruction which, upon any Measure of Congress to this Effect, requird the Delegates of that Colony to repair to their provincial Convention. These Gent. accordingly declard that they shoud consider their Colony as unrepresented untill they receivd the directions of their principals who were then sitting at Annapolis. Yesterday the Sense of that Convention was made publick; they approve of the Conduct of their Delegates in Dissenting from the preamble & the Resolution—they repeat & enforce their former Instructions—declare that they have not lost sight of a Reconciliation with Great Britain; & that they will adhere to the Common Cause & support it on the principles of the Union as explaind at the time of entering on the War. So much for Maryland.[2]

The General Assembly of Pensylvania is averse to any Change. The people of this Town assembled last Monday in the State house yard & agreed to a set of Resolutions in favour of a Change. Another body are signing a Remonstrance against the Acts of that Meeting and in Support of the Assembly. The Committee for the County of Philadelphia have unanimously Supported the Assembly & protested against any Change. It is supposed the other Counties will follow the Example & take a part in the dispute. Is it not to be feared that this spirit of Dissention will spread itself into the adjoining Colonies? But I intend to make no Reflections. The facts I have hinted at will be published—what relates to this City & the County of Phila. already are—and the Maryland Delegates have express directions to submit their Acts to the publick View. It may be Some days before they come to your Knowledge thro' the Channel of the Press. I coud say a great deal to you on this interesting Subject; but you are master of my sentiments which are not altered since you left me here.

I expect Mr Alsop this Evening & shall in that Case set out on Monday to visit my Family.[3] It is more than 9 months since I have seen my Children; & I have spent but about ten days in that time with Mrs. Duane.

I am my dear Sir, with the greatest Regard, Your affectionate & most Obed Servt,   Jas Duane

RC (NNC).
[1] In his reply to Duane written from New York on May 29, 1776, Jay observed: "So great are the Inconveniences resulting from the present Mode of Government, that I believe our Convention will almost unanimously agree to institute a better, to continue till a Peace with Great Britain shall render it unnecessary." Jay, *Papers* (Morris), pp. 269-70. Jay's draft of this reply, located in the Jay Papers, NNC, contains the following paragraph about John Alsop and Francis Lewis, which is crossed out in the draft and does not appear at all in the RC:

"Messrs. Alsop and Lewis start for Congress on Saturday next. The former of them has committed a piece of Imprudence or mercantile Finesse which I suspect will destroy the Confidence the People fixed on him. They say he asked six Shillings per pound for his Tea by the Quantity, on which the Retailor, not being able to make any Proffit if sold agreable to the Resolve of Congress, objected to taking it. To remove this objection, it is said, Mr. Alsop advised him to put it up in *paper Parcels* and by an extra Charge for *Paper*, obtain a reasonable Proffit. This Affair has made much Noise, and I believe will make more."

[2] See Carter Braxton to Landon Carter, May 17; and Thomas Stone to James Hollyday?, May 20, 1776.

[3] Duane left Congress on May 31, 1776, and did not return until April of the following year. Edward P. Alexander, *A Revolutionary Conservative: James Duane of New York* (New York: Columbia University Press, 1938), pp. 119, 124.

John Hancock to the Commanding Officer
in Philadelphia

Sir,   Philada. May 25th 1776
   As the Congress have desired the Battalions of Associators in &
near the City & Liberties to have their Battalions drawn out as
early as they can on Monday Morning, & propose with the Generals
now in Town to attend the Review at 9 O'Clock, I have it in Command to order you to draw out such of the Continental Troops as
have Arms, & form them in Battalion with the Associators aforesaid.[1]
   I am Sir you most obed. Sert,   J. H. Pt.

LB (DNA: PCC, item 12A). Addressed: "To the Commanding officer of the Continental Troops in Philada."
   [1] See *JCC*, 4:392–93. The next day Hancock sent the following additional instruction: "To prevent any mistake . . . I am to inform you that the Battalions
of Associators are to form distinct from your Corps, and to be solely Commanded
by their own officers. This you will please to Notice, and Post your Troops in
the Field in such order as not to Interfere with the Disposition of the City
Troops." PCC, item 12A; and *Am. Archives*, 4th ser. 6:577.

Secret Committee Minutes of Proceedings

                                                        May 25th. [1776]
   Issued an order in favor of Jonathan Hudson of Baltimore on the
Treasurers for 1333 1/3 dlls in part of his account of charges &
demurrage on ship Molly, Isaac Hudson Master, as per contract with
this Come. for which he is to be accountable.[1]
   Order on Robt. Towers for 75 lb powder in favor of J. Wilson
& Peter Chevalier, who are accountable for the same. Order on
R. Towers in favor of Come. of safety Philadelphia, for half ton
of powder for which they are to be accountable.

MS (MH).
   [1] On August 6 the committee paid Jonathan Hudson an additional $800 "in
part for damage &c on his ship Molly," which had been seized by Lord Dunmore's fleet and was later retaken by the Continental brig *Andrew Doria*. Journal
of the Secret Committee, fol. 90, MH; Clark, *Naval Documents*, 5:341, 6:895.
See also Secret Committee Minutes of Proceedings, March 14 and September 20,
1776.

Oliver Wolcott to Laura Wolcott

My Dear,   Philadelphia 25 May 1776
   By Oliver's Letter by D'Lucence I was glad to be informed that

you was well. I hope to have the Pleasure of seeing my Family this Summer. Mr. Huntington is now gone Home. He will Return in about a Forthnight. Mrs. Sherman is here and Mr. Sherman intends to go home with her as soon as Mr. Huntington comes back.[1] I do with less regret Submit to live here till the heat of Summer, as it will be then uncomfortable And tho it will [be] tedious travelling yet I had rather submit to that than live here in that Season. In about Two Months I may probably Return but which I may Vary upon Circumstances. Mr. Baldwin the Tutor is in Town who tells Me he will take Care and provide a good Place for Oliver. Perhaps he will take him into his own Rooms, however he says he will see that he Shall be well provided for. Mr. Pierpoints is a Very good Place but its Seems Oliver must remove from thence. Capt Mix is a Virtuous Family. His Son Oliver's Classmate it seems is but an Ordinary Lad. If he is to live with him I shall be averse to it and as he is his Classmate Should preferr that he would not live in the same House. The Lad is not that I know of Vicious but indolent and triffling and has a Town Acquaintance which it is not any advantage to a Child to be led into. But this must be left to yr Prudence. Mr. Baldwin I believe will Very cheerfully Assist him in any Things and he mentioned as tho he perhaps might live with Mr. Buksminster. I care not whether he lives in the Colledge or not, but let him have good company and such advantages as may be Necessary. It seems he maintains a good Character, and I hope he will keep it. If the Matter is not So fixd, with Regard to his living with Capt Mix, Oliver need but Wait upon Mr. Baldwin and he will tell him of his Lodgings—such as I do not doupt will be Very proper for him.

I wrote to you the 16t, 11t, and 4t instant. I shall Write to you once in a Week or ten Days while I am here. For News referr you to the Papers. G. Britain mean or rather the King of it to exert his utmost force agt. this Country and has infamously hired Mercenaries to Subdue us but I trust in God he will be defeated. I have No Apprehension that more than 30,000 at most including those already here will be employed in the Land Service. By the blessing of God I am Well. My Love to my Children and Friends. I am with the greatest Affection, yrs,   Oliver Wolcott

RC (CtHi).
[1] Samuel Huntington returned to Philadelphia soon after June 25 and Wolcott apparently left for home about June 28. See Wolcott to Laura Wolcott, June 25, 1776.

John Adams to James Sullivan

Dear Sir.[1]   Philadelphia May 26. 1776
Your Favours of May 9th and 17th are now before me;[2] and I

consider them as the Commencement of a Correspondence, which will not only give me Pleasure, but may be of Service to the public, as, in my present Station I Stand in need of the best Intelligence, and the Advice of every Gentlemen of Abilities and public Principles, in the Colony which has seen fit to place me here.

Our worthy Friend, Mr Gerry has put into my Hand, a Letter from you, of the Sixth of May, in which you consider the Principles of Representation and Legislation, and give us Hints of Some Alterations, which you Seem to think necessary, in the Qualification of Voters.

I wish, Sir, I could possibly find Time, to accompany you, in your Investigation of the Principles upon which a Representative assembly Stands and ought to Stand, and in your Examination whether the Practice of our Colony, has been conformable to those Principles. But alass! Sir, my Time is so incessantly engrossed by the Business before me that I cannot Spare enough, to go through so large a Field: and as to Books, it is not easy to obtain them here, nor could I find a Moment to look into them, if I had them.

It is certain in Theory, that the only moral Foundation of Government is the Consent of the People. But to what an Extent Shall We carry this Principle? Shall We Say, that every Individual of the Community, old and young, male and female, as well as rich and poor, must consent, expressly to every Act of Legislation? No, you will Say, this is impossible. How then does the Right arise in the Majority to govern the Minority, against their Will? Whence arises the Right of the Men to govern Women, without their Consent? Whence the Right of the old to bind the Young, without theirs?

But let us first Suppose, that the whole Community of every Age, Rank, Sex, and Condition, has a Right to vote. This Community is assembled—a Motion is made and carried by a Majority of one Voice. The Minority will not agree to this. Whence arises the Right of the Majority to govern, and the obligation of the Minority to obey? From Necessity, you will Say, because there can be no other Rule. But why exclude Women? You will Say, because their Delicacy renders them unfit for Practice and Experience, in the great Businesses of Life, and the hardy Enterprises of War, as well as the arduous Cares of State. Besides, their attention is so much engaged with the necessary Nurture of their Children, that Nature has made them fittest for domestic Cares. And Children have not Judgment or Will of their own. True. But will not these Reasons apply to others? Is it not equally true, that Men in general in every Society, who are wholly destitute of Property, are also too little acquainted with public affairs to form a Right Judgment, and too dependent upon other Men to have a Will of their own? If this is a Fact, if you give to every Man, who has no Property, a Vote, will you not make a fine encouraging Provision for Corruption by your fundamental Law?

Such is the Frailty of the human Heart, that very few Men, who have no Property, have any Judgment of their own. They talk and vote as they are directed by Some Man of Property, who has attached their Minds to his Interest.

Upon my Word, Sir, I have long thought an Army a Piece of Clock Work and to be governed only by Principles and Maxims, as fixed as any in Mechanicks and by all that I have read in the History of Mankind, and in Authors, who have Speculated upon Society and Government, I am much inclined to think, a Government must manage a Society in the Same manner; and that this is Machinery too.

Harrington has Shewn that Power always follows Property. This I believe to be as infallible a Maxim, in Politicks, as, that Action and Reaction are equal, is in Mechanicks. Nay I believe We may advance one Step farther and affirm that the Ballance of Power in a Society, accompanies the Ballance of Property in Land. The only possible Way then of preserving the Ballance of Power on the side of equal Liberty and public Virtue, is to make the Acquisition of Land easy to every Member of Society: to make a Division of the Land into Small Quantities, so that the Multitude may be possessed of landed Estates. If the Multitude is possessed of the Ballance of real Estate, the Multitude will have the Ballance of Power, and in that Case the Multitude will take Care of the Liberty, Virtue, and Interest of the Multitude in all Acts of Government.

I believe these Principles have been felt, if not understood in the Massachusetts Bay, from the Beginning: and therefore I Should think that Wisdom and Policy would dictate in these times, to be very cautious of making Alterations. Our People have never been very rigid in Scrutinising into the Qualifications of Voters, and I presume they will not now begin to be so. But I would not advise them to make any alteration in the Laws, at present, respecting the Qualifications of Voters.

Your Idea, that those Laws, which affect the Lives and personal Liberty of all, or which inflict corporal Punishment, affect those, who are not qualified to vote, as well as those who are, is just. But, so they do Women, as well as Men, Children as well as Adults. What Reason Should there be, for excluding a Man of Twenty Years, Eleven Months and Twenty seven days old, from a Vote when you admit one who is twenty one? The Reason is you must fix upon Some Period in Life, when the Understanding and Will of Men in general is fit to be trusted by the Public. Will not the Same Reason justify the State in fixing upon Some certain Quantity of Property, as a Qualification.

The Same Reasoning, which will induce you to admit all Men, who have no Property, to vote, with those who have, for those Laws, which affect the Person will prove that you ought to admit Women and Children: for generally Speaking, Women and Children have as good Judgment, and as independent Minds as those Men who are wholly destitute of Property: these last being to all Intents and Purposes as much dependent upon others, who will please to feed, cloath, and employ them, as Women are upon their Husbands, or Children on their Parents.

As to your Idea of proportioning the Votes of Men in Money Matters, to the Property they hold, it is utterly impracticable. There is no possible Way of ascertaining, at any one Time, how much every Man in a Community, is worth; and if there was, so fluctuating is Trade and Property, that this State of it, would change in half an Hour. The Property of the whole Community, is Shifting every Hour, and no Record can be kept of the Changes.

Society can be governed only by general Rules. Government cannot accommodate itself to every particular Case, as it happens, nor to the Circumstances of particular Persons. It must establish general, comprehensive Regulations for Cases and Persons. The only Question is, which general Rule will accommodate most Cases and most Persons.

Depend upon it, Sir, it is dangerous to open so fruitfull a Source of Controversy and altercation; as would be opened by attempting to alter the Qualifications of Voters. There will be no End of it. New Claims will arise. Women will demand a Vote. Lads from 12 to 21 will think their Rights not enough attended to, and every Man, who has not a Farthing, will demand an equal Voice with any other in all Acts of State. It tends to confound and destroy all Distinctions, and prostrate all Ranks, to one common Levell. I am &c

LB (MHi).
[1] James Sullivan (1744–1808), brother of Gen. John Sullivan, was a lawyer and member of the Massachusetts legislature, 1775–79, 1783–84, 1787–88. He served as a justice of the Massachusetts Superior Court of Judicature, 1776–82, and in 1782 was elected a delegate to Congress. *DAB.*
[2] Sullivan's May 9 and 17 letters to Adams are in the Adams Papers, MHi.

Commissioners to Canada
to John Thomas

Sir,   Montreal May 26th. 1776.
We are favoured with yours of yesterday from Chambly. We went to Sorel on purpose to learn the Conditions of our Army, and to know the Sentiments of the General officers respecting the future operations of the Campaign. We expected to have had the pleasure of meeting with you there; on our way to Sorel we were informed of your being taken ill with the Smallpox, and that you had left the

Camp. We hoped to have found you at Chambly; and to converse with you on the state of our Affairs in this Country was the principal end of our Journey thither: unluckily we passed you on the road. In the present situation of the Army we think it would be impracticable to occupy & fortify the post of Déchambault & Jacques Cartier. We are sorry to find so little discipline in the Army, and that it is so badly provided in every respect. We have some time since written pressingly to Congress for hard Money, without which we believe it impossible to relieve our wants: the most immediate & pressing necessity is the want of flour. We have advised Genl. Wooster to issue an Order to the town Major to wait on the Merchants or others having provisions or Merchandize for sale and request a delivery of What the soldiers are in immediate want of, & pledge the faith of the United Colonies for payment; & have given it as our Opinion, that on Refusal, our necessity requires, that force should be used to compel a Delivery. We have advised the Genl. to issue a similar order to Messrs. Price & McCarty. The Genl. has complied with our Advice in both instances, and yesterday Evening dispatched an Express to St Johns with a letter to those Gentn. We wrote to them by the same opportunity our sentiments. Flour is not to be procured in any considerable quantity on this Island. Unless immediate steps be taken to secure large quantities of Wheat, & have it ground up into flour with the utmost dispatch, the Army will be reduced to the greatest Streights for want of bread. We most earnestly intreat you to turn your attention to this matter, and to use all the means which your prudence will suggest to procure flour for the troops. None is to be expected, at least for some time, from over the Lakes. Our Soldiers will be soon reduced to the dreadful alternative of Starving, or of plundering the Inhabitants: the latter will surely happen, if our Troops should not be Supplied with bread in a regular way; their other immediate wants may in some measure be relieved by compelling a delivery of some Goods on the same terms with wheat & flour. This however we confess a Violent remedy, which nothing can justify, but the most Urgent Necessity, and therefore cannot be long pursued without drawing on us the resentment of the Inhabitants. In short, Sir, without a speedy supply of hard money it appears to us, next to impossible to remain in Canada, even if we had no enemy, but the Inhabitants to contend with.

We have already mentioned the bad discipline of the Army. It is no doubt in a great measure owing to the cause assigned in One of your letters, the short inlistments; but there appears to us other causes: the Officers are not sufficiently active, nor do they seem actuated by those disinterested principles & generous Sentiments, which might be expected from men fighting in so just & glorious a cause. We would not be understood to cast a general reflection.

There are many Officers we are satisfied, who act upon the noblest motives, but it gives us pain to assert on the best information, that there are several, whose conduct has too plainly proved them unworthy of the charactor & trust conferred on them by their countrymen. We have mentioned our sentiments with freedom. We shall always give our Opinions with the same; We mean not to dictate, but to advise with you & the Genl. Officers on the most effectual ways & means of extricating ourselves from our present difficulties, and promoting the Genl. service. As by this time the virulence of yr. disorder, we hope is abated, we recommend a meeting of the Genl. Officers at Chambly to consult about, & agree upon the future operations of the War in Canada. The inclosed copy of General Arnolds last letter will give you the best intelligence respecting the Affair at the Cedars, & the actual State of the Enemy & our forces on this Island. Colo. DeHaas marched yesterday evening from this town, at 6 oClock, with 400 Men to La Chine. We flatter ourselves we shall drive the Enemy off the Island, redeem our prisoners, & recover our post at the Cedars.

We are with sincere wishes for your speedy recovery, Sir, Yr. most Obt. hum Servts.   Samuel Chase

Ch. Carroll of Carrollton

RC (MHi). From the papers of Theodore Sedgwick, who at this time was secretary to General Thomas. In a clerical hand and signed by Carroll and Chase.

Joseph Hewes to Samuel Johnston

Dear Sir: Philadelphia, 26th May, 1776.

The prisoners sent under the direction of Colonel Haynes arrived here yesterday morning.[1] They are put into the jail of this city for the present. Mr. Haynes informs me he received £100, Virginia, at Williamsburg, and the like sum in Continental money in Maryland, for which he had drawn bills on the Treasury. I shall take care to see they are paid when they come to hand. I had advanced him $134, which I charge to our Province, and for which he will account with you.

The wagon with the medicines (of which I wrote to you by Mr. Luther) will set off in two or three days; it waits only to have them properly put up, which takes some time. Those things that are most useful are beginning to grow scarce.

On the 17th of this instant (being fast day), the Continental armed schooner Franklyn fell in with and took a transport ship of 300 tons burden, bound for Boston, having on board seventy-five tons (say, 1,500 barrels) of powder, one thousand arms, and sundry

other military stores. She has been carried in and the cargo safely
landed in Boston, the place of her destination. This we consider
a great acquisition.[2]

The Generals Washington and Gates are now here. They were
sent for in order that Congress might consult them on several matters respecting the present campaign, which is expected to be a very
warm one in every part of the Continent.

A deputation of the Six Nations of Indians came to town a few
days ago. They are to have an audience of Congress to-morrow,
previous to which the city battalions are to be drawn out and reviewed by the Generals, in order to give those savages some idea
of our strength and importance.[3]

I have not had the pleasure of hearing from any of my friends
at Halifax since the 22nd of April. I should be happy in receiving
an account of the proceedings of your Congress respecting public
matters.

Mr. Haynes, fearing he might get the smallpox, left town much
sooner than I expected, which prevents me from writing to any other
friend. Please give my compliments to Hooper, Penn, Harnett, etc.,
etc. I am respectfully, dear sir, Your most obedient humble servant,

Joseph Hewes.

MS not found; reprinted from *N.C. State Records*, 22: 969–70.

[1] These prisoners consisted almost entirely of officers of the loyalist force defeated at the battle of Moore's Creek Bridge in North Carolina in February 1776.
See *JCC*, 4:389, 392; and *Am. Archives*, 4th ser. 5:1005–6.

[2] For other accounts of the capture of the *Hope* by the *Franklin*, see Clark,
Naval Documents, 5:133–36, 141.

[3] See *JCC*, 4:392, 396–97.

Secret Committee Minutes of Proceedings

May 26th. 1776.

At a meeting of the Come. Prest. Mr Morris, Mr. Hewes, Mr Lee,
Mr. Bartlet & Mr. McKean. A Charter party with G. Mead & Co for
the ship Fanny was signd.[1] A letter from J. Langdon dated Portsmouth April 22d was read & enclosd the following Receit—Receivd
Cambridge March 27, 1776 of Capt. J. Langdon, by the hand of Mr.
Jeremiah Libbey 22 barrels, 4 half barrels, 111 quarter Casks, 88
kegs of 10 [lb.] each, one Cask containing twenty six pounds & 8
Casks 15 lb each, in the whole Six thousand two hundred & fifty one
pounds powder all in good order except three Casks of ten pounds
wch. are some thing wanting. Ezekl. Cheever Com[missar]y Artillery.[2]
Ordered that a vessel not drawing more than 13 feet water be hird
& loaded on continentl. Acct. to be dispatched to Cape Francois
under direction of a proper Supercargo who is to sell the vessel &

treat with M. D'Oraison of said place, for the vessel & Cargoe mentiond in his letter to the Congress dated 6th of April last, referrd by Congress to the Committee.[3]

MS (MH).

[1] See Secret Committee Minutes of Proceedings, May 2, 1776.

[2] For John Langdon's instructions to wagonmaster Jeremiah Libby, see Clark, *Naval Documents*, 4:468–69.

[3] The remainder of this entry pertains to orders on the Continental treasurers to pay accounts submitted to the committee for expenses incurred in obtaining, packing, and shipping small lots of arms and powder.

John Adams to Abigail Adams

May 27. 1776

I have three of your Favours, before me—one of May 7, another of May 9 and a third of May 14th. The last has given me Relief from many Anxieties. It relates wholly to private Affairs, and contains such an Account of wise and prudent Management, as makes me very happy. I begin to be jealous, that our Neighbours will think Affairs more discreetly conducted in my Absence than at any other Time.

Whether your Suspicions concerning a Letter under a marble Cover, are just or not, it is best to say little about it.[1] It is an hasty hurried Thing and of no great Consequence, calculated for a Meridian at a great Distance from N. England. If it has done no good, it will do no harm. It has contributed to sett People a thinking upon the subject, and in this respect has answered its End. The Manufactory of Governments having, since the Publication of that Letter, been as much talk'd of, as that of salt Petre was before.

I rejoice at your Account of the Spirit of Fortification, and the good Effects of it. I hope by this Time you are in a tolerable Posture of defence. The Inhabitants of Boston have done themselves great Honour, by their laudable Zeal, the worthy Clergymen especially.

I think you shine as a Stateswoman, of late as well as a Farmeress. Pray where do you get your Maxims of State, they are very apropos.

I am much obliged to Judge Cushing, and his Lady for their polite Visit to you: should be very happy to see him, and converse with him about many Things but cannot hope for that Pleasure, very soon. The Affairs of America are in so critical a State, such great Events are struggling for Birth, that I must not quit this station at this Time. Yet I dread the melting Heats of a Philadelphia Summer, and know not how my frail Constitution will endure it. Such constant Care, such incessant Application of Mind, drinking up and exhausting the finer Spirits upon which Life and Health so essentially depend, will wear away a stronger Man than I am.

Yet I will not shrink from this Danger or this Toil. While my Health shall be such that I can discharge in any tolerable manner, the Duties of this important Post, I will not desert it.

Am pleased to hear that the superiour Court is to sit, at Ipswich in June. This will contribute to give Stability to the Government, I hope, in all its Branches . . . .[2] But I presume other Steps will be taken for this Purpose. A Governor and Lt. Governor, I hope will be chosen, and the Constitution a little more fixed. I hope too that the Councill will this year be more full and augmented by the Addition of good Men.

I hope Mr. Bowdoin will be Governor, if his Health will permit, and Dr. Winthrop Lt. Governor. These are wise, learned, and prudent Men. The first has a great Fortune, and wealthy Connections, the other has the Advantage of a Name and Family which is much reverenced, besides his Personal Abilities and Virtues, which are very great.

Our Friend,[3] I sincerely hope, will not refuse his Appointment, for although I have ever thought that Bench should be fill'd from the Bar, and once laboured successfully to effect it, yet as the Gentlemen have seen fit to decline, I know of no Gentleman, who would do more Honour to the Station than my Friend. None would be so agreable to me, whether I am to sit by him, or before him. I suppose it must be disagreable to him and his Lady, because he loves to be upon his Farm, and they both love to be together. But you must tell them of a Couple of their Friends who are as fond of living together, who are obliged to sacrifice their rural Amusements and domestic Happiness to the Requisitions of the public.

The Generals Washington, Gates, and Mifflin are all here, and We shall derive Spirit, Unanimity, and Vigour from their Presence and Advice. I hope you will have some General Officers at Boston soon. I am, with constant Wishes and Prayers for your Health, and Prosperity, forever yours.

RC (MHi). Adams, *Family Correspondence* (Butterfield), 1:419–21.

[1] Abigail had correctly surmised that John had written the recently published pamphlet *Thoughts on Government*. See ibid., p. 404.

[2] Suspension points in MS.

[3] James Warren.

Commissioners to Canada to John Hancock

Sir   Montreal May 27. 1776.

We refer you to the inclosed letter from Genl. Thomas of the 20th instant for the reasons which induced him to order Colo. Maxwell to retreat from 3 Rivers to Sorel.[1] He has since given orders, as we are informed by Genl. Thompson's letter of the 20th to remove all the Artillery & Artillery Stores from the mouth of Sorel without the least consultation with the Genl. Officers. We have reason to beleive that there is not that good understanding & free communication of sentiments between the General Officers, which we think essential for the good of the service. General Thomas is now at Chambly under the Small pox; being taken with that disorder, he left the Camp at Sorel, & wrote to General Wooster to come and take the Command. When the interest of our Country, and the safety of your Army is at Stake we think it a very improper time to conceal our sentiments either with respect to persons or things. General Wooster is in our opinion unfit, totally unfit, to Command your Army & conduct the war; we have hitherto prevailed on him to remain in Montreal, his stay in this Colony is unnecessary & even prejudicial to our Affairs, we would therefore humbly advise his recall.

In our last we informed you of the deplorable state of the Army. Matters have not mended since we went to the Mouth of Sorel last week, where we found all things in confusion, there is little or no discipline among your Troops nor can any be kept up, while the practice of Enlisting for a twelve Month continues. The General Officers are all of this Opinion. Your Army is badly paid and so exhausted is your Credit, that even a Cart cannot be procured without ready Money or force. We will give you an instance of the lowness of your Credit. 3 barrels of gunpowder were ordered from Chambly to Montreal. This powder was brought from Chambly to a ferry about 3 Miles off, where it would have remained, had we not luckily passed by, and seeing the distress of the Officer, undertaken to pay ready and hard money for the hire of a cart to convey it to Longueul. The Army is in a distressed condition, and in want of the most Necessary articles. Meat, Bread, tents, Shoes, Stockings, Shirts &c. The greatest part of those who fled from Quebec left all their baggage behind them, or it was plundered by those whose times were out, & have since left Canada. We are informed by Colo. Allen that the Men, who from pretended indisposition had been excused from doing duty, were the foremost in the flight, and carried off such burthens on their backs as hearty & stout Men would labour under.

With difficulty 3 hundred tents and about 2 hundred Camp kettles were procured here, & sent to the Sorel for the use of the Army, and were delivered, as we are informed, to one Major Fuller, who acted in the room of Mr Campbell D.Q.M.G., who had joined the Army at the Sorel, but a day or two before our arrival there. Among other instances of mismanagement we give the following, Colo. Nicholson's regiment consisting only of one Hundred Men received 30 tents and 31 camp kettles, Colo. Porters Regt. not exceeding that number rec'd 56 Tents & 33 kettles.

Your Army in Canada does not exceed 4000. Above 400 are sick with different disorders. 3/4ths of the Army have not had the small Pox. The greater part of Greatons, Bonds, & Burrels Regts. have been lately innoculated. There are about Eight Tons of Gunpowder in the Colony. To evince the great distress we are reduced to for want of bread, we must inform you, that we were obliged to buy 30 Loaves of bread of our baker, to feed Colo. De Haas detachment, which entered this town Friday Night on their way to join General Arnold at La Chine and who could not be supplied by the Commissary; Such is our extreme want of flour, that we were yesterday obliged to seize by force 15 bbs to supply this garrison with bread; previous to this seizure a general order was issued to the town Major to wait on the Merchants or others having provisions or Merchandize for Sale, requesting a delivery of what our Troops are in immediate want of & requiring him to give a receipt expressing the quantity delivered, for the payment of which, the faith of the United Colonies is pledged by your Commissioners. Nothing but the most urgent necessity can justify such harsh measures, but men with arms in their hands will not starve, where provisions can be obtained by force: to prevent a general plunder which might end in the Massacre of your Troops & of many of the Inhabitants we have been constrained to advise the General to take this Step. We cannot conceal our concern that Six Thousand Men should be ordered to Canada without taking care to have Magazines formed for their Subsistance, cash to pay them, or to pay the Inhabitants for their Labour, in transporting the baggage, Stores, and provisions of the Army. We cannot find words strong enough to describe our Miserable Situation, you will have a faint Idea of it if you figure to yourself an Army broken and disheartned, half of it under innoculation or under other diseases, Soldiers without pay, without discipline and altogether reduced to live from hand to mouth, depending on the scanty & precarious Supplies of a few half Starved cattle & triffling quantities of flour which have hitherto been picked up in different parts of the Country.

Your Soldiers grumble for their pay; if they receive it, they will not be benefitted as it will not procure them the necessaries they stand in need of. Your Military chest contains but eleven thousand paper Dollars. You are indebted to your Troops treble that sum and to the Inhabitants above 15000 dollars. You have no adjutant General, a most important Officer, General Thomas appointed a Man totally unfit for the Office, as we are informed by General Thompson & Colo. Sinclair. On General Arnolds recommendation Colo. Antil now does that duty & We gave him Expectation of being paid. We are by no means proper judges of his abilities & fitness for that Station but we are informed, that it requires a Gentleman of great activity and abilities. You have no muster master, We have Authority only to fill up such Vacancys as may happen during our

Continuance in Canada. We met Mr. Flemming appointed by Congress Deputy Adjutant for this Colony, in [New York?], and Captn. Rensselaer the Deputy Muster Master passed Us on the Lake. In some few Instances it may be necessary to make new appointments. E.G. more Deputy Commissaries and Deputy, or Assistant Quarter Masters. Your Generals here have hitherto exercised that power.

The Detachment of 150 Men mentioned in our last to have been sent to the relief of the Cedars under the Command of Major Sherburne were intercepted; we were some time before we could learn the fate of both parties. General Arnold upon his arrival from Sorel set off with a party of 100 Men & took post and Entrenched at La Chine about 9 Miles from this City; Captn Young with a Small Detachment posted at Fort St. Ann on the end of this Island evacuted his post and retreated back leaving the provisions & Stores, on a report that some Indians were landed on the Island. His post might have been defended some days until relief could be sent. General Arnold was soon reinforced by part of Greatons Regt. & some other Troops. Colo. De Haas with 110 Riffle Men & 300 Musqueteers was despatched immediately from Sorel. By the best Intelligence we can get, the enemy are about Six hundred, abt 40 or 50 Regulars, 300 Inds. & 250 Canadians. They have the two pieces of Cannon taken from Colo. Bedels party and were Yesterday within three Miles of General Arnolds Camp, but finding he had been reinforced made a precipitate retreat. Colo. De Haas set off at Six oClock yesterday Morning to endeavour to cut off their retreat, & General Arnold was to follow in a few Minutes in persuit of them. We hope hourly to hear that our prisoners are liberated, & the Enemy routed. The Canadians being threatened to have their habitations destroyed by the Savages, thro' fear are induced to join the Savages. We have also a party of Canadians. We enclose You Copies of Letters from Genls Thomas, Arnold & Thompson [2] and are, Sir, with great Respect to yourself & the Congress, Yr. Most Obedt. Servants,   Samuel Chase

Ch. Carroll of Carrollton

May 28. 1776 Tuesday

General Arnold arrived on Sunday Evening with the Troops, at St. Anns just in time to see the Savages carrying off from an Island the last boat Load of our unhappy prisoners.[3] He had no Boats to follow them. He sent a Caghnawaga Chief to the Savages to inform them if they injured any of our Prisoners that he would destroy their Villages & follow them to the end of the Earth. They replied if he attempted to cross over or attack them that they would immediately kill all their prisoners & for that purpose had collected them together. A Council of war notwithstanding determined to attack them, & the Kings Troops in the morning. Lieut. Park was

sent by Captn. Forster to inform Genl. Arnold that the Savages
were determined to kill their prisoners if attacked, that he could
not control them & therefore from the Dictates of Humanity, he
would propose to release all our prisoners, on Condition that they
should not bear Arms agt. the King during the War, & that an
equal number of his Majesties Troops of the same Rank should be
returned in Exchange. This proposal was rejected by Genl. Arnold.
The inclosed is a Copy of the agreement entered into. This hypro-
critical, insidious, base & wicked Conduct of a British Officer needs
few Comments. The Governors, Agents & Officers of a British King
incite the Savages to join them in a war against these Colonies
without the least provocation or Injury. No cause of Quarrel Subsists between the Savages & the Colonies. If by the Chance of War
any of our Troops are made prisoners they are delivered by the
King's Officers into the Murderous hands of those Cruel & barbarous
savages; contrary to the practice & usage of every civilized Nation
in the World; the British Troops secure their safety by Threats from
the Savages to murder the Prisoners if attacked. Captn. Forster
alledged he had it not in his power to controul the Savages from
an act, which he declares to be opposite, & contrary to the humane
Disposition of the British Govt. & to all civilized Nations. If the
Commander of British forces cannot controul the Savages from
Committing acts of Cruelty & Barbarity, why do they incite them
to Arm agt. Us or act in Conjunction with Barbarians whose Savage
Customs they condemned? This same Conduct in the French during
the last War, was censured and execrated by the British Nation.
Captn. Forster had sufficient Influence over the Savages to induce
them to deliver up *their* prisoners (tho' our Troops surrendered to
him) in order to procure an Exchange of so many of the Kings
Troops now our prisoners, he could controul their will for the
Advantage of the British Nation, but had not the least Influence
over them to prevent the Murdering our people in Cold Blood.
The fear of the Indians of being attacked by our forces was only a
pretext, for Captn. Forster appears desirous of Commencing Hostilities before the Expiration of the time limited. Five or Six of
our prisoners were murdered by the Indians, in the most cruel
manner after the Surrender, The whole were Stripped, contrary to
the Terms of Capitulation, and drove in a Neck of Land: during a
very stormy & tempestuous Night. Colo. Reads & [Starks?] Regts.
arrived at St Johns Saturday Evening. The Letter from Genl.
Thomas to Genl. Wooster of which the enclosed is Copy, this
Minute came to hand.

RC (DNA: PCC, item 166). In a clerical hand and signed by Carroll and Chase.
Received and read in Congress on June 6, 1776. *JCC,* 5:420.
    [1] See *Am. Archives,* 4th ser. 6:592.
    [2] See ibid., pp. 588–97; and *JCC,* 5:420.

³ For an account of this entire affair, see Justin H. Smith, *Our Struggle for the Fourteenth Colony: Canada and the American Revolution*, 2 vols. (New York: G.P. Putnam's Sons, 1907), 2:367–80. See also *Am. Archives*, 4th ser. 6:595–600.

Benjamin Franklin to the Commissioners to Canada

Dear Friends,   N York May 27. 1776

We arrived here safe yesterday Evening, having left Mrs Walker with her Husband at Albany, from whence we came down by Land. We pass'd him on Lake Champlain; but he returning overtook us at Saratoga, where they both gave themselves such Liberties in taunting at our Conduct in Canada, that it came almost to a Quarrel. We continu'd our Care of her, however, and landed her safe in Albany, with her three Waggon Loads of Baggage, brought thither without putting her to any Expence, and parted civilly tho coldly. I think they both have excellent Talents at making themselves Enemies, and I believe, live where they will, they will never be long without them.

We met yesterday two Officers from Philadelphia with a Letter from the Congress to the Commissioners, & a Sum of hard Money.[1] I opened the Letter & seal'd it again, directing them to carry it forward to you. I congratulate you on the great Prize carry'd into Boston. Seventy-five Tons of Gunpowder is an excellent Supply; and the 1000 Carbines with Bayonets, another fine Article. The German Auxiliaries are certainly coming. It is our Business to prevent their Returning.

The Congress have advis'd the erecting new Governments, which has ocasion'd some Dissension at Philada.; but I hope it will soon be compos'd.

I shall be glad to hear of your Welfare. As to my self, I find I grow daily more feeble, and think I could hardly have got along so far, but for Mr Carroll's friendly Assistance & tender Care of me. Some Symptoms of the Gout now appear, which makes me think my Indisposition has been a smother'd Fit of that Disorder, which my Constitution wanted Strength to form completely. I have had several Fits of it formerly.

God bless you & prosper your Councils; and bring you safe again to your Friends & Families. With the greatest Esteem & Respect, I am, Your most obedt humble Servant,[2]   B Franklin

RC (NN).

[1] See John Hancock to the Commissioners to Canada, May 24, 1776.

[2] Franklin also wrote to General Schuyler this date relating an account of his journey and thanking the general and his wife for their assistance during his trip southward. Miscellaneous MSS, N.

Richard Henry Lee to Charles Lee

My dear Friend   Philadelphia 27th May 1776
    The inclosed intelligence lately received from England will give
you a better idea of the designs of our enemies than any we have
before received.
    In a letter I have seen from London of unquestionable authority
is the following paragraph. "A General of the first abilities & experience would come over if he could have any assurance from the
Congress of keeping his rank, but that being very high, he would
not submit to have any one but an American his Superior, and that
only in consideration of the confidence due to an American in a
question so peculiarly American. Let me have your opinion of this
matter. Prince Ferdinand's recommendation of the General mentioned above is in these words. 'Si l'on veut un Officier approuvé,
intelligent et brave; je ne scai si on peut trouver un autre qui le
vaille.' " [1]
    There is no person in America can answer this paragraph so well
as yourself. Our friend Gates who with Generals Washington and
Mifflin (the latter lately made a Brigadier and Mr. Gates a Major
General) are now here is of opinion that the Officer desiring to come
to America is Majr. General Beckwith. But this is mere conjecture,
founded on the Mans political principles and his abilities as a
Soldier. The papers I formerly sent you, with the evening post
now inclosed, will shew you the political convulsions of this Province, but I incline to think that this sensible spirited people will
not long be duped by Proprietary machinations whatever may be
the fate of Maryland. Apropos what do you think of the representative bodies of this latter Province? Of all the extraordinary Phe-
nomina of this extraordinary age, these are the most extraordinary!
Is the Convention of Maryland a Conclave of Popes, a mutilated
legislature or an Assembly of wise Men. By the manner in which
they dispense with oaths it wd. seem they conceived of themselves
as the first of these, for surely a mutilated legislature, an unorganized
Government, cannot do what these men by their Resolve of May the
15th have undertaken. Nor is their 2d resolve of the 21st better
founded, unless they can shew, which I believe is not in their power,
that the people had in contemplation these things when they chose
them and elected them accordingly.[2] What do these folks mean by a
"Reunion with G. Britain *on constitutional principles?*" I profess I
do not understand them, nor do I believe the best among them have
any sensible ideas annexed to these terms. But I have done with them,
being satisfied they will never figure in history among the Solons, Ly-
curgus's, or Alfreds. Our Commissioners in Canada seem to be on
the fright but I hope Thomas, Sullivan, Thomson &c. will restore

the spirits with our affairs in that Province. The disgrace apart, our late capture of the valuable Transport to the Eastward, much more than compensates for the loss before Quebec. The Continental armed Ship Franklin has certainly taken & secured a most valuable Transport with 75 Tons of Gun powder, 1000 stand of arms and a variety of other useful articles, valued at £50,000 this money.[3] The sensible and manly resolve of Virginia of the 15th instant has gladdened the hearts of all wise and worthy Men here.[4] It will powerfully contribute to sett things right in these Proprietary governments. We have here 4 Tribes of the Six Nations Indians and yesterday we had between 2 & 3 thousand men parading on the Common to their great astonishment and delight. We hope effectually to secure the friendship of their people.

Farewell dear Sir, and be assured you have my hearty wishes for success and happiness. Cant Clinton (if he is on Shore) be disturbed before the rest of his Mirmidons join him? My compliments to Gen. Howe.   Richard Henry Lee

RC (NjP).
  [1] Four delineated lines were left blank in MS at this point. For the letter "from London of unquestionable authority," written by Arthur Lee and dated February 13, from which the quoted passage was taken, see *Am. Archives*, 4th ser. 4:1126; and PCC, item 83, 1:5–8. See also Josiah Bartlett to John Langdon, May 21, 1776, note 2.
  [2] The May 15 and 21 resolves of the Maryland Convention are in *Am. Archives*, 4th ser. 5:1584–85, 1588–89.
  [3] The schooner *Franklin*, commanded by Capt. James Mugford, had captured the British transport *Hope* near Boston harbor on May 17. See Clark, *Naval Documents*, 5:134–35, 216–18.
  [4] See Lee to Edmund Pendleton, May 12, 1776, note 3.

Commissioners to Canada to Philip Schuyler

Dear sir   Montreal 28th May 1776

We leave open for Your perusal the enclosed letter & papers to Congress which we desire you to forward with all expedition after taking copies if you think proper.[1] Pray order the Royal Savage & the other vessel to be immediately Armed. We believe the Generals will find it very difficult to supply the Army here with flour, therefore whatever you can furnish send with the utmost expedition. Our Army is so weakened with the small pox and so badly provided in other respects that we are of Opinion if Carleton should be reinforced with three thousand Regulars it will not be in our power to continue in Canada much above three weeks, unless we should receive a considerable reinforcement of Men who have had the small Pox, flour and Cash.

The following articles are much wanted: 6000 pair of Shoes, do. Shirts, Bullet molds, lead for ball, Buck Shot, two coarse bolting mills. If the Congress should resolve to keep possession of what we hold in Canada, hard cash must be sent & paper money, of the latter the smallest bills will answer best. We think it will be highly prudent to forward on all the Battoes with the utmost dispatch to St Johns with Provisions. The two Pena. Regiments of Genl Sullivan's brigade most of whom it is said have had the smallpox Should be sent immediately to Canada. The New Engld Regiments had better we think remain on your Side the Lake. For if they should come into Canada they will most assuredly be obliged to innoculate or run the danger of losing great numbers by taking the small pox in the natural way. To prevent the infection from spreading is next to impossible.

Thursday a council of War will be held by the Genl. & Several field Officers at Chambly to consider of what is most eligible to be done in our present situation. We wait the result of their deliberations, & intend to bring it with us, as we propose Setting off from St Johns next Friday if the weather will permit & a boat can be got ready. With respects to your amiable family we are with sincere regard & esteem, Dr sir, Your most hum Servts.

Samuel Chase

Ch. Carroll of Carrollton

P.S. Colo. Allen desires his Compts. to you.

RC (NN). In a clerical hand and signed by Carroll and Chase.
[1] The "enclosed letter" of May 27–28 from the commissioners to President Hancock was forwarded by Schuyler to Congress with his letters of May 31 and June 1, 1776. See *JCC*, 5:420; and *Am. Archives*, 4th ser. 6:589–92, 639–40, 677–79.

Elbridge Gerry to Benjamin Lincoln

Dear sir   Philadelphia May 28th 1776

I received your Favour of the 17th per Mr Cabot & am very happy in the Intelligence it contain'd relative to the valuable Prize which has afforded Us so good a Supply of Ammunition, but cannot avoid mourning the Loss of Capt Mugford whom We are informed the Enemy boarded in a Day or two afterwards & slew with a great Loss on their Side.[1]

I observe what You say relative to the State of the Colony & hope it will be soon reinforced by the Levies lately ordered by Congress from the same & Connecticut, as well as by a good Major General & Brigadier which We shall this Day apply for to General Washington. We shall take particular Care that the powder due to the Colony be replaced out of the Prize Cargo—& as to the Shot, Shells, Carriages &c they are considered as continental altho being under Command of the General officer they will be naturally converted to the Defence of the Colony; I shall however endeavour to obtain an order for the Carriages to be given the Colony, but whether this is obtained or not I hope you will use them & mount as many Cannon as are necessary for the Defence of the Colony which General Ward will surely have no objection to. The Carbines for the Train shall be applyed for, at least a proportion of them altho I do not expect Congress will grant them.

I have inclosed to our worthy Speaker some Papers relative to Virginia & North Carolina's declaring for Independency to which beg Leave to refer You.[2]

The lucky Circumstance of repairing the Cannon ought to be published that all the Colonies may receive the Information; & that they may be usefull as soon as possible. I hope the Blacksmith who repairs them will be immediately orderd to employ a Number of Hands & finish them without Delay as the Expence will be same as in the slow Way in Which I am informed he is now going on. I think those that are not repaired ought to be removed from the Castle untill that can be done, since the Enemy may effectually disable them if that place should be again attacked before it is well fortified.

Pray let a Recommendation go to the Inhabitants of Boston to send their Salt into the Country as no advantage can accrue from its being in Boston & it is now become exceeding scarce & is almost essential to Existence.

Lead is wanted, and the Example of this City will undoubtedly be readily followed by the Inhabitants of Boston in selling to the assembly their Leaden spouts, Weights &c. Small Arms are wanted & an additional Price must obtain them as it has done Salt petre. Powder I think We cannot Want in future if the Manufactory of Salt petre is pursued. Woolen Goods Vizt Blankets, Coats, Vests & Hose, & also Shirting must be manufactured as it was the last year. Pray push these Matters as of the utmost Consequence as well as the Manufactory of Lead which goes on briskly at Virginia.

There is nearly 6 Months provision for an Army of 20000 Men in Massachusetts belonging to the Continent which is to remain there, excepting what may be wanted for the Ships of War, to supply the Army in that Department; so that We have Reason to suppose No Want will arise from that Quarter.

I shall be glad to be informed whether Capt Johnson who arrived with Arms for the Colony last Winter rendered an Acct. to whom the same were delivered in the Army; Vouchers I think should be produced of the Delivery of her Cargo that the Continent might be charged. Pray inform me likewise what is become of the Brigantine

which the Comme. sent for Powder to the West Indies commanded
by Capt Corbet, & whether Mr Shaw has delivered all the power for
the Sum of Money he recd.; I doubt not Care has been taken but
have not been able to be inform'd whether the Voyages succeeded.

My Regards to all Friends & beleive me to be sincerely sir your
Friend & huml sert,   Elbridge Gerry

RC (MeHi).
  [1] On the death of Capt. James Mugford, commander of the schooner *Franklin,*
see Clark, *Naval Documents,* 5:161–62.
  [2] In a brief letter of this date to Speaker Warren, Gerry inclosed several newspapers containing reports and resolves from Virginia and North Carolina. "Their
conventions have unanimously declared for independency, and have in this respect
exceeded their sister colonies in a most noble and decisive measure. I hope it
will be forthwith communicated to your honourable assembly, and hope to see
my native colony following this laudable example." Gerry to James Warren,
May 28, 1776, Austin, *Life of Gerry,* 1:180–81.

Richard Henry Lee to Thomas Ludwell Lee

My Dear Brother,[1]   Philadelphia, 28th May 1776
This is Post morning and I am obliged on a Committee of
conference [2] with the Generals Washington, Gates, & Mifflin by 9 on
the operations of this Campaign, so that I cannot possibly write to
many of my friends and particularly Colo Mason. Pray make my
compliments to him, let him have the news sent, and apologize for
me. Colo Nelson is not arrived, but I suppose he will by this day
sennight, about which time I shall sett out for Virginia, and after
resting at home a day or two, will attend the Convention at
Williamsburg.[3] The sensible and spirited resolve of my Countrymen
on the 15th has gladdened the heart of every friend to human nature
in this place, and it will have a wonderful good effect on the misguided Councils of these Proprietary Colonies.[4] What a scene of
determined rapine and roguery do the German treaties present to us,
and Ld Dartmouths answer to the Duke of Graftons motion, 16th
March, has shut the mouths of all Gapers after Commissioners.[5] The
transport Prize taken to the Eastward is extremely apropos. The
vessel and Cargo are valued at £50,000. We are not without hopes
of getting some more of the same flock, if fortune should have
separated them from the Shepherd, they will most probably fall.
This is the Campaign that we shall be most tried in probably, and
we should endeavour as far as human care can go to be more in-
vulnerable than Achilles, not exposing even the heel, where the
stake is so immense. We have not lately heard from Canada, but we
hope for better news soon than our last. A potent push will assuredly
be made there this Summer by our enemies, and if we can prevent

them from communicating with the Upper Country, and thereby debauching the Indians, we shall answer every good purpose there. The Roebuck is gone from here crippled, but the Liverpoole remains thinly manned and in want of provisions. It is to be hoped that the death of the King of Portugal will produce something in Europe favorable to us. Let no consideration interrupt your attention to the making of Common Salt, Salt Petre & Arms; and every kind of encouragement should be given to all sorts of useful manufacture.

Farewell my dear brother,   Richard Henry Lee.

[*P.S.*] Our brothers in London were well, the 13. Febry. last. I write Gen. Lee by this post—do see that the letter is forwarded from Williamsburg.[6]   R. H. Lee.

MS not found; reprinted from *NYHS Collections,* 5 (1872): 47–48.

[1] Thomas Ludwell Lee (ca. 1730–77), who represented Stafford County at the Virginia Convention then convened at Williamsburg, had been appointed on May 15 to the committee charged with drafting a declaration of rights and a plan of government for Virginia. *Appleton's Cyclopaedia of American Biography;* and *Am. Archives,* 4th ser. 6:1524.

[2] The May 29 report of the Committee of Conference, in Lee's hand, is in PCC, item 19, 6:185–87; and *JCC,* 4:399–401. For further information on the work of this committee, see *JCC,* 4:406–14.

[3] Although Thomas Nelson was not mentioned in the journals until June 12, he listed expenses for "Attendance from 9th June 76 till Aug. 11th, 62 days" in his later account with Virginia. Emmet Collection, NN. Lee left Philadelphia on June 13. See Lee to Washington, June 13, 1776.

[4] Lee had been at work for some time in the struggle to change "the misguided Councils of these Proprietary Colonies." The following undated note in the hand of Benjamin Rush among the Lee Family Papers, ViU, subscribed only "Wednesday evening" but obviously written on May 22, 1776, illustrates the shape of such activities.

"A Memorial will be presented by our assembly tomorrow to the Congress," Rush wrote, "praying an explanation of your resolve of the 15th instant. The Motion for the Application (which came from one of the Allens) Shews a design to enslave the people of Pennsylvania. I conjure you by your past & present affection for our common *mistress* not to desert us in this trying exigency. 4/5 of the inhabitants of our colony will fly to the *ultima ratio* before they will submit to a new government formed by the present Assembly. Please to circulate the papers you will receive herewith [*not found*] among all the Southern delegates tomorrow morning. Mr. Hews must not be neglected. Yours Affectionately, B R—h."

Rush's note had been prompted by the Pennsylvania Assembly's appointment on May 22 of a committee charged with drafting a memorial to Congress to clarify the May 15 resolve recommending new governments and to obtain "an Explanation in such Terms as will not admit of any Doubt, whether the Assemblies and Conventions, now subsisting in the several Colonies, are or are not the Bodies, to whom the Consideration of continuing the old, or adopting new Governments, is referred." The committee had been appointed in response to receipt of a petition from "the Inhabitants of the City and Liberties of Philadelphia," which had itself been a reaction to Congress' resolve of the 15th, and Rush obviously assumed that the assembly would the next day adopt a memorial to Congress prepared by the committee. Although his note betrays a sense of alarm, he had nothing to fear. The committee reported "an Essay" on May 24, which was "read by Order, and referred to further Consideration," but no further action was ever taken upon it. The campaign to overthrow proprietary government in Pennsylvania was already well under way, and even a series of petitions from several counties protesting Congress' resolution of May 15 could not divert the movement against the traditional order. Ironically, the next petition from Pennsylvania laid before Congress was not from the assembly but from the Philadelphia committee. Dated May 24 and signed by chairman Thomas McKean, it was elicited by the discovery "that the Assembly of this Province are about to present a Memorial to your honourable body, in consequence of a Remonstrance delivered to them from a number of the inhabitants of the City of Philadelphia, in which they are said to request an explanation of your resolve of the 15th instant." See *Pa. Archives,* 8th ser. 8:7516, 7519, 7521ff.; *JCC,* 4:390; *Am. Archives,* 4th ser. 6:560–61; and David Hawke, *In the Midst of a Revolution* (Philadelphia: University of Pennsylvania Press, 1961), pp. 156–57.

Rush's note to Lee, a patent attempt to ensure that Congress would ignore any such memorial from the assembly, is additional evidence that this movement was receiving important support from many delegates in Congress. The reference to Joseph Hewes is especially interesting since little other evidence survives to indicate that on this issue he might be enlisted to support the position taken by men of Rush's and Lee's persuasion.

[5] During a debate in the House of Lords on a conciliatory resolution offered by the duke of Grafton, Lord Dartmouth, former secretary of state for America, had declared that "this country cannot . . . consent to lay down our arms, or suspend the operations now carrying on, till the Colonies own our legislative sovereignty; and, by the acts of duty and obedience, show such a disposition as will entitle them to the favour and protection of the parent State." *Am. Archives,* 4th ser. 6:323.

[6] See Lee to Charles Lee, May 27, 1776.

Robert R. Livingston to Catharine Livingston

Dear Caty [1]   Philadelphia 28th May 1776.

I this day recd. your favour which tho' agreeable in itself was the more so for being the first from the manor since my departure which is now near a month & yet the post afforded daily or rather weekly oportunities of hearing from there. I am much obliged to you for the attention you shew to my wishes & wish I could requite it by any thing that would give you pleasure But these times afford little of this sort. We should prepare our selves for calamities by a confidence in heaven which will bear us thro' whenever they happen. We have reason to believe that our enemy will make great efforts this summer, I hope however by the blessing of God to see them repelled & this country after a Glorious struggle emancipated from the tyranny of an inhuman prince. But enough of politicks, only let me give you one caution before I leave it, never let your spirits forsake you, believe that many evils are incident to war but at the same time believe that a just cause can not fail of success.

As to your questions about the bath waters I hardly know how to answer them since I have been so much confined here as to have given them but little chance—however Philadelphia agrees very well with me which is much the same thing. I suppose you know that our little family is settled about two miles from Bristol. I visit it on Saturday & leave it on Monday. I am very happy that Peggy & Polly have an agreeable neighbourhood who are attentive to them in my absence.

You do wrong to tell me of the beauties of the Manor at a time when the remembrance of them only makes me regret my absence. As I am a farmer you should have said some thing of my domain— but I am unreasonable. I should rather thank you for what you have said than blame what you have not said. I am glad Janet is gone to Albany since it may tend to her amusement, but sorry that Angelica has left you, since it increases your solitude. By the pathetic appellation of poor Ann I fear she has not recovered her health, for which I should be extreamly sorrey since the goodness of her heart entitles her to every blessing.

If Gittys laziness is not invincible I may hope to hear from her: however I have little faith in modern miraclles. As for John I shall pass him by in silence—but of Dolly I have some hopes. I know Hannah means well, & I am affraid that from her according to the adage I must acceppt the will for the deed. Give my love to mama, she is three letters in my debt. May heaven bless you all & grant us a happy meeting.

N. B. I would have my wheat ground immediately and let my people eat the cornel for which there will be no vent. From your Aff. Brother,   Robt. R Livingston

RC (CtW).
[1] Livingston's sister, Catharine (1752–1849).

New Hampshire Delegates to Meshech Weare

Sir,   Philadelphia 28th May 1776

We have obtain'd an order for 10500 Dols. for defraying the expences of raising & advancing a months pay to the Regiment to be station'd at Portsmouth which we only wait for an opportunity to send forward.[1] Flour & salt Provisions may be supplied from Boston where a much larger Quantity was left by the Commisary Genl. than will be wanted by the troops station'd there. We are extreamly sorry that the Colony we have the Honour to Represent which has had so high a place in the esteem of the whole Continent, for its forwardness, & great exertions, in the Glorious Contest, in which we are now engag'd, shod. be lessen'd by the delay of the Regiment order'd last winter into Canada. Our misfortune in that Country is imputed to tardiness of that & two other N. England Regiments, if that Regiment had March'd at the time we expected, & frequently asserted, the evil might have been averted; we hope (for the Honor of the Colony) there will be a strict inquiry made and the cause of the delay fully investigated, that the Officers (if they are faulty) may be brought to justice.

The Convention of Virginia have instructed their delegates to use their endeavors that Congress sho'd declare the United Colonies a Free independent state, North Carolina have signified the same desires.[2] S. Carolina & Georgia will readily Acceed. The Proprietary Govts will be the last to agree to this necessary step, the disafected in them are now exerting themselves but their exertions are no more then the last strugles of expiring factions. We hope in a few months Civil Governments will be establish'd in all the United Colonies on a firm & permanent Basis. We shod be glad to know the sentiment of our Colony on the important subject of a total seperation from Great Britain. Let our own opinions be what they may, we think ourselves in duty bound, to act agreeable to the sentiments of our constituents.[3]

We are with great Respect, Your Most Obt Serts,

Josiah Bartlett

Wm. Whipple

RC (DLC). Written by Whipple and signed by Whipple and Bartlett.

[1] Although the resolution was passed on May 22, two weeks elapsed before the money was sent to New Hampshire. See *JCC*, 4:380; and Josiah Bartlett to Meshech Weare, June 14, 1776.

[2] These instructions were read in Congress on May 27. *JCC*, 4:397.

[3] On June 15, the New Hampshire Assembly instructed its delegates in Congress "to join with the other Colonies in Declaring *The Thirteen United Colonies, A Free & Independent State.*" *N.H. State Papers*, 8:149–50.

William Whipple to John Langdon

My Dear Sir,   Philadelphia 28th May 1776

Your two favors of 11th and 12th current came duly to hand.[1] I rejoice to find your ship the most forward of any except those at Providence, but I very much fear you'll still wait for guns if they are not to be had at Providence as I mentioned in my last. I have still kept off the appointment of an Agent in hopes of fixing the appointmt to your mind.[2] I have nominated the Captain who is unanimously accepted by the Committee, but the Sanction of Congress is still wanting which I think there is no doubt of. The attention of Congress has been taken up some days in conference with General Washington, as the plan of operations for this campaign.

So soon as that is finished and the conference with the Chiefs of the Six Nations, who are now here, naval matters will be attended to, but I shall be glad of an answer to one of my letters wherein I wrote freely of those you proposed for officers, before I nominate them.[3]

You are much mistaken if you supposed I meant to call in question your patriotism—my only design was to point out to you what might be the opinion of envy. I wrote from the sincerity of my heart, with the freedom of friendship; relying on your confidence and candor shall say no more on the subject.

I observe there is a number of sand bags on board the prize carried into Boston—will they not make hammocks? Bread and Salt, Salt provisions, will be furnished from Boston. I intended to have written several letters to my friends, but as the post goes out earlier than usual this morning have not time and am obliged to conclude this in a hurry. Yours &c,   Wm Whipple

Tr (DLC).
  [1] Langdon's May 11 letter has not been found, but his May 12 letter to Whipple is printed in Clark, *Naval Documents*, 5:62.
  [2] See Whipple to Langdon, April 29, 1776.
  [3] For further information on Langdon's nomination of officers, see Whipple to Langdon, April 20, 1776, note 1.

John Adams to Benjamin Hichborn

Dear sir   Philadelphia May 29. 1776
  Your agreable Favour of 20th May was handed me Yesterday,[1] and it gave me much Pleasure on various Accounts—one particularly as it gave me Evidence of your Existence, which for some Time past you have Suffered to remain problematical. I have long expected Letters from you, but yet I cannot find fault, because I believe I am much in your Debt. However, if you had considered the Situation I am in, Surrounded with Demands for all and more than all my Time, you would not have waited for regular Payments from me.

Am Sorry to see you complain of suspicions. I hoped they were forgotten. Indeed I think, that upon your Return they ought to have vanished. I have none, nor am I in the least degree afraid of censure on your Account nor of loosing a thread of Influence. Fortified in Innocence a Man should set groundless Censures at Defyance: and as to Influence the more a Man has of it, at least of such as mine, if I have any, the more unfortunate he is. If by Influence is understood the Power of doing Good to the public, or of serving Men of Merit, this Influence is devoutly to be wished by every benevolent Mind: but very little of this Kind of Influence has ever fallen to my share.

I wish I had enough of it, to serve the Interest of your Friend Russell whom I have ever esteemed as a Man of Honour, and Spirit, a Man of Business as well as an agreable Companion: But I fear it is not in my Power to give him any assistance. (The Agents, who have the Sales you mention, were appointed, by the marine Committee which was chosen in my absence, when I was at Watertown. Mr Hancock was appointed, for our Colony, and I Suppose the Agents have been recommended by him. But as it lay in a Department which I had no Right nor Duty to interfere in, I have never inquired, or known any thing of it. The marshalls to the Court of Admiralty, will be recommended probably by the Judges. I know nothing of those Matters and indeed I dont see that I can with Propriety intermeddle in those Matters. I have however shewn your Letter to some of my Colleagues, and will shew it to others, Mr Hancock particularly.) [2] If any opportunity should present of serving Mr Russell, I shall gladly embrace it.

I am much pleased with your Spirited Project of driving away the Wretches from the Harbour, and never shall be happy till I hear it is done, and the very Entrance fortifyed impregnably. I cant bear that an unfriendly Flagg or Mast should be in Sight of Beacon Hill.

You are shocked by Accounts from the Southward of a Disposition in a great Majority, to counteract Independence. Read the Proceedings of Georgia, South and North Carolina, and Virginia, and then judge. The Middle Colonies have never tasted the bitter Cup—they have never Smarted—and are therefore a little cooler—but you will see that the Colonies are united indissolubly. Maryland have passed a few excentric Resolves but these are only Flashes, which will soon expire. The Proprietary Governments are not only incumbered with a large Body of Quakers, but are embarrassed by a proprietary Interest—both together clogg their operations a little: but these cloggs are falling off, as you will Soon see.

I dread the Spirit of Innovation which I fear will appear in our new and numerous Representative Body.[3] It is much to be desired that their attention may at present be more fixed upon the defence of the Province and military operations, than upon opening sources of endless altercation. Unanimity in this Time of Calamity and Danger is of great Importance. You ask my sentiments of the political System to be adopted. My opinion I am very certain will not be followed. We have able Men in the Colony, but I am much afraid they will not be heard. I hope a Governor, and Lieutenant Governor will be chosen: and that they will be respectable for their Fortune, as well as abilities and Integrity if such can be found. The Judges I hope will be made independent both for the Duration and Emoluments of office. There is nothing of more importance than this: but yet there is nothing less likely to be done.

How the Representation will be Settled I cannot guess. But I really hope they will not attempt any material alteration in the Qualifications of Voters. This will open a Door for endless disputes—and I am much afraid for numberless Corruptions.

I wish I could be at Home, at this important Period. But you will remember that all the other Colonies have Constitutions to frame— and what is of infinitely great Delicacy, Intricacy, and Importance, the Continent has a Constitution to form. If I could be of some little use at home, I may be of more here at present.

You kindly and politely express a Concern for my Health, and if you have any Regard for me it is not without Reason. I have been here four Months, during which Time I have never once been on Horseback, and have found but little Time to walk. Such un-interupted Attention to Cares and Perplexities of various Kinds, is enough to destroy a more robust Body than mine. But I cannot excuse myself from these Duties, and I must march forward untill it comes to my Turn to fall. Indeed if a few Things more were fully accomplished, I should think it my duty to ask Leave of my Con-stituents to return home to my Garden.

The Moment I can see every Colony in Possession and actual Exercise of all the Powers of Government, and a Confederation well settled for all the Colonies under a Congress with Powers clearly defined and limited; and Sufficient Preparation and Provisions made for Defence against the Force which is coming against Us; that Moment I shall return to my family; from which I have been too long divorced. But whether my Constitution will hold out so long must be left to him that made it, to whose wisdom and goodness I chearfully Submit.

N.B. The Petition from the independent Corps, in Boston gave me great Pleasure and is much to their Honour. I did my Endeavour to get the Prayer granted, but it is at last left to the General.[4]

LB (MHi).
[1] Benjamin Hichborn (1746–1817), a Boston lawyer, was the ill-fated carrier of John Adams' controversial letters of July 24, 1775, to Abigail Adams and James Warren that were captured and published by the British. After escaping from the British, Hichborn returned to his legal practice and subsequently was one of the organizers of the Boston Independent Corps. His May 20 letter to Adams is in the Adams Papers, MHi. Shipton, *Harvard Graduates*, 17:36–44.
[2] Adams marked this part of the letter in parenthesis "a Mistake not copied."
[3] The Massachusetts General Court in May 1776 made representation in that body dependent on the number of qualified voters in a town. Under provincial law each town of 120 qualified voters had elected a maximum of two representa-tives with the sole exception of Boston, which elected four. Under the new law a town could send two representatives for its first 120 qualified voters and an additional representative for each additional 100 qualified voters. Under the new system Boston elected 12 representatives in the May 29 election. Western and rural towns immediately expressed their fears that this maneuver would lodge control of the government in the populous, eastern, commercial region. For further discussion of the impact of enlarged representation in the Massachu-setts House of Representatives, see Stephen Patterson, *Political Parties in Revolu-tionary Massachusetts* (Madison: University of Wisconsin Press, 1973), pp. 153–70; and Robert J. Taylor, *Western Massachusetts in the Revolution* (Providence: Brown University Press, 1954), pp. 35–36, 101, 140n.39.

[4] The Boston Independent Corps had apparently sent a petition to Congress requesting some of the arms recently recovered following the British evacuation of Boston, and since Washington was at this time in Philadelphia to confer on operations for the ensuing campaign, the petition was referred to him. Washington, however, sidestepped the issue, responding simply that "whatever decision Congress may come to [regarding 'the Arms lately taken'] . . . will be agreeable to me and be litterally complied with." Washington to John Hancock, June 3, 1776, Washington, *Writings* (Fitzpatrick), 5:96.

William Livingston to Henry Brockholst Livingston

Dr Brock,   Philadelphia 29 May 1776
   I believe your present Station will be very agreable to your mamma to whom I sent a Copy of General Schuylers Letter to me, & your original Letter to show her at the same time the great Regard the General expresses for you; & your own satisfaction with your present Situation.[1] You have it now in your Power to [see] much of our military operations in that Department & to acquire considerable Skill in the commissary Business in which the General is probably superior to every Man in America. By the Character he gives of the young Gentlemen who compose his family, you may see what Qualifications he deems essential. They are, says he all *virtuous* young men, *sober, industrious & secret.*
   I think I shall be able to procure the Cloth for the Coat; but as to the Buff colour'd Cloth for the waistcoat & Breeches, the Taylor gives me but poor Encouragement. But if they cannot be procured I will endeavour to supply the want of them with nankeen, which may answer for Summer. I hope you will make it your Business to please the General both out of Gratitude for his kindness to you & for your own sake, as it is in his Power & I dare say inclination to advance you. One very effectual way of pleasing him is to pay the closest Attention to Business, as he is a man of indefatigable Industry, & abhors an idle indisposition. Endeavour to make yourself master of every thing that is worth knowing, especially of the State of the Troops in your Department, the geography of the several passes or Posts they will occupy, so that if ever you should be sent to Congress upon public Business, which may possibly be the case, you may be prompt in answering any Questions that may be proposed on those Subjects. I am, your affect Father,   Wil Livingston.

RC (MHi).
   [1] For further references to Henry Brockholst Livingston's situation at this time, see John Jay to Philip Schuyler, May 5, 1776, note.

Caesar Rodney to Thomas Rodney

Sir,   Philadelphia May the 29th 1776
    You tell me you are proceeding on the Recommendation of Congress by way of Instruction to the members of the House for that county,[1] I fully approve the methods and hope You will proceed in the business Deliberately, Coolly and persuasively, but diligently. I don't doubt the Assembly will Act prudently. If otherwise, it will then be time Enough for the people to take the Matter up in another way. The Recommendation of Congress was certainly Meant to go to the Assemblies, Where there were such who had Authority to Set; and the people of this province haveing taken the matter up upon other Grounds have occationed verry great disturbance, Such as I would not wish to see in our Government. The Colonies of North-Carolina and Virginia have both by their Conventions for Independence by a Unanimus Vote, and have Instructed their members to move and Vote for it in Congress reserving to Each Colony the exclusive right to frame government for it's Self. The Convention of North-Carolina has appointed a Committee (of its own Body) to draw up and Report to them a plan of Government. South-Carolina and all the New-England Colonies have declared off some time Since. When these things are known to the people they will no doubt have great weight with them. I have not seen this day's paper yet, but imagine you'l have the doings of one or more of those Colonies published there. However Whether in the paper or not, You may depend on the whole of the above relation to be matter of fact. Coll. Dickinson's, Coll. Robertdoe's, Coll. Cadwallader's, Coll. Mckean's and Coll. MatLock's Battallions, three companies of Artillery & the Light-horse of the Militia; and Coll. Shee's and Coll. Magaw's Battalion's of the Continental Troops Were all Reviewed the day before Yesterday, on the Common, by the Congress, Generals Washington, Gates and Mifflin accompanied by a great number of other officers, most of the Assembly, the Presbiterian Clergey who were here at the Sinod—and 21 Indians of the Six Nations who gave the Congress a War-dance Yesterday. I Shall put on board John Morris Who is to leave town this day, two barrells of Rum, One of West-India, the other Philadelphia, one barrel of Muscavado Sugar, One hundred Weight of Loaf Sugar and twelve pounds of Bohea Tea. I Shall Send you a Bill of the Articles, hope they will Get safe down and that you will have Care taken of them. They are most abominable high. But having an Eye to havest as well as present Use, Could not do without them.
    Mr. Ball the Lieutt. is now fixed at Germantown. Since the return of the Liverpool into our Capes there has been another Attempt of the Committee of Safety here, to have Ball Exchanged for Captn. Budden, but Totally rejected by Congress.[2] Misses. Minchel just

now told me that Mr. Mark McCall's mother in Law is dying and that she was with her last night.

I have Made further Enquiry about your fifty pounds Sent by Parke, and Mr. Redwood Lets me know that he has not Recd or heard of it. That he has not recd a Letter from you any time within four Months past. Therefore it will be Expedient that You secure yourself in the best, and Quickest way you Can. I think his long Stay in Virginia is Something Suspecious.

With Respect to the twenty pounds you Recd of Rymear Williams, keep it till I Come home—perhaps I may be able to get down from our Assembly which Sets next Munday Week.

Would doctr. Tilton Think himself obliged, by an Appointment (in his Way) of forty dollars per month, in Virginia, or toward Canada? These things have frequently happened of late, and wou'd probably be in the power of a friend to Serve him.

Mr. Jourdan informs me, that McLean has lost the Letter I sent by him to Coll. Haslet.[3] I don't Recollect any thing verry Material in it—But that Evans the Contractor, had an application made to Congress to have the Troops Quartered at Some two places in the Government that he might the more Conveniently provide for them, otherwise he must decline the Contract—Which Congress absolutely Refused, for that it would be interfering with the business of the Coll., that they never will interfer with his duty but when it shall Evidently appear to them for the greater security and protection of the Government. I took the Liberty to tell Coll. Haslet that I did not doubt he would Study Mr. Evans Convenience (Especially as his providing for them wou'd be a Saving to the public) whenever he should think the safety of the Government wou'd not be En-dangered by it. I also mentioned to him (as my opinion) That if he Should Send all the Troops out of Kent, the Committee of *Safety* there, would Call upon him for the Arms lent, and put them into the hands of the Militia for the imediate protection of that County. I am Asstonished that McLean Should have Lost the Letter—but if it Should Contain any Matter of politic's (which I do not recollect it did) Shall be verry Angry, and Even Suspect some unfair play.

As I have now got to the End of my paper, Must Conclude, Yours &c,   Caesar Rodney

RC (PHi).
[1] See Thomas Rodney to Caesar Rodney, May 26, 1776, in Rodney, *Letters* (Ryden), p. 84.
[2] On this day Congress offered to exchange William Budden for John Draper. *JCC*, 4:398–99. See also *JCC*, 4:340, 345, 357; and John Hancock to Walter Stewart, May 9, 1776, note.
[3] Probably Rodney's May 23 letter to John Haslet, which has not been found, but see Haslet's undated response to it in Rodney, *Letters* (Ryden), pp. 86–87.

John Adams to Samuel Cooper

My dear sir   May 30th. 1776

Yours of the 20th was handed me by the last Post.[1] I congratulate you upon the first modern Election, on the last Wednesday in May, of Councillers as at the first. I could not avoid indulging myself yesterday, in Imagination with my Friends in Boston, upon an occasion so joyfull. I presume you must have had a very solemn and ceremonious Election, and wish that no Interruption may ever hereafter take Place, like that of the last year.

You have given me great Pleasure by your account of the Spirit and Activity of our People, their Skill and success in fortifying the Town and Harbour: But there are several Things still wanting, in my Judgment. I never shall be happy, untill every unfriendly Flagg is driven out of sight, and the Light House Island, Georges and Lovells Islands, and the East End of Long Island are secured. Fire Ships and Rafts will be of no service without Something to cover and protect them from the Boats of the Men of War. Gallies are the best Engines in the World for this Purpose. Coll Quincy has the best Idea of these Gallies, of any Man I know. I believe he has a perfect Idea of the Turkish, and Venetian Gallies. Some of these are large as British Men of War, but some are small. (I Sincerely wish, that at this Time he was a Member of one or the other House, because his knowledge and Zeal would be usefull. This however is none of my Concern. But his Knowledge in naval and marine affairs is not exceeded by any Man I know.)[2] Gallies might be built and armed with heavy Cannon, 36 or 42 Pounders, which would drive away a Ship of almost any Size, Number of Guns or Weight of Metal. The Dexterity of our People in Sea Matters must produce great Things, if it had any Person to guide it, and stimulate it. A Kind of dodging Indian Fight might be maintained, among the Islands in our Harbour, between such Gallies and the Men of War.

Whether you have any Person, Sufficiently acquainted with the Composition of those Combustibles, which are usually put into Fire Ships and Rafts I don't know. If you have not, it would be worth while to send some one here to inquire and learn. At least let me know it, and altho I have a demand upon me for an Hour, when I have a Minute to Spare, yet I will be at the Pains, tho I neglect other Things of informing my self as well as I can here, and send you what I learn.

We are making the best Provision we can, for the Defence of America. I believe We shall make Provision for 70,000 Men in the three Departments the Northern, including Canada, the middle, and the southern. The Die is cast. We must all be soldiers and fight pro Aris et Focis. I hope there is not a Gentleman in the Massachusetts Bay, not even in the Town of Boston, who thinks himself too good to take his Firelock and his Spade. Such imminent Dangers level all Distinctions. You must before now, have seen Some important Resolutions of this Congress,[3] as well as of Seperate Colonies. Before many Weeks you will see more.

Remember me with every sentiment of Friendship and Respect to all who deserve well of their Country. These are all my Friends, and I have, and will have no other. I am &c.

P.S. Gallies to be used mainly in Boston Harbour, the less they are the better provided they are large and strong enough to sustain the Weight of the Guns and the Shock of the Explosion. The Gallies first built in Delaware River, were too large to be handy and too small, to live and work in a Sea. We are building two of different Construction.[4] They are to carry two large Guns in the Stern and two in front—and five or six 3 Pounders on each side besides swivalls. They are built to put to sea, live and fight in a swell or a storm. They are narrow but almost 100 feet long.

LB (MHi).
   [1] Cooper's May 20 letter to Adams is in the Adams Papers, MHi.
   [2] Adams marked this portion of the letter in parenthesis "not sent."
   [3] Undoubtedly a reference to Congress' May 10 resolution and its May 15 preamble advising the colonies on instituting new governments. *JCC*, 4:342, 357–58.
   [4] Congress had authorized the construction of two gallies on April 13, 1776. *JCC*, 4:280.

Secret Committee Minutes of Proceedings

May 30th. 1776.

At a meetg. of the Come. Present Morris, McKean, Hewes, Lee & Bartlett. The followg. Letr. was wrote to the Captains, Osman, Harvey & Collins, whose vessels are now loaded on Acct. of the Continent. Sir, Philada. May 30th. 1776. We are informed the men of war have left our Capes. You are therefore to proceed to sea fast as possible, & we have sent to the Hornet & Wasp to keep a good lookout & give you timely notice to return if the Enemy comes back before you get out.[1]

MS (MH).
   [1] Two days later Robert Morris asked the Pennsylvania Committee of Safety to grant "a pass & Pilot" for the sloop *Peggy*, Capt. Thomas Patton, which was also "loaden for Acct of the Continent." Robert Morris to the Pennsylvania Committee of Safety, June 1, 1776. Clark, *Naval Documents*, 5:339. The *Peggy* was captured by the *Kingfisher* on July 3 off Cape Henlopen. Ibid., p. 901.

Secret Committee to William Hodge

Sir   Philadelphia 30th May 1776

As you are now bound on a voyage to Europe [1] with a view of procuring sundry articles that are wanted here and have expectations that your friend Mr Jean Wanderwoordt will supply such as we may desire provided he is assured of being duly paid the Cost with Interest for the Time he remains in advance, We the subscribers being a Quorum of the Secret Committee appointed by the Honble the Continental Congress and Authorized to procure from foreign Countries Supplies of Arms, ammunition and other Articles on the best terms we can being Sensible of your deserving Character and knowing that your attachment to the liberties of your Native Country intitle you to our confidence have concluded to Authorize and empower you to contract with any Person or persons in Europe for Ten thousand Stands of good Soldiers Muskets well fitted with good double bridled Gun Locks, and good Bayonets, 200,000 Gun Flints, One thousand Barrels of the best Pistol Powder, One thousand Barrels of the best Cannon Powder and for two fast sailing well armed Cutters such as you may think best calculated for a good and safe passage to this Country and for making good Cruizers on this Coast afterwards. You are to make your Contracts in writing, stipulate the prices not to exceed the Current rates for each Article, and make it your business to be well informed in this point. We are sensible that it is dificult to extract arms, and ammunition from many parts of Europe and that penalties are inflicted on such as are detected in doing it, consequently a premium beyond the first cost & Common Commissions must be allowed to those that undertake it, and in this respect we are rather at a loss how to limit you, being willing to allow what might be a reasonable compensation but unwilling to submit to extortion. However as it is not in our power to judge of this point with precision, we exhort you to make the best bargin you can for the Continent, and we conclude to allow you a Commission of 2 1/2 per Cent on the amount of the Invoice of the goods and on the cost and outfit of the Cutters, but you'l observe this Commission is the whole of what we are to pay you being the only compensation you are to expect for transacting this business, and expect and hope it will afford you a very handsome reward for your Services.

Our design is to pay for those Goods & Cutters by remitting to the Consignation of those that supply them Cargoes of this Country Produce such as Tobacco, Rice, Indigo, Skins, Furrs, Wheat, flour, Lumber, Iron &c, and we hereby pledge the Thirteen United Colonies for the punctual discharge of the debt or debts you may Contract in virtue of and in conformity with these orders, we agree to allow such rate of Interest as you may agree for not exceeding 5 per Cent on the amount of the debt or debts from the Time the goods are Shipped until payment is made, and this interest to cease on such partial Payments as may be made from Time to Time. In confirmation of these orders we deliver you herewith a Letter to your friend Mr. Jean Wanderwoordt attended with A Certificate of our being a Quorum of the Secret Committee properly authorized to transact such business for the Public, which you may avail yourself of with Mr. Wanderwoordt or any other Person necessary for the effecting the purchase.

It is our understanding that the goods you contract are to be at the risque of the Contractor until they are Shipped onboard and bills of Lading granted for them after which they become our risque and if the risque from that Time to the ending of the voyage can be covered by Insurance at A Premium not exceeding 20 per Cent we woud wish to have such part Insured as is to come from Europe direct out for this Coast the Insurance to be against all risques what ever at and from the Shipping Port to any place of delivery in the Thirteen United Colonies of America. When you have accomplished this business so far as to make the Contracts and purchase the Cutters you must cause to be shipped 3000 Stand of Arms, 600 barrels of Powder, 3000 Gun Locks, & 60,000 Gun Flints on board each Cutter, take bills of Lading deliverable to us in any part of the United American Colonies and dispatch them for this Coast. These Cutters must be well armed and manned. You should procure if possible Masters that are acquainted with the Sea Coast of America, men of intelligent understanding and firm minds well attached to the American Cause. Many such there are in Europe pining to return and serve this Country in the present glorious contest.

You will also pick up as many American seamen as possible, and if sufficient of those dont offer, compleat the Number with the best you can get, and in fitting these Vessels it will be well done to put on board each 3 or four Tons of Musket Balls suited to the bore of the 10,000 stand of Arms. As the operations of our enemies are uncertain it is hard for us to point out what part of the Coast these Cutters should push for. We believe the Inlets between New York & Virginia may be as safe as any. They must get into the first place of Safety they can and give us immediate advice by express of their arrival, and by these Vessels you'l transmit us any Public News or any useful intelligence in your power. The remainder of the goods we think it most prudent to order out in foreign bottoms to some of the Foreign Islands in the West Indies, where we can send for them with ease and tollerable security.

You will consult with your friends what Island may be safest to make use of, and also obtain recommendation to a proper house for receiving & reshipping the goods, transmitting us the name & address by the Cutters, and we shall send them funds to pay the freight and Charges. These goods going in neutral bottoms need only be insured against the Common risques of the sea &c. We are Sir, &c &c &c.

Tr (DNA: PCC, item 37).

[1] William Hodge's voyage ended prematurely when the brig *Polly* on which he took passage was captured by the *Orpheus* off Cape May on July 3. See Clark, *Naval Documents*, 5:901. For the new instructions the committee subsequently sent him, see Secret Committee to William Hodge, October 3, 1776.

Samuel Chase to Philip Schuyler

Dear Sir   Chambly May 31st. 1776, Fryday A.M. 11 o'Clock
    We leave this place in an Hour & if our Boat is ready leave Saint Johns tomorrow. I take my Chance of this reaching You before I have the pleasure to see You. Our affairs here grow every Hour more gloomy. On yesterday there was a Meeting of our Generals & greater part of our field officers. They resolved to make a Stand as long as possible at Sorel, & to attack Capt. Forster & his infernal Crew.[1] The Truce expires this Night. About 11 o'clock last Night an express arrived from Sorel, that Colo. [Shrieve?] had received Intelligence that a Body of Troops were passed De Chambault, & on their March. At 12 o'Clock, Genl. Thompson, Colos Sinclair [St Clair] & Maxwell, & Allen went off. We have at Sorel but 1100 effective Men.
    Genl. Arnold is gone about an Hour ago to attack Forster & take Care of our Troops at Montreal. To our other Distresses We have no Lead or Ball & no Medicine, tho' 1300 Sick of the Small pox.
    I think it absolutely necessary to send all the vessells & Boats You have immediately to Saint Johns—Some flour, et, et.
    By private Letters from N. Haven to Mr. Winslow We are informed 16,000 foreign Troops are on their passage for America, 12,000 to N. England, 4,000 to Canada. This is confirmed by a Letter from Bilboa, & by a Captain arrived at N. Haven.
    The Torries in Montreal gave out the same Intelligence some Time past.
    I beg You will give Us the utmost Dispatch over the Lakes, as I wish to be at Congress as soon as possible.
    It is a Million to a Shilling that General Thomas will die, Genl. Wooster leaves this place this Day. General Arnold is first in Command 'till Genl. Sullivan arrives. I esteem & respect both those Gentlemen, but neither of them are competent to the Supreme Command.
    I have no Expectation of keeping any footing in this Colony if 3 or 4,000 Troops are sent here within three weeks. We have great

Reason to believe a Reinforcement is arrived at Quebec. 14 Ships were there on Monday week.

I would say more, but I am called on for this Scrawl. Adieu. Your affectionate & Obedt. Servt.   Saml. Chase

[P.S.] Part of our heavy Cannon was carried yesterday [to] Saint Johns. The rest & our two Mortars go this [day] with great part of our powder.

Write to Genl. Washington & Congress, I believe Genl. Gates ought to be sent here immediately.

RC (NN).
[1] For the minutes of the council of war held at Chambly on May 30, 1776, see *Am. Archives,* 4th ser. 6:628.

Committee for Indian Affairs
to George Morgan

Sir,   Philadelphia 31 May 1776.
Two letters from the committee for Indian Affairs, with the papers inclosed in them, which were forwarded some weeks ago, we hope have come to your hands before this time, and will remove the difficulties you mention in your letter to col. Morris, of the 16th instant.[1] You may purchase a horse for capt. Whiteeyes, of a equal value with that taken from young Still. But we desire you to inquire into the right of Moses Watson to the latter, that he may be obliged to restore him, if wrongfully detained, or that mr Speare if he sold what was another's property, may reimburse the money. We shall be glad to receive the intelligence you expect to obtain, and we doubt not the continuance of your diligent attention to the affairs of your department. We are, Sir, Your humble servants,
                                                            G. Wythe
                                                            James Wilson
                                                            Edward Rutledge

RC (DLC). Written by Wythe and signed by Wythe, Rutledge, and Wilson. Endorsed by Morgan: "recd. July 22. G.M. Answerd July 26th."
[1] See Committee for Indian Affairs to George Morgan, May 11 and 14, 1776. Morgan's May 16 letter to Lewis Morris, which was referred to this committee on May 27, is in PCC, item 163, fols. 237–40, and *Am. Archives,* 4th ser. 6:474–75.

Elbridge Gerry to Joseph Palmer

Dear sir   Philadelphia May 31 1776
The Conviction which the late Measures of Administration have

brot to the Minds of doubting Persons has such an Effect, that I think the Colonies cannot long remain an independant depending People, but that they will declare themselves as their Interest & Safety have long required, entirely separated from the prostituted Government of G Britain. Upon this Subject I have wrote to our Friend Colo. Orne & beg Leave to refer You thereto.[1] The principal object of our Attention at this important Time I think should be the Manufacturing Arms, Lead & Cloathing, & obtaining Flints, for I suppose since the Measures adopted by North Carolina & Virginia that there cannot remain a Doubt with our Assembly of the propriety of declaring for Independency & therefore that our Tho'ts will be mostly directed to the Means for supporting it. Powder & Cannon are so successfully manufactured that if the Spirit continues with sufficient Encouragement for the Manufacturers I think We may be sure of full Supplies. With respect to Arms' then, is it not necessary that each assembly should give such Encouragement as will effectually answer the purpose? I was of Opinion last fall that twelve Dollars should be given for all that should be brot to the Commissary in Consequence of the Resolve then issued by the Court, but since that was not the opinion of the Members in General & We are now greatly in Want of this Article would it not be a good plan to exempt from the Duties of War all Manufacturers of fire arms, to give a premium to them for each Apprentice which they shall take & Journey Man that they shall employ, & thirteen or fourteen Dollars for all that shall be delivered agreable to the former Resolve in twelve Months. Surely when the Success of our Measures so much depend on obtaining this Article We shall not hesitate to give such Encouragement as will obtain it with as good Success as We have heretofore the article of Saltpetre.

Lead You have before attended to, & I hope You will pursue the plan of carrying on the Works at North Hampton. If a Manufacturer is Wanted I apprehend the Colony of Virginia will spare us one. They sent to Europe for several & are now successfully carrying on the Works in that Colony, pray my Dear sir pursue these objects as of the greatest Importance.

Flints I think must be imported, & Cloathing may be manufactured if the Inhabitants are timely apprized thereof. Would it not be well to recommend to them at large to exert themselves for obtaining by their manufactures a Sufficiency of Woolens & Linnens for the ensuing Year & also for the Assembly to cause a sufficient Number of Blankets, Coats &c to be made for the Soldiers agreable to the Method pursued the last Year? The Men must be well fed, cloathed, armed, & payed or You can never oblige them to do their Duty. Our Friends Majer Hawley, the Speaker [James Warren], Genl. Orne & Mr. Sullivan I think will assist & promote these Measures, if you think it convenient to suggest the same.

I hope that one or more Cannon Forges will be encouraged in our Colony, & with respect to Cloathing think that after this Year our Trade will plentifully supply us. I remain sir with sincere regard for yourself & Friends Your most obedt & very hum sevt,

                                                        Elbridge Gerry

P.S. If Manufacturers can be obtained without sending to Virginia It will save much Time & Expence, as the Works are far beyond the Allegheny Mountains.

RC (MeHi).
[1] Not found.

Joseph Hewes to Thomas Cushing

Dear Sir   Philadelphia May 31st 1776
    I have seen a Letter directed to my Colleague Mr. Hooper signed by Dorothy Forbes and Eliza. Murray of Brush Hill near Boston, they seem to be in a distressed situation themselves and say my friend Hoopers Mother is in danger of suffering also.[1] In his absense for he is now in North Carolina let me entreat the favour of you to enquire into the affairs & present situation of this Lady. I have been told she had £500 Sterling setled upon her during life and that it was in the hands of Mr. Irwin of Boston who I understand went off with the Kings Troops and carried this money with him which occasions her distress. I hope Irwin has left some estate behind and that you will endeavour to have as much of it secured as will satisfie that worthy old Lady for any demands she may have against it. I must also beg the favour of you to see that she gets into some proper place where she can be kept happy and that you will advance the Necessary sums for that purpose till your friend Hooper Arives here. I have put one hundred dollars into Mr. Hancocks hands, he will write to you to advance that sum to Mrs Hooper and if any thing further should be necessary to be done so as to make the remainder of her life easy and comfortable I doubt not you will do it and be assured you cannot lay greater obligation on your friend Hooper. The two Ladies whose names I mentioned above I suppose are relations or particular friends of Mrs. Hoopers, if any thing can be done to serve them I doubt not your humanity will prompt you to do it. I shall be glad to receive a line from you relative to these matters & am with great respect & esteem, Dear Sir, your mo. Obedt. hume Sert,   Joseph Hewes

RC (NjHi).
[1] Dorothy Forbes and Elizabeth Murray were the daughters of James Murray, a Massachusetts loyalist and Hooper's uncle by marriage, who had looked after

Hooper's mother and brothers in Boston after Hooper had moved to North Carolina in the early 1760's. Nina Moore Tiffany and Susan I. Lesley, eds., *Letters of James Murray, Loyalist* (Boston: Privately printed, 1901), pp. 114–17, 237. For a letter of April 2, 1776, from Hooper to Dorothy Forbes, written from Baltimore while he was on his way back to North Carolina to attend a session of the provincial congress, see ibid., pp. 237–40.

Marine Committee to Esek Hopkins

Sir In Marine Committee Philada. May 31 1776
   The Marine Committee have directed Captn. John Bradford their Agent in Massachusets Bay to send to this City from Newberry Port, One hundred & twenty Chaldron of Coal. You are hereby directed to send one of the Armed Vessels under your Command to that port, to take under Convoy and Conduct safe into Delaware Bay the Vessel or Vessels in which the said Coal may be Shipped.[1]
John Hancock Chairman

Tr (RHi).
[1] Hopkins ordered John Paul Jones, commander of the Continental sloop *Providence*, to escort the coal ships from Massachusetts. See Clark, *Naval Documents*, 5:509, 599.

Robert Treat Paine to Henry Knox

Dr Sr, Philada. May 31st 1776
   The Congress have ordered 40 Howitzers to be cast, in the direction of which I have some Concern, & shall esteem my self much obliged to you if you will send me the weight & the bore of the Iron Howitzers you have with you as also the diameter & depth of the Chamber & the length of the bore. My particular reason for these Queres is that a Workman with whom I have Conferred on the Subject differs much in his dimension & Weight from the discription Muller [1] gives of them as Commonly made in England. Your opinion of the most profitable Sizes of Howitzers will be very Acceptable. Two uses are proposed 5 or 6 inch Howitzers to play upon Troops with shells or Grape Shott & some of 8 or 10 inch to fire point blank at ships, at what distance will they drive a shell through the Side of a Ship. Please to inform me also the weight of the 24 pounders & also of the largest Cannon you have. We make good 18, 12, 9, & 4 pounders & when we have got a Sufficiency of these hope to make larger Sizes. The opinion I have of yr. understanding & Zeal in these matters induces me to write thus freely to you hoping you will with all Convenient Speed inform me of those matters & favour me with such further Observations as you May think of service in the affair.

Hoping yr Welfare in all things, I Subscribe with great Esteem yr
hble Servt,   R T P

P.S. Pray inform me whether they now cast Iron Cannon at the Air
Furnace in New York & of what Sizes & whether they can Cast Iron
Howitzers there (Brass we cant get) & whether they can bore Cannon
after they have Cast them.

FC (MHi).
   [1] At the bottom of the second page of this draft Paine had written and lined out
the following note: "Extracts from Mullers Treatise of Artillery, printed 1757,
page 132. Capt. Desagulier & my Self made several experiments with different
Chambers (of Mortars) which contained the Same."
   [2] On April 13 Congress had ordered the committee for casting cannon, of which
Paine was a member, to oversee the construction of 40 howitzers. See *JCC*, 4:55,
280. Knox subsequently wrote several letters discussing this topic. His letters to
Paine of June 10, 24, 29, and July 19, 1776, are in the Robert Treat Paine Papers,
MHi.

George Wythe's Draft Address to the Foreign Mercenaries

[May ? 1776] [1]
The delegates of the thirteen united colonies of America
to the officers and soldiers of

It is with no small pleasure, when in this first address we ever
made to you we must call you enemies, that we can affirm you to be
unprovoked enemies. We have not invaded your country, slaughtered
wounded or captivated your parents children or kinsfolk, burned
plundered or desolated your towns and villages, wasted your farms
and cottages, spoiled you of your goods, or annoyed your trade. On
the contrary, all your countrymen who dwell among us, were received as friends, and treated as brethren, participating equally with
our selves of all our rights, franchises and privileges. We have not
aided ambitious princes and potentates in subjugating you. We
should glory being instrumental in the deliverance of mankind from
bondage and oppression. What then induced you to join in this
quarrel with our foes, strangers to you, unconnected with you, and at
so great a distance from both you and us? Do you think the cause
you are engaged in just on your side? To decide that we might safely
appeal to the judicious and impartial—but we have appealed to the
righteous judge of all the earth, inspired with humble confidence and
well-grounded hopes, that the lord of hosts will fight our battles,
whilst we are vindicating that inheritance we own ourselves indebted
to his bounty alone for. Were you compelled by your sovereigns to
undertake the bloody work of butchering your unoffending fellow-

creatures? Disdain the inhuman office, disgraceful to the soldier. Did lust of conquest prompt you? The victory, unattainable by you if heaven was not against us, which we know of no good reason you have to expect, or we to dread, shall cost you more than the benefits derived from it will be equivalent to; since it will be disputed by those who are resolved inflexibly to live no longer than they can enjoy the liberty you are hired to rob them of, and who are conscious of a dignity of character, which a contempt of every danger threatening the loss of that blessing seldom fails to accompany. Were you tempted by the prospect of exchanging the land you left for happier regions,—for a land of plenty and abhorrent of despotism? We wish this may be your motive; because we have the means, and want not inclination, to gratify your desires, if they be not hostile, without loss to ourselves, perhaps with less expense, certainly with more honour and with more advantage to you than victory can promise. Numberless germans and other foreigners settled in this country will testify this truth. To give you farther assurance of it, we have resolved,

Mistake not this for an expedient suggested by fear. In military virtue we doubt not americans will prove themselves to be second to none; their numbers exceed you and your confederates; in resources they now do or soon will abound. Neither suppose that we would seduce you to a treacherous defection. If you have been persuaded to believe, that it is your duty, or will be your interest to assist those who prepare, in vain we trust, to destroy us; go on; and, when you shall fall into our hands, and experience less severity of punishment than ruffians, and savages deserve, attribute it to that lenity, which is never separate from magnanimity. But if, exercising your own judgments, you have spirit enough to assert that freedom which all men are born to, associate yourselves with those who desire, and think they are able to secure it, with all the blessings of peace, to you and your posterity.

MS (DLC). In the hand of George Wythe.

[1] Upon receiving copies of several treaties negotiated by George III with various German principalities for some 16,000 troops, Congress on May 21 appointed a committee to publish extracts of the treaties "and to prepare an address to the foreign mercenaries who are coming to invade America." The committee, consisting of John Adams, William Livingston, Richard Henry Lee, Jefferson, and Sherman, quickly distributed extracts of the treaties to various printers for publication, but no address to the foreign mercenaries was ever submitted to Congress for action.

On May 29, in anticipation that great exertions would be called for during the forthcoming campaign, a committee consisting of Jefferson, Samuel Adams, Edward Rutledge, and Wythe was appointed to prepare an address "to impress the minds of the people with the necessity of their now stepping forward to save their country, their freedom and property." As in the case of the former committee, no address from this committee was ever reported to Congress.

However, the papers of Thomas Jefferson, DLC, contain two draft addresses, in the hand of Wythe, that were undoubtedly prepared as a result of the appointment of these two committees, although Wythe was a member of only the second. Worthington C. Ford, the editor of the *Journals of the Continental Congress,* published Wythe's address "to the inhabitants of the . . . colonies" in a footnote to the journal entry for May 29, but he mistakenly associated the address "to the foreign mercenaries" with a committee appointed in August to stimulate desertions among the "Hessians" after they had arrived. See *JCC,* 4:369, 401–2, 5:707–9.

The present entry, which seems clearly related to the assignment given to the committee appointed on May 21, is reprinted here in order to place it in the context of the events that inspired it. Although Wythe was not a member of this committee, it seems likely that he drafted it at Jefferson's request, perhaps when the two men were collaborating on the address being prepared by the second committee, a conjecture that would account for the presence of both documents in Jefferson's papers. In any event, since Wythe left Philadelphia for Virginia in mid-June and did not return until September, he could not have been involved in preparing the address to the "Hessians" drafted by Jefferson which Congress adopted on August 27. Finally, the wording of the present address so directly reflects the conditions Congress faced at the end of May it seems highly improbable that Wythe could have drafted it for any purpose other than as a response to Congress' resolution of May 21.

John Adams to Isaac Smith, Sr.

Dear sir   Philadelphia June 1. 1776

Your favours of May 14 and 22d are now before me.[1] The first I shewed to Mr. Morris, as soon as I received it. The last contains Intelligence, from Hallifax of the Streights to which our Enemies are reduced, which I was very glad to learn.

I am very happy to learn from you and some other of my Friends that Boston is securely fortified; but still I cannot be fully satisfied untill I hear that every unfriendly Flagg is chased out of that Harbour.

Cape Ann, I am sensible is a most important Post, and if the Enemy should possess themselves of it, they might distress the Trade of the Colony to a great Degree. For which Reason I am determined to do every Thing in my Power to get it fortified at the Continental Expence. I cant be confident that I shall succeed but it shall not be my Fault if I dont.[2]

I am very glad you gave me your Opinion of the Utility of that Harbour and of the Practicability of making it secure, because I was not enough acquainted with it before to speak with Precision about it.

Your Observations upon the oppressive severity of the Old Regulations of Trade in subjecting Ships and Cargoes to Confiscation for the Indiscretion of a Master or Mariner, and upon the Artifice and Corruption which was introduced respecting Hospital Money, are very just: But if you consider the Resolution of Congress, and that of Virginia of the 15th of May, the Resolutions of the two Carolinas and Georgia, each of which Colonies, are instituting new Governments, under the Authority of the People; if you consider what is doing at New York, New Jersey, Pensilvania, and even in Maryland, which are all gradually forming themselves into order to follow the Colonies to the Northward and Southward, together with the Treaties with Hesse, Brunswick and Waldeck and the Answer to the Mayor &c. of London; I believe you will be convinced that there is little Probability of our ever again coming under the Yoke of British Regulations of Trade. The Cords which connected the two Countries are cutt asunder, and it will not be easy to splice them again, together.

I agree with you, in sentiment, that there will be little Difficulty in Trading with France and Spain, a great deal in dealing with Portugal, and some with Holland. Yet by very good Intelligence I am convinced, that there are great Merchants in the United Provinces and even in Amsterdam, who will contract to supply you with any Thing you want, whether Merchandize or military Stores by the Way of Nieuport and Ostend, two Towns which are subject to the Empress of Austria, who has never taken any public Notice of the Dispute between Britain and Us, and has never prohibited her Subjects from supplying us with any Thing.

There is a Gentleman, now in this City, a Native of it, and a very worthy Man who has been lately in those Towns as well as Amsterdam, who informs me that he had many Conversations there, with Merchants of figure, and that they assured him they should be glad to contract to furnish us with any Supplies, even upon Credit, for an Interest of four Per Cent.

Other Intelligence to the same Purpose, with Additions of more Importance, has been sent here. But the Particulars may not be mentioned.

Europe seems to be in a great Commotion; altho the Appearance of a perfect Calm is affected, I think this American Contest will light up a general War. What it will end in, God alone knows, to whose wise and righteous Providence I chearfully submit, and am with great Esteem and Respect for the Family, your Friend & servant.

LB (MHi). Adams, *Family Correspondence* (Butterfield), 2:1–2.

[1] Isaac Smith's letters of May 14 and 22 are in Adams, *Family Correspondence* (Butterfield), 1:409, 413–14. In his letter of May 22, Smith refers to the reception of letters from Adams dated April 29 and May 6, 1776, neither of which has been found.

[2] On March 23 Adams had been appointed to the committee to supervise the fortification of ports. *JCC*, 4:233. Subsequently the committee asked Washington to appoint engineers to inspect the ports of Cape Ann, Mass., and New London, Conn. See Committee on Fortifying Ports to George Washington, April 14; and Washington's letters to the committee of April 22 and June 8, 1776, in Washington, *Writings* (Fitzpatrick), 4:504, 5:109–10.

Oliver Wolcott to Laura Wolcott

My Dear,   Philadelpa 1 June 1776
I Wrote to you the 25 and 16 last which I hope you have recd.[1]
It is now a long time which I have been here, and I do most sincerely
Wish to return to the Pleasures of a domestick rural Life, such a Life
as Poets and Wise men have always with so much Propriety praised.
Here I see but little except human Faces which I know not, and
numerous Pyles of Building, which have long since Satiated the
Sight, and the street rumble is farr from being musical. But as I was
not sent here to please myself, I shall cheerfully yeild to my Duty,
convinced of this Truth, that the Noise and Bustle of this World are
the best Lessons to teach a man how few are it's Injoyments.

You See by the Papers that our inverterate Foes threaten us with
a large Armament this Summer, tho I rather think their Land Forces
will not probably be more than about Thirty Thousand. These may
be principally employed in Canada, N York and that Provence.
These exertions of our Enemies will call for the like on our part. A
Considerable Augmentation therefore will likely be made to our
Army for the Canada and other Services and the Troops will be
raised at the eastward. The Disadvantage which the Enemy are
under in carrying on a War at such a Vast Distance is Very great
and if they fail of any considerable success this summer, it may go
near to put an End to the Controversy. I think We have no Reason
to be discouraged. Our Cause is just. We may therefore Hope God
will as he has done appear to Vindicate it. Our Resources are
Numerous.

By Olivers Letter by Delucence I learn that you was well and the
Family, which was a great Satisfaction to Me to hear. My Freinds at
Litchfeild Write to Me but seldom, so that I know but little about
them. I mentioned to you in my last that I hoped to Visit my
Family the latter End of the Next Month, which I still purpose.
It will be more agreable to my Colleuges to go home then than
earlier; and as it will give me an Oppertunity of being out of this
City in the hottest Season Shall Submit to it. By the Blessing of
God I Still injoy Health. May the best of Heavens Blessings be
your Portion. My Love to my Children and be assured that I am
yours Affectionately,   Oliver Wolcott

P.S. Since I Wrote my Letter recd. Letters from Dr. Smith, Mr.
Champion, Mr. Lyman. I am glad to hear that you and Family are
well but as the Post goes out immediately I shall not be able to
Write further, but shall Send againe by the next Post.

RC (CtHi).
[1] See Wolcott's letters to Samuel Lyman, May 16, note, and to Laura Wolcott,
May 25, 1776.

John Adams to Henry Knox

Dear Sir   Philadelphia June 2. 1776
    Your esteemed Favour of the 16 of May, came to my Hand a few
Days ago.[1]
    You have laid me under obligations, by your ingenious observa-
tions upon those Books, upon military Science, which are necessary
to be procured in the present Circumstances of this Country. I have
been a long Time convinced of the utility of publishing American
Editions of those Writers, and that it is an object of sufficient
Importance, to induce the public to be at the Expence of it. But
greater objects press in such Numbers, upon those who think for the
public, as Ld Drummond expresses it, that this has been hitherto
neglected. I could wish that the Public would be at the Expence
not only of new Editions of these authors, but of establishing
Accademies, for the Education of young Gentlemen in every Branch
of the military Art: because I am fully of your sentiment, that We
ought to lay Foundations, and begin Institutions, in the present
Circumstances of this Country, for promoting every Art, Manufacture and Science which is necessary for the Support of an independent State. We must for the future Stand upon our own Leggs or
fall. The Alienation of affection between the two Countries, is at
length, so great, that if the Morals of the British Nation and their
political Principles were much purer than they are, it would be
scarcely possible to accomplish a cordial Reunion with them.
    The Votes of the Congress and the Proceedings of the Colonies
seperately must before this Time have convinced you, that this is
the sense of America, with infinitely greater Unanimity, than could
have been credited by many People a few Months ago. Those few
Persons indeed, who have attended closely to the Proceedings of the
several Colonies, for a Number of years past, and reflected deeply
upon the Causes of this mighty Contest, have foreseen, that Such an
unanimity would take Place as soon as a Seperation should become
necessary. These are not at all surprised while many others really
are and some affect to be astonished at the Phenominon.
    The Policy of Rome, in carrying their Arms to Carthage, while
Hannibal was at the Gates of their Capitol, was wise and justified by
the Event, and would deserve Imitation if We could march into the
Country of our Enemies. But possessed as they are of the Dominion
of the Sea, it is not easy for Us to reach them. Yet it is possible that
a bold attempt might succeed. But We have not yet sufficient Confidence in our own Power or skill, to encourage Enterprizes of the
daring, hardy Kind—such often prosper and are always glorious. But
shall I give offence if I say, that our Arms have kept an even Pace
with our Councils? that both have been rather slow and irresolute?
Have either our officers or Men, by Sea or Land, as yet discovered

that exalted Courage, and mature Judgment, both of which are necessary for great and Splendid Actions? Our Forces have done very well, considering their poor Appointment and our Infancy. But I may say to you that I wish I could see less attention to Trifles, and more to the great essentials of the service, both in the civil and military Departments.

I am no Prophet, if We are not compelled by Necessity, before the war is over, to become more Men of Business and less Men of Pleasure. I have formed great Expectations from a Number of Gentlemen of Genius, Sentiment, and Education, of the younger sort, whom I know to be in the Army, and wish that Additions might be made to the Number. We have had Some Examples of Magnaminity and Bravery, it is true, which would have done Honour to any Age or Country. But these have been accompanied with a want of Skill and Experience, which intitles the Hero to Compassion, at the same Time that he has our Admiration. For my own Part I never think of Warren or Montgomery, without lamenting at the same Time that I admire, lamenting that Inexperience to which, perhaps they both owed their Glory.[2]

LB (MHi).
[1] Knox's May 16 letter to Adams is in the Adams Papers, MHi.
[2] Adams also wrote a letter this day to Abigail commenting on the availability of spring fruit and vegetables and announcing that he had begun to maintain a letterbook to preserve his correspondence. See Adams, *Family Correspondence* (Butterfield), 2:3.

Joseph Hewes to Samuel Purviance, Jr.

Sir   Philadelphia 2d June 1776

I have received your favours of the 24th & 28th ulto. With respect to the former, I wish you could collect all the Accounts that are yet unpaid for the two Vessels Fitted out by you & Mr Lux and settle them in such manner that the Marine Committee may have nothing further to do with them than to order payment.[1] As the Iron was taken without Mr Ridglys consent you must settle that matter in the best & easiest manner so as to give Satisfaction. All the men belonging to the Hornett & Wasp at the time of their Arival here have been discharged at their own request, being at that time very sickly. Some few of them may have entered again on board some of the Vessels for ought I know, however, you Are requested by the Marine Committee not to Advance any thing for any of them. I read your last letter to that board who desired me to inform you that Cannon had been contracted for in this Colony for all the Frigates, but as there is no certainty of geting them in any reasonable time they wish you to get them for the Frigate you are building.[2] If I can get the dimen-

sions of them to send by this Post you shall have them enclosed, if
not I will send them by the next. I suppose it will be more convenient for you to get the Cannon from Mr. Hughes's works than from
any other place. The Committee intend to have all the Frigates
fitted out as fast as possible and desire your board to furnish every
thing for the one under your care, your precaution in keeping a
guard I think a good one.

I am with much respect, Sir, your mo. Obedt Servt,

                                                    Joseph Hewes

RC (MdHi).
    [1] The sloop *Hornet* and schooner *Wasp*. See Clark, *Naval Documents*, 3:218, 607,
773–74; Benjamin Harrison to Wilson Miles Cary, December 10; John Jay to Lewis
Morris, December 20, 1775; and letters of both the Naval Committee and Hewes
to Samuel Purviance, Jr., January 6 and 29, 1776.
    [2] The *Virginia* (so named by Congress on June 6). *JCC*, 5:422–23.

Richard Henry Lee to Landon Carter

Dear Sir,   Philadelphia 2d June 1776
    Since the establishment of our Westmoreland Rider, I conclude
the papers come so regularly into your neighborhood from this City,
as to render it the less necessary to repeat in letters what you will
find exactly detailed in the Gazette. I cannot help congratulating
you on [. . .] Virginia has obtained by the resolve of Convention on
the 15th of last month. A Gentleman of the first understanding here,
and of very moderate passions, said on reading the resolve "Virginia
has determined like a brave, sensible and injured people." Still the
views of interested, weak, and wicked men, obstruct the public service in these proprietary governments. The infamous treaties with
Hesse, Brunswick, &c. (of which we have authentic copies) and the
Ministerial reply to Graftons motion leave not a doubt but that our
enemies are determined upon the absolute conquest and subduction
of N. America. It is not choice then, but necessity that calls for Independence, as the only means by which foreign Alliance can be obtained; and a proper confederation by which internal peace and
union may be secured. Contrary to our earnest, early, and repeated
petitions for peace, liberty and safety, our enemies press us with war,
threaten us with danger and Slavery. And this not with her single
force but with the aid of Foreigners. Now, altho we might safely
venture our strength circumstanced as it is, against that of Great
Britain only, yet we are certainly unequal to a Contest with her and
her Allies without any assistance from without, and this more
especially, as we are incapable of profiting by our exports for want
of Naval force. You seem to apprehend danger from our being aided

by despotic States, but remember that France assisted Holland without injury to the latter. [Nor will?] the help we desire put it, by any means, [in] the power of France to hurt us tho she were so inclined. Supplies of Military Stores and Soldiers Clothing, Ships of war to cover our Trade and open our Ports, which would be an external assistance alltogether, could never endanger our freedom by putting it in the power of our Ally to Master us, as has been the case where weak States have admitted powerful Armies for their Defenders.[1] When last we heared from Canada, our forces that had retreated from Quebec, on the arrival of succors, had fixt at De Chambaud, or Falls of Richlieu, about 30 miles above Quebec, and were strongly fortifying there. If they can maintain that Post, which commands 8 tenths of Canada, we shall do almost as well as if we had Quebec, as we [there]by effectually cut off all communication with the upper Country, or Western Indians, and prevent the West Indies receiving supplies from that fertile Province. We are making the best preparation to meet the numerous foreign Mercinaries with which we are to be invaded this Campaign. This expence of G. Britain this summer is estimated at 10 millions, exclusive of the ordinary expences. With half her Trade subducted, with a debt of 140 millions, how can she go on? The Dutch begin to fear for their money in English funds, and say they wd. give 30 per Cent discount to have it withdrawn. Franklin the late Governor of New Jersey, you will see by the inclosed paper, is endeavoring to bring himself under the notice of Congress, and I believe he will effect it now, as the plan of calling an Assembly by a Kings Governor [. . .] the Resolve of the 15th cannot [. . . .][2]

I hope to be in Virga. in 10 or 12 days, [when] I shall endeavour to visit Sabine Hall.

I am, with great esteem, dear Sir your affectionate and obedient servant   Richard Henry Lee

P.S. We have just seen a petition from London to the King [asking?] in m[. . .]ng & moving language that he wd. let explicit terms [of] justice precede the operation of Arms in America. His ans[wer is] that he is sorry for the rebellion, but that force on his part & sub[mission] on ours is all he proposes. This is the substance of his Tyrannic answer to the most sensible & humane Address that Modern times has produced.[3]

RC (CCamarSJ).
    [1] Some of Carter's views on this subject have been preserved in the note he wrote on the cover of this letter: "This Gentleman [i.e., Lee] is a correspondent but so late in his replys that I almost forget what I wrote to him. I see he says I am apprehensive that by courting foreign assistance, they who assist us will demand terms equally injurious; and Puts me in mind of France who assisted Holland.

But he should consider the claim of France on America which was mostly taken from her. Now the case was different as to Holland. But he seems to hint we dont want any internal assistance but only as to trade &c. If we dont, I hold no argumt. At least I see, tho he does not [c]are to own it. He agrees that our independance is by compulsion. If that is granted I hold no argument there neither. All that I urged was that the Pure British Constitution was not to be so reprobated as Common Sense had done it."

² William Franklin's May 30 proclamation calling for the general assembly to meet on June 20 was cited by the New Jersey Provincial Convention as justification for their June 14 order for his arrest. See *Am. Archives*, 4th ser. 6:626, 967–68; Jonathan Dickinson Sergeant to John Adams, June 15, note; and John Hancock to John Witherspoon, June 19, 1776.

³ The March 22 "Address and Petition of the Lord Mayor, Aldermen, and Commons of the City of London" and the king's reply are in *Am. Archives*, 4th ser. 5:462–63.

William Whipple to Joshua Brackett

My Dear Sir   Philadelphia, 2nd June, 1776

I am much obliged by your favor of the 21st ult. I must confess that I something wonder that people should move their families and effects into town just at this time, when Britain is collecting her whole strength, aided by every possible Foreign power, she can engage and determined to push the war with the utmost fury. I by no means think she will be able to execute her plans, but still I think it would be prudent for people who move there effects into the country to secure them from danger, to let them remain while the danger continues. My greatest objection to these movings is, that if there should be an alarm, people will be engaged about their goods when they should have arms in their hands to oppose the enemy. As every thing depends on this summer's campaign, every nerve should be exerted and if we are successful, which by divine assistance I am in no doubt of, our enemies will not be able to support the war another year. The terms on which Britain has taken troops of the German States will undoubtedly render her contemptible in the eyes of all Europe.¹

Tr (MH).

¹ In addition to this fragment of Whipple's letter, the following extract and summary of additional subjects Whipple discussed was printed in a 1967 auction catalog describing the letter. " 'You want to know when another name is to be adopted instead of the United Colonies; the free Independent States of America is the common toast in this City & I hope ere long will be established by Congress. . . .' Mentions his brother's problems, naval action on the Delaware river, and vessals arriving from the West Indies with ammunition and supplies." *Parke-Bernet Galleries Catalog*, no. 2569 (May 16, 1967), item 66.

William Whipple to John Langdon

My Dear Sir,   June 2d [1776]

Your favor of the 20th came to hand Yesterday.[1] I think I mentioned to you in a former letter,[2] that I supposed there wod be a considerable alteration in the wages of the officers in the naval department, the principle offices higher & the warrant & petty officers considerably lower. As there is the highest probability that will be the case you no doubt will be careful of the encouragement you give those when you ingage them. I told you in my last that Congress were ingaged in a Conference with the Genl. on the necessary operations for the present Campaign. This Business is not yet finish'd nor do I think will be this week & Congress have determined to do no other business 'till that is compleated. So soon as that is done naval matters will be attended to. I wish you had talk'd with some of those Gentn. you propose for officers. My objection still remains to him you mention for 1st Leut.; it is meerly on accot of his unsteadyness that I object to him & that must remain until his nature is changed, however if you are fond of having him appointed I'll give up my opinion. Rob. Parker I've a very good opinion of, & shod be very fond of serving [him] but am somthing doubtful whether he wod make a good subordinate officer even if he wod accept. Shores Wheelwright, & Follet I have a very high opinion of as resolute enterprising men. I shall be glad you'll talk with them or such of them as you think will best answer the purpose. There will be time enough for you to answer this before it will be necessary to fill up the commissions as there is no guns yet & I fear they are still to be made. For my part I have no views whatever in this appointment but the publick good but if there shod be any worthy men who wod be willing to enter in to the service that cannot be provided for in this ship I will do my endeavor to get such places for them as will be most agreeable in some other, & no doubt some may be provided for in this way.

Have not yet had an opportunity to send the money but have a prospect of one in a few days. Here is a report that Col. Beedle who was posted at a place called the Cedars some distance above Montreal is cut off by a party of the 8th regt and Indians that came down the St. Lawrence, also Major Sherburne who endeavored to support him. This story comes in so loose a way and at the same time so different from the accounts we have just before rec'd from Canada that I do not credit it; however it may be true; we must expect to meet with some hard rubs.[3] A brig in the Service of the Continent arrived a few days since with Some powder and arms. Several French vessels have also arrived here lately with sugar, molasses, coffee &c.

The Agent is not yet appointed. I still intend to insist on my first proposal. My regards to your friends and accept the best wishes of, your assured friend,   Wm Whipple

FC (Capt. J. G. M. Stone, Annapolis, Md., 1973); endorsed: "J. Langdon June 2d, sent off 4th." Tr (DLC). FC incomplete; last paragraph and signature taken from Tr.
¹ John Langdon's May 20 letter to Whipple is in Clark, *Naval Documents*, 5:159–60.
² See Whipple to Langdon, May 7, 1776.
³ See Josiah Bartlett to John Langdon, June 3, 1776.

John Adams to Abigail Adams

Philadelphia June 3. 1776 [1]

The last Evening, Mess. Adams, P[aine] and G[erry] and my self, by Agreement waited on the P[resident] at his House, in order to accompany him to the Generals, to request that Gates and Mifflin might be sent immediately, to take the Command at Boston.[2] The P. we found very ill of a violent fitt of the Gout, unable to go abroad. At our Disire, he sent a Card to the G. requesting his Company, who soon afterwards came. This Conversation would make a Figure in History. It turned upon the general State of Affairs in the military Departments, and the Characters of the principal Officers in the Army. I dont think it prudent to commit to Writing the Particulars.

But a few Reflections that occurred, may be safely written. One is this.

There is so much of Accident in the Appointment of Officers, even where they are chosen by the People or their Representatives, and their Characters are of such vast Importance, after they are appointed, and in Times like these when there are so many Jealousies, Envys, and Distrusts abroad from whence so many Calumnies arise, that it is absolutely necessary to support the Characters of Officers whenever you can, to be silent when you cannot, untill you are furnished with sufficient Evidence of their Faults and Guilt, and then censure, and punish.

LB (MHi). Adams, *Family Correspondence* (Butterfield), 2:5–6.
¹ There is no evidence that a copy of this letter was ever sent; and it was not enumerated in a list of letters that John later provided Abigail. See Adams to Abigail Adams, June 26, 1776.
² On this point, see Massachusetts Delegates to George Washington, May 16; and Samuel Adams to Horatio Gates, June 10, 1776.

John Adams to Patrick Henry

My dear Sir.   Philadelphia June 3. 1776
I had this Morning the Pleasure of yours of 20 May.[1] The little
Pamphlet you mention is nullius Fidius, and if I should be obliged
to maintain it, the World will not expect that I should own it. My
Motive for inclosing it to you, was not the value of the Present, but
as a Token of Friendship—and more for the Sake of inviting your
Attention to the subject, than because there was any Thing in it
worthy your Perusal. The Subject is of infinite Moment, and perhaps
more than Adequate to the Abilities of any Man, in America. I know
of none so competent, to the Task as the author of the first Virginia
Resolutions against the Stamp Act, who will have the Glory with
Posterity, of beginning and concluding this great Revolution. Happy
Virginia, whose Constitution is to be framed by so masterly a Builder.
Whether the Plan of the Pamphlet, is not too popular, whether the
Elections are not too frequent, for your Colony I know not. The
Usages and Genius and Manners of the People, must be consulted.
And if annual Elections of the Representatives of the People, are
sacredly preserved, these Elections by Ballott, and none permitted to
be chosen but Inhabitants, Residents, as well as qualified Freeholders
of the City, County, Parish, Town, or Burrough for which they are to
serve three essential Prerequisites of a free Government, the Council
or middle Branch of the Legislature may be triennial, or even
Septennial, with out much Inconvenience.
I esteem it an Honour and an Happiness, that my opinion so
often co-incides with yours. It has ever appeared to me, that the
natural Course and order of Things, was this—for every Colony to
institute a Government—for all the Colonies to confederate, and
define the Limits of the Continental Constitution—then to declare
the Colonies a sovereign State, or a Number of confederated Sovereign
States—and last of all to form Treaties with foreign Powers. But I
fear We cannot proceed Systematically, and that We shall be obliged
to declare ourselves independent States before We confederate, and
indeed before all the Colonies have established their Governments.
It is now pretty clear, that all these Measures will follow one
another in a rapid Sucession, and it may not perhaps be of much
Importance, which is done first.
The Importance of an immediate application to the French Court
is clear, and I am very much obliged to you for your Hint of the
Rout by the Mississippi.[2]
Your Intimation that the session of your Representative Body
would be long gave me great Pleasure, because We all look up to
Virginia for Examples and in the present Perplexities, Dangers and
Distresses of our Country it is necessary that the Supream Councils
of the Colonies should be almost constantly sitting. Some Colonies

are not sensible of this and they will certainly Suffer for their Indiscretion. Events of such magnitude as those which present themselves now in such quick succession, require constant Attention and mature Deliberation.

The little Pamphlet you mention which was published here as an Antidote to the Thoughts on Government and which is whispered to have been the joint Production of one Native of Virginia and two Natives of New York, I know not how truly, will make no Fortune in the World. It is too absurd to be considered twice. It is contrived to involve a Colony in eternal War.

The Dons, the Bashaws, the Grandees, the Patricians, the Sachems, the Nabobs, call them by what Name you please, Sigh, and groan, and frett, and sometimes Stamp, and foam, and curse—but all in vain. The Decree is gone forth, and it cannot be recalled, that a more equal Liberty, than has prevailed in other Parts of the Earth, must be established in America. That Exuberance of Pride, which has produced an insolent Domination, in a few, a very few oppulent, monopolizing Families, will be brought down nearer to the Confines of Reason and Moderation, than they have been used. This is all the Evil, which they themselves will endure. It will do them good in this World and every other. For Pride was not made for Men only as a Tormentor.

I shall ever be happy in receiving your Advice, by Letter, untill I can be more compleatly so in seeing you here in Person, which I hope will be soon. I am with Sincere Affection and Esteem, dear sir, your Friend and very humble servant.

LB (MHi).
[1] Henry's May 20 letter is in Adams, *Works* (Adams), 4:201–2.
[2] Henry had suggested that the Mississippi River might provide the best route for American ambassadors to reach French officials in the West Indies. Ibid., p. 201.

Josiah Bartlett to Mary Bartlett

My Dear,   Philadelphia June 3rd. 1776
Last Saturday I recd your 2nd letter Dated 17th May and am very thankful to hear that you and my family are well and that my friend Lieut Pearson is Recovering his health again. I hope this will find you and yours well as it leaves me and that we may all retain our health till by the leave of Providence we meet again in Safety.

This is the 4th letter I have wrote you from this place, beside the one I wrote by Col. Gale, the Dates are May 18th, 21st & 28th,[1] all which I hope are come safe to hand, that of the 21st I sent by the way of Portsmouth, the other two directed to be left at Newbury

Port. I want much to know whether those sent to Newbury come Seasonably to you. The post takes your letters from Newbury sometimes on Tuesday & the next Saturday week they arrive here. The weather here pleasant and Seasonable tho, two nights last week so cold I am told there was a white frost here.

All last week there was plenty of green peas in the market here— Strawberries and Cherries just begin to be brought in. We have recd. certain intelligence that Brittain is Determined to use her utmost endeavors this year to Subdue us. The Congress have Determined to oppose them with all their power and have agreed to send 8 Regiments of Militia of 750 men each to joyn our army in Canada: one of the Regiments is to be raised in the western parts of our Province, four in Massachusetts, 2 in Connecticut, & one in N.Y.— and 25 thousand men more are to be raised between New Hampshire & Maryland viz in Mass, Conn, N.Y., N.J., Penn & Maryland for the Defense of the Sea Coasts.[2] As to the Enemy attacking this place I am in no fear of it, Nay I rather wish it for the Difficulties will be so great that I am almost sure they must be Defeated. It is said that Canada & New York will be their principal objects, tho it is likely they will make attacks on some other places. I hope the Americans will play the man for their country & for their all, and that kind Providence will give us success & victory that the wickedness and villany of our Enemies will fall on their own heads, and that America may be forever seperated from the Tyranny of Brittain.

French vessels frequently arrive here. Two came up to this city yesterday their loading chiefly Cotton, molasses, sugar, coffee, Canvass &c. Last Saturday an American vessel arrived from the French West Indies with 7400 lb. of powder, 149 stand of arms, beside a large quantity of other articles. I hope you wont fail to write to me every week for receiving letters from you is next to seeing you.

Tell Polly & Lois I recd. their's and am glad to hear they are well. Remember my love to them & to all the children. Give my regards to Mr. Thayer, Lieut Pearson, Capt Calef, James Procter and All my friends. I am yours &c,   Josiah Bartlett

P.S. I shall for the present write to you by Tuesdays post which will convey them to Newbury the next Friday week. This goes off this Day the 4th & I expect will get to Newbury the 14th & to you the 15th. The same day I expect to Receive yours which will leave Newbury to Day or tomorrow morning.
I am now well.   J. B.

Tr (Mrs. Rodney M. Wilson, Kingston, N.H., 1975).
   [1] Only Bartlett's May 18 letter has been found.
   [2] For the resolutions raising troops for the coming campaign, see JCC, 4:410–13.

Josiah Bartlett to John Langdon

My dear Sir,   Philada. June 3rd 1776.
Yours of the 21st ulto is come to hand. I hope you have had good luck in launching the Ship. The Circumstances of affairs in Canada and the certainty of a large body of Hessians &c being hired and designed soon to attack the United Colonies has so engrossed the attention of Congress to be prepared for them, that it is not possible to get them to attend to smaller matters. The affair of the Agency lays dormant. Capt. Thompson is nominated by the Marine Committee for the command of your ship but not yet confirmed by Congress.[1] The Generals Washington, Gates, and Mifflin are here to consult the operations of the war for this year. Congress have resolved that eight regiments of Militia to consist of 750 Men each forthwith be raised and sent into Canada 'till the first of December, to be raised in the Western part of New Hampshire one Regiment, 4 Massachusetts, 2 Connecticut & one New York.[2] I expect 25 thousand more men will be ordered to be raised for the same time for the defence of the Sea Coasts from New Hampshire to Maryland inclusive. In short Sir, this will be the trying year, and if possible they must be hindered from getting any Foothold this Season; if that can be done, I think the day will be our own, and we be forever delivered from our British Tyranny.
Yesterday one of the Continental vessels that were sent out for necessaries arrived here. She brought 7400 lbs of powder, 149 **Arms** being all she could procure. The rest of her Cargo, canvas &c &c. She had like to have been taken by the Liverpool in this Bay, but two of the small continental vessels took her and a French schooner under their protection and the Liverpool did not think proper to engage them. Several French vessels from the West Indies have arrived here with Molasses, Coffee, Linen &c. One of them was taken by a man of war who examined all the Cargo and finding no arms or Military Stores, and not being willing to affront the French, ordered her forthwith to proceed for France (where she pretended to be bound) having previously taken out the American master & put him on board the man of war; at night she shifted her course and came in here. I shall inclose a paper containing the Virginia and North Carolina Resolves concerning Independance. This province, New Jersey, and the Delaware Counties will soon take up Government, entirely under the people. New York and Maryland it is thought will soon follow. The constitution of Government that South Carolina has formed for themselves you have no doubt seen. Virginia, North Carolina & Georgia were forming theirs when the last accounts left them.
This moment an express has arrived from Albany with the Copy

of a Letter from General Sulivan Dated Ticonderoga May 27th informing that it was reported there by a man from Canada that Col. Bedel's regiment & an hundred men with Major Sherburn who were posted at a place called the Cedars above Montreal were attacked by the Soldiers from Niagara & Detroit with some French & Indians and were all cut off, but no particulars.[3] Hope it will not prove so bad as reported; You will be likely to hear more before you receive this, if it is true.

By a St. Kitts Newspaper this moment recd. there is the address of the City of London to the King on American Affairs presented to him the 22nd of March & by his Answer we see he will have absolute submission or nothing.[4] You will soon see it in the publick prints.

I am Sir, your friend and servant,   Josiah Bartlett

Tr (MH).
[1] Thomas Thompson was appointed "captain of the frigate built in New Hampshire" on June 6. *JCC*, 5:422.
[2] See *JCC*, 4:410–11.
[3] Probably Sullivan's May 27 letter to Philip Schuyler, which was one of the "Sundry letters received by General Washington" that were laid before Congress on this day. *JCC*, 4:411; and *Am. Archives*, 4th ser. 6:609–10.
[4] The Address of the City of London of March 22, 1776, and the king's response are in *Am. Archives*, 4th ser. 5:462–63.

Committee of Secret Correspondence to William Bingham

Sir [1]   Philada June 3d 1776

You are immediately to repair on Board the Sloop Hornet, Wm Hallock Esqr Comr, bound to Martinico.[2] On your Arrival deliver the Letter you are entrusted with to the General there & show him your Credentials.

You are earnestly to endeavor to procure from him Ten Thousand good Musquets, well fitted with Bayonets.[3] If he cannot or will not supply them, you are to request his Favor & influence in procuring them in that or any other Island if to be had. We propose to pay for them by remitting the Produce of this Country with all possible Dispatch to any Island that may be agreed on. You are to take especial Care, that the Musquets you send are good. We direct you to send 2500 of them by the Hornet on her Return & the Remainder in Parcels not exceeding 1000 in swift sailing, well appointed Vessels, with Directions to the Masters to put into the first Port within the united Colonies, where they can safely land. We desire you to obtain from the General if possible a French Man of War or Frigate to convoy these Vessels so far that they may be out of the Course of the British Ships that are cruizing in the West

Indies. You are carefully to publish all the Papers delivered to you by us for that Purpose & disperse them as much as you can throughout the Dutch, English & French West Indies, having first obtained the General's Permission to do so in the Latter.

You must with the greatest Prudence endeavor to discover either by Conversation with the General or others the Designs of the French in assembling so large a Fleet with a great Number of Troops in the West Indies & whether they mean to act for or against America. You are to convey to us the speediest Intelligence of any Discoveries you may make on this Head.[4]

You are to continue at Martinico untill we recall you & are to cultivate an intimate & friendly Correspondence with the General & other Persons of Distinction there, that you may be enabled to procure all the usefull Intelligence you can. You are immediately on your arrival to inform Silas Deane Esqr of it & desire him to address to you his Dispatches for us.

Your Letters to him are to be directed under Cover to Mess Saml & J H Delap at Bourdeaux or to Monsr Dubourg at Paris. Whenever you obtain any Intelligence which you think of such Importance, that it ought to be immediately conveyed to us, You are to charter a fast sailing Vessel, if no other opportunity offers & Send her to this Continent, with such Directions to the Master as are herein before mentioned.

You are to observe the strictest Secrecy & not to discover any Part of the Business you are Sent upon to any Persons, but those to whom you are under an absolute Necessity of communicating it, in the Transaction thereof. It will readily occur to you that an Appearance of Commercial Views will effectually cover the Political; therefore you will make frequent Enquiries amongst their Merchants what Articles of this Country's Produce are most wanted in the Islands & You must consider yourself as authorized by the United Colonies to engage for the Payment of the 10,000 Musquets in Such Articles deliver'd at Martinico (or any other Island they may fix on) as fast as they can be introduced. The Exports shall be made from the Continent on the first Advice of your having succeeded & as our Ships are liable to Capture, when one is taken another shall be dispatched untill the entire Payment is made agreable to your Contract.

When you write to Mr Deane desire him to put his current Dispatches addressed to you, under Cover to the General, but when he has any particular Matters to communicate either to Congress, Yourself or to Us, that he thinks should not be risqued through that Channel for fear of Inspection let him procure a Mercht in France to put such Dispatches directed for you under Cover to a Mercht in Martinico with an express Injunction to deliver them into your own Hands; and when you have made acquaintance with an established

Merchant of good reputation in Martinico, you had best name him to Mr Deane, that he may so address his Dispatches without the Intervention of a Merchant in France.

We shall from Time to Time furnish you with Intelligence of what is passing on this Continent in order that you may not only make good use thereof in the West Indies, but also transmit the same to Mr Deane. It is of great Importance that He should be fully & frequently advised of what passes & as you may often have earlier & fuller Intelligence by means of News Papers & private Letters, than our Avocations will permit us to give, You will be on the Watch; send all Advices forward to Mr Deane marking what you receive from us, what from private Letters, what from public Papers & what from 'Hearsay & always distinguishing between what you think can be depended on & what is doubtfull. In short Sir, you are to be constantly on the Watch, & give to Mr Deane & us every Information that you think connected with the Interest or that can be improved to the Advantage of the United Colonies.

You may possibly find it necessary or usefull to visit Guadaloupe, St Eustatia or other foreign Islands. If you do, always take Passage in Foreign Vessels & dont be long absent from Martinico at any one Time, as our Dispatches will be directed thither.

Should you at any time during your Stay in the West Indies have an opportunity to contract on Reasonable Terms for Arms, Ammunition or other Articles wanted here, give us Information thereof & you shall be instructed on that Head; in the mean time you will encourage as many private Adventurers as you can, by holding up the high Prices we give, the low Price of our Produce, & as we have Cruizers on this Coast to watch the Enemies Tenders, Cutters &c, small Vessels have a good Chance of getting safe in & out of the Bays, Rivers & Inlets on our Coast.

As we have already many Cruizers & are daily adding to the Number, you will take proper opportunities of sounding the Genl, & learn from him whither he could admit Prizes made by our Cruizers to be sent in & protected there untill proper Opportunities offered for bringing them to the Continent. But this being a Matter of great Delicacy you must introduce it as a Thing of your own & not as any Part of your Instructions.

Dated at Philadelphia, this 3d Day of June 1776.

      B Franklin   John Dickinson

     Benja Harrison   Robt Morris

RC (PHi). In a clerical hand, and signed by Dickinson, Franklin, Harrison, and Morris.

 [1] William Bingham (1752–1804), Philadelphia merchant and secretary to the Committee of Secret Correspondence, was appointed by the committee as agent to Martinique, where he remained gathering intelligence and arranging com-

mercial transactions for both Congress and his business partners Thomas Willing and Robert Morris until 1779. His later public career, which eventually took him to the United States Senate in 1795, included service as a delegate to Congress, 1786–88. See Robert C. Alberts, *The Golden Voyage: The Life and Times of William Bingham, 1752–1804* (Boston: Houghton Mifflin Co., 1969). Because of the comparative secrecy in which the committee conducted its activities at this time, few documents pertaining to the early work of its agents abroad survive, but for Bingham's own "clear and succinct Account of My Agency during my Residence in this place [Martinique]," see his lengthy letter to Congress of June 29, 1779, ibid., pp. 454–63. His agency has been discussed at length in Margaret L. Brown, "William Bingham, Agent of the Continental Congress in Martinique," *PMHB* 61 (January 1937): 55–87. Although his earliest reports are not known to survive, some of the intelligence contained in his letters to Congress of August 4, 15, and 26, 1776, can be obtained from the committee's letter of September 21 to him. See Committee of Secret Correspondence to William Bingham, September 21, 1776. See also Josiah Bartlett to William Whipple, August 27, notes; and William Hooper to Jonathan Trumbull, Jr., August 28, 1776, note.

² Bingham did not actually set sail for the West Indies until July 3. For information on the problems that contributed to delaying his departure, see Alberts, *The Golden Voyage*, pp. 5–9. See also Marine Committee to Lambert Wickes, June 10, 1776.

³ These instructions were written in consequence of a resolution of Congress passed on May 18 following receipt of intelligence sent by John Langdon. *JCC*, 4:366.

⁴ That Bingham was assured of French cooperation when he arrived in Martinique can be conjectured from the committee's response to his August 4 report, in which he was instructed to "signify" their gratitude to the governor "for his disposition to favour Our Commerce in Port and protect it at Sea." See Committee of Secret Correspondence to William Bingham, September 21, 1776.

Committee of Secret Correspondence to William Bingham

Sir,   Philada June 3d 1776

We deliver you herewith two Letters from the secret Committee of Congress,[1] one directed to Messr Adrian Le Maitre & Mr Richard Harrison at Martinico, whereby they are directed to pay the Net Proceeds of a Cargo of Provisions Consign'd them per the Sloop Fanny, Capt Britton, to our Order & We have endorsed on said Letter that the Payment is to be made to You. The other Letter is directed to Mr Richd Harrison directing him to pay to our Order the Net Proceeds of another Cargo of Provisions Consign'd him per the Sloop Peggy, Capt Patton, which we have also endorsed to you.

We hope both these Cargoes may arrive safe & thereby afford you the intended Supply of Money. In that Case you must detain what may be sufficient for your present Expences & apply the Remainder to Payment for the Ten Thousand Stand of Arms you are directed to procure; but should things be so circumstanced that You cannot procure those arms nor any Part of them, you may then only take up so much of the Money as may be necessary for your present Expences & direct the Gentn to whom the Cargoes are consigned to pursue the orders they received from the secret Committee & to dispatch the two sloops as quick as they can under Convoy of Capt Hallock in the Hornet. On the Contrary if you take up the whole Money & Send the Muskets by the Hornet you may order the two Sloops to be sent away without any Goods or you may Send a Part of the Muskets by each as you shall judge may be best.

We are, Sir, Your obedt hble servts,

B Franklin   John Dickinson

Benja Harrison   Robt Morris

RC (PPAmP). In a clerical hand, and signed by Dickinson, Franklin, Harrison, and Morris.

[1] See the Secret Committee's letters of June 3 to Adrien Le Maitre and Richard Harrison and to Richard Harrison.

Committee of Secret Correspondence to Richard Harrison and Adrien Le Maitre

Gentn[1]   Philada. June 3d. 1776

In Consequence of the annexed letter of order from the Secret Committee of Congress[2] We desire You to Account with Wm. Bingham Esqr. the bearer hereof for the Amount of the Cargo mentioned therein and either pay him the whole or any part of the money or do with it what he may desire for the Public Service of this Continent.[3]

We are sirs, Your hble servants,

B Franklin   Robt Morris

Benja Harrison   John Dickinson

RC (PPAmP). Written by Morris and signed by Dickinson, Franklin, Harrison, and Morris. Addressed: "To Messrs. Richd Harrison & Adrien Le Maitre, Merchts., Martinico."

[1] Richard Harrison (1750–1841), merchant of Maryland and Virginia, had recently removed to Martinique where he served several years as an agent for Congress and for Virginia before returning to reestablish commercial operations in Alexandria, Va. He subsequently operated as unofficial consul at Cadiz, 1780–86, and was auditor of the United States Treasury, 1791–1836. See James Madison, *The Papers of James Madison*, ed. William T. Hutchinson and William M. E. Rachal (Chicago: University of Chicago Press, 1962–), 2:252–53; and John R. Sellers et al., comps., *Manuscript Sources in the Library of Congress for Research on the American Revolution* (Washington: Library of Congress, 1975), items 21, 577. Little information on Le Maitre has been found beyond his business relationship with Harrison at Martinique.

[2] See the Secret Committee's letter to Harrison and Le Maitre of this date and

also the Committee of Secret Correspondence's second letter to William Bingham of this date.

³ Another letter of this date from the Committee of Secret Correspondence, nearly identical to the document printed here but addressed solely to Richard Harrison, is in the Dreer Signers Collection, PHi.

Secret Committee to
Adrien Le Maitre and Richard Harrison

Gentn   Philada. June 3d. 1776

We wrote you the 2d Ulto. by the Sloop Fanny, Capt Wm Britton, which we hope will get safe.[1] At that time we directed how you were to dispose of the Net Proceeds of the Cargo Consigned you by said Sloop and probably you may have complyed with those orders before this reaches you. If so, its well, but if those orders are not executed and you remain possessed of the Net Proceeds of said Cargo when you receive this letter, We desire that in such case you may pay the same to the order of Benjn. Harrison, Benjn. Franklin, John Jay, Thos. Johnston junr, John Dickinson & Robt Morris Esquires or any three of them who are a Committee of Congress that send a young Gentn to your Island on business and expect he will have Occasion for the Money. You are also to Comply with their instructions respecting the dispatch of the Sloop Fanny. We are sirs Your obedt Servants,

B Franklin	Thos M:Kean
Robt Morris	Josiah Bartlett
Richard Henry Lee	Joseph Hewes

RC (PPAmP). Written by Robert Morris and signed by Bartlett, Franklin, Hewes, Lee, McKean, and Morris. Addressed: "To Messrs Adrien Le Maitre & Rd Harrison, Merchants, Martinico."

¹ Not found. The sloop *Fanny* was condemned as a prize in Nova Scotia in July. See Clark, *Naval Documents*, 5:1121–22, 6:277. See also Secret Committee Minutes of Proceedings, May 2, 1776.

Secret Committee to Richard Harrison

Sir   Philada. June 3d. 1776

We have already wrote you of this date by the Sloop Peggy, Capt Patton, and directed how you shou'd apply the Net Proceeds of that Cargo unless you received other Orders from us.

But shou'd you receive this letter in time it will be delivered you by a Young Gentleman[1] who will be authorized by another Committee of Congress to receive & dispose of the Net proceeds of said

Cargo. Therefore we hereby Authorize & direct you to pay the said net proceeds to such person & in such manner as may be ordered by Benjn. Harrison, Benjn. Franklin, John Jay, Thos. Johnston junr, John Dickinson & Robert Morris Esquires or any three of them and also to comply with their orders respecting the dispatch of the Sloop but if this letter does not arrive in time you will of Consequence follow the directions we have given. Sir, Your hble Servants,

Thos M:Kean	Robt Morris
Josiah Bartlett	B Franklin
Joseph Hewes	Richard Henry Lee

RC (PHi). Written by Robert Morris and signed by Bartlett, Franklin, Hewes, Lee, McKean, and Morris.

[1] William Bingham. See the second letter of the Committee of Secret Correspondence to Bingham of this date.

John Hancock to George Washington

Sir,   Philadelphia June 3d. 1776.

I am extremely sorry it is not in my Power to wait on you in Person to execute the Commands of Congress. But being deprived of that Pleasure by a severe Fit of the Gout, I am under the Necessity of taking this Method to acquaint you, That the Congress have directed me in their Name, to make the Thanks of that body to you, for the unremitted Attention you have paid to your important Trust; and in particular for the Assistance they have derived from your military Knowledge & Experience, in adopting the best Plans for the Defence of the United Colonies.

Tomorrow Morning I will do myself the Honour of sending you, all such Resolves of Congress, as any Ways relate to the operations of the ensuing Campaign.[1]

Having therefore fully accomplished that View of Congress in requesting your Attendance in this City, I am commanded to inform you that they submit to your Choice the Time of returning to Head Quarters; well knowing you will repair thither, whenever the Exigency of Affairs shall render your Presence there necessary.

With the most ardent Wishes, that you may be crowned with Success equal to your Merit and the Righteousness of our Cause, I have the Honour to be, with the highest Esteem and Regard, Sir, your most obedt. & very hble Sevt,   John Hancock Presidt

RC (DLC). In the hand of Jacob Rush and signed by Hancock.

[1] See the various resolutions concerning military affairs passed by Congress between May 22 and June 3 in *JCC*, 4:375, 380, 388, 410–11, 412–14.

Massachusetts Delegates to the
Massachusetts Council

Sir   Philadelphia June 3d 1776
    We received your Favour of the 10th May with the Inclosures,[1]
& having communicated such a part thereof as was necessary to
Congress, beg Leave thro You to inform the honorable Assembly
that the Sum of 30,000 Dollars is ordered to be sent them for the
purpose of exchanging it for Specie. We inclose a Copy of the
Resolve by which It will appear how the latter is to be disposed of,[2]
& think it will be necessary to place to the account of the united
Colonies the Sum mentioned in your Letter as delivered to Colo.
Porter, & any other Sums of Money that may be delivered in Conse-
quence of the Resolve aforsd, since the Colony is charged with the
Sums advanced it by Congress.
    We find in an Account sent by the General Court to General
Washington & by him transmitted to Congress a Charge of 3000 lbs
of Powder delivered by Governor Trumbull on Account of the
Colony more than is contained in the Account You inclosed Us;
And as the General is now here & informs Us that he shall write to
General Ward Directions to deliver to the Colony the whole of the
Powder which is due from the Continent, We inclose the last mentioned Account & Vouchers to be adjusted accordingly.
    We shall send forward the Money mentioned above & 21000 Dol-
lars granted by Congress for raising the two Battalions lately ordered
to be raised in Massachusetts Bay[3] & are sir with great Respect for
yourself & the honorable Assembly, your most huml servants. At
the Desire & in behalf of the Delegs. of Massachusts. Signed,
                                                       John Hancock

RC (M–Ar). Written by Elbridge Gerry and signed by John Hancock. Addressed:
"To The Honorable The President of the Council of Massachusetts Bay To be
Communicated to the Honorable Assembly, Watertown."
    [1] James Otis, Sr., had informed the Massachusetts delegates of efforts to collect
specie for the army in Canada and had enclosed an account of powder "delivered
out of the Colony Magazine" to the Continental Army while it was at Cambridge. Otis to the Massachusetts Delegates, May 10, 1776, PCC, item 65, 1:85–86;
and *Am. Archives,* 4th ser. 6:419.
    [2] See *JCC,* 4:318–19, 397.
    [3] See *JCC,* 4:380.

Willing, Morris & Co. to William Bingham

Sir   Philada. June 3d. 1776
    You will find enclosed herein a Copy of our letter to Mr. Saml.
Beall[1] respectg the Adventure in Powder under his management in

which we have interested you to the Amount of Five hundred pounds Sterlg & as it is most likely he will come out with his Goods Via Martinico we hope You will have the pleasure of seeing him there. If he comes out to St Eustatia lodge orders for you to be informed of it & as you will have frequent intelligence from us & the best opportunitys for Shipping Goods We hope this adventure may be brought to a happy Conclusion for us all. If you think proper to write to Mr Beall address him under Cover to Messrs. Delap at Bourdeaux & if you hear any thing of him do not fail to advise us. As you are likely to remain sometime in the West Indies it may probably fall in Your way to make Connections with some good Houses that will Ship West India Produce this way & have in return the produce of these Colonies, we shall be ready to transact such business & will Credit you half the Coms. on the Sale of their Goods that is on any parcells you procure to our address.

You may probably have it in your Power to purchase some Linnens or other European Manufactures on a Credit untill we can have time to remit You produce to pay for them. If so we agree to be half Concerned with you in such Adventures and you may Ship back by the Hornet some Packages of such Goods to the Amot of £1000, or Fifteen hundred pounds this Cury Value Consigning the same to us. We will sell them to the best advantage free of Coms., you charging no Coms. on the purchase nor on the Sale of the returns which we shall ship to you directly in this Country produce, and in this way we will keep up a Constant intercourse with You. If you cannot get goods on Credit We must furnish You with Effects to make such purchases & for this & other purposes Youl keep us constantly informed of what is passing in the mercantile line. Wishing You a pleasant & successfull Voyage, We are, Sir, Your obedt hble servts,

Willing, Morris & Co.

RC (DLC). Written by Robert Morris.
[1] Probably Willing, Morris & Co.'s letter to Samuel Beall of March 6, 1776. See Clark, *Naval Documents*, 4:199–201.

John Adams to Hugh Hughes

Sir   Philadelphia June 4. 1776
Yours of May 29 came safe to Hand, and am much pleased to find that your Citizens have behaved with so much Wisdom, Unanimity, and Spirit.[1] Yet I was disappointed that you did not inclose their Votes.

I am very glad Mr J[2] is with you, and hope he will be of great Service there but will he not be for making your Governor and Councillors for Life or during good Behaviour? I should dread such a Constitution in these perilous Times, because however wise and brave and virtuous these Rulers may be at their first appointment, their Tempers, and Designs will be very apt to change, and then they may have it in their Power to betray the People, who will have no Means of Redress. The People ought to have frequently the opportunity, especially in these dangerous Times, of considering the conduct of their Leaders, and of approving or disapproving. You will have no safety without it.

The Province of Pensilvania is in a good Way, and will soon become an important Branch of the Confederation. The large Body of the People will be possessed of more Power and Importance, and a proud Junto of less: and yet Justice will I hope be done to all.

I wish you Happiness, Promotion, and Reputation in the service, and am, with much Respect, your servant

LB (MHi).
[1] Hughes had informed Adams that New York citizens had met and instructed the provincial convention "on that most important of all sublunary affairs, in order that application may be made to your honorable House." Hughes to Adams, May 29, 1776, Adams Papers, MHi. On May 29 the "General Committee of Mechanicks in union, of the City and County of New York" had sent a petition to the New York Provincial Convention urging them to instruct the New York delegates in Congress "to use their utmost endeavours in that august assembly to cause these United Colonies to become independent of Great Britain." *Am. Archives,* 4th ser. 6:614–15.
[2] Probably John Jay.

John Adams to Richard Lee

Sir[1]   Philadelphia June 4. 1776

Your Favour of 18 May,[2] inclosing the momentous Resolution of your wise and patriotic Convention,[3] together with the American Crisis came duely to Hand, and yesterday, I had the Pleasure of receiving the Proceedings of the House of Burgesses. I thank you, sir, for both these esteemed Favours.

Is it not a little remarkable that this Congress and your Convention should come to Resolutions so nearly Similar, on the Same day, and that even the Convention of Maryland should, in that critical Moment, have proceded so far as to abolish the oaths of allegiance, notwithstanding that Some of their other Resolves are a little excentric?

Your Resolution is consistent and decisive, it is grounded on true Principles which are fairly and clearly stated, and in my humble opinion the Proviso which reserves to yourselves the Institution of your own Government is fit and right, this being a Matter of which the Colonies are the best Judges, and a Priviledge which each Colony ought to reserve to it self. Yet after all I believe there will be much more Uniformity in the Governments which all of them will adopt than could have been expected a few Months ago.

The Joy and Exultation which was expressed upon that great occasion did Honour to their good sense and public Virtue. It was an important Event at a critical Time, in which the Interest and Happiness of themselves and their Posterity, was much concerned.

Hopkins's Fleet has been very unfortunate: a dreadful sickness had raged among his Men, and disabled him from putting more than two of his Vessells to sea. To what Place they are gone I know not—Perhaps to cruise for Transports.

I am, sir, with great respect, your most humble servant

LB (MHi).
¹ Richard Lee (1726–95), Virginia planter, served several terms as a burgess from Westmoreland County before 1775, was a member of the Virginia Convention in 1775–76, and subsequently was elected several times to the House of Delegates. Edmund Jennings Lee, ed., *Lee of Virginia, 1642–1892* . . . (Philadelphia: Privately printed, 1895), pp. 287–90.
² This letter is printed as Richard Henry Lee to John Adams, May 18, 1776, in Adams, *Works* (Adams), 9:374.
³ The Virginia Convention's May 15 resolution on independence. *Am. Archives,* 4th ser. 6:1524.

John Hancock to Certain Colonies

Gentlemen,   Philada. June 4th. 1776.

Our Affairs are hastening fast to a Crisis; and the approaching Campaign will in all Probability determine for ever the Fate of America.

Such is the unrelenting Spirit which possesses the Tyrant of Britain and his Parliament, that they have left no Measure unessayed, that had a Tendency to accomplish our Destruction. Not satisfied with having lined our Coasts with Ships of War to starve us into a Surrender of our Liberties, and to prevent us from being supplied with Arms & Ammunition, they are now about to pour in a Number of foreign Troops; who from their Want of Connections and those Feelings of Sympathy which frequently bind together the different Parts of the same Empire, will be more likely to do the Business of their Masters without Remorse or Compunction.

By the best Intelligence from Canada it appears, that our Affairs in that Quarter wear a melancholy Aspect. Should the Canadians & Indians take up Arms agt. us (which there is too much Reason to fear) we shall then have the whole Force of that Country to contend with, joined to that of Great Britain, & all her foreign auxiliaries. In this Situation what Steps must we pursue? Our Continental

Troops alone are unable to stem the Torrent; nor is it possible at this Day to raise & discipline Men ready to take the Field by the Time they will be wanted.

From the Secrecy with which the Ministry carry on their Machinations, we neither know their Views, or how near our Enemies may be. Perhaps at this Moment they are landing on some Part of our Country.

In this difficult & trying Situation of our Affairs, the Congress have come to the enclosed Resolves, which I have it in Command to transmit you by Express, containing Matters of the greatest Importance, and to which I beg Leave to request your Attention. You will there find, the Congress have judged it necessary to call upon the Militia at this alarming Crisis.[1]

Should the united Colonies be able to keep their Ground this Campaign, I am under no Apprehensions on Acct. of any future one. We have many Disadvantages at present to struggle with, which Time and Progress in the Art of War, will remove. But this Circumstance should rouse us to superior Exertions on the Occasion. The Militia of the United Colonies are a Body of Troops that may be depended upon. To their Virtue their Delegates in Congress, now make the most solemn Appeal. They are called upon to say, whether they will live Slaves, or die Freemen. They are requested to step forth in Defence of their Wives, their Children, their Liberty, and every Thing they hold dear. The Cause is certainly a most glorious one and I trust every Man in the Colony of New Hampshire,[2] is determined to see it gloriously ended, or to perish in the Ruins of it.

In short on your Exertions at this Critical Period, together with those of the other Colonies, in the Common Cause, the Salvation of America now evidently depends. Your Colony, I am persuaded, will not be behind hand. Exert therefore every Nerve to distinguish yourselves. Quicken your Preparations, and stimulate the good People of your Govt.—and there is no Danger, notwithstanding the mighty Armament with which we are threatened, but you will be able to lead them to Victory, to Liberty & to Happiness.

I have the Honour to be Gent., your most obedt & very hble Serv.

J. H. Prst.

LB (DNA: PCC, item 12A). Addressed: "The Honble Convention of New Hampshire. The Honble Assembly of Massachusetts Bay. The Honble Govr. Trumbull. Honble Convention of New York. Honble Convention of New Jersey. Honble Assembly of the Govt. of New Castle, Kent & Sussex on Delaware. Honble Convention of Maryland."

[1] See JCC, 4:410-15. This day Hancock also wrote a letter to Paymaster General William Palfrey, commending to his attention "Col. [Daniel] Roberdeau of this City . . . a Gentleman distinguished for his Benevolence towards all Men . . . a zealous American, and a Friend of mine." Palfrey Papers, MH.

[2] Or any one of the other six provinces to which a copy of this letter was directed.

John Hancock to the Pennsylvania Assembly

Gentlemen,   Philada. June 4th 1776.

By the Resolves sent herewith, which I do myself the Honour of inclosing in Obedience to the Commands of Congress, you will perceive they have judged it necessary to call upon the Militia at this alarming Crisis.[1]

We have too much Reason to believe, the whole Force of Great Britain, aided by foreign Auxiliaries, will be exerted agt. us the ensuing Campaign. In this Case, the Continental Troops disperssd thro' such a Number of Colonies, will be totally inadequate to our Defence. Nor is it possible at this Day, to raise & discipline Troops ready to take the Field by the Time they will be wanted.

Our Country however is not destitute of Resources. The Militia of the United Colonies are a Body of Troops that may be depended upon. To their Virtue, their Delegates in Congress now make the most solemn Appeal. They are called upon to say, whether they will live Slaves, or die Freemen. They are requested to step forth in Defence of their Wives, their Children, their Liberty, & every Thing they hold dear. The Cause is certainly a most glorious one; and I hope every Man in the Colony of Pennsylvania is determined to see it gloriously ended, or to perish in the Ruins of it.

In short, on your Exertions at this critical Period, together with those of the other Colonies, the Salvation of America now evidently depends.

I shall only add, that from your Zeal & Ardor in the American Cause, I have the greatest Reason to hope, you will pay that immediate Attention to the enclosed Resolves, which your own Situation in particular, & the Public Good so evidently require.

I have the Honour to be Gentlemen, your most obedt. & very hble Ser.   J. H. Prst.

LB (DNA: PCC, item 12A).
[1] See *JCC,* 4:412–13.

Joseph Hewes to Samuel Johnston

Dear Sir   Philadelphia 4th June 1776

Your favour by Allen McDonald Esqr. I have received. He and all those that came with him as prisoners are confined in the Jail of this City.[1] I have not seen him or any of them, it is not in my power to do them any kind of service, Congress will not suffer them to go out on parole 'till they hear further from North Carolina or perhaps 'till the British Troops have left the Province. Many of our Prisoners

have broke their parole and gone off which will make those poor
devils you sent and all taken hereafter fare the worse. As I cannot
serve them I do not visit them, to hear their complaints and have
no power to relieve would be disagreable.

"I shall write you again in a few days," you say. You told me the
same when you enclosed me your Resolutions respecting your Officers & your Independance.[2] Not one line have I received on public
matters from any part of the province since Hoopers Letter from
Halifax of the 22d of April 'till yesterday I recd. a Letter from
Penn dated the 20th of May informing me your Congress had broke
up, and postponed the forming a constitution till November. He
says you have resolved to emit £500,000. This is a very large sum
and if I am not very much mistaken will ruin the Country. I wish it
had been less and that you had ordered a considerable sum to have
been sent from hence in Continental money. This would have found
its way out of the Country again, I wish the other may not like a
deluge overflow the whole Country and sink it to perdition.

I wrote to you some time ago by Mr Lowther who I expect is at
Edenton 'ere this time. I have been impatiently waiting for some
days past for the Medicines I wrote to you about. They are now
ready and my Waggon will set off with them to day. The Instruments
are not yet made. They must be sent by some other oppertunity. The
fellow that drove your Waggon and with whom you engaged, will
return to you as driver to mine. Gen. Washington is now here. He
has been confering with Congress on a general plan of defense. An
Express arrived yesterday with an Account that five Men of War
had just arrived at Sandy Hook. Our Affairs in Canada are in a very
bad way. The army there is mostly down with the Small Pox, the
greatest part of Howes Army is expected there. We shall probably
be driven out of that Country, tho shall not give it up if we can help
it. We Are about to Order 6000 Militia to march from the New
England Provinces into it. We ought to have 10,000 men there already. We have 10,000 men at New York & shall order 15,000 more
from the Militia to take post there. A flying Camp of 10,000 Militia
is to be formed immediately some where near this City to be in
readiness to March wherever the enemy may land. These 31,000
Militia men are only on paper at present. I am something doubtfull
such numbers will not turn out especially in or near harvest time.

A West India paper that came yesterday contains a petition from
the Lord Mayor, Aldermen &c of London to his Majesty the purport
of which is to implore his Majesty to give to the inhabitants of the
American Colonies a clear and explicit account of the terms of such
a reconciliation as would be acceptable to him before he proceeded
with his dreadfull Armament to Shed any more of the Blood of his
people. He answers he shall take the most effectual methods to
reduce his rebellious subjects to obedience and a proper sense of

their duty and then will exercise his Clemency & Mercy, no terms
whatever are to precede the Chastisement. Nothing but a total unconditioned submission will satisfie the Tyrant.

I shall Order my Waggoner to call at Col Jones's and if he finds
no directions from you respecting the Medicines, he will carry them
to Edenton. He carries [a packet directed] to you & Robert Smith.
It contains one doz. pair of Womens Shoes, some News papers,
pamphlets, Magazines &c. &c. My Compliments to Mrs. Johnston &
family. I am with respect & esteem, Dear Sir, Your mo Obed Servant,

                                                                          Joseph Hewes

RC (PHC).
    ¹ See Hewes to Samuel Johnston, May 26, 1776, note 1.
    ² See Samuel Johnston to the North Carolina delegates, April 13, 1776, in *N. C.
Colonial Records,* 10:495. For the April 12 resolution of the provincial congress
authorizing the North Carolina delegates "to concur with the delegates of the
other Colonies in declaring Independency and forming foreign alliances," see
ibid., p. 512. It was presented to Congress on May 27. *JCC,* 4:397. For Congress'
action on the provincial congress' resolutions about "Officers," see Hewes to
Samuel Johnston, April 30, 1776, note 3.

Robert R. Livingston to John Jay

Dear John   4th June 1776 Philadelphia
    I own I was very much mortified at not hearing from you nor can
I yet quite forgive your neglect since it takes but little time to write
when the pen is only copying from the heart. I am very sorry that
we are not to have the pleasure of Mrs. Jays company but greatly
rejoyced at the prospect of her recovery about which from your
Letter to Duane I had some uneasy apprehentions.

    We have been for some days past occupied in settling a plan of
defence. The attachment which some people have for Canada have
left us very defenceless. However I have contrived to lessen the
number after much altercation & settle our own quota much to my
satisfaction at 3750 men who are to be drafted from the militia 3000
of them to serve at New York.¹ This I hope will not prove very
burthensome as a large proportion may be taken from the City where
I suppose many of the Citizens are unemployed. What I want you
particularly to attend to is to endeavour to get volunteers for Canada
if possible from the Green Mountain boys by offering higher pay
than the Continent allows, the expence of which will be very
triffling to the Colony. What makes me wish it most is in order to
frustrate the schemes of some people here who affect to consider
them as no part of our Colony, & to assert that they never did nor
ever will act under our convention. They even introduced a motion
founded on this supposition; however I treated them so roughly as

prevented their proceeding & has silenced them for the present.[2] The force ordered for our defence at New York is 25000 so that I hope we shall be able to give an enemy a pretty warm reception. I wrote to you about Gallies but I have got the Congress to take it upon themselves, & the Genl. has power to build as many as he thinks proper.[3] We have recd. an answer of the King to the livery of London, which I hope will be productive of very good affects since it takes away all hopes of accommodation & shews that nothing less will do them absolute submission. It comes in very happy time for this place, in which the people were very unfortunately divided between the advocates for the old & new government.

I learn from the paper the steps you have taken to collect the sentiments of the people, I wish to be with you a while, but do not know whether it is absolutely necessary, & I am unwilling to leave this till it is. I hope you are laying the foundation for a better form than I have yet seen, & inculcating the proper principles you can not begin too early to point out both men & measures.

Morris they tell me flourishes as much as ever. As you are either too lazy or too cautious engage him to write with as much freedom as he speaks. I have heard Mr. S——,[4] does he not look very high? Clinton is not come. Send him on if you see him. I am, Dear John, Your Aff. Freind,   Robt R Livingston

RC (Windsor Castle: The Royal Archives). Addressed: "To Coll. John Jay, New York. Per favour of Majr. Genl. Gates."
[1] See *JCC,* 4:410–12.
[2] See the report relating to New York's jurisdiction over "the New Hampshire grants," which Congress ordered tabled on May 30, in *JCC,* 4:405.
[3] See *JCC,* 4:406–7; and Robert R. Livingston to John Jay, May 21, 1776.
[4] Apparently John Morin Scott.

New Hampshire Delegates to Meshech Weare

Sir   Philaa 4th June 1776

We wrote you the 28 Ulto since which Congress have Resolv'd to send a farther Reinforcement into Canada. 750 men including officers will be requir'd of our Colony to serve as Militia until the 1st Decr. the officers to be Commissioned by the Colony. It is absolutely necessary our posts shod. be Supported in that Country for shod. the Enemy get possession we shall certainly have a long & troublesome war on our hand; but if we are successfull which by proper Exertions & divine assistance there is no doubt of, this Campaign will place us out of the Reach of their Mallace. You will soon receive the Resolution respecting this reinforcement from the President.[1]

The money mention'd in our last is not Yet gone forward not having had an opportuny but hope shall have in a few days.

We are with great Respect, Your Most obt Sevts,

Josiah Bartlett

Wm. Whipple

RC (MeHi). Written by Whipple and signed by Whipple and Bartlett.

[1] The New Hampshire legislature voted to raise this additional force on June 14, 1776. *N. H. State Papers,* 8:148. See also John Hancock to Certain Colonies, this date.

Oliver Wolcott to Roger Newberry

Sir,[1]   Philadelpa 4t June 1776

Your kind favour of the 20t came safe. Nothing gives Me more pleasure than Letters from my Freinds. They would out of meer Charity Write oftner to Me, if they knew the Satisfaction which it gave Me. If I do not always [make] a speedy Acknowledgment I hope it will not be imputed to any Want of Inclination to do it.

I am glad to be informed by you that People seem determined in supporting the mighty Cause upon the Decision of which the Fate of this and future Generations depend. Your Observations that a Regard ought to be had to the Expectations of the People are just, and as the Appeal is made to them as to the Justice and Propriety of publick Measures, any Information to one who must think that his Services in some good Degree must depend upon an Observance of popular Opinions, will be advantagious not for the Reason for which this kind of Knowledge is often Sought for a personal Account, but to prevent him from adopting ineffectual and consequently pernicious Measures. You can easily conceive that in this long extended Continent Very different Customs prevail but I trust that there will be no further Augmentation in the Officers Wages, indeed I am sure there will not, tho' some of the Southern Colonies have enlarged them at a colonial Expence.

The Prisoners have been treated by us with great Indulgence, I see by the papers what has been done with McKay and Skeene. You will observe a Code of Laws published for the Regulation of Prisoners which if duly attended to, I hope will be effectual.[2]

You Mention to Me the hard Fate of Col Enos. I believe his Character from what I had before heard, had suffered unjustly. Dr. Smith an ill Natured Man, in his Oration on the Death of Genl. Montgomerry, went out of the way to asperse him. He had not the Thanks of the Congress for his performance, nor was it published at their Desire. Col Enos' Freinds made this as one objection against his Sermon, that he had Scandalisd a man who had been Acquitted

by a Court Martial.[3] I [receive] the Hartford Paper Very un-
steadily (I know not for what Reason); if you will send one to me
enclosed, in which his Case is stated I will comply with Your and
his Request.

By every Intelligence you perceive that the Decision of the present
Controversy must be made by the Sword only. This, together with
the untoward State of our Affairs in Canada has induced the Congress
greatly to enlarge their Milatary Force by calling in the Aid of the
Militia to serve till the first of December, six Thousand of which
are proposed to be sent to Canada, 750 Men from N Hamshire, 2000
from Massachusetts, 1500 from Connecticut and 750 from N York
forming 6 Battalions, under 2 provincial General Officers from Connecticut and Massachusetts, the whole Appointment &c by their
Assembly.[4] Canada is a Very important Object, our possession of
that Country is Very necessary, and I am sorry our Affairs there have
not been more regarded. This measure therefore hope will be tho't
necessary tho' I can conceive a dificulty in carrying it into Execution
—but We must exert ourselves this summer, as every Thing which
is Amiable in life, We may Suppose in a good Degree depends upon
the Events of it. If We can hold out this Season without having any
deep Impressions made upon Us, I hope it may go near to End the
Controversy, and may a most merciful God grant that this may be
the Case. The Other Method for Strengthening our Army in N York
and for the Security of the Middle Colonies may be best, but I can
claim but Very little Honor in promoting it. To be sure I think the
Requisition upon our Colony is unreasonable and I apprehend
cannot be complied it. The Plan adopted is this, to Send 2000 Men
from Massachusetts, I mean Militia, 5500 from Connecticut, 3000 in
New York and 3300 from the Jerseys, these for the N York Station,
to be under provincial Genl. Officers, one from Connecticut, to
serve till the 1st Decr. and under the Genl. of the Army—for
Pensilvania &c a flying Camp of 10,000 to be raised, 6000 Pensilvania,
3400 Maryland and 600 Delaware to serve as above.[5] I will not
trouble you with a detail of my Reasons why I do not Approve of
this measure in its Latitude. I agree that We must exert every Nerve,
but I fear this Scheme Will not improve our Strength for a general
defence—but as in such a Vicissitude of affairs it is difficult to form
Opinions which may be relied upon and as Mine is pretty Singular
in this Case, and as Genls. Washington, Gates and Mifflin who are
here have recommended it, it becomes on many Accounts improper
for me publickly to censure the Measure, tho I imagine the Colony
will. I told the Congress they might be absolutely Assured that the
above Number of men could not be sent from our Colony. I tho't it
impolitick to ask of a People an Exertion which they were incompe-
tent to; it gave offences and carryed with it an Idea of Desperation.
We could not absolutely say where Assistance might be most Wanted;

perhaps at R Island, every Man would fight when the War was bro't near him, but would reluctantly be drawn into such a length of service especially such Numbers. I told them that I had heard the Colony had it in consideration to raise a Battalion for their own Defence and that I hop'd they would do it and that it would be taken into continental Pay &c. I think such a Battalion should in the present Exigency be raised, and they might as occasioned required, to be employed if necessary on acco. of an attack agt other Colonys but as no direction of that kind has been given We could not Very Seriously ask for Such an Establishment. I find I am running along with telling you my own opinion instead of other Peoples, but as I observed, tho I think We must Submit to the fullest Exertion this Summer, yet our People are so Situated as that they can from their Homes go and afford Succor either to the Eastward or Westward when Attackd and I think that would be better than to carry them all to one place. I think about half that Number as directed taken thro might have been sufficient—the Report called for eight more Regiments. I hope no mans Heart will fail under the present tryals. I am most sincerely sorry for the distresses of my Country but let a man Consider that every thing which he holds dear is at Stake. That a Conquest by our Enemies ensures Slavery and Misery thro endless Generations. Is this a Patrimony which We must leave our Children? God Forbid! No he who sitteth in the Heavens, who holds Empires in his hands, who holds the Tyrant Worms of this earth, in utter dirision, he will Crush the Power of the Oppressor, he will Vindicate the Cause of the righteous, he will preserve his People like a Flock, and by the Arm of his Power make them to know their Almighty Deliverer—While the Malice of the oppressor shall cease and he who fears not the Justice of God shall perish for ever. I firmly believe this Country will be saved. Let us take up the Resolution of Joab, play the Man for the Cities of our God; and let God do as it pleases him. Upon looking back I find I have wrote a long and incoherent letter, but this is a Priviledge in Writing to a Friend to Say any thing as it occurs to the mind I trust your Prudence with it, as well as Candor. This Colony Jurisdictions I hope will get all established. This I think is extremely Necessary. For News refer you to the Prints. My best Compliments to Mrs. Newbery, Dr Wolcott, his Family, and my Friends. I am Sir, with true Regard, your most humble Servant and Kinsman,

Oliver Wolcott

P.S. In a few days an Address to the Colonies will be published.[6]

RC (NjR: Elsie O. and Philip D. Sang deposit, 1972).

[1] Although unaddressed, Wolcott's references to "Mrs. Newbery" and to his "kinsman" strongly suggest that the recipient was Wolcott's nephew Roger Newberry (1735–1814), a Windsor, Conn., lawyer and merchant who served as an

officer in the Connecticut militia from 1775 until the end of the war and was later a probate judge and a member of the Connecticut legislature. Henry R. Stiles, *The History and Genealogies of Ancient Windsor, Connecticut,* 2 vols. (Hartford: Case, Lockwood, and Brainard Co., 1892), 2:520.

[2] On May 21 Congress approved a series of resolutions concerning the treatment of prisoners. See *JCC,* 4:370–73.

[3] For further information about Roger Enos, as well as Smith's oration, see Wolcott to Laura Wolcott, March 19, 1776, note 2.

[4] See *JCC,* 4:410.

[5] See *JCC,* 4:412–13.

[6] Anticipating the difficulties the colonies might experience in meeting the latest call for militia support, Congress resolved on May 29 "that an animated address be published to impress the minds of the people with the necessity of their now stepping forward to save their country, their freedom and property." Although there is no evidence that such an address was ever approved or published, a fragment in George Wythe's hand, which was probably a committee draft, is in the Thomas Jefferson Papers, DLC, and is printed in *JCC,* 4:401–2.

John Hancock to George Washington

Sir,   Philadelphia June 5th. 1776.

The Congress having this Day made several Promotions in the Army of the United Colonies, and established some Rules for the future Direction of the Deputy Commissaries general, Deputy Quarter Master General &c I do myself the Pleasure to enclose you a Copy of the same.[1]

I delivered Col. Reed his Commission, & have sent Mr. Whitcomb, Mr. Mercer & Mr Moyland theirs.[2]

Should you stand in Need of any more blank Commissions, they shall be immediately forwarded, on your letting me know it. I entirely forgot to make Enquiry into the Matter while you was in this City.

Having Nothing further in Charge from Congress at this Time, I beg Leave to assure you that I am, with the greatest Respect and Esteem, Sir, your most obedt. and very hble Sevt.

John Hancock Presidt

June 6.

P.S. This Morning two small Privateers arrived here after a very successful Cruise, having taken three West India Ships with 22,420 Dollars on Board, 1052 Hhds & Trs. [Tierces] of sugar, 70 Pipes best Madeira Wine, and a Variety of other Articles. The Captain and Owner this Moment called to acquaint me, the Money is now in this City, and have generously made an offer of it to the Congress.

I have this Morning advanced thirty Dollars to Fessenden in Part of his Account, which you will please to deduct on Settlement.

RC (DLC). In the hand of Jacob Rush and signed by Hancock.

[1] See *JCC,* 5:418–20.

² This day Hancock also wrote a letter to Joseph Reed, informing him of his appointment as adjutant general and directing him "to take the earliest opportunity of repairing . . . to Head Quarters at New York." PCC, item 12A; and *Am. Archives*, 4th ser. 6:713–14. On June 6 Hancock informed Hugh Mercer of his appointment as brigadier general and directed him "immediately on Receipt hereof, [*to*] set out for Head Quarters at New York." Allyn K. Ford Collection, MnHi; and *Am. Archives*, 4th ser. 6:723. Hancock also wrote to Stephen Moylan on the sixth to apprise him of his appointment as quartermaster general. PCC, item 12A; and *Am. Archives*, 4th ser. 6:723. Attached to the letter to Moylan is the following note: "N.B. A similar Letter of same Date enclosing a Commission was sent at same Time to Brigadr. General Whitecombe, at Watertown."

Robert Morris to Silas Deane

Dr. Sir,   Philada. June 5th. 1776

I had great satisfaction in receiving your favours of the 26th April & 3d May¹ from B[ermuda] as I think there was little risque in the rest of your Voyage & I flatter myself you have arrived safe previous to this date.

I extracted from your letter of the 26th all the parts that related to the Public & laid them before Congress. Those extracts are Committed but no report is yet brought in. I am on the Committee and we are to meet tomorrow morning but whether they will determine to benefit by your usefull hints or not I cannot yet tell.²

You have mixed business & Politics in your letter which is a bad example and I must try to avoid it, therefore this letter must be Confined to the latter.

This goes by Wm Bingham Esqr. a Young Gentln who has for sometime acted as Secretary to the Committee of Secret Correspondence. He carrys with him triplicates of your Credentials & instructions, the Duplicates went by another Conveyance and each of these as well as yourself having an exceeding good Chance to arrive safe I think it needless to send you any more. Mr Bingham now goes out to Martinico in order to procure some Arms from the Governor & with another view that I need not mention as he will write to you. You can send advices under Cover to him but you'l remember he is a *Young* tho' a Worthy Young Man. The papers he carrys will give you the Public News, the worst part of which is an appearance of great division amongst ourselves especially in this Province; however I believe the King has put an effectual stop to those divisions by his Answer to an Address of the Ld Mayor & Aldermen &c the [22] ³ of March, as His Majesty has there totally destroyed all hope of Reconciliation. I confess I never lost hopes of reconciliation untill I saw this Answer which in my opinion breaths nothing but Death & Destruction. Every body see it in the same light and it will bring us all to one way of thinking, so that you may soon expect to hear of

New Governments in every Colony and in Conclusion a declaration of Independancy by Congress. I see this step is inevitable and you may depend it will soon take place. Great Britain may thank herself for this Event, for whatever might have been the original designs of some Men in promoting the present Contest I am sure that America in general never set out with any View or desire of establishing an Independant Empire. They have been drove into it step by step with a reluctance on their part that has been manifested in all their proceedings, & yet I dare say our Enemies will assert that it was planned from the first movements. The Dogs of Warr are now fairly let loose upon us. We are not dismayed but expect to give a good Account of the Numerous hosts of Foes that are coming to Slaughter us, especially your Hessians, Hanoverians, Waldeckers &c. Our Climates will most probably handle them pretty severely before they get seasoned and our Troops are pretty well prepared for their reception but the Fortune of Warr being ever uncertain God only knows what may be the Event.

Our affairs in Canada have been badly managed by Your Countryman Genl Worster but I hope Genl. Thomas & your Friend Arnold will invigorate them. However I dont think we have any occasion to hold that Country, if we maintain the passes on the Lakes it is sufficient for our purposes and the Garrison that defend those passes will always be ready to rush into Canada if the Enemy quit it, so that a good Force well posted for this purpose may keep Mr. Burgoyne with his 10,000 men uselessly employed the whole year without any expence of ammunition or loss of Men on our side unless they attack exceedingly to their own disadvantage. Genl. Washington has taken post at New York. He has lately been here attended by Genl. Gates & Genl. Mifflin and the plan of operations has been fully settled in several Conferences between them & a Committee of Congress appointed for that purpose & in Consequence of the arrangements made we shall have not less than 30,000 men ready to take the Field, so divided & posted as to oppose the Enemys attacks wherever made.

Genl. Lee commands to the Southward and I fancy that department will be well defended. We are to have a flying Camp of 10,000 men here the Commander of which is not yet named. Genl. Washington at New York, Gates at Boston, Thomas in Canada & each of these are well supported by able General officers and we hope a Sufficient number of Troops. We are better supplyd with Powder than formerly; our Mills make it fast & some of the Colonies have had great success in making Salt Petre. Arms we are most in Want of, but our manufactorys of them improve & increase daily. In short it appears to me We shall be able to baffle all attempts of our Enemy, if we do but preserve Union amongst ourselves. I dont mean the Union of the Colonies, but union in each Colony. The former is safely fixed on a broad & firm basis, the latter had been greatly threatned. The necessity of assuming new Governments has been pretty evident for sometime and the Contest is who shall form them & who upon such a Change shall come in for the Power. The divisions woud probably have run very high particularly in this Province, had not His Majesty determined so peremptorily that there can be no reconciliation but through the door of abject Submission. This seems to bend all mens minds one way and I have no doubt but Harmony will be restored & our united efforts exerted to defend our Country & its freedom in which God grant Success to an injured & oppressed People.

One of our Cruizers has lately taken a Valuable Prize & carried her safe into Boston with 1500 bbls Powder, 1000 stand of arms & a variety of other articles on board, & the two New York Pilot Boats that were fitted out as Privateers from hence have taken three large ships bound from Jama. to London with 1052 hhds Sugar, 260 Puncheons Rum, 300 Casks Piemento, 22000 hard Dollars, 70 Pipes Madeira Wine & a Number of other Valuable Articles. I fancy many more West India Men will be taken this Summer & probably Great Britain may have cause to repent of the prohibitory act, especially as they have much more property to loose than we have.

We have a Number of the Six Nation Indians now in this City[4] upon the most Friendly terms and I hope shall be able to Continue them in our Friendship altho I do very much suspect, that if we evacuate Canada, the Indians & Canadians will be prevailed on to Act against us. However if the passes on the Lakes are well fortifyed & Guarded we need not mind or fear them.

Our Money holds its Credit but we must not Issue too much of it. Therefore when we find the Circulation begins to Clog we must borrow it in & Fund it. Pray what think you of Negotiating with Holland for a loan of Specie & how shall we offer them Security for at present I doubt if any Power in Europe will Trust us but probably after the Next Campaign they may think better of our Credit. Commodore Hopkins has fallen short of Expectation & his Fleet which might have performed most signal service under an Active Vigilant Man, have been most useless. He remains with the Alfred at Rhode Island & the rest are gone & going on separate Cruizes after Transports &c.

Our Frigates are nearly ready but their Guns are not yet finished. We shall be carefull who are trusted to Command them and from these we may expect good Services. This Navy must be increased & you must Contrive to make it known that Noble encouragement is given to Seamen of all Nations that will enter into the American Service. I have not time to enlarge & therefore Conclude with ass[uring you] of that true esteem with which I am, Your Friend & Servant,   R. M.

RC (CtHi). Endorsed: "Recd. the 19 & forwarded the 21 Sepr. 1776 by Yr most obt Hble Svts., S. & J.H. D[elap]."

¹ For Deane's letter of April 26, see *NYHS Collections* 19 (1886): 134n. His May 3 letter is in the Robert Morris Papers, DLC.

² Morris' lengthy extract, containing Deane's description of conditions at Bermuda and recommending that Congress outfit privateers there and utilize the island as a base for disrupting Britain's West India trade, is in PCC, item 58, fols. 353–56. It was referred on May 30 to the committee "appointed to consider of the fortifying . . . ports on the American coast . . . for the protection of our cruizers, and the reception of their prizes," which submitted a report on June 6. Although the report was ordered "to lie on the table," its substance was apparently incorporated into a resolution of the same day instructing the Secret Committee to send two supply ships to Bermuda and the Marine Committee "to take such measures as they may think proper for purchasing, manning, arming and fitting at the said islands two sloops of war for the service of the United Colonies."

The decision to combine instructions to two separate committees in a single resolution was probably a result of the fact that at about the same time the report on Deane's letter was completed, another letter pertaining to Bermuda was received from the Committee of Cumberland County, New Jersey. Little else seems to have come from Deane's recommendations, for on August 2 Congress passed a resolution having the effect of rescinding the June 6 instructions to the two committees. See *JCC*, 4:233, 406, 5:417, 421, 423–24, 626.

³ Blank in MS.

⁴ See *JCC*, 4:392, 396–97, 410, 412, 5:421, 430–31.

Caesar Rodney to Thomas Rodney

Sir,   Philadelphia June 5th 1776.

I am glad you are so well Secured as to Parke. Tho you and David Gordon have been to View the place, Do Suppose it will hardly be Necessary to Confirm the Bargain before you See me at Newcastle on Tuesday, which is the day of the Assembly's Meeting.

The Petition of the Lord, Mayor and City of London to the King, and his Answer will Convince those people (Who have opposed the Resolution of Congress) of their Error; if they be open to Conviction it certainly will—You will have it in this day's paper. Remember me to all at home. As I Expect to see you in a few days, Shall say no more than that I am, Yrs.   Caesar Rodney

RC (MWA).

William Whipple to John Langdon

Dear Sir,   Philadelphia 5th June 1776.

This goes by express early tomorrow morning. It is determined in Committee this evening to urge the appointment of the Captain for your ship tomorrow. There is no doubt but what Thompson will be the man.[1] If you and he will talk with Such persons as you think proper for Lieuts and marine officers and let me know who will accept, I will have them commissioned. It's idle to have the Commissions filled up before we know whether they will be accepted or not. You may engage the master and all warrant and petty officers that you think necessary as soon as you please. I know of no objection to the men being shipped, only the uncertainty when the guns will be ready. Just received advice that two small privateers belonging to this place have taken three Jamaica men with very valuable cargoes, 24000 dollars in specie.[2] The money is arrived at Egg Harbor but the ships are sent to the Eastward. I fear they will fall into the hands of the enemy—now is the time to pick up homeward bound West India men. It's now 12 o'clock; high bed time. Good night,   W Whipple

Tr (DLC).
    [1] See JCC, 5:422.
    [2] See John Hancock to Philip Moore and James Craig, June 13, 1776.

Samuel Adams to James Warren

My dear sir   Philada. June 6 1776
    I have for some time past been expecting to visit my Friends in New England, which has made me the less sollicitous of writing to them, but Business of the most interesting Importance has hitherto detained me here. Our Affairs in Canada have of late worn a displeasing Aspect,[1] but Measures have been adopted which I trust will repair Misfortunes and set Matters right in that Quarter. This will, in my opinion, be an important Summer, productive of great Events which we *must* be prepard to meet. If America is virtuous, she will vanquish her Enemies and establish her Liberty. You know my Temper—Perhaps I may be too impatient. I have long wishd for the Determination of some momentous Questions. If Delay shall prove mischeivous, I shall have no Reason to reflect upon my self. Every one here knows what my Sentiments have been. However, tomorrow a Motion will be made,[2] and a Question, I hope, decided, the most important that was ever agitated in America. I have no Doubt but it will be decided to *your* satisfaction. This being done, Things will go on in the right Channel and our Country will be saved. The Bearer waits. Adieu,   S A

[*P.S.*] Let me intreat you, my Friend, to exert your Influence to prevent unnecessary Questions in the Assembly which may cause Contention. Now if ever Union is necessary. Innovations may well enough be put off, till publick Safety is secured.

RC (MHi).
    [1] Robert Treat Paine noted in his diary for this day: "Confirmation of the bad news of the loss of Col. Beadle's Co. at the Cedars above Montreal. P.M. walked in Company to Proprietors Gardins." MHi.
    [2] Richard Henry Lee's motion on independence, foreign alliances, and confederation. *JCC*, 5:425–26.

Josiah Bartlett to Nathaniel Folsom

Dear Sir   Philadelphia June 6th 1776
    I have Enclosed to you a News paper Containing the address of the City of London to the King and his answer by which we see what we have to Depend on from the ruling powers of Brittain.[1]
    The affair of Declaring these Colonies Independant States and absolved from all allegiance to the Crown of Brittain must soon be Decided. Whatever may be the opinion of the Delegates of New Hampshire on that matter They think it their Duty to act agreable to the minds of their Constituents and in an affair of that Magnitude Desire the Explicit Directions of the Legislature of the Colony and that it may be forwarded to us as soon as possible.
    Last Monday we had an account that Col Bedel with 300 or 400 men were Cut off at the Cedars above Montreal. We have Since had news that our people &c got the advantage of the Enemy in the action and had Killed & taken a considerable number. I believe there is nothing to be Depended on in Neither Report.
    Two Privateers from this place have taken 3 Large Sugar Ships with above 1000 Hogsds of sugar &c &c &c, also Twenty-four Thousand Dollars in Specie; if they are not retaken before they get in to Port it will be a fine Prize.[2]
    Please to give my best regards to the Council and assembly of New Hampshire & Believe me to be your friend & Humble Servt,
                                                                    Josiah Bartlett

[*P.S.*] Please to Convey my letter to Mrs. Bartlett.

RC (NN).
    [1] See Bartlett to John Langdon, June 3, 1776, note 4.
    [2] See also John Hancock to Philip Moore and James Craig, June 13, 1776.

Elbridge Gerry to James Warren

Dear sir   Philadelphia June 6th 1776
    I am favoured with yours of the 20th of May[1] & have attended to your observations on the office of Paymaster General which with You I think ought to be annihilated & a Paymaster substituted in each

Department. The Congress however have previously adopted another Mode & have appointed Gentlemen in two Departments under the Title of Deputy Paymaster Generals, thinking it necessary that there should be but one General officer to fill each of the offices of Commissary, Paymaster, Quarter Master, Muster Master & Adjutant, to whom it is intended that others of the same Denomination should be Deputies & Subordinate to the General officers for the purpose of obtaining returns of the Affairs of the army thro out the Continent. Indeed the Deputy paymasters Generals are excused from making such Returns to their superior officer & only make them to Congress, but I cannot consent to propose an office for my Friend which is denominated lower than One already discharged by him with Credit & Dignity unless particularly desired, & must therefore be contented to wait for some thing that in the Course of our affairs may offer more agreably.

The 2 Instant We received a Letter inclosing sundry others sent by General Schuyler to General Washington dated 27th May at Albany, & in one wrote by General Sullivan to G Schuyler at Ticonderoga he says that the Commissary at St John's had just arrived & informed him that the Kings Troops stationed at Detroit had come down with a Number of Indians making in the Whole about 1000 & attacked a party of our Men at the Cedars abt. 30 Miles from Montreal & cut them all off, also that Major Sherbune and another party of abt 150 sent to reinforce them were cut off to a Man; the Account appeared to Congress very imperfect but gave Room to fear that some unfortunate Event had taken Place; but Mr Payne Author of Common Sense shewed me a Letter from Albany dated the 30th May which came to Hand yesterday & was wrote by Mr Walker who is a Gentleman of Education, wherein he says that our Troops at the Cedars hearing of a Party of Regulars & Indians coming to attack them gave them Battle & entirely routed them having killed & taken Prisoner a considerable Part thereof. From these different accounts every one is left to form his own opinion, & We hope that the latter will prove true since it is 3 days later than General Schuyler's, but do not choose to place too much Dependance on it altho the Chance preponderates somewhat in our Favour.

A privateer owned by some Gentlemen in this City is arrived at Egg Harbour with the agreable advice of her having taken in Company with another small privateer from the same place three homeward bound Jamaica Men with 1100 hhds Sugar, 140 Puncheons Rum, 70 Pipes Madeira, 24000 Mexico Dollars &c &c &c & sent them to Dartmouth in Massa Bay. The privateers took out the Specie & divided it between them half of which is now on the Road to this place. This may be depended on as a Fact.[2]

The Answer of the King to the London Petition has given the Coup de Grace to all Expectations of Reconciliation in the middle Colonies & I think will produce excellent Effects from the observations to be made in this City but it is much [to be] regretted that their Knowledge was so shallow as not to have discovered the Designs of the Ministry which were equally apparent to every discerning Person in the Beginning of the present Year.

Congress have voted but 6000 Men for Canada & 2000 Indians if the General can obtain them instead of 10000 Men which I mentioned to Colo Orne as intended to reinforce the Army, having left out 2000 after the same were agreed to in a Com. of whole House. The Army at N York is to be reinforced to the Number of 25000 & a flying Camp at the Jerseys of 10000. General Whitcomb is appointed a Brigadier, Colo Mercer another, & Colo Reed Adjutant General.[3]

Pray inform me whether We cannot fix out a privateer or two & send for some Woolens & Linnens on the Coast of England? Two fishing Schooners with eight Guns each & forty Men would bring Us three or four rich Londoners in three or four Months Time, And I think We want Spirit if the same is not attempted. I will readily be concerned but cannot add as the Express is waiting being, sir, your sincere Friend & hum sevt,   Elbridge Gerry

RC (DLC photostat).
    [1] This letter is in C. Harvey Gardiner, ed., *A Study in Dissent: The Warren–Gerry Correspondence, 1776–1792* (Carbondale: Southern Illinois University Press, 1968), pp. 24–25.
    [2] See also John Hancock to Philip Moore and James Craig, June 13, 1776.
    [3] See *JCC*, 5:419–20.

John Hancock to Thomas Cushing

Dear Sir,   Philada. June 6th. 1776.
    I have just Time to acquaint you of the Success of two Privateers fitted out from this Port a few Months ago. They have taken three West India Ships loaden as per inclosed Invoice. The Dollars are actually safe landed at Egg Harbour in the Colony of New Jersey, and are on their Way to this City. The Captains of the Privateers thought it best to take the Money into their own Care; and for Fear any Accident should happen to either and the whole be lost or retaken, they divided the Money between them, and are now both arrived.

The Prizes are sent to New England where it is hoped they will get in safe.

By the next Post, I will do myself the Pleasure of writing more fully. I am, Sir, Your's sincerely,   John Hancock

[*P.S.*] The Capt has this Moment come in, & informs me that the Money is now in this City, & offers it to Congress.[1]

RC (MHi). In the hand of Jacob Rush and signed by Hancock.
    [1] See Hancock to Philip Moore and James Craig, June 13, 1776, note.

Robert Morris to Silas Deane

Dear Sir,   Philada June 6th. 1776
   I have already wrote you a Political letter[1] & intend this as
Commercial. Since you left us the Men of Warr have given us an
opportunity of trying the use of our Galleys or Gondolas. The Roebuck of 44 Guns & Liverpool of 26 Guns came up the River opposite to Wilmington Creek for fresh Water, our little fleet attacked
them there but not knowing their own Strength or not having
sufficient Confidence in it, they kept at too great a distance the first
day, but the second they begun to know themselves a little better
and attacked them again very Smartly. They drove the Roebuck
inshoar & with good management might have taken her, however
they greatly damaged that Ship & obliged both her & the Liverpool
to push back again to the Capes & from there to Sea leaving behind
them a Transport Brigts which our People took from them. All
this youl think has little to do with Commerce but thats a mistake
for in Consequence of this Action all the Fleet of Merchantmen have
got safe out to sea, several vessels have got safe in and we have some
trade revived & Consequently a better prospect of making remittances to you than at the time you Sailed. Our Cruizers are also got
out and I expect will be very serviceable and continue increasing
their number & shall Constantly go on making additions to our
Navy but we want our Seamen home again. The Congress has Voted
a Bounty of Eight Dollars to be paid to the Owners of every Vessell,
for each Seaman they bring in over & above the proper Number
that navigates the Vessell which youl make known all over Europe
if you can & Seamens wages in the Merchants Service here is now at
16 Dollars per Month.[2] The Polly, Capt McFadden, has been long
detained & the Rascall of a Captn left her and persuaded the Seamen to do the same. She is now Commanded by Capt Philip Lacey
and I hope is got out to Sea before this date. The Contractors for
Indn Goods will Continue making remittances in the best manner
they can and I will by a future Conveyance furnish you a full State
of what has been done but at present I really have not time. The
Scarcity of Goods all over this Continent affords a fine opportunity
to private adventurers, but the difficulty at present is how to Continue remittances during the Summer. You know it is farr more
difficult than it will be during Winter. I therefore propose that you
Shou'd engage Messrs Delap or some other good House of reputation & Capital to ship any quantity of Woolens & Linens, Pins,
needles, &c &c suited for the Consumption of this Country that you
Can possibly prevail on them to send either on your & our Account
in halves, or on your, their & our Acct. In Thirds. Let the Goods
be shipped immediately in French Ships as French property to
Martinico & Consigned to the Friend or Correspondent of those that

ship them with orders to reship the same from Martinico for our address home. Let the shippers there apply to Mr. Bingham or Mr. Richd Harrison at Martinico as they will always know of the best Conveyances and I will take care there shall be such very frequently the ensuing Fall, probably in Armed Ships of Warr, sufficient to defend themselves. You may depend the Goods if once introduced here will sell for immense proffits and at the same time be most usefull to America. The persons who engage in this business must put Confidence in us for they must trust us but you can enter into any obligations they may think necessary that we will most faithfully remit with the utmost expedition our third of the Cost & your & their share of the proceeds. The goods will Command instant pay and we will not detain it one moment. I think also that you might get the whole Risque Insured either in France or Holland from France to Martinico. You need only Insure against the Common dangers of the Sea, from Martinico here. All Risques of Sea & Capture or Seizure is not worth more than 8 to 10 per cent but the Trade will afford you to give 50 per cent if needfull or more and I woud wish the whole adventure to be Insured in this way. If you find it needfull send for my Brother Tom & let him join you in the Securitys to [. . .] that Ships the Goods and if you can not prevail with any one House to go sufficient lengths engage several of them prevailing on each to go as farr as possible for if you ship the Value of several hundred thousand pounds Sterlg. the Goods will all sell well, however if you can send us in this way £20 to £50,000 sterling it will yield Fortunes to us all, and you may depend on my utmost exertions to get the Goods safe in, to sell them well and to make speedy remittances. This affair deserves your utmost exertions to Accomplish it & under that recommendation I leave it with you being, Dr. sir, Your affectionate Friend & Servant,

Robt Morris

RC (CtHi).
[1] See Morris to Deane, June 5, 1776.
[2] For Congress' resolution on this subject of April 17, 1776, see *JCC,* 4:289–90.

Secret Committee Minutes of Proceedings

June 6th. 1776.

At a meeting of the Come. Present Morris, Alsop, Hewes, Lee, Bartlett, McKean, Lewis. The proposals of Mr. Merckle to this Come. were considrd & rejected.[1] An acct of Messrs. King & Harpers for the Brigantine Cornelia with a protest was exhibited & read together with the Charter party for sd. Brigantine. Orderd that the sd. papers be reserved for future consideration. Copy of an agreemt.

proposd to be made with Peter & Isaac Wicoff was read, orderd to be transcribd & executed at the next meeting. Order on the Treasurers in favor of Jams. Latimer, Jona. Rumford, Elias Boys, Ferguson Mcilvain & Robt. Briges for 2720 dlls being for 4 months freight of ship Liberty charterd by this Come.

MS (MH).
[1] See *JCC*, 4:403; and Secret Committee Minutes of Proceedings, June 27, 1776.

John Hancock to the Colonies

Gentlemen,   Philada. June 7th. 1776.
   I am commanded by Congress to transmit you the enclosed Resolves, and to request your immediate Attention to the same.[1]
   The Article of Lead is so essentially necessary to us at this Juncture, and is withall so scarce, that no Pains should be spared to procure it. The Situation of the United Colonies will be extremely deploreable if we depend entirely upon the Importation of it. Every People should have, within themselves, all the Means of Self Defence. To the Bounty of Providence we owe it, that America has these in the greatest Plenty. Let us not therefore be wanting to ourselves, but faithfully and dilligently cultivate those Means; and I trust we shall, ere long, baffle the most malicious Schemes of our enraged & implacable Enemies.
   You will readily perceive the great Importance of the enclosed Resolve, wherein the Congress earnestly recommend to you to remove every Thing out of the Way, that could enable our Enemies to prosecute their Plans of Violence agt. us. It is indeed so apparently the Advantage of Individuals to remove their Stock & grain, that in this Instance, their Interest, & that of the Public are one & the same.
   I have the Honour to be, Gentlemen, you most obed. & very hble Svt.   J. H. Prest.

LB (DNA: PCC, item 12A).
[1] See the June 3 resolves respecting lead mines and the removal of "stocks, grain, and meal" from areas threatened by British invasion in *JCC*, 4:413–14.

John Hancock to George Washington

Sir,   Philadelphia June 7th. 1776.
   The enclosed Letter from the Commissioners in Canada, I am commanded by Congress to transmit to you. The Contents of it are truly alarming. Our Army in that Quarter is almost ruined for Want

Richard Henry Lee's Draft Resolution on Independence

of Discipline, and every Thing else necessary to constitute an Army, or to keep Troops together. The Congress, in this Situation of our Affairs, have resolved that Genl. Wooster be recalled from Canada. I am therefore to request, you will immediately order him to repair to Head Quarters at New York.[1]

Yesterday I sent off an Express to Genl. Mercer with Orders to set out directly for Head Quarters, and at the same Time enclosed his Commission.

I enclose you a Resolve respecting Docr. Potts's appointment in Canada. You will please to give him Orders to go, either into Canada or to Lake George, as you may think most proper.[2]

I have the Honour to be, With every Sentiment of Regard & Esteem, Sir, your most obedt. & very hble Ser.

John Hancock Presidt

RC (DLC). In the hand of Jacob Rush and signed by Hancock.

[1] See Commissioners to Canada to Hancock, May 27–28, 1776; and *JCC*, 5:420–21. Washington ordered Wooster to report to New York in a brief note written on June 9. Washington, *Writings* (Fitzpatrick), 5:112n, 114. Wooster subsequently demanded a congressional investigation of his conduct as commander of Continental forces in Canada. Congress granted Wooster's wish and entrusted the inquiry to the committee appointed on June 24 to investigate the American debacle in Canada. On August 17 this committee submitted a report, in which Congress concurred, stating "that nothing censurable or blameworthy appears against Brigadier General Wooster." See *JCC*, 5:480, 664–65; and Wooster to Hancock, June 26, 1776, in *Am. Archives*, 4th ser. 6:1081.

[2] On June 6 Congress decided to employ Dr. Jonathan Potts "as a physician and surgeon in the Canada department, or at Lake George," on the understanding that he was not to supersede Dr. Samuel Stringer, the hospital director and chief physician and surgeon for the Northern Army. *JCC*, 5:424. For Washington's prior recommendation of Potts to Congress, see Washington, *Writings* (Fitzpatrick), 4:520–21. Stringer had described some of the shortcomings of his medical establishment in a May 10 letter to Washington. *Am. Archives*, 4th ser. 6:417–18.

Thomas Jefferson's Notes of Proceedings in Congress

In Congress. [June 7–28, 1776][1]

Friday June 7. 1776. The Delegates from Virginia moved in obedience to instructions from their constituents that the Congress should declare that these United colonies are & of right ought to be free & independant states, that they are absolved from all allegiance to the British crown, and that all political connection between them and the state of Great Britain is & ought to be totally dissolved; that measures should be immediately taken for procuring the assistance of foreign powers, and a Confederation be formed to bind the colonies more closely together.

furnished to J. M. by Mr. Jefferson in his hand writing; as
a copy from his original notes.

In Congress. Friday June 7. 1776.

The delegates from Virginia moved in obedience to instructions from their constituents that
the Congress should declare that these United
colonies are & of right ought to be free & independant states, that they are absolved from all
obedience to the British crown, and that all
political connection between them & the state
of Great Britain is & ought to be totally dissolved: that measures should be immediately taken for procuring the assistance of
foreign powers, & a Confederation be formed
to bind the colonies more closely together.

The house being obliged to attend at that
time to some other business, the proposition was
referred to the next day when the members
were ordered to attend punctually at ten
o'clock.

Saturday June 8th they proceeded to take it
into consideration, and referred it to a Committee of the whole, into which they immediately
resolved themselves, and passed that day &
Monday the 10th in debating on the subject.

It was argued by Wilson, Robert R. Livingston, E. Rutlege, Dickinson & others.

1

Thomas Jefferson's Notes of Proceedings in Congress

The house being obliged to attend at that time to some other business, the proposition was referred to the next day when the members were ordered to attend punctually at ten o'clock.

Saturday June 8. They proceeded to take it into consideration and referred it to a committee of the whole, into which they immediately resolved themselves, and passed that day & Monday the 10th in debating on the subject.

It was argued by Wilson, Robert R. Livingston, E. Rutlege, Dickinson and others

That tho' they were friends to the measures themselves, and saw the impossibility that we should ever again be united with Gr. Britain, yet they were against adopting them at this time:

That the conduct we had formerly observed was wise & proper now, of deferring to take any capital step till the voice of the people drove us into it:

That they were our power, & without them our declarations could not be carried into effect:

That the people of the middle colonies (Maryland, Delaware, Pennsylva., the Jersies & N. York) were not yet ripe for bidding adieu to British connection but that they were fast ripening & in a short time would join in the general voice of America:

That the resolution entered into by this house on the 15th of May for suppressing the exercise of all powers derived from the crown, had shewn, by the ferment into which it had thrown these middle colonies, that they had not yet accomodated their minds to a separation from the mother country:

That some of them had expressly forbidden their delegates to consent to such a declaration, and others had given no instructions, & consequently no powers to give such consent:

That if the delegates of any particular colony had no power to declare such colony independant, certain they were the others could not declare it for them; the colonies being as yet perfectly independant of each other:

That the assembly of Pennsylvania was now sitting above stairs, their convention would sit within a few days, the convention of New York was now sitting, & those of the Jersies & Delaware counties would meet on the Monday following & it was probable these bodies would take up the question of Independance & would declare to their delegates the voice of their state:

That if such a declaration should now be agreed to, these delegates must ⟨now⟩ retire & possibly their colonies might secede from the Union:

That such a secession would weaken us more than could be compensated by any foreign alliance:

That in the event of such a division, foreign powers would either refuse to join themselves to our fortunes, or having us so much in their power as that desperate declaration would place us, they would insist on terms proportionably more hard & prejudicial:

That we had little reason to expect an alliance with those to whom alone as yet we had cast our eyes:

That France & Spain had reason to be jealous of that rising power which would one day certainly strip them of all their American possessions:

That it was more likely they should form a connection with the British court, who, if they should find themselves unable otherwise to extricate themselves from their difficulties, would agree to a partition of our territories, restoring Canada to France, & the Floridas to Spain, to accomplish for themselves a recovery of these colonies:

That it would not be long before we should receive certain information of the disposition of the French court, from the agent whom we had sent to Paris for that purpose:

That if this disposition should be favourable, by waiting the event of the present campaign, which we all hoped would be succesful, we should have reason to expect an alliance on better terms:

That this would in fact work no delay of any effectual aid from such ally, as, from the advance of the season & distance of our situation, it was impossible we could receive any assistance during this campaign:

That it was prudent to fix among ourselves the terms on which we would form alliance, before we declared we would form one at all events:

And that if these were agreed on & our Declaration of Independance ready by the time our Ambassadour should be prepared to sail, it would be as well, as to go into that Declaration at this day.

On the other side it was urged by J. Adams, Lee, Wythe and others

That no gentleman had argued against the policy or the right of separation from Britain, nor had supposed it possible we should ever renew our connection: that they had only opposed it's being now declared:

That the question was not whether, by a declaration of independance, we should make ourselves what we are not; but whether we should declare a fact which already exists:

That as to the people or parliament of England, we had alwais been independant of them, their restraints on our trade deriving efficacy from our acquiescence only & not from any rights they possessed of imposing them, & that so far our connection had been federal only, & was now dissolved by the commencement of hostilities:

That as to the king, we had been bound to him by allegiance, but that this bond was now dissolved by his assent to the late act of parliament, by which he declares us out of his protection, and by his levying war on us, a fact which had long ago proved us out of his protection; it being a certain position in law that allegiance & protection are reciprocal, the one ceasing when the other is withdrawn:

That James the IId never declared the people of England out of his protection yet his actions proved it & the parliament declared it:

No delegates then can be denied, or ever want, a power of declaring an existent truth:

That the delegates from the Delaware counties having declared their constituents ready to join,[2] there are only two colonies Pennsylvania & Maryland whose delegates are absolutely tied up, and that these had by their instructions only reserved a right of confirming or rejecting the measure:

That the instructions from Pennsylvania might be accounted for from the times in which they were drawn, near a twelvemonth ago, since which the face of affairs has totally changed:

That within that time it had become apparent that Britain was determined to accept nothing less than a carte blanche, and that the king's answer to the Lord Mayor, Aldermen & common council of London, which had come to hand four days ago, must have satisfied every one of this point:

That the people wait for us to lead the way ⟨in this step⟩:

That *they* are in favour of the measure, tho' the instructions given by some of their *representatives* are not:

That the voice of the representatives is not alwais consonant with the voice of the people, and that this is remarkeably the case in these middle colonies:

That the effect of the resolution of the 15th of May has proved this, which, raising the murmurs of some in the colonies of Pennsylvania & Maryland, called forth the opposing voice of the freer part of the people, & proved them to be the majority, even in these colonies:

That the backwardness of these two colonies might be ascribed partly to the influence of proprietary power & connections, & partly to their having not yet been attacked by the enemy:

That these causes were not likely to be soon removed, as there seemed no probability that the enemy would make either of these the seat of this summer's war:

That it would be vain to wait either weeks or months for perfect unanimity, since it was impossible that all men should ever become of one sentiment on any question:

That the conduct of some colonies from the beginning of this contest, had given reason to suspect it was their settled policy to keep in the rear of the confederacy, that their particular prospect might be better even in the worst event:

That therefore it was necessary for those colonies who had thrown themselves forward & hazarded all from the beginning, to come forward now also, and put all again to their own hazard:

That the history of the Dutch revolution, of whom three states only confederated at first proved that a secession of some colonies would not be so dangerous as some apprehended:

That a declaration of Independance alone could render it consistent with European delicacy for European powers to treat with us, or even to receive an Ambassador from us:

That till this they would not receive our vessels into their ports, nor acknowlege the adjudications of our courts of Admiralty to be legitimate, in cases of capture of British vessels:

That tho' France & Spain may be jealous of our rising power, they must think it will be much more formidable with the addition of Great Britain; and will therefore see it their interest to prevent a coalition; but should they refuse, we shall be but where we are; whereas without trying we shall never know whether they will aid us or not:

That the present campaign may be unsuccessful, & therefore we had better propose an alliance while our affairs wear a hopeful aspect:

That to wait the event of this campaign will certainly work delay, because during this summer France may assist us effectually by cutting off those supplies of provisions from England & Ireland on which the enemy's armies here are to depend; or by setting in motion the great power they have collected in the West Indies, & calling our enemy to the defence of the possessions they have there:

That it would be idle to lose time in settling the terms of alliance, till we had first determined we would enter into alliance:

That it is necessary to lose no time in opening a trade for our people, who will want clothes, and will want money too for the paiment of taxes:

And that the only misfortune is that we did not enter into alliance with France six months sooner, as besides opening their ports for the vent of our last year's produce, they might have marched an army into Germany and prevented the petty princes there from selling their unhappy subjects to subdue us.

It appearing in the course of these debates that the colonies of N. York, New Jersey, Pennsylvania, Delaware, Maryland & South Carolina were not yet matured for falling from the parent stem, but that they were fast advancing to that state, it was thought most prudent to wait a while for them, and to postpone the final decision to July 1. but that this might occasion as little delay as possible, a committee was appointed to prepare a declaration of independance. the Commee. were J. Adams, Dr. Franklin, Roger Sherman, Robert R. Livingston & myself. committees were also appointed at the same time to prepare a plan of confederation for the colonies, and to state the terms proper to be proposed for foreign alliance. the committee for drawing the Declaration of Independence desired me to do it. ⟨I did so⟩ it was accordingly done and being approved by them, I reported it to the house on Friday the 28th of June when it was read and ordered to lie on the table.[3]

MS (DLC). In the hand of Thomas Jefferson.

[1] The editor of the definitive edition of Jefferson's papers provided the following explanation of the MS printed here and under the dates July 1–4 and July 12–August 1, 1776, below. "MS (DLC); 20 numbered pages in TJ's hand. Another MS (DLC); in TJ's hand, consisting of 49 pages; this copy was transmitted to Madison by TJ on 1 June 1783 (but has now been placed with the Jefferson Papers in the Library of Congress) and was probably made on or shortly before that date. In the letter of transmittal TJ wrote: 'I send you inclosed the debates in Congress on the subjects of Independence, Voting in Congress, and the Quotas of money to be required from the states. I found on looking that I had taken no others save only in one trifling case. As you were desirous of having a copy of the original of the declaration of Independence I have inserted it at full length distinguishing the alterations it underwent.' This would seem to indicate that the Notes, as originally copied 'in form and with correctness,' did not contain a text of the Declaration. This is to be doubted. . . . The original notes or memoranda of debates from which the Notes were written are not known to be extant." Jefferson, Papers (Boyd), 1:327. For further analysis of Jefferson's notes, here presented in three entries, see ibid., pp. 299–329. For the crucial matter of the notes' literal accuracy and the date of their composition—it is known with certainty only that they were written sometime between August 1776 and June 1783—see also the following note.

[2] Since the Delaware Assembly did not take this action until June 15, it seems unlikely that this argument could have been advanced on June 8 or 10. It suggests rather that Jefferson was reconstructing this portion of the debate from memory rather than "written notes, taken by myself at the moment and on the spot," as he claimed in 1823. Jefferson, Papers (Boyd), 1:300–301. On this point misleading statements in other passages from the notes below are also pertinent. For example, because Pennsylvania approved new instructions for her delegates on June 8, it was not "Pennsylvania & Maryland" but rather New York and Maryland that were "tied up" after Delaware's action noted here. And in the second paragraph below, the reference to the king's response to the petition of the city of London—which Jefferson explicitly states "had come to hand four days ago"—is to news received in Philadelphia on June 2 or 3. See Richard Henry Lee to Landon Carter, June 2, note 3; Josiah Bartlett to John Langdon, June 3, note 4; and John Adams to Samuel Chase, June 14, 1776, note 4.

Other passages from Jefferson's notes that are inaccurate are found in the section printed under the date July 1–4, 1776. Long ago attention was drawn to the improbability of Jefferson's assertion that after the Declaration was "agreed to by the house," it was "signed by every member present except Mr. Dickinson," because there is no evidence that there was a signing of the Declaration by the delegates before August 2. Historians have failed to take issue, however, with Jefferson's casual reference to the time of day when the debate came to an end and the vote was taken on the Declaration—upon which rest nearly all traditional accounts that assert that the Declaration was approved late in the day. As Jefferson phrased the matter: "the debates having taken up the greater parts of the 2d. 3d. & 4th. days of July were, in the evening of the last closed." Although this assertion is difficult to square with the journals of Congress, which indicate that the Declaration was the second matter taken up after the delegates convened at approximately 9:00

A.M., and that they conducted a great deal of important business later during the day, no critical analysis of this passage has been made. It is clear now, however, from the evidence of the July 4 letters of Abraham Clark and of the committee appointed that day to confer on the defense of New Jersey and Pennsylvania, that the Declaration was approved in the morning, rather than in the evening as Jefferson implies. See Abraham Clark to Elias Dayton, July 4; and Committee of Congress to the Lancaster Associators, July 4, 1776.

Considering, then, those passages reviewed here that conflict with what is known about the events leading to adoption of the Declaration, it seems clear that Jefferson's notes—like all noncontemporary evidence—ought to be used with caution. Although undoubtedly based upon an earlier set of notes, they were surely put into their present form long after the proceedings reviewed actually occurred, at a time when some of the details of the events were no longer sharply etched in Jefferson's mind.

For a discussion of another passage from Jefferson's notes pertaining to their general credibility—suggesting that in one particular instance Jefferson rather than his critics was probably correct—see Jefferson's Notes of Proceedings in Congress, July 1–4, 1776, note 5.

[3] For the continuation of these notes, see Jefferson's Notes of Proceedings in Congress, July 1–4, 1776.

John Dickinson's Notes for a Speech in Congress

[June 8–10? 1776] [1]

Two Points recommended & enjoined by our Constituents.
1st. Defence.   2. Reconciliation.
On this Footing & with this View they have engaged in this Contest.
I shall consider the proposition in 3 Lights.
1st. As establishing an independent & seperate State & govt.
2d. As to the Right We have to take such a Step.
3d. As to the Policy of it—Bargain Difficult, already our Interest to support G.B.

As to the first, I would ask if such a Declaration does not necessarily involve in it an Assurance to foreign States, that during the Course of such a War We will maintain the Rights of Neutrality according to the well known Laws of Nations & consequently the free & equal admission of the ships & vessels of the belligerent Powers? If it does involve such an Assurance, does it not also involve in it necessarily an Engagement of Protection to the ships of such foreign Powers? If it does, can it be denied, that We assume a Sovereignty independent on & Separate from that of the Crown of G.B.? Is not this plainly to go beyond the Limits of the present War, and to make an Establishment for a Time of Peace with G.B. totally repugnant to our former Connection with her? Is not this to wound her vitally even in the Time of Peace, by totally rescinding her Authority to regulate our Commercial Intercourse with foreign Powers? An Authority which We have repeatedly declared was necessarily lodged in her?

In order to avoid these Conclusions will Gentlemen say—they do not mean such acts of Sovereignty. Let Us then honestly say so—& not give foreign Powers Reason to complain of our having deceived them. How then will our Proposal to them stand? That after our Reconciliation with G.B. which may perhaps be in a Year or two, We will not join our Armies or Fleets to G.B. so that we hold out the precarious profit of a few Months Trade as a Temptation to foreign Powers to come in a War with the first maritime Power in the world.

But in such a Case, how are We to prevent the Crown from procuring seamen or Soldiers who are Inhabitants of the Colonies? Shall We [withstand?] Attempts in Consequence of our Declaration? This would be an Act of Sovereignty in direct opposition to the Sovereign with whom We are reconciled.

But taking the proposition in the most limited Sense, without allowing the before mentioned to be fairly deduced from it, do We not [become?] an independent & separate State in the plainest Manner? The Power of declaring Peace or War is one of the highest Powers of Sovereignty. There cannot be a Sovereignty without it—if not lodged in the Crown or King of G.B. the Sovereignty is not vested in him; it is vested in Us.

2d. Point.

Our Right. Even those Delegates who are not restrained by Instructions have no Right to establish an independent seperate Government for a Time of Peace. Inter arma silent Leges. Our Business is defence. Celebrated Writers deny a Power to change a Government without a full & free Consent of the People plainly exprest. The Sense of America as exprest is for Reconciliation. What Evidence have We of a contrary Sense? Reason & Justice deny our Right—of such vast Importance to present & succeeding [generations?]. It is in vain to say all Ties are dissolv'd. It is begging the Question. We are now acting on a Principle of the English Constitution in resisting the assumption or Usurpation of an unjust power. We are now acting under that Constitution. Does that Circumstance prove its Dissolution?

But granting the present oppression to be a Dissolution, the Choice of [setting?], a Restoring it, or forming a new one is vested in our Constituents, not in Us. They have not given it to Us. We may pursue Measures that will force them into it. But that implies not a Right so to force them.

Should We be justified as to our Constituents at this Time to make a Declaration of Independence at this Time? Why then to take a step that inevitably leads to it? The first would be most becoming as being most candid.

3d. Point.

Policy.[2] It is Politic not to engage the Faith or Honor of a Nation farther than it may be their Interest to perform. G.B. is now our Enemy, but if France or the House of Bourbon attack her, embarrassed in her Contest with Us, it may become our true Interest to support her. Case of Holland with regard to Spain.

Where is the Necessity of such a Declaration? We appear strong enough to resist our Enemies this Campaign. Boston. North Carolina. It is a favorite Maxim with some, that our Commerce is so valuable, it will protect itself.[3] Let Us see whether We overrate it. At least do not let Us undervalue it, & go a begging round the World with it, to coax States into a War for it. We have opened our Ports. Let Us act with a dignified Reserve. Let us keep ourselves Masters of our own Conduct—& reserve our Favor for the friendly state that shall most deserve it. Otherwise We throw in our Neutrality with as much Indifference as the Statuary did the Statue of [Mercury?] to the purchaser of [Jupiter?].

By such a Conduct We shall not only act imprudently with Regard to foreign States, but with Respect to G.B.

Commissioners coming over. Many Friends there—a Clog upon Administration. We united—they divided. This measure will divide Us & unite them. Not a Man of the least Understanding there, but will be convinced from its Nature & Time that We take this step to render Reconciliation impracticable. As much so as a full Declaration of an seperate Commonwealth.

Then We shall be pushed by the united & reanimated Exertions of the whole Kingdom.

If We mean Independence, it is our Business to conceal our Meaning. Keep up the useful Opinion.

England, Holland & the Empire acknowledged the Duke of Anjou King of Spain while arming to dethrone him.

What Mortal can tell with Certainty that it will not be our best Interest to be reconciled to G.B.? It will depend on the Terms We can obtain. They are yet unknown.

We may perhaps get such as will render Us as independent, as wise & good Men would wish for—Our Internal Commerce—such a share of foreign [commerce]—Removal of Troops—Annual Assemblies—Councillors for Life—&c.

Do not let Us turn our Backs on Reconciliation till We find it a Monster too dreadful to approach. It will [be] a bargain—to procure the aid & naval protection of G.B. We may purchase it perhaps at a reasonable price—& in such Case would We be so unreasonable as to reject it?

We are seeking now for the protection of France &c. We must pay some price I suppose for that. Dont let Us make our Case desperate & have only one Bidder for our Friendship. A Man generally sells his Goods to the most profits when there are two or three Chapmen that bid for it. This procedure would be the more extraordinary at this time, as We are actually sounding the Disposition of a very great Power—looks like an Insult not to wait for his Decision. The Friendship of G.B. has many Circumstances to recommend it.

We shall have a limited Monarchy the easiest the World ever knew. A form approv'd by the greatest Geniuses that ever wrote on the subject. Tacitus.

[Limitations?] of Religion, Blood, Manners, Customs, [. . . .]

The first Naval Power in the World. States of Barbary, Spain, Portugal.

Stoppage of an immense & consuming Expense.

On the other Hand, Novelty of Government, Connections, Trade, Expense, Every Thing.

Commonwealth a Government the most subject to Convulsion. Rome, Greece, Holland. Switzerland preserved by its Neighbors.

The first political Wish of my Soul is for the Liberty of America. The next is for a constitutional Reconciliation with G.B. If We cannot obtain the first without relinquishing the second, Let us seek a new Establishment as the Pious Aeneas did.

Attolens humeris famam & fata Nepotum.[4]

MS (PHi). In the hand of John Dickinson. These notes are strikingly cryptic and are strewn with abbreviations which have been expanded without brackets in this text.

[1] At least two passages in these notes suggest that Dickinson wrote them at the beginning rather than near the conclusion of the debate on independence. First, in developing his "2d. Point," Dickinson refers to "those Delegates who are not restrained by Instructions." The passage implies that many delegates were still so restrained, suggesting the situation that existed in early June before the instructions of the Pennsylvania, Delaware, and Maryland delegates were changed. Second, in discussing "the Necessity of such a Declaration" under his "3d Point," Dickinson argues that "We appear strong enough to resist our Enemies this Campaign," an argument that he would have been less likely to employ after mid-June when the dismal facts concerning the rout of the American army from Canada became better known. Finally, although the evidence is only suggestive, the arguments developed in these notes better coincide with Jefferson's account of the debates of June 8 and 10 than those of July 1 and 2, the four days on which the principal debates on independence took place. See Thomas Jefferson's Notes of Debate, June 7–28 and July 1–4, 1776. For a comparison of the arguments developed in the present entry with those he articulated at the beginning of July, see John Dickinson's Notes for a Speech in Congress, July 1? 1776.

[2] At this point in the margin Dickinson penned the following cryptic remarks. "Committee of Supplies. Papers to be published in Canada. Papers to be sent to Europe. A [. . .] Address to People of Pennsylvania. Ordinance against Officers."

[3] At this point in the margin Dickinson wrote: "Amount of Money emitted in several Colonies."

[4] "Bearing aloft on his shoulders the fame and fortune of his descendants." Virgil *Aeneid* 8.731. Dickinson employed the same phrase again in 1782 when he wrote a "Vindication" of his conduct during 1776. The "Vindication," which was originally printed by Francis Bailey in his *Freeman's Journal, or the North-American Intelligencer*, January 1, 1783, appears as Appendix V in Charles J.

Stillé, *The Life and Times of John Dickinson, 1732–1808* (1891; reprint ed., New York: Burt Franklin, 1969), pp. 364–414. For Dickinson's retrospective review of the principal arguments against independence he had attempted to set forth in June–July 1776, see especially pp. 368–73.

John Dickinson to Thomas Willing

Saturday [June 8? 1776] [1]
Mr. Dickinson presents his Compliments to Mr. Willing, and begs Leave to inform him, that the public Business in a very particular Manner demands his Attendance this Morning, as a Matter of the last Importance is to be determined.

FC (PPL). In the hand of John Dickinson.

[1] Although the only specific evidence available for determining the date of this document is the word "Saturday," it is inviting to speculate that the "Matter of the last Importance" mentioned by Dickinson was the issue of independence, one on which he and Willing held similar views. If this conjecture is indeed true, the day Dickinson wrote this note would almost certainly have been June 8, because it was the only Saturday between the introduction of Richard Henry Lee's resolution on independence, on June 7, and its adoption, on July 2, that the issue was debated in Congress.

Elbridge Gerry to Samuel R. Gerry

Dear Brother   Philadelphia June 8 1776
I recd your Favour of May the 18th with the inclosed Letters & am sorry to find that the Enemy had disposed of your Vessel; but the Fortune of War is uncertain & We must be contented therewith. I think it a happy affair that Capt Mugford took the powder Vessal altho the Loss of so brave a Man is to be lamented. I am glad to find You are fortifying in Marblehead, pray give my Compliments to your Father Colo Glover & inform him that I wrote to Colo Orne [1] desiring that twenty good pieces Cannon may be obtained of the General Court & repaired for your Fortifications, which I think it will be adviseable for him to press as thereby the Town may be defended against Bomb Ketches & Ships of War. I am sorry to hear of the Conduct pursued with Respect to your Brother's Services in the Camp, but think he may make himself easy in the Matter, & that the Money will be obtained on my Return to the Colony. Your little Daughter I hope will recover Health & that the same will be confirmed to Mrs. Gerry, your Family & all Friends at Marblehead, to whom give my regards & believe me to be, yours sincerely,   Elbridge Gerry

[P.S.] I have just heard that Capt. James in your Father Glovers Brig was chased by the Man of War & ran on shore.[2] His Cargo will be saved but the Vessel lost. I hope she is insured. This happened at the Mouth of the Run.

RC (MHi).
¹ Not found.
² For further information on the fate of the snow *Champion*, see Henry Fisher to the Pennsylvania Committee of Safety, June 7, 1776, in Clark, *Naval Documents*, 5:414–15.

Elbridge Gerry to Joseph Trumbull

Dear sir,   Philadelphia 8th June 1776

Since You left this Place You have probably recd a Confirmation of the unwelcome News which then arrived from Canada, since which Mr. Moylan is appointed Quarter Master General & Colo Reed Adjutant General, General Whitcomb of Massa. & Colo Mercer of Connecticut Brigadiers, & the Appointment of Majir Generals are suspended for the present. General Worcester is also ordered to Head Quarters. I beleive We should have executed our Design of promoting You to Quarter Masr. General if it can be called a promotion, had not Congress been doubtful whether the place of so faithful a Servant could be immediately supplyed & had it not been urged (with what real Grounds You can best judge) that his Excelly. the General had mentioned the Gentleman who is appointed for this office while Dependance was placed on You in the other more important One. For my own part I could Wish the Alteration had taken Place as was proposed, but am doubtful whether Mr Livingston would not have obtained your Birth had You been appointed QM General which I should have considered as an Unfortunate Exchange. With Respect to Rank there will probably be no Opposition made to your having that of Colonel Whenever proposed & I shall be glad to know your Sentiments on the same.¹

You have doubtless heard of the Success of two small Privateers of this City in taking three homeward bound Jamaica Men with 1100 hhds Sugar, 140 puncheon Rum, 70 pipes Madeira Wine, 24000 Mexico Dollars &c &c &c. Half of the Money is on the Road from Egg Harbour & one of the prizes arrived here last Evening.

I am glad to inform You that the General is now authorized to establish Magizines of provissions & Military Stores as he shall judge expedient, & hope it will not be too late to retreive our affair in Canada.

Lord Dunmore We hear with his Regiment of Royal Africans is landed in an Island in the Susquehanna River, having been obliged to leave his former post from the fatal Sickness which prevailed in Camp, where were found 350 fresh Graves.

Pray inform me by the first oppertunity what General Officers are ordered to Massachusetts, & when they are to proceed beleiving me to be sincerely sir your Friend & humb ser., Elb Gerry

[*P.S.*] My Regards to General Gates, & other Friends.

RC (CtHi).
[1] In a June 9 letter to John Hancock, Joseph Trumbull threatened to resign as commissary general unless he was paid a commission on the purchase of supplies rather than a fixed salary. Congress responded on June 17 by raising his salary to $150 a month. Stephen Moylan's election as quartermaster general on June 5 had been with "the pay of 80 dollars a month, and the rank of colonel." See Trumbull to Hancock, June 9, 1776, in *Am. Archives*, 4th ser. 6:790–91; and *JCC*, 5:419, 451. See also Gerry to Joseph Trumbull, June 18, 1776. Trumbull remained commissary general until his resignation in August 1777, and he was appointed to the Board of War on November 27, 1777. *JCC*, 8:598, 9:971.

New York Delegates to the New York Convention

Dr Sir, Philadelphia 8th June 1776
Your Delegates here expect that the question of independance will very shortly be agitated in Congress. Some of us consider ourselves as bound by our instructions not to vote on that question & all wish to have your sentiments thereon.[1]

The matter will admit of no delay we have therefore sent an express who will wait your orders. We are Sir, With the greatest respt., Your Most obt Hum. Servts,

Wm. Floyd   Robt R Livingston

Henry Wisner   Frans Lewis

RC (MeHi). Written by Livingston and signed by Livingston, Floyd, Lewis, and Wisner. *Journals of N. Y. Prov. Cong.*, 1:488. Addressed: "To Nathaniel Woodhull, Esqr, Prest. of the Hon. the Convention of New-York."
[1] The New York delegates were bound by their April 22, 1775, instructions to work "for the preservation and re-establishment of American rights and priviledges, and for the restoration of harmony between Great Britain and the Colonies." See *JCC*, 2:15–16. Responding to this letter on June 11, the provincial congress confirmed that the delegates were not authorized "to give the sense of this Colony on the question of declaring it to be . . . an independent State; nor does this Congress incline to instruct you on that point; it being a matter of doubt whether their constituents intended to vest them with the power to deliberate and determine on that question." But the delegates were then told that although it would now be "imprudent to require the sentiments of the people relative to the question of Independence, least it should create division," the inhabitants of the colony would be consulted on this matter at "the earliest opportunity." Despite this assurance, the provincial congress never submitted this question to the people of New York; and in consequence the New York delegation abstained from voting when Congress approved Richard Henry Lee's reso-

lution in favor of American independence on July 2. Only after the New York Convention had approved the Declaration of Independence on July 9 were the New York delegates free to sign it. See New York Provincial Congress to the New York delegates, June 11, PCC, item 67, 1:228–31; *Am. Archives,* 4th ser. 6:814, 1392–96; New York Delegates to the New York Provincial Congress, July 2, 1776, note; and Bernard Mason, *The Road to Independence: The Revolutionary Movement in New York, 1773–1777* (Lexington: University of Kentucky Press, 1967), pp. 166–77.

Robert Treat Paine to John Griffith and Samuel Patrick

Sir,   Philada. June 8. 1776
The Committee for Contracting for the Casting Cannon have attended to yr proposals delivered them by Francis Lewis Esqr.[1] & make you the following Answer vizt. that they have not advanced Money to any Person till some Cannon were made, but to assist you in carying on the works they will immediately buy of you 100 Tons of Pigg Iron to ballast the Continental Frigates to be delivered where they are building & pay you £8 per Ton York Currency for the Same. They will buy of you the Cannon for said Frigates Vizt. 24 12-pdrs., 20 9-pdrs., & 8 4-pdrs., provided that you can get them done by the time they are wanted. The Cannon must be made 16 diameters of the Shot long & stand Sufficient proof & they agree that you Shall have 40£ Penn. Currency per Ton for them delivered at the Frigates & we likewise agree to take of you 50 shot to each Cannon being the same bargain we made with the others & will give you the Same Price. We will likewise furnish the Powder to prove the Cannon as soon as it shall be wanted, please to let us know immediately when you will undertake to get the Cannon ready, for it is necessary that they Should be made soon. Tho we do not engage with you for more Cannon than for the two Frigates, yet if you can make good Cannon especially of a large Size you need not fear being employ'd.

FC (MHi).
[1] See Samuel Patrick to Francis Lewis, May 12, 1776, in Clark, *Naval Documents,* 5:66.

Rhode Island Delegates to Nicholas Cooke

Sir,   Philadelphia June 8th 1776
That Correspondence between the Colony and its Delegates which by the Death of Mr. Ward and the great Inconveniency which attends Mr. Hopkins in Writing, hath for some Time past been in-

terrupted, We wish might be resumed. Mr. Hopkins gave the earliest
Notice, by Express, that our Brigade was put under continental Establishment,[1] and John Collins Esqr. informed the Assembly of the
Determination of Congress respecting the Cannon which were landed
at Newport by the Commander in Chief of the Continental Navy.[2]
Since that the Congress have order'd Six thousand of the Militia to
reinforce the army in Canada and keep up a Communication with
that Province.

Massachusetts are requested to furnish of their
Militia for that Purpose   3000 . . . 4 Battalls
Connecticut   1500 . . . 2 ditto
N. Hampshire   750 . . . 1———
N. York   750 . . . 1———

Thirteen thousand eight Hundred Militia are
order'd to reinforce the Army at N. York.
Massachusetts are requested to furnish
thereof   2000
Connecticutt   5500
N. York   3000
N. Jersey   3300

A flying Camp is ordered to be formed
to consist of Ten Thousand Militia,
and to be furnished as follows, from
Pennsylvania   6000
Maryland   3400
Delaware Government   600

The Congress have also empowerd Genl.
Washington to employ in Canada Indians   2000

John Hopkins and Samuel Tompkins are appointed to the Com-
mand of the Two Ships built in Providence; but which of the Ships
they are respectively to command is not yet determined. When it is
We shall give you Notice thereof as well as of every thing of Importance which passes the Congress. Please to desire the Committee
appointed to build the Ships in Providence, to transmit to the Marine
Committee of Congress, the Names of the Lieutenants and other
Officers they have appointed in Order that they may receive their
Commissions.[3]
By Letters from Canada to Congress it appears that our Affairs
there are in a bad Situation. Genl. Arnold in a Letter of the 27th
of May last informs that 500 of our Troops were taken Prisoners at
a Place above Montreal called the Cedars, by 50 Regulars, 300
Canadians and 250 Indians. We lost only 10 Privates and not one
Officer. Genl. Arnold writes that as soon as he had Intelligence of

this Defeat, he collected a Body of Men and determined to attack the
Enemy, but he could not get his Batoes ready early enough [for] his
Purpose, and that he had agreed with the Commander of the Enemy
Forces to an Exchange of Prisoners, Officer for Officer and Man for
Man. Foster, who commanded the Party of the Enemy, when he
became acquainted with Arnold's design to attack him, told him with
seeming Concern that if he did attack him his Indians would im-
mediately destroy every Prisoner, that it would be out of his Power
to prevent it &c &c. This did not check Genl. Arnold; but it seems
that his Batoes not being able to get to him seasonably put a Stop to
his Design. We are at a Loss how to account for this Capture of our
Men by a Body but a little superior to them in Numbers. In our
Detachment were Major Sherburn, and another Major and nine or
Ten Captains.[4]

Two Privateers fitted out from this Place have taken three valuable Ships bound to England from Jamaica. One of the Privateers
hath arrived at Egg Harbour, and sent to this City by Land 24,800
Dollars, the other Privateer with the Prizes were bound for Bedford.

We are with great Respect your Honor's most obedient humble
Servants,   Step Hopkins

William Ellery

RC (R-Ar). Written by Ellery and signed by Ellery and Hopkins.
  [1] See Stephen Hopkins to Nicholas Cooke, May 15, 1776.
  [2] See John Hancock to Esek Hopkins, May 7, 1776, note 2.
  [3] See JCC, 5:422–23. The Rhode Island "Committee . . . to build the Ships"
appointed commissioned officers for the frigates *Providence* and *Warren* without
reference to Congress. Clark, *Naval Documents*, 5:856n.2.
  [4] These "Letters from Canada," received by Congress on June 6, are listed in
JCC, 5:420. For Congress' action on the cartel between General Arnold and Capt.
George Forster, see JCC, 5:446, 454–58, 468, 475, 533–39, 601.

Edward Rutledge to John Jay

My dear Jay   Saturday Evg 10 o'clock [June 8, 1776]
I am much obliged to you for your Introduction of Mr.
Merckle—he will tell you what has been done in Consequence of it.[1]
I have shown him all the Civility in my Power. I fear in the present
Situation of Affairs we will not be able to give the Dutch much Security as will induce so cautious a Power to part with that which
they consider the first Blessing. The Congress sat till 7 o'clock this
Evening in Consequence of a Motion of R. H. Lee's resolving ourselves free & independent States. The Sensible part of the House
opposed the Motion. They had no Objection to forming a Scheme
of a Treaty which they would send to France by proper Persons, &
a uniting this Continent by a Confederacy. They saw no Wisdom in

a *Declaration* of Independence, nor any other Purpose to be answer'd by it, but placing ourselves in the Power of those with whom we mean to treat, giving our Enemy Notice of our Intentions before we had taken any Steps to execute them & there by enabling them to counteract us in our Intentions & rendering ourselves ridiculous in the Eyes of foreign Powers by attempting to bring them into an Union with us before we had united with each other. For daily experience evinces that the Inhabitants of every Colony consider themselves at Liberty to do as they please upon almost every occasion. And a Man must have the Impudence of a New Englander to propose in our present disjointed State any Treaty (honourable to us) to a Nation now at Peace. No Reason culd be assigned for pressing into this Measure, but the Reason of every Madman, a Shew of our Spirit. The Event however was that the Question was postponed. It is to be renewed on Monday when I mean to move that it should be postponed for 3 Weeks or a Month.[2] In the mean Time the plan of Confederation & the Scheme of Treaty may go on. I don't know whether I shall suceed in this Motion; *I think not,* it is at least Doubtful. However I must do what is right in my own Eyes & Consequences must take Care of themselves. I wish you had been here. The whole Argument was sustained on one side by R. Livingston, Wilson, Dickenson & myself, & by the Powers of all N. England, Virginia & Georgia on the other. Remember me to Morris affectionately. I wuld have wrote to him, but did not know of this Conveyance until a few Minutes ago, & am as you will see by this incorrect Letter too fatigued to hold my Pen any longer than whilst I tell you how sir truely I esteem & love you. Yours Affect,

E. Rutledge

RC (NNC).
[1] See Secret Committee Minutes of Proceedings, June 6, 1776, note.
[2] On Monday, June 10, Congress did in fact postpone until July 1 further consideration of Richard Henry Lee's resolution about independence. *JCC,* 4:425–29.

John Adams to Samuel Cooper

Dear Sir,   Philadelphia June 9. 1776

Yours of 27 May, recd yesterday.[1] I did not expect that our Army would have raised the Siege of Quebec, so soon, much less so unskillfully and so timorously. I cannot forbear these Epithets. But raising a siege in open day, and in the Face of an Enemy, was a Step, that nothing could justify, that I can think of.

The Small Pox is a terrible Enemy, but why could not this have been kept out of the Camp before Quebec, as well as out of the Camps at Cambridge and Roxbury? Provisions enough for the whole

Army twice told, have been sent into Canada and taken there from the Enemy. But all has been total Confusion there and still is so. We have no regular Returns nor any certain Information. Our People dont fight. The officers have had no Command—the Men no order. However, I hope, Things will be better. We are doing the best We can. When I say We I mean the Delegates from N. E. and Some few others. In Truth the Syren Voice of Reconciliation, which deluded the Town of Boston to its Ruin, the Winter before last, has deluded the Congress and the Colonies whom they represent, during the last Winter, and this has petrified Us, and Stupified Us.

The Causes of our Misfortunes and Miscarriages in Canada, are so numerous, are of so long standing, and have been so incessantly increasing, that it would take a long Letter to develop them.

1. The primary Cause has been the Diversity of Sentiments in Congress, concerning that Expedition, and the Indecision, or rather Fluctuation of our Councils in the Support and Prosecution of it. In the original Conception of the Design of Sending our Arms into that Province, nearly one half the Number of the Colonies were against it. Some thought it too great an undertaking—Some thought it too expensive—others thought it, or pretended to think it unnecessary. From this Variety of opinions, or some other unknown Cause, an opposition has taken Place to every Motion, and Projection for promoting and expediting the Service there.

2. Since the Death of Montgomery, We have had no General in Command there who Seems to have had a full and comprehensive View of the State of that Province, to have watched the Motions in every Part, or concerted his Measures with any System.

3. We have never had any regular Returns of Men, Arms, Cannon, Ammunition, Cloathing, Provisions, Money, or any Thing else.

4. We have never had a Commissary, Muster Master, Quarter Master, Principal, Deputy, or assistant, who has faithfully done his Duty.

5. We have never had Intelligence of the Truth of Facts, nor true Information concerning the Characters of officers or Men, every new Person from Canada, having generally contradicted the whole Story in every particular, of him who came before, both with respect to Men and Things, Characters and Facts.

6. The Want of Physicians, Surgeons, Apothecaries, Medicines, amputating and trepanning Instruments, has been a great Misfortune to the sick and wounded and discouragement to the Army.

7. Our Inability to procure hard Money for the Service in that Country, has impaired our Credit with the Canadians, and prevented our officers and Men from procuring such Articles of Cloathing, Provisions and other necessaries as were wanted.

8. The Small Pox, an unexpected Enemy, and more terrible than British Troops, Indians, or even Tories, invaded our Armies and defeated them more than once.

I believe you will think, Sir, that I have enumerated Causes enough to account without Recourse to any Thing more extraordinary, for all the Disasters in that Province.[2]

LB (MHi).

[1] Samuel Cooper's May 27 letter to Adams is in the Adams Papers, MHi.

[2] Adams' letterbook also contains the following fragment of an unfinished letter that he began this day. "The Intelligence from Canada is very discouraging. Every thing is in Confusion there. Men discontented, dispirited, naked, starved, Officers chagrined. Canadians disappointed, and intimidated. Commissioners not very judicious, or penetrating, haughty and condescending. Rather Men of Dissipation than Business." Adams to Unknown, June 9, 1776, ibid.

John Adams to William Cushing

Dear Sir   Philadelphia June 9. 1776

I had, yesterday, the Honour of your Letter of the 20th of May, and I read it, with all that Pleasure, which We feel on the Revival of an old Friendship when We meet a Friend, whom, for a long Time We have not Seen.[1]

You do me great Honour, Sir, in expressing a Pleasure at my appointment to the Bench; [2] but be assured that no Circumstance relating to that Appointment has given me so much concern, as my being placed at the Head of it, in Preference to another, who in my opinion was so much better qualified for it, and intituled to it. I did all in my Power to have it otherwise but was told that our Sovereign Lords the People must have it so.

When, or where, or how, the Secret Imagination Seized you, as you say it did, heretofore, that I was destined to that Place, I cant conjecture: nothing, I am Sure, was further from my Thoughts, or Wishes.

I am not a little chagrined that Sargeant has declined, having entertained great Hopes, from his Solid Judgment and extensive Knowledge. Paine has acted in his own Character, tho scarcely consistent with public Character, which he has been made to wear. At this, however, I am not much mortified, for the Bench will not be the less respectable, for having a little less Wit, Humour, Drollery, or Fun upon it—very different Qualities being requisite in that Department.

Warren has an excellent Head and Heart, and Since the Province cannot be favoured and honoured with the Judgment of regularly educated Lawyers I know not where a better Man could have been found. I hope he will not decline. If he should, I hope that Lovell or Dana will be thought of.

Your Appointment of Mr Winthrop,[3] whose Experience will be usefull in that Station and whose Conduct and Principles have deserved it, was undoubtedly very right and cannot fail to give universal satisfaction.

You shall have my hearty Concurrence in telling the Jury, the Nullity of Acts of Parliament, whether We can prove it by the Jus Gladii or not.

I am determined to live and die of that opinion, let the Jus Gladii say what it will. The System and Rules of the Common Law, must be adopted, I suppose, untill the Legislature shall make Alterations in Either, and how much Soever, I may, heretofore have found fault with the Powers that were, I suppose I shall now be well pleased to hear Submission inculcated to the Powers that be— because they are ordained for good.

It would give me great Pleasure to ride this Eastern Circuit with you, and prate before you at the Bar, as I used to do. But I am destined to another Fate, to Drudgery of the most wasting, exhausting, consuming Kind, that I ever went through in my whole Life. Objects of the most Stupendous Magnitude, Measures in which the Lives and Liberties of Millions, born & unborn are most essentially interested, are now before Us. We are in the very midst of a Revolution, the most compleat, unexpected, and remarkable of any in the History of Nations. A few Matters must be dispatched before I can return. Every Colony must be induced to institute a perfect Government. All the Colonies must confederate together, in some Solemn Compact. The Colonies must be declared free and independent States, and Embassadors must be Sent abroad to foreign Courts, to solicit their Acknowledgment of Us, as Sovereign States, and to form with them, at least with some of them commercial Treaties of Friendship and Alliance. When these Things shall be once well finished, or in a Way of being so, I shall think that I have answered the End of my Creation, and sing with Pleasure my Nunc Dimittis, or if it should be the Will of Heaven that I should live a little longer, return to my Farm and Family, ride Circuits, plead Law, or judge Causes, just as you please.

The Rumours you heard of a Reinforcement in Canada, and those you must have heard before now of many Disasters there, are but too true. Canada has been neglected too much, to my infinite Grief and Regret, and against all the Remonstrances and Entreaties, which could be made. This has been owing to Causes, which it would tire you to read, if I was at Liberty to explain them. However nothing on the Part of your Delegates will be wanting, to secure, with the Blessing of Heaven, a Redress of Fortune there. Dunmore is fled to an Island, having left behind him in their Graves most of his Negroes, and abandoned his Entrenchments in the Main. Our little fleet has had a shocking sickness, which has disabled so many Men, that the Commodore has sent out, on a Cruise two of his ships only. The Difficulty of defending so extended a Sea Coast is prodigious, but the Spirit of the People is very willing, and they exert themselves nobly in most Places. The British Men of War are distressed for Provisions and even for Water, almost every where. They have no Comfort in any Part of America.

My good Genius whispers me very often that I shall enjoy many agreable Hours with you, but Fortune often disappoints the Hopes which this Genius inspires. Be this as it may, while at a distance I shall ever be happy to receive a Line from you. Should be much obliged to you, for some Account of occurrences in your Eastern Circuit. Remember me, with every Sentiment of Respect to the Bench, the Bar, and all other Friends. I have the Honour to be with very great Respect, your affectionate Friend, and very humble servant,   John Adams

RC (MHi).
[1] William Cushing (1732/33–1810), a Scituate and Pownalborough, Mass., lawyer, was appointed in 1772 to the Massachusetts Superior Court of Judicature on which he served as chief justice from 1777 until he was named to the United States Supreme Court in 1789. Shipton, *Harvard Graduates*, 13:26–39; and *DAB*. Cushing's May 20 letter to Adams is in the Adams Papers, MHi.
[2] That is, the Massachusetts Superior Court of Judicature.
[3] Samuel Winthrop, who was appointed clerk of the Massachusetts Superior Court. See Adams to John Winthrop, May 6, 1776, note 1.

John Adams to James Warren

June 9. 1776

I shall address this to you as Speaker, but you may be Councillor, or Governor, or Judge, or any other Thing, or nothing but a good Man, for what I know. Such is the Mutability of this World.

Upon my Word I think you use the World very ill, to publish and send abroad a Newspaper, since the 29 May without telling Us one Word about the Election—where it was held—who preached the sermon—or &c &c.

I write this in haste only to inclose to you a little Treatise upon Fire ships [1]—it may be sending Coals to New Castle—But it appears to me of such Importance that I thought my self bound to procure and send it least this Art should not be understood among you. This Art carries Terror and Dismay along with it, and the very Rumour of Preparations in this Kind may do you more service than many Battallions.

I am not easy about Boston, and have taken all the Pains in my Power with G. Washington, to engage him to send G[ates] and M[ifflin] there, but he is so sanguine and confident that no Attempt will be made there that I am afraid his security will occasion one.

[*P.S.*] The News Papers inclosed, when you have read them, please to send them to the Foot of Penns Hill.[2]

RC (MHi). In Adams' hand, though not signed.
  [1] Presumably a copy of a five-page treatise, bearing the heading "To prepare a Fireship," which Adams copied in his letterbook immediately preceding this letter to Warren. Adams Papers, MHi.
  [2] That is, to Abigail Adams.

Samuel Adams to Horatio Gates

My dear sir   Philade June 10 1776
  Your Favor of the 8th Instant was brought to me by Express.[1] I am exceedingly concernd that a General officer is not yet fixed upon to take the Command of the Troops in Boston. Ever since the Enemy abandond that place I have been apprehensive that a renewed Attack would probably be made on some part of Massachusetts Bay. Your Reasons clearly show that it will be the Interest of the Enemy to make a grand push there if they are not properly provided for a Defence. Congress judgd it necessary that a Major & Brig Genl should be sent to Boston or they would not have orderd it three Weeks ago. The wish of the Colony with regard to particular Gentlemen has been repeatedly urgd, and I thought that an appointment which has been made since you left us would have given a favorable Issue to our request. The Necessity of *your* taking the Command in the Eastern District immediately has been in my mind most pressing since I have been informd by your Letter that your Intelligence in respect to the attack on the Massachusetts is direct & positive.[2]
  It will be a great Disappointment to me if General Mifflin does not go with you to Boston. I believe that to prevent the apparent necessity for this, Genl Whitcomb was thrown into View. He is indeed in many respects a good Man, but to the other I think the preference must be given.
  The Hint you gave me when I last saw you respecting the Enemies offers to treat, I have revolved in my Mind. It is my opinion that no such offers will be made but with a Design to take advantage by the Delay they may occasion. We know how easily our people, too many of them, are still amusd with vain hopes of Reconciliation. Such Ideas will, no doubt, be thrown out to them, to embarrass the Army as others have been; but I conceive that the General in Whose Wisdom & Valor I confide, will, without Hesitation employ all his Force to annoy & conquer immediately upon the Enemies Approach. We want our most stable Counsellors here. To send Gentlemen of *indecisive* Judgments to assist as field Deputies

would answer a very ill purpose. The sole Design of the Enemy is to subjugate America, I have therefore no Conception that any terms can be offerd but such as must be manifestly affrontive. Should those of a different Complexion be proposd, under the hand of their Commanding officer, the General will have the oppty. of giving them in to Congress in the space of a Day. This I imagine he will think it prudent to do. At the same time, I am very sure, he will give no Advantage to the Enemy, and that he will conduct our affairs in so critical a Moment in a Manner worthy of himself.

I am affectionately yours,   S A

FC (NN).
[1] Gates' letter to Adams of June 8, 1776, is in the Samuel Adams Papers, NN.
[2] Despite Adams' hopes, Congress decided on June 17 to appoint Gates to command the army in Canada. Artemas Ward remained in command of the Continental forces in Massachusetts. See JCC, 5:448; John Hancock to Artemas Ward, April 26, note 2; and Massachusetts Delegates to George Washington, May 16, 1776.

Josiah Bartlett to John Langdon

Dear Sir,   Philadelphia June 10th 1776.

Your's of the 27th ulto is come to hand and am glad to hear you have had so good luck in building and launching the ship; [1] I hope she will prove as good a ship as any of her bigness in the British Navy. Capt Thompson is appointed to the command of her, the other officers are not yet appointed. I hope the Captain will set about raising the men and that she will be fitted for sea as soon as possible.

I think with you that the brave Capt Mugford and the men on board the privateers at Boston fought gallantly and did honor to the country; but what shall we think of 500 of our men in Canada surrendering themselves prisoners to about the same number of the enemy. The accounts are very vague but thus much I believe is certain that almost the whole of Col Bedel's regt and 100 men with Major Sherburne of Rhode Island are prisoners to the enemy and by what at present appears surprising surrendered without much resistance, when so large an army of our men were so near to assist them.

It seems as if our men in Canada were struck with a panic. What else could be the reason of their running away from Quebec and leaving their cannon and sick and every thing behind without firing one musket. In short, I could never have believed that our men would be guilty of such conduct; however I hope and believe that when our army come to get settled and the officers and men reflect on what has passed, they will act with more spirit and retrieve their credit; the small pox among them is very frequent and very discouraging for which we must make proper allowance, but the conduct of the hardy sons of New Hampshire is truly mysterious.

You have no doubt heard of the two privateers from this place taking 3 large Jamaica ships very richly loaded. One of them is arrived here, the other two are said to be gone for New England. The cash amounting to 22400 dollars and the plate weighting 180 lb as near as I remember was taken on board the privateers and is safe arrived here. The Liverpool, man of war, lays at the Capes of Deleware and has taken 2, or 3 vessels lately—one with dry goods. I want much to have our ships fitted to drive her off or take her.

I shall enclose you a paper containing the Bill of Rights drawn up by Virginia.[2] You have seen the Virginia Resolves concerning Independence. I wish our Colony would give us Instructions on that head,[3] for whatever may be our private opinions, instructions from the Colony either requiring, or only authorizing us to vote in favor of it, if we should think it for the best would carry great weight with it. The Congress has been so taken up with very important business that the affair of Agency has not been mentioned since my arrival. When it does shall not be wanting in seconding Col Whipple.

By one of the enclosed papers you will see that the Assembly of this Province have given new Instructions to their Delegates.[4]

11th. By a letter just rec'd from Canada [5] it appears that our men had neither provision nor ammunition and that was the cause of their surrendering.

I am Sir, your most humble servant and what is more, Your sincere friend,[6]   Josiah Bartlett

Tr (DLC).
    [1] Langdon's May 27 letter to Bartlett is in Clark, *Naval Documents,* 5:265. See also William Whipple to Langdon, this date.
    [2] A draft of the Virginia declaration of rights, as reported in the Virginia Assembly on May 27, 1776, was printed in the *Pennsylvania Evening Post,* June 6, 1776.
    [3] See New Hampshire Delegates to Meshech Weare, May 28, 1776, note 3.
    [4] The revised instructions to the Pennsylvania delegates were approved by the Pennsylvania Assembly on June 8 and were printed in the *Pennsylvania Evening Post* the same day.
    [5] Probably the June 1 letter of Gen. John Sullivan, which was delivered to Congress on June 11 by Samuel Chase upon his arrival from Canada. See *JCC,* 5:431; and *Am. Archives,* 4th ser. 6:679–80.
    [6] On June 10 Bartlett also wrote a brief personal letter to his wife:
    "Yours of the 23d of May I Recd the 8th inst. and am glad to hear you are all well, that tho Sally has been unwell She is better, that Lieut Bearson is better. May Kind Providence preserve you all in health & safety till my return to you. I have had a very Severe Cold the latter End of last week but am now much better. This is the Sixth letter I have wrote you from this City Since my arrival; my last

was the 6th Inst. by Express to Exeter. I want to know how soon my letters by Newbury port get to you. I am Glad you find an oppertunity to send me a letter Every week; your letters leave Newbury Tuesday afternoon & I Receive them the next Saturday week.

"Last Thursday after Congress, I with 5 or 6 other Delegates walked about a mile & half out of the City to See the Proprietors Gardens. There are a great many Curious trees, Bushes, Plants &c. Among the rest the alois Plant is I think the most Curious. I Cannot Describe it as it is not like any thing I Ever Saw before. There are a number of Sweat & Sower orange trees, Lemmon trees, lime trees & Citron trees; the Same tree had some flowers, some small & some ripe fruit at the same time; the trees are about 8 or ten feet high Set in Boxes of Sand so that they can be removed in Cold weather into a hot house, so that they grow & bear fruit all the year round.

"I Remember my Love to you all & Remain yours &c." Josiah Bartlett to Mary Bartlett, June 10, 1776. Mr. Francis W. Bartlett, Kansas City, Mo.

John Hancock to George Washington

Sir,   Philadelphia June 11th [i.e. 10th] 1776 [1]

I am honoured with your Letters of 7th, 8th and 9th Instant. The two first I have read in Congress.[2] We have been two Days in a Committee of the Whole deliberating on three Capital Matters, the most important in their Nature of any that have yet been before us; & have sat till 7 O'Clock in the Evening each Day. That not being finished I judged best to return the Express. I shall press Congress as soon as possible to determine upon the several Matters you wish to be ascertained, and immediately transmit you the Result.

The Congress have agreed to settle the Mode of paying the Troops in the Eastern Department this Morning, and to proceed to the Appointment of a Deputy Paymaster General.[3]

The particular Mode of establishing Expresses is now under the Consideration of a Committee, and as soon as agreed, you shall know the Issue.

Altho Congress have not acted upon your Queries respecting the Indians, yet I will venture to give my opinion that Congress intended the Resolution of 25 May should be general and extend to the several Departments, and that the Resolution of 3d June goes only to the Number which the General shall be empowered to employ in Canada.[4] But I hope soon to give you a full Answer to all your Queries; and in future I will exert myself in Congress that your Applications may be considered as soon as received, and you punctually and regularly informed of the Result.

Inclosed you have a Resolve, whereby you will see, that all the Troops in the Middle Department are put upon the same Pay 6 2/3 Dollars as the Troops in the Eastern Department.[5]

I have sent you four Bundles of Commissions and will forward you more by next opportunity.

The enclosed from Mrs. Washington I wish [safe] to Hand. I have the Pleasure to acquaint you [she] is in fine Spirits and proposes paying you a [Visit] next Week. I sent her your Letter by the Express; and when you write, if you will please to put the Letter under my Cover, I will immediately deliver it.

I have the Honour to be with every Sentiment that Respect & Esteem inspire, Sir, your very hbe Sevt.

John Hancock Presidt

RC (DLC). In the hand of Jacob Rush and signed by Hancock.

[1] Both the location of this letter in Hancock's letterbook and his assertion that "this Morning" Congress resolved the issue "of paying the Troops in the Eastern Department" and decided to take up the question of appointing a deputy paymaster general indicate that he wrote this letter on June 10, not June 11. See *JCC*, 5:428.

[2] See *JCC*, 5:427. These letters are in PCC, item 152, 2:5–12, 17–20, and Washington, *Writings* (Fitzpatrick), 5:103–5, 107–9, 111–14.

[3] See *JCC*, 5:428; and Hancock to Ebenezer Hancock, June 13, 1776.

[4] See *JCC*, 4:395, 412; and Washington, *Writings* (Fitzpatrick), 5:108. For an explanatory resolution on the employment of Indians by Washington, which Congress passed on June 17, see *JCC*, 5:452.

[5] See *JCC*, 5:428.

Marine Committee to Lambert Wickes

Sir,   Philada June 10th 1776

We have received your Letter of the 6th & approve your Proceedings as therein represented & as you seem very desirous to make a Cruize, we have this day agreed to give up the Direction of the Ship Reprisal to a Committee of Congress, stiled the Committee of secret Correspondence. The Members are Benj Harrison, Benj Franklin, John Jay, John Dickinson, Thos Johnston & Robert Morris Esqrs, any three of them are a quorum.

This Committee are directed to dispatch one of our Cruizers to the West Indies & we understand they have already given the needfull Orders to Capt Wm Hallock of the Sloop Hornet, from whom we have just received Advice that Said Sloop is leaky & unfit to proceed on that Voyage. For this Reason your Ship is assign'd for that Service & you are hereby directed to receive from Capt Hallock the Letters & orders of Said Committee; Consider them as directed to yourself & obey them in every Particular.[1]

We hope this Voyage will afford you an opportunity of rendering essential Service to your Country & that you will bring us back a Parcell of fine Seamen & a Number of good Prizes.

A Supply of stores will be Sent you by the Wasp & we are, Sir,
Your hble Servts,

	John Hancock	Jona Sargeant
signed	Richd Henry Lee	Joseph Hewes
	Step Hopkins	George Read
		Wm Whipple

Tr (DNA: PCC, item 37).

[1] The Marine Committee's orders were delivered to Lambert Wickes by William Bingham, who was ordered this day by the Committee of Secret Correspondence to "take your Passage for Martinico on board the *Reprisal*." Clark, *Naval Documents*, 5:454. For Wickes' June 16 reply to the Marine Committee see ibid., p. 569. Wickes (1735?–77), a Kent Co., Md., ship captain, had received command of the Continental armed ship *Reprisal* in April 1776. After taking three prizes and repelling a British attack off Martinique, he returned in September with powder and muskets. In October 1776 he carried Benjamin Franklin to France, and during 1777 he took numerous prizes along the English and Irish coasts before his ship was lost in a storm off Newfoundland in October 1777. *DAB*.

William Whipple to John Langdon

My Dear Sir,   Philadelphia 10th June 1776

Your favor of the 27th May came duly to hand.[1] I heartily condole with you the loss of the brave Mugford, however we must submit to the divine will and rest assured that whatever is ordered by Providence is right. I have the pleasure to tell you, that Capt Thompson's appointment is confirmed by Congress; his commission will be sent him very soon. As he is appointed, he may with propriety join you in conferring with proper persons for Lieutenants and Marine officers, which I hope you will do and let me know who will accept those commissions. I have sometime ago given you my opinion of those you have mentioned; you may engage the master and other officers when ever you think it necessary; as I have before told you, it is very uncertain when you'll have the guns unless you can get them at Providence. I shall send you the blank warrants so soon as I can get them but I imagine the old forms will undergo a revisal. Congress never were so much engaged as at this time; business presses on them exceedingly. We do not rise some times till 6 or 7 o'clock—there is so many irons in the fire I fear some of them will burn. I congratulate you on the success you have had in building and launching the *Rawleigh*. I proposed her being called the New Hampshire, but could not obtain my wish; however I think this name will do very well. The name of every martyr to liberty ought to be perpetuated and then this name is in some measure a compliment to Virginia who you know is entitled to compliments from New England. I have done every thing in my power to forward the business of this ship, but I need not tell you how heavily business goes on here.

The matter of Agency, I have not had an opportunity to urge with a prospect of success; it therefore remains as it did, but hope it won't be long before there will be a fair opportunity; I shall still persist in my first proposal. The uncertainty of guns is the only reason you have not orders to ship men but as the Committee meets this evening I will endeavor once more to know their minds on this subject.

We have dismal accounts from Canada: 500 men taken by the enemy who consisted of about 40 regulars, 250 Canadians and 400 Indians. How so large a number as 500 could be taken by about 7 is very unaccountable, but so it is though we have no particular accounts how it happened. When the last express came off, General Arnold was near the enemy with about 1000 men—some messages had passed between him and a Capt Foster who commanded the party. Arnold was threatened if he attacked them they would murder all the prisoners. I am fearful his humanity got the better of his judgment. I hope shall be able to give you a more particular account of this affair before I close this.

One of the Jamaica ships taken by the Privateers from this place is arrived here; the other two have not yet been heard of. The money viz 20,000 dolls. is also in this city. Congress did not rise till 7 o'clock which prevented the Committee from meeting last evening. No accounts from Canada since the above. You say you want to be here for a short time; I hope you'll let me know about 2 or 3 weeks before you set out, that I may meet you half way. I hope my next will give some accounts more pleasing than is in my power at this time.

I am respectfully, yours,   W Whipple

[P.S.] I write to Col Weare by this post.[2] I shall be much obliged if you'll press an immediate answer. Col Bartlett sends you news papers.[3] I have had your carriage cleaned—it was in a dirty pickle— when I can spare time shall exercise it a little. I hope shall have it in my power to give you some agreeable tidings in two or three weeks.

W. W.

Tr (DLC).
    [1] An extract of Langdon's May 27 letter to Whipple is in Clark, *Naval Documents*, 5:264–65.
    [2] See New Hampshire Delegates to Meshech Weare, June 11, 1776.
    [3] See Josiah Bartlett to John Langdon, this date, notes 2 and 4.

Elbridge Gerry to James Warren

My Dear Sir,   Philadelphia, June 11, 1776.

Yesterday after a long debate the question of independence was postponed until the first July,[1] in order to give the assemblies of the middle colonies an opportunity to take off their restrictions and let their delegates unite in the measure. In the interim will go on plans for confederation and foreign alliance.[2]

If these slow people had hearkened to reason in time, this work would have long ere now been completed, and the disadvantage arising from the want of such measures been wholly avoided; but Providence has undoubtedly wise ends in coupling together the vigorous and the indolent; the first are retarded, but the latter are urged on, and both come together to the goal.

To the obstructions in council are owing in part our military misfortunes, which, however, we must use as fresh incitements to greater exertions.

Your sincere friend,   E. Gerry.

MS not found; reprinted from Austin, *Life of Gerry*, 1:191–92.

[1] See *JCC*, 5:428–29.

[2] Both the committee "to prepare and digest the form of a confederation" and the committee "to prepare a plan of treaties to be proposed to foreign powers" were appointed on June 12, 1776. *JCC*, 5:433.

Elbridge Gerry to John Wendell

Dear sir [1]   Philadelphia 11th June 1776

I recd. your Favours of the 21st & 27th May & Am obliged to You for the Intelligence therein contained; [2] It will afford me Pleasure to continue the Correspondence proposed, & from being apprized of the political Movements in your Colony as well as the principles productive of the same, I doubt not that Oppertunities will frequently offer of touching upon some thing that will add Harmony to the common Cause.

I agree with You with Respect to some Inconveniences that will arise from opening our Ports & am persuaded that had they continued open thro the Winter & been closed in the Spring a much larger Supply of Arms & Ammunition would have been introduced into the Colonies & less Advantages have been derived to the Enemy by Captures; but as it has happened the matter has been veiwed in a different light, & the Restrictions on Trade have been so pressingly felt by the Merchants & Farmers in the southern Colonies that it became necessary to adopt this Measure of opening the ports to quiet their Minds: notwithstanding which I believe little Trade will be carried on, unless in armed Vessels, untill it shall be better protected. With Respect to the French Nation their Interest seems to be connected with that of the Colonies under the present Situation of the latter, for if France can avail herself of their Trade It will greatly add to her Resources while G Britain's are proportionably weakened, & if she ever expects to rise superior to the latter there cannot be a more favourable Oppertunity for effecting it than is furnished by the present Contest. Great Care is certainly to be taken by the Colonies in forming such an Alliance, but so long as it is confined to Commerce & they grant only their Trade for a protection thereof, there cannot be Danger arising from the Connection, but, as it appears to me, there will be all the probability of immediately engaging France in a Rupture wth Britain, by which Means a Diversion will be made to her Arms in Europe & such a War carried on as will be most for the Interest of the Colonies.

I have attended to your Desire relative to the [. . .]³ It must be by your Brother Mr Wendell who is the present Agent in the Colony. In Massachusetts Bay the [. . . ,] but whether any provision is made in New Hampshire You can best determine; if not & the [. . .] is under the Direction of the Agent, Mr. Wendell. It must be [. . .] for the Congress have in most of the Colonies Agents of their own appointment, who were nominated agreable to order by the Marine Committee, but Mr. Langdon having been nominated for Portsmouth & an objection made on Account of his being a Member of Congress, the place is not yet filled from the Want of Oppertunity, & I think of Consequence Mr. Wendell continues their Agent untill a new appointment takes place. I see no objection to his Reappointment.

Our Affairs in Canada are at present unfortunate. I have never liked their appearance since my Arrival here & hope that a favourable Change will take place, but however it may happen We must use Misfortune as a Stimulus to new & greater Exertions.

I observe you have begun to Speculate in the papers & think You have made a good Exordium: I hope You will go on & successfully finish the Theme. The paper will undoubtedly prove a good one but the printers in our own Colony & this City generally furnish Us with One or two a Day which are as many as We can well peruse.

I observe what You hint relative to my Brother J.G.⁴ & shall attend thereto.

Pray inform Doctor Jackson that in April last I sent him by Mr Tileston of Boston 130 Dollars granted by Congress & shall be glad to know whether he has received it.

My Complimts to Miss Sally & all Friends & beleive me sir your sincere Freind & huml sert,   Elbridge Gerry

P.S. I hope soon to see your Colony following the others in declaring for Independence.

RC (PHi).
¹ John Wendell (1731–1808), although a native of Boston, had established himself as a merchant in Portsmouth, N.H. Shipton, *Harvard Graduates*, 12:592–97.
² A photostat of Wendell's letter of May 27 is in the Gerry Papers, DLC.
³ More than two dozen words have been inked out in the first half of this paragraph, which deals with Wendell's request for Gerry's support in securing his appointment as vendue master for New Hampshire to serve under his brother-in-law, Joshua Wentworth. When Wentworth, who was appointed provincial prize agent by General Washington, was replaced by John Langdon, Wendell's request became a dead issue. See ibid.; and Marine Committee to the Prize Agents appointed by George Washington, October 18, 1776, in Clark, *Naval Documents*, 6:1322–23.
⁴ In his May 27 letter, Wendell had commented that "I think the Disappointment that Brother J[ohn] Gerry mett with in his Regiment has been a Damage to him as it has soured & chagrined him, I hope you will find an Opening to provide for him, He is a Man of Discernment and good Conduct & wd make an Excellent Officer." Wendell to Gerry, May 27, 1776, Gerry Papers, DLC.

John Hancock to Certain Colonies

Gentlemen,   Philada. June 11th, 1776.
The Congress have this Day received Advices, and are fully convinced, that it is the Design of Genl. Howe to make an Attack upon the City of New York as soon as possible. The Attack, they have Reason to believe, will be made within ten Days. I am therefore most earnestly to request you, by Order of Congress, to call forth your Militia as requested in my Letter of the 4th Inst. and to forward them with all Dispatch to the City of New York; and that you direct them to march in Companies, or in any other Way, that will hasten their Arrival there.[1]

The important Day is at Hand, that will decide not only the Fate of the City of New York, but in all Probability, of the whole Province. On such an Occasion there is no Necessity to use Arguments with Americans. Their Feelings, I well know, will prompt them to their Duty, and the Soundness of the Cause, urge them to the Field.

The greatest Exertions of Vigour & Expedition are requisite to prevent our Enemies from getting Possession of that Town. I must therefore again most earnestly request you, in the Name and by the Authority of Congress, to employ every Mode in your Power, to send forward the Militia agreeably to the Requisition of Congress; and that you will do it with all the Dispatch which the infinite Importance of the Cause demands.

I have the Honour to be, Gentlemen, your most obed. & very hble Sert.   J. H. Prest.

LB (DNA: PCC, item 12A). Addressed: "The Assembly of Massachusetts Bay. The Assembly of Connecticut. The Convention of New York. The Convention of New Jersey."
[1] See *JCC*, 5:431.

John Hancock to the New York Convention

Gentlemen,   Philadelphia, June 11th, 1776.
Your Favour by Mr. Governeur Morris I had the Pleasure of receiving yesterday, and immediately laid the same before Congress.

By the inclosed Resolve, which I am commanded to transmit, you will perceive, they have come to a Resolution, that the Pay of the Troops in the Middle and Eastern Departments, shall hereafter be the same.[1]

Altho it is much to be wished, that the Pay of the Eastern Troops could have been reduced, yet as that Measure would naturally give great and general Disgust, and might be attended with the worst Consequences in our present Situation; the Congress chose rather to increase the Pay of the other Troops, than to run the Risque of breaking up the eastern army.

Every state or government should punctually perform the terms of enlistment, on which the soldier enters into service. In this view of the matter, it would have been neither honourable or equitable to have abridged the Pay of the Eastern Troops. Nor can any Reason be urged, why the other Troops, who do the same Duty and are exposed to the same Dangers, should not also receive the same Pay. The particular mode of enlisting the Pennsylvania and York Troops originated with their and your Delegates; and as they moved it, Congress could not but gratify them.

I am extremely happy that any Part of my Conduct should meet with the Approbation of the Convention of New York. I seek only to do my Duty, but find an additional Pleasure, if, in the Discharge of it, I merit the Praise of the worthy and the good. I have the Honour to be, with Respect, Gentlemen, your most obedt. and very hble Servt.   John Hancock Presidt

RC (N). In the hand of Jacob Rush and signed by Hancock. *Journals of the N.Y. Prov. Cong.,* 2:202. RC damaged; missing words supplied from Tr.

[1] Upon receiving Hancock's June 4 letter enclosing resolutions for the employment of 3,750 local militiamen in Canada and New York, the New York Provincial Congress deputed Gouverneur Morris to carry a letter to Philadelphia asking Congress to equalize the pay received by New York and New England troops. This request, which was also supported by Washington, led to the passage of the June 10 resolution on equal pay that Hancock forwarded in this letter. See *JCC,* 5:428; *Am. Archives,* 4th ser. 6:1377–81; Washington, *Writings* (Fitzpatrick), 5:108; and Hancock to Certain Colonies, June 4, 1776.

John Hancock to George Washington

Sir,   Philadelphia June 11th. 1776.
Your Favour of the 10th Inst containing the most interesting Intelligence was received this Day, and immediately laid before Congress.

In Order to expedite the March of the Militia destined for New York, I have sent, by Order of Congress, Expresses to the several Colonies that are requested to furnish Troops for that Place. Copies of my Letters on the Occasion, I do myself the Pleasure to enclose to you.

I am in Hopes, the alarming Situation of Affairs will induce the neighbouring Colonies to think of their Danger, and to adopt the only effectual Means of saving themselves from Destruction.

The Congress have this Day ordered Colonels Shee and Magaw with their Battalions to repair immediately to New York, and they are to begin their March tomorrow.[1]

Mr. Chace & Mr Carrol arriv'd this Day, by their Accott. there has been most shocking mismanagement in that Quarter. I hope our Affairs will soon be upon a more reputable footing.

I have the honour to be with Esteem, Sir, Your most Obedt Servt.
John Hancock Presidt

[*P.S.*] Please to order the two Letters for the Convention of New York to be Deliver'd.

RC (DLC). In the hand of Jacob Rush, with last two paragraphs, signature, and postscript by Hancock.
[1] See *JCC*, 4:431; and Washington, *Writings* (Fitzpatrick), 5:121.

Francis Lewis to Nathaniel Shaw, Jr.

Dr Sir,   Phila. 11th June 1776
We have this day per Post received a Letter from Mr. John Warder dated the 5 Inst advising that Capt. Serley of the Sloop Lucretia was so very Ill, that there was little probability of his proceeding on his Voyage. Should that be the case upon receipt of this as we learn that the Coast is clear we must beg you would endeavor to procure another Master and forward the Vessell with the utmost dispatch as she has a Valuable Cargo for Account of the Congress.[1] We are, Sir, your very Humble Servts,   Frans Lewis

RC (CtY). Written on behalf of the Marine Committee.
[1] Shaw, the Continental prize agent in Connecticut, subsequently informed Lewis, a member of the Marine Committee, "that Capt Serley has so farr Recovrd

his Health that [he] will Proceede in the Sloop as Soon as their is any Probability of Getting out." Clark, *Naval Documents*, 5:625–26; and *JCC*, 4:301.

Maryland Delegates to the Maryland Council of Safety

Gentlemen.   Phila. June 11th. 1776. Tuesday.

We have received your Letter by Mr Steward,[1] Also that by the Post of the 7th of this month.[2] We have confered with Mr Steward, assisted him in Changing his provincial Money for Continental and procured a recommendation from Mr Morris to those who have been concerned in fitting out the Gallies here to give him all the Information in their power respecting them. We shall make Application for the Arms lent the Congress but We do not see any probability of obtaining them, none having been made or having arrived but what were immediately disposed of among the Continental Troops. It seems to be taken for granted that our Province will not be attacked, and upon this Supposition We presume it will be thought unnecessary to strengthen Us even by returning the Warlike Stores which we lent when the Scheme for marching the Militia was agitated. We informed Congress of the Circumstances of our Province and of the Impossibility of marching the Militia out of the Province without their Consent; however our Quota for the flying Camp was struck at 3,400 as you will see by the resolve inclosed by the President, but it was not understood that the Militia were to be drafted or compelled to march.[3] And it is left altogether at large how they are to be collected. Some additions to the Resolutions on that Subject are talked of but not formally proposed. We are astonished at the ungenerous and malevolent Turn given to the Proceedings of our convention by that of Virginia—And hope they will be as unsuccessfull in their nefarious Attempt to stir up the People of Maryland against their representatives as they have hitherto been in their Endeavours to render the Councils of that Province suspected. We are excedingly sorry to observe this unfriendly Disposition in a Neighbouring Sister Colony, but hope there will be found spirit enough in the Convention of Maryland to resent this most nefarious Treatment in the Manner it deserves.

The Proposition from the Delegates of Virginia to declare the Colonies independent was yesterday after much Debate postponed for three Weeks, then to be resumed, and a Committee is appointed to draw up a Declaration to prevent Loss of time in Case the Congress should agree to the Proposition at the day fixed for resuming it. This postpone was made to give an Oppertunity to the Delegates from those Colonies, which had not as yet given Authority to adopt this decisive Measure, to consult their Constituents; it will be necessary that the Convention of Maryland should meet as soon as possible to give the explicit Sense of the Province on this Point. And we hope you will accordingly exercise your Power of convening them at such Time as you think the members can be brought together.[4] We wish to have the fair and uninfluenced Sense of the People we have the Honour to represent in this most important and interesting Affair And think it would be well if the Delegates to Convention were desired to endeavour to collect the opinion of the people at large in some Manner or other previous to the Meeting of Convention. We shall attend the Convention whenever it meets if it is thought proper we should do so. The approaching Harvest will perhaps render it very inconvenient to many Gentlemen to attend the Convention; This however must not be regarded when matters of such momentous Concern demand their deliberation. We beg you will inform Us as soon as may be of the Time you fix for the Convention to meet, and We should also be very glad to receive the Proceedings of the last session. We see with the deepest Concern the Attempts from various Quarters to throw the Province into a State of Confusion, Division & Disorder but trust the Exertions of those who are the true friends of Virtue & the American Cause will be adequate to the surrounding Difficulties & Dangers. From every Account and Appearance the King and his Ministers seem determined to hazard every thing upon the Success of the Sword; with out offering any Terms to America which she ought to accept. That Peace & Security which every virtuous man in this Country has so earnestly desired seems not attainable in the present disposition of the ruling powers of Britain. We wish we had any reason to suppose there was any foundation for what Mr Smith reports to have been told him by Capt Hammond & Ld Dunmore, but all Circumstances strongly oppose the Supposition of Commissioners, as Messengers of Peace. However we know not more of this matter than you & the publick do and it is impossible to speak certainly upon this or any other Subject without more full Information than we have. We will send the Gun Carriage, Instruments & paper by Mr Steward who informs us he has sundry Articles for the Province to be sent from hence. We begg to be informed frequently of the State of the Province and of your Proceedings: And assure you of our readiness to attend your Commands. Our hurry and necessary Attendance in Congress must apologize for this Scrawl. The Question for postponing the Declaration of Independence was carried by seven Colonies against five. We are with great Respect, Gent., Yr most Obt Sevts.

Mat. Tilghman

T. Stone

J. Rogers

RC (MdAA). Written by Stone and signed by Stone, Rogers, and Tilghman.
    [1] See *Md. Archives,* 11:458–59.
    [2] Undoubtedly the letter printed under the date June 8, 1776, in ibid., pp. 470–71.
    [3] See *JCC,* 4:412–13. The resolves pertaining to the mobilization of the militia were transmitted in Hancock's circular letter of June 4, 1776, and were received by the Maryland Council on June 9. Believing their authority "not being competent to order the marching of our militia out of the Province," the council immediately called a meeting of the Maryland Convention, which passed a series of resolutions on the subject on June 25. See John Hancock to Certain Colonies, June 4, 1776; *Md. Archives,* 11:474–75; and *Am. Archives,* 4th ser. 6:1487–89.
    [4] The delegates did not know, of course, that the council had already decided to convene the convention upon receipt of the resolves of June 3–4 pertaining to the militia, and consequently they discussed the matter again in their letter of June 15 after receiving notification from the council. See Maryland Delegates to the Maryland Council of Safety, June 15, 1776.

New Hampshire Delegates to Meshech Weare

Sir,   Philadelphia 11th June 1776
    We some time ago signified our wish, to know the sentiments of our Colony respecting Independence,[1] the Question has been agitated in Congress, a Resolution pass'd Yesterday,[2] to chose a Committee to prepare & bring in a Declaration for that purpose, on the first of July, by which time it is expected that all the Delegates who have not already been instructed will receive ample Powers. As this is a Subject of the greatest importance, we beg we may be furnish'd with the Sentiments of our Constituents as we wish to Act agreeable to them let our own be what they may. We shall be in full expectation of an answer by the return of post. We have the Honour to be, Your Most Obt Serts.   Josiah Bartlett

                                                            Wm. Whipple

RC (DLC). Written by Whipple and signed by Whipple and Bartlett.
    [1] See New Hampshire Delegates to Meshech Weare, May 28, 1776, note 3.
    [2] See *JCC,* 5:428–29; and Thomas Jefferson's Notes of Debates, June 7–28, 1776.

Oliver Wolcott to Laura Wolcott

My Dear,   Philidelpa. 11 June 1776
    I Wrote to you the 25 last and 1 instant which I hope you have recd., since which I recd. a Letter from Mr. Lyman of the 1 inst. by which I had the Very agreable news of your own and the Familys Wellfare. You Wrote to me for a piece of Linnen, which I have desired Capt Sheldon who is now here to procure. He has tryed but says it is scarcly to be had, which I easily beleive as I have for

some months understood that there was scarcly a piece to be had in this City, but shall endeavour to procure some for you as also some Handkercheifs, tho the scarcity and Dearness of those Articles are in the extreme. Other Articles at least Many are in more Plenty but every Thing bears an extravigant Price. I hope next Winter when our Coast cannot be so infested by Pirates Goods may be had in more plenty. I have just now recd. a Letter from Oliver. He tells me he is well, and has such Lodging as he thinks I shall approve of.

We expect dayly to hear further from our Enymies—they will give us what trouble they can this Summer. A Requisition of the Militia has been made to our Colony, I think much too large and what I apprehend cannot be complyed with. We seem at present to be in the midst of a great Revolution, which I hope God will carry us safe thro with. Pensilvania Assembly last Saturday rescinded their Instructions to their Delegates, and they now say that they expect No Reconciliation.[1] Much Wisdom and Firmness are requisite to conduct the Various and most important Matters which are necessary to be determined upon. This year will probably be productive of great and most interesting Consequences. And my Wish is that the Supreme Ruler of the Universe would guide every publick Measure.

By the Blessing of God I injoy Health which demands my Gratitude. The Service is hard, and affords but little Time for Excercise, but I hope before next month is out to be upon my Return to my Family whom I do most sincerely Desire to see. My best Regards to my Friends, such of them as have favoured me with their Letters shall acknowledge. I hope they will continue the same friendly Correspondence. My Love to my Children and Family, and Accept the tender Regards of him who always esteemed himself happy in your Affection.   Oliver Wolcott

RC (CtHi).
[1] See Delegates Certification of James Wilson's Conduct in Congress, June 20, 1776, note 3.

John Adams to Oakes Angier

Dear Sir   Philadelphia June 12, 1776
It was with great Pleasure, and perhaps some little Mixture of Pride, that I read your Name among the Representatives of Bridgwater, in the Boston Gazette.[1] I rejoiced to find that your Townsmen had so much Confidence in your Abilities and Patriotism, and that you had so much Confidence in the Justice of our Cause, and the Abilities of America to support it, as to embark your Fortune in it.

Your Country never Stood so much in need of Men of clear Heads and Steady Hearts to conduct her Affairs. Our civil Governments

as well as military Preparations want much Improvement, and to this
End a most vigilant Attention, as well as great Patience, Caution,
Prudence and Firmness are necessary.

You will excuse the Freedom of a Friend, when I tell you, that
I have never entertained any doubt that your political Principles and
public Affections corresponded with those of your Country. But you
know that Jealousies and Suspicions have been entertained & propa-
gated concerning you. These Jealousies arose, I am well perswaded
from an unreserved Freedom of Conversation, and a social Disposition, a little addicted to disputation, which was sometimes perhaps
incautiously indulged. Your present Situation, which is conspicious
and not only exposed to observation but to Misconstruction and
Misrepresentation, will make it necessary for you to be upon your
Guard.

Let me recommend to you, an observation, that one of my Colleagues is very fond of, "The first Virtue of a Politician is Patience;
the second is Patience; and the third is Patience." As Demosthenes
observed that Action was the first, second, and third Qualities of an
orator.

You will experience in public Life such violent, sudden, and unexpected Provocations, and Disappointments, that if you are not
now possessed of all the Patience of Job, I would advise you to acquire
it, as soon as possible. News, I can tell you none. I have written to
Coll Warren, Mr Sewall, and Mr Lowell, a few broken Hints, upon
subjects which I wish you would turn your Thoughts to. Be so good
as to write me, any Remarkables in the Legislature, or the Courts of
Justice. I am your Friend

LB (MHi).
    [1] Oakes Angier (1745–86), a Bridgewater, Mass., lawyer and former law clerk of
John Adams, had recently been elected to the first of four terms that he served in
the Massachusetts House of Representatives. Shipton, *Harvard Graduates*, 16:5–7.

John Adams to John Lowell

Dear Sir.[1]   Philadelphia June 12. 1776
    Yesterdays Post brought me a Newspaper of the 3d Inst, containing
a List of your House, and Board, and upon my Word I read it with
more Pleasure than I ever read any other List of the two Houses.
I dont believe the Records of the Province can shew, a more respectable set of Representatives or Councillors. Sergeant, Lowell,
Pickering, Angier are great Acquisitions in the House: so are
Dana, [2] and Sewall at the Board, not to mention many other very
respectable Characters among the new Members of each.

From this Collection of wise and prudent Men, I hope great

Things. I hope that the most vigorous Exertions will be made to put the Province in the best State of Defence. Every Seaport in it, ought to be fortified in Such a Manner that you may sett the Enemy at Defyance. To this End, large additions must be made to the Cannon of the Colony. I wish to know, whether, they are cast, at any Furnace in the Province, if not no Expence I think should be Spared to procure them. They are casting them Successfully in Maryland, Pensylvania, and Rhode Island. Another Article essentially necessary is that of Musquetts. I wish that every Man in the Province who can work about any Part of a Gun or Bayonnett was set to work. No Price should be thought extravagant.

Salt Petre it seems you are in a Way to procure in sufficient Quantities. But Sulphur and Lead I have not yet learnt to be made among you. I hope you will take effectual Measures to make Salt. You must do it. The other Colonies are too lazy and shiftless to do any thing untill you set them the example. The Defence of the Colony is the first object. The Second is the Formation of a Constitution. In this Business, I presume you will proceed Slowly and deliberately. It is a difficult work to atchieve and the Spirit of Levelling, as well as that of Innovation, is afloat. Before I saw, the List of the new Election I was under fearfull Apprehensions I confess. But my Mind is now at Ease, in this Respect. There are So many able Men in each House that I think they will have Influence enough to prevent any dangerous Innovations, and yet to carry any necessary and usefull Improvements.

Some of you must prepare your stomachs to come to Philadelphia. I am weary, and must ask Leave to return to my Family, after a little Time, and one of my Colleagues at least, must do the same, or I greatly fear, do worse. You and I know very well the Fatigues of Practice at the Bar: But I assure you, this incessant Round of thinking and Speaking upon the greatest Subjects that ever employed the Mind of Man, and the most perplexing Difficulties that ever puzzled it, is beyond all Comparison more exhausting and consuming.

Our affairs in Canada are in a confused and disastrous situation. But I hope they will not be worse. We have made large Requisitions upon you. How you can possibly comply with them I know not: but hope you will do as much as you can.

We have no Resource left my Friend, but our own Fortitude, and the Favour of Heaven. If We have the first I have no doubt We shall obtain the last. And these will be Sufficient. All Ideas of Reconciliation, or Accommodation seem to be gone with the years before the Flood.

I have nothing new to communicate, but what is in every Newspaper, and I began this Letter only to make my Compliments to you, and ask the Favour of your Correspondence, but have wandered, I know not whither. It is Time to subscribe myself your Friend & servant

LB (MHi).

[1] John Lowell (1743–1802), a lawyer in Newburyport and Boston, Mass., served several terms in the Massachusetts General Court. Following his election to the Continental Congress in 1782, he was appointed judge of the Confederation Congress' Court of Appeals on Admiralty Cases and subsequently became judge of the United States Court for the District of Massachusetts. Shipton, *Harvard Graduates,* 14:650–61; *DAB.*

[2] Adams also wrote to Francis Dana this day in a similar congratulatory vein, asking to be kept informed of Massachusetts' affairs and hinting at the work about to be undertaken on a declaration of independence. "We have greater things in contemplation than ever; the greatest of all which We ever shall have. Be silent and patient and time will bring forth, after the usual groans, throes, and pains upon such occasions, a fine child." Adams, *Works* (Adams), 9:395–96.

John Adams to David Sewall

Dear Sir   Philadelphia June 12 1776

In the Boston Gazette of the 3d Instant, I have the Pleasure to see your Name among the Councillors,[1] where I have wished to see it, for some Time. That refined Ingenuity and pertinacious Industry, which distinguished my Classmate at Colledge, and my Brother at the Bar, I am sure will be of great service to the Province, at the Councill Board, especially at this Time, when the public Stands so much in Need of the services of her best Men.

Your Mathematical and Philosophical Genius will be agreably entertained with Speculations for the Defence of Plans, and the Fortifications of the Harbours and Seaport Towns.

Let me Suggest to your Consideration two objects of Inquiry; the one is Row Gallies and the other is Fire ships. Row Gallies and Floating Batteries are Engines very formidable to Men of War, because they are so low and small that it is about impossible for a Man of War to bring her Guns to bear upon them so as to do Execution, and the great Weight of Mettal, which is carried by the heavy Cannon, on bord such Gallies and Batteries, tear the Ships to Pieces—and the shot is very sure.

Fire Ships and Rafts are the King of Terrors to Men of War, when so protected by Row Gallies and floating Batteries, that they cannot grapple them and anchor them by Means of their Boats, and Barges. I have inclosed to your excellent Speaker, a little Treatise upon the Art of making the Composition and constructing the Vessells.[2] There seems to be Something infernal in this Art. But our quondam Friend Jonathan used to quote from Mat. Prior "when it is to combat Evil, Tis lawfull to employ the Devil." There is no greater

Evil on Earth or under it than the War that is made upon Us. And
We have a Right, and it is our Duty to defend our selves, by such
Means as We have.

There are such Preparations of Vesseaux de Frizes, Fire Ships,
Fire Rafts, floating Batteries and Row Gallies in Delaware River,
that they would Spread Destruction through any British Fleet, that
should attempt to come up here. I wish that Similar Preparations
were made in every Seaport in the Mass. Bay.

After you have done every Thing that is necessary for the Defence
of the Colony, and her Sisters, I presume you will turn your
Thoughts to the Establishment of a permanent Constitution of civil
Government. The Board is so unwieldy a Body to conduct the Executive Part of Government, productive of so much Delay, and unnecessary Trouble, that you will no doubt, choose a Governor. Will
you give him a Negative upon your Laws, or only make him
Primus inter Pares, at the Board? I suppose the high, free Spirit of
our People will demand the latter. But, I must conclude my Letter,
by requesting the Favour of your Correspondence, and assuring you
that I am with great Esteem, your Friend and humble Servant

LB (MHi).
[1] David Sewall (1735–1825), a York, Mass., lawyer, sat in the Massachusetts
Council, 1776–78, and on the bench of the Massachusetts Superior Court of
Judicature, 1777–89. Shipton, *Harvard Graduates,* 13:638–45.
[2] See John Adams to James Warren, June 9, 1776, note.

Josiah Bartlett's Notes on the Plan of Confederation

[June 12–July 12? 1776] [1]
United Provinces proportion of 100000 Guilders viz.

		s	d
Gelderland	3612—	5:	0
Holland	58309—	1:	10
Zealand	9183—	14:	2
Friesland	11661—	15:	10
Overyssel	3571—	8:	4
Utrecht	5830—	17:	11
Groningen	5930—	17:	11

Each province sends as many Deputies as they please but however
many Deputies sent such province has but one vote. The Deputies
chosen for Different periods, some anually, some for life.

By the Albany plan		The present plan 5000 polls to a Delegate supposed	
New Hampshire	2	Do	5 near 1/6
Massachusetts	7	Do	18
Conecticut	5	Do	10—2/6
Rhode Island	2	Do	3
N York	4	Do	10—2/6
New Jersey	3	Do	6—3/4
Pensylvania	6	Do	15—1/2
Lower Counties	—	—	1 1/2
Maryland	4	Do	13
Virginia	7	Do	20 3/4
North Carolina	4	Do	10
South Carolina	4	Do	10
	48		124 1/2

Massach., Pensylvania, Virginia & Maryland. 66 Members, More than half the whole.

Remarks by G.W.[2]

Addition to 6th article

And the Delegates are to Bring with them to Every Congress an authenticated Return of the No. of the polls in their respective Colonies which is to be triennially taken in order that Each Colonies proportion of the General taxes may be Equitably affixed.

Art 7th

Each Colony shall choose what No. of Delegates the assembly or convention of such colony pleases not Exceeding
for any one Colony.

Art 8th

Each Delegate at the Congress shall have a vote in the first Instance in all Cases but if any Colony or Colonies are Dissatisfied with the majority of voices so taken the Colonies shall be Called seperately and Each Colony whatever its No. of Delegates may be, shall have only one vote as hath heretofore been customary in Congress.

MS (DLC). In the hand of Josiah Bartlett.

[1] Although no evidence survives to indicate precisely when Bartlett made these notes, it is probable that he prepared them for his use as a member of the committee "to prepare and digest the form of a confederation" to which he was appointed on June 12. To judge from comments he made in a letter to John Langdon—"the affair of voting . . . is not decided and causes some warm disputes" —Bartlett may have made particular use of them the week of June 17. The notes pertain to the issue of representation in Congress, which was ultimately incorporated in articles 16 and 17 of the committee draft submitted to Congress on July 12. See JCC, 5:433, 549–50; and Bartlett to John Langdon, June 17, 1776. See

also Josiah Bartlett's and John Dickinson's Draft Articles of Confederation, June 17–July 1? 1776, note 1.

[2] George Wythe, who was not a member of the committee on confederation, was undoubtedly the source of these comments, which are based on the plan of confederation Benjamin Franklin submitted to Congress on July 21, 1775. *JCC*, 2:197. It cannot be determined when Wythe, who returned to Virginia in mid-June, suggested these revisions of Franklin's plan or when or from whom Bartlett obtained them.

John Hancock to Thomas Cushing

Dear Sir,   Philadelphia June 12th. 1776.

By the enclosed List,[1] comprehending the Names of the Captains with their respective Vessels and the Number of Guns they mount, you will see we are taking every Step in our Power towards finishing the Business. I hope the Appointments will be agreeable. We have [done] every Thing we [can] to give Satisfaction.

The Money for your Purpose shall be sent off this week.[2] Being so extremely hurried at present in dispatching several Expresses, I have only time to assure you that, I am with respect, Yours sincerely,   John Hancock

P.S. Do Send me my Commissn. as Majr Genl.

I find I am left out of both House and Council, I can't help it, they have a right to do as they please, I think I do not merit such Treatmt. but my Exertions & my Life are & shall be at their Service.

RC (MHi). In the hand of Jacob Rush, with signature and postscript by Hancock.
[1] Printed in Clark, *Naval Documents*, 5:497.
[2] See Hancock to Thomas Cushing, June 16, 1776. See also Cushing to Hancock, May 17, 1776, ibid., p. 135.

Samuel Chase to Horatio Gates

My Dear Gates   Philadelphia. June 13th. 1776. Thursday Evening

I am compelled to leave this City early tomorrow. Mrs. Chase is extreamly ill.

We have laid before Congress the many and great abuses and mismanagements in Canada, and proposed such Remedies as We thought most expedient in our present Situation. A General is to be sent there with the powers of a Roman Dictator. Many of the Congress have cast their Eyes on You, and I doubt not You will be appointed to this great & important Command.[1] I am pleased with the Reflection that You will now have an Opportunity to render great Services to America, your Inclination and Abilities will have

Room for Exertion and Laurels are still to be reaped in Canada. You will have a respectable Army and every Measure, We can suggest, is taking to supply them with Necessaries.

I cannot but recommend to You the most unreserved and unlimited Confidence in General Schuyler. Be assured of his Integrity, Diligence, Abilities and Address. I know him well, and will be answerable for that Gentleman as for Myself. I know he is injured, basely traduced. If You have not a constant & friendly Intercourse with General Schuyler, You will fail in Canada. In a Word, inform him of every Doubt or Suspicion. He will show You his Conduct, evidenced by his Letters and Orders. You may show him this Letter and say it was my Request to You as his and your Friend, and as one of those in whom America reposes some Trust. Be attentive to this advice. More depends on it than I can explain in a Letter.

You will have the assistance of many able Officers in Canada. You are acquainted with General Sullivane. General Arnold is brave, active & well acquainted in that Country. He is acquainted with Men and Things. Desire him to shew You my Letter relative to Point Au Fer, and another, of my Suspicions of some people now in our Service. *Be extreamly cautious who you trust.* General Thompson has Sense to conceive and Spirit to execute. You may safely repose a Confidence in him. Colonel Sinclair [St. Clair] will be of great Service. He has prudence, bravery and a Knowledge of the Country. If he would accept I beleive he is the most proper person in Canada to be your adjutant General. Colonel Maxwell bears a high Character. Colo. Allen I know. His Vivacity & Spirit will be useful if properly directed. He will never turn his back on the Enemy. Colo. Dehaas is said to be an experienced officer. Colo. Drayton & Patterson have the Appearance of good officers. Colonels Wayne & Irvin are Gentlemen. There are many other Gentlemen in the Army there but I am not acquainted with them, or cannot at present recollect them. Mr. McCartey acts as Quarter Master. I rely on his integrity. He is a Man of Business, intimately acquanted with the Country and Language. Mr. Bonfield may be recommended to Mr. Trumbell as Deputy Commissary if he will accept. If Mr. Wells, who lived with Us and was acquainted with all affairs & acted as our Secretary should return to Canada, I beg Leave to mention him to your attention and Consideration. I left him in Albany.

I beg to hear from you as often as possible. Remember Me to all the Gentlemen I have before mentioned. Present my most respectful Compliments to Lord Sterling. Assure General Washington I entertain every Sentiment of Respect and Regard for him. Commend Me to your Lady, beg her to accept, with you, my warmest wishes & beleive Me to be in all the Vicissitudes of Life, Your Affectionate & Obedt. Servt.[2]   Saml. Chase

RC (MH).
[1] Chase and Charles Carroll of Carrollton attended Congress on June 11 to give an oral account of their mission to Canada, and on the following day they submitted a written report which was immediately taken into consideration in the committee of the whole. On June 17 Congress resolved "that an experienced general be immediately sent into Canada" and instructed General Washington to send Gates to take command of the forces there. See *JCC,* 5:431, 436, 448.

[2] The following day Charles Carroll of Carrollton, although not a delegate to Congress, sent a letter to Gates informing him that he would "probably be appointed to the chief command in Canada" and thereupon took the liberty to offer several suggestions pertaining to the Canadian command. Carroll's letter is printed in Kate Mason Rowland, *The Life of Charles Carroll of Carrollton, 1737–1832, with His Correspondence and Public Papers,* 2 vols. (New York: G.P. Putnam's Sons, 1898), 1:174–76.

John Hancock to the Cumberland County Committee

Gentlemen,   Philada. June 13th 1776
Your favour of June 8th Inclosing a resolution respecting the Powder stopt by you came safe to hand, and was Communicated to the Congress, in Consequence of which I have it in charge to Acquaint you that the two Parcels of Powder you Mention to have Stopd were Design'd for the use of the Inhabitants at Pittsburgh and our Friend Indians, and sent for that Purpose by Mr. Morris to Mr. Morgan the Agent, by Order of Congress. I am now to Request you upon receipt of this, that youl Please to Direct the said Powder to be forwarded with all Possible Dispatch to Mr. Morgan for the Purposes aforesaid, & I beg you will Direct the Waggoners to be as Expeditious as Possible.[1]
I am with Respect, Gentlemen, your very Hble. Servt.
John Hancock Presidt.

Tr (PWW).
[1] See *JCC,* 5:437; and Lewis Morris to Ephraim Blaine, May 14, 1776. The Cumberland County Committee's letter and proceedings with respect to the seizure of the gunpowder are in PCC, item 69, 1:133–35; and *Am. Archives,* 4th ser. 6:756.

John Hancock to Ebenezer Hancock

Dear Brother   Philadelphia June 13th. 1776
I have the pleasure to Acquaint you that the Congress have been pleased to Appoint you Deputy Pay Master General to the Continental Troops in the Eastern Department,[1] with a Sallary of Fifty Dollars a Month, which I hope will prove agreeable to you, and I

most earnestly Recommend to you a very close and strict Attention to the Business of your office. The Departmt. to which your Office extends, takes in the Colony of Massachusetts, New Hampshire, Rhode Island, & Connect., the Continental Troops in all those places fall under your Care.

I inclose you several Resolves of Congress respecting your office,[2] which I must direct that you closely Adhere to, and you are to obey all orders from General Washington, or the Commander in Chief for the time being in the Eastern Department. You will apply to the Commanding officer at Boston for a Centinel to be plac'd at the Door of your office by Night & Day.

Be carefull to make your Monthly Returns regularly to me. By next Post I shall transmit you the Pay list.

Inclos'd you have your Commissn.[3] I wish you happy, and am, Your huml Servt.   John Hancock Presidt.

[P.S.] Inform the Comandg officer in Boston of your appointt. The 150,000 Dollars mention'd in the Resolve is on its way under the Care of my Mr Sprigs, who will deliver it to you. Send me a Rect. for the money.

RC (MB).
    [1] See JCC, 5:432.
    [2] Passed by Congress on June 5. JCC, 5:418.
    [3] Located at MB, with signature by Hancock and attestation by Charles Thomson.

John Hancock to Thomas McKean

Sir   Philada. 13 June 1776
Your favr. rec'd this morng. & have only time to Tell you that the Powder & Lead is order'd under Guard of a Company of Troops, & that a Battaln. of Associators is order'd down to your assistance. I wish success. I have it in Command to Request that your Assembly would please to order the Commandg Officer to disarm all the disaffected in your Colony, which please to Communicate to the Assembly.[1]

Excuse me, as I am hurried, Steal time to write, & am most Respectfully, Your very huml svt,   John Hancock Prt.

RC (MH). Addressed: "To the Honl Thomas McKean Esqr. at New Castle."
    [1] See JCC, 5:436–37. This day McKean wrote two letters to Hancock. The first, written at two in the morning, reported that 1,000 armed tories had gathered in Sussex County to join with the British in an assault on three companies of Continental soldiers at Lewes. The second, written at seven in the evening, reported that the "insurgents" in Sussex had already dispersed but had denied that they were in league with the British or inimical to the American cause,

although the assembly had failed to discover why they had gathered together in the first instance. PCC, item 78, 15:57–60; and *Am. Archives,* 4th ser. 6:833.

John Hancock to Philip Moore and James Craig

Gentlemen,   Philada. June 13th. 1776.

I am directed by Congress to inform you, that the offer which the Owners made of the hard Money taken on Board their Prizes is accepted—and that you will please to apply to the Men for the Moiety belonging to them. The public Service calls for the Money as soon as it can possibly be had.[1]

Should the Men consent to let Congress have their Share, I will immediately give Draughts on the Treasury for the Amount.

It is the Request of Col. Roberdeau that the Money remain at Capt. Craig's until further Orders.

I beg Leave to thank you, and the Rest of the Owners for the Example of public Spirit, which you have, in the most unsolicited Manner, shewn upon this Occasion.

I have the Honor to be, Gentlemen, your most obedient & very hble Sert.   J.H. Prest.

LB (DNA: PCC, item 12A). Addressed: "Messrs. Moore & Craig, Agents &c."

[1] On June 12 Congress had accepted the offer of the owners of the Pennsylvania privateers *Chance* and *Congress* to exchange their "moiety" of the $22,000 in hard money taken by their vessels from the *Juno, Lady Juliana,* and *Reynolds* for the like amount in "continental dollars." *JCC,* 5:432. Accounts of the capture of these three ships by the *Chance* and *Congress* are in Clark, *Naval Documents,* 5:154, 379, 448. Philip Moore was one of the owners of the *Chance* and *Congress* when they were commissioned as privateers in April 1776. James Craig subsequently acquired part ownership of the *Chance.* Ibid., 4:774–75, 5:882.

John Hancock to the Pennsylvania Assembly

Gentlemen,   Philadelphia, 13th June, 1776.

The Congress have just received Advice, that a Number of Disaffected Persons have got together in *Sussex* County, in *Delaware* Government; that there is Reason to apprehend those deluded People are supplied with Arms and Ammunition from the Men of War of our Enemies, and mean to act in Concert with them. As it is of the utmost Importance, that such Insurrections be immediately quelled and totally suppressed, the Congress have come to the following Resolution:

That it be recommended to the Assembly of *Pennsylvania*, immediately to order a Battalion of the Provincial Rifle-Men, now at

Chester, to march to the Assistance of the Militia in *Delaware* Government.[1]

I doubt not you will see the Necessity of an immediate Compliance.

I have the Honour to be, Gentlemen, Your obedient humble Servant,   John Hancock, President

MS not found; reprinted from *Pa. Archives,* 8th ser. 8:7541.
[1] See *JCC,* 5:436.

John Hancock to Charles Preston

Sir   Philada. 13th June 1776

Your Letter of 3d Inst. I duly Rec'd, & immediately Sent to Capt Crawford the one you Inclos'd open for him. Capt Crawford will deliver you this, he agreeable to the Resolve of Congress proceeds to Reading to furnish the officers & Men with Money & to Determine the Rations to Mr Franks.[1] I dare Say a strict attention to the Parole in other instances will be observ'd by Capt Crawford, my Knowledge of & Reliance on your honour is such that I am Confident you will not suffer any Circumstances to take place that shall in the least Degree occasion an Alteration in the present Determination with respect to the Gentlemen who are prisoners. In any thing wherein I can promote the Ease & happiness of the Gentlemen consistant with my Scituation depend I will with pleasure do it, & you will please at any time to Communicate any Occurrencies to me.

I am, Sir, Your most Obedt sevt,   John Hancock Prt.

RC (PHi). Addressed: "To the Honl. Major Preston, Reading."
[1] The letter from Maj. Charles Preston—commander of the British garrison at St. Johns that surrendered to the Americans on November 2, 1775—requesting permission for Capt. John Crawford, "Paymaster to the Twenty-Sixth Regiment," to visit British prisoners at Reading, Pa., is in PCC, item 78, 18:61, and *Am. Archives,* 6:691. The "Resolve of Congress" referred to is in *JCC,* 4:371. David S. Franks had been granted permission by Congress on February 7, 1776, to victual the prisoners at Reading. *JCC,* 4:116.

Richard Henry Lee to George Washington

Dear Sir,   Philadelphia 13th June 1776

I am informed that a certain Mr. Eustace, now in New York, but some time ago with Lord Dunmore, is acquainted with a practise that prevailed of taking letters out of the Post Office in Virginia and carrying them to Dunmore for his perusal and then returning them to the Office again. As it is of the greatest consequence that this nefarious practise be stopt immediately, I shall be exceedingly obliged to you Sir for getting Mr. Eustace to give in writing all that he knows about this business, and inclose the same to me at Williamsburg. I wish to know particularly, what Post Offices the letters were taken from, by whom, and who carried them to Lord Dunmore. This day I sett off for Virginia,[1] where, if I can be of any service to you, it will oblige to command me. It is more than probable that Congress will order our friend Gates to Canada. His great abilities and virtue will be absolutely necessary to restore things there, and his recommendations will always be readily complied with. You will find that great powers are given to the Commander in that distant department. The system for Canada, adopted since the arrival of the Commissioners here, will I hope be of essential service to our affairs. All good Men pray most heartily for your health, happiness, and success, and none more than dear Sir Your affectionate friend and obedient Servant,   Richard Henry Lee

RC (DLC).
[1] Lee apparently carried with him a letter from John Rogers to Thomas Sim Lee, which was to be delivered to the latter at his Mellwood estate. Rogers' letter was chiefly personal in nature, but it contains the following comments on public affairs. "The Canada Commissioners are returned, our affairs there are not in a very promising scituation, but I am in great Hopes of their being very speedily put in a better state. The inclosed paper (if it comes to Hand before the Public Post) will inform of all the late intelligence in circulation of any consequence. If the Article respecting the King of France is to be relied upon I am inclined to think it will have a very considerable effect upon the Political World in general and upon America in particular." John Rogers to Thomas Sim Lee, June 12, 1776. Dreer Collection, PHi.
   George Wythe probably left Philadelphia with Richard Henry Lee. In a June 17 letter to Robert Carter of Nomini Hall, Wythe reported that "Col. Lee is so obliging as to take with him the stocking-Loom-needles, with some wire, which I brought for you from Philadelphia to Hooe's ferry, where I now am." Signers Collection, InU. Wythe's account with Virginia lists "Wages from 5 September, 1775, to 12 June, 1776, 281 days at 45s" for his services in Congress and indicates that he attended the Virginia convention "from Wednesday 27 June to the end of the session." Jefferson Papers, MHi.

Secret Committee Minutes of Procedings

June 13. 1776.
   At a meetg of the Come. Present Morris, Alsop, Hewes, Lewis, Bartlett. The papers relative to the seizure of the Brige. Cornelia by the Syren Man of war being producd &c considerd, Agreed that the follg. Acct. of the owners of sd. Brigantine be paid.[1]
   The Honble Cont. Congress to King & Harper, Drs.

For the Brigante. Cornelia taken by the Syren man of war 15
March last valued as per Charter party—   £650.
Hire due on sd. Brige. from 1st Feby to 15 March
is 1½ months at £120   180
                                                              ‾‾‾‾‾‾
                                                               £830.
Deduct 2 per Cent for underwriting as customary   13
                                                              ‾‾‾‾‾‾
                                                               817.

Order on the Treasurers for 2178 2/3 dollars, amt. of the above
Acct. A protest before Mat. Clarkson Not. Pub. of Bart. Gallate a
Mariner belonging to the Ship Grace under Charter party to this
Come. & taken on her passage to Virginia by the Dunmore Tender
sloop of war being read, Orderd That the value insurd on said ship
be paid together with 18 days freight both amountg. to £1082. Accordingly an order was drawn on the Treasurers in favor of the
Owners Elias Boys, Fergus McIlvain & Robert. Bridges for 2885 ⅓
dollars.[2] Agreemt. with P. & J. Wicoff was signd by the Come. A
Charter-party with Meredith & Clymer was signd by the Come. for
the Sloop Peggy.

MS (MH).
    [1] See Secret Committee Contract, February 1, 1776.
    [2] The ship *Grace* had been chartered by the committee in February and was
captured by the British in March. See Secret Committee Minutes of Proceedings,
February 27, 1776; and Clark, *Naval Documents,* 4:427, 5:481–85.

Secret Committee to the
Pennsylvania Committee of Safety

Gentn,   Philada. June 13th, 1776.
    The Congress having recd information of a dangerous Insurrection
of Tories in the Lower Counties, have directed me to send down immediately One Ton of Powder & a suitable quantity of Lead if to be
obtained. The Powder I have issued orders for, but Lead I have not,
nor do I know where to get it, unless upon this occasion you shou'd
think proper to spare a quantity for this service.[1]
    I have the honor to be, Gentn, Your obedt Servant,
                                    Robt. Morris,
                                    Chairman of the Secret Committee.

MS not found; reprinted from *Pa. Archives,* 1st ser. 4:773.
    [1] The Pennsylvania Committee of Safety responded immediately by ordering two
tons of lead to be delivered to the Secret Committee. *Am. Archives,* 4th ser. 6:1282.
See also John Hancock to Thomas McKean, this date, note.

John Adams to Samuel Chase

Dear Sir   Philadelphia June 14. 1776

Mr Bedford put into my Hand this Moment a Card from you,[1] containing a Reprehension for the past, and a Requisition for the Time to come. For the past I kiss the Rod: but from complying with the Requisi[ti]on, at least one Part of it, I must be excused. I have no objection to writing you Facts, but I would not meddle with Characters, for the World. A burn'd Child dreads the Fire. I have Smarted to[o] severely, for a few crude Expressions, written in a Pet, to a bosom Friend, to venture on such Boldnesses again. Besides if I were to tell you all that I think of all Characters, I should appear so ill natured and censorious, that I should detest my self. By my soul, I think very heinously, I cant think of a better Word, of some People. They think as badly of me, I suppose, and neither of us care a farthing for that. So the Account is ballanced and perhaps after all both sides may be deceived, both may be very honest Men.

But of all the Animals on Earth, that ever fell in my Way, your Trimmers, your double tongued and double minded Men, your disguised Folk, I detest most. The Devil I think has a better Title to those, by half, than he has to those who err openly, and are bare faced Villains.

Mr Adams ever was and ever will be glad to see Mr Chase, but Mr Chase never was nor will be more welcome than, if he should come next Monday or Tuesday fortnight, with the Voice of Maryland in Favour of Independence, and a foreign Alliance. I have never had the Honour of knowing many People from Maryland, but by what I have learnt of them and seen of their Delegates they are an open, sincere and united People—a little obstinate to be sure, but that is very pardonable when accompanied with frankness, from all which I conclude, that when they shall be convinced of the Necessity of those Measures, they will all be convinced at once, and afterwards be as active and forward as any, perhaps more so than most.

I have one Bone to pick with your Colony. I suspect they levelled one of their Instructions at my Head.[2] This is a distinction of which you may suppose I am not very ambitious. One of your Colleagues moved a Resolution that No Member of Congress should hold any Office under any of the new Governments and produced an Instruction to make him feel strong. I seconded the Motion with a trifling amendment that the Resolution should be that no Member of Congress should hold any office civil or military, in the Army or in the Militia under any Government old or new. This struck through the assembly like an Electric shock, for every Member was a Governor, or General, or Judge, or some mighty Thing or other in the militia or under the old Government or some new one. This was so important a Matter that it required Consideration, and I have never heard another Word about it.

The Truth as far as it respects myself is this. The Government of the Massachusetts without my Solicitation and much against my Inclination, were pleased sometime last Summer to nominate me to an office. It was at a Time, when offices under new Governments were not in much demand, being considered rather precarious. I did not refuse this office, altho by accepting it, I must resign another office which I held under the old Government, three Times So profitable, because I was well informed that if I had refused it no other Man would have accepted it, and this would have greatly weakened, perhaps ruined the new Constitution. This is the Truth of Fact. So that one of the most disinterested and intrepid Actions of my whole Life, has been represented to the People of Maryland to my Disadvantage. I told the Gentleman that I should be much obliged if they would find me a Man who would accept of my office, or by passing the Resolution, furnish me with a Justification for refusing it—in either Case, I would Subscribe my Renunciation of that office before I left that Room. ⟨*So much for Egotism.*⟩[3] Nay I would go further, I would vote with them, that every Member of this Congress should take an oath, that he never would accept of any office, during Life, or procure any office for his father, his Son, his Brother, or his Cousin. So much for Egotism.

McKean has returned from the Lower Counties with full Powers.[4] Their Instructions are in the same Words with the new ones to the Delegates of Pensilvania. New Jersey have dethroned Franklyn,[5] and in a Letter which is just come to my Hand from indisputable Authority, I am told that the Delegates from that Colony will "vote plump." [6] Maryland now stands alone. I presume She will soon join Company—if not she must be left alone.

LB (MHi).
    [1] Chase's brief note promising to be in Philadelphia "on Monday or Tuesday fortnight with the voice of Maryland in favor of independence and a foreign alliance," is in Adams, *Works* (Adams), 9:396n.
    [2] See John Adams to James Otis, Sr., April 29, 1776, note.
    [3] The remainder of this letter was probably added on June 16 or later. The following paragraph contains information that could not have been available to Adams earlier than the 16th, and his statement that the New Jersey delegates would join the other colonies in voting for independence is based upon a letter to him from Jonathan Dickinson Sergeant dated June 15. The two sentences following this deletion are written in a much smaller hand and are crowded into the space setting off Adams' concluding paragraph.
    [4] New instructions for the Delaware delegates to Congress were not voted by the Delaware Assembly until the afternoon of June 15, and McKean probably returned to Philadelphia on June 16. See John M. Coleman, *Thomas McKean, Forgotten Leader of the Revolution* (Rockaway, N.J.: American Faculty Press, 1975), pp. 165–66; and Rodney, *Letters* (Ryden), p. 92.

[5] The resolutions of the New Jersey Provincial Convention of June 14 and 15 which led to the removal of William Franklin from the governorship are in *Am. Archives*, 4th ser. 6:967–68.

[6] See Jonathan Dickinson Sergeant to John Adams, June 15, 1776.

Josiah Bartlett to Meshech Weare

Sir,   Philadelphia 14 June 1776

This goes by the Person who carries the Money mention'd in a former Letter which was order'd for the advance wages, and defraying the charges of raising the Regiment to be station'd at Portsmouth.[1] The Sum ordered is 10,500 Dols., 500 Dols of which Wm. Whipple has taken, which he desires may be replac'd out of the Treasury and charg'd to him. 10,000 dols. is in a Box directed to you, there is in the same Box 10,000 Dols. for John Langdon Esqr which please to advise him of.

We are with great respect, Your most obt Serts,

Josiah Bartlett

RC (DLC).

[1] See William Whipple to Meshech Weare, May 16, 1776.

John Hancock to Certain Colonies

Gentlemen,   Philada. June 14th. 1776.

Since my last I have Nothing further in Charge from Congress, except the enclosed Resolve to prohibit the Exportation of salted Beef & Pork, which I am to request you will have published in your News Papers as soon as possible.[1]

I am Gentlemen, your most obed. & very hble Sevt.

J. H. Prest.

LB (DNA: PCC, item 12A). Addressed: "Honble Convention of New Hampshire. Govr. Trumbull, Connecticut. Govr. Cooke Rhode Island."

[1] On June 9 Washington requested Commissary Joseph Trumbull to intercede with the New York Provincial Congress to secure a ban on the exportation of salted pork from the province. Trumbull did so, and on June 11 the provincial congress approved a two-week ban on the exportation of salted beef and pork and referred the matter to Congress. Congress responded on June 14 by passing the resolve restricting the export of salted beef and pork which Hancock enclosed in this letter. See *JCC*, 5:441; *Am. Archives*, 4th ser. 6:815–16, 1393–94; and Washington, *Writings* (Fitzpatrick), 5:120–21. Hancock wrote an identical letter to the New York Convention on June 15, with the following postscript: "You have also enclosed a Resolution of Congress respecting the disaffected persons in your Colony, to which I beg leave to call your attention." *Am. Archives*, 4th ser. 6:1412. Congress passed this resolution "respecting the disaffected persons in your

Colony" on June 14 in response to Washington's June 10 letter to Hancock. See *JCC,* 5:441; and Washington, *Writings* (Fitzpatrick), 5:121–22.

John Hancock to Esek Hopkins

Sir,   Philada. June 14th. 1776.
    Notwithstanding the repeated Efforts and Solicitations of the Marine Board to put the Continental Ships upon a respectable Footing, and to have them employed in the Service for which they were originally designed, they are constrained to say, that their Efforts & Solicitations have been frustrated & neglected in a Manner unaccountable to them; and in Support of their own Reputation they have been under the Necessity of representing the State of their Navy to Congress, and have informed them, that there has been a great Neglect in the Execution of their Orders; and that many and daily Complaints are exhibited to them agt. some of the Officers of the Ships, and that great Numbers of Officers & Men have left the Ships in Consequence of ill Usage, and have applied to the Marine Board for Redress. These, with many other Circumstances, have induced the Congress to direct you to repair to this City. And in Consequence of their Authority to me, I hereby direct you immediately on Receipt of this, to repair to the City of Philadelphia, and on your Arrival here to give Notice to me, as President of the Marine Board. The Command of the Ships will of Course devolve, in your Absence upon the eldest officer, to whom you will give the Command with this Direction however, that he take no Steps with Respect to the Ships till further Orders. And I further inform you, that by this Opportunity I write to Captains Saltonstal & Whipple immediately to repair to this City.
    As your Conduct in many Instances requires Explanation, you will of Course be questioned with Respect to your whole Proceedings since you left this City. I give you this Notice that you may come prepared to answer for your general Conduct.
    You will bring with you all the Instructions you have hitherto received from the Naval or Marine Board, all Letters & Papers relative to the Fleet, and your Proceedings, Journals, State of all the Ships, those in and out of Port, State of the Stores of every Kind, Provisions, List of the effective and non-effective Men, and in Short, every Thing relative to the Ships under your Command.
    As your Presence is immediately necessary here, I again repeat that on Receipt of this, and as soon as you can prepare, you proceed by Land to this City, there to wait the further Orders of Congress.[1]
    I am Sir your very hble Svt.   J. H. Prst.

LB (DNA: PCC, item 12A). Addressed: "To Esek Hopkins Esqr commanding the Continental Ships at Newport, or elsewhere."

[1] For additional details on the sources of congressional discontent with Commodore Hopkins, culminating in his censure in August 1776, see Thomas Jefferson's Notes on the Inquiry into Esek Hopkins' Conduct, August 12, 1776.

John Hancock to the Massachusetts Assembly

Honorable Gentlemen,   Philadelphia June 14th. 1776.

Your Letter from the Honble President of the Council was duely received. The Delegates of Massachusetts Bay, you may depend, will pay all the Regard and Attention in their Power, to the Instructions you are pleased to honour them with.[1]

In my Letter of the 4th of June, which I hope came safe to Hand, I enclosed you sundry Resolves of Congress, relative to supplying a Part of your Militia for the Defence of the Common Cause in the present critical State of our Affairs. On the 11th Inst., in Obedience to the Commands of Congress, I sent a second Express to the several Colonies that were to furnish Troops for the Defence of New York. This last was sent in Consequence of alarming Intelligence from Genl. Washington of an intended Attack on that City by Genl. Howe with all his Forces. To the Motives suggested in my Letters on the Occasion, I can only repeat, that it is the only Measure that can possibly save us from Destruction.[2]

I am extremely sorry to observe that our Affairs in Canada are on so bad a Footing. In Order however to retrieve our Misfortunes in that Quarter, a most important Step will be, to supply our Troops there with as much Gold and Silver as we can collect. You will therefore be pleased to send by Express, immediately on Receipt of this, all the hard Money in your Possession, to Genl. Schuyler, or to the Paymaster in Canada, Mr. Jona. Trumbull.

I do myself the Pleasure to transmit herewith the Sum of thirty Thousand Dollars in a small Box marked and numbered, which, you will please to use your best Endeavours, to have exchanged for Specie; and also, the Sum of twenty one Thousand Dollars, in a small Box marked and numbered, for the Use of the two Battalions to be raised in our Province, which you will please to improve accordingly. There are in this Box Massachusetts Bills equal in Value to 2725 3/4 Dollars, as per List enclosed.[3]

You will also be pleased to procure hard Money to the Amount of one Hundred Thousand Dollars if possible. For any Sum above the thirty Thousand Dollars now sent, which you may collect in Specie, your Bills on me, shall be duely honored. Or should you be so fortunate as to collect even more than one Hundred Thousand

Dollars in hard Money, your Bills on me for such over plus Money, shall be likewise duely honored.

Whatever further Sum you may collect, after you shall have forwarded all now in your Hands, you will be pleased to send immediately to Canada, if you should judge it so considerable as to be worth the Expence of transmitting.

I have the Honour to be with every Sentiment of Respect, Gentlemen, your most obed., and very hble Sevt.

John Hancock Presidt.

[*P.S.*] The Inclos'd Resolution respectg. the Prohibition on the Exportation of Salted Beef & Pork, I request the favr. you will please to order to be publish'd in all the News Papers.[4]

I have in Charge from Congress most earnestly to Solicit your Attention to the Article of hard Money, & to request you will issue such orders as may be effectual for obtaing a considerable quantity, & as often as a Sum worth Sending is in hand you would please to order it by Express to Canada.

Your Delegates, from the enhanc'd price of all Articles & the increase of Expences in this City, are reduc'd to the Necessity of Acquainting you that their Funds are exhausted; & to Solicit your Attention to them in ordering them such Sums of Money as you Judge necessary, this is the Request of the whole, by whose desire I mention it.[5]

RC (M–Ar). In the hand of Jacob Rush, with signature and postscript by Hancock.

[1] See James Otis, Sr., to the Massachusetts Delegates, May 10, 1776, in PCC, item 65, 1:85–86; and *Am. Archives,* 4th ser. 6:419.

[2] The Massachusetts Council subsequently reported to Hancock that the general court "voted to raise . . . five thousand men, to reinforce and cooperate with the Continental troops in Canada and New York." Massachusetts Council to Hancock, June 26, 1776, PCC, item 65, 1:89–90, and *Am. Archives,* 4th ser. 6:1087.

[3] See *JCC,* 4:397.

[4] See *JCC,* 5:441.

[5] On June 27 the Massachusetts Assembly ordered the payment of $400 to each of the Massachusetts delegates. *Am. Archives,* 5th ser. 1:294.

John Hancock to William Palfrey

Sir,   Philadelphia June 14th. 1776.

I received your Favour, enclosing your weekly Return to the eighth of June.[1]

The Congress having appointed Ebenezer Hancock Esqr Deputy Paymaster Genl. for the Eastern Department, it will no doubt give you Pleasure to find yourself relieved of so considerable a Part of your Burthen. I forward to him by this opportunity one Hundred and fifty Thousand Dollars for the Use of the Troops in that Department.

It is my opinion, you had better hire a Clerk immediately, and run the Risque of Congress making an Allowance for him. It is scarcely possible at this Time to get them to determine the Matter for you. A thousand Objects, infinitely more important, press on them, and demand an immediate Attention and Decision. Thus much you may depend upon, I will do all in my Power to prevail with them to make an adequate Allowance for a Clerk if you choose to employ one.

Should you incline to adopt my opinion in this Matter, Mr. Wynthrop, whom I expect every Hour, will be as fit a Person as you can find, or you shall do as you please.

I am, Sir, your most obedt. & very hble Servt.

John Hancock Presidt

[*P.S.*] I will Venture from the urgency of the case to Authorize you to Employ a proper person as Clerk, let him be on as easy terms as possible.

RC (MH). In the hand of Jacob Rush, with signature and postscript by Hancock.
[1] Paymaster General William Palfrey's latest extant letter to Hancock is dated June 3 and forwards a state of his accounts to the end of May. See *Am. Archives*, 4th ser. 6:692.

John Hancock to
the Pennsylvania Committee of Safety

Gentlemen,   Philad'a, June 14, 1776.

You will receive herewith from the commanding officer of the troops in the barracks, Mr. M'Lean, a prisoner who was sent hither by General Putnam in irons, for refusing to give his parole and for other misbehavior, the letter respecting him was referred to the committee appointed by Congress on prisoners, & the prisoner was committed to the charge of the Commanding officer in the barracks 'till the committee should report on his conduct, but as the troops are ordered from the barracks, I have it in command to request you to take charge of him, & have him safely kept agreeable to former resolutions of Congress, until the Congress shall take order concerning him.[1]

I am, Gentlemen, Your obedt humble servt,

John Hancock, Presidt.

MS not found; reprinted from *Pa. Archives*, 1st ser. 4:773.
[1] See *JCC*, 5:440. Gen. Israel Putnam's June 2 letter to Hancock about Lt. Neil McLean is in PCC, item 159, fol. 20; and *Am. Archives*, 4th ser. 6:683. McLean's

side of the story is given in his letter to Robert Morris, November 5, 1776, in PCC, item 78, 15:117–18; and *Am. Archives,* 5th ser. 3:515–17. For the committee's response to Hancock, see ibid., 4th ser. 6:1283.

John Hancock to Richard Peters

Sir,   Philada. June 14th. 1776.

I am to inform you that the Congress were yesterday pleased to appoint you Secretary to the Board of War & Ordnance, with a Salary of eight Hundred Dollars a Year.[1]

Should you accept the office, you will please to acquaint me with it: and, that you may enter upon your Duty, as soon as possible, you will apply to the Committee, who will give you necessary Directions.[2] The Gentlemen on the Committee are Mr. J. Adams, Mr. Sherman, Mr. Harrison, Mr. Wilson, Mr. Rutledge.

The Nature and Importance of the office are such, that the most constant Attendance, and unremitting Application, are indispensibly required, in the Execution of it.

I am, Sir, your most obedt. and very hle Sevt.   J. H. Prsit.

LB (DNA: PCC, item 12A).
[1] See *JCC,* 5:438. Richard Peters (1744–1828), a Philadelphia lawyer and captain in the city militia, became a member of the Board of War, 1777–81, and was a delegate to Congress, 1782–83. *JCC,* 5:438; and *DAB.* For the background and history of the Board of War, see Jennings B. Sanders, *Evolution of the Executive Departments of the Continental Congress, 1774–1789* (Chapel Hill: University of North Carolina Press, 1935), chap. 1.
[2] Peters' letter of acceptance, written this day, is in PCC, item 78, 18:65; and *Am. Archives,* 4th ser. 6:888.

John Hancock to Dudley Saltonstall and Abraham Whipple

Sir,   Philada. June 14th. 1776.

The present inactive State of the Navy of the United Colonies, the many Complaints exhibited to the Marine Board agt. some of the Officers of the Ships, and the daily Applications of both Officers & Men who have left the Fleet in Consequence of very severe Usage, have constrained the Marine Board to make a Representation of our Naval Concerns, to the Congress, which require a speedy Reform. And in Order that the true & just Reasons of this very great Uneasiness & Inactivity may be fully investigated, it is necessary that the Officers agt. whom Complaints have been lodged should be fully heard. I have it in Command therefore from Congress to direct you immediately upon Receipt of this, to repair to the City of Philada. by Land, and on your Arrival here to give Notice to me as

President of the Marine Board. The Command of the Ship will naturally devolve upon the next Officer. And you are to bring with you an exact State of the Ship under your Command, the List of the Men remaining, what Number of effective & noneffective, the State of the Stores of every Kind belonging to the Ship, and every Thing relative to your Ship.

As you will be called upon in general to answer for your Conduct since you left this City, I give you this Notice that you may come prepared for that Purpose.[1]

I am to repeat to you, that Congress expect your immediate Compliance with this Order, & am, Sir, your very hble Sev.

J. H. Prest.

LB (DNA: PCC, item 12A). Addressed: "To Captain Dudley Saltonstal of the Ship Alfred. To Cap. Abraham Whipple of the Ship Columbus."

[1] See JCC, 5:439. Saltonstall was reputed to have a "Rude Unhappy Temper," and Whipple had acquired a reputation in the Continental fleet for cowardice as a result of his behavior during the engagement with H.M.S. Glasgow in April 1776. (Early in May, however, a court-martial, which was held at Whipple's insistence, had found him guilty only of poor judgment.) Clark, Naval Documents, 4:1328–29, 1419–21, 5:152, 295. Saltonstall and Whipple arrived in Philadelphia on July 2, at which time Congress directed the marine committee "to enquire into the complaints against them." After examining "divers of the inferior officers" of the Alfred and the Columbus, the marine committee reported to Congress on July 11 "that the charge against Captain Saltonstal does not appear to the committee to be well founded, and that the charge against Captain Whipple amounts to nothing more than a rough, indelicate mode of behaviour to his marine officers." Congress thereupon directed the committee to order Saltonstall and Whipple to return to their ships and to admonish Whipple "to cultivate harmony with his officers." JCC, 5:507, 542–43. The RC of Hancock's letter to Saltonstall is in the Hoadley Collection, CtHi.

John Hancock to George Washington

Sir, Philadelphia June 14th. 1776.

I am extremely happy to have it in my Power to assure you that the several Matters referred to Congress in your Letters, will receive a speedy Determination. With great Pleasure I shall transmit you the Result, as soon as I am ordered.

I enclose to you, at this Time, sundry important Resolves, to which I beg Leave to refer your Attention.[1]

You will there perceive that Congress have ordered 9000 Dollars to be advanced to Col. Hand, which you will please to direct to be paid him out of the military Chest at New York. This Money is to be stopped out of the Pay of the Regiment.[2]

The establishing a War Office is a new and great Event in the History of America, and will doubtless be attended with essential Advantages when properly conducted & inspected. I hope the Committee will be ready in a few days to enter upon the Execution of their Duty. You will see the Outlines of this Office in the enclosed Resolves. Some further Regulations, it is more than probable, will be necessary in the Course of Time. The Congress have only laid a Foundation at present. It still remains, in a great Measure, to erect a System of Rules and Laws that will enable us to carry on our military operations with more Knowledge, Certainty, and Dispatch.

I have paid Capt Grier the 600 Dollars agreeably to the Order of Congress, which you will please to direct the Paymaster to deduct on Settlement.[3]

The shameful Inactivity of our Fleet for some Time past, the frequent Neglect or Disobedience of Orders in Commodore Hopkins, the numberless Complaints exhibited to the Marine Committee agt. him, and also against Captains Saltonstal and Whipple, have induced the Congress, in Consequence of a Representation from the Marine Committee, to order them to repair immediately to this City to answer for their Conduct. I have accordingly wrote them to set out on the Receipt of my Letters, and to repair here by Land as fast as possible. I hope soon to have our Ships on a more respectable Footing. No Efforts of mine shall be wanting to accomplish so desireable an Event.

I have sent the Resolves to the Convention of New York, which relate to them. The Prohibition on salted Beef and Pork, I have given Orders to be printed in all the Papers to the Eastward.

The Resolves respecting the Indians, I must ask the Favour of you to forward to Genl. Schuyler, with such Directions as you shall judge necessary.

I am to inform you that the Congress have appointed Ebenezer Hancock Esqr. Deputy Paymaster General for the Eastern Department. A Carriage with one Hundred and fifty Thousand Dollars for the Pay of the Troops in that Department, will set out tomorrow.

June 16th. A Waggon with about twenty two Thousand Dollars in Silver, and a Quantity of Continental Money, will set out tomorrow Morning for Canada. I have given Directions to call on you at New York, and must request you will order a Guard to proceed with it as fast as possible, the Rest of the Way.

I have the Honour to be, Sir, your most obed. & very hble Sevt.

John Hancock, Presidt

[*P.S.*] I Request the favr. you will please to give the necessary orders to the Commanding officer in the Eastern Departmt. & to my Brother respecting the Payment of the Troops.

RC (DLC). In the hand of Jacob Rush, with signature and postscript by Hancock.
    [1] These resolves, which were passed by Congress June 12, 13, and 14, dealt with rifle regiments, the creation of the Board of War, the investigation of Commodore

Hopkins, nonintercourse with the British, restraints on the exportation of beef and pork, and Canadian military operations. See *JCC*, 5:432, 434–35, 441–42.
² See *JCC*, 5:432.
³ See *JCC*, 5:438.

William Whipple to John Langdon

Dear Sir,   Philadelphia 14th June 1776

This accompanies the 10,000 dollars for the naval service mentioned in a former letter; I have put it in a box with some other money directed to Col Weare and wish it safe to hand; ¹ am sorry it was not in my power to send it sooner but hope the service will not suffer.

We have no news here, except from Canada which I suppose has reached you ere now. The Commissioners are returned from that country; it is expected that Genl Thomas is dead before this. If so the command devolves on Sullivan, but there will be another General Officer sent there—believe Gates will be the man.²

In haste, Yours,   Wm Whipple

Tr (DLC).
¹ See Josiah Bartlett to Meshech Weare, this date.
² On June 17 Congress directed Washington to send Gates "to take command of the forces" in Canada. *JCC*, 5:448.

John Adams to Peter Boylston Adams

My dear Brother   Philadelphia June 15. 1776

I have an Account of the Politicks of the Town of Braintree; but it is an imperfect one. I wish you would write me, a clear, and distinct one. . . .¹ I am told there was a Tie, between your Hon. Brigadier General and You, and that, in order to get a Decision in his Favour he was obliged to declare that he would leave the Board for the Sake of serving the Town.² I should be glad to learn a little of Motives and Politicks upon this Occasion.

How is it? You leave me in the dark: you dont tell me whether I have the Honour to be a select Man, or not, or who are select Men, nor any Thing about Town Affairs. . . . Do you think that, because I am half a thousand miles off, I never think about you and that I dont want to know this, and that and the other? I do, indeed. You may at any Time send a Letter to the Post Office in Boston, it will be brought to me free of Expence, to you, or me. . . . I am greatly at a Loss to account for the Conduct of your Hon. Councillor and gallant Brigadier, upon this Occasion. Pray explain it. Ask Mr. Norton[3]—what it means.

LB (MHi). Adams, *Family Correspondence* (Butterfield), 2:8–9.
   [1] Suspension points in MS, here and below.
   [2] Abigail Adams had informed John that Joseph Palmer had agreed to remain in the House of Representatives if elected, thus thwarting Peter's election. Abigail to John Adams, May 27, 1776, Adams, *Family Correspondence* (Butterfield), 1:416.
   [3] Probably Norton Quincy.

Elbridge Gerry to James Warren

Dear Sir   Philadelphia June 15th 1776
   Since my last nothing occurs new, save a Continuance of our Difficulties in Canada which are not hitherto abated. To cure them It must be first known what are the Causes; & the State physicians must be fully convinced of them before they can apply a Remedy, or perhaps the Demon will increase, & the saying of the poet will be verified in America "aegrescit medendo." [1] Congress are determined to search the wound & probe it to the Bottom & be assured that your Delegates will see it *layed open*, altho It may be uncertain but that the Causes existed in the Supineness of C——.[2] The Enquiries are plain in my own Mind & simply these: Why were not the Men ordered by Congress, raised, & what Colonies have been deficient? What are the Causes of these Deficiencies? Why have not the Supplies that were necessary been Sent to Canada & the Men been well payed, cloathed, armed, & fed? What officers have failed or been negligent in their Duty, & what has been the Cause of such Failure or Negligence? When these Inquiries are answered We shall be possessed of Documents for redressing the great Greivance of these Colonies relative to the Canada Expedition, upon which in my Opinion depends not only the Recovery of our Ground in that Colony but also the Success of our Arms in every Part of America. We must have vigourous Armies, or they may as well remain unlevied; & in order to then they must be well payed, appointed &c as beforementioned, & obliged to do their Duty.
   I expect soon that loan offices will be established & Commissioners appointed for borrowing Money for the Continent.[3] A Report is prepared for this purpose providing that there shall be four in Number & one in Massachusetts & that the Commissioners shall have $1/8$ per cent on all the Money borrowed, which perhaps will afford to each a Salary of £3 or 400 Sterling per Year out of which the Expence of a Clerk & office are only to be paid. I suppose the Delegates of the Colony will have the Nomination & [. . .] a *par-*

ticular Friend of mine who has also ever proved himself a true
Friend to America & evinced his abilities to serve her in such a Department will have my Vote & Little Interest in Congress: a Majority of the Mass Delegates there can be no Doubt of altho I have
never hinted the Matter to our Friend Mr. A——s.[4] Shall be glad
to know your Mind on the battalion Appointment.

I have wrote to my Brother in the House & inclosed him some
News papers to which beg Leave to refer You being Sir with Regards to all Friends yours most assuredly,   Elbridge Gerry

P.S. I think the House have acted Judiciously in not electing Members of Congress into the Council: perhaps it will be necessary to
pass a Resolve of both Houses inviting them to a Seat in either or
both whenever they shall return from their Congress & also to express their Sentiments on a Matter in Debate *without voting,* since
a Knowledge of the affairs of the Continent may enable them to
throw great Light on many Matters, & their being in the General
assembly may at the same Time afford useful Information at their
Return to Congress. I speek not for myself having a Seat independant of your Mightynesses.   ETG

[*P.S.*] I am very fond of the Ladies & therefore like them, have a
postscript containing the most important parts of my Letter. I beg
as a Matter of the greatest Moment that the General Assembly
would take particular Care of all their Military Stores of every Kind
& spare none out of the Colony untill they are fully supplied, [. . .]
upon the most pressing & apparent Necessity, & even then by Loan
only. Each Colony is acting on this plan & if Massachusetts is too
liberal, It will be soon drained of Arms, Ammunition, Tents, Cannon &c &c &c, which when once in possession of the Continent can
Never perhaps be again recovered. The Article of Saltpetre is so
plentifully manufactured that I think it will be well to offer to
Congress what can be spared for the Continent at the price given by
the Colony; the Quantity now in your Magazine will make upwards
of sixty Tons of Powder which with twenty Tons besides in the
Colony will be eighty; a sufficient Quantity at one Time. If then the
continent was to be supplyed at 7s per pound as the new Saltpetre
comes in, You will be at the Expence of 5s only for all that is used
by the Colony; which, if you think worthy of the attention of the
House, may with the first proposal be commuicated to Major
Hawley or some other Friend [. . .] to be moved accordingly.

Quære. Why are the Stocks on Martha's Vineyard & Nantucket
suffered to remain untill the Enemy are ready to take possession?
Surely the Inhabitants of those Islands if left to themselves will not
only be ruined, but give the Enemy such Supplies as may tend to
ruin the Continent.

RC (NjR: Elsie O. and Philip D. Sang deposit, 1972). Recipient identified from James Warren's July 7, 1776, letter to Gerry in Gerry Papers, DLC.

¹ Gerry's concern was that proposed remedies might do more harm than good, as in the case alluded to in the *Aeneid* where the patient worsened under the doctor's care. Virgil, *Aeneid,* 12.46.

² On June 24 Congress appointed a committee "to enquire into the cause of the miscarriages in Canada." *JCC,* 5:474.

³ The Continental Loan Office was not approved by Congress until October 3, 1776. Each state was authorized to appoint the commissioner for the state's loan office. *JCC,* 5:845–46.

⁴ Adams.

Robert R. Livingston to John R. Livingston

Dear John   Philadelphia 15th June 1776.

Mr. Wisener will bring you a letter from the chairman of the secret Committee of Congress ¹ remanding 20 tons of salt petre which was directed to be sent to Mr. Wiseners Mill & which by some mistake is gone to yours. I am sorry for this disappointment but hope you will make no difficulty in complying. Mr. Morris promisses me that he will when you inform him that your stock is nearly worked up endeavour to procure you an additional supply tho in the meanwhile more will probably arrive at New York. I wish you would converse very freely with Mr. Wisener on the subject of refining your salt petre & the manufacture of powder since he confessedly understands it well,² & Mr. Eves's powder is in very bad repute.³ [He will tell?] you of the person at New York that will [cast] brasses for you at 8s apiece. I hope to be home in 20 days so that I shall not think it necessary to enlarge. My health is much mended tho I begin to find that the warm wheather & a close attention to business will be no advantage to [*me*]. I shall therefore follow your advise & take a journey to the manor & back again. I am much of Dr. Lathams opinion with respect to inoculation. If I can think of it when the house is not too much engaged I will try & get something done in that matter. I know you are entitled to a longer letter but you can not conceive how reluctently one takes up the pen after the fatigue of body & mind which a whole days confinement to the Congress Chamber occasions. This must plead my excuse. Give my love to all the family & believe me to be, Your Aff. Brother,   R R Livingston

RC (DLC).

¹ Not found.

² See Henry Wisner to Benjamin Towne, December 21, 1775.

³ On June 7 Livingston, Robert Treat Paine, and Henry Wisner were appointed as a committee to investigate a "complaint . . . made with respect to the powder manufactured at Mr. O[swell] Eve's mill." No report about Eve's

powder mill at Frankford, Pa., has been found. However, on August 28 and September 2 Congress did pass resolutions governing the inspection of domestic and imported gunpowder. The August 28 resolutions, which dealt only with gunpowder manufactured in America, were also printed in broadside form. See *JCC*, 5:425, 440, 634, 713–14, 729, 6:1125. See also David L. Salay, "The Production of Gunpowder in Pennsylvania during the American Revolution," *PMHB* 99 (October 1975): 422–42.

Maryland Delegates to the Maryland Council of Safety

Gentn.   Phila. June 15. 1776.

Yours of the 10th Inst. was delivered to Us yesterday. It has happened very well that you have called a Convention on the 20th tho for the purpose of complying with the resolve of Congress We think your own powers are fully adequate.[1] It never was intended that any part of the militia was compellable to march out of the Provinces; nor do We know of any Power in ours, even tho the Convention was sitting to order the Militia upon Service out of the Province. It was intended that the flying Camp should be formed by voluntary Inlistments of the Militia and it was supposed that the People of the respective Provinces would readily and voluntarily march to the head Quarters of this flying Camp, which was ordered principally to defend the Middle Colonies. It will be necessary however to appoint officers, and give Directions to the body of militia when raised and this may be done by your Council or the Convention. We wrote you a few days ago requesting a Call of the Convention to deliberate upon Matters of the last Importance, and We are glad that an earlier Meeting than we expected will afford an Oppertunity to our Constituents to communicate to us the Sense of the Province upon the very interesting subjects mentioned in our Letter. The Session will be a very important one and We wish to attend, tho we know not whether it will be agreable to our Constituents to leave the Province unrepresented in Congress, it being a Matter of much Consequence to keep up the representation at this and all other times. We shall wait to hear from You and them upon this head, indeed we can't quit the Congress without Leave which will not be given here unless our Attendance in Convention is desired.[2] Mr. Tilghman left us yesterday, Mr Paca is here. We have nothing new since we last had the Honour of Addressing You. The Continental Proof of Cannon is two thirds of the Weight of the Ball, of Powder and two Balls, tho this is said to be less powder than is used for the purpose in England.

We are Gent., with much Respect, Yr most obt Sevts,

T. Stone

J. Rogers

[*P.S.*] We have sent by the Stage 4 Reams paper, a Box Instruments, & a Gun Carriage.

RC (MdAA). Written by Stone and signed by Stone and Rogers.
   [1] See *Md. Archives*, 11:474–75; and Maryland Delegates to the Maryland Council of Safety, June 11, 1776.
   [2] The Maryland Convention responded to this explanation by resolving on June 21 that the delegates "move Congress for permission to attend here, but that they do not leave the Congress without such permission, and with out first having obtained an order that the consideration of the questions of Independence, foreign alliance, and a further Confederation of the Colonies, shall be postponed until Deputies from this Province can attend Congress." *Am. Archives*, 4th ser. 6:1485. Nevertheless, only delegates Samuel Chase, Robert Goldsborough, Thomas Johnson, and Matthew Tilghman, all of whom were already in Maryland, attended the convention.

Jonathan Dickinson Sergeant to John Adams

Dear Sir   Burl[ingto]n 15 June 1776.
   Jacta est Alea. We are passing the Rubicon & our Delegates in Congress on the first of July will vote plump.[1] The Bearer is a staunch Whigg & will answer any Questions You may need to ask. We have been very busy here & have stole a Minute from Business to write this.
         In haste, Yours,   Jona D Sergeant

RC (MHi).
   [1] Sergeant's use of Caesar's exclamation upon crossing the Rubicon was apparently in response to the New Jersey Provincial Congress' June 14 resolution denouncing Gov. William Franklin's call, "in the name of the King of Great Britain," for a meeting of the provincial assembly on June 20. Sergeant, who was attending the provincial congress in Burlington, evidently interpreted this resolution as a strong indication of that body's willingness to support a declaration of independence, but not until June 22 did it actually authorize the New Jersey delegates in Congress to vote for independence. See *Am. Archives*, 4th ser. 6:1620–22, 1628–29.

Oliver Wolcott to Laura Wolcott

My Dear   Philidelpa 15 June 1776.
   I Wrote you the 11t by Capt Sheldon who I expected would have gone out of Town before now, but he has been detained by Reason of the Stage Boat's going off sooner than was expected. I therefore improve the oppertunity of Writing by the Post. The few Articles which you mentioned to Me I have not yet procured, perhaps I shall do it before Capt. Sheldon goes away. Linnens of the ordinary kind are 12/ per yard, the better sort 15/ and 20/. Capt. Sheldon prom-

Jonathan Dickinson Sergeant

ised me to get a piece for you last Winter at N York but it seems he
has failed of doing it. Every Thing here is sold at an extraordinary
Price. Nothing more so than Linnens and indeed scarcly any could
be had for several Months past. A few Dutch Linnens are lately
bro't in and sold at 12/ per yard, which nothing but necessity could
induce any one to purchase.

Nothing Very particular has Occured since my last. We have not
heard of any late Arrivals of Troops. Those lying at Cape Fear N
Carolina it is said are sickly, and have atcheived nothing of consequence. Col Allyn is there on Board of Parkers Fleet with 31 Men
of his.[1] One Peter Noble of Norfolk a Soldier taken with Allyn is
now in this City. He swam from the Fleet the 3d. May last.

We seem at present to be in the Midst of a great Revolution, which
will probably be Attended with most important consequences. Every
Thing is leading to the lasting Independancy of these Colonies.

I hope to Return by the Time I mentioned in my former Letters.
By the Blessing of God I have injoyed more Health than I had Reason
to expect since I have been here, considering the confined Life which
I am oblidged to lead. I Wrote you the 1t. inst which I hope you have
recd. My Love to my Children and My Freinds. And be assured that
I am with the sincerest Affection yours,   Oliver Wolcott

RC (CtHi).
    [1] Ethan Allen was a prisoner on board H.M.S. *Mercury.* See Clark, *Naval
Documents,* 5:175–76, 430, 673–75.

John Adams to Abigail Adams

June 16. 1776
    Yesterday was to me a lucky Day, as it brought me two Letters
from you, one dated May 27 and the other June 3d.

Dont be concerned, about me, if it happens now and then that you
dont hear from me, for some Weeks together. If any Thing should
injure my Health materially, you will soon hear of it. But I thank God
I am in much better Health than I expected to be. But this cannot
last long, under the Load that I carry. When it becomes too great
for my Strength I shall ask leave to lay it down and come home. But
I will hold it out a good while yet, if I can.

I am willing to take the Woodland Sister mentions, and the Watch
and the sword. As to the Lighter, it cost more than five hundred
Dollars in hard Cash.

I wish our Uncle [1] had as much Ambition, as he has Virtue and
Ability. A Deficiency of Ambition is as criminal and injurious as an
Excess of it. Tell him I say so. How shall We contrive to make so
wise and good a Man ambitious? Is it not a sin to be so modest. Ask

him how he can answer it? So! then it seems the Brigadier[2] was obliged to step down Stairs in order to keep my Brother, out of the lower Room. . . .[3] I am sorry for it.

Thanks for your Quotation from Sully. It is extreamly appropos.

I am very glad you are so well provided with Help. Give my Respects to Mr. Belcher, and his Family. Tell him, I am obliged to him for his Kind Care of the Farm. I wish I could go out with him, and see the Business go on, but I cant.

Thank your Father, and my Mother, for their kind Remembrance of me. Return my Duty to both.

Charles's young Heroism charms me. Kiss him. Poor Mugford. Yet glorious Mugford. How beautifull and sublime it is to die for ones Country. What a fragrant Memory remains!

The Rumour you heard of General Gates, will prove premature. I endeavoured both here and with the General, to have it so, and should have succeeded, if it had not been for the Loss of General Thomas. Cruel small Pox! worse than the sword! But now I fear We must part with Gates for the sake of Canada.[4]

Mrs. Montgomery is a Lady like all the Family, of refined Sentiments and elegant Accomplishments. Her Letter, as you quote it, is very pathetic.

Do you mean that our Plymouth Friends are in Trouble for a disordered son! If so, I am grieved to the Heart. God grant them Support under so severe an Affliction. But this World is a scene of Afflictions.[5]

Rejoice to hear that the Enemy has not fortified. Hope they will not be suffered to attempt it.

Dont think about my Cloaths. I do well enough in that Respect. As to your House at Boston, do with it, as you please. Sell it, if you will, but not for a farthing less than it cost me. Let it, if you please, but take Care who your Tenant is—both of his Prudence to preserve the House, and his Ability to pay the Rent.

Your Brother,[6] I hope will be promoted. He is fit for it, and has deserved it. If his Name comes recommended from the General Court, he will have a Commission for a Field Officer, and I will recommend him to the General for his Notice.

My Pupil, if he pleases, will do Honour to his Preceptor, and important service to his Country. I hope his Zeal and Fidelity will be found equal to his Abilities.[7]

I will endeavour to relieve your Head Ach if I can.

I send you all the News, in the Papers. Great Things are on the Tapis. These Throws will usher in the Birth of a fine Boy. We have no Thoughts of removing from hence—there is no occasion for it.

RC (MHi). Adams, *Family Correspondence* (Butterfield), 2:12–13.
   [1] Norton Quincy.

[2] Joseph Palmer. See John Adams to Peter B. Adams, June 15, 1776.

[3] Suspension points in text.

[4] On June 15 Robert Treat Paine recorded in his diary: "Very hot. P.M. Showers. Heard that Gen. Thomas died at Chamblee of the Small Pox." MHi. Gates was appointed to the Canadian command on June 17. JCC, 5:448.

[5] For further information on the Warrens' "disordered son," James Warren, Jr. (1757–1821), see Adams, *Family Correspondence* (Butterfield), 1:419n.7.

[6] William Smith, Jr. (1746–87).

[7] See Adams to Oakes Angier, June 12, 1776.

John Adams to James Warren

Dear sir   Philadelphia June 16. 1776.

Your Favours of June 2d and 5th are now before me.[1] The Address to the Convention of Virginia, makes but a Small Fortune in the World. Coll Henry, in a Letter to me, expresses an infinite Contempt of it, and assures me, that the Constitution of Virginia, will be more like the Thoughts on Government.[2] I believe, however, they will make the Election of their Council, Septennial. Those of Representatives and Governor annual. But I am amazed to find an Inclination So prevalent throughout all the southern and middle Colonies to adopt Plans, so nearly resembling that in the Thoughts on Government. I assure you, untill the Experiment was made, I had no adequate Conception of it. But the Pride of the haughty, must, I see come down a little in the South.

You Suppose "it would not do, to have the two Regiments you are now raising converted into continental Battallions." But why? Would the officers, or Men have any objection? If they would not, Congress would have none. Indeed this was what I expected, and intended when the Measure was in agitation. Indeed I thought, that as our Battallions with their Arms, were carried to N. York and Canada in the Service of the united Colonies, the Town of Boston, and the Province ought to be guarded against Danger by the united Colonies.

You have been Since call'd upon for Six Thousand Militia for Canada and New York—how you will get the Men, I know not.[3] The Small Pox, I Suppose will be a great Discouragement. But We must maintain our Ground in Canada. The Regulars, if they get full Possession of that Province, and the Navigation of St. Lawrence River above Dechambeault, at least above the Month of the Sorrell, will have nothing to interrupt their Communication with Niagara, Detroit, Michilimachinac; they will have the Navigation of the five great Lakes quite as far as the Mississipi River; they will have a free Communication with all the numerous Tribes of Indians, extending along the Frontiers of all the Colonies, and by their Trinketts and Bribes will induce them to take up the Hatchett, and Spread

Blood and Fire among the Inhabitants by which Means, all the Frontier Inhabitants will be driven in upon the middle settlements, at a Time when the Inhabitants of the Seaports and Coasts, will be driven back by the British Navy. Is this Picture too high coloured? Perhaps it is. But surely We must maintain our Power, in Canada.

You may depend upon my rendering Mr Winthrop, all the service in my Power.[4]

I believe it will not be long, before all Property, belonging to British Subjects, Whether in Europe, the W. Indies, or elsewhere will be made liable to Capture.[5] A few Weeks may possibly produce great Things. I am &c

RC (MHi). In Adams' hand, though not signed.

[1] Warren's June 2 and 5 letters to Adams are in the Adams Papers, MHi, and *Warren-Adams Letters*, 1:252–55.

[2] See Adams to Patrick Henry, June 3, 1776.

[3] See John Hancock to Certain Colonies, June 4, 1776. The Massachusetts General Court later complained to Hancock of the difficulty of raising the additional troops without the payment of a bounty. See Jeremiah Powell to John Hancock, June 26, and Benjamin Greenleaf to John Hancock, July 19, 1776, PCC, item 65, 1:89–90, 93–95; and *Am. Archives*, 4th ser. 6:1087, 5th ser. 1:459–60.

[4] See Adams to John Winthrop, May 6, 1776, note 1.

[5] Adams was subsequently a member of the committee appointed on July 17 "to bring in a resolution for subjecting to confiscation the property of the subjects of the crown of Great Britain, and particularly the inhabitants of the British West Indies, taken on the high seas, or between high and low water mark." The committee's report was read on July 19 and approved by Congress on July 24, 1776. *JCC*, 5:572, 591, 605–6.

John Hancock to Thomas Cushing

Dear Sir   Philada. 16 June 1776 Sunday

I am Reduc'd to the last moment, & even keep the Express to write this, that I have only time to inform you that I yesterday dispatch'd a Waggon with Money for my Brother who is appointed Depy Pay Mas Genl. in the Eastern Departmt. under the Care of my Mr Spriggs, & by the same Conveyance I forwarded a Box directed to you containg 20,000 Dollars for the Ships, which he will Deliver you. He will show you his written Directions; he will also deliver you a Box of Money directed for New Hampshire which the Delegates of that Colony request you will forward with the Inclos'd Letter.[1] I shall write you fully by the next Post, & also to Capt Bradford. I shall Send all the Warrants to your Sea officers &c. I want the recommendations for the Marine Officers &c. Next Monday Eveng. the Marine Board will perfect the most of the matters relative to the Ships, when you shall have the necessary Directions. I shall send you an order for what Provisions you may want to be taken from the Commissary's Store.

Your several favrs. to 6th June I have Rec'd, the last Inclosing my Commission as Major General, I beg you will make my Acknowledgments to the Gentlemen for the honour they have done me, & Assure them I will Endeavour to answer their Expectations.

In my last I Sent you a List of the Captains with the Names of the Ships as far as we had then proceeded, since which the following Appointments have been made,[2] Vizt.

> Israel Turner— 1st Lieutt. ⎫   For the Ship Hancock Com-
> Joseph Doble— 2d do. ⎬   manded by Capt. Manly.
> Mark Desmitt—3d do. ⎭
>
> Hector McNeil Captain ⎫   For the Ship Boston.
> John Brown   1st. Lieut ⎭

Thomas Grenell to the Command of the Frigate Montgomery at N York.

You will please to Send me a Rect. for the Money. Do Send me the Names of the other Lieuts.

McNeil & Brown are both here & will proceed down to you in a day or two.

Dr. Sir, I must beg of you in your own way to impress the Assembly with the importance of Answering Letters from Congress, we are in the Dark whether matters are Carried into Execution, pray let us hear constantly. If you can propose anything that I can serve young Mr. Avery in, I will with much pleasure endeavour to answer his & your wish.[3]

I am exceedingly hurried. Remember me to all Friends. I am very truly, Dr. Sir, Your faithfull friend & Sevt,   John Hancock

[P.S.] I have inclos'd in my Letter to the Assembly a Resolve, which I beg may be inserted in all the News papers immediately.

One Frederick Beck who guards the money, will have some demand, either you pay or I. I kept him here a few days.

We have wrote to the assembly to order us some money, be so good as to attend to it, & let us have some soon.

Mr Gill I find prints a News paper, please to ask him to Enter me for a paper & to Send it [to] me regularly here every week.

RC (MHi).

[1] See Josiah Bartlett to Meshech Weare, June 14, 1776.

[2] See JCC, 5:423, 444.

[3] On June 4 the Massachusetts General Court had appointed a "standing Committee of Correspondence" to communicate regularly with the Massachusetts delegates. Am. Archives, 5th ser. 1:267. For a lengthy extract from Cushing's June 24 reply to Hancock's letter, see Clark, Naval Documents, 5:706.

John Hancock to Daniel Roberdeau

Dear Sir   Philada 16th June 1776

The Continental Troops having left this City for New York, I am laid under the necessity to Request you will be so obliging as to order a Guard of Six Men with an officer of your Battalion of associators in whom you can confide to attend a Waggon of money from hence to New York on its way to Canada, your Guard to be Reliev'd at New York by a Guard which General Washington will appoint immediately on their Arrival at New York. I should be Glad the Guard might be at my house by 9 oClock tomorrow morng.[1]

I am with much Esteem, Sir, Your very huml sevt,

J H Pt.

LB (DNA: PCC, item 12A).

[1] On the following day Hancock wrote a letter to Capt. William Bradford, Jr., who had been appointed by Roberdeau to command the escort for the money ordered to General Schuyler, delivering "to your Charge Six Boxes of Money for the use of the Army in Canada" and urging him to "proceed with the Guard under your Command, & the Waggon of Money, with all possible Dispatch to the City of New York, & wait upon General Washington to whom you will Deliver your Charge, or Take his order respecting it." Hancock to William Bradford, Jr., June 17, 1776, Society Collection, PHi. Congress awarded Bradford "88 57/90 dollars" on July 23, 1776, for this mission. *JCC*, 5:603.

Josiah Bartlett

Josiah Bartlett's and John Dickinson's Draft Articles of Confederation

[June 17–July 1? 1776] [1]

[Josiah Bartlett's Draft]	[John Dickinson's Draft]

[Josiah Bartlett's Draft]

Articles of Confederation & perpetual union between the Colonies of New Hampshire &c in General Congress met at Philadelphia the   Day of 1776.

Art 1st. The name of this Confederation shall be the "United States of America."

Art 2nd. The Said Colonies unite themselves so as never to be divided by any act whatever ⟨of the Legislature of any Colony or Colonies or of the Inhabitants thereof,⟩ and hereby Severally Enter into a firm League of friendship with each other for their Common Defence, the Security of their liberties, & their mutual & General wellfare, binding the said Colonies ⟨all the inhabitants & their Posterity⟩ to assist one another ⟨with their lives & fortunes⟩ against all force offered to or attacks made upon them or any of them on ⟨pretence⟩ [Account] of Religion, sovereignty, trade, or any other pretence whatever ⟨and faithfully to observe & adhere to all and Singular the articles of this Confederation⟩.

Art 3d. Each Colony shall retain & Enjoy as much of its present laws, rights & Customs as it may think fit and reserve

[John Dickinson's Draft]

Articles of Confederation and perpetual Union between the Colonies of New Hampshire &c ⟨in General Congress met⟩ at Philadelphia the   Day of   1776.

Art.[1]. The Name of this Confederacy shall be "The United States of America."

Art.[2]. The said Colonies unite themselves ⟨into one Body politic⟩ so as never to be divided by any Act whatever ⟨of the Legislature of any Colony or Colonies, or of the Inhabitants thereof⟩, and hereby severally enter into a firm League of Friendship with each other, for their Common Defence, the Security of their Liberties, and their mutual & general Wellfare, binding the said Colonies ⟨and all the Inhabitants, & their Posterity,⟩ to assist one another ⟨with their Lives and Fortunes⟩ against all Force offered to or Attacks made upon them or any of them, on account of Religion, Sovereignty, Trade, or any other Pretence whatever, ⟨and faithfully to observe and adhere to all & singular the Articles of this Confederation⟩.

Art.[3]. [2] Each Colony shall retain and enjoy as much of its present Laws, Rights & Customs, as it may think fit, and reserves

to it self the Sole and Exclusive
regulation & Government of its
Internal Police (in all ⟨articles⟩
[matters] that shall not interfere
with the articles ⟨agreed upon
by⟩ [of] this Confederation).

to itself the sole and exclusive
regulation and Government of
its internal Police, in all Matters that shall not interfere with
the Articles ⟨agreed upon by⟩ of
this Confederation.

Art.[4].[3] No person in any
Colony living peaceably under
the Civil Government, shall be
molested or prejudiced in his or
her person or Estate for his or
her religious persuasion, Profession or practice, nor be compelled to frequent or maintain
or contribute to maintain any
religious Worship, Place of Worship, or Ministry, contrary to
his or her Mind, by any Law or
ordinance hereafter to be made
in any Colony different from
the usual Laws & Customs subsisting at the Commencement
of this War—provided, that such
person frequents regularly some
Place of religious Worship on
the Sabbath; & no religious Persuasion or practise for the Profession or Exercise of which,
persons are not disqualified by
the present Laws of the said
Colonies   respectively,   from
holding any offices Civil or military, shall by any Law or Ordinance hereafter to be made in
any Colony, be rendered a Dis-
qualification of any persons pro-
fessing or exercising the same
from holding any such offices,
as fully as they might have done
heretofore: Nor shall any further Tests or Qualifications concerning   religious   persuasion,
Profession or Practise, than such
as have been usually adminis-
tered in the said Colonies re-

spectively, be imposed by any Law or Ordinance hereafter to be made in any Colony; and whenever on Election or Appointment to any Offices, or on any other occasions, the Affirmation of persons conscientiously scrupulous of taking an Oath, hath been admitted in any Colony or Colonies, no Oath shall in any such Cases be hereafter imposed by any Law or Ordinance in any such Colony or Colonies, it being the full Intent of these united Colonies that all the Inhabitants thereof respectively of every Sect, Society or religious Denomination shall enjoy under this Confederation, all the Liberties and Priviledges which they have heretofore enjoyed without the least abridgement of their civil Rights for or on Account of their religious Persuasion, profession or practise.

Art 4th. No Colony or Colonies without the Consent of the ⟨union⟩ [United States assembled,] shall send any Embassy to or receive any Embassy from or Enter into any treaty [Convention] or Conference with the King or Kingdom of Great Brittain or any foreign prince or State nor shall any Colony or Colonies nor any servant or servants [of the United States, or] of any Colony or Colonies accept of any present, Emolument, office or tittle of any kind whatever from the King or Kingdom of G.B. or any foreign prince or State ⟨under any pretence whatever⟩ nor shall the ⟨union⟩

Art. [5]. No Colony or Number of Colonies without the Consent of the union shall send any Embassy to or receive any Embassy from, or enter into any Treaty, Convention or Conference with the King or Kingdom of Great Britain, or any Foreign Prince or State; nor shall any Colony or Colonies, nor any Servant or Servants of any Colony or Colonies, accept of any Present, Emolument, Office or Title of any kind whatever from the King or Kingdom of G.B. or any foreign Prince or State, Nor shall the Union of any Colony grant any Title of Nobility to any person whatsoever.

[United States assembled] or any Colony grant any title of nobility ⟨to any person whatsoever⟩.

Art 5th. No two or more ⟨of the⟩ Colonies shall Enter into any treaty, Confederation, alliance ⟨or agreement⟩ whatever between them ⟨on any pretence whatever,⟩ without the previous & free Consent & allowance of the ⟨union⟩ [United States assembled] specifying accurately the purposes for which the Same is to be Entered into & how long it shall Continue.

Art. [6]. No two or more Colonies shall enter into any Treaty, Confederation, or Alliance whatever between them without the previous and free Consent & Allowance of the Union, specifying accurately the purposes for which the same is to be entered into, and how long it shall continue.

Art 6th. The Inhabitants of Each Colony shall henceforth always have the Same Rights [Liberties] privileges [Immunities] & advantages in ⟨all Cases whatever in the other Colonies which they now have⟩ [the other Colonies, which the said Inhabitants now have, in all Cases whatever, except in those provided for by the next following Article.]

Art. [7]. The Inhabitants of each Colony shall henceforth always have the same Rights, Privileges and advantages in all Cases whatever in the other Colonies, which they now have.

Art 7th. The Inhabitants of ⟨all the united Colonies⟩ [each Colony] shall Enjoy all the rights [Liberties] Priviledges ⟨&⟩ imunities [and Advantages] in trade, navigation & Commerce in ⟨Every⟩ [any other] Colony and in going to & from the Same [from and to any Part of the World,] which the natives of ⟨Each⟩ [such] Colony Enjoy;

Art. [8]. The Inhabitants of all the united Colonies shall enjoy all the Rights, Liberties, Priviledges, Exemptions & Immunities in Trade, Navigation & Commerce in every Colony, and in going to & from the same, which the Natives of such Colony enjoy. ⟨No Colony shall assess or lay any Duties or Imposts on the Importation of the Productions or Manufactures of another Colony, nor settle or establish any Fees for Entries, Clearances, or any Business whatever relative to Importation or Exportation [. . . .]⟩

[Art. VIII]. Each Colony may assess or lay Such imposts or Duties as it thinks proper on importations ⟨from,⟩ or Exportations ⟨to, the Brittish Dominions or any foreign State, or the importation of the production or manufacture of Such Dominion, Kingdom or State from another Colony⟩ Provided Such imposts or Duties do not interfere with any Stipulation in ⟨any⟩ treaties hereafter ⟨made and⟩ Entered into by the ⟨whole Union⟩ [United States assembled] with the King or Kingdom of G.B. or with any foreign prince or State.

Art ⟨8th⟩ [IX]. No [standing] army or Body of forces shall be kept up by any Colony or Colonies in time of peace, Except such a number only as may be requisite to Garrison the forts necessary for the Defence of such Colony or Colonies, ⟨nor shall this be done without the Consent of the Union⟩; But Every Colony shall always keep up a well regulated & Disciplined Militia Sufficiently armed & accoutered, and shall provide & Constantly have ready for use, ⟨a proper quantity of Public Stores of Ammunition, field pieces, tents & other Camp Equipage⟩ [in public Stores, a due Number of Field Pieces and Tents, and a proper Quantity of Ammunition, and Camp Equipage.]

Art. [9]. Each Colony may assess or lay such Imposts or Duties, as it thinks proper, on Importations or Exportations ⟨to the British Dominions, or any foreign Kingdom or State, on the Importations of the productions or Manufactures of such [. . .] or any foreign Kingdom or State from another Colony⟩, provided such Imposts or Duties do not interfere with any Stipulations in Treaties hereafter entered into by the Union, with the King or Kingdom of G.B. or with any foreign Prince or State.

Art. [10]. No ⟨standing⟩ army or Body of Forces shall be kept up by any Colony or Colonies in Time of Peace ⟨or War without the Approbation of the Union⟩ except such a Number only as may be requisite to garrison the Forts necessary for the Defence of such Colony or Colonies; ⟨nor shall this be done without the Consent of the Union⟩ but every Colony shall always keep up a well regulated & disciplined Militia sufficiently armed and accoutred; and shall ⟨properly⟩ provide and constantly have ready for use a proper Quantity of public Stores of Ammunition, Field pieces, Tents, and other Camp Equipage. ⟨Each Colony shall also be constantly provided with public Stores of Ammunition not less than   pounds of lead powder &   pounds of leaden Ball for every Militia

Man in the Colony with good Tents sufficient for one third of the whole Militia of the Colony, and with   Field pieces not less than nor larger than   to every thousand Men of the Militia, and a proper Company of Officers   to every Train of Artillery, who shall be well exercised in the Management thereof.⟩

Art ⟨9th⟩ [X]. When troops are raised in any of the Colonies for the Common Defence the Commission officers proper for the troops raised in Each Colony Except the General officers shall be appointed ⟨in Such manner as shall be Directed by the Legislature of each Colony Respectively⟩ [by the Legislature of each Colony respectively, or in such manner as shall by them be directed.]

Art. [11].⁴ When Troops are raised in any of the Colonies for the Common Defense, the Commission Officers proper for the Troops raised in each Colony, except the General Officers, shall be appointed by the Legislature of each Colony respectively, or in such Manner as shall by them be directed. ⟨*It being the Intent of this Confederacy, Notwithstanding the Powers hereafter given to the Union in Genl. Congress, that all Resolutions of Congress for raising Land Forces, should be executed by the Legislature of each Colony respectively where they are to be raised, or by persons authorized by such Legislature for that purpose.*⟩

Art ⟨10th⟩ [XI]. All Charges of wars and all other Expences that shall be incurred for the [common Defence, or] general welfare and allowed by the ⟨union in General Congress⟩ [United States assembled] shall be Defreyed out of the Common treasury, which shall be supplied by the several Colonies in proportion to the Number of ⁵ in Each Colony a true account of which [distinguishing the white Inhabi-

Art. [12]. All Charges of War and all other Expences that shall be incurr'd for the general Wellfare and allowed by the Union in General Congress, shall be defrayed out of a Common Treasury, which shall be supplied by the several Colonies in proportion to the Number of ⁵ in each Colony, a true Account of which shall be triennially taken and transmitted to Congress. The Taxes for paying that proportion shall be

tants] shall be triennially taken
& transmitted to ⟨Congress⟩ [the
Assembly of the United States].
The taxes for paying that proportion shall be laid & Levied
by the authority & Direction of
the Legislature of the ⟨respec-
tive⟩ [several] Colonys [within
the Time agreed upon by the
United States assembled.] [7]

laid and levied by the Authority
& Direction of the Legislature
of the respective Colonies.[6]

Art. [13]. Every Colony shall
abide by the Determinations of
the Union in general Congress,
concerning the Losses, or Expences of ⟨any Contributions of
Men or Money⟩ every Colony in
the general Cause, and no Colony or Colonies shall in any Case
whatever endeavour by Force
to procure Redress of any Injury
or Injustice supposed to be done
by the Union to such Colony or
Colonies in not granting to such
Colony or Colonies such Indem-
nifications, Compensations, Ret-
ributions, Exemptions or Benefits of any kind, as such Colony
or Colonies may think just or
reasonable.

Art ⟨11th⟩ [XIII]. No Colony
or Colonies shall Engage in any
war without the [previous] Consent of the ⟨union⟩ [United
States assembled,] unless such
Colony or Colonies ⟨shall⟩ be
actually invaded by Enemies, or
shall have Received Certain advice of a Resolution being
formed by some nation of Indians to invade Such Colony or
Colonies and the Danger is so
imminent as not to admit of
a Delay till the other Colonies
Can be Consulted.[9]

Art ⟨12th⟩ [XIV]. A perpetual

Art. [14]. No Colony or Colonies shall engage in any War
⟨with any Nation of Indians⟩
without the Consent of the
Union,[8] unless such Colony or
Colonies be actually invaded by
Enemies, or shall have received
certain Advice of a Resolution
being formed by some Nation of
Indians to invade such Colony
or Colonies, and the Danger is
so imminent as not to admit of
a Delay, till the other Colonies
can be consulted.

Art. [15]. A perpetual Alliance

alliance offensive & Defensive is to be Entered into by the ⟨whole union⟩ [United States assembled] as soon as may be with the Six nations & all other [neighbouring] nations of Indians, their Limits [to] be ascertained, their lands to be Secured to them and not Encroached on, no purchases [of Lands, hereafter to be made of the Indians] by Colonies or private persons ⟨hereafter to be made of them⟩ before the Limits of the Colonies are ascertained to be ⟨held Good⟩ [valid:] all ⟨Contracts for⟩ [Purchases of] Lands not Included within those Limits where ascertained, to be made [by Contracts] between the ⟨whole Union in General Congress met, and the Great Council of Indians for the General Benefit & advantage of all the united Colonies, persons to be appointed by the union to reside among the Indians in proper Districts who shall take Care to prevent injustice in the trade with them and shall be Enabled at the Common Expence of the united Colonies by occasional supplies to relieve their personal wants & Distresses⟩ [United States assembled, or by Persons for that Purpose authorized by them, and the great Councils of the Indians, for the general Benefit of all the United Colonies.]

Art ⟨13⟩ [XV]. ⟨The union shall in a short time ascertain the Boundaries between Colony & Colony, where they Cannot agree among themselves Either in General Congress or by Erect-

offensive & defensive, is to be entered into by the Union as soon as may be with the Six Nations and all other Nations of Indians; [10] their Limits to be ascertained; their Lands to be secured to them, and not encroached on; [11] no Purchases by Colonies, or private persons hereafter to be made of them before the Limits of the Colonies are ascertained, to be held good; all Contracts for Lands not included within those Limits where ascertained, to be made between the whole Union in General Congress met, and the Great Council of Indians, for the general Benefit & Advantage of all the united Colonies. ⟨*Persons to be appointed by the Union to reside among the Indians in proper Districts, who shall take Care to prevent Injustice in the Trade with them and shall be enabled at the Common Expence of the united Colonies by occasional Supplies to relieve their personal Wants & Distresses.*⟩

Art. [16]. ⟨*The [. . .] of the Union shall in a short Time ascertain the Boundaries between Colony & Colony, where they cannot agree among themselves either in General Congress or by* ing some Court for that purpose and shall also in General Congress fix & assign reasonable limits towards the west to those Colonies the words of whose Charters extend to the great South Sea; upon thus ascertaining⟩ [When] the Boundaries of any Colony [shall be ascertained by Agreement, or in the Manner herein after directed,] all the other Colonies shall Guarantee to Such Colony the full & peaceable possession of, and the free & intire Jurisdiction in & over the territory included within Such Boundaries.

Art ⟨14th⟩ [XVI]. For the more Convenient management of the General Interest [of the United States], Delegates ⟨shall⟩ [should] be Annually appointed ⟨by⟩ [in such Manner as the Legislature of] Each Colony [shall direct,] to meet ⟨in General Congress in⟩ [at] the City of Philadelphia in the Colony of Pensylvania until otherwise ordered by ⟨Congress⟩ [the United States assembled;] which meeting shall be on the first Monday of November [in] Every year, with a power reserved ⟨in Each Colony to supersede the Deligates thereof⟩ [to those who appointed the said Delegates, respectively to recal them or any of them] at any time within the year and to send new Deligates in their Stead for the Remainder of the year. Each Colony shall support its own Deligates in ⟨Congress⟩ [a Meeting of the States, and while they act as Members of the Council of State, herein after mentioned].

erecting some Court for that purpose & shall also in General Congress fix and assign reasonable Limits towards the West to those Colonies the words of whose Charters extend to the South Sea, and⟩ When the Boundaries of any Colony shall be ascertained by agreement among themselves, in the Manner hereinafter directed, all the other Colonies shall garrantee to such Colony the full & peaceable Possession of and the free and entire Jurisdiction in & over the Territory included within such Boundaries.

Art. [17]. For the more convenient Management of the general Interests, Delegates shall be annually appointed by Legislature of each Colony or such Branch thereof as the Colony shall authorize for that purpose,[12] to meet in General Congress at the City of Philadelphia in the Colony of Pennsylvania untill otherwise ordered by Congress, which Meeting shall be on the first Monday in November in every Year, with a Power reserved to those who appointed the said Delegates, to supersede them or any of them, at any Time within the Year, and to send new Delegates in their Stead for the Remainder of the Year. *⟨If any Matter shall come to the Knowledge of a Colony, in Recess of Congress, and shall appear of such Importance as to require its assembling before the Day appointed, such Colony shall communicate the Business to the rest, & if a Majority of them shall agree, that the Congress ought* *to be assembled before the Day appointed, the Colony that gave the Intelligence may summon a Congress and appoint the Day & Place of Meeting.*⟩ Each Colony shall support its own Delegates in Congress,[13] and while acting as Members of the Co[un-ci]l of State.

Art. [18].[14] Each Colony shall have one Vote in Congress.

[Art XVIII]. The ⟨Congress⟩ [United States assembled shall] have the sole & Exclusive power & right of Determining on [Peace and] war Except in the Cases mentioned in the ⟨11th⟩ [thirteenth] article ⟨& peace &⟩ [—Of] Establishing rules for Deciding in all Cases, what Captures by land or water shall be Legal, ⟨and⟩ in what manner prizes taken by ⟨ships of war⟩ [land or naval Forces] in the service of the ⟨union⟩ [United States] shall be Divided ⟨& apportioned⟩ [or appropriated] Granting ⟨Commissions to the Commanders of ships or vessels of war &⟩ letters of marque & reprisal [in Times of Peace—] ⟨and authorising the supreme Legislative power in Each Colony to grant the same, under such Regulation as shall be made by the union, Establishing & regulating⟩ [Appointing] Courts for the trial of all Crimes, frauds & piracies Committed on the high Seas ⟨and⟩ [or on any navigable River, not within the Body of a County or Parish—Establishing Courts] for Receiving & Determining finally appeals in all ⟨maritime Causes

Art. [19]. The Congress shall have the sole and exclusive Power & Right of determining on War, ⟨except in the Cases mentioned in the Article [15]—see pa. 5 & first Art in this Copy⟩ and Peace,[16] establishing Rules for deciding what Captures by Land or Water shall be legal ⟨*in Time of War*⟩ and in what Manner Prizes shall be divided & appropriated; granting Commissions to the Commanders of Ships or Vessels of War, & Letters of Marque and Reprizal; establishing & regulating Courts for the Trial of all Crimes, Frauds & piracies committed on the high Seas, & for receiving & determining finally Appeals in all maritime Causes, sending and receiving Embassadors under any Character; entring into Treaties & Alliances; settling all Disputes and Differences now subsisting or that hereafter may arise between two or more Colonies concerning Boundaries, Jurisdictions, or any other Cause whatever; establishing a sameness of Weights & Measures throughout all the united Colonies; coining Money and regulating the Value thereof; superintending all In-under Such Regulations as may be made by the union;⟩ [Cases of Captures—] Sending & Receiving Ambassadors under any Character, Entering into treaties & alliances, Settling all Disputes & Differences now subsisting or that hereafter may arise between two or more Colonies concerning Boundaries, Jurisdictions or any other Cause whatever, Coining money & regulating the value thereof; ⟨Superintending all Indian affairs & regulating the trade with those nations,⟩ [Regulating the Trade, and managing all Affairs with the Indians—] Limiting the Bounds of those Colonies which by Charter [or] proclamation or under any pretence are Said to extend to the South Sea, and ⟨also of those that appear to have no Determinate Bounds,⟩ [ascertaining those Bounds of any other Colony that appear to be indeterminate —] assigning territories to new Colonies Either in lands to be thus seperated from Colonies & heretofore purchased [or obtained] by the Crown [of Great-Britain from the Indians] or hereafter to be purchased [or obtained] from ⟨the Indians and⟩ [them—] Disposing of all such lands for the general benefit of all the united Colonies, ascertaining Boundaries to Such new Colonies, within which forms of Government ⟨shall⟩ [are to] be Established, on the principles of liberty, ⟨and⟩ Establishing & regulating Post offices throughout [all] the united Colonies on the [Lines of] Communication from one Colony to another.[17]

dian Affairs, & regulating all Trade with those Nations; assigning Territories for new Colonies either in Lands to be separated from Colonies the words of whose Charters extend to the South Sea, or from the Colony of New York, heretofore purchased by the Crown, or Lands hereafter to be purchased from the Indians, & selling all such Lands for the general Benefit and advantage of all the united Colonies, ascertaining convenient and moderate Boundaries to such new Colonies, and giving proper Forms of Government to the Inhabitants within them upon the Principles of Liberty; and establishing and regulating Post-Offices throughout all the united Colonies.

The ⟨Congress⟩ [United States assembled] shall have ⟨power &⟩ authority for the Defence & ⟨Security⟩ [Welfare] of the united Colonies & Every of them to agree upon & fix the necessary Sums & Expences to Emit ⟨money or⟩ Bills [or to borrow Money] on the Credit of the united Colonies, to raise naval ⟨& land forces for those purposes, to make rules for governing & regulating such forces, to appoint General officers to Command them, and other officers necessary for managing the General affairs of the union under the Direction of Congress: To appoint a Council of Safety to act in the recess of Congress and such Committees & officers as may be necessary for managing the general affairs of the union under the Direction of the Congress while Sitting & in their recess of the Council of Safety; they may appoint one of their Number to preside & a Suitable person for secretary.⟩ [21]

The Congress shall have Authority to agree upon in the Manner herein directed proper Measures for the Defence & Security of the united Colonies & every of them against all their Enemies, and to carry the same into Execution so far forth as they are hereby permitted; to raise naval & land Forces for these purposes; [18] to emit Money or Bills of Credit; to make Rules for governing & regulating such Forces; [19] to appoint General Officers to command them; and other Officers necessary for managing the general Affairs of the Union under the Direction of Congress; [20] to commission other Officers appointed by Virtue of the Article preceding (see pa. 4. last art of this Copy); to appoint a Council of Safety to act in the Recess of Congress, and such Committees and Officers as may be necessary for managing the general Affairs of the Union, under the Direction of Congress while sitting, and in their Recess, of the Council of ⟨Safety⟩ State,[22] a Chamber of Accounts, an Office of Treasury, a Board of War, a Board of Admiralty, out of their own Body, and such Committees out of the same as shall be thought necessary.[20] They may appoint one of their Number to preside, and a suitable person for Secretary. The Chamber of Accounts, the Office of Treasury, the Board of War and Board of Admiralty, shall always act under the Direction of Congress while sitting, and in their Recess, under that of the Council of Safety.

But the ⟨Congress⟩ [United States assembled] shall ⟨not⟩ [never] levy or impose any taxes or Duties Except in managing the post offices [24] nor interfere in the internal Police of any Colony ⟨or Colonies⟩ any further than such Police may be ⟨expressly⟩ affected by [the Articles of] this Confederation [25] ⟨nor shall any alteration be at any time hereafter made in the terms of this Confederation, unless Such alteration be agreed to in General Congress by the Delegates of Every Colony of the union and be afterwards Confirmed by the Legislature of Every Colony.⟩

The ⟨Congress⟩ [United States assembled] shall never Engage the united Colonies in a war, [nor grant Letters of Marque and Reprisal in Time of Peace,] nor ⟨Conclude⟩ [enter into] any treaty or alliance ⟨with any other power nor raise land or naval forces, nor agree upon the Coining specie & Emitting the Same or any other money or Bills of Credit unless the Delegates of   Colonies freely Assent to the Same⟩.[28]

But the Congress shall never impose or levy any Taxes or Duties,[23] except in managing the Post offices, nor interfere in the internal Police of any Colony or Colonies, any farther than such Police may be ⟨expressly⟩ affected by this Confederation; nor shall any Alteration be at any Time hereafter made in the Terms of this Confederation or any of them,[26] unless such Alteration be agreed to in ⟨General Congress by the Delegates of every Colony of the Union and⟩ an Assembly of the United States and be afterwards confirmed by the Legislature of every Colony.

The ⟨Congress shall⟩ United States assembled shall never engage the United Colonies in a War, nor conclude any Alliance or Treaty [27] with any other Power, nor raise naval Forces, nor form a Resolution to raise land Forces, nor agree upon the coining Money & regulating the Value thereof, or the emitting Bills or borrowing money on the Credit of the United Colonies, unless the Delegates of nine Colonies freely assent to the same.[29] No Question on any other Point except for adjourning shall be ⟨put unless all the Colonies are actually represented in Congress when the Question is put⟩ determined unless the Delegates of seven Colonies vote in the affirmative.[30]

No person shall be capable of being a Delegate for more than three Years in any Term of six Years.

No person holding any Office

Art ⟨15th⟩ [XIX]. The Council of ⟨Safety⟩ [State] shall Consist of one Delegate from Each Colony ⟨of whom in the first appointment five shall be Determined by lot, to serve for one year, four for two years & four for three years and as the said terms Expire the vacancies shall be filled by appointments for three years from among the Delegates of those Colonies whose Delegates then go out of the Said office, and no person who has served the Said term of three years as a Councillor shall be Elected again untill after a respite of three years⟩ [to be named annually by the Delegates of each Colony, and where they cannot agree, by the United States assembled.]

⟨The Business & Duty of⟩ this Council ⟨of which   members shall be a Quorum shall be in Recess of Congress⟩ [shall have Power] to receive & open all letters Directed to the ⟨Congress⟩ [United States] and to return proper answers, but not to make any Engagements that shall be binding on the united ⟨Colonies or any of them⟩ [States —] to Correspond with the ⟨several assemblies, Colonial Councils & Committees of Safety, Governors & Presidents of Colonies and all persons acting under the authority of the Congress or of the Legislature of any Colony⟩ [Legislature of each

under the United States, for which he receives any pay or Fees by himself or another for his Benefit, shall be capable of being a Delegate.

Art. [20]. The Council of ⟨Safety⟩ State shall consist of one Delegate from each Colony,[31] ⟨of whom in the first appointment, five shall be determined by Lott to serve for one Year, four for two Years, and four for three Years, and as the said Terms expire, the Vacancies shall be filled by appointments for three Years, from the Delegates of those Colonies, whose Delegates then go out of the said offices; and no person who has served the said Term of three Years as a Councillor, shall be elected again until after a Respite of three Years⟩ annually to be named by the Delegates of each Colony, and where they cannot agree, by the Congress.

The Business and Duty of this Council, ⟨of which seven Members shall be a Quorum,⟩ shall be, ⟨in Recess of Congress⟩ To receive & open all Letters directed to the ⟨Congress⟩ United States, and to return proper Answers, but not to make any Engagements that shall be binding on the united Colonies, or any of them.

To correspond with the several Assemblies, Colonial Councils and Committees of Safety, Governors and Presidents of Colonies, and all persons acting under the Authority of the Congress, or of the Legislature of any Colony.

Colony, and all Persons acting under the Authority of the United States, or of the said Legislatures—To apply to such Legislatures, or to the Officers in the several Colonies who are entrusted with the executive Powers of Government, for occasional Aid whenever and wherever necessary—]

To give Counsel to the Commanding officers ⟨of the Land or naval forces in the pay of the Continent whenever it may be Expedient: Supply the Continental forces by Sea & land with all necessaries from time to time: to Expedite the coining or striking of money ordered by the Congress to be Coined or Struck and the Execution of such other measures as the Congress is hereby impowered to resolve upon and may by them be injoined; To transmit to the several Commanding officers, paymasters & commissaries from time to time such sums of money as may be necessary for the pay & Subsistance of the Continental forces & draw upon the treasurers for Such other Sums that may be appropriated by Congress and to order payment for such Contracts as the Said Council may make in persuance of the authority hereby given them; to take charge of all military stores Belonging to the united Colonies, to procure such further Quantities as may probably be wanted & to order any part thereof wheresoever it may be most requisite for the Common Service, to Direct the safe Keep-

To give Counsel to the Commanding officers of the Land and naval Forces in the Pay of the Continent whenever it may be expedient.

To supply the continental Forces by Sea and Land with all Necessaries from Time to Time.[32]

To expedite ⟨*the Coining or Striking Money ordered by the Congress to be coined or struck and*⟩ the Execution of such Measures as the Congress is hereby impowered to resolve upon, and may by them be injoined.

To transmit to the several Commanding Officers, Paymasters & Commissaries, from Time to Time, such Sums of Money as may be necessary for the Pay and Subsistance of the Continental Forces,[33] to draw upon the Treasurers for such Sums as may be appropriated by Congress, and to order Payment by them for such Contracts as the said Council may make in Pursuance of the Authorities hereby given them.[34]

To take Charge of all military stores belonging to the united Colonies, to procure such further Quantities as may probably be wanted, and to order any part

ing & Comfortable accommodation of all prisoners of war, to Contribute their counsel & authority toward raising Recruits ordered by Congress.) [35] To procure intelligence of the Condition & Designs of Enemies; to Direct military opperations by sea and land, not Changing any objects or Expeditions Determined on by Congress, unless an alteration of Circumstances which shall come to their Knowledge after the Recess of Congress shall make such Change absolutely necessary. To attend to the Defence & preservation of forts & Strong posts & to prevent the Enemy from acquiring new holds: to apply to the Legislatures or Such officers in the several Colonies as are Entrusted with the Executive powers of Government for the occasional aid of minute men & militia whenever & whereever necessary: In Case of the Death of any officer within the appointment of Congress to Employ a person to fulfil his Duties, until the meeting of Congress unless the office is of such a nature as to admit of a Delay of appointment untill such meeting, to Examine Public Claims & accounts and   [36]

thereof wheresoever it may be most requisite for the Common Service.[33]

To direct the safe keeping & comfortable Accommodation of all Prisoners of War.[33]

To contribute their Counsel & Authority towards raising Recruits ordered by Congress.[33]

To procure Intelligence of the Condition & Designs of Enemies.

To direct military operations by Sea and Land, not changing any Objects of Expeditions determined on by Congress, unless an Alteration of Circumstances which shall come to their Knowledge after the Recess of Congress, shall make such Change absolutely necessary.

To attend to the Defence and Preservation of Forts and strong Posts and to prevent the Enemy from acquiring new Holds.

To apply to the Legislatures or to such Officers in the several Colonies as are entrusted with the executive Powers of Government, for occasional Aid ⟨of *Minute Men & Militia*⟩ whenever & wherever necessary.

In Case of the Death or Removal of any Officer within the Appointment of Congress, to employ a person to fulfill his Duties, untill the Meeting of Congress, unless the Office be of such a Nature as to admit a Delay of appointment untill such Meeting.

⟨*To suspend any Officer in the Land or naval Forces.*⟩

To examine public Claims & Accounts and make Report thereof to the Congress.[37]

To superintend and controul or suspend all Officers civil & military acting under the Authority of the Congress.

To publish & Disperse authentic accounts of military opperations, to Summon a meeting of Congress at an Earlier Day than is appointed for its next meeting if any great & unexpected Emergencies should render it necessary for the Safety & welfare of the united Colonies or any of them; to propose matters for the Consideration of Congress, and lay before them at their next meeting all letters & advices Received by them with a Report of their proceedings, to appoint a proper person for their Clerk who shall take an oath of Secresy before he Enters on the service of his office, in Case of the Death of any member of the said Council immediately to apply to his Surviving Colleagues to appoint some one of themselves to be a member of said Council till the meeting of Congress, if only one survives to give him immediate notice that he may take his seat as a Councillor till such meeting. The Delegates while acting as Councillors to be supported at the expence of the union.

To publish & disperse authentic Accounts of military operations.

To summon a Meeting of Congress at an earlier Day than is appointed for its next Meeting, if any great & unexpected Emergency should render it necessary for the Safety or Wellfare of the United Colonies or any of them.

To prepare Matters for the Consideration of Congress & To lay before the Congress at their next Meeting all Letters & Advices received by them, with a Report of their proceedings.

To appoint a proper person for their Clerk, who shall take an Oath of Secrecy & Fidelity, before he enters on the Exercise of his Office.

Seven Members shall have power to act.

In Case of the Death of any Member of the said Council, immediately to apply to his surviving Colleagues to appoint some one of themselves to be a Member of the said Council till the Meeting of Congress. If only one survives, to give him immediate notice that he may take his Seat as a Councillor, till such Meeting.

⟨*The Delegates while acting as Members of the Council to be supported at the Expence of the Union.*⟩

Art [XX]. ⟨Any & every other of the Brittish Colonies on this Continent⟩ [Canada] acceeding to this confederation & entirely joyning in the measures of the united colonies shall be admitted [into] and Entituled to all the advantages ⟨& priviledges⟩ of this union. [But no other Colony shall be admitted into the same, unless such Admission be agreed to by the Delegates of nine Colonies.]

⟨Art⟩ These articles shall be proposed to the Legislatures of all the united Colonies to be by them Considered and if approved by them, they are advised to authorise their Delegates to ratify the same in ⟨Congress⟩ [the Assembly of the United States,] which being done ⟨the union so agreed to to be perpetual⟩ [the Articles of this Confederation shall inviolably be observed by every Colony, and the Union is to be perpetual: Nor shall any Alteration be at any Time hereafter made in these Articles or any of them, unless such Alteration be agreed to in an Assembly of the United States, and be afterwards confirmed by the Legislatures of every Colony].

Art. [21]. ⟨*Any & every other of the British Colonies on this Continent, acceding to this Confederation and entirely joining in the Measures of the united Colonies, shall be admitted & entitled to all the Advantages & Priviledges of this Union.*⟩[38] Canada acceding to this Confederation and entirely joining in the Measures of the United Colonies, shall be admitted into & entitled to all the Advantages of this Union. But no other Colony on this Continent shall be admitted into the same, unless such admission be agreed to by the Delegates of nine Colonies.

Art. [22].[39] These Articles shall be proposed to the Legislatures of all the united Colonies to be by them considered, and if approved by them they are advised to authorize their Delegates to ratify the same in Congress, which being done, the ⟨*Confederation and Union so agreed to is to be perpetual*⟩ ⟨*the foregoing*⟩ Articles of this Confederation shall be inviolably observed by every Colony, and the Union is to be perpetual.[40]

MS (Nh). In the hand of Josiah Bartlett. MS (PHi). In the hand of John Dickinson.

¹ Pursuant to Richard Henry Lee's motion of June 7 "that a plan of confederation be prepared and transmitted to the respective Colonies for their consideration and approbation," Congress resolved on June 11 to appoint a committee to draft such a plan and selected one delegate from each colony for this purpose the following day. (Since New Jersey was then unrepresented, however, the 13th member of the committee was not actually appointed until Francis Hopkinson arrived on June 28.) The members undoubtedly set to work almost at once on their assigned task, but very little evidence survives to reconstruct the story of how the Articles took form. Only committee members Josiah Bartlett, John Dickinson, and Edward Rutledge have left contemporary testimony pertaining to the committee's work, and their references to the subject are confined to a few points. Bartlett, for example, reported on June 17 that "The affair of voting, whether by Colonies as at present, or otherwise, is not decided, and causes some warm disputes"; and on July 1 he observed that after working on the plan "for about a fortnight at all oppertunities," including all day Saturday, June 29, "this Day after Congress we are to meet again when I Believe it will be fitted to lay before Congress." Rutledge, in a letter of June 29, explained that he had "been much engaged lately upon a plan of a Confederation which Dickenson has drawn," denouncing Dickinson for "the Vice of Refining too much" and for "the Idea of destroying all Provincial Distinctions and making every thing of the most minute kind bend to what they call the good of the whole." And Dickinson, in a July 1 speech before Congress opposing independence, mentioned the committee in a passage arguing that the step was unwise because no form of government had been agreed upon that would provide stability once independence was declared: "The Committee on Confederation dispute almost every Article—some of Us totally despair of any reasonable Terms of Confederation." See Josiah Bartlett to John Langdon, June 17, and to Nathaniel Folsom, July 1; Edward Rutledge to John Jay, June 29; and John Dickinson's Notes for a Speech in Congress, July 1, 1776.

Of the various papers produced by the committee in the course of their deliberations between June 12 and July 1, little more survives than the two documents printed here and the committee's draft in Dickinson's hand given to Secretary Thomson and reported to Congress on July 12. A few notes in Bartlett's hand pertaining to representation have been printed above under the date June 12, and two pages of Dickinson's notes incorporating revisions in his draft printed here are discussed in note 16 below.

From the two documents analyzed here, however, much of significance can be learned of the evolution of the Articles through committee. Dickinson obviously played the dominant role in creating the Articles, for his draft is heavily interlined and contains numerous deletions and marginalia. Photographs of pages one and three of the document can be examined in *A Rising People, the Founding of the United States, 1765–1789* (Philadelphia: American Philosophical Society, 1976), p. 234. It also appears that this document was Dickinson's second draft, and it was probably penned about the time Bartlett remarked to Langdon on June 17 that the committee had been disputing on "the affair of voting." As originally drafted, it included no article on voting; the numerous additions and deletions contained in it were obviously made over a period of several days. Dickinson's 18th article—"Each Colony shall have one Vote in Congress"—appears in the margin of the document; blanks left in the draft initially were undoubtedly filled in at a later date; and the last two paragraphs of the 19th article were certainly added later in direct response to a "Quære" Dickinson wrote but subsequently lined out in the margin. In sum, it seems highly likely that this document was the basic draft Dickinson employed in committee from about June 17 to July 1, and from which he copied the committee draft reported to Congress. Although the latter was not submitted to Congress until July 12, it seems unlikely that much time was devoted to it after the first. At that time the independence debate preempted the attention of Congress, and immediately thereafter the call for the Pennsylvania militia to meet the British military threat to New York and New Jersey dominated Dickinson's activities. It is not known when he gave the committee draft to Thomson, but he probably did not attend Congress after July 4, and he was already at Elizabethtown, N.J., at the head of his battalion, when it was .reported and read in Congress.

There is no evidence to indicate that Bartlett's manuscript is anything more than a clean copy of one of Dickinson's drafts. It is strikingly similar to the draft printed here, as Dickinson originally penned it and before making additions or deletions. The absence of both the fourth and thirteenth of Dickinson's articles suggests that Bartlett copied it from an earlier draft, probably at about the same time Dickinson made the draft printed here.

The double column format has been adopted here to facilitate examination of the alterations made in Dickinson's draft during the committee's deliberations. The document is also heavily annotated, and every attempt has been made to identify deletions made in committee through the conventional use of angle brackets and italic type. Deletions made in the ordinary course of composition have been ignored, except in a few cases in which the deleted words are revealing of Dickinson's thought. Dickinson did not number his articles, but numerals have been supplied in brackets to minimize confusion. *In the Bartlett draft, angle brackets and regular brackets have been employed unconventionally* to facilitate identification of variations between the manuscript and the committee draft reported to Congress on July 12. Thus, words appearing in Bartlett's manuscript but omitted from the committee draft are placed in angle brackets, and words substituted in or added to the latter appear in this text in regular brackets, with both in roman rather than italic type. For further discussion of some of the textual variations between these two documents, see Elwin L. Page, "Josiah Bartlett and the Federation," *Historical New Hampshire* (October 1947), pp. 1–6. The committee draft is in PCC, item 47, fols. 9–20, and *JCC*, 5:546–54.

Analyses of the Articles undertaken heretofore have of necessity focused on the evolution of the committee's plan through Congress after July 12 and on the struggle for ratification. Although only briefly concerned with the drafting of the Articles, the most thorough treatment of the committee's work is still Merrill Jensen, *The Articles of Confederation, an Interpretation of the Social-Constitutional History of the American Revolution, 1774–1781* (Madison: University of Wisconsin Press, 1940), chaps. 4 and 5. See especially pp. 130–39 for Jensen's analysis of the apportionment of powers and duties between the states and Congress that contains useful insights into the most difficult problem raised by the issue of confederation. It is apparent from the two documents printed here (see articles 19 and 20 of Dickinson's draft) that the allocation of powers was the most troublesome and time-consuming subject debated in the committee, and it was undoubtedly never resolved to the members' satisfaction before the pressure of events required submission of a draft plan of confederation to Congress.

Finally, there can be no doubt that the members of the committee began their work with a copy of Benjamin Franklin's proposed Articles of Confederation before them, for which see *JCC*, 2:195–99. Several passages from Franklin's plan can be found verbatim in the Bartlett and Dickinson drafts, and many others survive with only slight variations. Indeed, only the 4th, 7th, 8th, and 12th of Franklin's 13 articles are not conspicuously incorporated into the committee's work. See also Benjamin Franklin's Proposed Articles of Confederation, July 21, 1775.

  [2] At this point in the margin Dickinson penned the following "Quære." "The Power of Congress interf[erin]g in any Change of the Const[ituti]on? Also the Propriety of garranteeing the respective Constitutions & Frames of Government."

³ In the margin: "All this Article rejected." This rejected article provides striking evidence of the radical nature of Dickinson's efforts to vest substantial authority in Congress and impose explicit restrictions upon the states. Since the rights of persons were generally believed to be a local matter unrelated to the problem of constructing a confederation between independent states, it is not surprising that the article was rejected out of hand. No suggestion that this issue was germane to the work of the committee has been found in the writing of any other delegate, but Dickinson's continued concern for religious liberty can also be seen in the first query he appended to the committee's draft of the Articles reported to Congress: "Should not the first Article provide for a Toleration and agt. Establishments hereafter to be made?" See *JCC*, 5:547n.1.

⁴ In the margin Dickinson penned two paragraphs whose relationship to this article and to one another is not clear. Only the second—which has been printed in italic type in angle brackets—has been crossed out, but both were obviously superseded by the 11th article printed here. The first reads as follows. "When Troops are to be raised in any of the Colonies for the Common Defence, the Resolutions of the Union in General Congress for raising them, shall be executed by the Legislature of each Colony respectively where such Forces are to be raised, or by such persons as the said Legislatures shall authorize for that purpose, unless it be agreed by the Delegates of nine Colonies, that the Troops shall be raised immediately by the Union, without the Aid of the said Legislatures; and even in that Case, the Officers proper (front below)."

⁵ One line left blank in both the Bartlett and Dickinson drafts. In the committee draft submitted to Congress, Dickinson also left a large blank space when he initially penned this article but inserted the following words at a later time, and probably with a different pen: "Inhabitants of every Age, Sex and Quality, except Indians paying Taxes." See PCC, item 47, fol. 12; and *JCC*, 5:548.

⁶ Following this article Dickinson left a query in the margin: "The propriety of raising Troops in each Colony in due proportion to its share of Taxes, and the Number of Troops to be raised, and allowing Colonies to raise & pay Troops in Lieu of Taxes."

⁷ In the committee draft this paragraph is followed by a 12th article which differs only slightly from the 13th article of the Dickinson draft. See *JCC*, 5:548–49.

⁸ In the margin: "Q. How far the Expence of any War is to be defrayed by the Union?"

⁹ The committee draft here includes a section restricting the issuance of letters of marque, part of which appears in Bartlett's article 14. See *JCC*, 5:549.

¹⁰ In the margin: "Q. How far any Colony may interfere in Indian Affairs?"

¹¹ In the committee draft, Dickinson wrote "Art. 14th" in the margin at this point instead of at "A perpetual Alliance," the point at which the new article begins in both drafts printed here. The *JCC* text nevertheless actually follows the format of these earlier drafts, as Worthington C. Ford apparently decided to correct silently what he must have considered a slip of the pen by the author. Cf. PCC, item 47, fol. 13; and *JCC*, 5:549.

¹² In the margin: "Q. How Representation in Congress to be regulated? How many shall make a Quorum, save in the [Executive?]. . . .

"The Oath of every Delegate. What Points shall be determined by a Majority of the Colonies present, what by a Majority of all, or of two Thirds?

"If any Delegate may be allowed to vote by Proxy given to one of his Colleagues, or a Delegate of another Colony—if he is sick or absent?"

¹³ From the appearance of the MS it is obvious that Dickinson added the remainder of this sentence at a later date. This conclusion is also confirmed by Dickinson's use here of the term "Council of State," a term that was agreed upon relatively late in the committee's deliberations to replace "Council of Safety." After he originally wrote this article, Dickinson placed two queries in the margin

which he subsequently lined out, both of which employed the latter term. "If not supplied by Council of Safety?" and "If each Colony shall support its own Delegates while meeting as Members of the Council of Safety?"

[14] The placement of this article in the margin of the MS indicates that the provision was agreed to after Dickinson had penned this draft and that he used this copy of the document to incorporate changes later agreed to in committee.

[15] A reference to the 14th article of this draft.

[16] Although this Dickinson draft consists of 12 MS pages, two additional pages are located with the document. These 13th and 14th pages are actually two separate work sheets used by Dickinson in the course of composition, and they contain approximately two-thirds of the remainder of this article, much of which appears in the margin of Dickinson's draft. Apparently the document became too crowded to bear further interlineation, and he therefore resorted to additional sheets of paper in his efforts to improve the document.

[17] Seven clauses follow at this point in the committee draft, many of which appear later in this article in Bartlett's draft. See JCC, 5:551. The numerous variations in this article between Bartlett's draft and the Dickinson and committee drafts indicate that the attempt to specify the powers of Congress gave the committee great difficulty and consumed much of their time in the later stages of their deliberations.

[18] In the margin: "Q. To direct the Marches, Cruises & Operations of such Forces."

[19] In the margin: "Q. An Oath to be admd. to every Offr. in the Land & naval Forces & to every Soldier & Mariner to obey Congress & not to violate the laws or Rights & Liberties of any Colony?

"Q. The Power of Congress to erect Forts? establish Garrs. for the Genl. Wellfare & to call out the militia.

"Q. The Power of laying Embargos?

"Q. The Power of arresting, securing & trying persons in the service of the united Colonies?"

[20] Dickinson inserted regular brackets around this clause, apparently sometime later during the committee's deliberations.

[21] In the committee draft this sentence concludes: "Forces—To agree upon the Number of Land Forces to be raised, and to make Requisitions from the Legislature of each Colony, or the Persons therein authorized by the Legislature to execute such Requisitions, for the Quota of each Colony, which is to be in Proportion to the Number of white Inhabitants in that Colony, which Requisitions shall be binding, and thereupon the Legislature of each Colony or the Persons authorized as aforesaid, shall appoint the Regimental Officers, raise the Men, and arm and equip them in a soldier-like Manner; and the Officers and Men so armed and equipped, shall march to the Place appointed, and within the Time agreed on by the United States assembled." The committee draft also contains two additional paragraphs, on quotas for raising troops in the colonies and on "Weights and Measures," before continuing with the subject of taxes. See JCC, 5:551.

[22] In the margin: "Q. Powers of the Chamber of Accounts, Off. of Treasury, & Board of War and Admiralty. Need they be defined, as they are to act under the Congress & in their Recess under the Council of Safety?

"Q. Commrs. for Indian Affairs?

"Q. Need any of those be mentioned?"

[23] In the margin: "Q. If Congress may be allowed to impose any Duties for the Regulation of Trade or raising a Revenue for the general Benefit, provided they are equal & common to all the Colonies?"

[24] At this point Bartlett's draft contains a "Quere" in parenthesis: "whether or not on the Indians trade &c."

[25] The remainder of this sentence appears at the conclusion of article 20 of the committee draft.

[26] In the margin: "Q. If this part ought not to be transpos'd towards the End?"

[27] In the margin: "Q. Of a treaty of Peace?"

[28] In the committee draft this paragraph concludes: "nor coin Money nor regulate the Value thereof, nor agree upon nor fix the Sums and Expenses necessary for the Defence and Welfare of the United Colonies or any of them nor emit Bills, nor borrow Money on the Credit of the United Colonies, nor raise Naval Forces, nor agree upon the Number of Land Forces to be raised, unless the Delegates of nine Colonies freely assent to the same: Nor shall a Question on any other Point, except for adjourning, be determined, unless the Delegates of seven Colonies vote in the affirmative." In the committee draft two paragraphs restricting the eligibility of delegates to Congress and one on the publication of their journals of proceedings follow. See *JCC*, 5:552–53.

[29] In the margin: "Q. In what other Cases, such assent should be required?"

[30] Dickinson originally ended his draft at this point and placed a query in the margin on the subject of limitations on eligibility for election of delegates to Congress. He subsequently lined out the query and added the following two paragraphs of the article.

[31] In the margin: "Q. Oath of a Councillor?"

[32] In the margin: "Q. If these powers are not granted to the War Office & Admiralty."

[33] In the margin: "Same Quære."

[34] In the margin: "Q. If this is not too large a Power?"

[35] In the committee draft this sentence concludes: "and to direct military Operations by Sea and Land, not changing any Objects or Expeditions determined on by the United States assembled, unless an Alteration of Circumstances which shall come to the Knowledge of the Council after the Recess of the States, shall make such Change absolutely necessary."

From this point to the conclusion of the article the variations between this document and the committee draft are too numerous to annotate separately and clearly. See *JCC*, 5:553–54.

[36] At this point Bartlett left approximately one line blank.

[37] In the margin: "Q. If this power is not given to the Treasury."

[38] The two following sentences were written in the margin after the preceding passage was crossed out.

[39] In the committee draft this concluding paragraph does not appear as a separate article. It is clear from the MS, however, that Dickinson had written "Art" in the margin at this point and that the letters have been erased. See PCC, item 47, fol. 20; and *JCC*, 5:554. Whether the erasure was the work of Dickinson cannot of course be determined.

[40] Dickinson penned the following observations at the bottom of the page after the conclusion of this article.

"Q. The problem of proceedings of Congress every Month & the Yeas & Nays.

"Oath on Behalf of every Colony, all the Inhabitants & their posterity to observe & adhere to all the Acts of this Confederacy.

"Q. [. . . .] The Cons[titu]tion to be in Congress."

Josiah Bartlett to John Langdon

Dear Sir,   Philadelphia June 17. 1776.

Your favor of the [*June 3*] instant,[1] is come to hand and am sorry the news you mention from Quebeck is not true. Things have taken an extraordinary turn in that country. The behavior of Col Bedel and Major Butterfield is very extraordinary. No doubt you will hear the particulars before this reaches you. Dr Franklin, Mr Chase and Mr Caryl are returned from Canada; their account of the behavior of our New England officers and soldiers touches me to the quick. By their account never men behaved so badly—some regiments not having more than 100 men, when it was expected there were six times that number; stealing and plundering arms, ammunition, military stores &c and taking the battoes and running off. One man it is said stole six guns and to conceal them broke the stocks to pieces, cut up a tent to make a knapsack to carry off the barrels, locks &c—and all is said to be owing to the officers. Unless our men behave better we shall lose all our former credit and be despised by the whole Continent. This is the account here; I pray God, it may not be so bad as is represented.

The greatest care must be taken to have good officers—the fate of America depends on it. However I make no doubt as soon as the present Commanders have time, they will get things in a better regulation and that some examples will be made to deter others from such conduct. Poor General Thomas is dead and General Sullivan now commands in Canada; I expect soon General Gates will be ordered there.

As to Marine affairs brother Whipple will write you.[2] A Board of War is now appointed consisting of Mr J Adams, Mr Sherman, Col Harrison, Mr Wilson and E Rutledge.[3] I have taken every opportunity to mention to the members the affair of the agency and am surprised to find all of them agreeing that no member of Congress ought to be appointed to any post of profit under the Congress; so that as you are a Member, I am sure it will not go down, and I am by no means willing you should resign your seat here. As the affair of the ship will soon be finished and Col Whipple will be for returning to his family, my opinion is that it will be best for you to come here as soon as you and Col Whipple can agree on it and that the affair of the Agency be in the mean time left open. When you are here you will be better able to determine on several affairs.

The affair of a Confederation of the Colonies is now unanimously agreed on by all the members of all the Colonies.[4] A Committee of one from each Colony are to draw up the articles of confederation or a *Continental Constitution* which when agreed on by the Congress will be sent to be confirmed by the Legislature of the several Colonies. As it is a very important business and some difficulties have arisen, I fear it will take some time before it will be finally settled. The affair of voting whether by Colonies as at present or otherways is not decided and causes some warm disputes. The appointments of the officers of militia to be sent to Canada is with our Legislature and also the nomination of the field officers for the regt stationed in our Colony so that unless any objection is made, their nomination will be confirmed. I hope the greatest care will be taken in the appointment to get bold, resolute, intrepid and experienced persons.

The affair of taking the sugar ships has so animated the people here that they are now fitting out 5 or 6 privateers more here.

I should take great pleasure in recommending some active berth for you but while you continue a member of Congress it will not take effect. If you are absolutely determined to resign and should do it I make no doubt some place agreeable to you might be found and in that case you must see that another is appointed in your stead to come here in about a month to supply Col Whipple's place who is determined then to return. But it is my opinion you had better come here yourself at least once more. It is necessary however we should know your absolute determination as soon as possible.

Give my compliments to all enquiring friends. Major Patton, Mr Dean and Mrs Susy desire to be remembered to you.[5] I am Sir, your real friend,   Josiah Bartlett

Tr (DLC).

[1] See John Langdon to Bartlett, June 3, 1776, Clark, *Naval Documents*, 5:355–56.

[2] See William Whipple to Langdon, this date.

[3] See *JCC*, 5:434–35, 438.

[4] Bartlett was a member of the committee appointed on June 12 "to prepare and digest the form of a confederation to be entered into between these colonies." See *JCC*, 5:433; and Bartlett's Notes on the Plan of Confederation, June 12–July 12, 1776.

[5] Bartlett also wrote this day to his wife, but only a fragment of his letter is now extant. In the postscript, Bartlett noted, "I am in pretty good health. After I had wrote the inclosed letter to Levi I recollected that a vacation of the School would take place by the time the letter will arrive, if it Should not, you may Send it to him if you have an oppertunity or Keep it till he Comes home." Josiah Bartlett Papers, NhHi.

The letter to Levi, in the possession of Mr. and Mrs. Rodney M. Wilson, Kingston, N.H., is reproduced in the Josiah Bartlett Papers microfilm edition, NhHi. Writing to his son at school, Bartlett offered paternal advice and encouragement, urging him to "take Care to behave So as to have the good will of your Master & School mates that I may have the pleasure to hear of your good behavior and that you make a wise improvement of your time to gain learning that the Cost I am at for you may not be in vain."

John Hancock to Philip Schuyler

Sir   Philada. 17 June 1776

Inclos'd you have Invoice of three Boxes of Silver Dollars containing 21,725 ½ Dollars, also Invoice of three Boxes contg. 187,000 Paper Dollars which I wish safe to hand, for the use of the Army in Canada. More hard money will soon follow, & in a few days shall Send on some more Paper Money. I wish soon to hear a more favourable Accott. of our Affairs in Canada.

In a few days I shall write you, & Inclose you the Resolutions of Congress which are almost perfected & when Executed I think will much promote the general good, you shall have them as early as possible after they are Compleat.

I am in great haste, Sir, Your very huml Svt.

LB (DNA: PCC, item 12A). Addressed: "To General Schuyler, in his Absence, To Mr. Trumbull, Depy pay m[aste]r Genl. or Commandr. in Chief in Canada."

John Hancock to George Washington

Sir,   Philadelphia June 17th. 1776.

I wrote you by Express yesterday,[1] & inclosed you all the Resolutions of Congress to that Time, since which Nothing has occurred. This will be handed you by Captain Bradford, who has in Charge the Money destined for the Army in Canada, three Boxes of Silver Dollars containing 21,725 ½ and three Boxes of Paper Dollars containing 187,000.

I am to request you will please to discharge the Philadelphia Guard, and order a fresh Guard to proceed with the Money to General Schuyler, or the Paymaster Mr. Trumbull in such Manner as you shall judge best, and either in the same Waggon, or another, as you shall direct. Please to forward by the Officer of the Guard, the inclosed Letter.[2]

I have the Honour to be, Sir, your most obedt. and very hble Sevt.   John Hancock Presidt

RC (DLC). In the hand of Jacob Rush and signed by Hancock.
[1] See Hancock to Washington, June 14, 1776, to which Hancock added a postscript on June 16.
[2] Probably Hancock to Philip Schuyler, this date.

New York Delegates to the New York Provincial Congress

Sir.   Philadelphia June 17, 1776.

We were honoured by your favours of the 11th Instant. A resolution of Congress has passed agreeable to your intention restraining the exportation of salt Beaf & pork from any of these Colonies under the limitations mentioned in your resolve.[1]

We recd. great pleasure from knowing the sentiments of the hon. the Convention, relative to the important subject on which we thought it our duty to ask their opinion.[2] We are very happy in having it in our power to assure them, that we have hitherto taken no steps inconsistant with their intention as expressed in their letter, by which we shall be careful to regulate our future conduct. We remain Sir, With the greatest respect, Your's & the Conventions Most Obt & Hum Servts.

Fra. Lewis   John Alsop

Robt R Livingston   Wm. Floyd

Henry Wisner

RC (N). Written by Livingston and signed by Livingston, Alsop, Floyd, Lewis, and Wisner. Addressed: "The honble. Nathl. Woodhull, Presidt. of the provincial Congress, New York." Burnett, *Letters*, 1:494. RC damaged; missing words supplied from Tr.

[1] See *JCC*, 5:441. The provincial congress' two June 11 letters to the New York delegates are in *Am. Archives*, 4th ser. 6:814–16.

[2] See New York Delegates to the New York Convention, June 8, 1776, note.

George Walton to Lachlan McIntosh

Williamsburg, 17th June, 1776. Explains that he has been in ill health since leaving Georgia, but is sure that "I am not too late for the great American question—If a question now it may be called!" Reports that he has secured permission from the Virginia Convention for the recruitment of 300 Virginia men for McIntosh's battalion.[1] Concludes: "I shall set out after Dinner for Philadelphia, and having recovered my health considerably in this place, and, having also obtained fresh horses of my friends in this country, expect to be there in seven or eight days."

Abstracted from the *Macon Daily Telegraph and Confederate*, January 25, 1865.

[1] Lachlan McIntosh (1725–1806) had been appointed colonel of the first Georgia battalion in January 1776 and became a brigadier general in the Continental Army the following September. *DAB*.

William Whipple to Joshua Brackett

My Dear Sir,   Philadelphia 17th June 1776

I received Yours of the 3d inst by which I find you are mistaken with regard to the appointment of officers, for the Battallion. The Field officers are nominated by the Legislature of the Province. Blank commissions for all other officers, are sent to be fill'd up by the Legislature of the Province, so that in fact they have the appointment of all the officers. Of course application must be made to them.[1] Our affairs in Canada are in a miserable scituation. Col. Beedle's Regiment has most infamously Tarnish'd the Glory of the

New-Hampshire Troops who have ever before been high on the list of fame. In order to make you easey about the Manifesto as you call it, I just whisper you that a Committee are appointed to prepare a Declaration to be laid before the House on the 1st of July which no doubt will pass & I believe will meet with your approbation. You may expect it in abot a month from this time.

I suppose its a matter of indifference to you whether Mr. McCleur is settled or not, as I understand you have a Chaplain of your own. I hope your Gostly Father will so prepare your for your journey, that there will be no necessity of your stopping at the half way house.

I have no news to tell you; perhaps another week may produce some. Yours sincerely,   Wm Whipple

RC (MH).
  [1] For further information on the appointment of officers for the New Hampshire battalion, see Whipple to Meshech Weare, May 17, 1776.

William Whipple to John Langdon

My Dear Sir,   Philadelphia 17th June 1776
    The money mentioned in a former letter is gone forward to Boston. Mr Hancock has desired Mr Cushing to send it to New Hampshire. It is in a box directed to Col Weare.[1] I am glad you intend for Providence and heartily wish you may succeed in getting the guns there; if not, I don't know when you will have them but fear it will be a long time, for though two furnaces in this Province are employed making guns for the ships there are no more than two 12 pounders yet brought to town and but very few of the other sizes and if they were here I think there will be great difficulty in getting them to you. I sometime ago mentioned to the Chairman of the Secret Committee, what you propose respecting powder and am in no doubt, but you'll be supplied in season with that article; in short I am not concerned about any thing but guns and men. The Committee decline giving orders for shipping men, while the prospect of getting guns is at such a distance. I find there is no possibility of getting you appointed Agent while you have a seat in Congress and if you are not appointed I am apprehensive the present Acting Agent will be confirmed.[2] I have already told many of the members that you intended to resign your seat here. It's Col Bartlett's opinion, that you should come here; I don't know but it would be right for you to come. I should be exceeding glad to be at home for a few months; if this plan is agreeable to you. I shall like to set out about the middle of July, but as there will be time enough for you to answer this before I shall set out shall let it rest entirely on your

determination. If you do determine to resign shall have you appointed as soon as I know of your resignation. I must confess I am loath you should give up your seat, but if it's your choice, I hope you'll see that a proper person is appointed to supply your place. At all events it's probable I shall set out some time in July and if I can get a companion shall take your carriage; in that case should be glad to know if you'll have your trunk brought home. I mean to take your carriage unless you direct otherwise. You mention in some of your letters the appointment of two Agents; that I think would be unnecessary and improper, as one man could certainly do all the business. I hope your answer will be very explicit about your coming or resigning.

This day fortnight I expect the grand question will be determined in Congress, that being the day assigned to receive the report of a Committee who are preparing the Declaration. There is a great change here since my arrival as there was in New Hampshire between the time that the powder was taken from the fort and the battle of Bunker Hill. New Jersey have called a new Convention who are now setting. They have forbid the meeting of the Assembly who were called by the Governor's Proclamation and I hope my next will advise you of that govr's being seized which I think ought to have been done many months ago. Affairs go on here bravely as you'll see by the papers.

I wrote some time ago that blank warrants would be sent to you, but it seems the Committee have changed their minds and now say the names must be sent here. I am, &c,   Wm. Whipple

Tr (DLC).
[1] See John Hancock to Thomas Cushing, June 16, 1776.
[2] Joshua Wentworth had been appointed acting prize agent in New Hampshire by General Washington in 1775. See Stephen Moylan to Washington, October 13, 1775, in Clark, *Naval Documents*, 2:434; and Elbridge Gerry to John Wendell, June 11, 1776, note 3.

John Adams to Horatio Gates

My dear General   Philadelphia June 18. 1776
We have ordered you to the Post of Honour, and made you Dictator in Canada for Six Months, or at least untill the first of October.[1] We dont choose to trust you Generals, with too much Power, for too long Time.

I took my Pen, at this Time, to mention to you the Name of a young Gentleman, and to recommend him to your Notice and Favour. His Name is Rice.[2] This gentleman is the Son of a worthy Clergyman. He was educated at Harvard Colledge, where he was an officer of the Military Company, and distinguished himself as a soldier in the manual Exercises and Maneuveres. After he came out of Colledge he put himself under my Care as a Student of the Law. While he was in my office he was very usefull in the Neighbourhood in training the Companies of Militia there. He is a modest, sensible, and well read young Man, and a very virtuous and worthy one. In my Absence from home, after the Battle of Lexington, he applied for a Commission in the Army, and obtained a Place, in my opinion vastly below his real Merit; I mean that of Adjutant in General Heaths, now Coll Greatons Regiment. In this Capacity, he has continued, from his first Engagement which was immediately after the Battle of Lexington, untill this Time, and is now in Canada with his Regiment, and I have been informed by a Variety of officers, that he has behaved remarkably well. As you are going to Canada, with full Powers, I must beg the Favour of you to think of this young gentleman, inquire into his Character and Conduct, and if you can, consistently with the Public Service, advance him to Some Place more Adequate to his Abilities and Merits, and services, I should take it as a Favour.

I pray God to prosper you in Canada, and grant you a plentifull Crop of Laurells, and am your affectionate humble Servant,

John Adams

RC (NHi).
[1] See *JCC*, 5:448; and John Hancock to George Washington, this date.
[2] Nathan Rice (1754–1834).

Elbridge Gerry to Elisha Porter

Dear sir,[1]   Philadelphia June 18th 1776

I recd. your Favour of the 31st May per Mr Chase but have heard nothing of the other Letter which is mentioned therein. I am sorry to find the affairs of Canada in such a situation, but they will be soon assisted if in the Power of Congress to effect it. General Gates is ordered to the Command in Canada, 6000 Militia from Connecticut & Massachusetts & New Hampshire are soon to join Him, 21000 Dollars in Specie & part of 500,000 in Bills were sent from this City the 16th for Albany, the Commissary General is to undertake the supplying the Army, a Committee is appointed to provide Medicine & Cloathing, & a strict Scrutiny will be made into the Causes of the Miscarriages in that Department. I am greived at the Loss of General Thomas & think he was a brave officer & could wish to have recd a Better Account of another officer which You mention.

The persons which You mention at our old Lodgings were well a

short Time since, & your Desire of being remembred to them shall
be complied with.

Things are going on well in the Colonies with Respect to Independency, Confederation &c &c, & the Question relative to the
former is to be agitated in Congress the 1st July next.

General Washington is to be reinforced with 15000 men at New
York which will augment his Army to 25000 & a flying Camp is to be
posted in the Jerseys consisting of 10000 men more. You have
undoubtedly heard of the prize lately taken & carried into Boston
out of which were landed seventy five Tons of Powder, 1000 Arms
&c &c &c. Saltpetre is manufactured in Abundance; in the Massachusetts only by Mr Devens Account they have already delivered into
the Magazines *fifty Tons,* & have thirty Tons of Sulphur imported
& left in Boston. Three Mills are built there two of which turn out
upwards of 1000 each per Week. I hope the Disposition that has
appeared in some officers to censure others will cease, & that in Leiu
thereof a laudable Emulation will take place to excell in Discipline
& Valour, without which an Army must be disgraced. I sincerely
wish You success & happiness, & remain sir your Friend & hum ser,

Elbridge Gerry

P.S. Pray continue to give me the state of Things in Canada.

RC (MHi).
¹ Elisha Porter (1741/2–96), Hadley, Mass., lawyer and a member of the Massachusetts Provincial Congress in 1775, had been appointed colonel and commander of
a Massachusetts militia regiment sent to Canada in early 1776. His diary of the
Canadian campaign, January–August 1776, is in the *Magazine of American History*
30 (1893): 187–205. Shipton, *Harvard Graduates,* 15:96–100.

Elbridge Gerry to Joseph Trumbull

Dear sir,   Philadelphia June 18th 1776

I received your Favour of the 10th Inst., since which Mr Carol
& Chace have arrived here & given to Congress a lengthy Detail of
the confused State of Things in that Department. To rectifie Matters, General Gates to the Disapointment of the eastern District is
Ordered to the Command there, with suitable Powers to organize
where wanting & reduce to order the Army in that Country. Congress
see the Necessity of a full Enquiry into the Miscarriages that have
taken place, & a Scrutiny will be made into the Causes of the
Failure in the Lines ordered, as well as those of the Want of
provisions, Ammunition, Cloathing & pay. The Conduct of the
Officers will not pass unnoticed. 21000 Dollars in hard Money & part
of 500000 in Bills went off on Sunday Morning for Albany,¹ & the
necessary Powers are given to the Commissary General for enabling

him to throw in the necessary Supplies & continuing them.[2] Thirty Dollars per Month is also added to his Salary. The president promised to send me your Letter after he had perused it, but thro the Hurry of Business I suppose has omitted it.[3] Nothing new here unless an intercepted Letter sent to Congress by the Convention of Virginia, whereby it appears that the Design of the Enemy is to land some Regulars at Florida & join the Cherokees &c with Which they intend to attack the western Frontiers of Virginia, & the other southern Colonies; but I hope their Vile Designs will be frustrated.[4]

I hope the Difficulties in the Quarter Master's Office will cease, & that the Assistant which You mention will not be so regardless of the public Good as from a small Consideration to resign his office.

My best Regards to Generals Gates & Mifflin & believe me to be with Esteem sir your assured Friend & huml sert.

Elbridge Gerry

P.S. The Lower Counties it is said have given similar Instructions to the Delegates with Pennsylvania, & this Day the Conference of Committees of this Colony meets; every County having sent Members.[5] The middle Colonies will I think soon be vigourous.

RC (CtHi).
    [1] See John Hancock to Philip Schuyler, June 17, 1776.
    [2] See *JCC*, 5:451.
    [3] Undoubtedly Trumbull's June 17 letter to John Hancock, which was read in Congress on June 18 and is in the *Am. Archives*, 4th ser. 6:938–39. *JCC*, 5:459–60.
    [4] A May 19 letter of Henry Stuart, British deputy superintendent of Indian affairs for the southern department, which had been intercepted and first sent to Georgia Gov. Archibald Bullock. Stuart, in an attempt to buoy the spirits of Carolina and Virginia frontier inhabitants, had urged that they swear loyalty to the king and be prepared to join a combined British-Indian army which would soon march from West Florida to attack North Carolina and Virginia. For Stuart's letter and related documents, see *Am. Archives*, 4th ser. 6:1228–30.
    [5] The proceedings of the conference of Pennsylvania committees of safety, June 18–25, 1776, are in *Am. Archives*, 4th ser. 6:951–67. Robert Treat Paine had laconically reported this event in his diary: "Wrote to Dr. Cobb & Wife & Col Palmer. Committee of Conference sat Philada." Paine's Diary, June 18, 1776, MHi.

John Hancock to Certain Colonies

Gentlemen,   Philada. June 18th. 1776.

As it is impossible fully to ascertain the Strength of our Enemies, or the Force destined for the Attack of New York, it is incumbent on us to be prepared to defend ourselves agt. any Number of Troops that may be ordered agt. that Place. This, it is apparent, can never be effectually done, but by adopting the enclosed Resolve; wherein it is recommended by Congress to your Colony, to empower the

General at New York to call such Part of the Militia to his Assistance, as may be necessary to repel our Enemies.[1]

The great Advantages the American Cause will receive from the Civil Power thus lending its Aid to the Military, and acting in Conjunction with it, are too manifest to be mentioned. The whole Strength of a Colony may, by this Means, be drawn to a Point the Instant the Situation of Affairs shall render it necessary.

The Colony of Massachusetts Bay while the British Troops lay in Boston, passed a Resolve, at the Request of Congress, similar to that which they now recommend to you.

The Colony of New Jersey[2] will, I am persuaded, imitate their Example, on the present Occasion; & convince her Sister Colonies, that in Virtue and Love of her Country, she is determined to be exceeded by none.

I have the Honour to be, Gentlemen, your must obed. & very hble Servt.   J. H. Prest.

LB (DNA: PCC, item 12A). Addressed: "Honble Convention of New Jersey. Honble Convention of New York. Honble Assembly of Connecticut."

[1] See *JCC*, 5:452.

[2] Or "Connecticut" or "New York," depending on recipient.

John Hancock to John Haslet

Sir,   Philada. 18 June 1776

The Two Companies which were Station'd at Cape May being order'd to Join their Regiment & proceed to Canada, and the Service requiring a constant force there, I have it in Charge from the Congress to Direct that you immediately order Two Companies of the Battalion of Continental Troops under your Command to proceed to Cape May, there to protect the Inhabitants & the Navigation, & to do Duty untill the further order of Congress.[1]

I am Sir, Your most obedt servt.   J. H. Pt.

LB (DNA: PCC, item 12A). Addressed: "To Colonell John Haslett or officer Commanding the Battalion of Continental Troops in Delaware Government."

[1] See *JCC*, 5:452.

John Hancock to the
Pennsylvania Council of Safety

Sir   Philada. 18th June 1776

In Consequence of your Application to Congress respecting the further Exchange of Prisoners from the Ships of War, I am Authorized to inform you that the Congress are in Sentiment with you that it will be prejudicial to the general Service, and that they therefore Judge it improper that any further Exchange should take place, which you will please to Notice accordingly.[1]

I am Sir, Your most obed servt.   J. H. Pt.

LB (DNA: PCC, item 12A). Addressed: "To John Nixon Esqr., Chairman of the Council of Safety of Pennsylva., To be Communicated."

[1] See *JCC*, 5:460. The Pennsylvania Council of Safety's June 17 letter to Hancock concerning the exchange of captured British seamen in Philadelphia for American seamen imprisoned aboard H.M.S. *Liverpool* is in PCC, item 69, 1:141, and *Am. Archives*, 4th ser. 6:934–35.

John Hancock to George Washington

Sir,   Philadelphia June 18th. 1776.

You will see, from the inclosed Resolves, which I do myself the Pleasure of forwarding in Obedience to the Commands of Congress, that they have bent their whole Attention to our Affairs in Canada, and have adopted such Measures, as in their opinion, are calculated to place them on a better and more reputable Footing for the future.[1]

The most unfortunate Death of General Thomas having made a Vacancy in that Department, and the Service requiring an officer of Experience and Distinction, the Congress have thought proper to appoint General Gates to succeed him. And I am to request you will send him into that Province to take the Command of the Forces there as soon as possible; and that you direct him to view Point au Fer, and to order a Fortress to be erected there if he shall think proper.

My opinion on the Resolve of the 25th May was well founded; Congress having since determined, as you will find by a Resolve herewith transmitted, that you are to employ the Indians wherever you think their Services will contribute most to the Public Good.[2]

I shall write to the Colonies of New York, New Jersey, and Connecticut to request them to authorize you to call on their Militia if necessary. My Time will not permit me to do it now, as the Post will set out directly, and the enclosed Resolves were not passed till late yesterday Evening.

I have the Honour to be, Sir, your most obedt. and very hble Sev.   John Hancock Presidt

[*P.S.*] A Muster Master Genl. in the Room of Mr. Moylan will be appointed this Day or tomorrow—and a Deputy will afterwards be sent into Canada.[3]

I beg you will think of the Eastern Departmt. with Respect to General officers, when your very important Concerns will admit.

RC (DLC). In the hand of Jacob Rush, with signature and last paragraph of post-script by Hancock.

[1] See the extensive series of resolutions passed by Congress on June 17 concerning reinforcements for the northern army, military operations in Canada, and the disposition of prize cargoes, in *JCC*, 5:447–54.

[2] See *JCC*, 5:452; and Hancock to Washington, June 11, 1776.

[3] Muster-Master General Stephen Moylan having been appointed quartermaster general by Congress on June 5, his deputy Gunning Bedford was chosen to succeed him on June 18. *JCC*, 5:419, 460. Hancock's letter of this date to Bedford, inform-ing him of his promotion and ordering him to "immediately Repair to Head Quarters at New York," is in PCC, item 12A, and *Am. Archives*, 4th ser. 6:949. Another Hancock letter of this date, written to Pennsylvania commissary James Mease and directing him immediately to "purchase & forward to Stephen Moylan Esqr Quarter Master General in New York as much Cloth suitable for Tents as you can procure," is in PCC, item 12A, and *Am. Archives*, 4th ser. 6:949. See also *JCC*, 5:453.

Elbridge Gerry to Joseph Trumbull

Dear sir,   Philadelphia 19th June 1776

Since my last of the 17th Instant [1] I recd yours of the same Date & find that notwithstanding upwards of 27000 Men with their Arms, two Major Generals & all the Brigadiers are marched or ordered from the N England Colonies, the Request of Massachusetts for a single Brigadier to their Liking is not complied with. This I consider as a Hardship & shall in future pay a more particular Regard to the eastern Department & Boston (to which the Enemy will think themselves invited) than has heretofore taken place.

General Sullivans letter [2] relative to Canada looks more favourable than those before received, but it is very surprising that amongst all the Men of Sense sent into that Country there cannot be found two that agree in their Relations of Facts. Surely some strange Demon representing the Genius of the British Ministry has banished Truth from the Canadian Climes, but I doubt not that she will again return with her good Friend General Gates & give Us future Proofs of her being reinstated in that Quarter. You have now the Direction of the Commissary's Department in Canada & I hope things will be reduced to order in good Time. With Respect to your order for Flower, It will undoubtedly be complied with.[3] The Office of Muster Master General is not yet filled,[4] Your Brother shall be remembered.

This Day a Recommendation has passed Congress to all the assemblies & Conventions to provide a suit of Cloaths of which the Waist Coat & Breeches to be Buckskin, a Blanket, Hatt, 2 pair

Hose, 2 shirts & 2 pair shoes for each soldier enlisted from their Respective Colonies for the ensuing Campaign.[5] These are to be either manufactured or otherwise provided, & to be deposited in suitable places after being bailed & Invoiced Untill the Army shall need the same, when they are to be delivered to the Generals Order & deducted from the Pay of the Soldiers who shall receive them. I think the Army will by these Means be well provided by the Fall & in a great Measure by our own Manufactures. Jersey has behaved nobly with Governer Franklin [6] & in obtaining their Militia, & if I mistake not, that Colony, Pennsylvania & the lower Counties will under good Constitutions be soon as vigourous as any Colonies on the Continent. Mr Adams's & the Queen Club joyn in best Respects to yourself, Generals Gates, Mifflin &c &c &c. With sir your assured Friend & huml sert.   Elbridge Gerry

[P.S.] Pray order the inclosed to be deliverd.

RC (Ct).
    [1] Presumably Gerry's letter to Trumbull of June 18.
    [2] Apparently John Sullivan's letter to Washington of June 5–6, 1776, which was received in Congress on June 18. JCC, 5:459.
    [3] See JCC, 5:459–60.
    [4] Gunning Bedford had been appointed muster-master general on June 18. JCC, 5:460.
    [5] See JCC, 5:466–67.
    [6] See John Hancock to John Witherspoon, June 19, 1776.

John Hancock to Jonathan Trumbull, Sr.

Sir,   Philada. June 19th. 1776.
    The enclosed Resolves I do myself the Honour of transmitting in Obedience to the Commands of Congress, and beg Leave to request your immediate Attention to the same.[1]
    The Congress approve the Proposal in your Letter, and join in opinion with you, considering the very critical Situation of our Affairs in Canada, that it will be best to send the two Battalions into that Province, altho they were not raised with a View to that Department.[2]
    The late Act of your Assembly for engaging one third of the Militia in the Sea Coast, and one fourth in the interior Parts of your Colony for the Defence of your own & the neighbouring Colonies, falls far short of the Object Congress had in View by their Resolution of the third of June. I must therefore request you will adopt such Measures as in your Judgment will be most likely to comply with their Requisition of that Date.[3]
    I send herewith the blank Commissions to be filled up agreeably to the Resolve of Congress.

I am to request that you will deliver to the Agent of the Council of Safety of Pennsylvania the Cannon & Trucks ordered by Congress to be taken from thence—and also to inform you that the Congress expect this Resolution will be immediately complied with.[4]

I have the Honour to be, Sir, your most obed. & very hble Svt.

J. H. Prest.

LB (DNA: PCC, item 12A).
[1] See *JCC*, 5:447–48.
[2] See Trumbull's letter to Hancock of June 10 in *Am. Archives*, 4th ser. 6:797; and Hancock to the Connecticut and New Hampshire Assemblies, May 16, 1776, note 2.
[3] See *JCC*, 4:412; and Trumbull's letter cited above.
[4] See *JCC*, 5:445–46; and Hancock to Esek Hopkins, May 7, 1776, note 2.

John Hancock to George Washington

Sir,   Philadelphia June 19th. 1776.

Since my Letter on the 18th Inst. I have Nothing further in Charge from Congress that particularly relates to yourself, or the Army immediately under your Command.

I have wrote to the Conventions of the Jerseys and New York, and to the Assembly of Connecticut on the Subject of the Resolve Inclos'd in my last, and have pressed them to a Compliance with the Request therein contained.

Mr. Bedford who is appointed Muster Master General, I have directed to repair to Head Quarters immediately, and have delivered him his Commission. You will please to appoint a Deputy Muster Master General for the Department of Canada.

I do myself the Honour of writing to Govr. Trumbull by this Conveyance, and transmitting a Copy of sundry Resolves respecting his Government. I also forward him blank Commissions.

Your several Favours to the 17th Inst. have been duely received, and are at this Time before Congress. As soon as I have it in my Power, I shall, with particular Pleasure, transmit the Result.

The Carpenters mentioned in the Resolve of the 17th I shall send to Genl. Schuyler directly from this City.

I have the Honour to be, Sir, your most obedt. & very hble Servt.

John Hancock Presidt

[*P.S.*] The Inclos'd Resolves I Transmitt, to which I beg Leave to Refer you.[1]

I have been so Engag'd that I have not Oppory. to Confer with the other Delegates of Massachusetts on the Subject of your Letter, but beg leave to Refer the matter to you, fully Convinc'd that you will Send such officers as will effectually Execute your & our wish.[2]

I will do my self the honour to address you by next Post.

RC (DLC). In the hand of Jacob Rush, with signature and postscript by Hancock.

¹ These resolves, which were passed by Congress on June 18 and 19, concerned Gunning Bedford's appointment as muster-master general, authorization for Washington to appoint a deputy muster-master general to serve in Canada, the settlement of debts contracted by the army in Canada, the validity of certain officers' commissions issued by Gen. John Sullivan, and pay for Washington's army. *JCC,* 5:460, 463, 465.

² Apparently a reference to the need for appointing a commanding officer for the Continental forces in Massachusetts. See Massachusetts Delegates to Washington, May 16, 1776.

John Hancock to John Witherspoon

Sir, June 19. 1776

I had the honour of laying before Congress the letter from your convention with the papers enclosed, whereupon the Congress came to the above resolution, which you will please to forward to your Convention by the first opportunity.¹

I am, Sir, Your obedient humble servt.

John Hancock Prest.

RC (PPRF). In the hand of Charles Thomson and signed by Hancock.

¹ A June 18 letter to Hancock from Samuel Tucker, president of the New Jersey Provincial Congress, enclosing the provincial congress' proceedings respecting the arrest of Gov. William Franklin, is in *Am. Archives,* 4th ser. 6:967–68. Congress' resolve of June 19, agreeing to select a place of confinement for Franklin if the provincial congress "shall be of opinion that he should be confined," is in *JCC,* 5:465. The provincial congress thereupon examined Franklin on June 21 and decided, after he refused to respond to its questions and denied its authority, that he should be kept under guard somewhere outside the province. Congress concurred in this decision and on June 24 ordered Franklin to be placed in the custody of Connecticut Governor Trumbull. See *JCC,* 5:473; *Am. Archives,* 4th ser. 6:1010, 1627; and Hancock's letters to the New Jersey Provincial Convention and to Jonathan Trumbull, Sr., June 24, 1776.

Secret Committee Minutes of Proceedings

[June 19? 1776] ¹

At a meeting of the Committee—Present Morris, Alsop, Hewes, Lewis, Bartlet. The Comme. finding that the Owners of the Vessels freighted by this Come. & wch. have been taken think they have a right to the full valuation mentiond in the Charter partys, wherein no deduction has been stipulated, have now reconsiderd the justice of their claim [and] are of opinion they ought to be paid agreable to the letter of their charter partys.² The petition of S. Howell Blair Mcclenachan, J & P. Chevalier (Owners of Vessels charterd by this Come) praying an allowance to be made them for the detention of their vessels, in the river after they were loaded was read. Orderd That the Chairman direct them to state accounts of the allowance they think ought to be made them, to be considerd at next meeting.[3] Order on the Treasurers in favor of T. Yorke for 5000 dollars in part for the Brige. Hetty's Cargo & freight.[4] Do. in favor of Nathl. Greene & Co. for 10,000 dlls agreable to a Contract made with them 6th Feby. last.

MS (MH).
[1] Although this entry is undated, a congressional resolve of June 19 immediately precedes it in the journal of the Secret Committee.
[2] See Secret Committee Minutes of Proceedings, July 18, 1776.
[3] See ibid.
[4] On August 30 this committee presented the *Hetty*'s captain, Ephraim Doane, with a £75 reward for "having made three expeditions & successful voyages with said Brigantine to the W. Indies for Acct. of the Continent bringing in Arms & Ammunition." Journal of the Secret Committee, fol. 97, MH.

Delegates' Certification of James Wilson's Conduct in Congress

Congress Chamber Philadelphia the 20th June 1776

Whereas it has been represented to the Congress that Reports have been circulated concerning Mr. Wilson one of the Delegates of Pennsylvania to the Disadvantage of his Publick Character and that Misrepresentations have been made for his Conduct in Congress— [1]

We the Subscribers Members of Congress do therefore certify, that in a late Debate [2] in this House upon a Proposition to declare these Colonies free and independant States, Mr. Wilson after having stated the Progress of the Dispute between Great Britain and the Colonies, declared it to be his opinion that the Colonies would stand justified before God and the World in declaring an absolute Separation from Great Britain forever, and that he believed a Majority of the People of Pennsylvania were in Favour of Independance, but that the Sense of the Assembly (the only representative Body then existing in the Province) as delivered to him by their Instructions was against the Proposition, that he wished the Question to be postponed, because he had Reason to believe the People of Pennsylvania would soon have an Opportunity of expressing their Sentiments upon this Point,[3] and he thought the People ought to have an Opportunity given them to Signify their opinion in a regular Way upon a Matter of such Importance—and because the Delegates of other Colonies were bound by Instructions to disagree to the Proposition, and he thought it right that the Constituents of these Delegates should also have an Opportunity of deliberating on

James Wilson

the said Proposition and communicating their Opinions thereon to their respective Representatives in Congress. The Question was resumed and debated the Day but one after Mr. Wilson delivered these Sentiments, when the Instructions of the Assembly referred to were altered, and new Instructions given to the Delegates of Pennsylvania.[4] Mr. Wilson then observ'd that being un-restrained, if the Question was put he should vote for it; but he still wished a Determination on it to be postponed for a short time until the Deputies of the People of Pennsylvania who were to meet should give their explicit Opinion upon this Point so important and interesting to themselves and their Posterity; and also urged the Propriety of postponing the Question for the Purpose of giving the Constituents of several Colonies an Opportunity of removing their respective Instructions, whereby Unanimously [Unanimity] would probably be Obtained.

T. Stone	Samuel Adams	John Alsop
Edward Rutledge	John Hancock	Francis Lewis
Arthur Middleton	Wm. Whipple	Joseph Hewes
Thomas Willing	Thos. Jefferson	Robert Treat Paine
Francis Lightfoot Lee	Thos. Nelson Jun.	William Ellery
Robert Morris	Benja. Harrison	J. Rogers
John Adams	William Floyd	Henry Wisner
Step. Hopkins		

Tr (DLC). Endorsed: "Certificate of Sundry Members of Congress. Mr. Wilson."

[1] The "reports . . . circulated concerning Mr. Wilson . . . to the Disadvantage of his Publick Character" consisted of copies of letters from Robert Whitehill to friends, written from Philadelphia, June 10, 1776. Whitehill (1738–1813), who was one of the two "additional" representatives to the Pennsylvania Assembly elected from Cumberland County on May 1, 1776, had been in the assembly during the debates over revising the instructions to the Pennsylvania delegates in Congress on the issue of independence and apparently concluded that Wilson would be forced to relent in his opposition to independence if his Cumberland County constituents were acquainted with his conduct in Philadelphia. The FC of one of Whitehill's letters, which is among a collection of his papers discovered in 1975 in the possession of a descendant but now available at The Hamilton Library, PCarlH, reads as follows:

"As a Servant to the County of Cumberland I think I would be a Neglecter of my Duty to my Constituents if I did not take the Earlyest opertunity to warn them of their danger, from a gentn. who hath ben high in Estimation in the County I am now a Representative of.

"As matters of some importance not to a County nor province only, but of the greatest Consequence to all America I proceed to give you sir some Expressions from a worthy Deligate of one of the midle Colonies, in Congress, upon being asked June 8th how the debates on independance prospered, in Congress? Go said he & ask your friends Dickinson and Willson.

"This Same Gentleman June 9th asked another Delegate [how] Colonel Wilson behaved in Congress on the debate about independance and was answered—Col.

Wilson formerly Complained of being bound by instructions Contrary to his Judgment. I Expected yesterday (said he) to have heard him alter his tone as his instructions were Rescinded—but—I must say no more. I will never trust a Scotchman again. They Cannot be honest when liberty is in question. Your Conferrence of Committees must appoint New Deligates, or your province will be Ruined. And sir Exprissions of John Dickinsons in the House on the 7th of June which I heard from his own mouth, Confirm me in opinion that he, with all the other deligates of this province in Congress with him design to opose and obstruct Independance as he pledged himself to his honour, William Allen in particular, and the house in general, that as the debate would very soon Come on in Congress whither independance of the united Colonies should be Declared that he with the other Deligates of this Colonie would vote against it at all Events, as he had Considered Every argument both for and against and had Counted the Cost that there for as shuer as he was alive he would opose the mesure altho I the Day before heard him Solomnly Declare that he thought the time was Come for it. That the kings answer to the Lord Mayor, auldermen, and Comons of London, had Confirmed him that we never Could be united to Great brittain again—that the mercyles, implacabel and irreconcilable designs was now made manifest.

"Dear Sir I have not only heard but felt the weight of such language and if Ever people were sold it apears to me that we are. A Recomendation of Congress lies before the house to Rais 4500 troops of the malitia Imediatly, to be paid by Congress for the Security of the Colonies. On tuesdy we are to go into a Committee of the whole House to take up the s[t]ate of the province and I think we shall withdraw and Brake the house if we find it nessary so to do. Dickinson, Wilson, and the others, have Rendered them selves obnoctious to Every Whig in town, and Every Day of theyr Existance are losing the Confidence of the people.

"Sir I have wrote fully that you may acquaint our people in Cumberland of matters as they stand, and if the[y] are so incredulouse as still to opose their own salvation and bring their own and other peoples Ruin for want of positive proof, I Stand Ready, able, and willing to give Even that Satisfaction, for the interest, peace, and future happyness of my Countery. The honourable old Mr. Allen in private Conversation with me 8th of June after my informing him that a Great majority of our County were for independance, told me, if the[y] wer, he would not Chuse to Represent the County. I am sir your most Huml Servt."

Obviously smarting from Whitehill's attack, Wilson attempted to defend himself with an account of his position during the opening debates on independence in Congress, to which he obtained the signatures of 22 delegates certifying the accuracy of his summary.

Although several of Wilson's opponents signed the document, it appears that some of them did so because they believed that Wilson's maneuvers would only further discredit his leadership among many Pennsylvanians. At least Whitehill, who had returned home after the breakup of the assembly in mid-June, received testimony to this effect in a letter from Paul Fooks, dated Philadelphia, June 24, 1776. Whitehill Papers, PCarlH. Fooks, who obtained his information chiefly from Samuel Adams, explained the matter to Whitehill as follows:

"I write you this in a very great hurry not to Miss the opportunity therefore shall be more breif than I otherwise would chuse.

"I heard with concern that your Enemies had endeavoared to hurt your Interest here and in your County by making use of a Coppy of a Letter you wrote when here to some of your Freinds. I have not seen that coppy but am told that it concerned Mr. Willsons behavior in Congress on the subject of Independency, and its contents as mentioned to me by those to whoom Mr. Willson shewd it were exactly word for word what you were told in my house by a Gentleman who authorised and desired you to write it to your Freinds in Cumberland, that they might be informed of the truth of Mr. Willsons behavior on that subject which he declared then and still does he had from sure authority and if necessary will declare it

Publickly and in the most solemn manner. Mr. Willson I am inform'd shewd this Letter to the Congress and desired they would recollect what [h]is behavior had been during the Debate on Independency and woud testifie the same as none but them could clear his Character. This method was debated, found unparliamentary and droped, but renewed afterwards, and a Certificate was presented which expresses according to what Mr. Samuel Adams told me as near as I can recollect what follows, Vizt. that on the first day of the Debate Mr. Willson had declared that in his private Character he thought that Independency ought to take place, and that he beleived that many of the Pennsylvania Delegates were of the same opinion, but that in his Public Character he was bound by the Instructions of the Assembly the only representatives of the People of this Province to oppose it. This was on a Saturday, on which very day the Assembly then sitting recinded their Instructions and before the Congress broke up Mr. Willson was told of it, but he answerd that he had not yet received any information of it from the house, and the Debate was ajourned untill the Monday following when Mr. Willson Confest that he had given his private oppinion in favour of Independency and that tho he was convinced that the majority of his Constituents were of the same opinion yet he desired the determination of that matter might be postponed untill he could procure the further opinion of his Constituents in a fuller manner either By public meetings or otherwise. This Certificate some sign'd and others refused. Mr. Saml. Adams told him that this Certificate if published would rather hurt his Character with the People than be in his favour for that tho he had at first declared his private opinion to be for indepen[den]cy he availed himself of the instructions of Assembly to oppose it and afterwards when the Assembly had repeald their Instructions and left him to the free exercise of his Will he had only changed his ground and desired the decision might be postponed to a further time. Which behavior cannot certainly be regarded as in favour of Independency. All which will certainly appear in a full and clear light if considered by an unprejudiced mind. And will be proved if necessary. Mr. Adams told me that this Certificate could be no prejudice to you and more of Disservice to Mr. Willson than otherwise and that he had told him so.

"I have the pleasure to inform you that yesterday the Committy of Conference voted Independency to take place in this Province and are to send their resolve this day to the Congress desiring it may take place thro the united Colonies. This in my opinion is a Convincing prooff that they could no longer trust that important matter to Mr. Willson and the other Pennsylvania Delegates particularly as they have Determined that it shall be carried to Congress by a Committy of their own Members and not by any [of t]he Delegates of this Province. . . . Shew my Letter if you will but dont let anyone take Coppies for they should Change, Add or diminish."

For an explicit denunciation of Whitehill's letter, see James Wilson to John Montgomery, July 9, 1776. For additional information on Whitehill's public career, which found him repeatedly in opposition to Wilson, especially over ratification of the Constitution in 1787–88, and culminated in the United States Congress, 1805–13, see *Bio. Dir. Cong.*; Page Smith, *James Wilson, Founding Father, 1742–1798* (Chapel Hill: University of North Carolina Press, 1956), pp. 263, 270–72, 278, 303; and Merrill Jensen, ed., *The Documentary History of the Ratification of the Constitution* (Madison: State Historical Society of Wisconsin, 1976–), 2:733.

[2] The debate of June 7 on Richard Henry Lee's motion pertaining to independence.

[3] The Pennsylvania Assembly had already (on June 5) appointed a committee headed by John Dickinson to draft a new set of instructions for the Pennsylvania delegates in Congress. For a discussion of this move, and of Wilson's response in Congress to Lee's motion on independence, see David Hawke, *In the Midst of a Revolution* (Philadelphia: University of Pennsylvania Press, 1961), pp. 160–61. Hawke's discussion is based primarily upon the document printed in the present

entry, which he cites as an "unpublished manuscript in Library of Congress, quoted by Hampton L. Carson, *American Law Register,* 55 (1907), 38."

⁴ These instructions were approved on Saturday, June 8, 1776, and transcribed into the assembly's minutes of proceedings under the date June 14. See *Pa. Archives,* 8th ser. 8:7539, 7542–43.

John Hancock to William Palfrey

Sir,   Philada. June 20th 1776.

The Congress have ordered three Hundred Thousand Dollars for the Use of the Troops at New York, which I will do myself the Pleasure of forwarding, as soon as the Signers shall have compleated that Sum. I will, in the mean Time, make a Point of hurrying them, that I may send the Money as soon as possible.[1]

You will inform me what is your Determination as to an Assistant, or whether you have come to any Determination as to the Person. I expect to hear from you on the Subject by the next Post. I am in great Haste, your most obedt. & very hble Sevt.

John Hancock Presidt.

RC (MH). In the hand of Jacob Rush and signed by Hancock.

[1] See *JCC,* 5:465.

Robert Morris' Memorandum

In Congress, June 20th, 1776.

Robert Morris, one of the Delegates from the Province of Pennsylvania, reminded the Congress that the Assembly of said Province had adjourned on the 14th instant, without having been able to Carry into Execution the Resolves of Congress of the 3rd Instant for raising 6,000 Militia for establishing a flying Camp; and then informed the Congress that their said Resolve, not being directed in *Terms* to the Committee of Safety, but addressed to the *Colony,* the said Committee were in doubt whether it would be expected from them to execute the said Resolve, as they are in Recess of Assembly the Executive body of this Province.[1] He Also alledged that if the Congress expected the Committee to proceed in this Business it would be necessary or adviseable that they should recommend it expressly to them, for under the present Circumstances of the Province, he much doubted if they would be obeyed unless so authorized, and added that, if the Congress did not see proper to take further order in this matter, he hoped the Committee of Safety would always be held blameless, as they now gave Congress this necessary information for the express purpose of having an explicit declaration, if they were expected to act in this important business, which they were ready to undertake if so desired. This application was made by Mr. Morris as declared, by order of the Committee of Safety, and after a debate of Considerable length, and two Motions made and seconded, one was withdrawn, and the other determined in the Negative. In Consequence whereof, I have made this Memorandum immediately on the spot, to appear when it may be necessary, and to prevent blame being cast where it is not merited.

Signed, Robert Morris.

The above is a true state of Facts.

Signed,   Joseph Hewes,

          Edward Rutledge,   } Delegates in Congress.

          T. Hope [Stone].

MS not found; reprinted from *Minutes of the Provincial Council of Pennsylvania, from the Organization to the Termination of the Proprietary Government,* 10 vols. (Philadelphia: J. Severns & Co.; Harrisburg: Theo. Fenn & Co., 1851–53), 10:611–12.

[1] Congress resolved on June 3 that a flying camp of 10,000 men be established in the middle colonies, for which purpose Pennsylvania was requested to furnish 6,000 militia. Since the Pennsylvania Assembly had failed to act on the resolve before adjourning on June 14, the committee of safety, of which Morris was vice-president, requested advice on whether it should proceed to organize the Pennsylvania militia in accordance with the resolve of June 3. Morris' "Memorandum" documents Congress' inability to agree on a proper response to the Pennsylvania Committee of Safety, which had resolved on June 19 to seek such clarification from their delegates in Congress. Upon receiving Morris' "Memorandum," the committee simply read the document into their minutes of proceedings on June 21. See *JCC,* 4:412–13; and *Am. Archives,* 4th ser. 6:1286, 1288–89. The following day the committee of safety laid the issue before the "Conference of Committees" then sitting in Philadelphia to arrange the convening of a constitutional convention in July. On June 23 the "Conference" resolved to "recommend to the committees and associators of this province to embody 4,500 of the militia, which with the 1,500 men now in the pay of this province, will be the quota of this colony required by congress," and subsequently drafted a specific plan and a covering letter to be forwarded to the county committees throughout Pennsylvania. See *Pa. Archives,* 2d ser. 3:564–65, 572–74, 578–82.

Robert Treat Paine to Henry Knox

Dear Sr,   Philada June 20th. 1776.

I received yrs. of June 10th & hoped you would favour me with a perticular answer to my Letter to which I take the liberty to referr you.[1] You promised me a Communication of Some Experiments. I hope you will not forget it. I want much to hear the State of the Air furnace at N York. Congress have ordered some Iron feild peices to be cast & wish to know if they can be made at that Furnace. Pray be as perticular in your Answer to my first Letter as

you can & write me by the Post.[2] I sincerely wish Sr. you may find
satisfaction in yr Office. Honor & Victory if you are attacked. Yr
freind & Sevt,   R T Paine

RC (MHi).
    [1] See Paine to Henry Knox, May 31, 1776, note 1.
    [2] On June 17 Congress had ordered the Cannon Committee to acquire brass or
iron fieldpieces. *JCC,* 5:453. Knox's June 24 response is in Clark, *Naval Documents,*
5:710–12.

John Adams to Zabdiel Adams

My dear Sir   Philadelphia June 21. 1776
    Your Favour of the Ninth of this Month was delivered to me,[1]
Yesterday by Mr. Whitney, whose Health I hope will be fully restored by the Small Pox for which he was innoculated the day before.
Your Letter, Sir, gave me great Pleasure and deserves my most
hearty Thanks.
    I am fully with you in Sentiment, that altho the Authority of the
Congress founded as it has been, in Reason, Honour, and the Love
of Liberty, has been sufficient to govern the Colonies, in a tolerable
Manner, for their Defence and Protection: yet that it is not prudent,
to continue very long in the same Way. That a permanent Constitution should be formed, and foreign Aid, obtained. In these Points
and thus far the Colonies, and their Representatives the Congress
are extremely well united. But concerning a Declaration of Independency there is some Diversity of Sentiment. Two Arguments
only, are urged with any Plausibility against such a Measure. One
is that it will unite all the Inhabitants of G. Britain against Us. The
other, that it will put us too much in the Power of foreign States.
The first has little Weight in it, because the People of Great Britain,
are already as much united against Us, as they ever are in any
Thing, and the Probability is, that such a Declaration would excite
still greater Divisions and Distractions among them.[2]
    The second has less Weight still, for foreign Powers already know
that We are as obnoxious to the British Court as We can be. They
know that Parliament have in effect declared Us independent, and
that We have acted these thirteen Months, to all Intents and Purposes as if We were so.
    The Reports of fifty five Thousand Men, coming against Us, are
chiefly ministerial Gasconade. However We have reason to fear that
they will send several very powerfull Armaments against Us, and
therefore our most strenuous Exertions will be necessary, as well as
our most fervent Prayers. America is yet in her Infancy, or at least
but lately arrived to Man hood, and is inexperienced in the perplex-

ing Misteries of Policy, as well as the dangerous Operations of War.

I assure you, sir, that your Employment, in investigating the Moral Causes of our Miseries, and in pointing out the Remedies, is devoutly to be wished. There is no station more respectable; nor any so pleasant and agreable. Those who tread the public Stage, in Characters the most extensively conspicuous, meet with so many Embarrassments, Perplexities, and Disappointments, that they have often reason to wish for the peacefull Retreats of the Clergy. . . .[3] Who would not wish to exchange the angry Contentions of the Forum, for the peacefull Contemplations of the Closet. Where Contemplations prune their ruffled Wings and the free Soul looks down to pitty Kings? Who would not Exchange the discordant Scenes of Envy, Pride, Vanity, Malice, Revenge, for the sweet Consolations of Philosophy, the serene Composure of the Passions, the divine Enjoyments of Christian Charity, and Benevolence?

Statesmen my dear Sir, may plan and speculate for Liberty, but it is Religion and Morality alone, which can establish the Principles upon which Freedom can securely stand. . . . The only foundation of a free Constitution, is pure Virtue, and if this cannot be inspired into our People, in a greater Measure, than they have it now, They may change their Rulers, and the forms of Government, but they will not obtain a lasting Liberty. They will only exchange Tyrants and Tyrannies. You cannot therefore be more pleasantly, or usefully employed than in the Way of your Profession, pulling down the Strong Holds of Satan. This is not Cant, but the real sentiment of my Heart. Remember me with much respect, to your worthy family, and to all Friends.

LB (MHi). Adams, *Family Correspondence* (Butterfield), 2:20–21.

[1] Zabdiel Adams (1739–1801), Lunenburg, Mass., minister, was a cousin of John Adams. Shipton, *Harvard Graduates*, 14:377–83. Zabdiel's June 9 letter to John is in Adams, *Family Correspondence* (Butterfield), 2:6–8.

[2] For a further exposition of some of the arguments put forth against independence, see John Dickinson's Notes for a Speech in Congress, June 8–10? 1776.

[3] Suspension points in MS, here and below.

Board of War to George Washington

Sir   War Office Philada. 21st June 1776

The Congress having thought proper to appoint us to the Board of War & Ordinance, we do ourselves the Honour to transmit you the foregoing Extracts from their Proceedings establishing a War Office for the more speedy & effectual Dispatch of military Business.[1] You will perceive, on Perusal of the Extracts, that it will be necessary for you forthwith to furnish the Board with an exact State of the Army under your Command & every thing relative thereto. You will therefore be pleased, as speedily as possible, to give the necessary Directions for true & accurate Returns to be made to you, so as to enable you to give the Board the proper Information. As much depends on reducing into Method the Business recommended to our Notice, we beg you will forward all Measures conducive to this desirable Purpose by every Means in your Power. It is expected that in future, monthly Returns be regularly transmitted to the War Office that Congress may frequently have a full & general Knowledge of the true Situation of their Military Affairs without which it will be impossible to conduct them with Propriety & Success. We must further request that you will keep up a constant & regular Correspondence with us that we may cooperate with you in such Measures as may tend to advance the Interest of America in general & the particular Department committed to your Care. You will be pleased in the Returns of the several Regiments to mention the Colonies in which they were raised, the Times when & the Periods for which the Men were enlisted as it will be necessary for us to have sufficient Notice of these Matters that Congress may keep up the Army to its full Compliment.

We are your Excellency's most obedient & most hble Servants,

John Adams   Benja Harrison

Roger Sherman   James Wilson

Edward Rutledge

RC (DLC). In the hand of Richard Peters and signed by Adams, Harrison, Rutledge, Sherman, and Wilson. The surviving copies of this letter sent to Charles Lee (ScC) and to William Heath (DLC) suggest that it was a circular to all general officers.

[1] The Board of War and Ordnance was established by Congress on June 12, and its five members and secretary were elected the following day. *JCC*, 5:434–35, 438. Hoping to bring greater order and efficiency to military administration, Congress charged the board with keeping a register of officers and returns on the disposition of the land forces in all the colonies, maintaining accurate accounts of ordnance and supplies, superintending recruitment, caring for prisoners of war, and dispatching and preserving correspondence pertaining to military affairs. But as a standing committee of Congress with only limited authority to meet specific problems, the board remained a body for deliberation rather than effective action and the immensity of its task led to several reorganizations. For further discussion on the Board of War's development, see Jennings B. Sanders, *Evolution of the Executive Departments of the Continental Congress, 1774–1789* (Chapel Hill: University of North Carolina Press, 1935), chap. 1.

Benjamin Franklin to George Washington

Dear Sir   Philadelphia June 21, 76

I am [much] obliged by your kind Care of my unfortunate Letter, which at last came safe to hand.[1] I see in it a Detail of the mighty Force we are threatned with; which however I think it is not certain will ever arrive; & I see more certainly the Ruin of Britain if she persists in such expensive distant Expeditions, which will probably prove more disastrous to her than anciently her Wars in the Holy Land.

I return Gen. Sulivan's Letter enclos'd.[2] Am glad to find him in such Spirits, and that the Canadians are returning to their Regard for us. I am just recovering from a severe Fit of the Gout, which has kept me from Congress & Company almost ever since you left us,[3] so that I know little of what has pass'd there, except that a Declaration of Independence is preparing. With the greatest Esteem & Respect, I am, Dr Sir, Your most obedt & most humbl Servt. B F

FC (NN).

[1] Probably a letter from Arthur Lee dated February 13, 1776. See Josiah Bartlett to John Langdon, May 21, 1776, note 2. See also Washington, *Writings* (Fitzpatrick), 5:64–65.

[2] Sullivan's letter to Washington of June 5–6, 1776, which Sullivan had requested be forwarded to Congress, and which Washington had enclosed in his letter to Hancock of June 16, is in *Am. Archives*, 4th ser. 6:921–23. It was read in Congress on June 18. See *JCC*, 5:459; and Washington, *Writings* (Fitzpatrick), 5:142–43.

[3] Washington had been in Philadelphia from May 23 to June 4, 1776, to discuss the defense of the colonies.

Elbridge Gerry to John Wendell

Dear sir   Philadelphia 21st June 1776

Since my last of the 11th Instant your Favour of the 4th is come to Hand, & I fully agree in the Opinion You enjoy of the Lords protest & of their Intention in publishing the same. In this Way & by inserting in news Papers the Substance of their Debates, have the Opposition in both Houses pointed out to America the Line of Conduct proper for her to pursue since the Commencement of the present Contest by the stamp act, & by comparing these with Events We shall find that the Colonies have judiciously improved the salutary Hints.

I wrote You my Sentiments with Respect to the Appointment of [the] Vendue Master since which I find the Business is loosely conducted & that the Continental Agent under the Direction of the marine Board is to make sd Appointmt. If Mr. Wendell [1] thinks himself authorized as an agent established by the Commander in chief previous to the Continental Regulations of the Admiralty, to make a temporary provission in that office untill Congress shall confirm him agent for the Colony or supersede him by a new Appointment, my Sentiments were that your Business or Intention of obtaining the Office would be best accomplished by applying to him & I am still of the same Opinion as I can see no Impropriety at present in the Measure. Indeed Mr Wendell may think himself unsafe in adopting this Method without consulting General Washington, & be thus referred to Congress, & in this Case an Agent must be first nominated by the New Hampshire Delegates to the marine Board & appointed by Congress before the former can proceed to recommend to the Agent a suitable person as Vendue Master. When your Delegates shall have adopted this Measure I shall then mention You to the Members of the Board & press the Matter as far as it will be prudent to interfere in the affairs of a Sister Colony.

I observe what You propose relative to sharing any genteel place which I can procure for you, but at the same time that the principles from which yr proposal be made may be founded in Generosity, yet I cannot reconcile it to my Ideas of Justice & Honor to accept the Offer. The Trust reposed in me by the public was for the purpose of promoting the public Good, & the Salus populi is the object at which alone I mean to aim in conducting the Affairs of the public. If then an Business or Act is to be done in the Executive Department for which a Reward is to be granted, that Reward is always in a just Government determined previous to the Appointment of the Officer (unless prevented by the Hurry of Business or other particular Reasons) & made adequate to the Services to be done as well or equal on the part of the Government; & whenever this is not the Case either the Officer or the people is injudiciously injured or wilfully defrauded by the Government, And the Error ought to be rectified when the Discovery is made. If the Reward granted is only adequate to the Services of the officer in the Discharge of his Trust, surely it is inconsistent with Justice to deprive him of any Part thereof from a Consideration that the person so depriving him, had in the Discharge of his own Trust proposed him as a Candidate for the office to which he was afterwards appointed. If on the other Hand the Reward granted exceeds the Services of the officer because he but partially discharges his Duty, it is inconsistent with the principles of Honor as it appears to me to support him longer in office, since the public must be injured by Continuing him therein. If then any agreable Appointment is to be made in which You can serve the public & benefit yourself, I shall think it justifiable so far to indulge Friendship as to propose You for the Office, & shall consider the Advantages accruing from the same to be as justly your due as any Estate or Interest which is now in your own possession.

With Respect to Money You will not be able to hire any in these Colonies as a loan office will probably be soon opened by the Continent & large Sums borrowed for the Use of the same.[2]

My Regards to all Friends & believe me to be sir, your Friend &
hum sert,   Elbridge Gerry

RC (DLC photostat).
[1] That is, Joshua Wentworth. See Gerry to John Wendell, June 11, 1776, note 3.
John Langdon was appointed prize agent for New Hampshire on June 25. *JCC*,
5:478.
[2] Congress did not create a system of Continental loan offices until October 3,
1776. *JCC*, 5:845–46.

John Hancock to Certain Colonies

Gentlemen,   Philada. June 21t. 1776.
    I do myself the Honour of enclosing in Obedience to the Com-
mands of Congress, sundry Resolutions to which I beg Leave to
request your Attention.[1]
    I have only Time to observe, in general, that it is totally impos-
sible the American Troops should ever be on a respectable Footing,
or that they should render any very essential Services to their
Country, unless the United Colonies, on their Part, will take Care
to have them well appointed and equipped with every Thing necessary for an Army. In this View of the Matter, the enclosed Resolve
respecting the Mode of providing proper Cloathing for our Troops,
is most certainly of the greatest Importance; and I make no Doubt
will appear in the same Light to you, and claim your immediate
& closest Attention.
    I have the Honour to be, Gentlemen your most obed. & very hble
Sert.   J. H. Prest.

LB (DNA: PCC, item 12A). Addressed: "To the Convention of New York. The
Assembly of Connecticutt. The Assembly of Rhode Island. The Assembly of Mass-
achus. Bay. The Assembly of New Hampshire."
[1] See the resolves concerning clothing for the Continental Army, which were
passed by Congress on June 19, in *JCC*, 5:466–67.

John Hancock to the New York Convention

Gentlemen,   Philada. June 21t. 1776
    I am directed by Congress to forward to you the enclosed Re-
solves, by which you will perceive it is their Desire that another
Regiment should be raised in your Colony on Continental Establish-
ment.[1]
    The many ill Consequences resulting from a short Enlistment of
Troops, have induced the Congress to leave the Time of their
Service indefinite. By this Means, there will be no Danger of losing

their Services at a Time when their Discipline and Experience have qualified them to be of the greatest Use to their Country.

With Respect to the Field officers, as soon as I have the Honour to receive your Recommendations I will lay them before Congress, & immediately upon their Determination, transmit you the Commissions filled up accordingly.

Major Dubois by his Behaviour in Canada has justly merited the Notice of his Country. I am therefore to request you will be pleased to return his Name as one of the Field Officers of the Regiment, for the approbation of Congress.[2]

I have the Honour to be Gentlemen, your most obedt. & hb srt.

J. H. Prest.

LB (DNA: PCC, item 12A).

[1] See *JCC*, 5:471–72.

[2] The commissioners to Canada had recommended Lewis Dubois' promotion in their letter to Hancock of May 16, which was received on June 14, 1776. See *Am. Archives*, 4th ser. 6:482. Although Hancock solicited the convention's participation in naming officers for the new regiment, the arrival of more alarming news from Canada led Congress to appoint Dubois as colonel in command of this regiment on June 26, well before the convention had an opportunity to act on the president's letter. *JCC*, 5:481. For the storm of controversy which this action aroused in New York, see *JCC*, 5:602; and *Am. Archives*, 5th ser. 1:40, 201–4, 228–29, 393, 772, 774–75.

John Hancock to George Washington

Sir,   Philadelphia June 21t. 1776.

The Congress having the greatest Reason to believe there has been very gross Misconduct in the Management of our Affairs in Canada, have come to a Resolution to have a general Enquiry made into the Behaviour of the Officers employed on that Expedition. The Honour of the United Colonies, and a Regard for the Public Good, call loudly for such an Enquiry to be set on Foot. I am therefore directed to request, after having made the Enquiry, agreeably to the inclosed Resolve, you will transmit the Result, together with the Proofs to Congress.[1]

The Opinion, that an officer cannot be tried by a Court Martial after his Resignation, for Offences while he held a Commission—so dangerous to the Service—and particularly destructive in our Army, where the short Enlistment of the Troops might furnish Temptation to Crimes from the Prospect of Impunity—has been this Day reprobated by Congress.

I have wrote to the Convention of New York on the Subject of the enclosed Resolve respecting another Regiment to be raised in that Colony. The Terms on which the Commissions are to be granted are extremely well calculated to excite the officers to exert themselves to fill up their Companies.

I have likewise written to the respective Colonies, and have sent Copies of the enclosed Resolve recommending to them to provide Cloaths for the Troops of their Colonies. These, or such Articles of them as you shall want, the Congress have empowered you to draw for on the Assemblies & Conventions from Time to Time, as you shall judge necessary. I have represented to them that it is totally impossible the American Army should ever be on a respectable Footing, or that they should render such essential Services to their Country as we expect & desire, unless the United Colonies will, on their Part, take Care that they are well appointed & equipped with every Thing necessary for an Army.

Genl. Wooster, it is the Order of Congress, should be permitted to return to his Family.[2]

I have Deliver'd Mr. Vissher his Commissn. as Lieut Coll. in the Regimt. commanded by Coll. Nicholson, & directed him to wait on you upon his Arrival at New York.[3]

Apprehending that such of the Resolves of Congress as respect the Conduct of the Army are executed in consequence of orders issued by you, I have omitted Sending to Genl. Schuyler such as respect him, concluding that the Directions would go from you, but if it will be any way a Relief to you, I will Continue to forward them.

I have the honour to be, with much Esteem, Sir, Your most Obedt. hum sevt.   John Hancock Presidt

22d [June 1776]. Your Letter of 20th this moment came to hand, shall be laid before Congress on Monday.[4]

RC (DLC). In the hand of Jacob Rush, with last two paragraphs, signature, and postscript by Hancock.

[1] See *JCC*, 5:472. Washington soon decided that he was in no position to carry out this resolution, and on July 15 he entrusted the task to General Schuyler. Washington, *Writings* (Fitzpatrick), 5:281–82; and *Am. Archives*, 5th ser. 1:473. In the meantime, on June 24 Congress appointed its own committee "to enquire into the cause of the miscarriages in Canada," which eventually submitted several reports between July and October 1776. See *JCC*, 5:474, 524, 530, 592, 617–20, 623, 629, 633, 644–45, 741, 852–53. Two members of this committee—Thomas Jefferson and Robert Treat Paine—kept detailed notes of the testimony which they heard about the reasons for the American debacle in Canada. See Jefferson's "Notes of Witnesses' Testimony concerning the Canadian Campaign," July 1–27, 1776, Jefferson, *Papers* (Boyd), 1:433–54; and Paine's "Testimony Relating to the Expedition into Canada," undated MS, Robert Treat Paine Papers, MHi. Another document pertaining to this committee's work, in the hand of William Whipple and dated July 30, 1776, is in PCC, item 58, fols. 383–86. For some reflections on the American failure in Canada by a delegate who was not a member of this committee, see Samuel Adams' Notes on Military Operations in Canada, August 1, 1776.

[2] See *JCC*, 5:470.

[3] See *JCC*, 5:472.

[4] This letter is in PCC, item 152, 2:75–78, and Washington, *Writings* (Fitzpatrick), 5:159–61.

Thomas Jefferson to Benjamin Franklin

Th. J. to Doctr. Franklin   Friday morn. [June 21? 1776][1]
   The inclosed paper has been read and with some small alterations
approved of by the committee. Will Doctr. Franklyn be so good as
to peruse it and suggest such alterations as his more enlarged view
of the subject will dictate? The paper having been returned to me
to change a particular sentiment or two, I propose laying it again
before the committee tomorrow morning, if Doctr. Franklyn can
think of it before that time.

RC (PPAmP). Jefferson, *Papers* (Boyd), 1:404.
   [1] For the date of this letter, see Julian P. Boyd's explanatory note in Jefferson,
Papers (Boyd), 1:404–6, where he also discusses the "inclosed paper"—a draft
declaration of independence—that Jefferson sent with this letter to Franklin.

Rhode Island Delegates to Nicholas Cooke

Sir   Philadelphia June 21st. 1776
   Since our last the Time of Congress hath been principally taken
up in considering the Report of the Commissioners who have returned from Canada, and in devising and determining upon
Measures for securing our Posts, and supplying our Troops in that
Department with Cloathing and Provision. Our Accounts from
that Quarter are so various that We do not know which to depend
upon. General Sullivan's Letter of the 5th & 6th of June, an Extract of which was in last Monday's New-York Paper, gives us a
favorable, and Genl. Arnold's of the same Date an unfavorable
Account of the Situation of our affairs.[1] Indeed Sullivan was at the
Mouth of the Sorrel, and Arnold at Montreal. However We hope
that Genl. Gates who is appointed to the Command of the Northern
Army (Genl. Wooster is recalled and Genl. Thomas dead as you
have doubtless heard) will restore Order to our distracted Troops
and retrieve the Reputation of our Arms.
   The Grand Question of Independance was brot upon the Tapis
the Eighth Instant, and after having been cooly discussed, the
further Consideration thereof was on the 10th postponed for three
Weeks, and in the mean Time, least any Time should be lost in
Case the Congress should agree to the proposed Resolution of
Independance, a Committee was appointed to prepare a Declaration to the Effect of said Resolution, another a Form of Confederation, and a Third a Plan for foreign Alliances.[2]
   A Board of War & Ordnance is established, Post ordered to be
taken at Fort Stanwix; and, which ought to have been mentioned

in another Place, Genl. Washington is requested to cause an Inquiry to be made into the Conduct of the Officers in Canada &c.[3] Beside these a Number of Resolves have passed, some of which have been published in the News Papers and therefore it would be idle and unnecessary to repeat them, and others are at present to be kept secret, or relate to particular Persons or Things, are not of general Concern; the former we ought not and it is not worth while to mention the latter. A Resolve respecting Prisoners taken in Arms you may not have received. We therefore inclose it.[4] We are not a little Surprised that the Resolve of Congress for taking our Battalions into continental Pay had not reached you when Mr. Ward wrote Us. Mr. Hopkins dispatched it by an Express (Anthony) the 15th of May.[5] John Hopkins is appointed to the Command of the largest Ship, called Warren after Dr. Warren of glorious Memory, and Samuel Tompkins to the Command of the smallest called Providence.[6] We shall continue from Time to Time to give you an Account of such Resolves of Congress as we may be allowed, and think proper to communicate. But if We should not write so frequently as our Constituents may wish, We hope it will not be attributed to a Neglect of our Duty; but because We have nothing of Moment to communicate. Business doth not proceed so rapidly in Congress as in some other Assemblies. Matters of Importance sustain great Deliberations. We should be glad to be made acquainted with such of the Doings of the General Assembly as it concerns Us to know as soon as may be convenient, and are with great Respect, Yr Honours most Obedient, humble Servants,

William Ellery

P.S. The Post being just about to set out & Mr. Hopkins not being at his Lodgings this Letter therefore goes out without his Signature.

W E

RC (PPRF). Written and signed by William Ellery. Addressed: "To The Honble Nicholas Cooke Esqr, Governor of the Colony of Rhode Island &c."

[1] Washington transmitted these and other letters in his June 16 letter to Hancock. PCC, item 152, 2:37–62; and *Am. Archives*, 4th ser. 6:919–26.

[2] See *JCC*, 5:428–29, 431, 433.

[3] See *JCC*, 5:434–35, 442, 472.

[4] See *JCC*, 5:453.

[5] See Stephen Hopkins to Nicholas Cooke, May 15, 1776, note 2.

[6] See *JCC*, 5:422.

John Adams to Nathanael Greene

Dear sir.   Philadelphia June 22. 1776[1]

Your Favour of the second Instant[2] has lain by me, I suppose these Eighteen days, but I fear I shall often have occasion to make

Apologies for such omissions, which will never happen from want of Respect, but I fear very often for want of Time.

Your Reasoning, to prove the Equity and the Policy of making Provision for the Unfortunate officer, or soldier, is extreamly just, and cannot be answered, and I hope that when We get a little over the Confusions arising from the Revolutions which are now taking Place in the Colonies, and get an American Constitution formed, Something will be done. I should be much obliged to you for your Thoughts upon the subject. What Pensions shall be allowed or what other Provision made? Whether it would be expedient to establish an Hospital &c—it is a Matter of Importance, and the Plan should be well digested.

I think with you that every Colony should furnish its Proportion of Men, and I hope it will come to this. But at present, some Colonies have such Bodies of Quakers, and Menonists, and Moravians, who are principled against War, and others have such Bodies of Tories, or Cowards, or unprincipled People who will not wage War, that it is as yet impossible.

The Dispute is, as you justly observe, in all human Probability, but in its Infancy. We ought therefore to Study, to bring every Thing in the military Department into the best order. Fighting is not the greatest Branch of the Science of war. Men must be furnished with good and wholesome Provisions in Sufficient Plenty. They must be well paid. They must be well cloathed and well covered, with Barracks and Tents. They must be kept warm with Suitable Fuel. In these Respects, We have not been able to do so well as We wished. But, Why the Regiments have not been furnished with proper Agents, I dont know. Congress is ever ready to hearken to the advice of the General, and if he had recommended such officers, they would have been appointed. Collonells should neither be Agents, nor suttlers. Congress have lately voted that there shall be regimental Paymasters who shall keep the accounts of the Regiments. If any other Agent is necessary let me know it. Good officers are no doubt the Soul of an Army, but our Difficulty is to get Men. Officers present themselves in Supernumerary Abundance.

As to Pay there is no End to the Desire and Demand of it. Is there not too much Extravagance, and too little œconomy, among the officers?

I am much at a Loss, whether it would not be the best Policy, to leave every Colony to raise their own Troops, to cloath them, to Pay them, to furnish them with Tents, and indeed with every Thing but Provisions, fuel and Forage. The Project of abolishing Provincial Distinctions, was introduced with a good Intention, I believe, at first but I think it will do no good upon the whole. However, if Congress is to manage the whole, I am in hopes they will get into a better Train. They have established a War office, and a Board of War and ordinance, by means of which I hope they will get their affairs into better order. They will be better informed of the state of the Army and of all its Wants.

That the Promotion of extraordinary Merit, may give disgust to those officers is true, over whom the Advancement is made—but I think it ought not. That this Power may be abused, or misapplied, is also true. That Interest, Favour, private Friendship, Prejudice may operate more or less in the purest assembly, is true. But where will you lodge this Power? To place it in the General would be more dangerous to the public Liberty, and not less liable to abuse from sinister and unworthy Motives. Will it do, is it consistent with common Prudence to lay it down, as an invariable Rule, that all officers, in all Cases shall rise in succession?

I am obliged to you for your Caution not to be too confident. The Fate of War is uncertain—so are all Sublunary Things. But, We must form our Conjectures of Effects from the Knowledge we have of Causes, and in Circumstances like ours must not attempt to penetrate too far into Futurity. There are as many Evils, and more, which arise in human life, from an Excess of Diffidence, as from an Excess of Confidence—proud as Mankind is, their is more Superiority in this world yielded than assumed. I learned, long ago, from one of the greatest Statesmen this World ever produced, Sully, neither to adventure upon rash Attempts from too much Confidence, nor to despair of success in a great Design from the appearance of Difficulties. "Without attempting to judge of the future which depends upon too many Accidents, much less to subject it to our Precipitation in bold and difficult Enterprises, We should endeavour to subdue one Obstacle at a Time, nor Suffer our selves to be depress'd by their Greatness, and their Number. *We ought never to despair of what has been once accomplish'd.* How many Things have the Idea of impossible been annexed to, that have become easy to those who knew how to take Advantage of Time, opportunity, lucky Moments, the Faults of others, different Dispositions, and an infinite Number of other Circumstances.

I will inclose to you, a Copy of the Resolution establishing a Board of War and ordinance;[3] and as you may well imagine, We are all, inexperienced in this Business, I should be extreamly obliged to you for any Hints for the Improvement of the Plan, which may occur to you, and for any Assistance or Advice you may give me, as a private Correspondent in the Execution of it. It is a great Mortification to me I confess, and I fear it will too often be a Misfortune to our Country, that I am called to the Discharge of Trusts to which I feel myself so unequal, and in the Execution of which I can derive no assistance from my Education, or former Course of Life. But my Country must command me, and wherever she shall order me, there I will go, without Dismay. I am, Dear Sir, with the greatest Esteem, your humble servant.

LB (MHi).

¹ This Saturday, June 22, Congress did not sit, pursuant to its passage on June 20 of the following resolve: "That in order to give time to the several committees, to prepare for the house the matters referred to them, it be a standing rule of Congress, that adjournments from the Friday evening, be always to Monday morning, unless on any particular occasion, the Congress shall order otherwise." *JCC*, 5:468. Notwithstanding this effort to take more time from their routine daily deliberations, the delegates continued to meet on Saturdays more frequently than not during the ensuing months.

² Greene's June 2 letter to Adams is in the Adams Papers, MHi.

³ Adams was a member of the Board of War and Ordnance. *JCC*, 5:434–35, 438.

John Adams to Benjamin Kent

Sir   Philadelphia June 22. 1776

Your Letters of April 24 and May 26 are before me ¹—both dated at Boston, a Circumstance which alone would have given Pleasure to a Man who has such an Attachment to that Town, and who has sufferd so much Anxiety for his Friends, in their Exile from it.

We have not many of the fearfull, and still less of the Unbelieving among Us, how slowly soever, you may think We proceed. Is it not a Want of Faith, or a Predominance of Fear, which makes some of you so impatient for Declarations in Words of what is every day manifested in Deeds of the most determined Nature and unequivocal Signification?

That we are divorced, a Vinculo as well as from Bed and Board, is to me, very clear. The only Question is, concerning the proper Time for making an explicit Declaration in Words. Some People must have Time to look around them, before, behind, on the right hand, and on the left, then to think, and after all this to resolve. Others see at one intuitive Glance into the past and the future, and judge with Precision at once. But remember you cant make thirteen Clocks strike precisely alike, at the same second.

I am for the most liberal Toleration of all Denominations of Religionists but I hope that Congress will never meddle with Religion, further than to Say their own Prayers, and to fast and give Thanks, once a Year. Let every Colony have its own Religion, without Molestation.

The Congress ordered Church to the Massachusetts Council to be let out upon Bail. It was represented to them that his Health was in a dangerous Way and it was thought he would not now have it in his Power to do any Mischief. No Body knows what to do with him. There is no Law to try him upon, and no Court to try him. I am afraid he deserves more Punishment, than he will ever meet.[2] I am, your humble sevt.

LB (MHi).

[1] Benjamin Kent (1708–88), a Boston lawyer, was appointed attorney general for Suffolk County in 1776. Shipton, *Harvard Graduates*, 8:220–30. Kent's April 24 and May 26 letters to John Adams, in which he urged a declaration of independence and vociferously protested the release of Benjamin Church, are in the Adams Papers, MHi.

[2] On May 14 Congress had ordered the release of Benjamin Church on £1000 bail and directed that he be handed over to the Massachusetts Council. *JCC*, 4:350, 352. Church returned to Massachusetts in early June, but after narrowly escaping a lynch mob, he was returned to confinement until allowed to leave Massachusetts in January 1778. The ship in which he sailed disappeared without a trace. Shipton, *Harvard Graduates*, 13:395–97.

John Adams to Samuel H. Parsons

Dear sir.   Philadelphia June 22. 1776

Your obliging Favour of the third of June,[1] has been too long unanswered. I acknowledge the Difficulty of ascertaining the comparative Merit of officers, and the danger of advancing Friends, where there is no uncommon Merit. This danger cannot be avoided by any other Means, than making it an invariable Rule, to promote officers in succession. For if you make a King the Judge of uncommon Merit, he will advance favourites, without Merit, under Colour or Pretence of Merit. If you make a Minister of State the Judge, he will naturally promote his Relations, Connections and Friends. If you place the Power of judging of extraordinary Merit, in an assembly, you dont mend the Matter much. For by all the Experience I have had, I find that assemblies have Favourites as well as Kings and Ministers. The Favourites of assemblies, or the leading Members, are not always the most worthy. I dont know whether they ever are. Those leading Members have Sons, Brothers and Cousins, Acquaintances, Friends, and Connections of one sort or other, near or remote: and I have ever found, those Leading Members of assemblies, as much under the Influence of Nature, and her Passions and Prejudices, as Kings, and Ministers. The principal Advantage and Difference lies in this, that in an assembly, there are more Guards and Checks, upon the Infirmities of leading Members, than there are upon Kings and Ministers.

What then shall We say? Shall we leave it to the general and the Army? Is there not as much Favoritism, as much of Nature, Passion, Prejudice, and Partiality, in the Army, as in an assembly? As much in a General as a King or Minister?

Upon the whole I believe it wisest to depart from the Line of

Succession, as seldom as possible. But I cannot but think that the Power of departing from it at all, tho liable to abuses every where, yet safest in the Hands of an assembly.

But in our American Army, as that is circumstanced, it is as difficult to Settle a Rule of Succession, as a Criterion of Merit. We have Troops in every Province, from Georgia to New Hampshire. A Coll is kill'd in N. Hampshire—the next Coll in the American Army, to him, is in Georgia—must We send the Coll from Georgia, to command the Regiment in New Hampshire—upon his journey, he is seized with a Fever and dies—the next Coll is in Canada. We must then send to Canada, for a Coll to go to Portsmouth and as the next Coll to him is in South Carolina We must send a Coll from S. Carolina to Canada, to command that Regiment. These Marches, and Countermarches, must run through all the Corps of officers, and will occasion such inextricable Perplexities, delays, and Uncertainties, that We need not hesitate to pronounce it impracticable and ruinous. Shall We say then that succession shall take Place, among the officers of every distinct Army—or in every distinct Department?

My own private opinion is, that We shall never be quite right, untill every Colony is permitted to raise their own Troops, and the Rule of succession is established among the officers of the Colony. This, where there are Troops of several Colonies, serving in the same Camp, may be liable to some Inconveniences. But those will be fewer than upon any other Plan you can adopt.

It is right I believe, to make the Rule of Promotion among Captains and Subalterns, regimental only—and that among Field officers more general. But the Question is how general, it shall be? Shall it extend to the whole American Army? or only to the whole District, or Department? or only to the Army, serving at a particular Place?

That it is necessary to inlist an Army to serve during the War, or at least for a longer Period than one Year, and to offer some handsome Encouragement for that End, I have been convinced, a long Time. I would make this Temptation to consist partly in Money, and partly in Land, and considerable in both. It has been too long delayed—But I think it will now be soon done.

What is the Reason that New York must continue to embarrass the Continent? Must it be so forever? What is the Cause of it? Have they no Politicians, capable of instructing and forming the Sentiments of their People? Or are their People incapable of seeing and feeling like other Men. One would think that their Proximity to New England, would assimilate their opinions and Principles. One would think too that the Army would have some Influence upon them. But it seems to have none. N. York is likely to have the Honour of being the very last of all in imbibing the genuine

Principles and the true system of American Policy. Perhaps she will never entertain them at all.

I am, with much Respect, your Friend and servant.

LB (MHi).

¹ Samuel H. Parsons (1737–89), a Connecticut lawyer and friend of Adams' since their student days at Harvard, was appointed a colonel in the Continental Army in September 1775 and promoted to brigadier general on August 9, 1776. Shipton, *Harvard Graduates*, 14:50–73. Parsons' June 3 letter to Adams is in the Adams Papers, MHi.

John Hancock to James Athearn

Sir   Philadelphia 22d June 1776

Two Privateers from this City having Taken Three Jamaica Ships, one of which being Arriv'd at your Island, & another at Cape Ann, the Owners Vizt. Philip Moore, Archibald Mercer, & John Donaldson of this City Merchts. Visit our Province to Attend the proper Adjustmt. of the Concerns of the Vessells, and being Strangers in our parts, I most earnestly Recommend them to every Civility and Notice in your power, and Request you will give them every Advice and assistance they may need.¹ They are Gentn. of Reputation, & warmly Attach'd to our Cause, & as such are entitled to the Notice of all Good Men. I beg you will introduce them to your & my Connections. I would just mention that the Specie & Plate found on board these Ships was landed in this City, and Congress having great Occasion for the hard Money, made Application to the Owners, & they very generously furnish'd it, which Congress look'd upon as of essential Service. I shall write you further by Mr Bant who sets out from this City to morrow.²

I am Dr Sir, Your very hum svt,   John Hancock

[*P.S.*] I shall be Glad you would introduce the Gentlemen to the Judge of the Court.

RC (MBNEH). Addressed: "James Athearn Esqr. & other well Dispos'd Gentn," at "Marthas Vineyard."

¹ See Hancock to Philip Moore and James Craig, June 13, 1776, note. James Athearn (1724–1814), a holder of some minor judicial offices in Dukes Co., Mass., had already served several terms in the Massachusetts Provincial Congress. L. Kinvin Wroth et al., eds., *Province in Rebellion: A Documentary History of the Founding of the Commonwealth of Massachusetts, 1774–1775*, 4 vols. (Cambridge: Harvard University Press, 1975), 4:2828.

² This day Hancock also wrote brief letters to his brother, Deputy Paymaster General Ebenezer Hancock, forwarding "the Pay Roll of the Continental Army, it being necessary for you in your new Department," and to Commissary General Joseph Trumbull, apparently enclosing Congress' June 19 resolves on clothing for the Continental Army. See PCC, item 12A; *Am. Archives*, 4th ser. 6:1021; and *JCC*, 5:466–67.

William Whipple to John Langdon

Dr Sr.   Philada 22d June [1776]
Agreeable to Your request in Your favor of the first inst[1] I have applyed to the Chairman of the secret Committee to know if you shod have Liberty to pay for the Brig. that was taken, in answer to which he says the Charter Party & accots must be before the Committee e're they can give orders for the payment. By continual application & importunities I have at last prevail'd on the Marine Committee to consent to your shipg men.[2] The warrents will be fill'd up as soon as you send the names. I expected to send you the Blank warrent but the Commte have changed their minds about that matter aledging it will be necessary to have the names enter'd in the office. Therefore the sooner you send them the sooner they will be return'd. I am endeavoring to persuade the Committee to order those Guns at Providence for your ship as she is so much more forward than any but am not certain of success. If I do not succeed in this plan shall endeavor to get the first that is made here but how to get them from this place to you is a difficulty that I don't know at present how to surmount, however shall continue to do every thing in my power that you may be furnish'd with guns the want of which I am fully sensible will be the sole cause of the detention of the ship.
You say you find the Commte at Providence has Liberty to appoint Leiuts &c. I must confess I don't know from whence they got that power but am sure it was not from the Marine Committee or from any man or body deriving their authority from Congress nor is there any one officer appointed for either of the ships at Providence except the Captains.[3]
The govt of Philadelphia are all afloat, but they are in a fair way to get things all right. The post is just going off so can't add, save that I am, with respect, yours,   Wm Whipple

FC (Capt. J. G. M. Stone, Annapolis, Md., 1973); Tr (DLC). FC incomplete; last paragraph and signature taken from Tr.
    [1] An extract of Langdon's June 1 letter to Whipple is in Clark, *Naval Documents,* 5:333–34.
    [2] Two additional sentences appear at this point in the Tr. "You accordingly have authority from them to enter seamen on board the Rawleigh, and get her manned as soon as you can. I shall send you next post a copy of the order from their Minutes, also an order for the provisions."
    [3] For further information on the appointment of officers for the Continental ships under construction in Rhode Island, see Rhode Island Delegates to Nicholas Cooke, June 8, 1776, note 3.

John Adams to William Gordon

Dear Sir,   Philadelphia June 23. 1776
Your agreable Favour of May the first has lain by me neglected, not for Want of Inclination to answer it, but for Want of Time.[1]

You have deserved highly of this Country, Sir, by Setting So
amiable and laudable an Example of public Spirit in Signing the
Subscriptions for Fortifications. With great Pleasure I have learn'd
that the Harbour is pretty well secured. I hope, in a Post or two,
to be informed that every hostile Ship is either burnt, sunk or
driven out of the Harbour.

I am obliged to you, Sir, for your Solicitude for the Credit of the
American Currency. It is a subject of great Importance. That milled
Dollars are esteemed better, is Proof of an Apprehension, that the
Paper will depreciate, rather than a certain Evidence that it has
depreciated. The Rise of Goods, in Consequence of the Scarcity
and the Demand, makes an Appearance of Depreciation in the
Currency greater than it is. However, I candidly acknowledge that
neither the increasing Scarcity of Goods, nor the increasing Demand for Goods for the Use of Armies, are Sufficient to account in
my Mind for the Rise of Labour, the Produce of Lands, Manufactures and every Necessary of Life, as it is in the Eastern Colonies,
without Supposing that the Currency has Somewhat depreciated.

But you must not Say, that a milled Dollar is better than a Paper
Dollar. It is an offence against the Public, which ought to be
punished, and the criminality of it must be ascertained, and punished, to give or take a farthing more for Silver than Paper.

That it is Time to put a Stop to Emissions of American Paper
Dollars, I have been convinced, some time. We must attempt other
Ways and Means of Supply. I know of but one Method, and that is to
borrow American Bills, and to give in Exchange for Them Notes
of the Treasury upon Interest. There will be two Difficulties attending this. One will be the Rate of Interest. In my opinion We
shall not be able to borrow at an Interest lower than six per cent.
But some Gentlemen will be obstinately set against an Interest so
high as that. Another Difficulty will be to establish proper Funds
for the prompt Payment of the Interest, without which the Continental Credit will not be Supported. However all Difficulties give
Way, before the spirit of Americans, whose Vigour, Fortitude and
Perseverance will be increased by those Revolutions in Government which are now taking Place in all the Colonies.

Unlocated Lands and Quit Rents may be Some Resource, but not
very Soon. We may lay our account for Taxes, heavy Taxes for
many years.

We expected before this Time to have had the Sense of our
Province upon Declarations of Independency, Confederation, and
foreign Alliances. But I begin to Suspect that your Delegates must
have the Honour of declaring your Sense without your possitive
orders. This will be no Hardship to me, who have been at no loss
about the Sense of my Constituents, for a long time, upon these
great subjects. I am &c

LB (MHi).
[1] Gordon's May 1 letter to Adams is in the Adams Papers, MHi.

John Adams to John Sullivan

Dear Sir.   Philadelphia June 23d. 1776
   Your agreable Favour of May the fourth has lain by me unanswered, till now.[1] The Relation of your Negociations at New
York, in order to convince the People of the Utility and necessity
of instituting a new Government, is very entertaining, and if you
had remained there a few Weeks longer, I conjecture you would
have effected a Change in the Politicks of that Region. Is it Deceit,
or Simple Dulness in the People of that Colony, which occasions
their excentric and retrograde Politicks?
   Your late Letter from Sorell gave us here many agreable Feelings.[2] We had read Nothing, but the dolefull, the dismall, and
the horrible from Canada for a long Time.
   The Surrender of the Cedars, appears to have been a most infamous Piece of Cowardice. The officer, if he has nothing to say for
himself more than I can think of, deserves the most infamous
Death. It is the first Stain upon American Arms. May immortal
Disgrace attend his Name and Character. I wish however, that he
alone had been worthy of Blame.
   We have thrown away Canada, in a most Scandalous Manner.
   Pray did not opening the Trade to the upper Country, and
letting loose the Tories bring upon Us so many Disasters? For Gods
Sake explain to me, the Causes of our Miscarriages in that Province.
Let us know the Truth which has too long been hidden from Us.
   All the military affairs in that Province have been in great Con-
fusion, and We have never had any proper Returns or regular
Information, from thence. There is now a Corps of officers, who
will certainly Act with more System and more Precision and more
Spirit. Pray make Us acquainted with every Thing that is wanted,
whether Men, Money, Arms, Ammunition, Cloathing, Tents, Barracks, Forage, Medicines or whatever else. Keep Us constantly
informed—give Us Line upon Line. I fear their is a Chain of
Toryism, extending from Canada, through N. York and N. Jersey
into Pensilvania, which conducts Misrepresentation and false Information, and makes Impression here upon credulous, unsuspecting,
ignorant Whiggs. I wish it may not have for its Object, Treasons
and Conspiracies of the deeper Die.
   There is a young Gentleman bred at Colledge and the Bar, an
excellent soldier, a good scholar, and a virtuous Man, in your
Brigade, who deserves a station far above that in which he Stands,
that of Adjutant to C[olonel] Greatons Regiment. Any Notice you
may take of him will be gratefully acknowledged by me as well as
him.[3]

Pray let me know the state of the Small Pox, an Enemy which we have more cause to fear than any other. Is it among our Troops? Is it among the Canadians, I mean the Inhabitants of the Country? Can no effectual Means be used to annihilate the Infection? Cannot it be kept out of the army? The New England Militia will be of no Use, if they came in ever so great Numbers, if that distemper is to Seize them, as soon as they arrive.

LB (MHi).
[1] Sullivan's May 4 letter to Adams is in the Adams Papers, MHi, and Sullivan, *Letters* (Hammond), 1:194–96.
[2] Undoubtedly Sullivan's letter to George Washington of June 5–6, 1776. See Benjamin Franklin to George Washington, June 21, 1776, note 2.
[3] Undoubtedly Nathan Rice. See also Adams to Horatio Gates, June 18, 1776.

John Adams to Cotton Tufts

My dear Friend   Philadelphia June 23d. 1776
It is with Shame, and Confusion of Face, that I acknowledge that your agreable Favour of April the twenty sixth,[1] came duely to my Hand and has laid by me unanswered to this Time. There has been as much Folly and Inattention to my own Pleasure, and Interest, in this Negligence as there is of Ingratitude to you, for in the sincerity of my Heart I declare, that none of the Letters of my numerous Correspondents, contain more important Information or more sensible Observations, than yours.

In a Letter I received last night from Boston, I have the Pleasure to learn that your Ideas of fortifying the Harbour have been adopted, and by the next Post or two I hope to be informed that every hostile ship is made to scamper.

The Danger, you apprehend, that our Armies will be thinned by the Freedom of Trade is real, but perhaps the Restraints laid upon it, by our Enemies may correct the Error, if it is one. The Voice of the People was so loud for it, that it was adopted altho some Persons thought it dangerous, and none expected any great Advantage from it before the next Winter.

You mention Independence and Confederation. These Things are now become Objects of direct Consideration. Days, and Times, without Number, have been spent upon these Subjects, and at last a Committee is appointed to prepare a Draught of Confederation, and a Declaration that these Colonies are free States, independent of all Kings, Kingdoms, Nations, People, or States in the World. . . .[2]

There has been the greatest Scarcity of News for the last Fortnight, which has ever happened since the War commenced. . . . I make it a constant Practice to transmit to my Family, all the News Papers, where I presume you get a Sight of them. You will find by them, the Course of political Causes and Effects in this Colony. The Assembly [were] necessitated to rescind their Instructions, and [became] so obnoxious, and unpopular, among the Inhabitants their own Constituents for having ever passed them, as to be obliged to die away, without doing any Thing else, even without Adjourning, and give Place to a Conference of Committees and a Convention. Every Part of the Colony is represented in this Conference which is now sitting, and is extremely unanimous, spirited, zealous, and determined. You will soon see Pensilvania, one of the most patriotic Colonies. New Jersey is in a similar Train. The Delaware Government the same.

Maryland is a little beside itself I think, but presently it will blaze out like a Fire ship or a Volcano. New York still acts in Character, like a People without Courage or sense, or Spirit, or in short any one Virtue or Ability. There is neither Spunk nor Gumption, in that Province as a Body. Individuals are very clever. But it is the weakest Province in point of Intellect, Valour, public Spirit, or any thing else that is great and good upon the Continent. It is incapable of doing Us much good, or much Hurt, but from its local situation. The low Cunning of Individuals, and their Prostitution plagues Us, the Virtues of a few Individuals is of some Service to Us. But as a Province it will be a dead Weight upon any side, ours or that of our Enemies.

LB (MHi). Adams, *Family Correspondence* (Butterfield), 2:21–23.
   [1] See Adams, *Family Correspondence* (Butterfield), 1:393–96.
   [2] Suspension points in MS, here and below.

John Adams to John Winthrop

Dear sir   Philadelphia June 23. 1776
   Your Favour of June the first is now before me.[1] It is now universally acknowledged that we are and must be independant states. But Still objections are made to a Declaration of it. It is said, that such a Declaration will arouse and unite Great Britain. But are they not already aroused and united, as much as they will be? Will not such a Declaration arouse and unite the Friends of Liberty, the few such who are left, in opposition to the present System? It is also Said that Such a Declaration will put us in the Power of foreign States. That France will take Advantage of us, when they see We cant recede, and demand Severe Terms of Us. That she and Spain

too, will rejoice to see Britain and America, wasting each other. But this Reasoning has no Weight with me, because I am not for soliciting any political Connection, or military assistance, or indeed naval, from France. I wish for nothing but Commerce, a mere Marine Treaty with them. And this they will never grant, untill We make the Declaration, and this I think they cannot refuse, after We have made it.

The Advantages, which will result from Such a Declaration, are in my opinion very numerous, and very great. After that Event, the Colonies will hesitate no longer to compleat their Government. They will establish Tests and ascertain the Criminality of Toryism. The Presses will produce no more Seditious, or traiterous Speculations. Slanders upon public Men and Measures will be lessened. The Legislatures of the Colonies will exert themselves, to manufacture Salt Petre, Sulphur, Powder, Arms, Cannon, Mortars, Cloathing, and every Thing, necessary for the Support of Life.

Our civil Governments will feel a Vigour, hitherto unknown— our military operations by Sea and Land, will be conducted with greater Spirit. Privateers will Swarm in great Numbers. Foreigners will then exert themselves to supply Us with what we want. Foreign Courts will not disdain to treat with Us, upon equal Terms. Nay further in my opinion, such a Declaration, instead of uniting the People of Great Britain against Us, will raise Such a Storm against the Measures of Administration as will obstruct the War, and throw the Kingdom into Confusion.

A Committee is appointed to prepare a Confederation of the Colonies, ascertaining the Terms, and Ends of the Compact, and the Limits of the Continental Constitution, and another Committee is appointed for Purposes as important.[2] These committees will report in a Week or two, and then the last finishing Stroke will be given to the Politicks of this Revolution. Nothing after that will remain, but War. I think I may then petition my Constituents for Leave to return to my Family, and leave the War to be conducted by others, who understand it better. I am weary, thoroughly weary, and ought to have a little Rest.[3]

I am grieved to hear, as I do from various Quarters of that Rage for Innovation, which appears, in So many wild Shapes, in our Province. Are not these ridiculous Projects, prompted, excited, and encouraged by disaffected Persons, in order to divide, dissipate, and distract the attention of the People, at a Time when every Thought should be employed, and every Sinew exerted, for the Defence of the Country? Many of the Projects that I have heard of, are not repairing, but pulling down, the Building, when it is on Fire, instead of labouring to extinguish the Flames. The Projects of County Assemblies, Town Registers, and Town Probates of Wills, are founded in narrow Notions, Sordid Stingyness and profound Ignorance, and tend directly to Barbarism. I am not solicitous who takes offence at this Language. I blush to see such Stuff in our public Papers, which used to breath a Spirit, much more liberal.

I rejoice to see, in the List of both Houses, so many Names, respectable for Posts and Learning. I hope their Fortitude and Zeal will be in Proportion. And then, I am Sure, their Country will have great Cause to bless them. I am, Sir, with every sentiment of Friendship and Veneration, your affectionate and humble servant,

John Adams

RC (MHi).
    [1] Winthrop's June 1 letter to Adams is in the Adams Papers, MHi.
    [2] Apparently the committee "to prepare a plan of treaties to be proposed to foreign powers," of which Adams was a member. *JCC*, 5:431, 433.
    [3] In his letterbook Adams had completed this paragraph with the following clause: "unless the General Court will send my Wife and Children to me, and in that Case, I should be as happy here as any where."

William Whipple to Joshua Brackett

Dear Sir   Philaa 23d June 1776
    I received Yours of the 11th inst; that part of it respecting the Surgeon I answered in my last. I now send you the resolutions of Congress respecting Captures. There are some few resolves that are not in the pamphlet which I shall send you very soon. I hope it wont be long ere there will be one for confiscating West India Property, at present You'll find Captures are confined to British property, but I think all ships bound from the West Indies to Britain are British property.[1] There will be a tryal soon in this City of this sort; the Proceedings & determination I'll endeavor to transmit to you. Whats to be done with all the Scotch men? There's a report here another of those transports is taken & carried into Connecticut. The truth of this (if true) will soon reach you. I am truely sorry for the disgrace of American Arms in Canada more perticularly so, as it falls cheifly on the New-Hampshire Troops, that is Col. Beedles Regiment. This Col. & his Major deserves the severest punishment that can be inflicted by a Court Martial;[2] the Col. for leaving his post when he expected an attack, the Major for not defending the post, which he might have done with great ease 'till the arrival of the reinforcement. In short if these men had behav'd as they Ought there is no doubt but the whole party (of the enemy) wod have fallen into our hands. This wod have settled the matter with the Indians, none of them wod ever have dar'd to appear against us again, whereas we may now expect great numbers of them will join the Enemy. The inclosed paper gives you Major Shurburnes accot. which I believe may be depended on, by

all accots from Canada this Gentn has behav'd well. Beedle & his Major are to have a Trial, but I fear the sentence will not be equal to their deserts. A report prevails here that a most vile Deep laid plot was yesterday discover'd at New York, I have not been able to assertain the perticular facts, perhaps I shall before I close this, which will be tomorrow, however 40 persons are apprehended & secur'd, among them is the Mayor of the City. What baseness are our Enemies not capable of, who wod wish to be connected with a people so destitute of every Vertue, God forbid it shod ever be the fate of America.[3]

24th 11 O'Clock at night. I have heard nothing perticular about the affair at York; expect soon to have the whole of it. Yours,

Wm. Whipple

RC (DLC).

[1] See John Adams to James Warren, June 16, 1776, note 5.

[2] Col. Timothy Bedel and Maj. Isaac Butterfield were cashiered from the army on August 1, 1776. See *Am. Archives,* 5th ser. 1:747–48, 801.

[3] For further information on this plot, which has generally been associated with the name of one of the detected conspirators, Thomas Hickey, see *Am. Archives,* 4th ser. 6:1084–86, 1108–9, 1119–20; and Douglas S. Freeman, *George Washington, a Biography,* 7 vols. (New York: Charles Scribner's Sons, 1948–57), 4:115–21.

James Wilson to William Thompson

My dear General [1]   [June 23–24? 1776][2]

I have been *favoured* with many Letters from you since you left New York.[3] I place an Emphasis upon the Word "favoured" to show that I mean it not as an Expression of Course. You know I have many Reasons, arising from public Considerations, to wish to hear frequently from you; I can assure you that those Reasons receive much additional Strength from the Part, which, I feel, I take in every Thing relating to yourself. When Letters come from Canada, I derive peculiar Satisfaction if I have one from you. If I have none, I feel somehow disappointed. It is easy to conceive how much your Attention must be constantly employed in the Duties of your office; especially when it is considered in what Confusion and Distraction the Affairs of Canada have been for a considerable Time before your Arrival in that Department. I know you can appropriate only a few Moments to writing Letters. Let me claim a Share of those few.

But I have much Occasion to make an Apology for myself. A long Time has elapsed since I have written to you. But, to say Truth, this Place is not so fruitful of Subjects as that where you are. The material Proceedings of Congress relating to the Operations of the War are communicated officially by the President. Intelligence from

Europe and from the different Parts of the united Colonies you receive sooner from New York than you could from Philadelphia. I have had it in View for some Time past to write you very fully and particularly concerning the State of this Province, its Parties, and its Politics; but even here Difficulties have occurred. Our Affairs have been in such a fluctuating and disordered Situation, that it has been almost impossible to form any Accurate Judgment concerning the Transactions as they were passing, and still more nearly impossible to make any probable Conjectures concerning the Turn that Things would take. Matters are, however, now, in all Likelyhood, approaching to a Crisis; and some Opinion can be given of the Manner, in which they will be conducted, and the Issue, in which they will terminate. I shall therefore embrace this Opportunity of giving you an Account of what has been done, and of what, in all Probability, will be done. I shall occasionally intrude upon you my own Sentiments concerning the different Measures, of which I shall have Occasion to take Notice.

On the 15th of May last a Resolution passed in Congress mentioning, in the Preamble, that it was necessary that every Kind of Authority under the Crown should be totally suppressed, and all the Powers of Government exerted under the Authority of the People, and recommending it to the respective Assemblies and Conventions of the united Colonies, where no Government sufficient to the Exigencies of their Affairs had been hitherto established, to adopt such Government as shall, in the Opinion of the Representatives of the People best conduce to the Safety and Happiness of their Constituents in particular, and America in General.

Concerning this Resolution many different Opinions were entertained. Some thought the Government of Pennsylvania sufficient for the Exigencies of its Affairs: Others were of contrary Sentiments upon this Point. Those others divided in their Opinions concerning the *Mode* of adopting a new Government. Some said that the Assembly were adequate to the Purpose of adopting a new Government; others, that they were adequate to the Determination of the Question, whether a new Government was necessary or not, but could not constitutionally adopt one without new Powers from the People, others, that they were adequate to neither. A Number of the Inhabitants of Philadelphia met at the State-House upon the Occasion. You have, perhaps, seen their Resolutions in some of the Newspapers. One of them was, "That the Committee of the City and Liberties of Philadelphia be directed to send the Resolution of Congress to the several Committees throughout the Province, and call together a Number from the Committee of each County, to hold a provincial Conference, in order to determine upon the Number of which the Convention for framing a new Government should be composed, and the Manner in which they should be elected." This Measure has accordingly been taken. A Conference of Committees consisting of above one hundred Members, met here on the 18th of this Month, and are now setting. They have fixed the Number of Representatives, in the Convention which is to be called, to eight for each County, and the same Number for the City and Liberties of Philadelphia, who are likewise to vote in the Election for Members of the County at large. The 8th of next Month is appointed for the Election; and the 15th for the Meeting of the Convention in this City.

To return to the Assembly—They admitted the new Members, chosen on the first Day of May last, to their Seats in the House, without taking the Oath of Allegiance; and dispensed with that Oath upon all other Occasions. After they had sat a considerable Time, their Number became so small that a Quorum of the House could not be made up; so that they adjourned without doing any Thing concerning the Resolution of Congress beforementioned.

FC (PHi).

[1] William Thompson (1736–81), Carlisle, Pa., farmer, surveyor, and justice of the peace, had commanded a battalion of riflemen organized and sent to Massachusetts in 1775. He was elected brigadier general on March 1, 1776, and ordered to New York in command of reinforcements being sent to Canada. On June 8, 1776, he was captured during the ill-fated attack on Three Rivers that he commanded, and although paroled and permitted to return to Pennsylvania soon afterwards, he was not exchanged until 1780. *DAB*.

[2] The assignment of this date rests upon Wilson's references in this letter to the activities of the "Conference of Committees" which sat in Philadelphia June 18–25, 1776, to make preparations for convening a constitutional convention the following month. Since the date for convening the convention was decided by the conference on June 23, a decision that Wilson reported to Thompson, it seems clear that Wilson wrote this letter on June 23 or 24. For the "Proceedings of the Conference of Committees," see *Pa Archives*, 2d ser. 3:555–82, especially pp. 565–69.

[3] Thompson's letters to Wilson of April 15 and 19, written from New York, and of May 6 and 19 and June 2, 1776, written after his departure, are in the James Wilson Papers, PHi.

John Adams to Samuel Chase

Dear sir.   Philadelphia June 24. 1776

I received your obliging Favour of the 21st this Morning, and I thank you for it. Dont be angry with me. I hope I shall attone for past Sins of omission soon.[1]

The Express which you mention brought us Such contradictory accounts, that I did not think it worth while to write to you upon it. In general, Sullivan writes that he was intrenching at the Sorell, that the Canadians expressed a great deal of Joy at his appearance, that they assisted him with Teams and with wheat, that he had

ordered General Thompson with 2000 Men to attack the Enemy,
consisting of about 300 according to his Intelligence at the Three
Rivers where they were fortifying, and from the Character of
Thompson and the goodness of his Troops he had much Confidence
of his success—that he hoped to drive away the Enemies ships
which had passed the Rapids of Richlieu. This Narration of Sullivans was annimating—But a Letter from Arnold of the same date,
or the next day rather, was wholly in the Dismalls.[2]

Gates is gone to Canada and We have done every Thing that you
recommended and more to support him. But for my own Part I
confess my Mind is impressed with other Objects the Neglect of
which appears to me to have been the source of all our Misfortunes
in Canada, and every where else. Make the Tree good and the
Fruit will be good. A Declaration of Independency, Confederation,
and foreign Alliances, in Season would have put a Stop to that
embarrasing opposition in Congress, which has occasioned us to do
the Work of the Lord deceitfully in Canada and elsewhere.

A Resolution of your Convention was read in Congress this
Morning, and the Question was put whether your Delegates sould
have leave to go home, and whether those great Questions should
be postponed, beyond the first of July. The Determination was in
the Negative.[3] We should have been happy to have obliged your
Convention and your Delegates. But it is now become public in the
Colonies that those Questions are to be brought on the first of
July. The lower Counties have instructed their Members, as the
assembly of Pensilvania have. Jersey has chosen five new Members,
all independant Souls, and instructed them to vote on the first of
July for Independence.

There is a Conference of Committees from every County in
Pensilvania, now Sitting in this City,[4] who yesterday voted that the
Delegates for this Colony ought on the first of July to vote for
Independence. This Vote was not only unanimous, but I am told
by one of them, that all the Members declared Seriatim that this
was their opinion, and the opinion of the several Counties and
Towns they represented, and many of them produced Instructions
from their Constituents to vote for that Measure. You see therefore
that there is such a universal Expectation that the great Question
will be decided the first of July, and it has been already so often
postponed, that to postpone it again would hazard Convulsions,
and dangerous Conspiracies. It must then come on and be decided.
I hope that before Monday Morning next, We shall receive from
Maryland, Instructions to do right.

Pray send me your Circular Letter and believe me your Friend
and svt.[5]

LB (MHi).
    [1] Chase had asked Adams to "write constantly" and reported on changing senti-
ments within Maryland on independence. "I am almost resolved not to inform

you, that a general Dissatisfaction prevails here with our Convention. Read the paper, & be assured Frederick speaks the Sense of many Counties. I have not been idle. I have appealed *in Writing* to the People. County after County is instructing." Chase to Adams, June 21, 1776, Adams Papers, MHi.

² See *JCC*, 5:459.

³ There is no mention of this motion or vote in the journals, but for the Maryland Convention's resolution, see Maryland Delegates to the Maryland Council of Safety, June 15, 1776, note 2.

⁴ For the minutes of this conference, see *Am. Archives*, 4th ser. 6:951–67.

⁵ On June 28 Chase acknowledged receipt of this letter and another of June 17 (not found), adding the following brief comment. "They were handed to Me in Convention. I shall offer no other Apology for Concluding, than that I am this Moment from the House to procure an Express to follow the Post with an Unan. Vote of our Convention for *Independence* &c. &c. See the glorious Effects of County Instructions—our people have fire if not smothered. Poor Genl. Thompson! I charge You to write to Me! *Now for a Government*." Chase to Adams, June 28, 1776, Adams Papers, MHi.

John Adams to Richard Devens

Dear sir   Philadelphia June 24. 1776

Your Favour of the Sixth of June, which came duely to my Hand, contains Information no less pleasing than Surprising. 102635 1/4 lb of Salt Peter actually made, recd and paid for by the Province, in so short a Time, is an abundant Proof that America never need to want that precious Commodity, any more. I have published your former Letters, and intend to do the same with this,¹ for the sake of informing other Colonies and exciting their Activity by your virtuous Examples. Connecticutt is not behind you. Letters Say that 30 Tons have been made there. I must beg the Favour of you to continue your Correspondence, and make me acquainted with the Quantities which may hereafter be brought in, and likewise the Progress that is made in the Powder Mills and Cannon Furnaces, and in the Manufacture of Fire Arms.

Flints begin to be wanted. Is there any of the Stone in our Prov.? Large Quantities are in N.Y. in the County of Orange. Who knows how to Split it into Size and shape. Sulphur and lead shd. not be neglected.

LB (MHi).

¹ Devens' June 6 letter to Adams is in the Adams Papers, MHi. An extract of the letter was printed in the *Pennsylvania Journal and the Weekly Advertiser*, June 26, 1776, under the title "Extract of a letter from the Commissary General of Massachusetts-Bay, dated Watertown, June 6, 1776."

John Adams to William Tudor

Dear sir   Philadelphia June 24. 1776

Your Favour of May 4th has lain by me, till this Time unanswered and I have heard nothing from you Since.[1] I have entertained Hopes of seeing you here before now, as I heard you intended Such an Excursion. I was much obliged to you, for your particular Account of Major Austin, and Mr Rice. The first I find has the Command of Castle William. The last is gone to Canada, where if he lives through the Dangers of Famine, Pestilence and the Sword, I hope General Gates will promote him. I have written to the General concerning him, recommending him to the Generals Notice and Favour, in as Strong and warm Terms, as I ever used in recommending any one. Rice has got Possession of my Heart, by his prudent, and faithfull Attention to the service.[2]

What is the Reason, that New York is still asleep or dead, in Politicks and War? Must it be always So? Cannot the whole Congregation of Patriots and Heroes, belonging to the Army, now in that Province, inspire it, with one generous Sentiment? Have they no sense? No Feeling? No sentiment? No Passions? While every other Colony is rapidly advancing, their Motions Seem to be rather retrograde. The timid and trimming Politicks of some Men of large Property here, have almost done their Business for them. They have lost their Influence and grown obnoxious. The Quakers and Proprietarians together, have little Weight. New Jerseys shews a noble Arder. Is there any Thing in the Air, or Soil of New York, unfriendly to the Spirit of Liberty? Are the People destitute of Reason, or of Virtue? Or what is the Cause?

I agree with you, in your Hopes, that the Massachusetts will proceed to compleat her Government. You wish me to be there, but I cannot. Mr Bowdoin or Dr Winthrop, I hope, will be chosen Governor. When a few mighty matters are accomplished here, I retreat like Cincinnatus to the Plough and like Sir William Temple to his Garden; and farewell Politicks. I am weary. Some of you, younger Folk, must take your Trick and let me go to Sleep. My Children will Scarcely thank me for neglecting their Education and Interest so long. They will be worse off than ordinary Beggars, because I shall teach them as a first Principle not to beg. Pride and Want, though they may be accompanied with Liberty, or at least may live under a free Constitution, are not a very pleasant Mixture, not a very desirable Legacy, yet this is all that I shall leave them. Pray write as often as you can to your,

John Adams

[P.S.] It is reported here that Coll Read is intended for the Governor of New Jersey. I wish with all my Heart, he may. That Province is a Spirited, a brave and patriotic People. They want nothing, but a Man of sense, and Principle at their Head. Such an one is Read. His only fault is that he has not quite Fire enough. But this may be an Advantage to him as Governor. His Coolness, and Candour, and goodness of Heart, with his abilities will make that People very happy.

RC (MHi).
¹ Tudor's May 4 letter to Adams is in the Adams Papers, MHi.
² See Adams to Horatio Gates, June 18, 1776.

Josiah Bartlett to Mary Bartlett

My Dear   Philadelphia June 24 1776
Your Letter of the 8th Inst. inclosed in one of Pollys, & yours of the 10th Inst. inclosed in one of Major Philbricks Came to hand Saturday the 22nd Inst. with the inclosed, and am happy to hear you & the family are well; yours that you say you sent the 7th by the way of Portsmouth is not arrived; you may Depend that they Come the Quickest by the way of Newbury.

I am Glad to hear that the Sickness is abated with you; it is a pretty healthy time in this City at present, but as the hot weather has come on for about a week & no rain the air seems to Stagnate, & if it should hold Dry, will I fear produce Sickness, I have for 2 or 3 Days past in the afternoon rode Back a mile or two & the very air of the Country seems reviving. As to what you mention of the Skirmish of the men of war & the Gondaloes, it was Below the Boom Batteries &c &c made for the Defence of this City; they are not above 8 miles below the City, as being the most Convenient place to Stop the ships. I am not under the least fear of their being able to penetrate to this place, so you may make your self quite Easy about me, on that account.

I am sorry to hear the frost has done damage with you: hope it has not Killed all the Beans &c. The Corn will Commonly grow again. How is the flax in General like to be; what are like to be the Crops of hay with you; how is the winter & sumer Grain like to be &c. Please to write me what is like to be the Success of the farming Business this year. Mowing English Grass was finished last week here.

As to news we have none Except the taking to 2 Scotch Companys of highlanders in the transports coming to Boston which you will see the accounts of before this reaches you. The affair of the New Hampshire regiment at the Cedars in Canada, surrendering to the Enemy is a most Scandalous Business; Major Sherburne who went from Montreal with 110 men to reinforce Col. Bedels Regiment at the Cedars, is now here & gives a very particular account of it; the infamous Scandalous Behavior of some of the officers has brought Disgrace on the Province which will be very hard ever to wipe off.

I have been for about a week on a Committee of one member

from Each Colony to form a Confederation or Charter of firm & Everlasting Union of all the United Colonies.[1] It is a matter of the greatest Consequence & requires the greatest Care in forming it. When it is agreed to by the Committee, it will be laid before the Congress & when they have agreed to it, it will be sent to Each Colony to be by them ratified & Confirmed. May God grant us wisdom to form a happy Constitution, as the happiness of America to all future Generations Depend on it.

I am in pretty good health Except something of a Cough that holds me Ever Since the Cold I mentioned to you, but hope it will go off in a little time. Remember my love to all the Children; particularly tell Polly I Recd hers, and hope she had a pleasant jorney to Newbury & back & found her Brother well. I suppose Levi will be at home by the time this reaches you as (if I am not mistaken) the vacation begins the first of July.

I hope Kind Providence will order all things for the best, and if sometimes affairs turn out Contrary to our wishes, we must make our Selves Easy & Contented, as we are not Certain what is for the best. I am Sincerely, yours,   Josiah Bartlett

RC (NhHi).
[1] See Bartlett's Notes on the Plan of Confederation, June 12–July 12, 1776; and Josiah Bartlett's and John Dickinson's Draft Articles of Confederation, June 17–July 1? 1776.

John Hancock to the
New Jersey Provincial Convention

Gentlemen,   Philadelphia June 24th. 1776.
Your Favour respecting the proper Measures to be taken with your late Governor William Franklyn Esqr came to Hand on Saturday the 22d Inst. But as the Congress did not sit on that Day, I could not lay it before them till Monday.

I now do myself the Honour of enclosing to you the Resolves of Congress, which they have this Day passed with Regard to the Treatment of him. You will there perceive, the Congress have directed him to be sent to Connecticut, under a Guard.[1]

I shall write to Govr. Trumbull to treat him as a Prisoner, should he refuse to give his Parole in Writing.

I have the Honour to be, Gentlemen, your most obed and very hble Servt.   John Hancock Presidt

[P.S.] The other Resolves, herewith transmitted, are of such a Nature, that no Arguments are necessary to enforce them.[2] You will be pleased to attend to them as soon as possible.

RC (NN). In the hand of Jacob Rush and signed by Hancock.
[1] See JCC, 5:473. New Jersey Provincial Convention President Samuel Tucker's

June 21 letter to Hancock is in *Am. Archives,* 4th ser. 6:1010. See also Hancock to John Witherspoon, June 19, 1776.

[2] Presumably the resolves on allegiance, treason, and counterfeiting passed by Congress this day. *JCC,* 5:475–76.

John Hancock to Jonathan Trumbull, Sr.

Honble Sir,   Philada. June 24th. 1776

The Convention of New Jersey having declared their late Govr. Wm. Franklyn Esqr a virulent Enemy to the United Colonies, and that he be confined in such Place & Manner as the Continental Congress shall direct, I do myself the Honour of transmitting you the enclosed Resolutions with Respect to him.

Should he give his Parole in Writing you will, in that Case, be pleased to send him to any Part of the Colony, which you shall judge most proper. But should he refuse to give his Parole in Writing I am to request you will proceed agt. him agreeably to the Resolves of Congress relative to Prisoners in that Predicament.[1]

I have the Honour to be, Sir, Your most obedt. & very hble Servt.

J. H. Prest.

LB (DNA: PCC, item 12A).

[1] See *JCC,* 5:473. Connecticut Governor Trumbull's July 6 reply to this letter is in *Am. Archives,* 5th ser. 1:45.

Charles Thomson to Richard Peters

Sir,   June 24. 1776

I have it in command to request you would please to send me what public Letters are in your office that they may be transcribed. Please to examine whether you have not among the letters one from brigr. general Arnold of the 27 May with a cartel for exchange of prisoners entered into between him & Capt Forster.[1]

I am Sr, Your humble servt,

Chas Thomson, secy of Congress

RC (DNA: PCC, item 78).

[1] Benedict Arnold's letter of May 27, 1776, to the Canadian Commissioners and the "cartel" for exchange of prisoners arranged between Arnold and Capt. George Forster are in *Am. Archives,* 4th ser. 6:595–97.

William Whipple to John Langdon

Dr Sr   Phila. 24th June 1776

Your two favors of the 10th inst one dated at Boston & the other at Portsmouth came duly to hand. I inform'd you in my last which went by Saturdays post, that the Marine Committee desire you would ship your men so soon as you can. They also direct me to desire You'll provide six months wet Provisions, & four months Dry, this stock to be keep good. You'll apply to the Commasary at Boston for the Provisions (that is the Beef, Pork, & Bread or flouer) he has orders to supply you. As for Guns, that matter remains as when I wrote you last. I cannot prevail with Gov. Hopkins to consent to part with those at Providence. I tell him Your ship will make a cruize of three months if she has guns, before either of the Providence ships can be got to sea, but he insists that those ships are as forward as Yours. I believe the Guns must go from hence. There is a probability that enough for one ship will be in town in about 10 days, & You may depend I shall exert every nerve to get the first for you.

I am just come from the Marine Commite & have once more got their Unanimos consent to nominate you for agent.[1] I think there is no doubt but you'll be appointed, but believe it will be in expectation that you resign Your seat in Congress, which I have assur'd all that I have mentioned the matter to that you are determined on. I suppose a list of offices are on the way here. I shall dispatch them as soon as they arrive.[2]

There has been a most hellish conspiracy at New York;[3] we have not the particulars of it yet, but by the best information I can get, the plan was to assassinate the General, blow up the magazine and spike the cannon; this was to be done on the arrival of the enemy it's supposed. However there is a full discovery of the whole plot and a considerable number, say 30, or 40 of the infernal villains seized and I hope justice will be done to them.

Governor Franklin is seized by the Convention of New Jersey and is to be confined in Connecticut.[4] The middle Colonies are getting in a good way. Next Monday being the first of July, the grand question is to be debated and I believe determined unanimously. May God unite our hearts in all things that tend to the well being of the rising Empire.

Yours very sincerely,   Wm Whipple

[P.S.] Col. Bartlett desires his regards, but is too lazy to write.

FC (Capt. J. G. M. Stone, Annapolis, Md., 1973); Tr (DLC).
   [1] Congress appointed Langdon prize agent the next day. JCC, 5:478. Josiah Bartlett also revealed a mixed reaction to Langdon's appointment. "I know not whether to congratulate or condole with you on your appointment to the Agency, as your acceptance of that office must vacate your seat in Congress, and tho' I did what was in my power to procure that Birth for you, as I knew it was your desire, and that you would perform the business well, yet I must confess it gave me no pleasure when I knew on what conditions only you must have it—resigning your seat here."

Bartlett to Langdon, June 26, 1776, Sparks Collection, MH; and Burnett, *Letters,*
1:511.
    [2] FC ends here.
    [3] See Whipple to Joshua Brackett, June 23, 1776, note 4.
    [4] See John Hancock to the New Jersey Convention, this date.

George Clinton to John McKeeson

Dear Sir,   Philadelphia, 25th June, 1776
    On Friday last the Congress passed a resolve for raising a regiment
of Continental troops in our Colony, and although the augmentation
of the army appeared necessary, yet the raising a whole regiment
in the Colony of N. York at this time might not (perhaps) have been
ordered, were it not with a view of providing for those officers who
have much merit, from reëngaging in the service of their country
last fall, after the surrender of Montreal, and continuing through a
most fatiguing and dangerous campaign in Canada during the winter.[1]
    Major Duboys is highly recommended to Congress as well by the
general officers as the committee who lately returned from Canada,
(as I am informed,) and I doubt not but he will be appointed colonel
of the regiment, especially as rank as well as merit entitles him to it.
The Congress having heretofore left the appointment or recommendation of the officers of new levies with the Provincial Congress, in
which the same are raised, and being therefore loath now to break
through this rule, is (I am informed,) the only reason why the
officers to this regiment are not appointed here. It will be wise,
therefore, to take special care to make the appointments so as to give
no just cause of complaint by appointing the officers according to the
rank they bear in the arrangement made by General Montgomery
at Montreal, on their reëngaging in the service until the 15th of
April ultimo, except where real and extraordinary merit, or the
contrary, may warrant a deviation from this general rule.
    Enclosed I send the arrangement made by General Montgomery
of the officers in my brother's regiment; and have noted such as are
already provided for in the regiment to be recruited in Canada by
Colo. Nicholson. I also enclose you a list of the officers in Colo.
Nicholson's regiment, as those who are already provided for by appointments in that regiment, can have no pretensions to any appointment or promotion in this, they having been provided for
while it was uncertain whether any more troops would have been
raised. General Montgomery's faith to his officers, also reëngaged in
the service at Montreal, will not be kept unless the appointments in
this regiment are made agreeable to this arrangement, as thereby
many officers acquired new and higher rank in their respective regi-

ments than what they had by the printed arrangements made by Congress last summer. My reasons for mentioning this is, because your Congress may not have heard of such new arrangement, and by taking up the old one might do injustice to those who the Congress have in view more particularly to provide for. Capt. Bruyn, I believe, is the oldest captain who continued in Canada; and from my brother's character of him, well deserves the post which his rank will entitle him to. He is a young man of education and fortune, and bears an unblemished character. I wish and believe young Platt may be properly provided for in this regiment; he was with Major Duboys and Capt. Bruyn at Point Lacoy, at the engagement between our people and a number of Canadians, in which the latter was defeated, and behaved well, as Major Duboys can testify.

We have just received the disagreeable intelligence from Canada, of the defeat of part of our army under Genl. Thompson, and of his being taken, &c. &c. which you must have had before it reached us.[2] We seem unfortunate in that quarter; but we must learn to bear the sound of bad as well as good news; indeed, it would be unreasonable to expect the chance of war always in our favour.

We have nothing new here worth communicating; whenever we have, you may expect to hear from me. I mean this scroll for my friends Treadwell and Hubbel, as well as you, not having time to write to either of them. My best compliments to them, and believe me to be, Yours, most affectionately,   Geo. Clinton.

P. S. Please to forward the enclosed to Mrs. Clinton. I can't find any such stockings as you mentioned yet. I can get green thread German Town stockings, but very dear. Will they do?

MS not found; reprinted from George Clinton, *Public Papers of George Clinton, First Governor of New York, 1777–1795, 1801–1804*, ed. Hugh Hastings and J. A. Holden, 10 vols. (New York and Albany: Wynkoop Hallenbeck Crawford Co. et al., 1899–1914), 1:239–41.
  [1] See *JCC*, 5:471–72. See also John Hancock to the New York Convention, June 21 and 26, 1776.
  [2] Letters from Generals Arnold, Sullivan, and Thompson describing the latest American reverses in Canada were transmitted to Congress by Washington in his June 23 letter to Hancock. See PCC, item 152, 2:89–102; and *Am. Archives*, 4th ser. 6:1035–39.

Elbridge Gerry to Horatio Gates

Dear General   Philadelphia June 25th 1776
    Since I had the pleasure of seeing You in this Place the affairs of Canada having been evidently suffering from Want of an experienced officer to take the Command; & your Appointment to that

Department is considered as a happy Circumstance, notwithstanding the eastern Colonies greatly need your Assistance. I hope the Campaign will terminate with Honor & Happiness to Yourself & Country, & if any Services can be rendered from this Quarter by giving You Information of the Measures here adopted, the Causes & moving principles thereof, or by promoting in Congress such other Measures as You shall find necessary for the Service, It will give me Pleasure to have a Share therein.

The Conference Committee amongst other Things reported the Expediency of appointing to each Regiment a Paymaster, Whose Duty they said You would take an opportunity of describing & communicating to Congress. The Matter has since layed on the Table; & only waits your Sentiments thereon to be carried into Execution.[1] I am very fond of the Measure as It will save an Infinitude of Trouble, by opening a Channel thro Which all Payments to the Soldiery will regularly pass whether consisting of Money payed out of the Chest, Cloathing, Arms, Accoutrements, or sutling Accounts; & when any Thing is wanted for the Comfort of the Army an order from the General on the paymaster General for a suitable Sum in Favour of the regimental Paymaster will enable the latter to communicate immediate assistance to each Soldier without the possibility of any Loss to the Continent: further when the paymaster General discharges himself It will appear what Sum the regimental paymasters have recd & these together with the amount of Cloathing before mentioned must be deducted from the pay Rolls whether payed immediately to the Men or other persons in their Behalf, & the Commanding officer without any further Trouble than an Occasional Warrant can always be sure of having his Men punctually payed & well supplied with other Necessaries, which is the Life of an Army.

I think We are in a fair Way to a speedy Declaration of Independency & Confederation, & other Measures that depend on Secrecy for Success, & Congress having yesterday passed Resolves for capitally punishing Spies that shall be found in or about any of the Camps or Fortifications of the united Colonies; & recommended to the Assemblies to make provision for punishing all Inhabitants, & other persons receiving protection in any of the Colonies, who shall be found affording aid or Comfort to the King of G Britain or other Enemies of the united States of America;[2] It appears to me that little will remain to be done, but an attention to the Supplies, Appointments & Discipline of the Army, all of which are of the utmost Importance. With Respect to the first the Soldiers must be each payed, cloathed, armed, & fed or they can never be made to do their Duty, & the plans on Foot for borrowing, securing the Currency & obtaining large Sums by Loan, also for manufacturing & otherwise obtaining Cannon, Arms, Ammunition & Cloathing, together with the great Ease in

obtaining provissions will I hope be timely & effectually carried into
Execution & have a happy Effect. The appointments of the Army
are Matters of interesting Consequences, & notwithstanding every
precaution of the Congress & the Assemblies to choose good officers,
yet Time & Experience will alone enable them to distinguish those
that are prolific with Conduct, Virtue & prowess suitable for their
respective Places.

Discipline is the last, but not the least Important object of Attention, & I shall be glad of your explicit Sentiments on the same. I
cannot conceive Why We may not by setting out Right soon make
Soldiers equal to any that the World affords. For surely Men inspired with the principles of Liberty & enthusiastically engaged in
its Defence afford as good Materials as can anywhere be found for
this purpose. And in the first place I put it down as a settled fixed
principle that they must be inlisted for the War let the Necessary
Encouragement be what it may, which I am happy to find the Generals agreed in & I think most of the Members of Congress. We can
easily look over the Statutes of Britain & other Regulations relative
to the Army & find how far the same are applicable to our own
Forces, & to promote the Measure the Sentiments of Military Gentlemen must be collected & amongst other[s] I know of None that I
shall more depend on than those which You shall have an Oppertunity to express.

I intended to have troubled You with only a Line or two, but
being now on the second sheet find it high Time to inform You that
Your Friends here are well & joyn in due Regards to General Miflin,
Trumbull & others, with sir, your assured Friend & hum sevt,

Elbridge Gerry

RC (NHi).
¹ Congress returned to this subject and authorized the appointment of regimental paymasters for continental units on July 16. See *JCC,* 5:564.
² See *JCC,* 5:475–76. But capital punishment of spies was not formally approved
in Congress until August 21. Ibid., p. 693.

Elbridge Gerry to Joseph Trumbull

Dear sir   Philadelphia June 25. 1776
I am favoured with yours of the 22d & am glad to find that our
Friend the General intends to take with him the Paymaster &
military Chest into Canada, where I doubt not he will make the
best Use of It. I observe You wish to have authenticated Copies
of Certain Resolutions of Congress which is surely reasonable, & the
Secretary informs me that he sent forward to You all that respect
the Commissary's office. I do not conceive that any things further
are necessary to be passed, but if You think otherwise, point them
out & a proper attention shall be paid thereto. You are greatly

misinformed with respect to your being ill used *in* Congress & out, by some who want to transfer the Office to other Hands. What is done out of Doors I know not, but your Conduct in Congress has been as highly approved as any officer's in the Service. With Respect to Mr L. perhaps he is stung with Disapointment,[1] but I assure You whatever may be his Desires relative to supplanting you It will never be effected; but by your *own Resignation,* which he may hope to bring about by such Detestable Conduct as You mention, can he alone effect his Purpose. However I trust You will be so far on your Guard as to treat with sovereign Contempt the Men & Measures that are calculated to counteract the most salutary Plans for establishing the Liberties of America. With respect to the Commissions allowed by the secret Committee, upon Enquiry I find that 5 per Cent is allowed for sales & Returns, & when it is considered that a Cargo to Europe must be sold by a Factor whose Commission will amount to 2 1/2 percent You will readily allow that the remainder is but a reasonable allowance for the Trouble of loading a Vessel when the Cargo is to be first collected, shipped & dispatched, the Accounts abroad liquidated, & on the Return of the Vessel the Cargo to be stored & delivered as well as the Accounts at Home relative to Voyage to be arranged & adjusted. I think You will find this to be a true state of the Case altho I have not had Time to be fully informed of the Matter. If it is otherwise I am very certain it will not be approved by Congress. Application has been lately made by a Mr Wharton who supplyed the Troops while in this City, for the Commissaryship of the flying Camp to be posted in the Jerseys. He offers to furnish the provissions at 8 1/2d per Ration & it has been said in Congress that this is much cheaper than the Rate at which the Army is now supplyed, but without sufficient Evidence to support the assertion.   Upon the Whole the Matter is deferred until the Generals opinion can be obtained, for two Reasons; first because many Members are doubtful whether the Affairs of the Army will go on as smoothly in a complicated Way of supplying as when the whole (excepting What respects the southern District) is under the Direction of the Commissary General, & in the next place the Oeconomy of the proposal does not clearly appear & remains to be ascertained by the General & the Commissary. Pray attend to the Matter & give me your Sentiments as soon as possible, & also the Generals.

I have been sometime attentive to the Article of Cloathing & think the Mode adopted will answer the purpose, especially since it is intended to pursue the plan hinted in the late Conference of Appointing regimental paymasters who are to receive the Cloathing, as well as Moneys that shall be advanced to their respective Regiments & see that the proper Stoppages are made from the Muster Roll.

The plot that You mention is alarming, but no more than I

have for a long Time expected. Provission is this Day made for capitally punishing Spies that may be found in or about any of the Camps or Fortifications of the united Colonies, & the Inhabitants residing in any of the Colonies or Persons transiently passing thro the same are considered as protected by & as owing allegiance to such Colony, & it is recommended to them to pass Laws for punishing such of the aforesd Inhabitants or persons as shall hereafter be found affording aid or Comfort to the King of G. Britain or any others of the Enemies of the united States of America.²

A number of Tents purrchased for & paid for by the Colony of Massachusetts Bay have been illegally detained at New York; this is a Mode of proceeding which I did not expect, & it will never be submitted to by any Colony on the Continent.³ Congress have ordered a Letter to be wrote to the Quarter Master directing him to deliver them packed as he received them without Delay. I hope never to see an Instance of the kind again in an American Army established to defend the Liberties of the Country. Had they not been in the utmost Need of them at Massachusetts & proper Application had been made they would have been spared, but neither of these is the Case at present & they must go on at all Events. I remain Sir with true regards to all Friends, your Friend & hum ser,   Elbridge Gerry

[P.S.] The Jersies have appointed five new Delegates & high charged them with Instructions for Independance. Pray inform me how the Troops come in; the Confer[ence] of Committees are attentive to the Pennsylvanians Forces.⁴

RC (Ct).
   ¹ Undoubtedly Walter Livingston, who ultimately submitted his resignation as deputy commissary general in a September 7 letter to John Hancock. See *Am. Archives,* 5th ser. 2:220–21; and Gerry to Joseph Trumbull, September 12, 1776.
   ² *JCC,* 5:475–76; and William Whipple to Joshua Brackett, June 23, 1776, note 3.
   ³ See John Hancock to George Washington, this date, note 3.
   ⁴ See Robert Morris' Memorandum, June 20, 1776, note.

Elbridge Gerry to James Warren

My Dear Sir,   Philadelphia, June 25, 1776
   I am favoured with your very agreeable letter of 10th June,¹ and am in hopes congress will soon render it unnecessary to take further measures preparatory to the declaration of independence. New-Jersey has appointed five new delegates, and instructed them to vote in favour of the question, and it appears to me there is not even a doubt of any colony on the continent except New-York and Maryland. These will not impede us a moment. I do not

affirm that either of these are of the neuter gender, but on the other hand am persuaded the people are in favour of a total and final separation, and will support the measure, even if the conventions and delegates of those colonies vote against it.

Since my first arrival in this city the New-England delegates have been in a continual war with the advocates of proprietary interests in congress and this colony. These are they who are most in the way of the measures we have proposed, but I think the contest is pretty nearly at an end, and am persuaded that the people of this and the middle colonies have a clearer view of their interest, and will use their endeavours to eradicate the ministerial influence of governours, proprietors and jacobites, and that they now more confide in the politics of the New-England colonies than they ever did in those of their hitherto unequal governments.

Your's as ever,   E. Gerry.

MS not found; reprinted from Austin, *Life of Gerry*, 1:193–94.
[1] Perhaps James Warren's letter dated June 12, 1776, in *Am. Archives*, 4th ser. 6:829–30.

John Hancock to Certain Colonies

Gentlemen,   Philadelphia June 25th. 1776.
Since my last of the 21t Inst. I have Nothing further in Charge from Congress, except the enclosed Resolves, which are so full and explicit that I need not enlarge.[1]

You will perceive, they are calculated to prevent Insurrections and to introduce good Order, and Obedience to Laws thro-out the United Colonies; Objects of the greatest Importance in our present Situation: since all internal Convulsions, while they weaken the Force & Springs of Government, must necessarily render its Operations agt. foreign Enemies, less vigorous and decisive.

I have the Honour to be, Gentlemen, your most obed. & very hble Sev.   J. H. Prest.

LB (DNA: PCC, item 12A). Addressed: "To The Convention of New Hampshire. The Assembly of Massachusetts Bay. The Assembly of Rhode Island. The Assembly of Connecticut. The Convention of New York."
[1] See the resolves on allegiance, treason, and counterfeiting passed by Congress on June 24 in *JCC*, 5:475–76. This day Hancock also sent an almost identical letter to the Maryland Convention. Red Books, MdAA.

John Hancock to Certain Colonies

Gentlemen,   Philada. June 25th. 1776
The Congress have this Day come to the enclosed Resolves, which

I have the Honour of transmitting in Obedience to their Commands.[1] You will there find they have come to a Resolution to augment the Number of Men destined for Canada, four Thousand. I am therefore to request you will send immediately one Regiment [2] of your Militia by Way of Augmentation of the Troops destined for that Department—and at the same Time earnestly to entreat you, to be expeditious in raising & equipping your Troops, and to provide them with Cloaths, Tents, and other necessary Camp Equipage, for which the United Colonies will engage to reimburse you.

In my Letter of the 4th Inst. in which were enclosed sundry Resolves of Congress with Regard to your sending a Part of your Militia into Canada, I took the Liberty of suggesting every Thing that occurred, to urge you to a speedy Compliance with the same. If the Complexion of our Affairs in that Quarter, was disagreeable at that Time, it has since altered extremely, and become much more alarming. The Arrival of Genl. Burgoyne with a large Reinforcement, the Defeat of Genl. Thompson with the Troops under his Command, and his being made Prisoner, are so many striking Circumstances that render it absolutely necessary to be more expeditious in our Preparations for the Defence of that Province, as well as to increase our Force there.

The present is not a Time for Delay. Every Thing we have a Right to expect from that Quarter, depends on Expedition. Without it, we shall inevitably be ruined. Remember, your own Safety, & the Security of Canada, are exactly one & the same Thing. If our Enemies are not opposed at a Distance, we must engage them in our Borders. One Idea should be for ever on our Minds—that in the Conduct of Political Affairs, every Moment is precious. A Week—a Day—even an Hour has often proved decisive; and by an Attention thereto, the Liberties of a Country have been either established, or destroyed, for ever.

I must repeat again to you that in all human Probability, the Fate of America will be determined the ensuing Campaign. Much depends on your Colony. I cannot therefore help once more pressing you to be expeditious in equipping & sending forward your Troops. As an additional Encouragement, the Congress have resolved that a Bounty of ten Dollars be given every Soldier who shall enlist for three Years.[3]

May the Great Disposer of all human Events, animate & guide your Councils, & enable you so to determine, that you may not only establish your own temporal Peace and Happiness, but those of your Posterity. Forgive this passionate Language. I am unable to restrain it—it is the Language of the Heart.

I have the Honour to be, Gentl. your most obed. & very hble Sert.   J. H. Prest.

LB (DNA: PCC, item 12A). Addressed: "To Convention of New Hampshire. Assembly of Masstts Bay. Assembly of Connecticut."
    [1] See *JCC*, 5:478–79.
    [2] The requisition on Massachusetts was for two regiments.
    [3] According to the journals, Congress did not formally adopt this measure until June 26. *JCC*, 5:483.

John Hancock to Jonathan Trumbull, Sr.

Honble Sir,   Philada. June 25th 1776.
    The Congress being informed by Letter from Genl. Washington, that Genl. Schuyler and the other Commissioners for Indian Affairs, had come to a Determination of taking into Continental Pay, the Mohekan & Stockbridge Indians, I am directed by Congress to request you will give Orders to have a Stop put to raising them as soon as possible, & that no Proceedings be had by the Commissioners till the further Direction of Congress.[1]
    I have the Honour to be, Sir, your most obedt. & very hble Sert.
                                                                        J. H. Prest.

LB (DNA: PCC, item 12A).
    [1] On June 3 Congress had authorized Washington "to employ in Canada a number of Indians not exceeding two thousand." Washington subsequently transmitted this resolution to General Schuyler and urged him and the commissioners of Indian affairs for the northern department to "pursue such Measures for the Purpose, as to you may seem best for securing their [i.e., the Indians'] Friendship and Service." In consequence of this resolve Schuyler and the commissioners devised a plan for raising two companies of "Mohekander and Connecticut Indians." However, when Washington was informed of this plan, he immediately suspected that it would not "answer the Views of Congress." This was so, he thought, because although the two tribes Schuyler intended to use "live within the Government of Connecticut, and are to be considered in the same Light with it's Inhabitants," the Indians whom Congress expected to employ under the June 3 resolution "were not Livers among us, and were of hostile Character or doubtful Friendship." Washington's interpretation of Congress' intent was confirmed by a June 24 congressional resolve forbidding "the raising the companies of Mohickan and Stockbridge Indians." See *JCC*, 4:412, 5:473; *Am. Archives*, 4th ser. 6:910–16; and Washington, *Writings* (Fitzpatrick), 5:102–3, 162–63, 172, 185. For Governor Trumbull's July 6 reply to Hancock promising compliance with Congress' June 24 resolve, see *Am. Archives*, 5th ser. 1:42–43.

John Hancock to George Washington

Sir,   Philadelphia June 25th 1775 [*i.e.* 1776].
    Your Favour of the 21st Inst. by Mr. Bennet with the Enclosure were duely received and laid before Congress, as you will perceive by the enclosed Resolves, to which I beg Leave to request your Attention.[1]

Altho the Commissioners have undoubtedly mistaken the Intention of Congress, yet the Terms, in which the Resolve is conceived, viz. "That the General be empowered to *employ in Canada* a Number of Indians not exceeding two Thousand," may at first View seem to confine their Employment to the Limits of that Province, and to give a Latitude of Construction as to the Place in which they are to be raised. And in this Sense they must have been understood by Genl. Schuyler and the other Commissioners. I am however to request, you will give Orders to have a Stop put to raising the Mohickan & Stockbridge Indians as soon as possible.[2] I shall write Governor Trumbull to the same Purpose.

The Conduct of the Quarter Master General in detaining the Tents sent from this Place to Massachtts. Bay, is a Stretch of office, which, however well meant, is certainly a very extraordinary one. You will therefore be pleased to order them to be delivered up and forwarded to the Massachusetts Bay, as soon as possible.[3]

The other Resolves, herewith transmitted, calculated to suppress Insurrections, and to promote good Order and Obedience to Laws in the United Colonies, are so full and explicit, that I need not enlarge. It is sufficient to observe, that internal Convulsions do always extremely weaken the Force and Springs of Government, and must necessarily render its operations against foreign Enemies less vigorous and decisive.

Applications having been made to Congress with Regard to Victualling the flying Camp, I am directed to request you will inform them what is the Cost of a Ration as furnished by the Commissary General.[4]

The several Matters in your Letters are before a Committee. The Proposal respecting a Troop of Horse is liked; and as soon as the Committee brings in their Report, and it is considered, you shall be made acquainted with the Result.

I have the Honour to be, Sir, your most obedt. & very hble Servant,   John Hancock Presidt

RC (DLC). In the hand of Jacob Rush and signed by Hancock.
    [1] These resolves, passed by Congress on June 24, dealt with the enlistment of Indians in Continental service; rifle company accounts; allegiance, treason, and counterfeiting; and the cost of rations. *JCC,* 5:473–77.
    [2] Washington so ordered Schuyler on June 27. Washington, *Writings* (Fitzpatrick), 5:185.
    [3] See *JCC,* 5:474.
    [4] For Washington's reply to this inquiry, see Washington, *Writings* (Fitzpatrick), 5:190–91.

Joseph Hewes to Samuel Purviance, Jr.

Sir,   Philadelphia 25th June 1776
    Your favour of the 21st I laid before the Marine Committee last

Evening and in answer thereto I have now to inform you, that when Congress appointed the Captains for the Frigates[1] it was agreed that the Rank should be setled hereafter, and that the Captains should only at present be Certified of their appointment. Captain. Nicholson has been strongly recommended, and Congress has a high opinion of his abilities and merit and I have no doubt of his standing pretty high in rank. The Marine Committee will pay great attention to the recommendations of Capt. Nicholson and your board of Commissioners for building the Frigate, but when you recommend two Gentn. for Sea Lieutenants it would be well to get such of your delegates as may be in your province to Join in such recommendation. I believe it will be agreeable to the Committee that Captain Nicholson should recommend all the Warrant Officers, in this however you can also Join, and the Committee will immediately transmitt the Warrants filled up agreeable to such recommendation. The Marine Officers for your Ship will be appointed to day, their names you have below, the sooner Capt. Nicholson engages all the Warrant & petty officers the more agreeable it will be to the Committee who wish to have the Ships ready soon as possible.[2] I fear many of them will wait for Guns & Anchors.

I am in haste, Sir, Your mo. Obed huml Serv,

Joseph Hewes

John Stewart, Captain
Tho. Pownal, first Lieut.   } Marines
Richd. Harrison, Second Lieutn. }

N.B. These Gentlemen were strongly recommended by the delegates of your Province & I hope they will be agreeable to all.

RC (MdHi).
[1] Done on June 6. *JCC,* 5:423.
[2] See *JCC,* 5:478.

Maryland Delegates to Matthew Tilghman

Sir,   Philada. 25 June 1776
Since writing the Enclosed[1] the post arrived from York and brought a letter from General Sullivan to the Congress giving a Melancholy account of another unfortunate event in Canada. General Thompson who was ordered with a party of two thousand Men to dislodge the English forces at the Three Rivers was attacked by General Burgoine and totally routed. Thompson and Several others are taken prisoners, and about one hundred and fifty of his men killed, the rest returned to the Sorel. The letter Says further (I

think) Arnold had abandoned Montreal, and that upon the whole our affairs in Canada bear a most unpromiseing aspect. This bad news is in Some measure Counterballanced by more agreeable Intelligence from Boston, the publick papers from thence inform us that the English Ships of War are all driven away from the Boston Harbour and private letters Say that five transports with Scotch Troops have been taken lately and carried into the Eastern Ports. The post is just Setting off and will not allow me to be more particular. We shall by the next opportunity transmit to you a more full and satisfactory Account.

A report prevails here, which is believed to be true, that a most diabolical plot to assasinate the General at York, blow up the Magazine, and Spike the Cannon has lately been discovered, many people it is Said have been thrown into prison, and some remain under guard, among the rest is the Mayor of the City.

What with External and internal Enemies we fancy we Shall very Shortly have our hands full of business.

We are Sir, with Great Esteem, yr. Most Obedt. Servant,

J Rogers

Tr (MdAA). Addressed: "The Honourable Matthew Tilghman, Esquire, President of the Maryland Convention."
[1] Not found.

Oliver Wolcott to Laura Wolcott

My Dear,   Philidelpa. 25t June 1776

I Wrote to you last Saturday and informed you that I had been unwell since which I find myself much better, but as my Health is rather low and Other Reasons strongly Urge Me to Return to my Family, I purpose therefore to Set out for home in a few days.[1] I have not been so ill as to be in the least confined, but a long Attention to Business of the Sendentary Kind has produced a Relaxation which nothing but a Journey can Cure. Mr. Huntington I hear is on the Way, he will likely be in this Morning.[2] Mr. Sherman puts in to Return but as he went home about Two Months ago, I think I have a prior and better Right.

Wishing you, my Family and Freinds the Blessing of the Almighty, I Subscribe myself with the tenderest Affection yrs,

Oliver Wolcott

RC (RPJCB).
[1] Wolcott probably left Philadelphia on June 28, since his letter of July 1 to Matthew Griswold, written from New York while en route home, discussed proceedings that transpired in Congress on June 27. His 1776 accounts with the state of Connecticut indicate that for this period of service he eventually collected

£163.16.0—"To my Attending Congress from the 4t of January 1776 to the 4t July 1776 inclusive, being 182 days at 18s per day." These inclusive dates undoubtedly included Wolcott's travel time. Revolutionary War Collection, Ct. See also Wolcott to Matthew Griswold, July 1, 1776.

² Samuel Huntington had returned to Connecticut around May 25. See Wolcott to Laura Wolcott, May 25, 1776. Huntington's appearance at the Connecticut Assembly was reported by Eliphalet Dyer in a June 25 letter to Joseph Trumbull: "Any Addition to our representation in Congress is in Vain to be hoped for or expected. The Governor pressed the Matter on the Assembly repeatedly at the last Sessions but to no purpose. The Lower house said they expected Mr Huntington every day & when he came they should be thoroughly Acquainted with every thing Necessary & then would determine. At length he Arrived but he seemed Very dull. Believe no Information of Consequence was gained from him. He soon went to Norwich dozzed about a While returned as far as Hartford two or 3 days after our special assembly set, seemed much Unconcerned at What was doing here or at Congress, set off on his Journey Southward. The Assembly quite Content to Submit their All to their Triumvirate for fear it might Cost them a great more if they should make an Addition." Joseph Trumbull Papers, Ct.

John Adams to Abigail Adams

June 26. 1776

I have written so seldom to you, that I am really grieved at the Recollection. I wrote you a few Lines, June 2. and a few more June 16. These are all that I have written to you, since this Month began. It has been the busyest Month, that ever I saw. I have found Time to inclose all the News papers, which I hope you will receive in due Time.

Our Misfortunes in Canada, are enough to melt an Heart of Stone. The Small Pox is ten times more terrible than Britons, Canadians and Indians together. This was the Cause of our precipitate Retreat from Quebec, this the Cause of our Disgraces at the Cedars. I dont mean that this was all. There has been Want, approaching to Famine, as well as Pestilence. And these Discouragements seem to have so disheartened our Officers, that none of them seem to Act with Prudence and Firmness.

But these Reverses of Fortune dont discourage me. It was natural to expect them, and We ought to be prepared in our Minds for greater Changes, and more melancholly Scenes still. It is an animating Cause, and brave Spirits are not subdued with Difficulties.

Amidst all our gloomy Prospects in Canada, We receive some Pleasure from Boston. I congratulate you on your Victory over your Enemies, in the Harbour. This has long lain near my Heart, and it gives me great Pleasure to think that what was so much wished, is accomplished.

I hope our People will now make the Lower Harbour, impregnable, and never again suffer the Flagg of a Tyrant to fly, within any Part of it.

The Congress have been pleased to give me more Business than I am qualified for, and more than I fear, I can go through, with safety to my Health. They have established a Board of War and Ordinance and made me President of it,[1] an Honour to which I never aspired, a Trust to which I feel my self vastly unequal. But I am determined to do as well as I can and make Industry supply, in some degree the Place of Abilities and Experience. The Board sits, every Morning and every Evening. This, with Constant Attendance in Congress, will so entirely engross my Time, that I fear, I shall not be able to write you, so often as I have. But I will steal Time to write to you.

The small Pox! The small Pox! What shall We do with it? I could almost wish that an innoculating Hospital was opened, in every Town in New England. It is some small Consolation, that the Scoundrell Savages have taken a large Dose of it. They plundered the Baggage, and stripped off the Cloaths of our Men, who had the Small Pox, out full upon them at the Cedars.

RC (MHi). Adams, *Family Correspondence*, 2:23-24.
[1] See *JCC*, 5:434-35, 438.

George Clinton to John McKesson

Dear Sir,   Philadelphia, 26th June, 1776

The enclosed I wrote yesterday morning, since which the board of war reported the necessity of sending more troops into Canada to reinforce our army there, and among other things, the necessity of immediately appointing the officers in the regiment ordered to be raised in New York, that they might immediately set about recruiting the regiment; and at the same time reported a list of the officers, taking them in rank as arranged by General Montgomery at Montreal; which report the Congress have confirmed, and made the appointments accordingly.[1] I should have had no objections to this had it been done before the resolve of last Friday, directing your Congress to recommend the officers for this new regiment, as in that case it might have saved you from troublesome application and blame; but as that resolve was transmitted to your Congress some time ago, at least three days, and you may have proceeded to the appointment of new officers, as thereby directed, I could not approve of this new step; especially as I can not think it will much hasten the recruiting the regiment, and at any rate, I think the recruits yet to be raised can not be got ready in time to save Canada.[2] However, I did not choose strenuously to oppose a measure which many thought essentially necessary. If it is wrong, we are not to blame. I have not time to add any thing further, nor have I any thing new worth communicating.

Yours affectionately,   Geo. Clinton

MS not found; reprinted from George Clinton, *Public Papers of George Clinton, First Governor of New York, 1777–1795, 1801–1804,* ed. Hugh Hastings and J. A. Holden, 10 vols. (New York and Albany: Wynkoop Hallenbeck Crawford Co. et al., 1899–1914), 1:241–42.

[1] See *JCC,* 5:479.

[2] See also John Hancock to the New York Convention, June 21 and 26, 1776.

Benjamin Franklin to Benjamin Rush

Dear Doctor,   Manor of Moreland, at Mr Duffield's, June 26. 76

I have just received the enclosed Letters by the Chevalier Kermorvan.[1] By the Conversation I have had with him he appears to me skilful in his Profession. I hope in a few days to be strong enough to come to town & attend my Duty in Congress. In the mean time I could wish you to introduce the Gentleman where it may be proper and that you would translate the Passage relating to him that I have mark'd in M. Dubourg's Letter, and show it with what you have received to the same purpose from the same Friend. As I think Philada should be better fortify'd than it yet is, I hope some Use will be made of this Gentleman's Talents as an Engineer for that End. With great Esteem, I am, Dear Doctor, Your affectionate Friend & most obedient Servant,   B Franklin

[*P.S.*] Respects to Mrs. Rush.

RC (DNA: PCC, item 82). Endorsed: "Read 28th June before Bd War."

[1] Letters from General Washington of June 21 and from General Wooster of June 26 introducing the chevalier Jean de Kermorvan were read to Congress on June 26 and referred to the Board of War for further consideration. On June 28 Congress adopted a report recommending that the Pennsylvania Committee of Safety employ him in laying out fortifications on the Delaware River, and on July 16 appointed him an engineer in the Continental service with the rank of lieutenant colonel. *JCC,* 5:480, 490, 565; and Washington, *Writings* (Fitzpatrick), 5:164.

John Hancock to the New York Convention

Gentlemen,   Philada. June 26th 1776.

You will perceive, from the enclosed Resolves, which I do myself the Honour of transmitting in Obedience to the Commands of Congress that they have appointed not only the Field officers in the Regiment to be raised in your Colony, but likewise a Number of the Subalterns.[1]

The Reasons that induced Congress to take this Step, as it is a Deviation from Rule, should be particularly mentioned. I am therefore directed to inform you, that in Consequence of their being furnished with a List of the Officers who had served in Canada, and the Rank to which they were entitled, they have been enabled to appoint, and in Fact, have only appointed, such as were originally recommended & appointed by the Provincial Congress of your Colony, and have served faithfully both the last Summer Campaign, and through the Winter. It is therefore apprehended the Congress have only prevented [2] you in their Appointments, and that the same Gentlemen would have met with your Approbation for their Services to their Country. Added to this, the last Intelligence from Canada, shewing our Affairs to be in the most imminent Danger, rendered the utmost Dispatch necessary, that not a Moment's Time might be lost.

The other Officers of the Battalion, I am to request you will be pleased to appoint, and to exert every Nerve to equip the Battalion as soon as possible. As an additional Encouragement, the Congress have resolved, that a Bounty of ten Dollars be given every Soldier who shall enlist for three Years.[3]

I have the Honour to be, Gentlemen, your most obed and very hble Ser.   J.H. Prest.

LB (DNA: PCC, item 12A).
    [1] See JCC, 5:481.
    [2] Used here in the sense of *anticipated*.
    [3] See JCC, 5:483. The New York Convention, after protesting against what it regarded as congressional usurpation of its right to nominate officers for New York troops, agreed to accept the appointments Congress had already made for the new regiment and asked Congress to select the rest of the officers for this unit. See New York Convention to Hancock, July 11, 1776, in PCC, item 67, 1:232–35, and *Am. Archives*, 5th ser. 1:1395–96.

John Hancock to George Washington

Sir,   Philadelphia June 26th. 1776.
    You will perceive by the enclosed Resolves, which I do myself the Honour of transmitting in Obedience to the Commands of Congress, and to which I beg Leave to request your Attention, that they have come to a Resolution to augment the Number of Troops, destined for the Northern Department, four Thousand.[1]
    It is scarcely necessary to mention the Motives on which they acted, or to explain the Propriety of the Measure. The Arrival of Genl. Burgoyne with a large Reinforcement—the known Character of that Officer for Action and Enterprize—the Defeat of General Thompson with the Troops under his Command, and his being made Prisoner, are so many Circumstances, that point out

the absolute Necessity of being more expeditious in our Preparations for the Defence of that Province, and of encreasing our Force there. In this Light I have represented the Matter to [the] Convention of New Hampshire, and the Assemblies of Massachussetts Bay, and Connecticut, to whom I have wrote by this Express, in the most pressing Language, urging them to send forward their Militia. As an additional Encouragement, the Congress have resolved that a Bounty of ten Dollars be given every Soldier who shall enlist for three Years.

I have also wrote to the Convention of New York on the Subject of the enclosed Resolve; and have delivered Col. Dubois, Col. Bruyn, and Major Goforth, their Commissions.

Should you be able, consistent with the Safety of New York, to afford any Assistance to the Canada Department, I am to request you will do it, and give such Directions, as you think will promote the Public Service.[2]

You will please to give Coll. Dubois the necessary Directions respecting the Raising his Regiment, he will wait on you immediately on his Arrival at New York.

I have the honour to be with Esteem, Sir, Your most Obedt Servt.

John Hancock Presidt.

[P.S.] I must Request the favr. of you to order a fresh Express to proceed with the Inclos'd Letters to the Northern Colonies.[3]

RC (DLC). In the hand of Jacob Rush, with concluding paragraph, signature, and postscript by Hancock.

[1] These resolves, dealing with reinforcements for the American army in Canada and the appointment of officers for Col. Lewis Dubois' battalion, are in *JCC*, 5:479, 481, 483.

[2] Washington replied on June 29 that owing to troop shortages in his own army at New York he was unable "to afford the least assistance to the Canada Department." Washington, *Writings* (Fitzpatrick), 5:199.

[3] See Hancock to Certain Colonies, June 25, 1776.

New Hampshire Delegates to Meshech Weare

Sir   Philadelphia 26th June 1776

The repeated Misfortunes our army in Canada have met with, make it necessary that a Strong reinforcement should be sent there as Speedily as possible. The many Disadvantages we shall Labour under by the Enemies being in full Possession of that Country, & the Lakes, is so obvious, it is needless to mention them.

By the last accounts Genl. Burgoyne with a strong army, was as high up the St Laurence as the three Rivers, where he had defeated a detachment of 2000 men under Genl. Thompson & taken him Prisoner. Sickness and other disasters have much dispirited our men, unless they are speedily supported by a strong reinforcement its uncertain what will be the consequence. The New England Colonies & New-York will be more immediately affected by our misfortunes there, then the other Colonies; & from their Scituation its likely will be able to afford the earliest assistance. For these reasons Congress have come to the Resolutions that are transmitted to you by the President Requesting that a Regiment in addition to that which was some time ago Requested, may be sent with all Possible dispatch from our Colony to join the Army in Canada.[1] If these troops can be rais'd soon it will have a tendency to raise the spirits of those already in that Country, and will in our opinion, be the only method of securing the frontiers of our Colony at the expence of the Continent. We shall be exceedingly glad to know from time to time, how you suceed in raising these Troops; it wod also be very agreeable, & serviceble, could we be inform'd of other Public transactions, in the Colony. Please to send by first opportunity a Copy of President Cutts Commission, also any Papers shewing Govr Wentworths authority, for Granting Lands westward of Connecticut River.[2] We understand Mr Langdon intends to resign his seat in Congress; if that shod be the case we hope some body will be immediately appointed in his Room.[3]

We have the Honour to be, With Great Respect, Sir, Your Most Obt. Serts.   Josiah Bartlett

                                                             Wm. Whipple

RC (PPRF). Written by Whipple and signed by Bartlett and Whipple.

[1] See John Hancock to Certain Colonies, June 25, 1776.

[2] The New Hampshire delegates were undoubtedly seeking these documents bearing on their colony's claims to the New Hampshire Grants as a consequence of the petition that had been presented to Congress on May 8, 1776, by Capt. Heman Allen. Although Congress sidestepped a final determination on the issue, a resolve of June 4 granted Allen "leave to withdraw the petition . . . he representing that he has left at home some papers and vouchers necessary to support the allegations therein contained." Bartlett and Whipple undoubtedly wished to be well prepared when the petition was resubmitted. See JCC, 4:334–35, 337, 405, 416.

Allen's petition is in Am. Archives, 4th ser. 4:702–5. See also the letter of transmittal covering the petition and the committee of Congress' draft resolution recommending that the "petitioners, for the present submit to the government of New York," which had been tabled on May 30, 1776, in PCC, item 40, fols. 1–7.

[3] John Langdon notified Whipple of his resignation from Congress in a letter of July 1, 1776. See Clark, Naval Documents, 5:846. Matthew Thornton, Langdon's replacement, was not appointed to the New Hampshire delegation until September 12 and did not take his seat in Congress until November 4, 1776. See N.H. State Papers, 8:333; and JCC, 6:920.

Secret Committee to Thomas Mumford

Sir   Philada. June 26th. 1776

We have received your favour of the 7th Inst. & thank you for the usefull advices therein. We have not time at present to Answer your said letter the present being only to request you will deliver or Cause to be delivered unto Capt Jno. Lawrence of New Haven or to Capt Jno. Paul Jones or either of them on their order as much of the Continental Gun Powder now under your care, as they may require not exceeding One Ton in the whole for which you'l please to transmit us a receipt & keep a duplicate for Your Voucher.[1] We are sir, Your very hble servts.

By order of the Secret Committee,

Robt Morris Chair Man

RC (Ronald von Klaussen, state of Florida, 1976). Written and signed by Robert Morris.

[1] This day Congress authorized the Marine Committee "to purchase the armed brig *Catharine* . . . as she now lies in Connecticut" and ordered the Secret Committee to supply one ton of powder. *JCC*, 5:482, 484.

New York Delegates to the New York Provincial Congress

Gentlemen,   Philadelphia 27th June, 1776.

We doubt not but before this you have received our President's letter, informing you that this Congress have appointed the officers for the regiment directed to be raised in our Colony, by the resolve passed on Friday last and then transmitted you; but as we conceive the appointment of officers by this Congress for new levies to be raised in a particular Colony, is contrary to the ordinary practice, and may therefore be considered as in some measure infringing on the rights of the Colony, we beg leave, as far as we are able, to explain the reasons of Congress for taking this step, and our conduct therein.[1]

On receiving the late intelligence from Canada, respecting the repulse of the detachment of our army commanded by Gen. Thompson, at Three Rivers, &c. the despatches containing this account, with the state of our army in Canada, were referred to the board of war, who, the same day, reported the necessity of reinforcing our army there with four regiments, &c.; that to be raised in our Colony to be one; to expedite the raising of which, an arrangement of the officers was also reported and agreed to by Congress. We objected to this measure, and thought it our duty to withhold our assent, not only because it was, as we conceived, introducing a new precedent which might give offence, but might interfere with appointments which you might probably have made for the same regiment, in consequence of the former resolves. The pressing occasion and necessity of despatch were urged to support the measure; and it was alleged that as these appointments were made of particular persons who had merited it by former service, it interfered with no former rule; and even should the appointments be continued to the Provincial Congress, it would in this case only create unnecessary delay, as the same persons must be appointed by them to answer the design and meaning of this Congress expressed in their former resolve. We were persuaded, nay we are morally certain, considering the busy season of the year, which will enhance the wages of labourers, and the numbers of militia now in the service, that this regiment can not possibly be raised in time to answer the end for which it is more particularly designed; and should our affairs in Canada grow worse, as we have reason to apprehend from present appearances, we feared lest delay, though unavoidable, and every misfortune which may befal our army in Canada, for want of a proper reinforcement, might by some be imputed to our Colony, notwithstanding your utmost exertions to carry in execution this impracticable and, as we conceive, ineffectual measure. We judged it, therefore, most prudent only to mention our reasons for withholding our assent, without making a more pointed and strenuous opposition to the measure, thereby leaving the Colony in such a situation as not to incur any blame on this occasion.

We are, gentlemen, With the highest respect, Your most obedt.

Geo. Clinton,

Fras. Lewis,

Wm. Floyd.

Henry Wisner,

John Alsop.

MS not found; reprinted from *Journals of N.Y. Prov. Cong.*, 2:238.

[1] See *JCC*, 5:471–72, 479, 481. See also John Hancock to the New York Convention, June 21 and 26, 1776.

Secret Committee Minutes of Proceedings

June 27. 1776.

Come. met. Present Morris, Alsop, Hewes, Bartlett, Lewis. A Contract with Tho. Yorke was signed by the Come. The Chairman was directed to order Messrs. Jenifer & Hooe of Virga. to send up to the head of Elk river 300 hhds tob. purchd by 'em on acct. of this Come. in order that it may be exported from Delaware Bay.

Letter from Mr Merkle now at N. York was read & considerd by the Come. Orderd that the Chairman write to Mr. Merkle & propose a Contract with him for supplyg. goods from Germany, agreable to the terms proposd in his letter to the amount of £30 or 40000 stlg. for wch. he is to be pd. here in money or produce of the Country.[1]

Issued an order on the Commissary to deliver J. Maxwell Nesbitt & Co. 125 lb powdr. agreable to an order of Congress this day.[2]

MS (MH).
[1] On July 19 Congress resolved "That the Secret Committee be empowered to contract with Mr. Mirtle for the importation of goods to the amount of £30,000 sterling, at his risque, and £15,000 sterling, at the risque of the United States of America," and on July 30 the Secret Committee signed a contract with Amsterdam merchant Johann Philip Merkle "for importing sundry goods from Holland." *JCC*, 5:592; and Journal of the Secret Committee, fol. 88, MH.

Merkle subsequently proved to be a great disappointment to Congress. For information on preparations associated with his voyage to Europe, see the July 30, 1776, letters of the Committee of Secret Correspondence to Steven Cleveland and of Robert Morris to John Bradford. For his introduction to Congress by John Jay and his ultimate failure to deliver the materials contracted for, see Jay, *Papers* (Morris), 1:270n.2; letters of March 7 and October 7, 1777, from the commissioners at Paris to Congress, in Wharton, *Diplomatic Correspondence*, 2:278, 405; and the commissioners' letter to Merkle of April 13, 1778, PCC, item 84, 1:133.

[2] See Congress' resolve of June 25, *JCC*, 5:478.

John Hancock to the the Pennsylvania Committee of Safety

Gentlemen   Philadelphia June 28th. 1776

The Congress wishing to be fully possessed of the Abilities of Monsr. Le Chevalier de Kermovan, and in order to form a proper Judgment they request you would Employ him in planning & laying out the Fortifications ordered at Billingsport on the Delaware, and you will please accordingly to give him Notice & Employ him as early as possible.[1]

I am Gentn., Your most Obed. servt.

John Hancock Prest.

Tr (PHarH).
[1] See *JCC*, 5:490–91. Washington introduced the chevalier de Kermorvan and Jean Arthur Marie de Vermonet to Congress in his June 21 letter to Hancock. PCC, item 152, 2:85; and Washington, *Writings* (Fitzpatrick), 5:164. Kermorvan, who also came equipped with letters of introduction from Barbeu-Dubourg to Benjamin Franklin and to Benjamin Rush, was appointed by Congress on July 16 as an engineer in the Continental Army with the rank of lieutenant colonel. Vermonet, a lieutenant in the French army, received an appointment as brevet captain in the Continental Army on July 29. See *JCC*, 5:565, 613–14; *Am. Archives*, 4th ser. 6:1040, 1726n; and André Lasseray, *Les Français sous les treize étoiles (1775–1783)*, 2 vols. (Mâcon and Paris: Imprimerie Protat frères, 1935), 1:120–22, 2:480–81. See also Benjamin Franklin to Benjamin Rush, June 26, 1776.

Joseph Hewes to James Iredell

Dear Sir   Philada. 28th June 1776

I have to thank you for two Letters, and believe me I do it most heartily; [1] you are almost the only Correspondent I have in No.

Carolina, but more of this next oppertunity, at present I confine my self to news. Burgoyne with a large force is arived in Canada. Genl Sullivan sent 2000 Men under Genl. Thompson to engage a party of the Kings Troops that were about forty Miles below head quarters towards Quebec but unluckily the evening before Thompson came up with them they had been reinforced by Burgoyne with several regiments just arrived. Notwithstanding the superiour force Thompson engaged them, was repulsed with the loss of 150 men killed & taken prisoners. In the retreat Thompson & five or Six officers were taken prisoners by a party of Canadians who tho they were supposed to be our friends found this a lucky time to make their peace with the strongest party. Our whole army are retreated to the Isle a Noix a little on this side St. Johns, 1500 of them have the Small Pox, out of three Regiments not more than fifty able to bear Arms, we hope to keep possession of the Lakes. A damnable Plott has been discovered in New York, there hellish Tories had concerted a plan to Murder General Washington & Several other Generals, Blow up the Magazine & Spike up all the cannon, they waited only for the Arival of the Kings Troops when this plan was to have been executed. The General has not yet got to the Bottom of this affair. Many persons are taken up and imprisoned, some persons of Note among them, the Mayor of the City, the famous Major Rogers &c. &c., it is said Govr. Tryon is concerned, but he is safe on board a Kings Ship at Sandy Hook, so much for the dark side. Things go a little better in another Quarter, our Continental Vessels of war & some Privateers have taken lately at different times & places Six large Transport Ships from Scotland having in all near 600 of Frasiers Regiment of highlanders on board with their Baggage, Arms, provisions &c. An express that came half an hour ago informs that he saw upwards of 200 of these march out of Boston in order to be confined in the Jails in the Country. He says they are fine Men, have all New regimentals, Scarlet faced with blue, he came out he says with them and heard Many of them curse most bitterly both King & Parliament for deceiving them. They had been told not a Rebel would be found on the Sea Coast, that they had all fled fifty or sixty miles back in the Country and that they were sent here to enjoy the Lands which the Rebells had forsaken, they did not expect any thing else, & had brought their Wives in order to set down quiet &c.[2] Governor Franklyn is taken into custody and sent Prisoner to Connecticut.

On Monday the great question of Independancy and Total Seperation from all political intercourse with Great Britain will come on, it will be carried I expect by a great Majority and then I suppose we shall take upon us a New Name. My Complimts. to Mr Johnston, I recd. a line from him from Halifax by the return Waggons, also one from Edenton by Williams who is the bearer of this. I have not [time] to write him now, shall do it by Post on Tuesday, he must consider this as written to him also, my Compliments to the Ladies. I am Dr Sir, Your mo. Obed hum Ser,

Joseph Hewes

RC (NcD).

[1] Letters from Iredell to Hewes of April 29 and June 9 are in *N.C. Colonial Records,* 10:1035–37, 1038–40.

[2] Accounts of the capture of these Highland troops are in Clark, *Naval Documents,* 5:293, 423, 434–36, 448–49, 563, 577–83, 618, 686–88.

John Penn to Samuel Johnston

Dear Sir   Philada. June 28th. 1776

I arrived here several days ago in good health & found Mr. Hewes well. I am truly sorry to inform you that our affairs are in a bad situation in Canada. I fear by the time you receive this our army will have left that Country. Unfortunately for us the small pox has gone through our Troops there, which has in some measure occasioned our misfortunes. I expect we shall be able to make a stand at the lakes. General Burgoin with a very considerable force arrived in Canada some time ago. He lately made Prisoners Brigad General Thompson and several other officers tho' we had but few men killed or taken at the time. A dangerious plot has lately been discovered at New York. The design was to blow up the Magazine and kill General Washington, a large number are under confinement some of note. Governor Tryon is at the bottom, several of the General's Guard were bribed, it seems when the whole is made known we shall be much surprised. The famous Rogers that was so active last war is one of the number & now confined.

The first day of July will be made remarcable; then the question relative to Independance will be ajitated and there is no doubt but a total seperation from Britain will take place. This Province is for it; indeed so are all except Maryland & her people are coming over fast, I shall be much obliged to you to give the inclosed letters passes and when you have an opportunity to let me know what is doing in the busie world your way. I am with great respect, Dear Sir, Your mo. obt. Servt.   John Penn

[*P.S.*] Please to give my Complts. to your Lady & Miss Peggy. J. P.

RC (PHi).

John Penn to Unknown

Dear Sir   Philada. June 28th. 1776

Agreeable to my promise I write this in hopes you may receive it, tho' I much fear by the time it gets to hand our Army will have left Canada. Our misfortunes there are in a great measure owing to the small pox, which has gone through all the Troops. I understand that we shall be able to make a stand at the lakes should it happen as I suspect. General Burgoin with several thousands arrived in Canada some time ago. He soon after made Prisoners General Thompson and severall other officers with him tho' we lost very few men either killed or taken at the time. Thompson was an inhabitant of Pennsylva. A very dangerous plot has lately been discovered at New York. The design was to blow up the magazine and kill General Washington. A large number were concerned, some of note, several of the General's guard were bribed, Governor Tryon is at the bottom. We do not know the whole of this affair as it is not made known yet. The general knew of the design for several days before he apprehended any of the persons concerned, in order that he might discover the whole end of their views, the principals were all taken at the same time by different officers so that they were totally unprepared either to escape or to make an excuse. The famous Rogers that was so much talked of last war is in confinement. The first day of July will be an era of great importance as that is the day for debating the great and important question of Independance and from what I have seen there is no doubt but a total seperation between Britain & her Colonies, that were, will take place as all the Provinces but Maryland are for it, and the Inhabitants there are coming over fast. I wish things may answer our expectation after we are Independant. I fear most people are too sanguine relative to commerce, however it is a measure our enemies have forced upon us. I dont doubt but we shall have spirit enough to act like men; indeed it could no longer be delayed. In haste I remain with great respect, Dear Sir, You mo. obt. Servt,

John Penn

Eleven oclock at night. Should any thing happen your way do write as I wish to hear as often as I can. Yrs,   J. P.

RC (Nc–Ar).

John Hancock to the Maryland Convention

Gentlemen,   Philadelphia. June 29th. 1776.
    You will perceive, by the enclosed Resolves, which I do myself the Honour of transmitting in Obedience to the Commands of Congress, that they have judged it necessary to augment the Continental Forces with a Battalion composed of Germans, to be raised in your Colony and Pennsylvania,[1] and to be employed in

such Manner, as will be most likely to defeat the Designs of our Enemies, and to promote the Cause of American Liberty.

In Order to compleat the Rifle Regiment at New York, the Congress have likewise determined that six Companies be raised for that Purpose—two in your Colony, and four in Viriginia.[2] I am therefore to request, by Order of Congress, you will be pleased to appoint the Officers, and forward with all possible Expedition, the raising the Companies, agreeably to the enclosed Resolves.[3]

I have the Honour to be, Gentlemen, your most obedt. and very hble Ser.   John Hancock Presidt

[*P.S.*] The Five Thousand Dollars your Delegates have Rec'd of me, and Inclos'd you have their Receipt.

RC (MdAA). In the hand of Jacob Rush, with signature and postscript by Hancock.

[1] See *JCC*, 5:487–88. This day Hancock also sent a letter to the Pennsylvania Committee of Safety enclosing the same resolves. PCC, item 12A; and *Am. Archives*, 4th ser. 6:1132. For Pennsylvania's response to this request, see ibid., p. 1294; and for Maryland's see ibid., 5th ser. 1:31–32.

[2] According to the president's letterbook, Hancock sent a similar letter to the Virginia Convention this day. PCC, item 12A; and *Am. Archives*, 4th ser. 6:1132.

[3] See *JCC*, 5:486.

John Hancock to George Washington

Sir,   Philadelphia June 29th. 1776.

I do myself the Honour of transmitting sundry Resolves, respecting the further Augmentation of the Continental Forces.[1] The Congress have thought it expedient, to order a German Battalion to be raised, as soon as possible, to be employed in such Manner, as will be most likely, to defeat the Designs of our Enemies, and to promote the Cause of American Liberty.

Your Favour of the 27th Inst. with its several Enclosures, came to Hand yesterday.[2] As the Congress will not sit this Day, I shall take the earliest Opportunity, on Monday, of laying their important Contents before them.

The Loss of Canada is, undoubtedly, on some Accounts, to be viewed in the Light of a Misfortune. The Continent has been put to great Expence in endeavouring to get Possession of it. It is highly probable too, that our Enemies will receive additional strength, both of Men and Supplies from it. Yet, on the other Hand, there is a Mixture of good Fortune attending it. That our Army should make so prudent a Retreat, as to be able to save their Baggage, Cannon, Ammunition, sick &c from falling into the Hands of the Enemy, is a Circumstance, that will afford a partial Consolation and reflect Honour upon the Officers who conducted it. Considering the superiour Force of the British Troops, and a Retreat as unavoidable, every Thing has been done, which, in such a Situation, could be expected. In short, Sir, I am extremely glad, our Army is likely to get safe out of Canada.

I am to request you will please to order Col. Stephenson, & one other Field Officer of that Corps, to repair to this City, to confer with the Delegates of Virginia and Maryland, on the most proper Steps, to fill up the Companies, as expeditiously as possible.[3] If there are any Subaltern Officers of that Corps, whom you can recommend it is the Desire of Congress, they should be promoted in Preference to those now to be taken into Pay.

I have the Honour to be, Sir, your most obedt. hble Sevt.

John Hancock Presidt

11 oClock. I have this moment Rec'd your favr. of 28th which shall be laid before Congress. I have also Rec'd by Post a Letter from Brigadr. General Whitcomb Returning his Commission, & desiring to be Excus'd on Accot. of Age & a Diffidence of not being able to answer the Expectation of Congress.[4]

The Inclos'd Copy of a Letter came to my hands, which I thought best to Transmit you. I am, yours,   J Hancock Pt.

RC (DLC). In the hand of Jacob Rush, with signature and postscript by Hancock.
    [1] See *JCC,* 5:486–88.
    [2] Two letters of the 27th from Washington, with their several enclosures, are in PCC, item 152, 2:103–22; and *Am. Archives,* 4th ser. 6:1000, 1101–9. Washington observed of the letters from Generals Arnold, Schuyler, and Sullivan and other American officers in Canada (enclosed in his first June 27 letter): "They will give a further account of the melancholy situation of our affairs in Canada, and show that there is nothing left to save our Army there but evacuating the country." *Am. Archives,* 4th ser. 6:1101.
    [3] Hugh Stephenson was appointed colonel in command of the rifle regiment that Congress ordered to be raised on June 27. *JCC,* 5:486.
    [4] Washington's letter to Hancock of June 28 is in PCC, item 152, 2:123–30; and Washington, *Writings* (Fitzpatrick), 5:190–94. The refusal of John Whitcomb, a general in the Massachusetts militia, to accept the commission as brigadier general in the Continental Army that Congress bestowed on him on June 5 is remarked on in Artemas Ward to Washington, June 23, *Am. Archives,* 4th ser. 6:1041; and Washington to Ward, July 1, 1776, Washington, *Writings* (Fitzpatrick), 5:210.

Francis Lewis to Nathaniel Shaw, Jr.

Dr. Sir   Phila. 29th June 1776.

I have been duly favored with your Letter of the 19th Inst. with a list of the Numbers of 70 bbls Flour landed out of the ship Mary, Capt. Kennedy.[1] Youl please to observe that this Flour is shiped on the Continental Account and therefore should be sold on their account and the Committee for those transactions are made sincible by contracts executed to the Eastwd that Flour Yields an advanced price there. Agreeable thereto youl please to dispose of those 70 bbls and transmit me the Account that I may lay it before the Committee, the weight & Fare of each bbl is mark'd upon the head.

I am sorry to find that Capts. Sarly & Kennedy are still detained in your harbor by the ships of War. I hope they will embrace the first good opportunity for going to sea. I expect there is another Sloop and Ship (ere this) in your harbor laden from Nw York for the Continental Account. Pray communicate this to the Capts. Sarly & Kennedy and that I have received Capt Sarleys letters, that they must waite with patience & take the first favourable opportunity.

The other parts of your Letter I communicated to the President in Congress, who promised me he would furnish you with the Agents appointmt and printed Instructions, that relative to the Seamen shall lay before the Marine Committee at their stated meeting on Monday next.[2]

I shall be always glad to render you any services here & am, Dr. Sir, Your very Humble Servt,   Fra Lewis

RC (CtY).
[1] This letter from Shaw, the Continental prize agent in Connecticut, is in Clark, *Naval Documents,* 5:625–26.
[2] Despite the fact that Shaw was appointed prize agent on April 23, he had not received official notice of the appointment by June 19 when he wrote to Lewis. Ibid; and *JCC,* 4:301.

Edward Rutledge to John Jay

My dear Jay   Philadelphia, June 29, 1776
I write this for the express Purpose of requesting that if possible you will give your Attendance in Congress on Monday next. I know full well that your Presence must be useful at New York, but I am sincerely convinced that it will be absolutely necessary in this City during the whole of the ensuing Week. A Declaration of Independence, the Form of a Confederation of these Colonies, and a Scheme for a Treaty with foreign Powers will be laid before the House on Monday. Whether we shall be able effectually to oppose the first, and infuse Wisdom into the others will depend in a great Measure upon the Exertions of the Honest and sensible part of the Members. I trust you will contribute in a considerable degree to effect the Business and therefore I wish you to be with us. Recollect the manner in which your Colony is at this Time represented.

Clinton has Abilities but is silent in general, and wants (when he does speak) that Influence to which he is intitled.[1] Floyd, Wisner, Lewis and Alsop though good Men, never quit their Chairs. You must know the Importance of these Questions too well not to wish to [be] present whilst they are debating and therefore I shall say no more upon the Subject.

I have been much engaged lately upon a plan of a Confederation which Dickenson has drawn.[2] It has the Vice of all his Productions to a considerable Degree; I mean the Vice of Refining too much. Unless it is greatly curtailed it never can pass, as it is to be submitted to Men in the respective Provinces who will not be led or rather driven into Measures which may lay the Foundation of their Ruin. If the Plan now proposed should be adopted nothing less than Ruin to some Colonies will be the Consequence of it. The Idea of destroying all Provincial Distinctions and making every thing of the most minute kind bend to what they call the good of the whole, is in other Terms to say that these Colonies must be subject to the Government of the Eastern Provinces.[3] The Force of their Arms I hold exceeding Cheap, but I confess I dread their over-ruling Influence in Council, I dread their low Cunning, and those levelling Principles which Men without Character and without Fortune in general Possess, which are so captivating to the lower Class of Mankind, and which will occasion such a fluctuation of Property as to introduce the greatest disorder. I am resolved to vest the Congress with no more Power than what is absolutely necessary, and to use a familiar Expression to keep the Staff in our own Hands, for I am confident if surrendered into the Hands of others a most pernicious use will be made of it.

If you can't come let me hear from you by the Return of the Post.[4] Compliments to Livingston and G. Morris. God bless you. With Esteem and affection, Yours,   E. Rutledge

RC (NNC). Jay, *Papers* (Morris), 1:280–81.

[1] Although the precise day Clinton left Philadelphia is not known, he apparently remained until near the end of the first week in July. His account for service in the Continental Congress indicates that he claimed compensation for the period May 10, 1775, to July 12, 1776, which undoubtedly included travel time from and to New York. See *Stan V. Henkels Catalog*, no. 1343 (January 17, 1924), item 129. It is also known that on July 12 General Washington directed a letter to him at New Windsor. *Am. Archives*, 5th ser. 1:227.

[2] Rutledge was a member of the committee appointed on June 12 to draw up a plan of confederation. *JCC*, 5:433.

[3] Perhaps one feature of the proposed Articles of Confederation that Rutledge found objectionable at this stage was a clause in the committee's draft vesting either "Congress or . . . some Court for that purpose" with authority to settle boundary disputes which states themselves could not resolve. In any case this clause did not appear in the draft articles that were finally submitted to Congress on July 12. See the 13th article of Josiah Bartlett's Draft Articles of Confederation, June 17–July 1? 1776.

⁴ "Your friendly letter," Jay subsequently wrote in response to this letter from Rutledge, "found me so engaged by plots, conspiracies, and chimeras dire, that though I thanked you for it in my head I had no time to tell you so either in person or by letter. Your ideas of men and things (to speak mathematically) run, for the most part, parallel with my own; and I wish Governor Tryon and the devil had not prevented my joining you on the occasion you mentioned. How long I may be detained here is uncertain, but I see little prospect of returning to you for a month or two yet to come. We have a government, you know, to form; and God only knows what it will resemble. . . . My compliments to Messrs. Braxton, Lynch, and such others as I esteem—of which number rank yourself, my dear Ned, among the first." John Jay to Edward Rutledge, July 6, 1776, John Jay, *The Correspondence and Public Papers of John Jay*, ed. Henry P. Johnston, 4 vols. (New York: G.P. Putnam's Sons, 1890–93), 1:68–70.

John Adams to Cotton Tufts

Dear Sir   Philadelphia June 30th. 1776

Your Favour of the 17th I received by Yesterdays Post.¹ Am much obliged, to you for your judicious Observations of the Spirit of Commerce and Privateering, and many other Subjects, which I have not Time to consider, at present. I mean [not] to express my Sentiments of them in this Letter.

You tell me a Plan is forming for immediately erecting a Foundery. I wish you would oblige me so much as to write me, who the Persons are who have laid this Plan:² whether it is to be carried on by the Public or by private Persons—who are the Undertakers— where the Foundery is to be—whether it is a brass or an Iron Foundery or both? In short what the Plan is in all its Particulars . . . .³ Are there any Artists sufficiently skilled with you? Have you Iron, or Ore, suitable to make Iron, proper for Cannon. Where shall you get Brass? Has Mr. Aaron Hobart of Abington done any Thing at casting Cannon. Has he an Air Furnace? Where does he get his Iron? And where, his Skill and Knowledge?

There are several other Subjects of Inquiry that occur to my Mind, which are of no small Importance.

Musquetts and Bayonnetts are excessively wanted in all the Colonies. Twelve Months ago We were distressed, to a Degree that Posterity will scarcely credit for Powder. This is now over. Now Arms are almost in as much Demand. The Convention of Virginia have taken as bold a Step to get Arms as the Massachusetts did to get Salt Petre. They have passed an ordinance for paying out of the public Treasury Twenty Dollars for every Musquet and Bayonnett which shall be made in the Colony for a year. Pensilvania makes very good Guns and in considerable Numbers. I fear the Massachusetts, in the Multiplicity of their Cares, have not done so much as they might in this Way. I am sure that Province upon a proper Exertion of its Ingenuity and Policy, as well as the Wit and Dexterity of her Tradesmen might make a vast Number of Arms annually. I want to be informed, what Number is now made Weekly or Monthly in the Province. How many are made by Mr. Orr; how many by Pratt, how many by Barrett of Concord, and how many by Pomroy of Northampton. . . . I sincerely wish that the Province would undertake in a public Capacity to encourage this Manufacture, and that they might do it with as much Wisdom and Spirit, and then I know they would have as much success as they had in the Manufacture of Salt Petre.

There are several other Articles which deserve the public Attention.

Flints begin to be wanted, and I am convinced that those Colonies abound with the proper Flint Stone, and that nothing is wanting but a little Attention to find it, and a little skill, to brake it into the proper Sizes and Shapes. Orange County in New York abounds with it, and the People there use no other flints. I wish the general Court would set a Committee to search for it, or recommend it to the select Men of the Towns to look for it.

Sulphur is an Object which lies in your Way as a Philosopher and a Physician. . . . It is to be found any where in the Province. Our Province has an Advantage of all others, in one Respect, the Division of it into Towns which are incorporated Bodies Politick and have public Officers and frequent public Meetings, gives the General Court Power, by ordering the select Men to call Town Meetings and to insert any subject in the Warrant, to diffuse and circulate any Information or Instruction and a Spirit of Inquiry into the whole Mass of the People at once. If some such Method was taken it is very likely that Sulphur Ore might be found in Plenty.

Lead is another Thing of great Importance, and there certainly is a great Quantity of the Ore in the Towns of Northampton and Southampton. It is a Pity that Something cannot be done to set the Manufacture agoing.

In one Word, my Friend, I cannot think that Country safe, which has not within itself every Material necessary for War, and the Art of making Use of those Materials. I never shall be easy, then, untill We shall have made Discoveries of Salt Petre, Sulphur, Flynts, Lead, Cannon, Mortars, Ball, Shells, Musquetts, and Powder, in sufficient Plenty, so that We may always be sure of having enough of each.

Another Thing my Heart is set upon is Salt. Pray inform me, what has been done with you towards the Manufacture.

The Intelligence you give me of your Success, in ferretting away, the Men of War, is some Consolation for the melancholly Accounts We have from Canada. It proves that Coll. Quincy was right when

he wrote me, that with Powder and heavy Cannon, he would undertake to make Prisoners at Discretion of the Army in the Town
and the fleet in the Harbour as he did last Summer.

I am &c.

LB (MHi). Adams, *Family Correspondence*, 2:24–26.
[1] Tufts' June 17 letter to Adams is in Adams, *Family Correspondence*, 2:17–19.
[2] See Tufts to Adams, July 25, 1776. Ibid., p. 61.
[3] Suspension points in MS, here and below.

Thomas Jefferson to the President of the Virginia Convention

Honble. Sir   [ca. June 30, 1776][1]

I this day received information that the Convention had been
pleased to reappoint me to the office in which I have now the
honor to be serving them and through you must beg leave to
return them my sincere thanks for this mark of their continued
confidence.[2] I am sorry the situation of my domestic affairs renders
it indispensably necessary that I should sollicit the substitution of
some other person here in my room. The delicacy of the house
will not require me to enter minutely into the private causes
which render this necessary: I trust they will be satisfied I would
not have urged it again were it not necessary. I shall with chear-
fulness continue in duty here till the expiration of our year by
which time I hope it will be convenient for my successor to attend.[3]

FC (DLC). Jefferson, *Papers* (Boyd), 1:408. That this letter was intended for Edmund Pendleton, president of the Virginia Convention, is clear from the substance of Jefferson's remarks.
[1] This conjectural date is based on Jefferson's July 1 letter to William Fleming,
which indicates that he had already received notice of his reelection to the Virginia delegation. See Jefferson to William Fleming, July 1, 1776.
[2] On June 20 the Virginia Convention decided to reduce its congressional delegation from seven to five, and reelected Jefferson, Francis Lightfoot Lee, Richard
Henry Lee, Thomas Nelson, and George Wythe to serve for the next year beginning August 11. Benjamin Harrison and Carter Braxton were not reelected. *The
Proceedings of the Convention of Delegates, Held at the Capitol, in the City of
Williamsburg. In the Colony of Virginia, On Monday, the 6th of May, 1776* (Richmond: Ritchie, Trueheart & Du-Val, 1816), p. 58; and *Am. Archives*, 4th ser.
6:1582. For further comments on the election, see Edmund Randolph to Jefferson,
June 23, and William Fleming to Jefferson, July 27, 1776, in Jefferson, *Papers*
(Boyd), 1:407, 475.
[3] Jefferson remained in Congress until September 2, but not until October 10,
1776, was Benjamin Harrison elected to replace him. *Journal of the House of
Delegates of Virginia. Anno Domini, 1776* (Williamsburg: Alexander Purdie, 1777),
pp. 7–8.

Francis Lightfoot Lee to Richard Henry Lee

Dear Brother,   Philadelphia June 30th. 1776
    Our affairs in Canada are at length brot to a conclusion, and we have now to contend with all the bad consequences which have been apprehended from the Enemy's being in possession of that Country. You will see by the papers that Genl. Thomson was sent with 2000 men to dislodge a party of the Enemy at Trois Rivieres, but Genl. Burgoine having arrived with a considerable body of troops, our men were obliged to retreat with the loss of 150, leaving the Genl. & a few others in captivity. Burgoine pursued his advantage, and our Generals found it absolutely necessary to retire out of the Country with their sick & dispirited Army. The accounts of Burgoine's force are from 8 to 10,000. We cou'd not muster above 3000, all the rest being in the small pox. Our Army, being 7000 brot off all their artillery, stores, baggage & provisions; having destroyed all the forts & bridges behind them. They are now at Crown Point, where they propose to make a stand against Burgoine's Army, assisted by Canadians & Indians, by keeping the mastery of Lake Champlain, if possible which is much to be doubted, as he has bro't with him a great number of vessells ready framed. At New York Genl. Washington has not 19000 men, & 50 of Howe's fleet are now at the hook. None of the militia is yet come in, & Genl. Washington is apprehensive they will not, till it is too late, and there is reason to fear they will never join the Army at Crown Point for fear of the small pox, or if they do, that they will be rendered useless by it. Add to all this, that it is certain great numbers in the Province of N York will join the Enemy. A horrid plot was lately discoverd in the City, to deliver up our Army to the Enemy by spiking the Cannon & blowing up the Magazine & some say to assassinate the Genl. We have not yet the particulars but many are in goal. They had debauched two of the Genl's guards, one of whome is executed.[1] Thus you have a full view of the situation of our affairs, from which I dare say you will agree with me, that we are in a most perilous state, from which nothing but some extraordinary event, can extricate us. We have advice, that the crew of one of the Ships that sailed from this port last winter, loaded by the Congress, confined the Capt. & carried her into Bristol and discover'd the signals by which all the other ships were to distinguish their friends from their Enemies upon their arrival on this Coast. I have nothing to ballance this dismal Acct., but that we have taken about 700 of Frazer's highlanders; & that depending on the goodness of our Cause, we have not lost our spirit.

July 1st. This day the resolve for independency was considered

& agreed to in Comtee of the whole, two dissentients S. Carolina & Pensylvania. N. York did not vote, not being empower'd. Tomorrow it will pass the house with the concurrence of S. Carolina. The Pensylvania delegates indulge their own wishes, tho they acknowledge, what indeed everybody knows, that they vote contrary to the earnest desires of the people.

This morning a unanimous vote of the Maryland Convention was brot to Congress, empowering their delegates to concur in all points with Congress. All the Colonies have declared their sense, except N. York, whose new Convention, now choosing, is to do the business. We expect you will join us in August, as soon as Government is settled;[2] indeed it will be necessary as Col. Braxton talks of going away in 3 weeks, & I suppose Col. Harrison will go early in August, which will leave us a bare representation. 3 or 4 months will in a great measure decide the fate of America. Tho I think, if our people keep up their spirits, & are determined to be free; whatever advantages the Enemy may gain over us This summer & fall; we shall be able to deprive them of in the winter, & put it out of their power ever to injure us again. Yet I confess I am uneasy, least any considerable losses on our side, shou'd occasion such a panick in the Country, as to induce a submission. The evil is coming, which I always dreaded, at the time when all our attention, every effort shou'd be to oppose the Enemy, we are disputing about Government & independence. My best respects to all friends, & believe me upon all occasions your most afft. friend & bror. Francis Lightfoot Lee

[P.S.] Will you do the needfull, with respect to Mr. Lee's estate, before you return? I think Tom Belfeild will be as good a manager, as you can get.

RC (ViHi).
¹ Thomas Hickey, a member of Washington's guard, was court-martialed for sedition, mutiny, and recruiting men for the enemy and was executed on June 28. Many of the rumors generated by his arrest, including that of an assassination plot, were not supported by the charges of his conviction. See Washington, *Writings* (Fitzpatrick), 5:182; and William Whipple to Joshua Brackett, June 23, 1776, note 3.
² Richard Henry was at this time in Williamsburg attending the Virginia Convention. His letter of June 29 to Gen. Charles Lee, in which he reported that "I shall return to Chantilly in a few days and remain there until the last of August, when I go to Philadelphia," is in Richard Henry Lee, *The Letters of Richard Henry Lee*, ed. James C. Ballagh, 2 vols. (New York: Macmillan Co., 1911–14), 1:203–5.

Samuel Adams to Perez Morton

My dear sir, Philada June   1776
When I was at Watertown in August last the General Assembly

being then sitting, a Croud of Business prevented our coming to
an Agreement respecting an Allowance adequate to your Services
in the Secretaries office or even conversing upon the Subject.[1] I
have been very easy about it, because I have never had the least
Doubt of your Integrity and Honor. Publick Affairs have demanded
so much of my Attention here that I have scarcely had Time to
spend a Thought on my domestick Concerns. But I am apprehensive that Mrs Adams will soon be in Want of Money for her
Support, if that is not already her Case. I shall therefore be much
obliged to you if you will let her have such a part of the Fees you
may have receivd as you can conveniently spare, Her Receipt shall
be acknowledgd by me. And as I foresee that I shall not have the
opportunity of visiting my Friends in New England so soon as I
have intended, you will further oblige me by sending me an Account
of the Monies paid into the office together with your own opinion
of what may be a reasonable and generous Allowance for your
Service.

I am with great Esteem & Affection, your Friend & hbl servt.

FC (NN).
    [1] Perez Morton was the deputy secretary of the Massachusetts Council, 1775–76,
and served under the chronically absent secretary, Samuel Adams. See John Adams
to Perez Morton, November 24, 1775, note 1. Morton's petition to the Massachusetts
General Court for allowances for his services was read in the House of Representatives on June 7, 1776, but action on it was postponed. *A Journal of the Honorable
House of Representatives of the Massachusetts-Bay* . . . (Boston: Powars and Willis,
1776), p. 48.

Thomas Jefferson's Proposed Resolution

[ante July 1776][1]
    To prevent every danger which might arise to American free-
dom by continuing too long in office the members of the Continental Congress, to preserve to that body the confidence of their
friends, and to disarm the malignant imputations of their enemies,
It is earnestly recommended to the several Provincial Assemblies or
Conventions of the United colonies, that in their future elections
of delegates to the Continental Congress one half at least of the
persons chosen be such as were not of the delegation next preceeding, and the residue be of such as shall not have served in
that office longer than two years. And that their deputies be chosen
for one year, with powers to adjourn themselves from time to time
& from place to place as occasions may require, and also to fix
the time & place at which their Successors shall meet.

MS (DLC). Jefferson, *Papers* (Boyd), 1:411.
    [1] This resolve is not mentioned in the journals, but Jefferson's use of the terms

Provincial Assemblies and *United colonies* suggests that he drafted it before the vote was taken on Richard Henry Lee's motion on independence, which was scheduled for July 1, 1776. It is interesting to note, however, that the words *colony* and *colonies* are found in the report of the committee on rules—of which Jefferson was a member—that was submitted to Congress on July 10 and adopted on the 17th, and several other uses of these words can be found in the journals of Congress well after July 2 or 4, 1776. See *JCC*, 5:521–22, 532–33, 541, 564, 573–74, 623.

John Adams to Archibald Bulloch

Dear sir.   Philadelphia July 1. 1776
Two Days ago I received your Favour of May 1st.[1] I was greatly disappointed, Sir, in the Information you gave me, that you should be prevented from revisiting Philadelphia. I had flattered my self with Hopes of your joining us soon, and not only affording us the additional Strength of your Abilities and Fortitude, but enjoying the Satisfaction of Seeing a Temper and Conduct here, somewhat more agreable to your Wishes, than those which prevailed when you was here before. But I have since been informed, that your Countrymen have done themselves the Justice to place you at the Head of their Affairs, a Station in which you may perhaps render more essential service, to them and to America, than you could here.

There seems to have been a great Change in the sentiments of the Colonies, since you left us, and I hope that a few Months will bring us all to the same Way of thinking.

This morning is assigned for the greatest Debate of all.[2] A Declaration that these Colonies are free and independent states, has been reported by a Committee appointed some weeks ago for that Purpose, and this day or Tomorrow is to determine its Fate. May Heaven prosper the new born Republic—and make it more glorious than any former Republics have been.

The Small Pox has ruined the American Army in Canada, and of Consequence the American Cause. A series of Disasters has happened there; partly owing I fear to the Indecision at Philadelphia, and partly to the Mistakes or Misconduct of our officers, in that Department. But the Small Pox, which infected every Man we Sent there compleated our Ruin, and have compell'd us to evacuate that important Province. We must however regain it, sometime or other.

My Countrymen have been more successfull at sea, in driving all the Men of War compleatly out of Boston Harbour, and in making Prizes of a great Number of Transports and other Vessells.

We are in daily Expectation of an Armament before New York,[3] where, if it comes the Conflict must be bloody. The object is great

which We have in View, and We must expect a great Expence of
Blood to obtain it. But We should always remember, that a free
Constitution of civil Government cannot be purchased at too dear
a Rate; as there is nothing on this Side of the new Jesusalem, of
equal Importance to Manklind.

It is a cruel Reflection that a little more Wisdom, a little more
Activity, or a little more Integrity would have preserved Us Canada,
and enabled Us to Support this trying Conflict at less Expence of
Men and Money. But irretrievable miscarriages ought to be lamented
no further, than to enable and Stimulate us to do better in future.

Your Colleagues Hall and Gwinn,[4] are here in good Health, and
Spirits, and as firm as you your self could wish them. Present my
Compliments to Mr Houstoun. Tell him the Colonies will have
Republics, for their Government, let us Lawyers and your Divine [5]
say what we will. I have the Honour to be, with great Esteem and
Respect, Sir, your sincere friend, and most humble Servant.

LB (MHi).

[1] Bulloch's May 1 letter to Adams, explaining his appointment as president of
Georgia, is in the Adams Papers, MHi.

[2] Adams played a prominent role in this debate, apparently delivering the principal response to John Dickinson's lengthy speech in opposition to independence.
As Adams explained in his autobiography: "No Member rose to answer him: and
after waiting some time, in hopes that some one less obnoxious than myself, who
had been all along for a Year before, and still was represented and believed to be
the Author of all the Mischief, I determined to speak.

"It has been said by some of our Historians, that I began by an Invocation to
the God of Eloquence. This is a Misrepresentation. Nothing so puerile as this fell
from me. I began by saying that this was the first time of my Life that I had ever
wished for the Talents and Eloquence of the ancient Orators of Greece and Rome,
for I was very sure that none of them ever had before him a question of more
Importance to his Country and to the World. They would probably upon less
Occasions than this have begun by solemn Invocations to their Divinities for
Assistance but the Question before me appeared so simple, that I had confidence
er ough in the plain Understanding and common Sense that had been given me,
to believe that I could answer to the Satisfaction of the House all the Arguments
which had been produced, notwithstanding the Abilities which had been displayed
and the Eloquence with which they had been enforced. Mr. Dickinson, some years
afterwards published his Speech. I had made no Preparation before hand and
never committed any minutes of mine to writing." Adams, *Diary* (Butterfield),
3:396–97. See also John Dickinson's Notes for a Speech in Congress, this date.

[3] Robert Treat Paine noted in his diary for this day: "Fine showers. Genl.
Howe's Army arrived at Sandy Hook." MHi.

[4] Lyman Hall and Button Gwinnett.

[5] John J. Zubly. See Zubly to Archibald Bulloch and John Houstoun, November 10? 1775.

John Adams to Samuel Chase

Dear Sir   Philadelphia July 1. 1776

Your Favour by the Post this Morning gave me much pleasure,[1] but the generous and unanimous Vote of your Convention,[2] gave me much more. It was brought into Congress this Morning, just as We were entering on the great Debate.

That debate took up the most of the day, but it was an idle Mispence of Time for nothing was Said, but what had been repeated and hackneyed in that Room before an hundred Times, for Six Months past.

In the Committee of the whole the Question was carried in the affirmative and reported to the House. A Colony desired it to be postponed untill tomorrow.[3] Then it will pass by a great Majority, perhaps with almost Unanimity: yet I cannot promise this. Because one or two Gentlemen may possibly be found, who will vote point blank against the known and declared sense of their Constituents. Maryland, however, I have the Pleasure to inform you, behaved well: Paca, generously and nobly.

Alas Canada! We have found Misfortune and disgrace in that Quarter. Evacuated at last. Transports arrived at Sandy Hook, from whence We may expect an Attack in a short Time, upon New York or New Jersey, and our Army not so strong as we could wish. The Militia of New Jersey and New England, not so ready, as they ought to be.

The Romans made it a fixed Rule never to send or receive Embassadors, to treat of Peace with their Enemies, while their affairs were in an Adverse and disastrous situation. There was a Generosity and Magnanimity in this, becoming Freemen. It flowed from that Temper and those Principles, which alone can preserve the Freedom of a People. It is a Pleasure to find our Americans of the same Temper. It is a good Symptom, forboding a good End.

If you imagine that I expect this Declaration will ward off Calamities from this Country, you are much mistaken. A bloody Conflict We are destined to endure. This has been my opinion, from the Beginning. You will certainly remember my declared opinion was, at the first Congress, when we found that we could not agree upon an immediate Non Exportation, that this Contest would not be Settled without Bloodshed, and that if Hostilities Should once commence, they would terminate in an incurable Animosity, between the two Countries. Every political Event Since the 19th of April 1775 has confirmed me in this opinion. If you imagine that I flatter myself, with Happiness and Halcyon days, after a Separation from Great Britain, you are mistaken again. I dont expect that our new Government will be so quiet, as I could wish, nor that happy Harmony, Confidence and affection between the Colonies, that every good American ought to study, labour, and pray for, a long time.

But Freedom is a Counterballance for Poverty, Discord, and War, and more. It is your hard Lott and mine to be called into Life, at such a Time. Yet even these Times have their Pleasures.

I am your Friend and Servant

LB (MHi).
¹ Undoubtedly Chase's letter to Adams of June 28. See Adams to Chase, June 24, 1776, note 5.
² The June 28 resolution of the Maryland Convention authorizing its delegates to vote for independence is in *JCC*, 5:504.
³ According to Thomas Jefferson, Edward Rutledge of South Carolina moved to postpone the vote. See Jefferson's Notes of Proceedings in Congress, July 1–4, 1776.

Josiah Bartlett to Nathaniel Folsom

Dear Sir   Philadelphia July 1st 1776

Your favor of the 15th ulto is come to hand. I am glad to hear that Harmony Subsists in our colony in the Grand American Cause; we are now Come to the time, that requires harmony, togather with all the wisdom, prudence, Courage, & resolution we are masters of, to ward off the Evils intended by our implacable Enemies. The utmost power of Brittain will be Exerted I believe in a short time; if the Americans behave with their usual Spirit, I make no Doubt we shall Defeat them, and fully Establish our freedom. But if they all behave as it is said Major Butterfield & his men did in Canada to their Eternal Disgrace, *Death*, nay what is tenfold worse, *unconditioned absolute Slavery* will be our portion; But reason, faith, Enthusiasm or something tells me, this last can never be.

I am Glad to hear our Colony has Continued the price of Salt petre for another year & that a powder mill is likely to be soon Erected and that you have given a Bounty for making fire arms; Quere whither offering 12 or 13 Dollars for Every good musket & Bayonet made in the Colony & Delivered within a year would not answer a very good purpose.

The giving a Bounty of twenty Dollars to the men for Canada will be a heavy Expence to the Colony, as I fear the Continent will not be willing to refund it;¹ yet as it is absolutely necessary for the Defence of the Colony to Keep a Strong army at the lakes or in Canada, it may be prudent to give that Bounty if the men Could not be raised without, of which the Colony are the best Judges. But I am sorry to hear that the Colony have Determined to keep up Col Gilmans Regiment in the pay of the Colony. The Design of raising the Continental Regiment was for the relief of the Colony and that Portsmouth might be Defended at the Expence of the Continent, and I was in hopes those men we had there would be immediately put on the Continental Establishment (as has been Done in several other Colonies) and others inlisted to make them up to a full Regiment; by that means the heavy Expence of maintaing those men would be saved to the Colony. But if they are kept in pay & another Regiment is raised beside, I fear when it is known it will be thought to be more than is necessary, and possibly the Continental Regiment will be ordered or at least a Considerable part of it to some other place and the Colony reap no advantage by raising them. If it be necessary for the public Safety I am willing to spare neither Cost nor pains; yet as almost Every Colony have raised men for their Defence at the Expence of the Continent, I should be sorry to loose the Benefit the Congress Designed us. I would not have you think by what I have wrote that I mean to Censure what you have Done; you may & no Doubt have good reason for it; But as things appear to me and as other Colonys have Done, I should not have thought best to keep any men at Portsmouth in the pay of the Colony, as I believe one full regiment will be Quite sufficient unless in Case of an attack when the militia will be called in.

The whole Congress are unanimous for forming a plan of Confederation of the Colonies. A Committe of one from Each Colony, have been upon it for about a fortnight at all oppertunities; last Saturday the Committe spent the whole Day on it, this Day after Congress we are to meet again when I Believe it will be fitted to lay before Congress.[2] When the Congress will model it to their minds I know not. Before it is in force it will be laid before all the Legislatures of the Colonies and Receive their Sanction. It is a Business of the greatest importance as the future happiness of America will Depend on it in a great measure; and you may Easily see the Difficulty to frame it so as to be agreable to the Delegates of all the Different Colonies & of the Colonial Legislatures also; for without the unanimous Consent of all it Cannot be Established.

May the Supreme Disposer of all Events overrule this and all our affairs for the happiness & Safety of America. Mr Dickenson the Pensylvania farmer is one of the Committee.

The Resolve of our Colony with regard to our Conduct in the affair of Independency Came to hand on Saturday,[3] very Seasonably, as that Question was agreable to order this day taken up in a Committee of the whole House & every Colony fully represented; Thus much I can inform you that it was agreed to in Committee & I make no Doubt but that by next post I shall be able to send you a formal Declaration of Independency Setting forth the reasons &c. By letters from General Lee we are informed that Genl. Clinton with above 50 Sail of Ships &c were before Charlestown South Carolina,[4]

and by an Express from Genl Washington it appears that Genl
Howe with near 100 Sail is at Sandy Hook so that we may soon
Expect news of Consequence.[5] Genl Sullivan had retreated with
our army as far as Nut Island. I hope Sir you will Excuse the
Erasements and interlinings &c &c as I have not time to Copy or
Correct this Long Epistle. Believe me to be your friend and Humble
Servant,   Josiah Bartlett

RC (PHi).
   [1] Meshech Weare's June 17 letter to John Hancock informing Congress of the
steps New Hampshire was taking to reinforce the army is in PCC, item 64, fols.
9–11, and *N.H. Provincial Papers*, 8:151–52.
   [2] For Bartlett's work on this committee, see Josiah Bartlett's and John Dickinson's
Draft Articles of Confederation, June 17–July 1? 1776, note 1.
   [3] The June 15 resolution of the New Hampshire Assembly urging a declaration
of independence is in *N.H. Provincial Papers*, 8:149–50.
   [4] General Lee's letter of June 6 to Hancock, enclosing a June 4 letter of John
Rutledge to Lee announcing the arrival of the British fleet off Charleston, was
read in Congress on June 27. *JCC*, 5:485. The letters are in PCC, item 158, 1:65–68,
73–76, and *Am. Archives*, 4th ser. 6:720.
   [5] General Washington's June 29 letter to Hancock is in PCC, item 152, 2:135–38,
and Washington, *Writings* (Fitzpatrick), 5:199–200.

Josiah Bartlett to John Langdon

Dear Sir,   Philadelphia July 1st 1776.
   Yours of the 14th ulto is now before me.[1] I am truly sorry that
guns &c for the ships cannot be got as soon as wanting; but so it
happens. The Committee appointed for that purpose have not been
able to procure them yet. As to naval affairs I must refer you to
brother Whipple who continues of the Marine Committee alias
Board of Admiralty and who will while here inform you from time
to time what is to be done in your department as Agent for New
Hampshire.
   I am sorry to hear our Colony have determined to keep up the
provincial regiment at Portsmouth in the pay of the Colony, besides
the Continental regiment. The design of raising that regt. was to
ease our Colony of that expense and I expected they would have
been immediately put on the Continental establishment and our
Colony eased of the burden. The cost of maintaining Col Gilman's
regt with the bounty given to the men going to Canada with our
other expenses will be very great, and where we can save cost
consistent with the public safety we ought to do it; in short in my
opinion it will be no advantage to us, for when it is known that
our harbor is defended by our own forces, it is very probable the
Continental regt may be ordered some where else, which would not
be the case if they were wanted as was expected for the Colony's

defence. I have the highest opinion of Dr Brackett but think he would not accept of the appointment of Surgeon to the Continental regt especially as it may possibly be ordered to some distant place and I fear he would take it as an affront to offer it to him. New Jersey have appointed a new set of Delegates consisting of five; among them is Dr Witherspoon.

The affair of Independency has been this day determined in a Committee of the whole House; by next post I expect you will receive a formal declaration with the reasons; the Declaration before Congress is, I think, a pretty good one. I hope it will not be spoiled by canvassing in Congress. Genl Lee by express informs us that 55 ships with Genl Clinton were before Charlestown, South Carolina; Genl Washington by express this day informs us that Genl Howe with near 100 sail were at Sandy Hook, so that we may soon expect serious work. Before this reaches you, you will hear that Genl Sullivan has evacuated Canada and is at present at Isle Noix and I expect soon to hear he is at Crown Point; the time is now at hand, when we shall see whether America has virtue enough to be free, or not.

Sir, you will excuse the erasements and many other defects in this scrawl as I have not time to copy or correct it.

I am Sir your friend &c,   Josiah Bartlett

P.S. The transport with Highlanders that was taken by the Cabot and afterward retaken, is taken a second time by Capt Barron and carried into Jamestown, Virginia; she had 212 soldiers on board, being the whole of the soldiers in two transports taken by the Cabot; the other transport contained the officers of both and was retaken by the Cerberus, man of war, and afterward taken again by the Schuyler and Montgomery & carried into New York.

Tr (DLC).
[1] An extract of Langdon's June 14 letter is in Clark, *Naval Documents*, 5:523.

John Dickinson's Notes for a Speech in Congress

[July 1, 1776][1]

Arguments against the Independance of these Colonies—In Congress.

The Consequences involved in the Motion now lying before You are of such Magnitude, that I tremble under the oppressive Honor of sharing in its Determination. I feel Myself unequal to the Burthen assigned Me. I believe, I had almost said, I rejoice, that the Time is approaching, when I shall be relieved from its Weight. While the

Trust remains with Me, I must discharge the Duties of it, as well
as I can—and I hope I shall be the more favorably heard, as I am
convinced, that I shall hold such Language, as will sacrifice any
private Emolument to general Interests. My Conduct, this Day, I
expect will give the finishing Blow to my once too great, and my
Integrity considered, now too diminish'd Popularity. It will be my
Lott to [Prove?] that I had rather vote away the Enjoyment of
[. . .] than the Blood and Happiness of my Countrymen [2]—too
fortunate, amidst their Calamities, if I prove a Truth known in
Heaven, that I had rather they should hate Me, than that I should
hurt them.[3] I might indeed, practise an artful, an advantageous Reserve upon this Occasion. But thinking as I do on the subject of
Debate, Silence would be guilt. I despise its Arts—I detest its Advantages. I must speak, tho I should lose my Life, tho I should lose
the Affections of my C[ountrymen]. Happy at present, however, I
shall esteem Myself, if I can so rise to the Height of this great
argument, as to offer to this Honorable Assembly in a fully clear
Manner, those Reasons that have so invariably fixed my own Opinion.

It was a Custom in a wise and virtuous State, to preface Propositions in Council, with a prayer, that they might redound to the
public Benefit. I beg Leave to imitate the laudable Example. And
I do most humbly implore Almighty God, with whom dwells Wisdom itself, so to enlighten the Members of this House, that their
Decision may be such as will best promote the Liberty, Safety and
Prosperity of these Colonies—and for Myself, that his Divine Goodness may be graciously pleased to enable Me, to speak the Precepts
of sound Policy on the important Question that now engages our
Attention.

Sir, Gentlemen of very distinguished Abilities and Knowledge
differ widely in their Sentiments upon the Point now agitated. They
all agree, that the utmost Prudence is required in forming our
Decision—But immediately disagree in their Notions of that Prudence, Some cautiously insisting, that We ought to obtain That
previous Information which We are likely quickly to obtain, and to
make those previous Establishments that are acknowledged to be
necessary—Others strenuously asserting, that tho regularly such Information & Establishment ought to precede the Measure proposed,
yet, confiding in our Fortune more boldly than Caesar himself, We
ought to brave the Storm in a Skiff made of Paper.

In all such Cases, where every Argument is adorn'd with an Eloquence that may please and yet mislead, it seems to me [the proper
method of?] discovering the right Path, to enquire, which of the
parties is probably the most warm'd by Passion. Other Circumstances
being equal or nearly equal, that Consideration would have Influence with Me. I fear the Virtue of Americans. Resentment of the

Injuries offered to their Country, may irritate them to Counsels &
to Actions that may be detrimental to the Cause they would dye to
advance.

What Advantages? 2. 1. Animate People. 2. Convince foreign
Powers of our Strength & Unanimity, & aid in consequence thereof.

As to 1st—Unnecessary. Life, Liberty & Property sufficient Motive.
General Spirit of America.

As to 2d—foreign Powers will not rely on Words.

The Event of the Campaign will be the best Evidence. This
properly the first Campaign. Who has received Intelligence that
such a Proof of our Strength & daring Spirit will be agreeable to
France? What must she expect from a People that begin their Empire in so high a stile, when on the Point of being invaded by the
whole Power of G.B. aided by [formidable foreign?] aid—
unconnected with foreign Power? She & Spain must perceive the
imminent Danger of their Colonies lying at our Doors. Their Seat
of Empire in another world. Masserano.[4] Intelligence from Cadiz.

More respectful to act in Conformity to the views of France. Take
advantage of their Pride, Give them Reason to believe that We
confide in them, desire to act in conjunction with their Policies &
Interests. Know how they will regard this ⟨new Star⟩ Stranger in
the States of the world. People fond of what they have attained in
producing. Regard it as a Child—A Cement of affection. Allow
them the glory of appearing the vindicators of Liberty. It will
please them.

It is treating them with Contempt to act otherwise. Especially
after the application made to France which by this time has reach'd
them. Bermuda 5 May.[5] Abilities of the person sent. What will
they think, if now so quickly after without waiting for their
Determination—Totally slighting their sentiments on such a
prodigous [. . .]—We haughtily pursue our own Measures? May they
not say to Us, Gentlemen You falsely pretended to consult Us, &
disrespectfully proceeded without waiting our Resolution. You must
abide the Consequences. We are not ready for a Rupture. You
should have negotiated till We were. We will not be hurried by
your Impetuosity. We know it is our Interest to support You. But
we shall be in no haste about it. Try your own strength & Resources
in which you have such Confidence. We know now you dare not look
back. Reconciliation is impossible without declaring Yourselves the
most rash & at the same Time the most contemptible Thrasos [6]
that ever existed on Earth. Suppose on this Event G.B. should offer
Canada to France & Florida to Spain with an Extension of the old
Limits. Would not France & Spain accept them? Gentlemen say
the Trade of all America is more valuable to France than Canada.
I grant it but suppose she may get both. If she is politic, & none

doubts that, I averr she has the easiest Game to play for attaining both, that ever presented itself to a Nation.

When We have bound ourselves to an eternal Quarrel with G.B. by a Declaration of Independence, France has nothing to do but to hold back & intimidate G.B. till Canada is put into her Hands, then to intimidate Us into a most disadvantageous Grant of our Trade. It is my firm opinion these Events will take Place—& arise naturally from our declaring Independance.

As to Aid from foreign Powers. Our Declaration can procure Us none this Campaign tho made today. It is impossible.

Now consider if all the advantages expected from foreign Powers cannot be attained in a more unexceptionable manner. Is there no way of giving Notice of a Nation's Resolutions than by proclaiming it to all the world? Let Us in the most solemn Manner inform the House of Bourbon, at least France, that we wait only for her Determination to declare an Independance. We must not talk generally of foreign Powers but of those We expect to favor Us. Let Us assure Spain that we never will give any assistance to her Colonies. Let France become Guarantee. Form arrangements of this Kind.

Besides, first Establish our governments & take the Regular Form of a State. These preventive Measures will shew Deliberation, wisdom, Caution & Unanimity.

Our Interest to keep G.B. in Opinion that We mean Reunion as long as possible. Disadvantage to administration from Opposition. Her Union from our Declaration. Wealth of London &c pour'd into Treasury. The whole Nation ardent against us. We oblige her to persevere. Her Spirit. See last petition of London. Suppose We shall ruin her. France must rise on her Ruins. Her Ambition. Her Religion. Our Danger from thence. We shall weep at our victories. Overwhelm'd with Debt. Compute that Debt 6 Millions of Pa. Money a Year.

The War will be carried on with more Severity. Burning Towns. Letting Loose Indians on our Frontiers. Not yet done. Boston might have been burnt. What advantages to be expected from a Declaration? 1. Animating our Troops. Answer, Unnecessary. 2. Union of Colonies. Answer, Also unnecessary. It may weaken that Union—when the People find themselves engaged in a [war] rendered more cruel by such a Declaration without prospect of End to their Calamities by a Continuation of the War. People changeable. In Bitterness of Soul they may complain against our Rashness & ask why We did not apply first to foreign Powers. Why We did not settle all Differences among ourselves. Take Care to secure unsettled Lands for easing their Burthens instead of leaving them to particular Colonies. Why not wait till better prepar'd. Till We had made an Experiment of our Strength. This [probably?] the first Campaign.

3. Proof of our strength & Spirit.[7] France & Spain may be alarm'd & provoked. Masserano. Insult to France.[8] Not the least Evidence of her granting Us favorable Terms. Her probable Conditions. The Glory of recovering Canada. She will get that & then dictate Terms to Us.

A *Partition* of these Colonies will take Place if G.B. cant conquer Us. Destroying a House before We have got another. In Winter with a small Family. Then asking a Neighbor to take Us in. He unprepared.

4th. The Spirit of the Colonies calls for such a Declaration. Answer, not to be relied on. Not only Treaties with foreign powers but among Ourselves should precede this Declaration. We should know on what Grounds We are to stand with Regard to one another.

Declaration of Virginia about Colonies in *their Limits*.

The Committee on Confederation dispute almost every Article—some of Us totally despair of any reasonable Terms of Confederation.

We cannot look back. Men generally sell their Goods to most Advantage when they have several Chapmen. We have but two to rely on. We exclude one by this Declaration without knowing What the other will give.

G.B. after one or more unsuccessful Campaigns may be enduc'd to offer Us such a share of Commerce as would satisfy Us—to appoint Councillors during good Behaviour—to withdraw her armies—in short to redress all the Grievances complained of in our first Petition—to protect our Commerce—Establish our Militias. Let Us know, if We can get Terms from France that will be more beneficial than these. If We can, let Us declare Independance. If We cannot, let Us at least withhold that Declaration, till We obtain Terms that are tolerable.

We have many Points of the utmost moment to settle with France —Canada, Acadia, Cape Breton. What will Content her? Trade or Territory? What Conditions of Trade? Barbary Pirates. Spain. Portugal. Will she demand an Exclusive Trade as a Compensation or grant Us protection against piratical States only for a share of our Commerce?

When our Enemies are pressing us so vigorously, When We are in so wretched a State of preparation, When the Sentiments & Designs of our expected Friends are so unknown to Us, I am alarm'd at this Declaration being so vehemently prest. A worthy Gentleman told Us, that people in this House have had different Views for more than a 12 month. Amazing after what they have so repeatedly declared in this House & private Conversations—that they meant only Reconciliation. But since they can conceal their Views so dextrously, I should be glad to read a little more in the Doomsday Book of America—Not all—that like the Book of Fate might be too dreadful.

Title page—Binding. I should be glad to know whether in 20 or 30 Years this Commonwealth of Colonies may not be thought too unwieldy—& Hudson's River be a proper Boundary for a separate Commonwealth to the Northward. I have a strong Impression on my Mind that this will take place.

MS (PHi). In the hand of John Dickinson. Endorsed: "Arguments agt. the Independance of these Colonies—in Congress." For additional notes appearing at the end of this MS, see the following entry. These notes are strikingly cryptic and are strewn with abbreviations which have been expanded without brackets in this text.

[1] This document was identified and dated by John H. Powell in 1941, and no documents have since been discovered that challenge his assessment. "Speech of John Dickinson Opposing the Declaration of Independence, 1 July, 1776," *PMHB* 65 (October 1941): 458–81. Powell relied heavily upon Burnett's *Letters* and drew particularly from both John Adams' letter to Samuel Chase of this date and his autobiographical recollections. In this context, a well known passage from Adams' autobiography merits reprinting. "I am not able to recollect, whether it was on this [July 1], or some preceeding day, that the greatest and most solemn debate was had on the question of Independence. The Subject had been in Contemplation for more than a Year and frequent discussions had been had concerning it. At one time and another, all the Arguments for it and against it had been exhausted and were become familiar. I expected no more would be said in public but that the question would be put and decided. Mr. Dickinson however was determined to bear his Testimony against it with more formality. He had prepared himself apparently with great Labour and ardent Zeal, and in a Speech of great Length, and all his Eloquence, he combined together all that had before been written in Pamphlets and News papers and all that had from time to time been said in Congress by himself and others. He conducted the debate, not only with great Ingenuity and Eloquence, but with equal Politeness and Candour: and was answered in the same Spirit." Adams, *Diary* (Butterfield), 3:396; Burnett, *Letters*, 1:521–23.

Powell also made three other attempts to tell the story of the events of July 1, the last of which contains a critical analysis of Adams' reliability when reporting on his clashes with Dickinson. For Powell's final reflections on the subject, as well as on the initial estrangement between the two men that occurred the previous summer, see his two essays "'A Certain Great Fortune and Piddling Genius,'" and "The Day of American Independence," in John H. Powell, *General Washington and the Jack Ass, and Other American Characters, in Portrait* (South Brunswick, N.J.: Thomas Yoseloff, 1969), pp. 86–175, 314–23.

[2] At this point Dickinson wrote in the margin: "Drawing Resentment one proof of Virtue."

[3] In the margin: "Where Men differ, on which side is Passion?"

[4] Filipe Ferrero de Fiesco, prince de Masserano, Spanish ambassador to the court of St. James's. It is not known just what Dickinson knew of Spanish policy at this time or how he learned of the ambassador's activities in London, but it seems likely that Arthur Lee was his principal source of information on the response of European powers to the American rebellion. Although Americans hoped that both France and Spain would provide them aid and were led to believe this by Beaumarchais, Dickinson feared that it was hazardous to depend upon such assurances. For a second reference to Masserano in this speech, see note 8 below.

[5] Perhaps a reference to Silas Deane's arrival at Bermuda en route to France. Letters from Deane written from Bermuda on May 3 had already been received in Philadelphia. See Robert Morris to Silas Deane, June 5, 1776.

[6] Thraso was the name of a bragging soldier in Terence's comedy *The Eunuch*.

⁷ In the margin: "Even the mere Title of Royalty not assumed without consulting other Powers [. . . . all actual sovereignty?]."

⁸ At this point Powell wrote a lengthy note speculating on Dickinson's understanding of deteriorating Spanish-Portuguese relations and their possible impact on Spanish policy toward Britain. "Speech of John Dickinson," pp. 476–78n.100. Unfortunately, the entire discussion rests upon a misreading of Dickinson's notes and seriously distorts his simple point that it would be premature to act on independence until Congress had learned what reception Silas Deane had met in Europe.

In reconstructing Dickinson's speech, Powell supplied many connectives in brackets to cast it in the form of complete sentences. Thus he printed this passage as follows—brackets omitted: "France & Spain may be alarm'd & provoked with each other; Masserano was an insult to France." It seems clear, however, that Dickinson actually believed (1) that France and Spain might be alarmed and provoked with Congress, not with each other; and (2) that Congress' failure to await a response to the Deane mission, not Masserano's appointment, was an insult to France. In the MS "Masserano" appears at the end of a line; the following passage begins a new one. See also note 4 above.

John Dickinson's Notes on Arguments Concerning Independence

[July 1? 1776]

1st argument. Foreign States will not assist Us, untill We declare Independence. No Instance of it. Elizabeth helping Holland. Holland confederated with England. Answer. States governed by Interests. Elizabeth did not openly assist Holland till She was on the Point of *War* with Spain. Holland would not treat with Parliament when it had *conquered*—[. . . .] Charles 1st complained of French Embassadors corresponding with Parliament. Richelieu assisted Parliament.

It will convince People of England We are united—Whereas the Ministry tell them some of Us are afraid of Independence. Answer. The King's Speech expressly charges Us *all* with aiming at it.

2d. Joy in Virginia on Declaration—the same in every part of America. The Spirit of the People. Blood. Fires. Answer. Raised too much by Resentment.

3d. It will accelerate the People of the Colonies in establishing their Governments. Answer. People are going on as fast as they can.

4th. It will hasten the suppression of Toryism—ascertaining Offenders, trying them; prevent publication of Tory [declarations?]. Answer. That purpose will be effectually answered by establishing Governments.

5th. The People expect it. Answer. Let them know it is only deferred till a Confederation or a Treaty with Foreign Powers is concluded.

6th. The Army have set their Hearts upon it. It will encourage them. Answer. Terrible Enforcement of an Argument.

MS (PHi). In the hand of John Dickinson. These notes were written horizontally across the bottom of the last page of the notes printed in the preceding entry. Although it is not known for what specific purpose he drafted them, it is obvious they are epitomes of Dickinson's responses to the various arguments he had encountered in support of declaring independence.

John Hancock to George Washington

Sir,   Philadelphia July 1t. 1776.
    This will be delivered to you by Monsr. Antoine Felix Wiebert, a French Gentleman, who brings such ample Recommendation of his Skill, as an Engineer, that the Congress are desirous of having him placed in a Situation, where he may have it in his Power to shew it.[1] And, indeed, this is all he requests himself; being very willing, after his Abilities shall be put to the Trial, that his future Character and Promotion in the American Army, should depend on the Proofs he may give of his Capacity and Qualifications. I am therefore to request you will employ him in such Way, as you shall judge, will best conduce to the Good of the Service, and answer Monsr. Wiebert's Desire.[2]
    I have the Honour to be, Sir, your most obedt. & very hble Servant,
                                                    John Hancock Presidt

RC (DLC). In the hand of Jacob Rush and signed by Hancock.
    [1] Concerning Wiebert, see JCC, 5:477, 481; Washington, Writings (Fitzpatrick), 5:200, 221; and André Lasseray, Les Français sous les treize étoiles (1775–1783), 2 vols. (Macon and Paris: Imprimerie Protat Frères, 1935), 2:485–87. On August 14, 1776, Congress made Wiebert an "assistant engineer, with the rank and pay of lieutenant colonel" in the Continental Army. JCC, 5:656.
    [2] Hancock wrote another letter to Washington on this day in which he informed the general that Maj. Robert Rogers had arrived in Philadelphia in the custody of a Continental officer and was "under Guard at the Barracks." Washington Papers, DLC; and Am. Archives, 5th ser. 1:1. On July 6 Congress ordered Rogers, who had been arrested on account of his suspicious conduct, to be sent to New Hampshire "to be disposed of as the government of that state shall judge best," but Rogers escaped before this order could be carried out. JCC, 5:523; Washington, Writings (Fitzpatrick); William Ellery to Benjamin Ellery, July 10; and Josiah Bartlett to John Langdon, July 15, 1776. For further information about Rogers, see Richard Smith's Diary, September 20, 1775, note 3.

Thomas Jefferson's Notes of Proceedings in Congress

[July 1–4, 1776][1]
On Monday the 1st of July the house resolved itself into a commee.

of the whole & resumed the consideration of the original motion
made by the delegates of Virginia, which being again debated
through the day, was carried in the affirmative by the votes of N.
Hampshire, Connecticut, Massachusets, Rhode island, N. Jersey,
Maryland, Virginia, N. Carolina, & Georgia. S. Carolina and
Pennsylvania voted against it. Delaware having but two members
present, they were divided: the delegates for New York declared
they were for it themselves, & were assured their constituents were
for it, but that their instructions having been drawn near a twelvemonth before, when reconciliation was still the general object, they
were enjoined by them to do nothing which should impede that
object. They therefore thought themselves not justifiable in voting
on either side, and asked leave to withdraw from the question,
which was given them. The Commee. rose & reported their resolution
to the house. Mr. Rutlege of S. Carolina then requested the determination might be put off to the next day, as he believed his
collegues, tho' they disapproved of the resolution, would then join
in it for the sake of unanimity. The ultimate question whether the
house would agree to the resolution of the committee was accordingly postponed to the next day, when it was again moved and S.
Carolina concurred in voting for it.[2] In the mean time a third
member had come post from the Delaware counties and turned the
vote of that colony in favour of the resolution. Members of a different sentiment attending that morning from Pennsylvania also,
their vote was changed, so that the whole 12 colonies, who were
authorized to vote at all, gave their voices for it; and within a few
days [3] the convention of N. York approved of it and thus supplied
the void occasioned by the withdrawing of their delegates from the
vote.

Congress proceeded the same day to consider the declaration of
Independance,[2] which had been reported & laid on the table the
Friday preceding, and on Monday referred to a commee. of the
whole. The pusillanimous idea that we had friends in England
worth keeping terms with, still haunted the minds of many. For
this reason those passages which conveyed censures on the people of
England were struck out, lest they should give them offence. The
clause too, reprobating the enslaving the inhabitants of Africa, was
struck out in complaisance to South Carolina & Georgia, who had
never attempted to restrain the importation of slaves, and who on
the contrary still wished to continue it. Our Northern brethren also
I believe felt a little tender under those censures; for tho' their
people have very few slaves themselves yet they had been pretty
considerable carriers of them to others. The debates having taken
up the greater parts of the 2d 3d & 4th days of July were, in the
evening of the last closed.[4] The declaration was reported by the

commee., agreed to by the house, and signed by every member
present except Mr. Dickinson.[5] As the sentiments of men are known
not only by what they receive, but what they reject also, I will state
the form of the [6] declaration as originally reported. The parts struck
out by Congress shall be distinguished by a black line drawn under
them; & those inserted by them shall be placed in the margin or in a
concurrent column.

A Declaration by the representatives of the United States of
America, in General Congress assembled

When in the course of human events it becomes necessary for one
people to dissolve the political bands which have connected them
with another, and to assume among the powers of the earth the
separate & equal station to which the laws of nature and of nature's
god entitle them, a decent respect to the opinions of mankind requires that they should declare the causes which impel them to the
separation.

We hold these truths to be self evident: that all men are created
equal; that they are endowed by their creator with {certain} [7] inher-
ent and inalienable rights; that among these are life, liberty & the
pursuit of happiness: that to secure these rights, governments are
instituted among men, deriving their just powers from the consent
of the governed; that whenever any form of government becomes
destructive of these ends, it is the right of the people to alter or to
abolish it, & to institute new government, laying it's foundation on
such principles, & organising it's powers in such form, as to them shall
seem most likely to effect their safety & happiness. Prudence indeed
will dictate that governments long established should not be changed
for light & transient causes; and accordingly all experience hath
shewn that mankind are more disposed to suffer while evils are
sufferable than to right themselves by abolishing the forms to which
they are accustomed. But when a long train of abuses & usurpations
[begun at a distinguished period and] pursuing invariably the same
object, evinces a design to reduce them under absolute despotism it
is their right, it is their duty to throw off such government, & to
provide new guards for their future security. Such has been the
patient sufferance of these colonies; & such is now the necessity
which constrains them to {alter} [expunge] their former systems of
government. the history of the present king of Great Britain is a
history of {repeated} [unremitting] injuries & usurpations, [among
which appears no solitary fact to contradict the uniform tenor of
the rest but all have] {all having} in direct object the establishment
of an absolute tyranny over these states. to prove this let facts be
submitted to a candid world [for the truth of which we pledge a
faith yet unsullied by falsehood.]

He has refused his assent to laws the most wholsome & necessary for the public good.

He has forbidden his governors to pass laws of immediate & pressing importance, unless suspended in their operation till his assent should be obtained; & when so suspended, he has utterly neglected to attend to them.

He has refused to pass other laws for the accomodation of large districts of people, unless those people would relinquish the right of representation in the legislature, a right inestimable to them, & formidable to tyrants only.

He has called together legislative bodies at places unusual, uncomfortable, and distant from the depository of their public records, for the sole purpose of fatiguing them into compliance with his measures.

He has dissolved representative houses repeatedly [& continually] for opposing with manly firmness his invasions on the rights of the people.

He has refused for a long time after such dissolutions to cause others to be elected, whereby the legislative powers, incapable of annihilation, have returned to the people at large for their exercise, the state remaining in the mean time exposed to all the dangers of invasion from without & convulsions within.

He has endeavored to prevent the population of these states; for that purpose obstructing the laws for naturalization of foreigners, refusing to pass others to encourage their migrations hither, & raising the conditions of new appropriations of lands.

He has {obstructed} [suffered] the administration of justice [totally to cease in some of these states] {by} refusing his assent to laws for establishing judiciary powers.

He has made [our] judges dependant on his will alone, for the tenure of their offices, & the amount & paiment of their salaries.

He has erected a multitude of new offices [by a self assumed power] and sent hither swarms of new officers to harrass our people and eat out their substance.

He has kept among us in times of peace standing armies [and ships of war] without the consent of our legislatures.

He has affected to render the military independant of, & superior to the civil power.

He has combined with others to subject us to a jurisdiction foreign to our constitutions & unacknoleged by our laws, giving his assent to their acts of pretended legislation for quartering large bodies of armed troops among us; for protecting them by a mock-trial from punishment for any murders which they should commit on the inhabitants of these states; for cutting off our trade with all parts of the world; for imposing taxes on us without our consent;

for depriving us {in many cases} of the benefits of trial by jury; for transporting us beyond seas to be tried for pretended offences; for abolishing the free system of English laws in a neighboring province, establishing therein an arbitrary government, and enlarging it's boundaries, so as to render it at once an example and fit instrument for introducing the same absolute rule into these {colonies} [states]; for taking away our charters, abolishing our most valuable laws, and altering fundamentally the forms of our governments; for suspending our own legislatures, & declaring themselves invested with power to legislate for us in all cases whatsoever.

He has abdicated government here {by declaring us out of his protection & waging war against us.} [withdrawing his governors, and declaring us out of his allegiance & protection.]

He has plundered our seas, ravaged our coasts, burnt our towns, & destroyed the lives of our people.

He is at this time transporting large armies of foreign mercenaries to compleat the works of death, desolation & tyranny already begun with circumstances of cruelty and perfidy {scarcely paralleled in the most barbarous ages, & totally} unworthy the head of a civilized nation.

He has constrained our fellow citizens taken captive on the high seas to bear arms against their country, to become the executioners of their friends & brethren, or to fall themselves by their hands.

He has {excited domestic insurrections amongst us, & has} endeavored to bring on the inhabitants of our frontiers the merciless Indian savages, whose known rule of warfare is an undistinguished destruction of all ages, sexes, & conditions [of existence.]

[He has incited treasonable insurrections of our fellow-citizens, with the allurements of forfeiture & confiscation of our property.

He has waged cruel war against human nature itself, violating it's most sacred rights of life and liberty in the persons of a distant people who never offended him, captivating & carrying them into slavery in another hemisphere or to incur miserable death in their transportation thither. This piratical warfare, the opprobrium of *infidel* powers, is the warfare of the *Christian* king of Great Britain. Determined to keep open a market where *Men* should be bought & sold, he has prostituted his negative for suppressing every legislative attempt to prohibit or to restrain this execrable commerce. And that this assemblage of horrors might want no fact of distinguished die, he is now exciting those very people to rise in arms among us, and to purchase that liberty of which he has deprived them, by murdering the people on whom he also obtruded them: thus paying off former crimes committed against the *Liberties* of one people, with crimes which he urges them to commit again the *lives* of another.]

In every stage of these oppressions we have petitioned for redress in the most humble terms: our repeated petitions have been answered only by repeated injuries. A prince whose character is thus marked by every act which may define a tyrant is unfit to be the ruler of a {free} people [who mean to be free. Future ages will scarcely believe that the hardiness of one man adventured, within the short compass of twelve years only, to lay a foundation so broad & so undisguised for tyranny over a people fostered & fixed in principles of freedom.]

Nor have we been wanting in attentions to our British brethren. We have warned them from time to time of attempts by their legislature to extend {an unwarrantable} [a] jurisdiction over {us} [these our states.] We have reminded them of the circumstances of our emigration & settlement here, [no one of which could warrant so strange a pretension: that these were effected at the expence of our own blood & treasure, unassisted by the wealth or the strength of Great Britain: that in constituting indeed our several forms of government, we had adopted one common king, thereby laying a foundation for perpetual league & amity with them: but that submission to their parliament was no part of our constitution, nor ever in idea, if history may be credited: and,] we {have} appealed to their native justice and magnanimity {and we have conjured them by} [as well as to] the ties of our common kindred to disavow these usurpations which {would inevitably} [were likely to] interrupt our connection and correspondence. They too have been deaf to the voice of justice & of consanguinity, [and when occasions have been given them, by the regular course of their laws, of removing from their councils the disturbers of our harmony, they have, by their free election, re-established them in power. At this very time too they are permitting their chief magistrate to send over not only souldiers of our common blood, but Scotch & foreign mercenaries to invade & destroy us. These facts have given the last stab to agonizing affection, and manly spirit bids us to renounce for ever these unfeeling brethren. We must endeavor to forget our former love for them, and to hold them as we hold the rest of mankind enemies in war, in peace friends. We might have been a free and a great people together; but a communication of grandeur & of freedom it seems is below their dignity. Be it so, since they will it. The road to happiness & to glory is open to us too. We will tread it apart from them, and] {we must therefore} acquiesce in the necessity which denounces our [eternal] separation {and hold them as we hold the rest of mankind, enemies in war, in peace friends}!

We therefore the representatives of the United States of America in General Congress assembled do in the name, & by the authority of the good people of these [states reject & renounce all allegiance & subjection to the kings of Great Britain & all others who may hereafter claim by, through or under them: we utterly dissolve all political connection which may heretofore have subsisted between us & the people or parliament of Great Britain: & finally we do assert & declare these colonies to be free & independant states,] & that as free & independant states, they have full power to levy war, conclude peace, contract alliances, establish commerce, & to do all other acts & things which independant states may of right do. And for the support of this declaration we mutually pledge to each other our lives, our fortunes & our sacred honour.

We therefore the representatives of the United States of America in General Congress assembled, appealing to the supreme judge of the world for the rectitude of our intentions, do in the name, & by the authority of the good people of these colonies, solemnly publish & declare that these United colonies are & of right ought to be free & independant states; that they are absolved from all allegiance to the British crown, and that all political connection between them & the state of Great Britain is, & ought to be, totally dissolved; & that as free & independant states they have full power to levy war, conclude peace, contract alliances, establish commerce & to do all other acts & things which independant states may of right do. And for the support of this declaration, with a firm reliance on the protection of divine providence we mutually pledge to each other our lives, our fortunes & our sacred honour.[8]

MS (DLC). In the hand of Thomas Jefferson. A continuation of Jefferson's Notes of Proceedings in Congress, June 7–28, 1776.

[1] For a detailed analysis of the notes printed in this entry, see Jefferson, *Papers* (Boyd), 1:327–29.

[2] In the margin beside this sentence, Jefferson wrote "July 2."

[3] Jefferson inserted an asterisk at this point in the MS referring to the date he wrote in the margin, "July 9."

[4] Contrary to this explicit statement, it now seems clear that the debate on the Declaration was brought to a close in the morning rather than "in the evening" of July 4. See Committee of Congress to the Lancaster Associators, July 4, 1776, note 2.

[5] The credibility of Jefferson's notes has long been in question because of this passage indicating that on this day the Declaration was signed and John Dickinson was in attendance. While the consensus of authorities at present is that there was no general signing of the Declaration until August 2, the matter of Dickinson's attendance merits reassessment. It has long been assumed, on the authority of Thomas McKean, that Dickinson and Robert Morris, both opponents of independence, did not attend Congress on July 4, deliberately absenting themselves

so that Pennsylvania's vote could be cast in favor of independence. As McKean long afterward explained: "The State of Pennsylvania on the 4th. of July (there being five members present, Messrs. Dickinson and Morris, who had in the committee of the whole voted against Independence were absent) voted for it; three to two, Messrs. Willing and Humphries in the negative. Unanimity in the thirteen States, an all important point on so great an occasion, was thus obtained; the dissention of a single State might have produced very dangerous consequences." See Burnett, *Letters*, 1:534–45.

Despite McKean's precise explanation of the behavior of the Pennsylvania delegates, there is good reason to believe that his memory failed him on this point, and that Dickinson and Morris may have actually been in Congress on July 4. It should be noted, at any rate, that Dickinson's name appears as a member of the committee appointed that day to confer on the defense of New Jersey and Pennsylvania and that Morris was explicitly ordered by Congress that morning to inquire into a matter related to a vessel employed by the Continental Navy. It is of course possible that both these actions involving the two men could have been taken in their temporary absence, but it seems more likely that McKean's account of Pennsylvania's vote on independence pertains to the vote of July 2 on Richard Henry Lee's resolution rather than the vote on the Declaration on July 4. McKean related his version of this vote twice, in 1796 and in 1813, the first of which is known to be in error on the subject of the weather. Thus McKean wrote "On the 4th (which was a rainy day) Messrs. Dickinson and Morris were absent," but it is beyond doubt that although it rained for several hours in Philadelphia on July 2, July 4 was a clear day.

If, therefore, McKean is wrong about Dickinson's presence on July 4, it would be a great irony that Jefferson's credibility was long questioned because of this particular passage from his notes but escaped challenge on other points analyzed in this volume, such as the time of day the Declaration was adopted, now believed to be in error. See Jefferson's Notes of Proceedings in Congress, June 7–28, note 2; and Committee of Congress to the Lancaster Associators, July 4, 1776, note 2.

[6] For a discussion of the significant alterations that Jefferson made in this paragraph, see Jefferson, *Papers* (Boyd), 1:328n.15.

[7] The words appearing in these brackets, here and below, Jefferson wrote in the margin, indicating their placement with carets.

[8] For discussion of a controversial statement about the signing of the Declaration that Jefferson later wrote on a separate slip and inserted at this point in the MS, see Jefferson, *Papers* (Boyd), 1:301–8. For the continuation of these notes, see Jefferson's Notes of Proceedings in Congress, July 12–August 1, 1776.

Thomas Jefferson to William Fleming

Dear Fleming   Philadelphia. July 1. 1776.

Your's of 22d June came to hand this morning and gratified me much as this with your former contains interesting intelligence.[1]

Our affairs in Canada go still retrograde, but I hope they are now nearly at their worst. The fatal sources of these misfortunes have been want of hard money with which to procure provisions, the ravages of the small pox with which one half of our army is still down, and an unlucky choice of some officers. By our last letters,[2] Genl. Sullivan was retired as far as Isle au noix with his dispirited army and Burgoyne pursuing him with one of double or treble his numbers. It gives much concern that he had determined to make a stand there as it exposes to great danger of losing him and his army; and it was the universal sense of his officers that he ought to retire. Genl. Schuyler has sent him positive orders to retire to Crown Point but whether they will reach him time enough to withdraw him from danger is questionable. Here it seems to be the opinion of all the General officers that an effectual stand may be made and the enemy not only prevented access into New York, but by preserving a superiority on the lakes we may renew our attacks on them to advantage as soon as our army is recovered from the small pox and recruited. But recruits, tho long ordered, are very difficult to be procured on account of that dreadful disorder.

The Conspiracy at New York is not yet thoroughly developed, nor has any thing transpired, the whole being kept secret till the whole is got through. One fact is known of necessity, that one of the General's lifeguard being thoroughly convicted was to be shot last Saturday.[3] General Howe with some ships (we know not how many) is arrived at the Hook, and, as is said, has landed some horse on the Jersey shore. The famous Major Rogers is in custody on violent suspicion of being concerned in the conspiracy.

I am glad to hear of the Highlanders carried into Virginia. It does not appear certainly how many of these people we have but I imagine at least six or eight hundred. Great efforts should be made to keep up the spirits of the people the succeeding three months: which in the universal opinion will be the only ones in which our trial can be severe.

I wish you had depended on yourself rather than others for giving me an account of the late nomination of delegates.[4] I have no other state of it but the number of votes for each person. The omission of Harrison and Braxton and my being next to the lag give me some alarm. It is a painful situation to be 300. miles from one's country, and thereby open to secret assassination without a possibility of self-defence. I am willing to hope nothing of this kind has been done in my case, and yet I cannot be easy. If any doubt has arisen as to me, my country will have my political creed in the form of a 'Declaration &c.' which I was lately directed to draw. This will give decisive proof that my own sentiment concurred with the vote they instructed us to give. Had the post been to go a day later we might have been at liberty to communicate this whole matter.

July. 2. I have kept open my letter till this morning but nothing more new. Adieu.   Th. Jefferson

Reprinted from Jefferson, *Papers* (Boyd), 1:411–13.

[1] Fleming (1736–1824), Cumberland County lawyer and judge, member of the Virginia House of Delegates, 1776–81, and delegate to Congress, 1779, was a representative to the Virginia conventions in 1775 and 1776. *Bio. Dir. Cong.* His June 22 letter is in Jefferson, *Papers* (Boyd), 1:406.

² For the several letters relating to Canadian affairs that were read in Congress this day, see *JCC*, 5:503.

³ See Francis Lightfoot Lee to Richard Henry Lee, June 30, 1776, note 1.

⁴ See Jefferson to the President of the Virginia Convention, June 30, 1776, note 2.

Edward Rutledge to John Morgan

My dear Doctor   July 1. 1776.

As three of my young Countrymen are so principled in the Cause of Liberty as to undertake a Journey to New York for the purpose of yielding their Assistance to repel the Attacks of the Enemy, I have taken the Liberty of troubling you with a Letter of Introduction and trusting in your Friendship for me beg Leave to recommend them to your particuler Notice. I do not know how I could draw their Characters better than by saying that they are Gentlemen; nor could you desire a better Inducement to shew them Civilities than knowing they are my Friends. Should the Fortune of War occasion any Accident to befal them I know your Humanity will afford them every Relief. Our Compliments to Mrs. Morgan. Yours Sincerely & affectionately,   Edward Rutledge

RC (PHi). Addressed: "Doctor Morgan at New York. Favored by Messrs Smith, [Harleston?] & Burrows."

Oliver Wolcott to Matthew Griswold

Sir,   N York 1 July 1776

Your Honor's Favr of the 17t last have recd. and think the Requisition for men of our Colony unreasonable and can assign no other Reason for it's being done,¹ only that Favours are Apt to be asked of those who are supposed to be well inclined to grant them. What Exertions may be necessary no one can say in the present uncertainty of affairs. You will sir, be informed by the Papers of the Arrival of a large Fleet last Saturday at the Hook off this City. The taking the Cannon from N London is unhappy and founded in a Mistake of the Congress.² Commodore Hopkins said he left 36 heavy Cannon which were supposed to be 18 pounders and upwards at N London. Mr. Collins from N port said the same. The Congress said that if 14 were ordered from thence 22 heavy Cannon would be left, which was as much as could be spared for that Harbor and would be sufficient, but by Gov. Trumballs Letter to Congress this Acco. is contradicted. The Result is a Request to Gov. Trumbull to make a Return of the Number and Size of the Cannon there, which implys and was intended as a suspension of the Order in Case the Congress had been misinformed. The Committee of Congress have reported that N London Harbour ought to be fortified with 22 heavy Cannon at a continental Charge still going on the same Idea.[3] This Report I suppose will be Accepted. Mr. Hopkins I think is an odd man. I met him and Capt Salstonstall on Saturday going to the Congress who had sent for them.[4] Mr. Hopkins affected to be ignorant or did not really know what kind of Cannon had been left at N London. He never has made any Regular Return of the Cannon he had taken, and is tho't to have been Very difficient in many parts of his duty.

I am on my Way home for the Recovery of my Health and to see my Family. For three Weeks past have been much unwell, owing I suppose to a too long confined Way of living. Am now much better, and I hope a short Course of Exercise will restore me.

Before I left Philadelphia We had an Acco. that a fleet of about 50 Transports lay off Charlestown S Carolina. Undoptedly Clintons Troops were on Board them. Genl. Lee is now there.

Please sir to present my best Regards to my sister and your Family, and Accept this hasty Sketch from sir, your most humble Sevt.   Oliver Wolcott

RC (PHi).
[1] Jonathan Trumbull's letter of June 17, which was read in Congress on June 27, is in PCC, item 66, fols. 185–87, and *Am. Archives*, 4th ser. 6:944–45. On June 2 Congress had requested Connecticut to supply 1,500 militiamen for the army in Canada and on the following day requisitioned an additional 5,500 to reinforce Washington at New York. See *JCC*, 4:410, 412, 5:447.
[2] For information on Congress' request for cannon, see John Hancock to Esek Hopkins, May 7, 1776, note 2.
[3] For the recommendations of the committee on harbor fortifications, which were submitted to Congress on June 24, see *JCC*, 5:476.
[4] On June 13 Congress had directed the Marine Committee to call Commodore Esek Hopkins and Capts. Dudley Saltonstall and Abraham Whipple to Philadelphia to answer complaints about their conduct. *JCC*, 5:439. For the congressional examination that followed, see Thomas Jefferson's Notes on the Inquiry into Esek Hopkins' Conduct, August 12, 1776.

John Adams to Samuel Cooper

Dear Sir,   Philadelphia July 2. 1776
Your obliging Favour of 17 June is now before me.[1] It contains an elegant and masterly Narration of the late Expedition against the British Men of War, in Nantaskett Road, and its happy and glorious Event. I am a little mortified however that my good Friends and Neighbours the Militia of Braintree, Weymouth and Hingham, did not execute their Part with So much activity, as they ought. But the very Post which brought us this agreable Intelligence from Boston, brought Us from Canada, the melancholly Tidings

that our Army had evacuated Canada, with such a Complication of Circumstances, of Famine, Pestilence, Distress, Defeat, and Disgrace, as are sufficient to humble a prouder Heart than mine.

The Small Pox is an Enemy more terrible in my Imagination, than all others. This Distemper will be the ruin of every Army from New England if great Care is not taken. I am really Sorry that the Town of Boston attempted to clear itself of the Infection. I cannot but wish that an innoculating Hospital was set up in every Town in New England. But if this is not done, I am sure that some Hospitals ought to be erected in Some convenient Places.

Between you and me, I begin to think it Time for our Colony to think a little more highly of itself. The military operations have been at least as well conducted, under our own officers, when left to themselves, as any others. You and several others of my best Friends have been pressing for a Stranger to command in Boston, and from two political Motives, I have been pressing for it too. The one was this, the People, and the Soldiery, at Boston, would not be so likely to respect a general from among themselves, as a Stranger. The other was that the People of the Southern and middle Colonies would have more Confidence in one of their own officers, than in one from New England. And in Case of any Thing Unlucky I had rather hear them groan for one of their own, than scold or curse at a New England man.

The Reverse of Fortune in Canada, and the Arrival of the Hallifax Fleet, at Sandy Hook have now removed all Expectation of having such an officer Sent to Boston as We wished, and therefore I wish that some Massachusetts Man will command at Boston.

Since the above was written, I have recd a Letter from Braintree containing a very circumstantial Relation of the Expedition against the Men of War,[2] by which I find that my Neighbours were not in fault. They were becalmed and by that unforeseen and unavoidable Accident, retarded and belated. I am &c.

LB (MHi).
[1] An extract of Cooper's June 17 letter, which is in the Adams Papers, MHi, is in Clark, *Naval Documents*, 5:577–79.
[2] See Mary Palmer to John Adams, June 15, 1776, Adams, *Family Correspondence* (Butterfield), 2:9–12.

Josiah Bartlett to Mary Bartlett

[*Philadelphia*] *July 2nd 1776.* "I shall write here Some things that you or the Children may have a Curiosity to Know altho of no great importance. . . . A few Days ago I rode out about 6 miles to Germantown before Breakfast for exercise. I went in to See the Brittish Museum so Called. It is a house Built on purpose to pre-

serve all the natural Curiosities that Can be Collected from all parts
of the world as Birds, beasts, fish, Shells, Snakes, plants & a great
many other Curiosities. Among them there was a Shark, a Crocodile,
a Cat fish, a Dog fish, a Sea porcupine, a Creature Called a Hog in
armour, 2 ostrich's Eggs which were perfectly round & of the Colour
of Ivory and I Guess would hold a pint & an half Each. There was a
great many other Creature of a Strange make from any thing I Ever
Saw before & whose names I have forgot as I had but a little time
there. Snakes Skins Stuft among them a Small Alligators Skin &c &c
&c." Reports availability of some fruits and vegetables at Philadelphia
and prices of a few articles of clothing.

RC (NhHi). Page one of four-page letter missing.

Elbridge Gerry to James Warren

Dear sir,   Philadelphia 2d July 1776
    I have only Time to inform You that Yesterday was agitated in
Congress the great Question of Independancy, & as the Facts are as
well known at the Coffee House of the City as in Congress I may go
on to inform You that in a Committee of the Whole House It was
carryed by nine Colonies.
    I remain sir with due Regards, your assured Friend & huml serv,
                                                      Elbridge Gerry

RC (Facsimile, Austin, *Life of Gerry*, following p. 196).

Joseph Hewes to Samuel Purviance, Jr.

Dear sir,   Philadelphia, 2d July, 1776.
    When I wrote to you last, I believe I mentioned to you only two
lieutenants for the ship.[1] It was a mistake. Three are allowed to
each of the frigates, so that, when Capt. Nicholson sends up a
recommendation for sea officers, he should put down three lieutenants. Part of General Howe's army is arrived at Sandy Hook. We
must expect warm work in that quarter in a few days.
    I am, with respect, sir, Your most obedient servant,
                                                      Joseph Hewes.

MS not found; reprinted from Robert Purviance, *A Narrative of Events which
occurred in Baltimore Town during the Revolutionary War* (Baltimore: Jos.
Robinson, 1849), p. 198.
[1] See Hewes to Samuel Purviance, Jr., June 25, 1776.

Marine Committee to John Barry

Sir   Philada. July 2nd. 1776

As we find our coast is now lined with Men of War of too great force for you to cope With, We think it can be of little use for you to remain cooped up at Cape May, and as the frigate You are to command is not yet launched,[1] her guns & anchors not yet ready, We think it a piece of justice due to your Merit to allow you to make a cruize in the Lexington for one or two Months, in hopes that fortune may favour your industry and reward it with some good Prizes. We send you a printed copy of the resolves of Congress respecting Prizes,[2] by which you will learn what to take and what to let pass, a list of the Agents you have already, and to them your prizes must be addressed. We think North Carolina is likely to remain unmolested by the Men of Warr, and, if so, your prizes may probably get safe in there. Cape May or Egg Harbour may also be safe places, however you must use your own discretion in this respect.

If you gain any intelligence during this cruize that you think may be useful, convey it to us as soon as possible. Capt Robinson of the Sloop Sachem has also liberty to make a cruize and probably it may be advantageous that you go in concert.[3]

Wishing you success & honor, We are sir Your Friends, (Signed by the Marine Committee).   Copy J Hancock

Tr (PHi). Endorsed: "Copy from the Original. July 13, 1776. T[imoth]y Matlack, Sec[retar]y Mar[ine] Com[mittee]."

[1] The frigate in question was the *Effingham,* which Barry had been appointed to command on June 6. See *JCC,* 5:423; and John Hancock to Thomas Cushing, June 12, 1776.

[2] For information about the publication of Congress' April 3, 1776, resolves on prize ships, see *JCC,* 6:1119–20. See also *JCC,* 4:253–54.

[3] This day Francis Lewis, a member of the marine committee, wrote a letter to Capt. Thomas Grenell, commander of the frigate *Montgomery,* of which only this extract has been found: "I received your letter of the 25th ultimo, which I shall lay before the marine committee when next they meet; and shall urge the requisitions you make and have no doubt of their being complied with." *Journals of N.Y. Prov. Cong.,* 2:504; and *JCC,* 5:444.

New York Delegates to the New York Provincial Congress

Gentlemen   Philadelphia 2d July 1776.

The important Question of Indepency was agitated yesterday in a Committee of the whole Congress, and this Day will be finally determined in the House. We know the Line of our Conduct on this Occasion; we have your Instructions, and will faithfully pursue them. New Doubts and Difficulties however will arise should Independency be declared; and that it will not, we have not the least Reason to expect nor do we believe that (if any) more than one Colony (and the Delegates of that divided) will vote against the Question; every Colony (ours only excepted) having withdrawn their former Instructions, and either positively instructed their Delegates to vote for Independency; or concur in such Vote if they shall judge it expedient. What Part are we to act after this Event takes Place; every Act we join in may then be considered as in some Measure acceding to the Vote of Independency, and binding our Colony on that Score. Indeed many matters in this new Situation may turn up in which the Propriety of our voting may be very doubtful; tho we conceive (considering the critical Situation of Public Affairs and as they respect our Colony in particular invaded or soon likely to be by Powerful Armies in different Quarters) it is our Duty nay it is absolutely necessary that we shoud not only concur with but exert ourselves in forwarding our Military Operations. The immediate safety of the Colony calls for and will warrant us in this. Our Situation is singular and delicate No other Colony being similarly circumstanced with whom we can consult. We wish therefore for your earliest Advice and Instructions whether we are to consider our Colony bound by the Vote of the Majority in Favour of Indepency and vote at large on such Questions as may arise in Consequence thereof or only concur in such Measures as may be absolutely necessary for the Common safety and defence of America exclusive of the Idea of Indepency. We fear it will be difficult to draw the Line; but once possessd of your Instructions we will use our best Endeavours to follow them.[1]

We are with the greatest Respect your Most Obedt Servts.

Geo. Clinton. John Alsop.

Henry Wisner. Wm. Floyd.

Fras. Lewis.

MS not found; reprinted from Burnett, *Letters*, 1:524–25, where it is described as "in the writing of George Clinton."

[1] The New York Convention, which had adjourned from New York City on June 30 in response to the arrival of British troops off Staten Island, took up this letter on July 9 when it reconvened at White Plains. At that time it approved the decision of Congress to declare independence and authorized the New York delegates "to consent to and adopt all such measures as they may deem conducive to the happiness and welfare of the United States of America." *Am. Archives*, 5th ser. 1:1387–91.

Henry Wisner to the
New York Provincial Congress

Gentlemen,   Philadelphia, July 2d, 1776.
Since Writeing the enclosed, the question of independance has Been put in Congress, and carried in the affirmative without one dissenting vote. I therefore beg your answer as quick as possible, to the enclosed.[1]
I am, with due regard, your humble servant,
                                                            Henry Wisner.

MS not found; reprinted from Burnett, *Letters*, 1:525.
[1] See New York Delegates to the New York Provincial Congress, this date.
Wisner himself took a seat in the New York Convention at White Plains on July 23. It is not known what day he left Philadelphia, but he subsequently submitted a claim for £102 8s for his "Services as a Delegate at the Continental Congress from May 22 to July 22 . . . and 2 Days more for going home from the White Plains." *Am. Archives*, 5th ser. 1:1432; and Henry Wisner Account, August 13–15, 1776, Miscellaneous MSS, N.

John Adams to Abigail Adams

                                                 Philadelphia July 3. 1776
Your Favour of June 17 dated at Plymouth, was handed me, by Yesterdays Post. I was much pleased to find that you had taken a Journey to Plymouth, to see your Friends in the long Absence of one whom you may wish to see. The Excursion will be an Amusement, and will serve your Health. How happy would it have made me to have taken this Journey with you?
I was informed, a day or two before the Receipt of your Letter, that you was gone to Plymouth, by Mrs. Polly Palmer, who was obliging enough in your Absence, to inform me, of the Particulars of the Expedition to the lower Harbour against the Men of War. Her Narration is executed, with a Precision and Perspicuity, which would have become the Pen of an accomplished Historian.[1]
I am very glad you had so good an opportunity of seeing one of our little American Men of War. Many Ideas, new to you, must have presented themselves in such a Scene; and you will in future, better understand the Relations of Sea Engagements.
I rejoice extreamly at Dr. Bulfinches Petition to open an Hospital. But I hope, the Business will be done upon a larger Scale. I hope, that one Hospital will be licensed in every County, if not in every Town. I am happy to find you resolved, to be with the Children, in

the first Class.[2] Mr. Whitney and Mrs. Katy Quincy are cleverly through Innoculation, in this City.

I have one favour to ask, and that is, that in your future Letters, you would acknowledge the Receipt of all those you may receive from me, and mention their Dates. By this Means I shall know if any of mine miscarry.

The Information you give me of our Friends refusing his Appointment, has given me much Pain, Grief and Anxiety. I believe I shall be obliged to follow his Example.[3] I have not Fortune enough to support my Family, and what is of more Importance, to support the Dignity of that exalted Station. It is too high and lifted up, for me; who delight in nothing so much as Retreat, Solitude, Silence, and Obscurity. In private Life, no one has a Right to censure me for following my own Inclinations, in Retirement, Simplicity, and Frugality: in public Life, every man has a Right to remark as he pleases, at least he thinks so.

Yesterday the greatest Question was decided, which ever was debated in America, and a greater perhaps, never was or will be decided among Men. A Resolution was passed without one dissenting Colony "that these united Colonies, are, and of right ought to be free and independent States, and as such, they have, and of Right ought to have full Power to make War, conclude Peace, establish Commerce, and to do all the other Acts and Things, which other States may rightfully do." You will see in a few days a Declaration setting forth the Causes, which have impell'd Us to this mighty Revolution, and the Reasons which will justify it, in the Sight of God and Man. A Plan of Confederation will be taken up in a few days.

When I look back to the Year 1761, and recollect the Argument concerning Writs of Assistance, in the Superiour Court, which I have hitherto considered as the Commencement of the Controversy, between Great Britain and America, and run through the whole Period from that Time to this, and recollect the series of political Events, the Chain of Causes and Effects, I am surprized at the Suddenness, as well as Greatness of this Revolution. Britain has been fill'd with Folly, and America with Wisdom, at least this is my Judgment. Time must determine. It is the Will of Heaven, that the two Countries should be sundered forever. It may be the Will of Heaven that America shall suffer Calamities still more wasting and Distresses yet more dreadfull. If this is to be the Case, it will have this good Effect, at least: it will inspire Us with many Virtues, which We have not, and correct many Errors, Follies, and Vices, which threaten to disturb, dishonour, and destroy Us. The Furnace of Affliction produces Refinement, in States as well as Individuals. And the new Governments we are assuming, in every Part, will require a Purification from our Vices, and an Augmentation of our Virtues or they will be no Blessings. The People will have unbounded Power. And the People are extreamly addicted to Corruption and Venality, as well as the Great.[4] I am not without Apprehensions from this Quarter. But I must submit all my Hopes and Fears, to an overruling Providence, in which, unfashionable as the Faith may be, I firmly believe.

RC (MHi). Adams, *Family Correspondence* (Butterfield), 2:27–28.

[1] See Mary Palmer to John Adams, June 15, 1776, Adams, *Family Correspondence* (Butterfield), 2:9–12.

[2] Abigail and the Adams children were inoculated by Thomas Bulfinch in July. See Abigail Adams to John Adams, July 13–14, 1776, ibid., pp. 45–47.

[3] James Warren had refused an appointment as justice of the Massachusetts Superior Court of Judicature.

[4] The following sentence was apparently inadvertently omitted in the RC and is here taken from the LB in the Adams Papers, MHi.

John Adams to Abigail Adams

Philadelphia July 3d. 1776

Had a Declaration of Independency been made seven Months ago, it would have been attended with many great and glorious Effects. . . .[1] We might before this Hour, have formed Alliances with foreign States. We should have mastered Quebec and been in Possession of Canada. . . . You will perhaps wonder, how such a Declaration would have influenced our Affairs, in Canada, but if I could write with Freedom I could easily convince you, that it would, and explain to you the manner how. Many Gentlemen in high Stations and of great Influence have been duped, by the ministerial Bubble of Commissioners to treat. . . . And in real, sincere Expectation of this Event, which they so fondly wished, they have been slow and languid, in promoting Measures for the Reduction of that Province. Others there are in the Colonies who really wished that our Enterprise in Canada would be defeated, that the Colonies might be brought into Danger and Distress between two Fires, and be thus induced to submit. Others really wished to defeat the Expedition to Canada, lest the Conquest of it, should elevate the Minds of the People too much to hearken to those Terms of Reconciliation which they believed would be offered Us. These jarring Views, Wishes and Designs, occasioned an opposition to many salutary Measures, which were proposed for the Support of that Expedition, and caused Obstructions, Embarrassments and studied Delays, which have finally, lost Us the Province.

All these Causes however in Conjunction would not have disappointed Us, if it had not been for a Misfortune, which could not be foreseen, and perhaps could not have been prevented, I mean the

Prevalence of the small Pox among our Troops. . . . This fatal
Pestilence compleated our Destruction. It is a Frown of Providence
upon Us, which We ought to lay to heart.

But on the other Hand, the Delay of this Declaration to this
Time, has many great Advantages attending it. The Hopes of Reconciliation, which were fondly entertained by Multitudes of honest
and well meaning tho weak and mistaken People, have been gradually and at last totally extinguished. Time has been given for the
whole People, maturely to consider the great Question of Independence and to ripen their Judgments, dissipate their Fears, and al-
lure their Hopes, by discussing it in News Papers and Pamphletts,
by debating it, in Assemblies, Conventions, Committees of Safety
and Inspection, in Town and County Meetings, as well as in private
Conversations, so that the whole People in every Colony of the 13,
have now adopted it, as their own Act. This will cement the Union,
and avoid those Heats and perhaps Convulsions which might have
been occasioned, by such a Declaration Six Months ago.

But the Day is past. The Second Day of July 1776, will be the
most memorable Epocha, in the History of America. I am apt to
believe that it will be celebrated, by succeeding Generations, as the
great anniversary Festival. It ought to be commemorated, as the
Day of Deliverance by solemn Acts of Devotion to God Almighty. It
ought to be solemnized with Pomp and Parade, with Shews, Games,
Sports, Guns, Bells, Bonfires and Illuminations from one End of
this Continent to the other from this Time forward forever more.

You will think me transported with Enthusiasm but I am not. I
am well aware of the Toil and Blood and Treasure, that it will cost
Us to maintain this Declaration, and support and defend these
States. Yet through all the Gloom I can see the Rays of ravishing
Light and Glory. I can see that the End is more than worth all the
Means. And that Posterity will tryumph in that Days Transaction,
even altho We should rue it, which I trust in God We shall not.[2]

RC (MHi). Adams, *Family Correspondence* (Butterfield), 2:29–31.
  [1] Suspension points in MS, here and below.
  [2] For the provenance and publication history of this celebrated letter, see Adams,
Family Correspondence (Butterfield), 2:31n.9.

John Hancock to
Certain Pennsylvania Committees

Gentlemen,   Philada. July 3d. 1776.
You are so well acquainted with the critical and alarming State of
our public Affairs, that it is unnecessary to use Arguments to press

you to a Compliance with any Resolves of Congress calculated to promote the Cause of Liberty in the United Colonies of America.

I am therefore to request by order of Congress that the Troops, you are raising to form the flying Camp, may be sent to the City of Philada. with the utmost Expedition.[1]

That they may arrive the sooner, it is the Desire of Congress you will send them by Battalions, or Detachments of Battalions, or Companies as fast as raised.

I am persuaded the Comee. of   [2] will strain every Nerve to comply with this Requisition of Congress, with all the Dispatch which the infinite Importance of the present Situation of Affairs requires.

I have the Honour to be, Gentlemen, your most obed. & very hble Serv,   J. H. Prst.

LB (DNA: PCC, item 12A). Addressed: "To the Comee of Philadelphia. Comee of Chester County. Comee of Bucks County. Come. of Berks County. Come. of Northampton County. Come. of Lancaster County. Come. of York County. Come. of Cumberland."

[1] See *JCC*, 4:400, 412–13, 5:508.

[2] Blank in MS left for insertion of name of appropriate Pennsylvania committee, depending on recipient. The responses of several of the committees to this appeal are in PCC, item 69, fols. 149, 154, 157, 161, 169, 185–86.

John Witherspoon to the
New Jersey Provincial Congress

Sir   Philadelphia July 3. 1776

This afternoon Mr Philip Livingston of New York told me that one of our Delegates at Burlington desired him to tell me that Mr. [William] Franklin was carried no further than Hackinsack & refused to go any further. I spoke to Mr Hancock a few minutes after who gave me the enclosed Letter to you [1] & expressed great Surprise that the Guard we sent with him had not proceeded Straightaway to Gov. Trumbull. Possibly you may have already taken order in this Matter; if not I hope it will be done immediately.

The Congress this Day read your Letter & ordered a Battalion to march to Monmouth & have also directed that the Militia of three Counties of Pensilvania intended for part of the flying Camp should rendevous at Brunswick & be there as soon as possible.[2] I am Sir Your most obedt, humble Servant,   Jno Witherspoon

RC (MeHi).

[1] Possibly a copy of John Hancock to the New Jersey Provincial Convention, June 24, 1776.

[2] In reality Congress only agreed to ask the Pennsylvania Committee of Safety

to send such troops "as they can spare" to Monmouth County, New Jersey. *JCC*, 5:508. Congress took this step in response to a July 2 letter from John Covenhoven, vice president of the New Jersey Provincial Congress, reporting a gathering of armed tories in Monmouth. PCC, item 68, fols. 161, 164; and *Am. Archives*, 5th ser. 1:1–2. For further details about this episode, see *Am. Archives*, 4th ser. 6:1633, 1636–37, 5th ser. 1:37, 139.

Abraham Clark to Elias Dayton

My Dear friend,   Phila. July 4th. 1776.
   Our Seeming bad Success in Canada, I dare say gives you great uneasiness. In Times of danger, and under misfortunes, true Courage and Magnanimity can only be Ascertained. In the Course of Such a War we must expect some Losses. We are told a Panick Seized the Army. If so it hath not reached the Senate. At the Time our Forces in Canada were retreating before a Victorious Army, while Genl. Howe with a Large Armament is Advancing towards N. York, Our Congress Resolved to Declare the United Colonies *Free and independent States.* A Declaration for this Purpose, I expect, will this day pass Congress, it is nearly gone through, after which it will be Proclaimed with all the State & Solemnity Circumstances will admit. It is gone so far that we must now be a free independent State, or a Conquered Country.[1]
   I can readily guess at your feelings upon hearing that Genl Howe with 130 Transports are between N. York & the Hook. This was our last Acct., no express hath come in this morning. All seems Uncertainty where they will Land, I assure you I don't feel quite reconciled at being here and the Enemy by my door at home. All reports Agree that New Jersey is all in motion to meet the Enemy in Case they pay our Province a Visit, or to Assist N. York as Occasion may require. Had Genl. Howe Landed his forces as soon as he Arrived he might have Carried all before him. Possibly while I am Writing this he may be reaping the Fruits of a Victory. This seems now to be a trying season, but that indulgent Father who hath hitherto Preserved us will I trust appear for our help, and prevent our being Crushed; If otherwise, his Will be done.
   I have no Particular News more to Communicate. No news from Your family to send. I wrote you the day before I left home. I am Among a Consistory of Kings as our Enemy Says. I assure you Sir, Our Congress is An August Assembly—and can they Support the Declaration now on the Anvil, they will be the greatest Assembly on Earth.
   As I am not Able to Communicate to you any thing but what the Public Papers will Announce, you will readily perceive I mean to let you know you are not forgot by me. Tho' I address my self to

you Sir, yet I mean to include my much esteemed friend Mr Caldwell in it.

We are now Sir embarked on a most Tempestious Sea, Life very
uncertain, Seeming dangers Scattered thick Around us, Plots
Against the Military, and it is Whispered, Against the Senate. Let
us prepare for the worst, we can Die here but once. May all our
Business, all our purposes & pursuits tend to fit us for that important event. I am Dr sir, Yours & Mr Caldwells most Obedient &
Huml Servt.   Abra. Clark

RC (PHi). Addressed: "To Elias Dayton Esqr., Colonel of the third battalion of
N. Jersey Forces, at Johns Town, Mohawk River, or Crown Point, to be forwarded
to their Station from Albany."
  [1] Clark was a member of the delegation elected by the New Jersey Provincial
Congress on June 22 and empowered to join with other delegates "in declaring the
United Colonies independent of Great Britain, entering into a Confederacy for
union and common defense, [and] making treaties with foreign nations for commerce and assistance." Am. Archives, 4th ser. 6:1628–29. In an earlier letter to
Dayton, Clark had observed of this election: "The Continental Congress are to
determine next Monday upon Independency. I am going among them to Morrow.
We have a New set of Delegates—Judge Stockton, Francis Hopkinson, Doctor
Witherspoon, John Hart & myself. We have raised 5 battalions to go to N. York,
they are now nearly raised & will I expect begin to March to Morrow. Mr. [Wil-
liam] Livingston was appointed to Command them, after Joseph Read [Reed], Who
was first Appointed had declined. Mr. Livingston hath declined he told me yesterday, and seems much Chagarened at his being left out of Congress, and there is
not wanting some who endeavour to persuade him that it was through my means
to Supplant him, which was far from true. I used my Endeavours to get him continued in, and it is much against my Will that I am Appointed." Clark to Elias
Dayton, June 26, 1776, Sparks Papers, MH. Jonathan Dickinson Sergeant, who was
not a member of the new delegation, also made some pertinent comments about
this election. "I have declined being appointed anew to the Continental Congress
for reasons which I have not Room to explain (this being the only white piece of
Paper in Bristol). However You will have a sound Delegation & they were instructed to vote right. . . . I am confident it is better that I stay in the Colony
for the present than in the Continental Congress. . . . The People of this Colony
were quite in the dark as to the Sentiments of the Delegates till lately. Our new
ones I trust will not deceive us; but lest they should I wish I could secretly learn
their Conduct whenever they may by any Means be found tripping. The others
were spoilt among You & I hope You will think this hint worth attending to."
Sergeant to Samuel Adams, June 24, 1776, Samuel Adams Papers, NN.

Committee of Congress to the
Lancaster Associators

Gentlemen,[1]   Philadelphia, July 4th, 1776,
  The Congress this morning [2] directed us to confer with the Committees of Safety and Inspection, and the Field Officers now in
town, about the proper mode of collecting the militia of this province, in order to form a flying camp, to cover Pennsylvania and

Philadelphia, July 4th, 1776,

GENTLEMEN,

THE Congrefs this morning directed us to confer with the Committees of Safety and Infpection, and the Field Officers now in town, about the proper
mode of collecting the militia of this province, in order to form a flying camp, to
cover Pennfylvania and New-Jerfey, from the Attacks of the Enemy, who have
landed on Statten-Ifland, and will probably direct their March this Way, if they
fhould imagine the Attempt on New-York too hazardous. Neceffity obliges us to
difpenfe with forms, and to avail ourfelves of the advantage, which we may rea-
fonably hope from your being affembled : We, therefore, moft earneftly requeft
you immediately to collect the Forces of your feveral Counties, and march them
down to Brunfwick, where the Congrefs will furnifh them with provifions, and
allow them Continental pay.

Men who-have the fafety of their country at heart, need no other incentive to the
greateft exertions, than fuch as arifes from its danger; for which reafon, we have
thought it neceffary barely to inform you of the fact; with this addition, that the
Militia of New-Jerfey are already, for the moft part, in New-York; fo that that
province will be defencelefs without your timely aid.

We are Gentlemen, your moft obedient humble fervants,

B. FRANKLIN,   ROBT. R. LIVINGSTON, ⎫
F. HOPKINSON, J. DICKINSON   ⎬ Committee of CONGRESS:
                                    ⎭

To the Committee of Affociators, ⎫
        at Lancafter.   ⎬

GENTLEMEN,

WE beg your moft ferious attention to the contents of the within letter, and
by the defire of the Committee of Congrefs, fignify to you our approbation thereof, and that it is our opinion only the four thoufand five hundred men
are meant by the Committee. It is hoped thofe volunteers who have engaged to
ferve in the flying camp, will march immediately the nigheft way to Brunfwick, in
New-Jerfey, and that regular mufter-rolls will be kept by the colonels of the feveral battalions.

As foon as a company is formed, it is expected it will march without waiting
for the battalion. As there is to be a conference between the Delegates of New-
York, New-Jerfey, and Pennfylvania, and the Committee of Safety, with this
Committee, and the Field-Officers of the five battalions of this city and the liberties, to-morrow morning, at the State-Houfe, at feven o' clock, we will let
you know the refult of their confultation.

Signed by Order of the Committee,

THOMAS M'KEAN, *Chairman:*

Philadelphia, Committee-Chamber, July 4th, 1776:

To the Convention of Affociators, of the ⎫
Province of Pennfylvania, at Lancafter.   ⎬

Committee of Congress Letter of July 4, 1776

New-Jersey, from the Attacks of the Enemy, who have landed on Statten-Island, and will probably direct their March this Way, if they should imagine the Attempt on New-York too hazardous. Necessity obliges us to dispense with forms, and to avail ourselves of the advantage, which we may reasonably hope from your being assembled: We, therefore, most earnestly request you immediately to collect the Forces of your several Counties, and march them down to Brunswick, where the Congress will furnish them with provisions, and allow them Continental pay.[3]

Men who have the safety of their country at heart, need no other incentive to the greatest exertions, than such as arises from its danger; for which reason, we have thought it necessary barely to inform you of the fact; with this addition, that the Militia of New-Jersey are already, for the most part, in New-York; so that *that* province will be defenceless without your timely aid.

We are Gentlemen, your most obedient humble servants,

B. Franklin,   Robt. R. Livingston,⎱
                                       ⎰ Committee of Congress
F. Hopkinson, J. Dickinson   ⎰

RC (DLC). Addressed: "To the Committee of Associators, at Lancaster." Distributed as a broadside with a letter of recommendation from the Philadelphia Committee of Safety (see illustration). The delegates' letter was drafted by Robert R. Livingston, for the text of which see below, note 2.

[1] In order to facilitate formation of the flying camp of militiamen from Delaware, Maryland, and Pennsylvania, which Congress had authorized on June 3 and for which additional instructions were issued on July 3, the New York, New Jersey, and Pennsylvania delegates were ordered on July 4 to confer with certain Pennsylvania political and military authorities "on the best means of defending the colonies of New Jersey and Pennsylvania." *JCC*, 4:412–13, 5:508, 516. Apparently operating under a sense of great urgency, the delegates involved met, approved a letter drafted by Robert R. Livingston explaining their plans, arranged to have it printed, and dispatched a rider to Lancaster with copies of it, all before the day was out. Furthermore, they held a conference the following morning at seven o'clock at which several decisions were reached that were immediately laid before Congress and endorsed in the form of a series of resolutions that were soon after distributed as a broadside and inserted in the Philadelphia newspapers. See *JCC*, 5:519–20; and, for the proceedings of the conference of July 5, *Am. Archives*, 5th ser. 1:14–15. Christopher Marshall is the authority for the statement that Livingston's letter was dispatched to Lancaster the night of July 4. "An express was sent off . . . near ten o'clock by request of a Committee of Congress, with a letter to the meeting of officers at Lancaster, in order to request them to expedite the six thousand men appointed to compose the Flying Camp. . . . The said Committee of Congress requested this Committee [i.e., the Philadelphia Committee of Safety] to meet a Committee of the members of New York, Jerseys, Lower Counties, officers of the Five Battalions and Safety, at seven to-morrow morning, at the State House, to take into consideration what may be necessary to be done in this critical situation." William Duane, ed., *Extracts from the Diary of Christopher Marshall, kept in Philadelphia and Lancaster, during the American Revolution, 1774–1781* (Albany: Joel Munsell, 1877), p. 82.

[2] This statement, that Congress "this morning" directed the committee to confer with the several groups specified, provides the best evidence available for deter-

mining the approximate time at which the Declaration of Independence was adopted, a question that has long puzzled scholars and remained unanswered until the significance of this letter was discovered.

It has traditionally been believed that Congress devoted most of July 4 to the final debate on the Declaration and that it was adopted late in the day. The evidence for this belief is from the hand of the author of the Declaration himself— as Jefferson explained the matter in his famous notes: "The debates having taken up the greater parts of the 2d. 3d. & 4th days of July were, in the evening of the last closed. The declaration was reported by the commee., agreed to by the house, and signed by every member present except Mr. Dickinson." Although Jefferson's statement does not fit easily with the evidence available in Secretary Thomson's journal, and despite the fact that the Declaration was not signed until August 2, no effort has been made heretofore to challenge Jefferson's claim that the final debate on the Declaration consumed most of July 4 and the vote on its adoption was not taken until "the evening."

The puzzling aspect of Jefferson's version is that according to Thomson the delegates failed to adjourn soon after finishing work on the Declaration. Thus we find that *after* the decisions were made to have the Declaration printed, distributed, and proclaimed, Congress subsequently took up no fewer than fourteen additional matters of business before finishing their day, the third of which was the appointment of the committee that wrote the letter printed here. And since examination of all available evidence provides no reason to doubt that the committee had indeed been appointed "this morning," and considerable time undoubtedly elapsed between adoption of the Declaration and the appointment of the committee, one is forced to the conclusion that the vote on the Declaraion was probably taken sometime before 11:00 A.M.

Livingston's draft of the letter provides independent confirmation of the date and authenticity of the broadside, and Abraham Clark's letter of this date to Elias Dayton provides additional support for the conclusion stated above. Clark, explaining Congress' recent work on the Declaration, wrote: "Our Congress Resolved to Declare the United Colonies Free and independent States. A Declaration for this Purpose, I expect, will this day pass Congress. It is nearly gone through, after which it will be Proclaimed with all the State and Solemnity circumstances will admit." Clark's statement that "It is nearly gone through" is, of course, the passage that takes on special meaning in the light of the committee's letter and the circumstances reviewed above.

Starting then with the journals of Congress and adding to them the evidence of both Livingston's and Clark's letters, it seems clear that when the delegates convened at approximately 9:00 A.M. very little work remained to be done on the Declaration, that it was completed in perhaps less than two hours without much additional controversy, and that Congress then proceeded to several other pressing matters, which consumed the greater part of their time this memorable day.

Because of the uncommon interest that traditionally has been directed at the events of July 4, 1776, the complete text of Livingston's draft of this letter is also provided here as follows: "Philadelphia 4th July 1776. Gent. The Congress this morning directed us to confer with the committtees of safety & inspection & the field Officers now in town, about the proper mode of collecting the militia of this province, in order to form a camp which will cover Pensilvania & New Jersey from the attacks of the enemy, who have landed on Staten Iland, & may probably direct their march this way if they should imagine the attempt on New York too hazardous. Necessity obliges us to dispence with form, & to avail ourselves of the advantages which we may reasonable hope from your being assembled. We therefore most earnestly request you immediately to collect the forces of your several counties, & march them down to Brunswick, where the Congress will order them to be properly furnished with provisions. Men who have the welfare of their country at heart need no other incentive to the greatest exertions thereon than such as arise from its danger, for which reason we have thought it necessary barely to inform you of the fact—with this addition, that the Militia of New Jersey are already for the most part in New York, so that that province will be defenceless without your timely aid. We remain Gent. &c." Sol Feinstone Collection, DLC microfilm.

[3] The Lancaster County Committee's response of July 6 to this appeal is in PCC, item 69, fol. 149.

Benjamin Franklin and James Wilson to Jasper Yeates

Sir   Philada. 4th July 1776

The Congress have appointed you one of the Commissioners of Indian Affairs in the middle Department; and we are desired to inform you of your Appointment.[1] A Treaty is to be held on the 20th of this Month at Pittsburgh. The Congress hope you will attend on that Occasion. This may be attended with Inconvenience to your private Affairs; but your Regard for the Public will, we know, prevail over any Consideration of this Nature. You will hear farther from us in a few Days. We are, Sir, Your very humble Servts,

B Franklin

James Wilson

RC (PHi). Written by Wilson and signed by Franklin and Wilson.

[1] See JCC, 5:517. The following day Franklin and Wilson sent a nearly identical letter to John Montgomery, the other appointee as commissioner for Indian affairs in the middle department. Franklin Collection, ICHi.

John Hancock to the Maryland Convention and the Delaware Assembly

Gentlemen,   Philada. July 4th. 1776.

The Congress have this Day received Intelligence which renders it absolutely necessary that the greatest Exertions should be made to save our Country from being desolated by the Hand of Tyranny. Genl. Howe having taken Possession of Staten Island, and the Jersey being drained of their Militia for the Defence of New York, I am directed by Congress to request, you will proceed immediately to embody your Militia for the Establishment of the flying Camp, and march them with all possible Expedition, either by Battalions, Detachments of Battalions, or by Companies, to the City of Philadelphia.[1]

The present Campaign, I have no Doubt, if we exert ourselves properly, will secure the Enjoyment of our Liberties for ever. All Accounts agree that Great Britain will make her greatest Effort this Summer. Should we therefore be able to keep our Ground, we shall afterwards have little to apprehend from her. I do therefore most ardently beseech & request you, in the Name and by the Authority of Congress, as you regard your own Freedom, and as you stand engaged by the most solemn Ties of Honour to support the Common Cause—to strain every Nerve to send forward your Militia. This is a Step of such infinite Moment, that in all human Probability, your speedy Compliance will prove the Salvation of your Country. It is impossible we can have any higher Motives to induce us to act. We should reflect too, that the Loss of this Campaign, will inevitably protract the War; and that in Order to gain it, we have only to exert ourselves, and to make Use of the Means which God & Nature have given us to defend ourselves. I must therefore again repeat to you, that the Congress most anxiously expect & request you will not lose a Moment in carrying into Effect this Requisition, with all the Zeal, Spirit, & Dispatch, which are so indispensibly required by the critical Situation of our Affairs.[2]

I have the Honour to be, Gentlemen, your most obed., & very hble Ser.   J. H. Pst.

LB (DNA: PCC, item 12A).

[1] See *JCC*, 5:509. Washington transmitted this "Intelligence" to Congress in his July 3 letter to Hancock. PCC, item 152, 2:149–52; and Washington, *Writings* (Fitzpatrick), 5:214–16.

[2] Also on this day Maryland delegates William Paca, John Rogers, and Thomas Stone signed a receipt stating that they had received "of the Honble John Hancock an order on the Treasurers for five thousand Dollars to be transmitted to the Convention or Council of Safety of Maryland for raising four German Companys directed by Congress to be raised in the Province." Red Books, MdAA. See also Hancock to the Maryland Convention, June 29, 1776.

Aside from its bearing upon the measures being taken for raising German troops in Maryland, this document confirms the presence in Congress of John Rogers this day, a fact that takes on additional significance because Rogers, who was not among the delegates Maryland elected this same day to new terms, left Philadelphia before the Declaration was signed on August 2 and did not become a "Signer" because he never returned to Congress. As a result, he has remained a man comparatively forgotten among the participants in this memorable day's events in Congress.

John Hancock to George Washington

Sir,   Philadelphia July 4th. 1776.

The enclosed Resolves, to which I must beg Leave to refer your Attention, will inform you of the Steps Congress have taken to establish the flying Camp.[1] To the unhappy Confusions, that have prevailed in this Colony, must principally be ascribed the Delays that have hitherto attended that salutary Measure. However I flatter myself Things will now take a different Turn, as the Contest

President John Hancock

to keep Possession of Power is now at an End, and a new Mode of Government, equall to the Exigencies of our Affairs will be adopted, agreeable to the Recommendation of Congress to the United Colonies.

I am directed to request you will appoint a proper officer for the Command' of the flying Camp; and also persons to supply them with Rations.

I have wrote to the severall Committees, and press'd them to forward their Troops with the utmost Dispatch.[2]

I have the Honour to be, with perfect Esteem, Sir, Your most obedt. Servt.   John Hancock Presidt

RC (DLC). In the hand of Jacob Rush, with concluding paragraph, closing, and signature by Hancock.
   [1] See *JCC,* 5:508–9.
   [2] Hancock also sent a letter this day to the Pennsylvania Committee of Safety, asking the committee to send Washington as many flints as it could spare. Record Group 27, PHarH; *JCC,* 5:516–17; and Washington, *Writings* (Fitzpatrick), 5:113, 215.

Robert Morris to the
Pennsylvania Committee of Safety

Gent'n: July 4th, 1776.
   The Congress passed a Recommendation this day,[1] Requesting a Conference of the Committee of Safety, the Committee of Inspection of this City, the Delegates of New York, New Jersey, & Pennsylvania, and the Commanding Officers of the Association, to devise the most expeditious mode of raising & marching the Militia of this Province to the Assistance of the Neighbouring Colonies.

I am, Gent'n, Your obed't Serv't, Sign'd,   Rob't Morris.

MS not found; reprinted from *Minutes of the Provincial Council of Pennsylvania from the Organization to the Termination of the Proprietary Government,* 10 vols. (Philadelphia: J. Severns & Co.; Harrisburg: Theo. Fenn & Co., 1851–53), 10:631.
   [1] See *JCC,* 5:516; and Committee of Congress to the Lancaster Associators, this date, note 1.

Robert Treat Paine's Diary

[July 4, 1776]
Cool.[1] The Independance of the States Voted & declared.

MS (MHi).
   [1] This was the fourth consecutive day Philadelphians had enjoyed a respite from

Philad.ª July the 4th 1776

Sir I have inclosed you a Summons directed to the Sheriff to ~~call~~ Summon the Member for our County to meet in Assembly at Newcastle on the 22d day of this Instant. which I hope you will have put into his hands as soon as possible after it comes to Yours — I arrived in Congress (tho detained by Thunder and Rain) time Enough to give my Voice in the matter of Independence — It is now determined by the Thirteen United Colonies without even one desenting Colony — We have now Got through with the Whole of the declaration, and Ordered it to be printed. so that You will soon have the pleasure of Seeing it — Hand-bills of it will be printed. and Sent to the Armies, Cities, County Towns &c.— To be published or rather proclaimed in form — — Don't neglect to attend Closely and Carefully to my Harvest and You'l oblige

Yours &c.

Caesar Rodney

Caesar Rodney's July 4, 1776, Letter to His Brother Thomas

the hot spell they had experienced the last two weeks of June. Paine's weather comments the preceding three days were as follows: July 1—"Fine showers." July 2—"Rain'd hard. Cool'd the air much." July 3—"Cool day."

Caesar Rodney to Thomas Rodney

Sir,   Philada. July the 4th 1776
    I have inclosed you a Summons directed to the Sheriff to Summon the Member for our County to meet in Assembly at Newcastle on the 22d day of this Instant which I hope you will have put into his hands as soon as possible after it Comes to Yours. I arrived in Congress (tho detained by thunder and Rain) time Enough to give my Voice in the matter of Independence.[1] It is determined by the Thirteen United Colonies with out even one disenting Colony. We have now Got through with the Whole of the declaration and Ordered it to be printed, so that You will soon have the pleasure of seeing it. Hand bills of it will be printed and Sent to the Armies, Cities, Countys, Towns &c—to be published or rather proclaimed in form. Don't neglect to Attend Closely and Carefully to my Harvest and You'l oblige, Yours &c,   Caesar Rodney

RC (CCamarSJ).
    [1] The circumstances behind Rodney's last minute appearance in Congress were described by Thomas McKean many years later as follows. "On Monday the 1st. of July the question was taken in the committee of the whole when the State of Pennsylvania (represented by seven Gentlemen then present) voted agt. it. Delaware (having then only two Representatives present) was divided; all the other States voted in favor of it. Whereupon, without delay I sent an Express (at my private expence) for your honored Uncle Caesar Rodney Esquire, the remaining member for Delaware, whom I met at the State-house door, in his boots and spurs, as the members were assembling; after a friendly salutation (without a word on the business) we went into the Hall of Congress together and found we were among the latest: proceedings immediately commenced, and after a few minutes the great question was put; when the vote for Delaware was called your uncle arose and said: As I believe the voice of my constituents and of all sensible and honest men is in favor of Independence and my own judgment concurs with them, I vote for Independence, or in words to the same effect." McKean to Caesar A. Rodney, September 22, 1813, Burnett, Letters, 1:534. For an analysis of several conflicting accounts of Rodney's ride to Philadelphia, see William Baskerville Hamilton, Anglo-American Law on the Frontier: Thomas Rodney & His Territorial Cases (Durham: Duke University Press, 1953), pp. 21–22.

James Wilson to the Pennsylvania Committee of Safety

Gentlemen   Philada 4th July 1776
    I beg Leave to recommend to you the following Gentlemen as officers of a Company in the German Regiment.[1]

Conrad Schneider—Captain
Jacob Stadler—1st Lieutt.
Jacob Foreman—2d Lieutt.
George Harmony—Ensign

They are recommended to me from Cumberland; and I am informed will be able to raise a Company immediately in that County. I am, with much Esteem, Gentlemen, Your very hble Servt,

James Wilson

RC (NN).
[1] For the creation of the German battalion, authorized according to a resolution of May 25, 1776, see *JCC*, 4:392, 5:454, 487–88. See also *JCC*, 5:571, 590.

John Adams to Mary Palmer

Miss Polly   Philadelphia July 5. 1776

Your Favour of June 15, 1776 [1] was handed to me, by the last Post. . . .[2] I hold myself much obliged to you for your Attention to me, at this Distance, from those Scenes, in which, altho I feel myself deeply interested, yet I can neither be an Actor nor Spectator.

You have given me (not withstanding all your modest Apologies) with a great deal of real Elegance and Perspicuity, a minute and circumstantial Narration of the whole Expedition to the lower Harbour against the Men of War. It is lawfull you know to flatter the Ladies a little, at least if Custom can make a Thing lawfull: but, without availing myself in the least degree of this Licence, I can safely say that from your Letter and another from Miss Paine to her Brother, I was enabled to form a more Adequate Idea of that whole Transaction, than from all the other Accounts of it, both in News papers and private Letters which have come to my Hands.

In Times as turbulent as these, commend me to the Ladies for Historiographers. The Gentlemen are too much engaged in Action. The Ladies are cooler Spectators. . . . There is a Lady at the Foot of Pens Hill, who obliges me, from Time to Time with clearer and fuller Intelligence, than I can get from a whole Committee of Gentlemen.

I was a little mortified, at the unlucky Calm, which retarded the Militia from Braintree, Weymouth and Hingham. I wished that they might have had more than half the Glory of the Enterprize. However, it satisfies me to reflect, that it was not their Fault but the fault of the Wind that they had not.

I will inclose to you a Declaration, in which all America is remarkably united. . . .[3] It compleats a Revolution, which will make as good a Figure in the History of Mankind, as any that has preceeded it—provided always, that the Ladies take Care to record the Circumstances of it, for by the Experience I have had of the other Sex, they are either too lazy, or too active, to commemorate them.

A Continuance of your Correspondence, Miss Polly, would much oblige me. My Compliments to Papa, and Mamma and the whole Family. . . . I hope they will see more serene Skies. I begin now to flatter my self, however, that you are situated in the safest Place upon the Continent.

Howes Army and Fleet are at Staten Island. But there is a very numerous Army, at New York and New Jersey, to oppose them. Like Noahs Dove, without its Innocence, they can find no Rest.

I am, with much Respect, Esteem and Gratitude, Your Friend and humble Servant,   John Adams

RC (PHi). Adams, *Family Correspondence* (Butterfield), 2:34–35.

[1] Mary Palmer (1746–91) was the daughter of Adams' old friend Joseph Palmer. See Adams, *Family Correspondence* (Butterfield), 1:18n.8, and 2:9–12.

[2] Suspension points in MS here and below.

[3] Presumably a copy of the broadside edition printed by John Dunlap and issued this day. For a facsimile reproduction, see Julian P. Boyd, *The Declaration of Independence: The Evolution of the Text as Shown in Facsimiles of Various Drafts by its Author, Thomas Jefferson* (Washington: Library of Congress, 1943), plate 10.

John Adams to Joseph Ward

Sir
                                                          Philadelphia July 5. 1776
Yours of the 16 June, and that of the 20th of the same Month, are before me.[1] I congratulate you on those happy Events which are the Subjects of them.

It is very true that We have disagreable Accounts from Canada. Our Army has retreated from that Country. Where they will make a stand I know not. Weakened and dispirited as they are, both with the Small Pox and with several Defeats, I fear they will retreat not only from St Johns and Isle au Noix but from Crown Point at least as far as Ticonderoga.

Many Gentlemen here, who are good Americans, say, that this is good Fortune—because the Distance to Canada is so great, and the Expences of Supporting an Army there so enormous, that We are better out of it than in it. I am not of this opinion myself, but We must acquiese in the Dispensation, let it be good or evil.

The Small Pox has been our most fatal Enemy. Our People must reconcile themselves, to inocculating Hospitals.

I am Sorry to hear of General Wards ill Health, and hope for his Speedy Recovery. I should be Sorry to hear of his leaving the Army.

You are Still impatient for a Declaration of Independency. I hope your Appetite will now be Satisfyed. Such a Declaration passed Congress Yesterday, and this Morning will be printed.

LB (MHi).
    [1] Ward's letters are in the Adams Papers, MHi. An extract of the June 16 letter
is in Clark, *Naval Documents*, 5:562–63.

Abraham Clark to William Livingston

Sir,   Phila. July 5th. 1776
    I enclose a Declaration of Congress, which is directed to be Pub-
lished in all the Colonies, And Armies, and which I make no doubt
you will Publish in your Brigade.[1]
    Part of the Pennsylvania Forces Marched this day to the assistance
of New Jersey, and the Principal part of the strength of Pennsylvania I
expect will soon be on their March to your Aid. We can't Account
for the Scarceness of intelligence. No Express hath been sent by the
Genl. since the beginning of this Week. All the News we get comes
by Private hands. Some think the Expresses are intercepted, or the
Communication across Hudsons River cut off. I am in hopes to Mor-
rows Post will give a full Acct. of the Armies.[2] I am, Sir, Your Hum.
Servt.   Abra. Clark

P.S. By a Person this day from the Lower Counties in Jersey we are
informed, a Vessel with Arms & Ammunition pursued by a Man of
War Run on shore at or near Egg Harbour, from which was taken
about 200 half Barrls. of Powder & some Arms before the Man of
Wars boats drove them off & took possessn. After getting Possn. they
set the Vessel on fire, or by some means or other, the Powder left on
board took fire and blew them up about 50 in Num[be]r. This Acct.
Comes so well Authenticated that it is not doubted as to the truth.[3]
                                                                      A.C.

RC (MHi).
    [1] Livingston, who had been chosen second brigadier general of the New Jersey
militia by the New Jersey Provincial Congress in October 1775, had recently
declined the provincial congress' offer of the command of the province's militia
"destined for New York." *Am. Archives*, 4th ser. 3:1248, 6:1626, 1629.
    [2] This day Congress resolved to establish expresses between Philadelphia and
New York so that Washington could "send off despatches to Congress every day."
JCC, 5:522.
    [3] For another account of this incident involving the New York vessel *General
Putnam*, see Clark, *Naval Documents*, 5:991–92.

Elbridge Gerry to James Warren

Dear Sir,   Philadelphia, July 5, 1776.
    I have the pleasure to inform you that a determined resolution of
the delegates from some of the colonies to push the question of in-

dependency has had a most happy effect, and after a day's debate all the colonies excepting New-York, whose delegates are not empowered to give either an affirmative or negative voice, united in a declaration long sought for, solicited and necessary, the declaration of independency.

New-York will most probably on Monday next, when its convention meets for forming a constitution, join in the measure, and then it will be entitled the unanimous declaration of the thirteen United States of America.[1]

I enclose you a copy of the declaration for yourself, and another for major Hawley, and offer you my sincere congratulations on the occasion, and I pray that we may never want the divine aid, or the spirit and the means to defend it.

Your, &c.   Elbridge Gerry.

MS not found; reprinted from Austin, *Life of Gerry*, 1:202–3.

[1] See New York Delegates to the New York Provincial Congress, July 2, 1776, note.

John Hancock to the New Jersey Convention

Gentlemen,   Philada. July 5th. 1776.

You will perceive by the enclosed Resolve that the Congress have judg'd it necessary to remove the Prisoners from your Colony to York Town in Pennsylvania, and have directed me to request you to carry the same into Execution immediately. Their Vicinity to our Enemies—and the opportunity of deserting to them, or keeping up a Communication dangerous to the Interest of these United States, rendered this Step not only prudent but absolutely necessary.[1]

I do myself the Honour to enclose, in Obedience to the Commands of Congress, a Copy of the Declaration of Independence, which you will please to have proclaimed in your Colony in such Way & Manner as you shall judge best.[2]

The important Consequences resulting to the American States from this Declaration of Independence, considered as the Ground & Foundation of a future Government, will naturally suggest the Propriety of proclaiming it in such a Mode, as that the People may be universally informed of it.

I have the Honour to be, Gentlemen, your most obed. and very hble Serv.   J. H. Prest.

LB (DNA: PCC, item 12A).

[1] See *JCC*, 5:523; and *Am. Archives*, 4th ser. 6:1640.

[2] See *JCC*, 5:516. Hancock also enclosed a copy of the Declaration in a letter he wrote this date to "Col. [John] Haslet, or Officer commanding the Battalion of Continental Troops in Delaware Government," who was ordered to station a

company of his battalion at Lewistown and to take the remainder of his unit to Wilmington "and there remain until the further Order of this Congress." PCC, item 12A; *Am. Archives*, 5th ser. 1:11; and *JCC*, 5:520.

John Hancock to the Pennsylvania Committee of Safety

Gentlemen,   Philadelphia July 5th. 1776.
    I do myself the Honour to enclose, in Obedience to the Commands of Congress, a Copy of the Declaration of Independence; which I am directed to request, you will have proclaimed, in your Colony, in the Way and Manner, you shall judge best.

The American States being now for ever divided from those who wished to destroy them, it has become absolutely necessary for their Security and Happiness to adopt some Government of their own. In this View of the Matter, the important Consequences, flowing from a Declaration of Independence, considered as the Ground & Foundation thereof, will naturally suggest the Propriety of proclaiming it in such a Mode, that the People may be universally informed of it.

I have the Honour to be, Gent, your most obed. hbe Ser.
John Hancock Presidt

RC (PHi). In the hand of Jacob Rush and signed by Hancock.

John Hancock to John Bradford and Daniel Tillinghast

Sir,   Philada. July 6th. 1776
    As I purpose writing you fully on the Subject of Marine Affairs some Time in the Course of next Week, I shall only enclose at present a Resolve of Congress,[1] directing you to send the Arms taken out of the Scotch Transports, to Genl. Washington at New York: and indeed, this is all I have Time to do now, being in great Haste,[2] Sir, your most obed. & very hble Sevt.   **J. H. Prest.**

LB (DNA: PCC, item 12A). Addressed: "To Mr. John Bradford Agent in Massachusetts Bay. Mr. Danl. Tillinghast Agent in Rhode Island."
  [1] See *JCC*, 5:524. Bradford and Tillinghast were Continental prize agents. *JCC*, 4:301. Hancock added the following postscript to his letter of this date to Bradford: "Inclos'd is a Declaration for your Amusement." Chamberlain Collection, MB.
  [2] This day Hancock also wrote a letter to Paymaster General William Palfrey, commending to his attention Capt. Alexander Graydon of the Third Pennsylvania Battalion, "a very promising young Gentleman of genteel manner and amiable

Character and the Son of a very wealthy Woman in this City of my Acquaintance," and requesting "you will shew him all the Civilities in your Power and
introduce him to such officers as you think it will give him pleasure to be
acquainted with." *T. F. Madigan's Autograph Bulletin* (n.d., 320 items), item 54.

John Hancock to William Cooper

My Dear Sir,   Philada., 6 July, 1776
    Could you exactly know my particular Scituation, and how much
of the Day and Night I devote to the Execution of publick Business,
I am Confident you and my Friends would readily excuse my not
writing. I am really so greatly Engag'd, and Business fast increasing
in my Department that I have not a moment to myself. My Friendship, however, is as strong, my Zeal as great, and my Reliance, under
God, that my Country will be Sav'd as firm as ever. I hope we shall
be a free and happy people, totally unfetter'd, and Releas'd from
the Bonds of Slavery, That we may be thus free, Congress have done,
and will still do, more, to promote it. Inclos'd you have the Declaration of Independence, to which Refer you. I write the Assembly,
and it is the wish of Congress the Declaration may be proclaim'd
in the *State* of Massachusetts Bay.
    I can't add, pray have me Remembred in strong terms of Affection
to your worthy Brother the Doctor and present him with one of the
Inclos'd.
    Remember me to all my Friends. The Revd. Mr. Whitney is at my
house and has gone through the Small Pox by Inoculation very
finely. Miss Katy Quincy is also here. She has been Inoculated, and
has it exceeding full, but is upon the Recovery, she will have enough
to Convince her Friends she will not Take it again.
    Two Days ago a Brig of ours with Powder and Arms arriv'd off
these Capes and was Chac'd by a Man-of-war, they Ran her on shore
at Egg harbour, and our people began unloading her, and after
Taking out some Arms and 250 half Barrs. Powder they discover'd a
Number of Boats full of Men from the Ships of war approaching
them. Our People finding it necessary to quit the Vessell, and determining she should not fall into the Enemy's hands, laid a long
train whereby to Blow her up; the Men from the Boats boarded her,
gave three Cheers, and immediately the Ship Blew up, and Destroy'd in a moment 50 or 60 of The Man-of-war's men and sent
them to ———— Heaven, I hope. the Man-of-war for want of hands
eno' to do mischief was oblig'd to go in pursuit of more; thus
they see it is Dangerous to be too meddling in other Men's affairs,
they had better quit, but if they will be so foolish they must abide
the Consequence.
    Mrs Hancock, who is in a *tolerable good way*, Joins me in best

Compliments to Mrs. Cooper, Miss Judith and all your Connections. My good wishes attend Mr. Oliver Wendell and Lady, in short I wish to be Remembred to every Friend.

I write in great haste, do let me hear from you. I wish you happy and am your Real Friend and hum. sert.

Reprinted from *Proceedings of the Massachusetts Historical Society* 60 (January 1927): 112–14.

John Hancock to James Mease

Sir,   Philada. July 6th. 1776.

You are hereby required to pay to Cap William Kilsay commanding a Company of New Jersey Militia one Month's Pay in the following Proportions the said Capt Kilsay to be accountable agreeable to a Resolve of Congress of this day,[1] viz.

To one Captain
  Two Lieutenants
  One Ensign
  Four Sergeants
  Four Corporals
  Fifty one Privates.

To each of the above gentlemen one Months Advance Pay agreeable to the established Pay. By order of Congress.

John Hancock Pret.

LB (DNA: PCC, item 12A). Addressed: "To Mr. Com[issar]y & Paymaster Mease."
[1] See *JCC*, 5:524.

John Hancock to Philip Schuyler

Sir   Philadelphia July 6. 1776.

The Bearer hereof Capt. Thomas Casdrop, with fifty fine Fellows, Ship Carpenters are Engaged in the Continental Service & Ordered to proceed from hence with the Utmost Expedition for Albany, there to put themselves under Your Direction. The Design of Engaging these People at the Very High Wages the Congress have contracted to pay, is to have the service of building Gallies, Floating Batteries &c. on the Lakes, faithfully, ably & Expeditiously executed.[1]

The Men have signed Articles which the Captain will shew You, And It is the Intention of Congress that they should be Immediately employed in this Essential service. Your Excellency will therefore Give Captn. Casdrop the Necessary Instructions & You may depend on his Compliance.

You will consider him in Rank as a Captain in the Army & Order the Rations, Rum & Necessary Stores to be supplyed to him & his Men. You will provide Smiths & Iron Work & in Short all Kinds of Materials & stores that may be necessary to Enable him to perform this Service He is engaged in; he will make Returns of his Men Monthly, in order to have two thirds of their Wages paid to their Attornies here, these must be regularly certified by the proper Officers. I have the Honor to remain, Sir, Your Obedient servant.

John Hancock

Tr (NN).

[1] See *JCC*, 5:450, 466, 508–9. This day Hancock also sent a letter to Washington, asking him to extend his assistance to Captain Casdrop in the event Casdrop "should find it safe & Convenient to call at New York in order to procure water Conveyance." Washington Papers, DLC; and *Am. Archives*, 5th ser. 1:33.

John Hancock to Certain States

Honble Gentlemen,   Philada. July 6th. 1776.[1]

Altho it is not possible to foresee the Consequences of Human Actions, yet it is nevertheless a Duty we owe ourselves and Posterity in all our public Counsels, to decide in the best Manner we are able, and to trust the Event to that *Being* who controuls both Causes and Events so as to bring about his own Determinations.

Impressed with this Sentiment, and at the same Time fully convinced that our Affairs may take a more favourable Turn, the Congress have judged it necessary to dissolve all Connection between Great Britain & the American Colonies, and to declare them free and independent States, as you will perceive by the enclosed Declaration, which I am directed by Congress to transmit to you, and to request you will have it proclaimed in your Colony in the Way you shall think most proper.

The important Consequences to the American States from this Declaration of Independence, considered as the Ground & Foundation of a future Government, will naturally suggest the Propriety of proclaiming it in such a Manner, that the People may be universally informed of it.[2]

I have the Honour to be, with great Respect, Gentlemen, your most obed. & very hbl Svt.

J. H. Prst.

LB (DNA: PCC, item 12A). Addressed: "Honble Convention of New York. Honble Assembly of Masstts. Bay. Govr. Trumbull. Govr. Cooke. Assembly of New Hampshire." Endorsed: "N.B. A Resolve to engage 50 Ship Carpenters was sent to Govr. Coke."

[1] Hancock sent an identical letter to the Maryland Convention on July 8. Purviance Papers, MdHi. In a postscript to the RC of his letter of July 6 to the New Hampshire Assembly Hancock noted: "Major Rogers of your Colony is now here.

The Congress have order'd that he be Sent to New Hampshire, to be Dispos'd of as that Government shall Judge best." Sang Deposit, NjR; and *JCC*, 5:523. He also wrote this postscript to the RC of his July 6 letter to Governor Cooke: "The Inclos'd to Mr. Green please to order to be Deliver'd to him." United States Historical MSS., InU; and *JCC*, 5:524.

[2] Another letter of the sixth from Hancock to "Genl. [Artemas] Ward, or Officer Commanding the Continental Troops at Boston," giving instructions for proclaiming the Declaration of Independence, is in PCC, item 12A, and *Am. Archives*, 5th ser. 1:34.

John Hancock to George Washington

Sir,   Philadelphia July 6th. 1776.

The Congress, for some Time past, have had their Attention occupied by one of the most interesting and important Subjects, that could possibly come before them, or any other Assembly of Men.

Altho it is not possible to foresee the Consequences of Human Actions, yet it is nevertheless a Duty we owe ourselves and Posterity, in all our public Counsels, to decide in the best Manner we are able, and to leave the Event to that Being who controuls both Causes and Events to bring about his own Determination.

Impressed with this Sentiment, and at the same Time fully convinced, that our Affairs may take a more favourable Turn, the Congress have judged it necessary to dissolve the Connection between Great Britain and the American Colonies, and to declare them free & independent States; as you will perceive by the enclosed Declaration, which I am directed to transmit to you, and to request you will have it proclaimed at the Head of the Army in the Way you shall think most proper.

Agreeable to the Request of Congress, the Committee of Safety of this Colony have forwarded to you ten Thousand Flints; and the Flints at Rhode Island are ordered to be sent to you immediately.[1]

It is with great Pleasure I inform you, that the Militia of this Colony, of Delaware Government, and Maryland are, and will be every Day in Motion to form the flying Camp; and that all the Militia of this Colony will soon be in the Jersey, ready to receive such Orders as you shall please to give them.

I have wrote to Governor Cooke to engage immediately and send forward as fast as possible, fifty ship Carpenters to General Schuyler for the Purpose of building Vessels on the Lakes. Fifty are already gone from hence on that Business.

The Congress having directed the Arms taken on Board the Scotch Transports to be sent to you, I have wrote to the Agents in Rhode Island and Massachusetts Bay to forward them immediately.

The enclosed Copy of a Letter from Mr. Green I am directed to forward by Congress,[2] with a Request that you will order such Parts of the Stores therein mentioned to New York as you shall judge proper.[3]

I have the Honour to be, Sir, with perfect Esteem, your most obedt. & very hble Servt.   John Hancock Prest.

RC (DLC). In the hand of Jacob Rush and signed by Hancock.
[1] See *JCC*, 5:516; and Washington, *Writings* (Fitzpatrick), 5:215.
[2] Thomas Green's letter informed Congress, in Washington's words, "of the Arrival of Capt. Chase with a Valuable Cargo at Providence." *JCC*, 5:524; and Washington, *Writings* (Fitzpatrick), 5:239–40.
[3] This day, at the request of Hancock, Jacob Rush wrote Washington a brief letter acknowledging receipt of the general's July 4–5 letter to Hancock. Washington Papers, DLC; and *Am. Archives*, 5th ser. 1:34. Washington's letter is in PCC, item 152, 2:159–66, and Washington, *Writings* (Fitzpatrick), 5:218–24.
The Board of War also directed a brief inquiry to Washington this day on the subject of "what provision has been made in the Continental Army for sergeant-majors, drum and fife-majors, and quartermaster-sergeants." See *Am. Archives*, 5th ser. 1:33.

Robert R. Livingston to John Jay

Dear John   [July 6, 1776][1]
I have but a moments time to answer your letter. I am mortified at the removal of our convention. I think as you do on the subject. If my fears on account of your health would permit I shd. request you never to leave that volatile politician a moment.[2] I have wished to be with you when I knew your situation. The Congress have done me the honour to refuse to let me go. I shall however apply again to day. I thank God I have been the happy means of falling on a expedient which will call out the whole militia of this country in a few days—tho' the Congress had lost hopes of it from the unhappy dispute & other causes with which I will acquaint you in a few days.[3] We have desired a Genl to take the Command. I wish Mifflin may be sent for very obvious reasons.[4] If you see [him] tell [him] so from me. I have much to say to you but [not a] moment to say it in. God be with you. Yours &c.   Robt R. Livingston

RC (NNC). Addressed: "To Coll. John Jay, New York."
[1] This date has been assigned on the basis of the postmaster's stamp on this letter: "Phila. July 6."
[2] Earlier in the month Jay had written Livingston from New York: "I returned to this City from Elizt. Town, & to my great mortification am informed that our Convention influenced by one of G[ouverneur] Morris' vagrant Plans have adjourned to the White Plains to meet there tomorrow." Jay to Livingston, July 1, 1776, Jay, *Papers* (Morris), 1:281–82. In the same letter Jay observed of fellow New York delegate Philip Livingston, who had recently been granted permission by the New York Provincial Congress to return to Philadelphia: "I wish Mr. Ph. Livingston could have been prevailed upon to stay here a little longer. I exhausted all my

Rhetorick on the occasion but in vain. Nor did he assign a better Reason for leaving the Province, than he *would* go to Philadelphia." Ibid., p. 282. Livingston arrived in Philadelphia no later than July 3. See John Witherspoon to the New Jersey Provincial Congress, July 3, 1776. Although Burnett was unable to find any evidence of Livingston's attendance in Congress between March 1 and early July 1776, two accounts of his with the New York Provincial Congress and the New York Convention provide new—and sometimes contradictory—evidence on this subject. The first shows that he received " £ 38.8" for "24 Days Attendance at the Continental Congress from the 17 March to the 9 Apl.," 1776, and the second that he was paid $772 "For his Allowance for expenses attending Congress from 11 June to the 20 Decr. [*1776*] . . . at 4 Dols. per Day." See Philip Livingston, Account with the New York Provincial Congress, June 26, 1776, Huntington Manuscripts, CSmH; and Account with the New York Convention, March 11, 1777, Betts Collection, CtY. Yet the second account cannot be accepted as an accurate record of Livingston's attendance in Congress because the journals of the Provincial Congress indicate that he was in New York throughout most of June 1776. See *Am. Archives*, 4th ser. 6:1403, 1431.

³ See Committee of Congress to the Lancaster Associators, July 4, 1776, note 1.

⁴ A few days later Washington appointed Gen. Hugh Mercer commander of the flying camp, thereby disappointing Livingston's hope that this post would go to Gen. Thomas Mifflin instead. Washington, *Writings* (Fitzpatrick), 5:250.

Robert Treat Paine to Joseph Palmer

July 6, 1776.

It is our unhappiness, in this time of danger, to have too many Calvinistic politicians, who seem to think their country will be saved by good words and warm faith, without concomitant exploits; if it did not proceed from a defect in human nature, I think we should not find it in so many places. I have a long time thought that the manufacture of arms and ammunition was an essential object of attention, and have accordingly applied myself most intensely to it, and I hope with good effect. . . .¹

The day before yesterday the declaration of American independency was voted by twelve colonies, agreeable to the sense of the constituents, and New-York was silent, till their new convention (which sits next week) express their assent, of which we have some doubt. Thus the issue is joined; and it is our comfortable reflection, that if by struggling we can avoid that servile subjection which Britain demanded, we remain a free and happy people; but if, through the frowns of Providence, we sink in the struggle, we do but remain the wretched people we should have been without this declaration. Our hearts are full, our hands are full; may God, in whom we trust, support us.

MS not found; reprinted from extract in *New York Review and Atheneum Magazine* 2 (May 1826): 449–50.

¹ Ellipsis in Tr.

Secret Committee to Thomas Mumford

Sir   Philada. July 6th. 1776

Your favour of the 26th Ulto came duely to hand, and we readily agree that you may dispose of the Six barrells of Montserat Sulphur to Messrs. Wales & Elderkin in order to keep their Powder Mill going, but you must fix the price with them as we neither know the Cost or Value of that Sulphur not having received any such here, nor have we ever as yet any Invoice, so that we are even at a loss to know what we must charge Messrs. Wisner & Livingston for the quantity delivered to them & hope you will assist us in this point. Indeed we wish to see the Invoice soon as Convenient. We rec'd the enclosed letter for You a few days since from St Eustatia & in taking off the Cover which was directed to the Secret Committee, the Seal of your letter inside stuck to it so that both came off together, which you'l not blame us for. You'l find herein all the papers that were enclosed except Capt Palmers bills of Loading for 50 half & 240 Quarter bbls of Powder shipped by your Friends at St Eustatia for this place which we have received safe & shall duely note the same in your Account. Your said Friends appear to be attentive good Men, deserving of the Confidence you repose in them. The freight of this Powder is fixed in St Eustatia at four Dollars for every hundred wt which is very dear, but we suppose you must pay the same for the 250 half barrells, unless the Owners of the vessell shoud agree to take less. We will hereafter give orders respecting that Powder & such other Quantitys as may arrive & are sir, Your obedt. hble servts. By order of the Secret Committee,

                                              Robt Morris, Chair Man

RC (Robert J. Sudderth, Jr., Lookout Mountain, Tenn., 1974). Written by Robert Morris.

John Adams to Abigail Adams

                                              Philadelphia July 7. 1776

I have this Moment folded up a Magazine, and an Evening Post [1] and sent it off, by an Express, who could not wait for me to write a single Line. It always goes to my Heart, to send off a Packett of Pamphletts and News Papers, without a Letter, but it sometimes unavoidably happens, and I suppose you had rather receive a Pamphlet or News Paper, than nothing.

The Disign of our Enemy, now seems to be a powerfull Invasion of New York and New Jersey. The Hallifax Fleet and Army, is arrived, and another Fleet and Army under Lord How, is expected to join them. We are making great Preparations to meet them, by marching the Militia of Maryland, Pensilvania, and New Jersey, down to the Scene of Action, and have made large Requisitions upon New England. I hope for the Honour of New England, and the Salvation of America, our People will not be backward in marching to New York. We must maintain and defend that important Post, at all Events. If the Enemy get Possession there, it will cost N. England very dear. There is no danger of the Small Pox at New York. It is carefully kept out of the City and the Army. I hope that your Brother and mine too will go into the Service of their Country, at this critical Period of its Distress.

Our Army at Crown Point is an Object of Wretchedness, enough to fill a humane Mind, with Horror. Disgraced, defeated, discontented, dispirited, diseased, naked, undisciplined, eaten up with Vermin—no Cloaths, Beds, Blanketts, no Medicines, no Victuals, but Salt Pork and flour. A Chaplain from that Army, preached a Sermon here the other day, from "cursed is he, that doth the Work of the Lord, deceitfully."

I knew better than he did, who the Persons were, who deserved these Curses. But I could not help myself, nor my poor Country any more than he.

I hope that Measures will be taken to cleanse the Army at Crown Point from the small Pox, and that other Measures will be taken in New England, by tolerating and encouraging Inoculation, to render that Distemper less terrible.

I am solicitous to hear, what Figure, our new Superiour Court made in their Eastern Circuit. What Business they did? Whether the Grand Juries, and petit Juries, were sworn. Whether they tried any Criminals? or any civil Actions. How the People were affected at the Appearance of Courts again. How the Judges were treated, whether with Respect, or cold Neglect &c.

Every Colony, upon the Continent will soon be in the same Situation. They are erecting Governments, as fast as Children build Cobb Houses. But I conjecture they will hardly throw them down again, so soon.

The Practice We have hitherto been in, of ditching round about our Enemies, will not always do. We must learn to Use other Weapons than the Pick Axe and the Spade. Our Armies must be disciplined and learn to fight. I have the Satisfaction to reflect, that our Massachusetts People, when they have been left to themselves, have been constantly fighting and skirmishing, and always with success. I wish the same Valour, Prudence, and Spirit had been discovered every where.[2]

RC (MHi). Adams, *Family Correspondence* (Butterfield), 2:37–38.
 ¹ Presumably the *Pennsylvania Magazine: or, American Monthly Museum;* and the *Pennsylvania Evening Post,* July 6, 1776, which contained the first newspaper printing of the Declaration of Independence.
 ² Adams wrote a second letter this day to Abigail, discussing "Epistolary Style" and urging her to have the children practice and master writing skills. Adams, *Family Correspondence* (Butterfield), 2:39–40.

John Adams to Joseph Reed

Dear Sir.   Philadelphia July 7 1776
   Yesterday your Favour of the 4th Instant was handed me by the Post. Am much obliged to you for it, and will give all the attention I can to its Contents. Am not certain that I know the Gentleman who you recommend by the Name of Henshaw—but I believe I do.¹ There are several very worthy Men of that Name: which of them this is, I am not clear. The Difficulty is that we dont know what vacancies there are, to which Congress may with Propriety promote such officers. If the general should recommend him to any advancement, he would readily have it. But if any Individual Member here should move for his Promotion without a Recommendation from Head Quarters, a suspicion would arise that he did not stand well there. Does he come to New York as Lt. Coll of a Regiment of Militia, or in what Capacity. Should be obliged to you for his Christain Name, and for a Hint of any Vacant Place to which he may be promoted. Nothing in my Power shall be wanting to serve a worthy Man and a usefull officer.
   Your description of the Force of the Enemy and your own weakness, is indeed allarming. The Importance of the Post you hold is very great; and it must be maintained and defended at all Events.
   Congress have already ordered three of the Battallions at Boston, to N. York, and tomorrow will order the other two.² The two Pensilvania Battallions are ordered to N. York, and Measures have been taken to send all the Militia of Pensilvania, who can be armed to N. York and N. Jersey. Maryland is requested to send along their Proportion of the flying Camp. I hoped that the Militia from New England would have been with you before this Time, at least a considerable Part of them. You will Soon see Some of them I think. I have the Pleasure to agree perfectly with you, that now is the golden opportunity, for Sending into New York, Troops from every Quarter. The General may rely upon it, that no Tenderness for my own Province, nor any other Consideration shall induce me, to throw the least Impediment in the Way of any Measure that shall be proposed for that Purpose. I have even promoted the order

for calling away the five Battallions from Boston, altho I know not how the numerous Fortifications there are to be garrisoned, or even the Continental Stores to be defended.

There really is a Strong, an earnest, and sincere desire, here, to do every Thing to forward the Militia from every Quarter. I wish their was as laudable a Spirit to give Bounties in Money, and Land, to Men, who would inlist during the War. But there is not. Congress offers Ten dollars Bounty to inlist for three years, when New Jersey, New York, Connecticut, Mass. Bay and New Hampshire are voting six, Eight, or Ten Pounds a Man to serve for Six Months. This Economy at the Spigot, and Profusion at the Bung will ruin us. Do for Gods Sake Coll Reed convince our Southern Brethren that the Common People and even Common Soldiers are rational Creatures, and that they can see, hear, and feel.

My Heart bleeds in every Veign of it, for New York and the Army in it: But there is another Scene more affecting Still. The Army under Schuyler and Gates is an object miserable enough to affect less feeling Hearts than yours or mine. An Army, disgraced and dispirited, with repeated defeats; devoured with Vermin; without a Second Shirt, or pair of Hose, without Beds, or Blanketts, diseased with the Small Pox, and nothing to eat, but Salt Pork and flour—incapable of succour, by fresh Recruits, because such as have had the Small Pox are not to be found, and such as have not, would only bring fresh Wretchedness among them! What shall we do? Is it possible to cleanse that army from Infection? Without this, I fear, our Hopes in that Quarter are but delusions.

After all I am not disconcerted by all these Confusions, because I have expected them these twelve Months, and because I have known our affairs in a situation much worse than they are even now. A fatal Delusion, from fond Hopes of Reconciliation, entertained, fostered and cherished, against the clearest Evidence, which is ever to be expected in such Cases, has held us back, from making such Preparations for our better Security as were in our Power. These Hopes are now extinguished, and I think that more Vigour will take Place and another winter will greatly befriend us. The golden opportunity however, is irretreivably lost. Canada is our Enemy, and We are now compleatly between two Fires. I expect an horrid Carnage upon our Frontiers, and a great Deal of Desolation upon the Sea Coast, but I hope still that We shall come out of the Furnace of Affliction, double refined. I am with great Respect,

LB (MHi).
[1] It is probable that the person Reed had recommended in his July 4 letter to Adams, which is in the Adams Papers, MHi, was Joseph Henshaw (1727–94), Boston and Leicester, Mass., merchant and lieutenant colonel of militia. Shipton, *Harvard Graduates*, 12:268–71.

[2] On July 8 Congress authorized General Washington "to call to his assistance, at New York, such of the continental regiments in the Massachusetts bay, as have not already received orders to march to Ticonderoga." *JCC*, 5:527.

John Adams to James Warren

Dear Sir   Philadelphia July 7. 1776
Congress has been pleased to establish a War office, and have done me the Honour to make me a Member of that Board, which lays me under obligation to write you upon the Subject of Flints.

Congress has impowered and directed the Board to employ a Number of Persons, wherever they can find them, to manufacture Flints, and also to enquire in the Several Colonies, for the proper Flint Stone.[1]

It would be unpardonable Negligence in Us, in our Circumstances, to depend upon Supplies from abroad, of any Articles necessary to carry on the War; Materials for the Manufacture of which are afforded by our own Country in Sufficient Plenty. This is the Case of Flint Stone. It is affirmed by Gentlemen of undoubted Credit, that large Quantities of the genuine Flint Stone are found in Orange County, in the Government of New York, and it is reported that other Quantities are found in various other Parts of the united American States. Congress is determined to leave no proper Measures unessayed, to discover the Truth, and to obtain Information in what Parts of America this Kind of stone is to be found and in what Quantities.

To this End the Board of War and ordinance is directed to invite the assistance of the Several Legislatures of all the States in Union, in promoting an Inquiry.

I am directed by the Board to request you to lay this Letter before the Legislature of the Massachusetts Bay, and to ask their Attention to this Subject and that they would be pleased to appoint a Committee of their Body, or take any other Measures which they may think proper and effectual for inquiring whether there is any Quantity of this necessary stone, in their Country, in what Counties or Towns of it it lies, and whether there are any Persons who have ever practiced the Art of making the Flints into suitable sizes and shapes for military service. And it is further requested, that after a proper Enquiry shall have been made, the Result of it, be reported to the Board of war and ordinance, at the War office, in Markett Street near the Corner of fourth Street Philadelphia.

I have the Honour to be &c.

LB (MHi).
[1] See *JCC*, 5:517.

Committee of Secret Correspondence
to Silas Deane

Sir   Philadelphia, July 8th 1776.

With this you will receive the Declaration of the Congress for a final separation from Great Britian. It was the universal demand of the people, justly exasperated by the obstinate perseverance of the Crown in its tyrannical and destructive measures, and the Congress were very unanimous in complying with that demand. You will immediately communicate the piece to the Court of France, and send copies of it to the other Courts of Europe. It may be well also to procure a good translation of it into French, and get it published in the gazettes.

It is probable that, in a few days, instructions will be formed in Congress directing you to sound the Court of France on the subject of mutual commerce between her and these States.[1]

It is expected you will send the vessel back as soon as possible,[2] with the fullest intelligence of the state of affairs, and of everything that may affect the interest of the United States. And we desire that she may be armed and prepared for defence in her return, as far as the produce of her cargo will go for that purpose.

The Committee have sent Mr. William Bingham to Martinico, where he is to reside in character of a merchant, and occasionally correspond with you. As we shall endeavor, by small armed vessels, to keep up a constant communication with that Island, we desire you would, from time to time, convey to and through him such information as you shall judge proper. He is a discreet young gentleman and worthy of confidence.

You will see in the newspapers that we have been obliged to quit Canada for the present. It was too bold a thing to block up Quebec a whole winter with an army much inferior in numbers to the garrison, and our troops sent too late to support them, not having had the small pox, have been much disabled by that distemper. But neither this disaster, nor the landing of an army in our neighborhood, have in the least dispirited the Congress, as you may perceive by our declaration being subsequent to both.

With great esteem, we are, sir, Your very obedient servants,

B. Franklin

Robert Morris

MS not found; reprinted from *North American and United States Gazette* (Philadelphia), October 12, 1855.

[1] Undoubtedly a reference to the work of the committee appointed on June 12 "to prepare a plan of treaties to be proposed to foreign powers." The committee did not submit its report to Congress until July 18, however, and a "plan" was not adopted until September 17. *JCC*, 5:431, 433, 575–89, 768–79. The "plan" and in-

structions of Congress were not sent to Deane until October 23. See Committee of
Secret Correspondence to Deane, October 23, 1776.

   [2] Capt. Peter Parker and the *Dispatch*, which carried the original of this letter,
were captured on July 22, 1776. Clark, *Naval Documents*, 5:1183n. But a copy of
the letter, from which this transcript was made in 1855, was enclosed in the August
7 dispatch of the Committee of Secret Correspondence to Deane printed below.

Elbridge Gerry to Joseph Trumbull

Dear sir   Philadelphia 8th July 1776
   I recd your Letters of the 3d & 5th Instant [1] & suppose e'er this
reaches You, that the General at the Head of his Army will cause
the Declaration of Independance to be published & read. May
Providence succeed our Endeavours to maintain & support it, & We
keep up to the Character of Men.
   Inclosed is the Saturday Evening's Post [2] by Which You will see
the Measures pursuing to defend the Jersies & Pennsylvania.
   I think it not improbable that the French intend a Blow in the
West Indies on it's being ascertained that the united States of
America are declared free & independant, & that this Event ought
to be communicated to their Governors & Commanders there with-
out Delay.
   Your Letters relative to General Gates & Avery on one side &
General Schuyler & Livingston on the other have been received.
Congress have the Matter under Consideration & what will be the
Result I know not; I shall use my little Influence to detach the
latter generally from the affairs of Canada or the Army at St Johns,
as a Measure essentially necessary to the well being of the same &
to make it successfull in that Quarter.
   A formal Declaration is to be made of Independance at the
State House this Day & the burning of the Kings Arms is to succeed
it. I understand that the Committee of Safety of the Colony, Com-
mittee of Inspection of the City, & officers of the Battalions of the
City & Liberties have ordered the Measure, & think it spirited.
   I remain sir your Friend & humble sert.   Elbridge Gerry

[P.S.] Pray send a List of Rations allowed to all officers from a
Major General downwards & also to Staff officers. They are not all
to be found on the Journals.
   Since writing the above Congress have determined that General
Schuyler is to have the Command & General Gates to continue there
under him, & the Commissary General to have the whole Care of
supplies & appointing or displacing Deputies for that purpose. [3] I
wish bad Consequences may not attend the first Measure but greatly
fear it.

RC (DLC photostat).
    [1] Photostats of Trumbull's July 3 and 5 letters to Gerry are in the Gerry Papers, DLC.
    [2] The *Pennsylvania Evening Post* of July 6, 1776, which also contained the Declaration of Independence.
    [3] See *JCC*, 5:526–27. See also John Hancock to Horatio Gates, this date.

John Hancock to Horatio Gates

Sir,   Philadelphia July 8th. 1776.
    The Congress being informed by Letter from General Schuyler to General Washington, which was laid before them at the Request of the former, and by your own Consent, that a Difference of Opinion had arisen between General Schuyler & yourself, with Regard to the Command of the Army in the Northern Department, they immediately took the Matter into Consideration, and have this Day come to the inclosed Resolution, which I do myself the Honour of transmitting in Obedience to their Commands.[1]
    You will there perceive that Congress are of Opinion, your Command was totally independent of Genl. Schuyler, while the Army was in Canada, but no longer, and indeed, the Terms in which the Resolve, relative to your Appointment, is conceived, seem to shew that this was their Intention. You were expressly, by that Resolve, to take the Command of the Troops *in Canada,* Words which strongly imply, that they had no Design to divest Genl. Schuyler of the Command while the Troops were on *this Side Canada.* I am however to inform you, that Congress highly approve your Resolution and Magnanimity that the public Service should receive no Detriment from any Difference of opinion on the Occasion. It is their most earnest Desire you will go on to act in the same Manner, and cultivate Harmony in all your military operations. A good Understanding and mutual Confidence are so essentially necessary in Order to give Success to our Measures, that I am convinced, they will take Place on all Occasions, between you.
    He deserves most of his Country, and will undoubtedly meet with the greatest applause, in whatever Rank or Station he may be, who renders her the most useful and signal Services. I have the Honour to be, Sir, with great Respect & Esteem, your most obed & very hble Ser.   John Hancock Presidt

RC (NHi). In the hand of Jacob Rush and signed by Hancock.
    [1] See *JCC*, 5:526. For accounts of this dispute between Generals Gates and Schuyler, see Schuyler to Washington, July 1, and enclosures, in *Am. Archives,* 4th ser. 6:1199–1203; and Washington to Hancock, July 4–5, and to Schuyler, July 11, 1776, in Washington, *Writings* (Fitzpatrick), 5:222–24, 257. See also *JCC*, 5:448; and Jonathan G. Rossie, *The Politics of Command in the American Revolution* (Syracuse: Syracuse University Press, 1975), pp. 103–11.

John Hancock to Philip Schuyler

Sir,   Philada. July 8th. 1776.
   In Consequence of your Letter to Genl. Washington stating that
a Difference of Opinion had arisen between Genl. Gates and yourself with Regard to the Command of the Troops in the Northern
Department, I am to inform you, that Congress have this Day taken
the Matter into Consideration, and directed me to transmit the enclosed Resolution.
   You will there perceive that it was the Intention of Congress to
give Genl. Gates the Command, while the Troops were in Canada,
but no longer. As they think it expedient he should still continue to
act with you, I am most earnestly to recommend to you to cultivate
a Harmony in your military operations.
   The Congress highly approve of your Patriotism and Magnanimity in not suffering any Difference of Opinion to hurt the public
Service.
   A mutual Confidence & good Understanding are, at this Time,
so essentially necessary, that I am persuaded, they will take Place on
all Occasions between yourself and Genl. Gates, and that by your
joint Exertions in the Cause of Freedom, your Country will receive
the most essential Benefits.
   I have the Honour to be, with great Respect, Sir, your most
obedt. & very hble Ser.   J. H. Prst.

LB (DNA: PCC, item 12A).

John Hancock to George Washington

Sir,   Philadelphia July 8th. 1776.
   I do myself the Honour of enclosing sundry Resolves of Congress,
to which I beg Leave to refer your Attention, and which are so
explicit, that I need not enlarge.[1]
   In obedience to the Commands of Congress, I have wrote to Gen-
erals Schuyler & Gates, and have recommended a mutual Confi-
dence and Harmony in their military operations. Their joint La-
bour & Exertions are requisite in that Quarter; nor have I the least
Doubt, but they will act on all Occasions with the most perfect
Unanimity.
   You will please to appoint suitable Places of Rendezvous for the
Battalions raising for Canada, and communicate the same to the
Assemblies of New Hampshire, Massachusetts Bay, Connecticut, &
New York, and also to issue Orders for supplying the Men with
Rations, Tents, Month's Advance Pay and other Necessaries.[2]

I am pressed for Time, can only Add that I am most truly, Sir,
Your most Obedt & hume servt,   John Hancock Presidt

[*P.S.*] The Inclos'd please to forward to Genl. Schuyler & Genl.
Gates.

RC (DLC). In the hand of Jacob Rush, with closing, signature, and postscript by
Hancock.

¹ These resolves, passed by Congress this day, dealt with the controversy between
Gates and Schuyler, the powers of the commissary general, the appointment of a
deputy quartermaster general for the flying camp in New Jersey, and authorization
for Washington to use Continental units in Massachusetts to reinforce his army
in New York, to employ certain New England Indian tribes, and to issue appropriate orders to new units for Canada. *JCC,* 5:526–28.

² This day Hancock also wrote to Pennsylvania Commissary and Paymaster James
Mease ordering him to "pay one Months Advance to such of the Militia as will
engage to serve in the flying Camp." PCC, item 12A; *Am. Archives,* 5th ser. 1:116;
and *JCC,* 5:528. Hancock also sent a letter on this date to Gen. Daniel Roberdeau
"to direct that you do not order Captain [Richard] Peters out of this City his
Service being necessary as Secretary to the War Office." PCC, item 12A; and *Am.
Archives,* 5th ser. 1:116.

Joseph Hewes to Samuel Johnston

Dear Sir   Philadelphia 8th July 1776
    I have received your favours of the 23d of May, 6th & 11th of
June, the first of these came last to hand.¹ I have not had an oppertunity to forward your Letter to Elmsley, Tryon is not to be
trusted with it. I shall send it by some Vessel bound to France or
Spain, I cannot find out any other way of conveyance, and that is
very precarious.
    I shall endeavour to get for you a proper Account of the Linnen
Manufactory here. I have been several times at it, but have not
hitherto been fortunate enough to meet with any of the directors. I
expect in the course of our political convulsions with Great Britain
I shall be rendered incapable of holding any share in any public
Manufactory for want of Stock, I will think of it when I get home
which I hope will be towards the latter end of August.
    I received a Letter from your Committee of Secrecy, War and
intelligence respecting the expediency of Fortifying the harbour of
Cape Lookout. I laid the matter before a Committee of Congress
appointed to consider what places were proper to be Fortifyed, but
before they consider & make report thereon it is absolutely Necessary they should have a plan or Map of the harbour with proper
explanations and discriptions. These should be taken by an engineer on the spot who should form a plan of the Fortifications necessary to be made and the expence that would attend it. I have wrote

to Mr. Harnett twice on this subject [2] but as I have reason to believe many Letters Miscarry I now mention the matter to you, in hopes you will endeavour to prevail on the Council of Safety to get the matter done as early as possible. I find a disposition in most of the Members of Congress to grant to our Province all that can be reasonably expected. It is not in their power to assist us at present with Cannon but as several Forges are beginning to Cast twelve & eighteen pounders I hope towards Winter they will not only have it in their power but be heartily disposed to assist us with some heavy pieces to put into such places as may be thought Most advisable. This is all you can expect, it is all that is done in the like cases. The works must be done At your own expence, or by such Continental Troops as may be in the province for the time being. I give you this as my opinion, perhaps they may do more for our Province, it stands high in Rank and high in estimation. I wish it may be able to support its good Character in future.

A hellish plott has been lately discovered at New York to Murder Genl. Washington and some other officers of the first rank, blow up the Magazine & spike up the Cannon. The persons employed had it in charge & have actually inlisted a number of Men for the Kings Army. It was to have been put in execution on the first arrival of the Army from Halifax. One of Genl. Washingtons guards has been put to death for being concerned in it. The Mayer of the City & some others are Confined, I believe many of them are guilty. It is said the matter has been traced up to Govr. Tryon.

What is become of my friend Hooper, I expected to have seen him here 'eer now, otherwise I should have wrote to him respecting some of his connexions at Boston who are like to suffer by having property in the hands of Tories that fled from that Country.[3]

My friend Penn came time enough to give his vote for independance. I send you the declaration inclosed. All the Colonies voted for it except New York, that Colony was prevented from Joining in it by an old Instruction, their Convention meets this day and it is expected they will follow the example of the other Colonies.

I had the weight of North Carolina on my Shoulders within a day or two of three months, the service was too severe. I have sat some days from Six in the morning till five, & sometimes Six in the afternoon without eating or drinking. My health was bad, such close attention made it worse, I nevertheless obstinately persisted in doing my duty to the best of my Judgment and abilities and attended Congress the whole time, one day only excepted. This I did contrary to the repeated solicitations of my friends, some of whom I believe thought I should not be able to keep Soul and body together 'till this time. Duty, inclination and self preservation call on me now to make a little excursion in the Country to see my Mother, this is a duty which I had not allowed my self time to perform during almost nine months that I have been here.

General Howe with his Army are in the Neighbourhood of New York, sometimes on Shore on Staten Island, and sometimes on board the Fleet. It is thought he has not more than Seven or eight thousd. Men with him. He is waiting for Lord Howe's Fleet to arive, when he expects to be Joined by twenty thousd. Men. All the Regiments on Continental pay that were raised in this Province are now at New York and on the lakes. Six thousand Militia from this province & three thousand four hundred from Maryland will march in a Few days towards New York. The Jersey Militia are all in Motion. I fear these Colonies will suffer greatly for want of Labourers to get in the harvest. Some people are of opinion that many fields of wheat will remain unreaped and be totaly lost.

Our Northern Army has left Canada and retreated to Ticonderoga and Crown Point. The small Pox has made great havock among them. Several Regiments had not well men enough to Row the Sick over the Lakes, men were draughted from other Regiments to do that Service. In short that Army has melted away in as little time as if the destroying Angel had been sent on purpose to demolish them as he did the Children of Israel. We are endeavouring to get the Lakes fortified in the best manner we can to prevent Burgoyne from passing them and entering the Colonies on that side.

A paper has been privately laid on the Congress Table importing that some dark designs were forming for our destruction, and advising us to take care of ourselves. Some were for examining the Cellars under the Room where we set. I was against it and urged that we ought to treat such information with Contempt and not show any marks of fear or Jealousy. I told some of them I had almost as soon be blown up as to discover to the world that I thought my self in danger. No notice has been taken of this piece of information which I think was right. I enclose you a resolve of Congress which please to forward to your Council of safety,[4] I also enclose a letter to Mr. Burke. If you can do any thing for the Gentlemen who subscribe it I hope you will do it, they are my friends and friends to America. I sent you a Commission of this kind some time ago, you have not mentioned it in any of your Letters. I will trespas no longer on your patience. Remember me to your family and Connections and be assured that I am with affection and regard, Dear Sir, Your most Obed Sevt,   Joseph Hewes

P.S. I copy no Letters, take them with all their imperfections.

RC (PHC).
[1] An extract from Johnston's May 23 letter is in Clark, *Naval Documents*, 5:223.
[2] Not found.
[3] On this point, see Hewes to Thomas Cushing, May 31, 1776.
[4] Probably the July 4 resolution calling upon "the several assemblies, conventions and committees, or councils of safety, and . . . the several commanding officers of the continental troops" to proclaim the Declaration of Independence. See *JCC*, 5:516.

Thomas Jefferson to Richard Henry Lee

Dr Sir   Philadelphia July 8th. 1776
    For news I refer you to your brother who writes on that head. I enclose you a copy of the declaration of independence as agreed to by the House, and also, as originally framed. You will judge whether it is the better or worse for the Critics. I shall return to Virginia after the 11th of August.[1] I wish my successor may be certain to Come before that time, in that case, I shall hope to see you and Mr. Wythe in Convention, that the business of Government, which is of everlasting Concern, may receive your aid.[2] Adieu, and beleive me to be Your friend & Servant,   Thomas Jefferson

Tr (ViHi). Jefferson, *Papers* (Boyd), 1:455–56.
    [1] See Jefferson to the President of the Virginia Convention, June 30, 1776, note 3.
    [2] In his response of July 21 Lee informed Jefferson that he planned to meet Gorge Wythe "at Hooes ferry the 3d of September . . . unless some pressing call takes me to Congress sooner." Jefferson, *Papers* (Boyd), 1:471.

Secret Committee to Nathaniel Shaw, Jr.

Sir,   Philadelphia July 8th 1776
    We have recd your favr. of the 24th Ulto. Inclosing General Lewis's Rect for 9645 lb of Gun Powder which shall be duly noted to your account. We received the Powder you imported into this place & applied it to the use of the Continent. Therefore you will retain the 1500 lb Continental Powder now in your possession in part payment, and as your Colony have also some Demand on the Continent for powder supplied on a requisition of his Excellency General Washington you'll oblige us by procuring an Accot of that quantity & transmit it with your own Accot, and as we have Powder in Rhode Island &c we will try to ballance those Accots. by causing the Powder to be delivered you.[1]
    We are sir your obdt, Hb Servts. By order & in behalf of the Secret Comtee.   Signed Robt Morris Chairman

Tr (CtY).
    [1] Shaw's reply of July 31 is in Clark, *Naval Documents*, 5:1305.

William Whipple to Joshua Brackett

My Dear Sir,   Philad 8th July 1776, 10 O'Clock PM
    Notwithstanding I was disappointed by not receiving a line from you last post I cannot forbare communicating the Pleasure I

know you will enjoy on Receipt of the enclos'd Declaration. It was this day publishd in form at the State House in this City, & is to be publish'd at the Head of the Army at New-York on Thursday next. We are now free from those Cursed Shackles that has embaresed all our affairs ever since the Commensement of the war. I already feel myself Lighter & I am in no doubt this step will give vigor to every measure which shall be here after persu'd. Yours,

Wm. Whipple

RC (DLC).

William Whipple to John Langdon

My Dear Sir, Philadelphia 8th July 1776.

Yours of the 24th ulto I've rec'd.[1] It grieves me that the frigates cannot be got to Sea, which I am sensible they might before this, had proper attention been paid to cannon in season. I have been a long time endeavouring to draw the attention of the Committee to the regulation of the Navy but hitherto without success. The present establishment certainly needs amendment, but business is so exceedingly pressing that it's impossible to form a judgment when it will be done. In my opinion a purser is a necessary officer, but as no provision is made for a purser, I think it necessary you should appoint a Steward. I submit it to you whether it would not be best to appoint a man that would do for a purser, as the wages at present are much higher than will be allowed for Stewards if Pursers are established. I must refer you to the papers for news as time just now is very precious. The *Declaration* will no doubt give you pleasure. It will be published next Thursday at the head of the Army at New York. I am told it is to be published this day, in form in this city.

As I am obliged to catch leisure minutes to write, perhaps something may turn up between this and to morrow morning. If so shall give it you. Govr Hopkins who has the direction of matters respecting the cannon at Providence, promises me that he will order the cannon for the Rawleigh to be sent from thence immediately, provided the Committee there think that the furnaces will be able to cast more for those ships by the time they will be ready to receive them. So you may expect to hear from thence on this Subject.

General How has landed part of his army on Statten Island which you know was not in General Washington's power to prevent. However the Jersey and Pennsylvania militia with 3000 from Maryland are now on their march and will soon form a very formidable army on this side Hudson's River and General Washington has by this time got 20,000 men at York including the militia of York and

Connecticut. I cannot help flattering myself that all this, with the smiles of Providence, will enable us to give a good account of these fellows before the campaign is over. I assure you the people here begin to feel themselves. Govr Franklin is sent to Connecticut for his good behavior.

I am with great truth, sincerely yours,   Wm Whipple

[*P.S.*] I hope you'll take care that the Declaration is properly treated. Col Bartlett desires his complmts and that you'll excuse his writing as he is much engaged.²

Tr (DLC).
    ¹ An extract of Langdon's June 24 letter to Whipple is in Clark, *Naval Documents*, 5:704–5.
    ² Langdon had also written a letter to Josiah Bartlett on June 24; for an extract see ibid., p. 704.

John Adams to Samuel Chase

Dear sir.   Philadelphia July 9. 1776
    Yours of the 5th came to me the 8th.¹ You will see by this Post that the River is past and the Bridge cutt away. The Declaration was yesterday published and proclaimed from that awfull Stage in the State house yard, by whom do you think? By the Committee of Safety,! the Committee of Inspection, and a great Crowd of people. Three cheers rended the Welkin. The Battallions paraded on the common, and gave Us the Feu de Joy, notwithstanding the Scarcity of Powder. The Bells rung all Day, and almost all night. Even the Chimers Chimed away. The Election for the City was carried on amidst all this Luxury, with the Utmost Decency, and order. Who are chosen I cant Say; but the List was Franklin, Writtenhouse, Owen Biddle, Cannon, Schlosser, Matlack and Khull. Thus you See the Effect of Men of Fortune acting against the Sense of the People.
    As soon as an American Seal is prepared,² I conjecture the Declaration will be Subscribed by all the Members, which will give you the opportunity you wish for, of transmitting your Name, among the Votaries of Independence.
    I agree with you, that We never can again be happy, under a single Particle of British Power, indeed this sentiment is very universal. The Arms are taken down from every public Place.
    The Army is at Crown Point. We have sent up a great Number of Ship wrights to make a respectable Fleet upon the Lakes.
    We have taken every Measure to defend New York. The Militia are marching this day, in a great Body from Pensilvania. That of Jersey has behaved well, turned out universally. That of Connecticutt, I was told last night, by Mr. Huntingdon, were coming in the

full Number demanded of them, and must be there before now. We shall make it do, this year, and if We can Stop the Torrent, for this Campaign, it is as much as We deserve for our Weakness and sloth, in Politicks, the last. Next year We shall do better. New Governments will bring new Men into the Play, I perceive, Men of more Mettle.

Your Motion last fall for sending Embassadors to France, with conditional Instructions, was murdered, terminating in a Committee of Secret Correspondence, which came to nothing.[3]

Thank you for the Paper and Resolves. You are attoning for all past Imperfections, by your Vigour, Spirit, and Unanimity.

Send along your Militia for the flying Camp. Dont let them hesitate about their Harvest. They must defend the Field, before they can eat the Fruit. I shall inclose to you, Dr. Price.[4] He is an independent, I think.

My Compliments to Mr. Johnson, Mr. Carroll, and all your Friends whom I have the Honour to know, and believe me to be, &c.

LB (MHi).

[1] In his July 5 letter, Chase touched on most of the major issues then being confronted in Congress. "I hope eer this Time the decisive blow is struck. Opposition, Inhumanity and Perfidy have compelled Us to it. Blessed be Men who effect the Work, I envy You! How shall I transmit to posterity that I gave my assent? Cursed be the Man that ever endeavors to unite Us. I would make *Peace* with Britain but I would not trust her with the least particle of Power over Us, she is lost to every virtue & corrupted with every vice.

"I am distressed for our army, I suppose at Crown Point; dont neglect to build vessells to keep the Command of the Lakes, if you do the British Army in Canada will not injure Us this Summer, & in the Winter You may regain that Country.

"I am miserable when I reflect on the Consequences of a Defeat at N. York. . . .

"If We should be endangered this Summer from the addition of foreigners to the National Strength of Gt. B., what blame is justly imputable to those who have neglected to provide for Assistance in Time. You know in November last I was for sending Ambassadors to France with conditional Instructions. I gave the Motion to Mr Lynch; I am told he starved the Matter.

"I have sent You our Paper and some Resolves of our Convention—do they not do Us Honor.

"Mr Paca will show You the News from Virginia, desire him to send Me Dr. Prices observations on Civil Liberty & the proceedings of the Committees of Penna." Adams Papers, MHi.

[2] Adams was a member of the committee appointed on July 4 "to bring in a device for a seal for the United States of America." *JCC*, 5:517–18.

[3] Adams' reference to Chase's "Motion last fall for sending Embassadors to France, with conditional Instructions," is suggestive of the origins of the Committee of Secret Correspondence. But no other evidence on this subject has been found, and, except for Chase's July 5 letter and Adams' explanation here, Chase's role would not be suspected, since he had been absent from Congress for nearly three weeks when the committee was appointed on November 29, 1775. See, however, Committee of Secret Correspondence to Arthur Lee, November 30, 1775, note 1.

[4] Richard Price (1723–91), English clergyman and well-known friend of America.

DNB. His *Observations on the Nature of Civil Liberty* had recently been reprinted by John Dunlap in Philadelphia. For citations to the several 1776 American reprintings of this celebrated pamphlet, see Charles Evans, *American Bibliography*, 12 vols. (Chicago: Privately printed, 1903–34), nos. 15030–34.

Samuel Adams to Joseph Hawley

My dear Sir,   Philade July 9 1776

I should sooner have acknowledgd the Receipt of your several Letters dated at Northampton & Springfield the 17th and 22d of May,[1] had I not expected that before this Time I should have had the pleasure of seeing and conversing with you—but Business here has been so pressing and important, that I have not thought it consistent with my Duty as yet to absent my self.[2]

Our repeated Misfortunes in Canada have greatly chagrind every Man who wishes well to America. I dare not at present communicate to you what I take to have been the real Causes of these Disasters. Some of them indeed must be obvious to any Man who has been attentive to that Department. Our secret Enemies have found Means to sow the Seeds of Discord & Faction there and Heaven has sufferd the small Pox to prevail among our Troops. It is our Duty to try all Means to restore our Affairs to a good Footing but I despair of that being effected till next Winter. To be acting merely on the defensive at the Time when we should have been in full possession of that Country is mortifying indeed. The Subject is disgusting to me—I will dismiss it.[3]

How is arrivd, as you have heard, with his Troops at New York. The People in this Colony & the Jerseys are in Motion and if the New England Militia joyn our Army with their usual Alertness & Spirit, I have no doubt but the Enemy will meet with a warm Reception. A few days may probably bring on an Event which will give a favorable Turn to our Affairs.

The Congress has at length declared the Colonies free and independent States. Upon this I congratulate you, for I know your heart has long been set upon it. Much I am affraid has been lost by delaying to take this decisive Step. ⟨*It is my opinion that if it had been done Nine months ago, when*⟩ we might have been justified ⟨*in doing it*⟩ in the Sight of God and Man, thos[e] Months ago. If we had done it then, in my opinion Canada woud this time have been one of the united Colonies; but "Much is to be endurd for the hardness of Mens hearts." We shall now see the Way clear to form a Confederation, contract Alliances & send Embassadors to foreign Powers & do other Acts becoming the Character we have assumd. Adieu my Friend. Write to me soon.

                                                                                S A

FC (NN).
[1] Hawley's letters to Adams of May 17 and 22 are in the Samuel Adams Papers, NN.
[2] Samuel Adams did not leave Philadelphia until August 12. See John Adams to Abigail Adams, August 12, 1776.
[3] For further evidence that Adams was greatly concerned over recent events in Canada, see Samuel Adams' Notes on Military Operations in Canada, August 1, 1776.

Samuel Adams to John Pitts

My dear Sir   [c. July 9, 1776][1]
You was informd by the last Post that Congress had declared the thirteen united Colonies free & independent States. It must be allowd by the impartial World that this Declaration has not been made rashly. The inclosd Catalogue of Crimes of the deepest Dye, which have been repeatedly perpetrated by the King will justify us in the Eyes of honest & good Men. By multiplied Acts of Oppression & Tyranny he has long since forfeited his Right to govern. The Patience of the Colonies in enduring the most provoking Injuries so often repeated will be a Matter of Astonishmt. Too Much I fear has been lost by Delay, but an accession of several Colonies has been gaind by it. The Delegates of every Colony were present & concurrd in this important Act; except those of N Y who were not authorizd to give their Voice on the Question, but thcy have since publickly said that a new Convention was soon to meet in that Colony & they had not the least Doubt of their acceding to it. Our Path is now open to form a plan of Confederation & propose Alliances with foreign States. I hope our Affairs will now wear a more agreable Aspect than they have of late.   S A

FC (NN).
[1] Although this letter was printed under the date July 17 in Adams, *Writings* (Cushing), 3:300–301, it was undoubtedly written before news of New York's endorsement of the Declaration of Independence reached Philadelphia on July 15. Indeed, it seems more likely that it was written relatively soon after the printed Declaration became available for distribution. Unless the recipient copy of the letter eventually comes to light, however, it is unlikely that the precise day Adams wrote it can be determined. It is suggestive nevertheless that his concluding reference to a plan of confederation and foreign alliances is similar to the comment he made on the same subjects in his letter of July 9 to Joseph Hawley.

Abraham Clark to Samuel Tucker

Sir,   Philadelphia July 9th. 1776.
Your Letter of the 6th Inst. wherein you mention the want of Amunition was yesterday before Congress. Upon Motion of your

Delegates four Tons were Ordered to be sent immediately, on Continental Acct. for the use of the Militia who March out to guard the Province untill the Flying Camp is formed, or for the use of the flying Camp if not expended before they take the field.[1] I have the Pleasure to assure you Congress pay particular Attention to the Defence of New Jersey, and hitherto have denied us nothing which we have Asked for that Purpose. They look upon our Province in great danger of being ravaged by the Enemy, and it is hoped you will not esteem it so far free from danger as to make your Continuing together unnecessary. It is indeed a busy Season, but we have a busy Enemy near us, and from the best intelligence Lord Howe is hourly expected to Arrive with 20,000 Troops. These with what have already arrived will make a formidable Army, and require the utmost exertion of the Middle Colonies to Oppose them. I expect the Militia of Phila. will begin to March to day—and from Accts. the Colony of Connectticut are sending forwards the strength of the Colony. I am, Sir, Your most Obedient, Humble Servt.   Abra Clark

RC (MeHi).
[1] See *JCC*, 5:525; and Samuel Tucker to John Hancock, July 6, 1776, in PCC, item 68, fols. 175, 177, and *Am. Archives*, 5th ser. 1:37–38.

John Hancock to Jacob Duché

Sir,   Philada. July 8th [*i.e.* 9] 1776.[1]
It is with the greatest Pleasure I inform you, that the Congress have been induced, from a Consideration of your Piety ⟨& *Religion*⟩, as well as your uniform & zealous Attachment to the Rights of America, to appoint you their Chaplain. It is their Request, which I am commanded to signify to you, that you will attend on them every Morning at nine O'Clock.

I have the Honour to be, Sir, with Respect, your most obedt. & very hble Sevt.   J.H. Prst.

LB (DNA: PCC, item 12A).
[1] According to the journals, Duché's appointment as chaplain of Congress was made on July 9. *JCC*, 5:530. Abraham Clark subsequently claimed that he was primarily responsible for this action. See Abraham Clark to James Caldwell, August 2, 1776.

John Hancock to James Mease

Mr. Mease,   Philada. 9th July 1776
The Quarter Master Genl. having wrote to Mr DeHaven for a Number of Waggons & Teams, & he having purchas'd them, & they

being wanted for immediate use, I must desire you to pay Mr. DeHaven the Amo. & Take his Bill on the Quarter Master Genl. which will Replace the money in your hands. The Owners of the Teams insisting on their pay & the Service Requiring their Setting off immediately induces me to Take this method, you will therefore please to pay it, & I will Indemnify you. The Bills on the Quar Master at New York will be Answer'd on Sight.[1]

I am Sir, Your very huml svt,   John Hancock

RC (Facsimile, William Brotherhead, *Centennial Book of the Signers* [Philadelphia: J.M. Stoddard & Co., 1875], p. 161).

[1] Hancock also wrote a brief letter this day to Ebenezer Hazard, the Continental postmaster in New York, informing him that as "it is Resolved in Congress that the Post Masters while in office be Excused from all Military Duty, you will therefore please to attend to the Duties of your office." Ebenezer Hazard Papers, PPAmP. See also *JCC*, 5:526.

John Hancock to Joseph Trumbull

Sir   Philada. 9th July 1776

I am so Engag'd in the Execution of the Resolves of Congress, that I have only time to Transmitt you the Inclos'd Resolutions respecting your Departmt. & indeed they are so Explicit as not to Require any Addition.[1]

I wish you happy, & am with Sentiments of Esteem, Sir, Your very huml sert,   J H Pt.

LB (DNA: PCC, item 12A).

[1] Hancock sent Commissary General Trumbull several resolves of July 6 and 8 pertaining to the commissariat, the most important of which declared "That the commissary general have full power to supply both armies, that upon the lakes as well as that at New York; and also to appoint and employ such persons under him, and to remove any deputy commissary, as he shall judge proper and expedient; it being absolutely necessary that the supply of both armies should be under one direction." This resolve was passed to settle a long-standing jurisdictional dispute between Trumbull and Walter Livingston, the deputy commissary general for the northern army, in which Livingston claimed virtual independence of Trumbull's authority, and was specifically occasioned by the opposition of Livingston and General Schuyler to Trumbull's effort to supplant Livingston with Elisha Avery, a deputy commissary of his own choosing. See *JCC*, 5:523, 527–28; *Am. Archives*, 4th ser. 6:1199–1201; Washington, *Writings* (Fitzpatrick), 5:223–24; and Jonathan G. Rossie, *The Politics of Command in the American Revolution* (Syracuse: Syracuse University Press, 1975), pp. 115–17. For the denouement of the conflict between Trumbull and Livingston, see Elbridge Gerry to Joseph Trumbull, September 12, 1776, note 2.

New Hampshire Delegates to Meshech Weare

Sir   Philadelphia 9th July 1776

Your highly Esteem'd favor of the 18 Ulto inclosing Instructions

to join with the other Colonies in Declaring these United Colonies,
Free & Independant States, came very Seasonably to hand.[1] As we
were so happy as to agree in sentiment with our Constituents it
gave us the greater Pleasure to Concur with the Delegates of the
other Colonies in the inclos'd Declaration, which was yesterday
Publish'd in form in this City and is to be Publish'd at the Head
of the Army at New-York next Thursday.

A plan of Confederation is now forming, which when finished
will be transmited to each Colony for their aprobation.

Major Rogers (whose Conduct it seems was Suspicious) was taken
up some time since by order of General Washington and sent under
Guard to this City. He Requested leave to go to England by way
of the West Indies but Congress not thinking it proper, have directed him to be sent to New-Hampshire to be dispos'd of as the
Authority there shall think Best.[2]

We have the Honour to be, with Great Respect, Your Most obt
Serts,   Josiah Bartlett

Wm. Whipple

RC (MH). Written by Whipple, and signed by Bartlett and Whipple.
[1] Weare's June 18 letter to Bartlett and Whipple enclosing the New Hampshire
Assembly's instructions on independence is in *Am. Archives,* 4th ser. 6:1029–30. See
also New Hampshire Delegates to Weare, May 28, 1776, note 3.
[2] See John Hancock to George Washington, July 1, 1776, note 2.

South Carolina Delegates to John Rutledge

Sir,   Philadelphia, July 9, 1776

Inclosed are the Resolutions of Congress respecting our Provincial Forces.[1] We wish they may be agreeable to your Excellency, to
our Assembly, and to the officers of our Army. If they are not, there
is nothing compulsory in them. Congress would not strictly comply
with the requests we were ordered to make on this subject lest
they should establish a precedent which might be injurious to the
general interest of America. We have therefore been obliged to vary
our application and to adopt such Resolutions as seemed most
conformable to the intentions of our Congress and most likely
to give satisfaction to the officers of our Army.

Inclosed also are some other occasional Resolutions of Congress
and a very important Declaration which the King of Great Britain
has, at last, reduced us to the necessity of making. All the Colonies
were united upon this great subject, except New York whose
Delegates were restrained by an instruction given several months
ago. Their Convention is to meet in a few days when, it is expected, that instruction will be immediately withdrawn and the

Declaration unanimously agreed to by the thirteen United States of America.

We have procured an order from Congress for three hundred thousand dollars for the payment and disbursements of our troops, which will be forwarded to you as soon as possible. Congress have also given directions to the commanding officer in Virginia about a fortnight ago to send forward five thousand pounds of gunpowder to our Colony.[2]

Every day now is likely to produce something important. We have heard of Clinton's arrival off Charles Town bar and most anxiously wait to know the event. General Howe's army from Halifax, said to contain 10,000 men, are arrived at Sandy Hook, a part of them are landed upon Staten Island. It is said he is waiting to be joined by 20,000 more who are coming from England in the fleet under Lord Howe, when it is expected that New York will become the scene of action. The Army under General Washington are in high spirits and the Militia have taken the field with an alacrity that does them honour. From these circumstances we still hope for a providential interposition and that the virtuous efforts of America will be crowned with deserved success.

With the greatest respect, we are your Excellency's most obedient servants,　Thomas Lynch　　Arthur Middleton

Edward Rutledge　　Thomas Heyward, Junior

Thomas Lynch, Junior

P.S. The express is to be paid for every day that he is detained in Carolina.

MS not found; reprinted from William E. Hemphill et al., eds., *Journals of the General Assembly and House of Representatives, 1776–1780* (Columbia: University of South Carolina Press, 1970), pp. 69–70.

[1] For these resolves, which were passed by Congress on June 18, see *JCC*, 5:461–63. See also *JCC*, 4:368, 393, 400; and *Am. Archives*, 4th ser. 5:577–79. For a number of other resolves enclosed with this letter, see *Journals of the General Assembly*, pp. 70–79. John Rutledge had been chosen "President and Commander-in-Chief" of South Carolina by the South Carolina Assembly on March 26, 1776. Ibid., p. 1.

[2] Congress gave this "order" and approved these "directions" on June 21 and 15 respectively. *JCC*, 5:444, 470.

James Wilson to John Montgomery

Dear Sir　　　　　　　　　　　　　　Philada 9th July 1776

I have been favoured with your Letter by Mr Smith. It gives me Pleasure to hear that the State of political Affairs in Cumberland County is beginning to mend. The People, I dare say, will, in a short Time, become sensible of the gross Impositions put upon them by a Set of Men, who have concealed the most factious and wicked Designs under the plausible Appearance of the warmest Attachment to the Interests of Liberty and of their Country. Such Men have double Guilt.

The Members chosen for this City are—Doctor Franklin, Mr Clymer, Mr Rittenhouse, Mr Owen Biddle, Fredrick Kuhl, Mr Schlosser, Mr Matlack and Mr Cannon. Those for the County are Col. Bull, Mr Antis, Harry Hill, —— Lollar, Archibald Thompson, Thos. Potts. The Rest I have forgot.[1]

It would give me peculiar Pleasure to be able to procure some Place suitable for Mr Buchannan: and I will seize the first favourable Opportunity that shall occur for that Purpose; though I must observe, at the same Time, that Places worthy of his Acceptance offer but seldom.

I have shewn Whitehill's Letter to the other Delegates of this Province.[2] They seem to think that it is not worth while to take public Notice of him. The greatest Kindness that can sometimes be shewn to such obscure and contemptible Wretches, is to bring them forth to public Views even though under the blackest Colours. He, and those who have employed him, will by and by become equal Objects of Indignation and Disdain.

Our Army in Canada have retreated to Crown Point. I have heard no Particulars from them since I had last the Pleasure of writing to you. All is still quiet at New York. The Militia are turning out in this City exceedingly well. I hope to hear from you soon, and am, with Compliments to all Friends, Dear Sir, Yours very sincerely

James Wilson

RC (ICHi).

[1] In addition to John Bull, Frederick Antis, Henry Hill, Robert Loller, and Thomas Potts, the County of Philadelphia elected Edward Bartholomew, Joseph Blewer, and William Coates to the Pennsylvania Convention that convened in Philadelphia on July 15, 1776. Wilson was apparently mistaken about the election of Archibald Thompson. See *Ar. Archives*, 5th ser. 2:1.

[2] For the letter of Robert Whitehill, and a discussion of Wilson's response to it, see Delegates' Certification of James Wilson's Conduct in Congress, June 20, 1776, note 1.

John Adams to Abigail Adams

June [*i.e.* July] 10. 1776

You will see by the Newspapers, which I from time to time inclose, with what Rapidity, the Colonies proceed in their political Maneuvres. How many Calamities might have been avoided if these Measures had been taken twelve Months ago, or even no longer ago than last December?

The Colonies to the South, are pursuing the same Maxims, which have heretofore governed those to the North. In constituting their new Governments, their Plans are remarkably popular, more so than I could ever have imagined, even more popular than the "Thoughts on Government." And in the Choice of their Rulers, Capacity, Spirit and Zeal in the Cause, supply the Place of Fortune, Family, and every other Consideration, which used to have Weight with Mankind. My Friend Archibald Bullock Esq. is Governor of Georgia. John Rutledge Esq. is Governor of South Carolina. Patrick Henry Esq. is Governor of Virginia &c. Dr. Franklin will be Governor of Pensilvania. The new Members of this City,[1] are all in this Taste, chosen because of their inflexible Zeal for Independence. All the old Members left out, because they opposed Independence, or at least were lukewarm about it. Dickinson, Morris, Allen, all fallen, like Grass before the Scythe notwithstanding all their vast Adventages in Point of Fortune, Family and Abilities.

I am inclined to think however, and to wish that these Gentlemen may be restored, at a fresh Election, because, altho mistaken in some Points, they are good Characters, and their great Wealth and numerous Connections, will contribute to strengthen America, and cement her Union.

I wish I were at perfect Liberty, to pourtray before you, all those Characters, in their genuine Lights, and to explain to you the Course of political Changes in this Province. It would give you a great Idea of the Spirit and Resolution of the People, and shew you, in a striking Point of View, the deep Roots of American Independence in all the Colonies. But it is not prudent, to commit to Writing such free Speculations, in the present State of Things.

Time which takes away the Veil, may lay open the secret Springs of this surprizing Revolution. . . .[2] But I find, altho the Colonies have differed in Religion, Laws, Customs, and Manners, yet in the great Essentials of Society and Government, they are all alike.

RC (MHi). Adams, *Family Correspondence* (Butterfield), 2:42–43.

[1] For a complete list of delegates to the Pennsylvania Constitutional Convention, see *Am. Archives*, 5th ser. 2:1–2.

[2] Suspension points in MS.

John Adams to Samuel Cooper

Dear Sir   Philadelphia July 10. 1776

Your last Letter relates to a Subject of the last Importance to America.[1] The Continental Currency is the great Pillar, which Supports our Cause, and if that Suffers in its Credit, the Cause must Suffer: if that fails the Cause must fail.

The Subjects of Coin and Commerce are the most nice, and

intricate of any within the compass of political Knowledge, and I am very apprehensive We Shall Suffer Some Inconveniences, from our Inexperience, in this Business. However, in Circumstances like ours, we should expect and be prepared in our Minds to suffer Inconveniences in every Particular Department of our affairs. We must try Experiments—and if one fails, try another, untill we get right.

Whether We can with Propriety, order in all the Colonial Currencies is an important Question. Will it not be interfering too much with the internal Polity of particular States? Can any one of them be a free state if they have not the Management of their own Coin, and Currency, which is but a Representation of Coin, as that is a sign of wealth?

That it will be dangerous to proceed much farther in Emissions, is to me probable, that it will be ruinous to go so far, as our occasions will call for in the Prosecution of this War, I am certain, and therefore I am convinced that the sooner, we begin to borrow Money, upon an Interest and to establish Funds and levy Taxes, to pay that Interest, the better, because I would not venture to try the Continental Credit so far, as to endanger a general Depreciation of the Bills. It would be better Policy to emit a less Quantity than the Credit of the States would bear, than to emit So much as to depreciate it.

We Shall very soon begin to borrow, and we shall continue to emit, untill We get enough, upon Loans to ensure the demands of the Public service. We shall not go beyond four Per cent, and Surely any Man who has the Bills, had better lend them at that low Interest than Keep them at none at all. The Monied Men will see their Interest in lending because the least Excess in an Emission of Paper Currency, becomes a Tax upon them. It is an Ease, and a Profit to Debtors, and a Loss to Creditors.

Is our Province about framing a new Constitution, or not? I should advise them to proceed cautiously, for the Eyes of the whole Continent are fixed upon them, and Some Colonies are waiting to copy their Model. I am.

LB (MHi).

[1] Undoubtedly Cooper's June 17 letter to Adams, Adams Papers, MHi.

John Adams to William Tudor

Dear Sir   Philadelphia July 10. 1776

Yours of the 7th instant I received Yesterday.[1] I wish to see you here for Several Reasons. But particularly, to hear your observations upon the Articles of war. I am perfectly of your opinion, that they must be amended, for the value of an Army depends upon its Discipline. The Discipline of Rome and Britain, occasioned the Tryumphs of their Arms.

I am Sorry you are tired of your situation in the Army. Without Command or even Rank, you have in your office of Judge Advocate as good an oppertunity to make yourself acquainted, with the whole Army, the World, and the Art of War, as you could in any other. Rank, without Command, is, in my Eyes, rather ostentatious, vain and despicable, than any advantage to a gentleman. You are pleased to ask my Advice, and I am very willing to give it. I would not by any Means advise you to continue in your present situation, longer, than this year. But I hope you will not leave the army this Campaign. This is the most critical, and hazardous summer, We ever Saw, or I think shall see. Serve it out, and then resign. You will be wanted in your own Country, and you cannot be desired to serve longer, without Promotion. With your Education, and Fortune you will be able to serve your Country at home with great Advantage. But if Promotion in the military Line is your Wish, I should think the General would readily recommend you to be a Field officer in some of the vacant Regiments. I wish our Massachusetts officers had better Educations, and more Capacity and Spirit, than I fear some of them have, and I wish to introduce you and other gentlemen of the younger Sort, who have Foundations laid on which any Superstructure may be built, into the Army. But I cannot wish you to forego, better Prospects of serving yourself and your Country too at home.

Somehow or other, Massachusetts Gentlemen have been neglected. Tudor, Austin, Osgood, Ward, Smith, Price, and many others might be mentioned who need not give Place to others of their Age in the Army. But others not their Superiours, have found better Fortune. There is a base Jealousy of the Massachusetts in more Places than one. I Said a Jealousy, I meant an Envy. I dont blame the Massachusetts Generals, for resigning, one after another. They have had Reason.

RC (MHi). In Adams' hand, though not signed.
[1] Tudor's July 7 letter to Adams is in the Adams Papers, MHi.

John Adams to Joseph Ward

Sir   Philadelphia July 10th. 1776

Yours of 1 July came duely to Hand.[1] The Establishment of the War office as you observe has given me Work enough—more than I have a Relish for, and of a Kind not very suitable to my Taste, but must acquiesce. Shoud be greatly obliged to any officer of the Army for a Hint of any Improvement in the Plan, and for any assistance in the Execution of it.

The continual Reports of our Disasters in Canada have not intimidated the Congress: on the Contrary in the midst of them, more decisive steps have been taken than ever, as you must have seen, or will see before this reaches you. The Romans never would send or receive an Ambassador to treat of Peace when their affairs were in an Adverse situation. This generous Temper is imitated by the Americans.

You hear there is not Candor and Harmony between Some of the Members of this Body. I wish you would mention the Names and Particulars of the Report—the Names I mean of the Members between [whom] it is reported there is not Candor and Harmony. The Report is groundless. There is as much Candor and Harmony between the Members as generally takes Place in assemblies, and much more than could naturally be expected in such an assembly as this. But there is a Prospect now of greater Harmony than ever. The principal object of dispute is now annihilated, and several Members are left out.

In making a Return of your Division of the Army, pray give us the Name and Rank of every officer. We want to make an army List for Publication.

LB (MHi).
¹ Ward's July 1 letter to Adams is in the Adams Papers, MHi.

Committee of Secret Correspondence to Samuel and J. H. Delap

Gentn   Philada. July 10th. 1776

You will receive this by the Brigantine Dispatch, Capt Peter Parker, & with it some letters for Silas Deane Esqr. which being of considerable Consequence We beg you will cause them to be sent or delivered to him with the utmost Expedition and we make no doubt he has left his address with you shou'd he have left Bourdeaux.

You will find herein an Invoice & bill of Loading for some Goods we have shipped onboard this Brigt. Consigned to you for Sale. These Goods youl please to receive & make the most advantageous Sales of them that your market will admit.

Capt Parker has orders to arm & fit out the Dispatch in a Warlike manner and we hope you will advise & assist him in doing it. You'l please to procure him the assistance of the most skillful Persons, Tradesmen &c for doing that business & supply him with money to purchase Cannon, Swivels, Howitzers, Musquets, Powder, Balls &c.

He must fit her in a very compleat manner & must have plenty of
these kind of Stores. He is also to procure as many Seamen as he
possibly can to come with him in this Brigt. in which we also pray
for your assistance & that you will furnish with money to pay advance wages for Provisions and a New Suit of Sails all which we
hope he will soon get Compleated with your assistance. When you
have paid all charges & Expences relative to this Vessell, whatever
ballance remains from the Sale of her Cargo you'l please to Invest
in the purchase of some Brass Field Pieces, Six & four pounder, & if
you can procure them, good Soldiers muskets, Gun Locks, Powder
or Salt Petre, or if you cannot ship such articles, you may then Invest the said Ballance in Blankets and other Woolen Goods suitable
for wear in a Cold Climate and whatever you buy, ship onboard the
said Brigt. Dispatch for address of the Committee of Secret Correspondence on Account & Risque of the United States of America
and enclose to them an Invoice & bill of Loading for the same. It is
necessary that Capt. Parker make dispatch in fitting the Brigt. and
getting her ready for Sea & that you also compleat your business for
her soon as you can but she is not to Sail untill Mr. Deane sends his
dispatches for those are the most immediate object of the present
Voyage. Therefore if Mr. Deane is not at Bourdeaux you will please
to keep him well informed when the Brigt. will be ready to return &
the Moment his dispatches come to your hands deliver them to Capt
Parker with an injunction to Sail immediately for this Coast agreable to his orders. Shou'd Mr. Deane be in Bourdeaux Capt. Parker
must be directed by him entirely in all his proceedings and if Mr.
Deane desires any Goods to be Shipped onboard the Dispatch they
must be received onboard. In short the Captain is ordered to receive onboard all Goods you recommend. Therefore you'l please to
Ship any you may have or that Mr Deane may order & inform Mr
John Danl Schweighauser of Nantes that he may Ship any he has
for Account of this Continent. We hope you will assist in making it
known that great Wages & encouragement are given to Seamen in
America & the Seamen of every Country will be alike Welcome. We
shall have frequent opportunitys of addressing you & remain,
Gentn, Your obedt Servants

FC (DNA: PCC, item 37). In the hand of Robert Morris.

Committee of Secret Correspondence
to Peter Parker

Sir   Philada. July 10th 1776
   The Brigt Dispatch of which you are hereby appointed Com-

mander in the Service of the United States of America, being now ready for Sea, You are to proceed immediately onboard said Brigantine for the Port of Bordeaux in France & on your arrival there deliver the dispatches given you herewith to Messrs Saml. & J. H. Delap, Merchts of that place. You are to consider their letter's directed to those Gentlemen as very important and must deliver them yourself soon as possible. You must have them Slung at Sea with a heavy weight ready to throw overboard & sink them in case you shou'd be unfortunately taken by the Enemy, but to avoid that danger you must make it a standing rule to run from every Vessell you see at Sea. The Dispatch is well found with plenty of sails, rigging, Stores & materials. You will therefore make good use of them and endeavour to make a short passage by a dilligent attention to winds and weather carrying at all times as much Sail as is proper.

The Goods we have caused to be shipped onboard this Brigt are Consigned to Messrs. Delap to whom you are to deliver the same & when this is done you must immediately set about arming the Brigt with Eight or Ten four pounder Cannon, as many Swivels, Blunderbusses, Cohorns, Howitzers & Muskets as you think proper, but take care that the Cannon &c are of the best & handsomest, fit for ships use. You may if you think proper fit her with Close quarters & mount some Guns in the Cabin, Steerage & Fore Castle, or you may Mount the whole on Deck, and if she will bear more than Ten Cannon you may buy them. You must procure a suitable quantity of Powder & Ball for the Cannon, Arms &c with Cartridges, Cartridge Paper & all necessary apparatus thereto. You will Compleat this business with Expedition and procure the best advice & assistance in doing it. Messrs Delap will recommend you to proper People for that purpose & they will supply you with Money to pay the Cost. You must Ship as many Seamen as you can possibly get, especially American Seamen or those that have been much Connected in this Country but you are not to Confine yourself to those above. We are in Want of Seamen and you may bring People of all Countrys or Nations that are willing to enter into the American Service. You must make it known in the best manner you can that great Wages & encouragements is now given to Seamen in every part of America both for the Publick & for Merchant Service. You are therefore to bring over not only sufficient for your own Compliment which as an armed Vessel ought be Thirty or forty, but as many as you can Conveniently give Ship room to and you may Contract with them for such reasonable Wages as may be satisfactory to them. If any Masters or Mates Want passages home you are to Accomodate them free of any Charge to them. You must lay in sufficient of Provisions and allow each man plenty but suffer no waste. You are to receive from Messrs. Delap any Goods they may desire to Ship or from any other persons Goods that Messrs. Delap approve of being

Shipped onboard and when you are ready for departure you are to wait on those Gentln for their dispatches and when you receive the same, with their approbation for your departure you are then to make the best of your way back for this Coast. You know how it is lined with British Men of Warr at present, and it is not possible for us to say what port may be safest by the time you return, but as we expect you will be well Armed & manned you need not fear small Vessells, and by keeping Constantly a hand at each Mast head to look out we think you may avoid all large ones especially as we expect the Dispatch will be a Flyer, and in France you might get another Compleat suit of Sail for her. You must therefore put into the first safe port you can any where in the United States of America & by the time you return you may expect to meet with some of our own Frigates, Galleys & Cruizers. Little Egg Harbour or Cape May will probably be as secure as any other places.

We deliver you herewith a Commission, a list of agents for Prizes, & the Resolves of Congress respecting Captures [1] by which you will learn how to Conduct yourself in this respect. Your business however is not to Cruize but to make quick passage, but if you meet any prizes on your return so much the better provided you do not loose time in seeking them, and in case of Capture you must send them in to some of the agents, who will do the needfull for all Concerned. We expect you will be carefull of the Brigt,[2] her Stores & Materials, dilligent in making dispatch both at Sea & in port, faithfull in the discharge of your Duty, and the moment you raise any port in America come or send the dispatches Express to the Committee of Secret Correspondance. We are sir, Your Hble servants

P.S. Shoud you meet Silas Deane Esqr. who lately went from this place for Bourdeaux, you may Consult with and be advised & directed by him in all things relative to your business with the Brigt Dispatch.

FC (DNA: PCC, item 37). In the hand of Robert Morris. Addressed: "Capt Peter Parker, No. 2."
   [1] See *JCC*, 4:230–32, 252–54, 300–301.
   [2] Parker and the *Dispatch* were captured on July 22. Clark, *Naval Documents*, 5:1183n.

William Ellery to Benjamin Ellery

Dear Brother,[1]   Philadelphia July 10th 1776

I am extremely obliged to you for your repeated Favours, and am glad to find that amidst your Misfortunes, and our common Calamities you preserve so much Fortitude of Mind. We have lived to see a Period which a few years ago no human forecast could have imagined. We have lived to see these Colonies shake of[f], or rather declare themselves independent of a State which they once gloried to call their Parent—I said *declare* themselves independent; for it is One Thing for Colonies to declare themselves independent, and another to establish themselves in Independancy. For this Establishment the Congress are exerting every Nerve, and I rejoice to see this as well as the other American States ready to execute their Measures. Six hundred of the Associators of this State have already marched and Thousands are preparing to march to the Jersey. The Lower Counties are ready to send forth the Troops they can spare to oppose the Army under Genl. Howe, and Maryland will soon furnish its Quota of the Flying Camp. I wish it may be feasible to attack the British Forces before the Reinforcement or rather the Army shall arrive—By the best Accts We can get, 20,000 Troops may be daily expected. A great Stroke will be struck in a short Time. The Events of War are uncertain. God send the Victory. We have nothing New. I send you inclosed the News-Paper of this Day, in which you will take Notice that the Declaration of *Independency* was proclaimed at the State-House; but it is not published that the late King's Arms were taken from thence and the Court House that Morning and were burned that evening near the Coffee House. What a surprizing Alteration hath taken Place here in the Course of a few Months! However there are still in this State, as well as in Jersey, the Lower Counties, Maryland and New York a Number of Tories who will show themselves should Howes Army be successful. I am as much afraid of those villains as of the British Troops with their mercenary Auxiliaries—A good Lookout is constantly kept and any Rising of them will be immediately surpressed. Major Rogers who was under Guard here made his Escape last Evening. He may do Mischief, if he should not be taken. I shall agreeable to your Desire write to a certain Gentleman, by the Bearer of this. As we have nothing New to communicate do not write to the Colony. I am determined to write to the Governor every Fortnight whether We have any Thing New or not, and oftner if any Thing material should in the mean Time occur. I wrote to him last Saturday [2] and shall in Course write to him next Saturday Week. By calculating you will know when to wait upon him for News. I shall write to you as I have Opportunity and hope you will continue your Favours to yrs,   W. E.

[*P.S.*] My Love to your Wife & Children.

MS not found; reprinted from *PMHB* 10 (October 1886): 320–21.

[1] Benjamin Ellery (1726–97), William's elder brother, resided in Newport, R.I., where he generally remained aloof from public affairs during the revolutionary era and instead devoted most of his attention to tending the fortune he had inherited from his first wife, Lucy Barron Vassall. Shipton, *Harvard Graduates*, 12:131–33.

[2] Not found.

John Hancock to William Palfrey

Sir,   Philada. July 10th. 1776.

I am to inform you, that Congress in Consideration of your Zeal, and Attachment to the Liberties of America, have tho't proper to give you the Rank of Lieutenant Colonel in the Continental Army.[1]

You will please to acquaint me whether General Washington ever delivered a Commission to Mr. Harrison, or to Mr. Bailer in Consequence of their Appointment. If he has, I will forward one to you. But if they have not received Commissions, you will in that Case, like them, take your Rank without a Commission.

I have the Honour to be, Sir, your most obed., & very hble Sert.

J. H. Prest.

LB (DNA: PCC, item 12A). Addressed: "Wm Palfrey Esqr, Paymaster Genl., New York."

[1] See JCC, 5:529.

John Hancock to George Washington

Sir,   Philadelphia July 10th. 1776.

The enclosed Letter from Mr. Ephraim Anderson, I am directed to transmit by Order of Congress.

As Mr. Anderson appears to be an ingenious Man, and proposes to destroy the British Fleet at New York, the Congress are willing to give him an Opportunity of trying the Experiment, and have therefore thought proper to refer him to you.[1]

The Event only can shew, whether his Scheme is visionary, or practicable. Should it be attended with Success (and the very Chance of it is sufficient to justify the Attempt) the infinite Service to the American States arising therefrom, cannot be described. Or should it fail, our Situation will be, in every Respect, the same as before.

Many Things seem highly probable in Speculation, which however cannot be reduced to Practice. And on the other Hand, Experiment has shewn, that many Things are extremely practicable, which our most accurate Reasonings had taught us to believe were impossible.

I have the Honour to be, Sir, with the greatest Respect, your most obed. & very hble Servt.   John Hancock Presidt.

RC (DLC). In the hand of Jacob Rush and signed by Hancock.

[1] For Ephraim Anderson's July 9 letter to Congress, see Washington Papers, DLC; and Clark, Naval Documents, 5:1017n.2. Anderson, adjutant to the Second New Jersey Battalion, discussed the progress of his plan to destroy the British fleet at New York with fire ships in his July 19 and 31 letters to Hancock. PCC, item 78, 1:11, 19; and Clark, Naval Documents, 5:1143, 1308. See also Washington, Writings (Fitzpatrick), 5:275, 343–44.

Arthur Middleton to William Henry Drayton

My dear friend [1]   Philadelphia July 10th 1776
I have written you a Sheet full of Stuff, but as I never like to do
things by halves must keep it, endeavour to add to it, & send it by
some future opportunity.

This is barely to acknowledge your favour of the 3d May, with the
charge under a prosperous Seal. The plant which you have been
nursing has thriven amazingly, its roots have reach'd this place &
sprung up in full vigour. I send you the fruit plucked from 12 of the
Branches, & have the pleasure to tell you that the 13th is in full
Blossom. My Sentiments upon this subject you shall have soon, in
the meantime enjoy the delicacies of this forbidden fruit, if it has
any.[2]

30,000 men soon to be before N York—10,000 with Burgoyne in
Canada—& Clinton's armament to the Southwd. These are alarming
Considerations—but "fortes Fortuna" my friend & this Campaign
will bring us near the goal. My anxiety for my dear Country whose
fate may by this time be determined, has almost deprived me of my
Senses, therefore Excuse this Scrawl from your Affecte.

[*P.S.*] I take the Liberty of inclosing Two Letters for Mr. Gadsden.[3]
The gentleman to whom they are directed is gone hence & as I know
not how to get them to him not knowing the road he took, please to
deliver them to Mr. G. with my Comps. Remember the word is "aut
Cæsaries aut nulli."

RC (ScU photostat). In Middleton's hand, though not signed.
   [1] William Henry Drayton (1742–79), a South Carolina lawyer who had recently
been elected chief justice of the province, served as a delegate in Congress, 1778–79.
DAB; and *Bio. Dir. Cong.*
   [2] In this allegorical paragraph, the "plant," "fruit," and "13th branch" are obviously the issue of independence, the Declaration of Independence, and the state
of New York.
   [3] Not found.

Caesar Rodney to Thomas Rodney

Sir,   Philadelphia July the 10th 1776
You mention in your last that Mr. Wells is discharged the Service.
Coll. Haslet has not as Yet Reported that matter to Congress. When
he does I Shall attend to what you have said on that head.

With respect to the other matters you sent me, I am of Opinion
that any good Effect which might flow from them must be Local, I
mean that it would be Confined principally to the Inhabitants of
that County. And on the other hand, at a time of Such Eminent
Danger, when Powerfull Armies are Actually Knocking at our Gates,

And the Serious attention of Every friend to American Liberty is Employed in giving that manly opposition to those Vile Invaders of their Just Rights, privaledges and property, Whether it would be prudent to hold out to the World Such numbers of Internal Enemies—Especially as by the manly and determined Spirit prevailing in the Congress their wings must and will be Clipped. The Declaration has laid the foundation—and will be followed by Laws fixing the degree of Offence, and punishment Suitable. Some people have done things, which if done in future nothing less than life will be Sufficient to Attone for. These Enemies to our Righteous Cause will (I apprehend) be Less on their Guard if they are not held up in that public way, than if they are—and Will undoubtedly meet their due Reward, provided you persue Steadily your line of Patriotism, and at the Same time keep a Watchfull Eye toward their Conduct in the pollitics of your County. These things Must and Will be Enquired into. But Sir, now is the time and Season that our open and avowed Enemies are pressing hard. They Call forth the attention and Utmost Vigilence of the Congress to that Point. They well know they have internal Enemies in disguise, And Whenever, by the blessing of God, their Virtuous Efforts Shall be Crowned with Success, They will imediately turn their thoughts toward those Sapper's of the Rights of Mankind. It is also the business of every Government so Soon as formed to take in hand that business. South Carolina has already Set them a Good Example.

I have sent you a pamphlet Called Observations on the Nature of Civil Liberty &c. wrote by Doctr. Price in England. It is an Excellent Peice and don't Doubt (properly used) will tend to Strengthen Your Patriotic or in other words Independent party. I have also directed one to Doctr. McCall as present.

The Militia of Pensylvania are beginning their March this day toward New York, and I do Suppose that by the last of this Week Generl. Washington will be Thirty Thousand Strong at Least. Coll. Haslet's Battalion (Except one Company Which [is] to Stay at Lewis) is ordered up to Wilmington, as a Security to Philadelphia,[1] in the Absence of their Militia as well as to the Lower Counties, And hopes for this Reason the Committee of Safety will permitted them to retain (while thus Employed) the Militia Arms belonging to the public.

Neither Betsey's or Sally's Shoes are yet done, tho the measures were sent as soon as I Got to town. I am Glad to find that You are of Opinion My Harvest will be down by the last of this Week. Pray do attend to it. Perhaps Wheat will bring something next year. I am Yours &c.   Caesar Rodney

RC (PPRF).
[1] See *JCC*, 5:520; and John Hancock to the New Jersey Convention, July 5, 1776, note 2.

James Wilson to Jasper Yeates

Dear Sir   Philada. 10th July 1776
I cannot have the Pleasure of going with you to Pittsburgh;[1] as Business of every Kind crowds exceedingly upon me here. Your own good Sense must, in a great Measure, be your Director in your Management of the Indians at the ensuing Treaty. I have the Minutes of a Number of Treaties at Carlisle. They will be of considerable Use in shewing you the Formalities practised with the Indians, and the Mode of Language adopted in Addressing them. I have also a great many Belts of Wampum. It will be proper to take them with you. You may, perhaps, have Occasion for them. Col. Montgomery of Carlisle is appointed a Commissioner. I presume he will attend the Treaty. I will write to you again in a Day or two; and am, Dear Sir, Your very affect & hble Servt.   James Wilson

RC (PHi).
[1] See Benjamin Franklin and James Wilson to Jasper Yeates, July 4, 1776.

John Adams to Abigail Adams

Philadelphia July 11. 1776
You seem to be situated in the Place of greatest Tranquility and Security, of any upon the Continent. . . .[1] I may be mistaken in this particular, and an Armament may have invaded your Neighbourhood before now. But We have no Intelligence of any such Design and all that We now know of the Motions, Plans, Operations, and Designs of the Enemy, indicates the Contrary. It is but just that you should have a little Rest, and take a little Breath.

I wish I knew whether your Brother and mine have inlisted in the Army, and what Spirit is manifested by our Militia, for marching to New York and Crown Point. . . . The Militia of Maryland, New Jersey, Pensilvania, and the lower Counties, are marching with much Alacrity, and a laudable Zeal, to take Care of Howe and his Army at Staten Island. The Army in New York is in high Spirits, and seems determined to give the Enemy a serious Reception.

The unprincipled, and unfeeling, and unnatural Inhabitants of Staten Island, are cordially receiving the Enemy, and Deserters say have engaged to take Arms. They are an ignorant, cowardly, Pack of Scoundrells. Their Numbers are small, and their Spirit less.

It is some Time, since I received any Letter from you; the Plymouth one was the last. You must write me, every Week by the Post. If it is but a few Lines, it gives me many Spirits.

I design to write to the General Court, requesting a Dismission, or

at least a Furlow. I think to propose that they choose four more
Members or at least two more, that so We may attend here in
Rotation. Two or three or four may be at home at a Time, and the
Colony properly represented notwithstanding. Indeed, while the
Congress were employed in political Regulations, forming the Sentiments of the People of the Colonies into some consistent System,
extinguishing the Remainders of Authority under the Crown, and
gradually erecting and strengthening Governments, under the Authority of the People, turning their Thoughts upon the Principles of
Polity and the Forms of Government, framing Constitutions for the
Colonies seperately, and a limited and defined Confederacy, for the
united Colonies, and in some other Measures, which I do not choose
to mention particularly, but which are now determined, or near the
Point of Determination, I flattered myself that I might have been of
some little Use here. But, now, these Matters will be soon compleated,
and very little Business will be to be done here, but what will be
either military or Commercial, Branches of Knowledge and Business, for which hundreds of others in our Province, are much better
qualified than I am. I shall therefore request my Masters to relieve
me.[2]

I am not a little concerned about my Health which seems to have
been providentially preserved to me, much beyond my Expectations.
But I begin to feel the disagreable Effects, of unremitting Attention
to Business for so long a Time, and a Want of Exercise, and the brac-
ing Quality of my Native Air: so that I have the Utmost Reason to
fear an irreparable Injury to my Constitution, if I do not obtain a
little Relaxation.

The Fatigues of War, are much less destructive to Health, than
the painfull laborious Attention, to Debates, and to Writing, which
drinks up the Spirits and consumes the Strength. I am &c.

RC (MHi). Adams, *Family Correspondence* (Butterfield), 2:43–44.
[1] Suspension points in MS, here and below.
[2] For Adams' proposals to the Massachusetts Assembly for rotating the delegates
to Congress, see Adams to John Avery, July 25, 1776. Adams did not leave Congress
until October 13, 1776.

John Hancock to George Washington

Sir,   Philada. July 11th. 1776.
I do myself the Honour to inform you, that your several Letters to
this Time, have been duely received in the Order of their Dates.
I now enclose sundry Resolves, to which I must beg Leave to re-
quest your Attention.[1]
Agreeable to the Resolve herewith transmitted, I have enclosed

Mr. Anderson's Letter to you, and wrote you on the Subject. He will present you the Letter himself.

The Postmaster having established a double Post in Obedience to the Resolve of Congress, a Post will, after Monday next, leave New York every Morning, subject however to be detained or hastened, whenever you think the Public Service requires it.[2]

It is with the greatest Pleasure I inform you, that the Militia of this Colony are in Motion from one End to the other. Several Companies marched yesterday; and a much greater Number, I expect, will now march every Day, until the whole are gone. A most laudable Spirit seems to have taken Place, and I am persuaded, our Exertions will exceed what I originally apprehended.

To that great and good Being who "poureth Contempt on Princes, and weakeneth the Strength of the mighty" I beg Leave most ardently to recommend you, and the Cause, you are entrusted to defend.

I have the honor to be with much Esteem, Sir, Your most obedt. hume Servt.   John Hancock Presidt

RC (DLC). In the hand of Jacob Rush and signed by Hancock.
[1] These resolves, which were passed by Congress on July 9 and 10, dealt with raising a Virginia rifle company, congressional military appointments, pay for Pennsylvania militiamen, and supplies for the flying camp in New Jersey. *JCC*, 5:529, 531.
[2] See *JCC*, 5:522; and Abraham Clark to William Livingston, July 5, 1776.

William Paca to William Livingston

Sir   Philad. 11 July 1776

Mr. Johnson is absent in Maryland. I therefore as directed opened yours.[1] Mr. Wright is the Son of Mr. Solomon Wright a gentleman of our Province who has ever been considered as an active & well affected Person in the American Cause. I know not the suspicious Circumstances you allude to But without the strongest Proofs I should not be inclined to question the Purity of Mr Wrights Intentions. I saw him here. He waited upon Mr. Bordley & myself to facilitate his Sale of the Bills of Exchange you mention. I know the Gentleman who furnished him with the Bills. He was recommended to us in Case he found difficulties in the Sale of his Bills. Mr. Wright not being satisfied with the Exchange here informed us of his Intention of going to New York to try the Exchange there. I must say I advised and remonstrated against it. Perhaps the suspicious Circumstances may arise merely from Indiscretion; however I may be deceived. I can only say if Mr. Wright has been dispatched upon any inimical Designs it is what I should never have conceived his Connections were capable of doing. I am, Sir, yr. hb Sert.

                                                          Wm Paca

RC (MHi).

[1] Livingston's letter to Thomas Johnson of July 10 is in the Livingston Papers, MHi. The following extract from it renders Paca's response self-explanatory. "A certain William Wright from Maryland was sent a Prisoner to me by the Committee of this County [Essex] for Examination. Many Suspicious Circumstances attend him. . . . he says . . . That he was bound to New York in order to sell Bills of Exchange, which he has with him to the amount of £1100 & upwards—but tho' a perfect Stranger he has neither Recommendation to any Gentleman there nor Pass. He says that he knows Mr. Paca, Mr. Boardley & yourself. . . . I am under necessity of detaining him till I hear from you. . . . We are within Sight of the Enemy, who lay as thick as Locusts along the Staten Island Shore, for several Miles."

Secret Committee Minutes of Proceedings

July 11th. 1776

The Come. met, present Messrs. Morris, Alsop, Lewis, Hewes & Bartlett. The follg. Acct. was producd to the Come.

The Hbl. Sect. Come. to J. Wilcocks

Dr. 1772 [i.e. 1776]—April 8th
to 147 lb G. powder at 5s————£36.15
Cr. by 75 lb G. Powder recd.
per Order of the Chairman————18.15
Ballance   £18

Orderd that the balance be paid. An order on the Treasurers in favor of sd. Wilcocks for 48 dlls balance of the above Acct.

Order on the Treasurers in favor of G. Mead & Co. for Dlls. 3370 1/3 being the amount of an Invoice of Goods purchasd by them & shipd. on board the Brigante. Freindship for Hispaniola on Contl. Acct.   Capt. Springs Acct. for storage of powdr. amount £19.9.2 1/2 being producd to the Come. Orderd that it be paid. Order on the Treasurers for 211 9/10 dlls in full for the same. A Charter party for the Brigantine Cornelia & Molly, Robt. Briges Owner, was signed by the Committee.[1] Do. for ship Olive branch, George Kennedy & W. McCullough Owners, was signed by the Come.

MS (MH).

[1] For information concerning the fulfillment of this contract, see Secret Committee Minutes of Proceedings, October 31, 1776.

John Hancock to the Lancaster County Committee

Gentlemen,   Philada. July 12th. 1776

The enclosed Resolve, which I have it in Charge from Congress to transmit, is so extremely explicit, that I have only to request you

will have it carried into immediate Execution with all the Dispatch
in your Power.[1]

I shall write to the Committee of Reading to remove the Prisoners
in that Place to your Town.

I have the Honour to be, Gentlemen, your most obed. & very hble
Svt.   John Hancock Presidt

RC (DLC). In the hand of Jacob Rush and signed by Hancock.

[1] This was Congress' July 10 resolve pertaining to British prisoners quartered at
Lancaster and the removal to Lancaster of prisoners in Reading. *JCC*, 5:531. See
also *Am. Archives*, 5th ser. 1:533. The first part of this resolve was inspired by a
July 7 letter to Hancock from George Ross, chairman of the Lancaster Committee.
Ibid., pp. 103–4.

Thomas Jefferson's Notes of
Proceedings in Congress

[July 12–August 1, 1776][1]

On Friday July 12 the Committee appointed to draw the articles
of confederation reported them and on the 22d the house resolved
themselves into a committee to take them into consideration. On the
30th and 31st of that month & 1st of the ensuing, those articles were
debated which determined the ⟨*manner of voting in Congress, & that
of fixing the*⟩ proportion or quota⟨*s*⟩ of money which each state
should furnish to the common treasury, and the manner of voting in
Congress. The first of these articles was expressed in the original
draught in these words. '*Art*. XI. All charges of war & all other expenses that shall be incurred for the common defence, or general welfare, and allowed by the United states assembled, shall be defrayed
out of a common treasury, which shall be supplied by the several
colonies in proportion to the number of inhabitants of every age,
sex & quality, except Indians not paying taxes, in each colony, a
true account of which, distinguishing the white inhabitants, shall be
triennially taken & transmitted to the assembly of the United states.'

Mr. Chase [2] moved that the quotas should be fixed, not by the
number of inhabitants of every condition, but by that of the 'white
inhabitants.' He admitted that taxation should be alwais in proportion to property; that this was in theory the true rule, but that from
a variety of difficulties it was a rule which could never be adopted
in practice. The value of the property in every state could never be
estimated justly & equally. Some other measure for the wealth of the
state must therefore be devised, some ⟨*measure of wealth must be*⟩
standard referred to which would be more simple. He considered the
number of inhabitants as a tolerably good criterion of property, and
that this might alwais be obtained. ⟨*yet numbers simply would not*⟩

he therefore thought it the best mode which we could adopt, with ⟨some⟩ one exception⟨s⟩ only. He observed that negroes are property, and as such cannot be distinguished from the lands or personalties held in those states where there are few slaves. That the surplus of profit which a Northern farmer is able to lay by, he invests in ⟨lands⟩ cattle, horses &c. whereas a Southern farmer lays out that same surplus in slaves. There is no more reason therefore for taxing the Southern states on the farmer's head, & on his slave's head, than the Northern ones on their farmer's heads & the heads of their cattle. That the method proposed would therefore tax the Southern states according to their numbers & their wealth conjunctly, while the Northern would be taxed on numbers only: that Negroes in fact should not be considered as members of the state more than cattle & that they have no more interest in it.

Mr. John Adams observed that the numbers of people were taken by this article as an index of the wealth of the state & not as subjects of taxation. That as to this matter it was of no consequence by what name you called your people, whether by that of freemen or of slaves. That in some countries the labouring poor were called freemen, in others they were called slaves; but that the difference as to the state was imaginary only. What matters it whether a landlord employing ten labourers in his farm, gives them annually as much money as will buy them the necessaries of life, or gives them those necessaries at short hand. The ten labourers add as much wealth annually to the state, increase it's exports as much in the one case as the other. Certainly 500 freemen produce no more profits, no greater surplus for the paiment of taxes than 500 slaves. Therefore the state in which are the labourers called freemen should be taxed no more than that in which are those called slaves. Suppose by any extraordinary operation of nature or of law one half the labourers of a state could in the course of one night be transformed into slaves: would the state be made the poorer or the less able to pay taxes? That the condition of the labouring poor in most countries, that of the fishermen particularly of the Northern states is as abject as that of slaves. It is the number of labourers which produce the surplus for taxation, and numbers therefore indiscriminately are the fair index of wealth. That it is the use of the word 'property' here, & it's application to some of the people of the state, which produces the fallacy. How does the Southern farmer procure slaves? Either by importation or by purchase from his neighbor. If he imports a slave, he adds one to the number of labourers in his country, and proportionably to it's profits & abilities to pay taxes. If he buys from his neighbor, it is only a transfer of a labourer from one farm to another, which does not change the annual produce of the state, & therefore should not change it's tax. That if a Northern farmer works ten labourers on his farm, he can, it is true, invest the surplus of ten men's labour in cattle: but so may the Southern farmer working ten slaves. That a state of 100,000 freemen can maintain no more cattle than one of 100,000 slaves. Therefore they have no more of that kind of property. That a slave may indeed from the custom of speech be more properly called the wealth of his master, than the free labourer might be called the wealth of his employer: but as to the state both were equally it's wealth, and should therefore equally add to the quota of it's tax.

Mr. Harrison proposed a compromise, that two slaves should be counted as one freeman. He affirmed that slaves did not do so much work as freemen, and doubted if two effected more than one. that this was proved by the price of labor, the hire of a labourer in the Southern colonies being from 8 to £12, while in the Northern it was generally £24.

Mr. Wilson said that if this amendment should take place the Southern colonies would have all the benefit of slaves, whilst the Northern ones would bear the burthen. That slaves increase the profits of a state, which the Southern states mean to take to themselves; that they also increase the burthen of defence, which would of course fall so much the heavier on the Northern. That slaves occupy the places of freemen and eat their food. Dismiss your slaves & freemen will take their places. It is our duty to lay every discouragement on the importation of slaves; but this amendment would give the *jus trium liberorum* to him who would import slaves. That other kinds of property were pretty equally distributed thro' all the colonies: there were as many cattle, horses, & sheep in the North as the South, & South as the North: but not so as to slaves. That experience has shewn that those colonies have been alwais able to pay most which have the most ⟨males⟩ inhabitants, whether they be black or white. And the practice of the Southern colonies has alwais been to make every farmer pay poll taxes upon all his labourers whether they be black or white. He acknoleges indeed that freemen work the most; but they consume the most also. They do not produce a greater surplus for taxation. The slave is neither fed nor clothed so expensively as a freeman. Again white women are exempted from labour generally, which negro women are not. In this then the Southern states have an advantage as the article now stands. It has sometimes been said that slavery is necessary because the commodities they raise would be too dear for market if cultivated by freemen; but now it is said that the labor of the slave is the dearest.

Mr. Payne urged the original resolution of Congress, to proportion the quotas of the states to the number of souls.

Dr. Witherspoon was of opinion that the value of lands & houses was the best estimate of the wealth of a nation, and that it was practicable to obtain such a valuation. This is the true barometer of wealth. The one now proposed is imperfect in itself, and unequal

between the states. It has been objected that negroes eat the food of
freemen & therefore should be taxed. Horses also eat the food of
freemen; therefore they also should be taxed. It has been said too
that in carrying slaves into the estimate of the taxes the state is to
pay, we do no more than those states themselves do, who alwais
take slaves into the estimate of the taxes the individual is to pay.
But the cases are not parallel. In the Southern colonies slaves pervade
the whole colony; but they do not pervade the whole continent.
That as to the original resolution of Congress to proportion the
quotas according to the souls, it was temporary only, & related to the
monies heretofore emitted: whereas we are now entering into a new
compact and therefore stand on original ground.

Aug. 1. The question being put the amendment proposed was
rejected by the votes of N. Hampshire, Massachusets, Rhode Island,
Connecticut, N. York, N. Jersey, & Pennsylvania, against those of
Delaware, Maryland, Virginia, North & South Carolina. Georgia
was divided.

The other article was in these words. 'Art. XVII. In determining
questions each colony shall have one vote.'

July 30. 31. Aug. 1. Present 41 members. Mr. Chase observed that
this article was the most likely to divide us of any one proposed
in the draught then under consideration. That the larger colonies
had threatened they would not confederate at all if their weight in
congress should not be equal to the numbers of people they added
to the confederacy; while the smaller ones declared against an union
if they did not retain an equal vote for the protection of their rights.
That it was of the utmost consequence to bring the parties together,
as should we sever from each other, either no foreign power will
ally with us at all, or the different states will form different alliances,
and thus increase the horrors of those scenes of civil war and bloodshed which in such a state of separation & independance would
render us a miserable people. That our importance, our interests,
our peace required that we should confederate, and that mutual
sacrifices should be made to effect a compromise of this difficult
question. He was of opinion the smaller colonies would lose their
rights, if they were not in some instances allowed an equal vote;
and therefore that a discrimination should take place among the
questions which would come before Congress. ⟨He therefore pro-
posed⟩ that the smaller states should be secured in all questions concerning life or liberty & the greater ones in all respecting property.
He therefore proposed that in votes relating to money, the voice of
each colony should be proportioned to the number of it's inhabitants.

Dr. Franklin [3] ⟨seconded the proposition⟩ thought that the votes
should be so proportioned in all cases. He took notice that the
Delaware counties had bound up their Delegates to disagree to this
article. He thought it a very extraordinary language to be held by

any state, that they would not confederate with us unless we would let them dispose of our money. Certainly if we vote equally we ought to pay equally: but the smaller states will hardly purchase the privilege at this price. That had he lived in a state where the representation, originally equal, had become unequal by time & accident he might have submitted rather than disturb government: but that we should be very wrong to set out in this practice when it is in our power to establish what is right. That at the time of the Union between England and Scotland the latter had made the objection which the smaller states now do. But experience had proved that no unfairness had ever been shewn them. That their advocates had prognosticated that it would again happen as in times of old that the whale would swallow Jonas, but he thought the prediction reversed in event and that Jonas had swallowed the whale, for the Scotch had in fact got possession of the government and gave laws to the English. He reprobated the original agreement of Congress to vote by colonies, and therefore was for their voting in all cases according to the number of taxables ⟨so far going beyond Mr. Chase's proposition⟩.

Dr. Witherspoon opposed every alteration of the article. All men admit that a confederacy is necessary. Should the idea get abroad that there is likely to be no union among us, it will damp the minds of the people, diminish the glory of our struggle, & lessen it's importance, because it will open to our view future prospects of war & dissension among ourselves. If an equal vote be refused, the smaller states will become vassals to the larger; & all experience has shewn that the vassals & subjects of free states are the most enslaved. He instanced the Helots of Sparta & the provinces of Rome. He observed that foreign powers discovering this blemish would make it a handle for disengaging the smaller states from so unequal a confederacy. That the colonies should in fact be considered as individuals; and that as such in all disputes they should have an equal vote. That they are now collected as individuals making a bargain with each other, & of course had a right to vote as individuals. That in the East India company they voted by persons, & not by their proportion of stock. That the Belgic confederacy voted by provinces. That in questions of war the smaller states were as much interested as the larger, & therefore should vote equally; and indeed that the larger states were more likely to bring war on the confederacy, in proportion as their frontier was more extensive. He admitted that equality of representation was an excellent principle, but then it must be of things which are co-ordinate; that is, of things similar & of the same nature: that nothing relating to individuals could ever come before Congress; nothing but what would respect colonies. He distinguished between an incorporating & a federal union. The union of England was an incorporating one; yet Scotland had suffered by that union:

for that it's inhabitants were drawn from it by the hopes of places & employments. Nor was it an instance of equality of representation; because while Scotland was allowed nearly a thirteenth of representation, they were to pay only one fortieth of the land tax. He expressed his hopes that in the present enlightened state of men's minds we might expect a lasting confederacy, if it was founded on fair principles.

John Adams advocated the voting in proportion to numbers. He said that we stand here as the representatives of the people. That in some states the people are many, in others they are few; that therefore their vote here should be proportioned to the numbers from whom it comes. Reason, justice, & equity never had weight enough on the face of the earth to govern the councils of men. It is interest alone which does it, and it is interest alone which can be trusted. That therefore the interests within doors should be the mathematical representatives of the interests without doors. That the individuality of the colonies is a mere sound. Does the individuality of a colony increase it's wealth or numbers? If it does; pay equally. If it does not add weight in the scale of the confederacy, it cannot add to their rights, nor weight in arguments. A. has £50. B. £500. C. £1000 in partnership. Is it just they should equally dispose of the monies of the partnership? It has been said we are independant individuals making a bargain together. The question is not what we are now, but what we ought to be when our bargain shall be made. The confederacy is to make us one individual only; it is to form us, like separate parcels of metal, into one common mass. We shall no longer retain our separate individuality, but become a single individual as to all questions submitted to the Confederacy. Therefore all those reasons which prove the justice & expediency of equal representation in other assemblies, hold good here. It has been objected that a proportional vote will endanger the smaller states. We answer that an equal vote will endanger the larger. Virginia, Pennsylvania, & Massachusets are the three greater colonies. Consider their distance, their difference of produce, of interests, & of manners, & it is apparent they can never have an interest or inclination to combine for the oppression of the smaller. That the smaller will naturally divide on all questions with the larger. Rhode Isld. from it's relation, similarity & intercourse will generally pursue the same objects with Massachusets; Jersey, Delaware & Maryland with Pennsylvania.

Dr. Rush [4] took notice that the decay of the liberties of the Dutch republic proceeded from three causes. 1. The perfect unanimity requisite on all occasions. 2. Their obligation to consult their constituents. 3. Their voting by provinces. This last destroyed the equality of representation, and the liberties of Great Britain also are sinking from the same defect. That a part of our rights is deposited in the hands of our legislatures. There it was admitted there should be an equality of representation. Another part of our rights is deposited in the hands of Congress: why is it not equally necessary there should be an equal representation there? Were it possible to collect the whole body of the people together, they would determine the questions submitted to them by their majority. Why should not the same majority decide when voting here by their representatives? The larger colonies are so providentially divided in situation as to render every fear of their combining visionary. Their interests are different, & their circumstances dissimilar. It is more probable they will become rivals & leave it in the power of the smaller states to give preponderance to any scale they please. The voting by the number of free inhabitants will have one excellent effect, that of inducing the colonies to discourage slavery & to encourage the increase of their free inhabitants.

Mr. Hopkins observed there were 4 larger, 4 smaller & 4 middlesized colonies. That the 4 largest would contain more than half the inhabitants of the Confederating states, & therefore would govern the others as they should please. That history affords no instance of such a thing as equal representation. The Germanic body votes by states. The Helvetic body does the same; & so does the Belgic confederacy. That too little is known of the antient confederations to say what was their practice.

Mr. Wilson thought that taxation should be in proportion to wealth, but the representation should accord with the number of freemen. That government is a collection or result of the wills of all. That if any government could speak the will of all it would be perfect; and that so far as it departs from this it becomes imperfect. It has been said that Congress is a representation of states; not of individuals. I say that the objects of it's care are all the individuals of the states. It is strange that annexing the name of 'State' to ten thousand men, should give them an equal right with forty thousand. This must be the effect of magic, not of reason. As to those matters which are referred to Congress, we are not so many states; we are one large state. We lay aside our individuality whenever we come here. The Germanic body is a burlesque on government: and their practice on any point is a sufficient authority & proof that it is wrong. The greatest imperfection in the constitution of the Belgic confederacy is their voting by provinces. The interest of the whole is constantly sacrificed to that of the small states. The history of the war in the reign of Q. Anne sufficiently proves this. It is asked Shall nine colonies put it into the power of four to govern them as they please? I invert the question and ask Shall two millions of people put it in the power of one million to govern them as they please? It is pretended too that the smaller colonies will be in danger from the greater. Speak in honest language & say the minority will be in danger from the majority. And is there an assembly on earth where this danger may not be equally pretended? The truth is that our proceedings will then be consentaneous with the interests of the majority, and so they ought to be. The probability is much greater that the larger states will disagree than that they will combine. I defy the wit of man to invent a possible case or to suggest any one thing on earth which shall be for the interests of Virginia, Pennsylvania & Massachusets, and which will not also be for the interest of the other states.

MS (DLC). In the hand of Thomas Jefferson. A continuation of Jefferson's Notes of Proceedings in Congress, July 1–4, 1776.
[1] For analysis of the notes printed in this entry, see Jefferson, *Papers* (Boyd), 1:327–29.
[2] For additional information on this debate, see John Adams' Notes of Debate, July 30, 1776.
[3] See also John Adams' Notes of Debate, August 1, 1776.
[4] See Benjamin Rush's Notes for a Speech in Congress, August 1, 1776.

Marine Committee to John Ashmead

Sir   Philada. July 12th 1776
    The Marine Committee having considered how necessary your attendance is in the Yard taking care of the Materials, and the Frigate of which you are Clerk, think proper to request that you will not go on the proposed expedition to the Jerseys, but that you remain to do your very necessary business.[1]
    You May shew this to your commanding officer to whom, it is hoped, it will prove a satisfactory reason for your stay.
    We are sir, Your hble servts.

Robt Morris	Geo. Read
Button Gwinnett	Arthur Middleton
Fras Lewis	

RC (CCamarSJ). In the hand of Timothy Matlack and signed by Gwinnett, Lewis, Middleton, Morris, and Read. Endorsed—"Agreed in Congress"—and signed by John Hancock.
[1] Ashmead, clerk of the frigate *Randolph*, was a member of a company of Quaker Light Infantry which was on its way to New Jersey to join the flying camp. Clark, *Naval Documents*, 5:1046n.3.

Secret Committee Minutes of Proceedings

July 12.[1776]
    A Contract was enterd into with Button Guinet [Gwinnett], of the province of Georgia, & an order in his favor was drawn on the Treasurers for 20,000 Dlls. to be by him laid out in the produce of

that Colony & exported to the W. Indies. The returns to be made in arms, Ammunition & goods suitable for the Indians in the southern parts of America.

MS (MH).

Thomas Stone to the Maryland Council of Safety

Gent.   Phila July 12th 1776.

Yours by Capt. Stricker was this morning delivered to me,[1] and I shall pay particular attention to its contents, tho I much fear our endeavour to procure an Engineer to suit your purpose will not be successful. Every man who ever fired a Cannon or was present at erecting any kind of fortification has been taken up for the Continental Service. There is no provision made here for quartering any troops which may pass through. Upon the first notice of Col Smallwoods approach I made enquiry of the State of the City Barracks, and find that there are some soldiers in them who have the Small pox of which I shall acquaint Col Smallwood before he gets into Town.

Indeed there is danger in almost every part of the City, and I shall advise him to halt his men upon the common for a while, until some safe place can be provided for their reception. They will feel severely the want of Tents of which there are none in the Continental Stores. I submit to your consideration if it would not be proper to have Tents immediately made, and sent after the Troops. They will probably be stationed at a place where no quarters can be had. I expect to see them tomorrow. Capt. Stricker will I think be appointed a field Officer in the German Battalion, for which I have no doubt but he is well qualified from what I have heard of him.[2] The militia of this Province are daily marching to Trent Town in the Jerseys, from whence they are to proceed to Amboy. This will be the rout of our Troops I presume. If Brigadier Dent should join the Regulars with the militia to be raised in your Province I dont know how it will be possible to settle the Rank of the Officers. As to keeping them distinct when they are to compose one Army, it seems to me to be impracticable. The rank of each Officer in the Army must be settled before Service is entered on, or the greatest confusion will probably take place. I ordered by Mr Stephen Steward a case of Instruments, some paper and a Gun Carriage. Be pleased inform me if you received them. Mr Alexander writes me that Dr Wisenthall wants the Instruments very much. Our affairs on the lake are far from being so prosperous as I wish them, tho' we have heard nothing certain from that quarter since our Army retreated to Crown Point. Considerable reinforcements are ordered & if they arrive in time I hope our Enemies will receive a Check. Gen. Howe remains on Staten Island exercising his men, and viewing the situation of the adjacent grounds. The inhabitants of the Island are generally Tories, who I suppose will assist him all they can without taking up arms, which I think few of them will do. Genl Washington and the Army under him are in good Spirits, and in strength daily increasing. We regret to hear of the arrival of a considerable reinforcement from Britain, daily will bring on a more intimate acquaintance between the two adverse Armies. May God send Victory to the Arm lifted in Support of righteousness, Virtue & Freedom, and crush even to destruction the power which wantonly would trample on the rights of mankind.

I am Gent. with most sincere esteem, Yr faithful & most humble Servt,   T. Stone.

[*P.S.*] Our Province is now unrepresented tho matters of the last consequence are coming on. I pray one of the Delegates may be desired to attend.

Mr Paca is out which occasions me alone to address you.

MS not found; reprinted from *Md. Archives,* 12:35–36.

¹ The council of safety's letter to the Maryland delegates of July 7 is in *Md. Archives,* 12:12.

² George Stricker was appointed lieutenant colonel of the German battalion on July 17. Samuel Chase's letter of July 8, 1776, to John Hancock recommending Stricker for this appointment is in PCC, item 42, fols. 9–12, and *Am. Archives,* 5th ser. 1:187. See *JCC,* 5:566, 571. See also Samuel Chase to the Maryland Council of Safety, July 30, 1776.

John Witherspoon to Benjamin Harrison

Philadelphia Friday July 12. 1776

Dr Witherspoons Complements to Col. Harrison. The Bearer of this is Mr Rowland Chalmers [Chambers] recommended by the provincial Congress of New Jersey as Paymaster to the 3300 Men raised in Jersey for the Army at N. York. He will be obliged to Col. Harrison if he is appointed to let him know as soon as possible the Condition of the Bond to be taken of him & the nature of the Security that no time may be lost in providing it.¹

RC (DNA: PCC, item 68).

¹ The New Jersey Provincial Congress' recommendation of Chambers is in *Am. Archives,* 4th ser. 6:1631–32. On July 16 Congress decided that Chambers' application for appointment as paymaster to the New Jersey forces in New York "cannot be complied with, as such an appointment would interfere with the duty of the pay master general, within whose department it properly lies." *JCC,* 5:564. This decision was based upon a report of the Board of War, of which Harrison was a member and in which capacity Witherspoon directed this letter to him. *JCC,* 5:438.

John Hancock to George Washington

Sir,   Philadelphia July 13th. 1776
I am to acknowledge the Receipt of your Favour of the 10th Inst., and to acquaint you, that it is under the Consideration of Congress.[1]

The enclosed Resolves I do myself the Honour to transmit, as necessary for your Information. I wrote to General Schuyler, and the Commissioners for Indian Affairs, respecting the same.[2]

In obedience to the Commands of Congress, I have enclosed you two Copies of sundry Resolves they have passed, relative to the Treatment of our Prisoners by Captain Foster in Canada. I am to request you will take the proper Steps to send one of them to General Howe, and the other to Genl. Burgoyne. I transmit also a third Copy for your own Use.[3]

Should the United States of America give their Sanction to the Jesuitical and villainous Distinction which Captain Foster adopts to justify his Conduct, there would be no End to butchering our Prisoners. They have therefore very properly reprobated it, and in the genuine Spirit of Freedom, resolved, that such Cruelty as shall be inflicted on Prisoners in their Possession, by Savages or Foreigners taken into Pay by the King of Great Britain, shall be considered as done by his Orders, and Recourse be immediately had to Retaliation. It is to be hoped, this Determination will have the desired Effect: and that for the future, such barbarous Scenes will never be acted under the Eye and Approbation of a British Officer. I say, under the Approbation of a British Officer: For there is the greatest Reason to believe, that Captain Foster engaged the Indians to join him, on the express Condition of giving up to them all such Prisoners as might fall into his Hands. His subsequent Conduct indeed renders this Conjecture more than probable.

I have the Honour to be, with perfect Esteem, Sir, your most obed. & very hble Sevt.   John Hancock Presidt

1 o'clock P.M. This Moment your Favour per Post of the 11th Inst. came to Hand. I shall lay it before Congress on Monday Morning.[4]

RC (DLC photostat). In the hand of Jacob Rush and signed by Hancock.
[1] This letter is in PCC, item 152, 2:189–96, and Washington, *Writings* (Fitzpatrick), 5:247–50.
[2] These resolves, which were passed by Congress on July 11, dealt with the defense of the Great Lakes. *JCC*, 5:542. Hancock's letter of this date to Schuyler, forwarding these resolves, is in PCC, item 12A, and *Am. Archives*, 5th ser. 1:253. Hancock's letter to the Indian commissioners has not been found.
[3] See *JCC*, 5:533–39; and Washington, *Writings* (Fitzpatrick), 5:279–81.
[4] Washington's letter to Hancock of July 11 is in PCC, item 152, 2:197–204, and Washington, *Writings* (Fitzpatrick), 5:251–55.
Later on the 13th Hancock also received a letter from Washington of July 12, announcing the arrival of Admiral Richard Howe's fleet at New York and request-

ing Congress to send "a Quantity of Musket powder and Lead" to the flying camp in New Jersey. PCC, item 152, 2:213–16; and Washington, *Writings* (Fitzpatrick), 5:264–65. This intelligence led to the convening of a special Sunday session of Congress on the 14th, at which several measures for supplying the flying camp were approved. *JCC*, 5:558–59.

Robert Treat Paine's Diary

[July 13, 1776]

Hot. Heard by Express that Lord Howe was arrived at Sandy Hook & that a 40 Gun Ship a 20 gun ship & 2 Tenders were gone up North River.[1] Frigate launched here.[2]

MS (MHi).

[1] See John Hancock to George Washington, this date, note 4.

[2] Undoubtedly the frigate *Delaware*. For information on the launching of the other frigate constructed at Philadelphia, the *Randolph*, which this day stuck on the ways but was nevertheless launched on the 14th, see Paine's Diary, July 14; and George Read to Gertrude Read, July 14, 1776. See also Clark, *Naval Documents*, 5:1046n.2 for some of the conflicting testimony that has been cited on this subject.

Josiah Bartlett to Mary Bartlett

My Dear   Philadelphia July 14th 1776

Yours of the 30th of June is Come to hand and I have had the pleasure of hearing from you & my other friends in New Hampshire Every week Since I arrived here, but very possibly our letters may not be so regular to & from Each other as they have hitherto been, as the Brittish fleet & army at Staten Island & Hudson's River will no Doubt Endeavor to hinder the Communication between the Eastern and Southern Colonies which perhaps they may in some measure Effect. I am sorry to hear their is like to be a Scarcity of Hay and must leave it to you with proper advice to Sell, fat or Exchange so many of my Cattle as you shall think proper and you will order all the Straw and fodder possible of Every Kind to be saved.

Last Evening an Express arrived from General Washington with some accounts that required our being Called togather this Day (tho Sunday) to give some immediate orders.[1] I Expect Every Body will be very much Engaged for sometime to come, some in taking Care of the harvest and many in opposing the several Brittish & German armies that are sent to Destroy & ravage the Country; But I hope & trust that the Supreme Disposer of all Events, who loveth Justice & hateth iniquity will Continue to favor our righteous Cause and that the wickedness of our Enemies will fall on their own heads.

I am glad to hear you & my family are well, I am so at this time & pray we all continue so till it shall please Providence to return me to you again in Due time.

I can inform you that the greatest preparations are making to oppose the Powerful army that are now or will soon be near New York. I hope it will be done Successfully; however that Depends on Divine Providence whose ways are unsearchable by human beings. I shall continue to write to you weekly unless I hear the communication is stopped. If it should for a short time I doubt not it will soon be opened again.

By Polly & Lois' letter I was informed of the misfortune Mr Wheeler &c &c &c met with in their party of pleasure in the great pond and am glad it was no worse; however this may show my children the dangers that are often run in such gay amusements; dangers at such times often little known & less thought of. Please to inform Major Philbrick I Recd his letter but have not time to write to him this week.

I am yours &c,   Josiah Bartlett

P.S.[2] There is a report that General Clinton who was sent to attack Charlestown in South Carolina in endeavoring to land was repulsed & drove back to the ships & that he had lost some of his ships. I wish it may prove true tho at present we have no certain account to be depended on.[3]

July 16th. Closed, now well. We have lately had Considerable rains here so that there is no want. The 14th was a very wet rainy day the whole of it.

Remember me to the Children and all friends.   J. B.

RC (MH).

[1] See John Hancock to George Washington, July 13, 1776, note 4; and JCC, 5:558–59.

[2] Whether Bartlett wrote the first paragraph of this postscript on July 15 or 16 can only be conjectured. Although its physical appearance suggests that the remainder of this letter was written at one sitting, the date "July 15th 1776" appears in Bartlett's hand at the bottom of the page, written upside down and probably with another pen. Several explanations accounting for this peculiarity can be imagined, but none seem more probable than that all three paragraphs of this postscript were written on July 16.

[3] Congress apparently did not receive official word of the British defeat from Charles Lee until July 19, 1776. JCC, 5:593. But Robert Treat Paine reported in his diary on July 18 that he had heard "News of our victory at Sullivans Island So. Carolina." MHi.

Abraham Clark to Elias Dayton

My Dear friend,   Eliza. Town July 14th. 1776.
I have not had the Pleasure of a Letter from you a long Time.
Yours of the 6th July to Mrs. Dayton I saw yesterday. I frequently
write, but fear you do not receive them.

Soon after my going to Congress at Phila. we had news of Genl.
Howes Arrival at Sandy Hook, and a few days after of his Landing
on Staten Island, and Surrounding it with his forces. From your
feeling for your Town & family when you first recd. this News, you
can form some Judgment of mine tho' I was much nearer to them. I
expected nothing less from this event, than Eliza. Town long Obnoxious to the Enemy, would be laid in Ashes, and indeed, had they
come over they would have met with no Opposition as our Militia a
few days before had Marched to New York by request of the Genl.
Few escaped from the Island, our friend Joshua Mersereau just
escaped them, and Saml. Dehart they took at the ferry, and Obliged
him to bring his family back from Eliza. Town where he had sent
them before. It is said they treat the people of the Island with great
kindness & tenderness. I continued at Phila. till Thursday last when
I returned homeward, We having first Obtained of Congress all the
Assistance they could afford for our Province. Near half the Militia
of Pennsyla. Chearfully offered to March to the Aid of this Province
and indeed, their Ardour was such Congress was Obliged to stop
part of the Militia of Phila. or the City would have been left wholly
defenseless. Part of the Pennsylvanians are at Amboy, and Many on
the road this way. More than 10,000 of them it is expected will in a
few days be here, and are to stay till a flying Camp of 10,000 men,
now raising in Pennsyla., Maryland & Delaware Counties, take their
place. I was yesterday at the Point, and could see near one hundred
of the Enemy Parading at Posts. They have taken up the draw
bridge to keep our people from Attacking them, and keep a guard
there behind a breast work made with the Planks of the bridge. We
have a breast work up the road near where Israel Arnet formerly
lived, extending across the road into the fields. Works is erected
from the Mouth of the Creek before the Point house to the East
Corner of the garden, two other works are erected & erecting further
Eastward. There is at the Point two of our Province field pieces
with part of the Artillery Company, and also the Cannon taken in
the Prize Ship. Two of our field pieces with 1/3 of the Artillery
Company is at New Blazeing Star, with a part of the Enemy in
sight across the Sound, two others of the field pieces at Newark
with 1/3 of the Company to keep of[f] their fears, the only enemy
in Sight. The Artillery Company from West Jersey is Stationed at
Amboy with only two pieces, being all that Company had. Altho'

the Enemy is in Sight at every pass to and from the Island, it is with great difficulty the Militia can be prevailed upon to stray from their farms at this busy season. It is a matter of great Surprize that the forces on the Island are Suffered to remain in quiet, where they are daily receiving Tory recruits, and An Army of near 20,000 from England is Expected hourly to Arrive to join them; and those on the Island, from the best Accounts Amount to About 10,000. A Vessel came up in the Narrows on Friday last Supposed to have Lord Howe on board from the Salute recd. from all the Shiping. If he hath arrived his Army is not far behind, which when Arrived with those on the Island will become formidable. The forces on the Island are dispersed in parties all round it, and I think might easily be dealt with. Capt McLeod said yesterday Our Generals deserved to be Damned if they did not Attack them on the Island before the reinforcements Arrived. On Friday two Men of War & some Tenders run up the North River as far as Kings Bridge and perhaps further as they went out of Sight Notwithstanding a fire from all our works; they recd. several Shot it is said into their Hulls, and had their rigging damaged.

Our Affairs to the Northward wear a bad Aspect; I am Surprized at our forces leaving Island Aux Noix as from the best intelligence recd they might easily have kept the Enemy out of the Lake, by keeping that Post, and it is said from good Authority that 3,000 could keep it against 30,000. The reasons for this Assertion are conclusive, but too long to give here.

In your Letter to Mrs. Dayton you desire Elias may be sent to you, but seem to leave the matter with Mrs. Dayton. You cannot think she would willingly consent to it, and at this Time under present Circumstances, I believe you would not desire it. She Asked my Advice, and I gave it for his not going much against Elias's inclination. The Navigation of Hudsons River now Stoped, and a passage to you almost impossible for him, at best very impracticable.

Mrs. Dayton hath removed part of your goods to Springfield, and herself and Children ready to follow as danger Approaches. She is in good Spirits, thinks she can flee faster than they can pursue.

As to the Plot in New York, I can inform you but little. The Mayor is Confined, One Forbes Appears to have been very Active in it, and all Centres in Governor Tryon, many have Absconded from New York; none in New Jersey are impeached, at least nothing proved Against them. Govr. Franklin is sent Prisoner to Harford in Connecticut. The Amboy Gentry are upon their parole at Trenton. Jouet at the Arrival of the Army run of[f] and hid himself at Schoolys Mountain but at request of his friends purposes to return. Mr. Chetwood put of[f] with his wife some where back, and is now it is thought, near his end by a fever Occasioned they say by the fright; he refuses to Doctor, and his wife in a state of deep Melancholy scarcely Speaking in a day.

Our Declaration of Independance I dare say you have seen. A few weeks will probably determine our fate. Perfect freedom, or Absolute Slavery. To some of us freedom or a halter. Our fates are in the hands of An Almighty God, to whom I can with pleasure confide my own; he can save us, or destroy us; his Councils are fixed and cannot be disappointed, and all his designs will be Accomplished.

My most cordial respects to my Friend Mr Caldwell, to whom I mean to address all my Letters on public affairs in Conjunction with your self as it is useless to tell you both the same Story in different Letters. Your families are well. I have nothing further Necessary to communicate, but that I am, most Affectionately yours,

Abra. Clark

RC (NN). Addressed: "To Elias Dayton Esquire, Colonel of a battalion of Jersey Troops, at the German Flatts."

John Hancock to Hugh Mercer

Sir, Philada. July 14th. 1776.

The Congress having been informed by Genl. Washington, that he had given the Command of the Flying Camp and Militia in New Jersey to you, and for that Purpose you was stationed in the Jerseys,[1] I have it in Charge from Congress to empower and direct you to march such of the Militia and Flying Camp to Brunswick, or other Places in the Jerseys, as you may, on all Occasions, judge necessary and most conducive to the public Service; provided it does not interfere with any prior Direction from Genl. Washington.

Four Tons of Powder were sent off to you, a few Days ago; and a large Parcel of Cartridges well balled, will be this Day forwarded to you for the Use of the Troops under your Command. Colonel Biddle, the Quarter Master Genl. has Orders to furnish all Necessaries. He will wait on you, and follow such Directions, as you may judge necessary to give him.

You will please to give me the earliest Intelligence of every Occurrence by Express, that it may be laid before Congress.

I most heartily wish Success to your Arms, & have the Honour to be, with much Esteem, Sir, your very hble Servt.

J. H. Prest.

LB (DNA: PCC, item 12A).

[1] See JCC, 5:558; and Hancock to Washington, July 13, 1776, note 4. Hugh Mercer (c. 1725–77), a Scottish Jacobite trained as a physician at the University of Aberdeen, came to Pennsylvania around 1747. After becoming acquainted with

Washington during the French and Indian War, he moved to Fredericksburg, Va., and resumed medical practice. Chosen as a colonel of militia by the Virginia Convention in January 1776, Mercer received an appointment from Congress on June 5 as brigadier general in the Continental Army, and shortly thereafter Washington made him commander of the flying camp in New Jersey. He died in January 1777 of wounds sustained at the battle of Princeton. *DAB*.

John Hancock to the Pennsylvania Committee of Safety

Gentlemen   Philadelphia July 14th. 1776.
I am directed by Congress most earnestly to request, you will supply the Flying Camp and Militia in the Jerseys, with as many Muskett Cartridges, with Balls therein, as you can possibly spare and send them forward with the greatest Dispatch.

The State of our Affairs will not admit the least Delay; nor need I use Arguments to induce you to an immediate Compliance with this requisition.

I am likewise to request, you will order all the British Officers Prisoners in this City, *immediately* to the respective places of their Destination. Their Ladies are not to go, until the Weather is fair.[1]

I have the Honour to be, Gentlemen, Your most obdt. & very hble Servt.   John Hancock Presidt.

[*P.S.*] The [*Secret*] Come. of Congress are instructed immediately to replace an equal Quantity of Powder to that deliver'd in Cartridges.[2]

Tr (PHarH).
[1] For Congress' resolves about "Musket Cartridges" and "British Officers," see *JCC*, 5:558–59. The committee's response to them is in *Am. Archives*, 5th ser. 1:1294–95.
[2] See *JCC*, 5:558. This day Hancock also wrote to Gen. Daniel Roberdeau and informed him of Congress' wish that "you will issue fresh orders & Exert yourself to forward the immediate march of the whole Militia destin'd for the Jerseys from this Colony." PCC, item 12A; *Am. Archives*, 5th ser. 1:326; and *JCC*, 5:559.

Robert Treat Paine's Diary

[July 14, 1776]
Very Rainy Day. Congress sat on the Express of last Evening.[1] A Frigate which Stuck yesterday launched to day.[2]

MS (MHi).
[1] See John Hancock to George Washington, July 13, 1776, note 4.
[2] See Paine's Diary, July 13, 1776, note 2.

George Read to Gertrude Read

My dear Gitty.   Philada. 14th May [*i.e.* July] 1776.[1]
I have your Letter of the 12th Instant inclosing one for Mrs. Thompson. You have certainly done very right as to our Man Thomas and he must not be suffered to return to the house again. I believe you must Apply to our Friend Doctor Way to find out a temporary Servant to supply Thos's place. I did expect to have been with you last Evening but was detained by a special call of the Marine Committee. This Morning there is a call of Congress, owing to a Letter by express from Genl. Washington, who writes that 2 Men of War & 3 Tenders passed N. York up the North river on Friday, notwithstanding a heavy fire from several Batteries, that a large Ship with a Flag at her fore topmast head had come up to the Fleet at the Narrows and was saluted, supposed to be Lord Howe (the Admiral's Ship).[2] We have no Accots. from the Army at the Lakes. Most of the companies of Militia of this city have proceeded to Trenton where they rendevous.

Your bror. George[3] came to Town last Evening and says his Battalion are on their way here, 2 companies of them will be in Town this morning. One of the smallest Frigates building here, called the Delaware, was launched yesterday and one of the largest was expected to have gone off the Stocks at the same time but cou'd not be moved owing to the misplacing of the Ways or some such cause, to the great disappointment of the Builder, John Wharton, and a numerous set of Spectators.[4] I went yesterday morning & was agreeably surprised to find that Mr. & Mrs. Biddle had set off the preceeding day to pay you a Visit. I was out at Mr. Gurneys all last Friday on Message from Mrs. Gurney the preceeding Night del[ivere]d to me in bed abt. 11 OClock. I inclose her letter for the singularity & behold the cause was none other than a Notice they had that some Associators were going about to collect Arms from the Non associators. Before I got there they were gone and the fright was over but I was kept the whole day. Mrs. Ross was in tolerable Spirits but complaining as usual. Mrs. Murray is still with them. As to my own health it is not so good as I cou'd wish. This day week I confined myself to the house and have taken some Bark that has relieved me & am now better and I shou'd have dined with Gurney today but the rain induced me to accept of a Seat in Mr. Braxton's Coach & I have been at Mr. Robt. Morris's Country house with a set of People who think & act alike, some Consolation in these times. As our Assembly are to meet to morrow Week I shall have a proper excuse to return to you the last of this. Be assured I wish it most sincerely. Preserve your Spirits and an equanimity of mind for your healths sake. Banish your fears, all may be right. A few Weeks will discover much, I hope in our favour. God preserve you and our little ones and believe me yours most Affectionately,   Geo. Read

[*P.S.*] I expect Mr. Rogers of Maryland will carry this; if you See him treat him as my old acquaintance. I am told the 2d Frigate was launched today. Tom & Jas. Read send their love to you.

RC (DeHi).
[1] Although Read clearly wrote "14th May 1776" the contents of the letter indicate that it was written on July 14. Read's references below to the passage of two British ships up the Hudson River, the arrival of Lord Howe at the Narrows, and the launching of the frigate *Delaware* are to events that took place on July 12 and 13, 1776.
[2] This unusual Sunday session of Congress was called on the receipt of Washington's July 12 letter to Hancock. *JCC*, 5:558; Washington, *Writings* (Fitzpatrick), 5:264–65.
[3] George Ross.
[4] See also Robert Treat Paine's Diary, July 13, 1776, note 2.

John Adams to Abigail Adams

Philadelphia July 15. 1776
My very deserving Friend, Mr. Gerry, setts off, tomorrow, for Boston, worn out of Health, by the Fatigues of this station. He is an excellent Man, and an active able statesman. I hope he will soon return hither. I am sure I should be glad to go with him, but I cannot. I must write to have the Guard relieved.

There is a most amiable, lawdable, and gallant Spirit prevailing, in these middle Colonies. The Militia turn out in great Numbers and in high Spirits, in New Jersey, Pensilvania, Maryland, and Delaware, so that We hope to resist Howe and his Mirimidons.

Independence is at last unanimously agreed to in the New York Convention. You will see by the Newspapers inclosed what is going forward in Virginia, and Maryland and New Jersey. Farewell! farewell, infatuated, besotted Stepdame. I have not Time to add, more than that I receive Letters from you but seldom of late. Tomorrows Post I hope will bring me some. So I hoped of last Saturdays and last Tuesdays.

Ever yours.

RC (MHi). Adams, *Family Correspondence* (Butterfield), 2:49–50.

John Adams to James Warren

Dear sir   July 15. 1776

I have Time only to tell you that I am yet alive, and in better Spirits than Health.

The News, you will learn from my very worthy Friend Gerry.[1] He is obliged to take a Ride for his Health, as I shall be very soon or have none. God grant he may recover it for he is a Man of immense Worth. If every Man here was a Gerry, the Liberties of America would be safe against the Gates of Earth and Hell.

We are in hourly Expectation of sober Work at New York. May Heaven grant Us Victory, if We deserve it; if not Patience, Humility, and Pennitence under Defeat. However, I feel pretty confident and Sanguine that We shall give as good an Account of them this Year as we did last. Adieu.

RC (MHi). In Adams' hand, though not signed.
[1] Robert Treat Paine noted in his diary entry for July 16: "Mr. Gerry set out for home." MHi.

Samuel Adams to Richard Henry Lee

My dear Sir   Philada. July 15 1776

I must acknowledge that when you left Congress, I gave you Reason to expect a letter from me before this Time. You will not, I am very certain, attribute my omission to the Want of a most cordial Esteem for you. The Truth is, I hardly know how to write without saying something of our Canadian Affairs; and this is a Subject so thoroughly mortifying to me, that I could wish totally to forget all that has past in that Country. Let me however just mention to you that Schuyler & Gates are to command the Troops to be employ'd there; the former, while they are without, and the latter, while they are within the Bounds of Canada. Admitting both these Generals to have the military Accomplishments of Marlborough and Eugene, I cannot conceive that such a Disposition of them can be attended with any happy Effects, unless Harmony subsists between them. Alas! I fear this is not the Case. Already Disputes have arisen, which they have referrd to Congress! And though they appear to treat each other with a Politeness becoming their Rank, in my Mind, Altercations between Commanders who have Pretensions so nearly equal, I mean in Point of *Command,* forebode a Repetition of Misfortunes. I sincerely wish my Apprehensions may prove to be groundless.

General Howe, as you have heard, is arrivd at New York. He has brought with him from 8 to 10,000 Troops. Lord Howe arrivd the last Week, and the whole Fleet is hourly expected. The Enemy landed on Staten Island. Nothing of Importance has been done, saving that last Fryday at about three in the Afternoon a 40 and a 20 Gun Ship with several Tenders, taking the Advantage of a fair & fresh Gale and flowing Tide, passed by our Forts as far as the Encampment at Kings bridge. General Mifflin who commands there in a letter of the 5 instant informd us he had twenty one Cannon planted and hoped in a Week to be formidable. Reinforcements are arrivd from N England, and our Army are in high Spirits. I am exceedingly pleasd with the calm & determind Spirit, which our Commander in Chiefe has discoverd in all his Letters to Congress. May Heaven guide and prosper him! The Militia of the Jerseys, Pennsylvania & Maryland are all in Motion. General Mercer commands the flying Camp in the Jerseys. We have just now appointed a Committee to bring in a Plan for a Reinforcement to compleat the Number of 20,000 Men to be posted in that Colony.[1]

Our Declaration of Independency has given Vigor to the Spirits of the People. Had this decisive Measure been taken Nine Months ago, it is my opinion that Canada would at this time have been in our hands. But what does it avail to find fault with what is past. Let us do better for the future. We were more fortunate than I expected in having 12 of the 13 Colonies in favor of the all important Question. The Delegates of N York were not enpowerd to give their Voice on either Side. Their Convention has since acceeded to the Declaration & publishd it even before they receivd it from Congress. So mighty a Change in so short a Time! N Jersey have finishd their Form of Government, a Copy of which I inclose. They have sent us five new Delegates, among whom are Dr. Witherspoon & Judge Stockton. All of them appear to be zealously attachd to the American Cause. A Convention is now meeting in this City to form a Constitution for this Colony. They are empowerd by their Constituents to appoint a new Committee of Safety to act for the present & to chuse new Delegates for Congress. I am told there will be a Change of Men, and if so, I hope for the better.

A Plan of Confederation has been brot into Congress wch I hope will be speedily digested and made ready to be laid before the several States for their Approbation.[2] A Committee has now under Consideration the Business of foreign Alliance. It is high time for us to have Ambassadors in foreign Courts. I fear we have already sufferd too much by Delay. You know upon whom our Thoughts were turned when you was with us.

I am greatly obligd to you for favoring me with the Form of Goverment agreed upon by your Countrymen.[3] I have not yet had time to peruse it, but dare say it will be a Feast to our little Circle. The Device on your great Seal pleases me much.

Pray hasten your Journey hither. Your Country most pressingly solicits, or will you allow me to say *demands* your Assistance here. I have written in great Haste. Adieu my dear Sir, and be assured that I am very affectionately, your Friend.   S A

RC (PPAmP).
    [1] See *JCC*, 5:561–62.
    [2] A draft plan of the articles of confederation was presented to Congress on July 12. *JCC*, 5:546.
    [3] Lee's letter to Adams of July 6, in which he enclosed a copy of Virginia's new constitution, is in Richard Henry Lee, *The Letters of Richard Henry Lee*, ed. James C. Ballagh, 2 vols. (New York: Macmillan Co., 1911–14), 1:207–8.

Josiah Bartlett to John Langdon

My Dear Sir,   Philadelphia July 15th 1776.
    Your's of the first inst is now before me and am obliged to you for your intelligence. The affair of the Agency you have heard is settled and in your favor and I hope another delegate will be appointed to attend Congress as you have resigned.[1]
    The marine affairs I shall leave to brother Whipple who will inform you from time to time what is to be done.
    The Congress and people here are engaged in making preparation for the reception of the British fleet and army in the neighborhood of New York. Lord Howe with the Germans &c is hourly expected. I pray God we may be able to give a good account of them. The confederation is agreed to by the Committee and is before Congress; when they will finish it is uncertain.[2] Two of the frigates here are launched. There is a report in town that General Clinton endeavored to land his men at South Carolina and was repulsed with loss. I know not the particulars and mention it only as a report. I hope you will excuse my not writing every week as brother Whipple has wrote you every thing of importance.
    Major Rogers was taken up by order of General Washington and having your letters of recommendation to us, the General ordered him to Congress to be examined and though no absolute proof was made of his ill designs, his conduct appeared so very suspicious that he was ordered to be sent to New Hampshire to be disposed of by our Legislature; but before he was sent off, he found means to make his escape and has not been retaken yet.[3]
    The Colony of New York have fully acceded to the Declaration of Independency so that it now has the sanction of the thirteen United States; the unparalleled conduct of our enemies have united the Colonies more firmly than ever.
    The Convention of this Colony are to meet here this day who will form a Constitution for the Colony and take upon them its Govt.

In the mean time the constitutions of Virginia and New Jersey are in this city. I shall send them forward, and the constitutions of the other Colonies as they are formed as possibly something may be taken from them to amend our own. Please to give my best regards to all friends and believe me to be, Your sincere friend &c,

Josiah Bartlett

P.S. Col Roberdeau is appointed a Provincial Brigadier General. Col Dickinson, Col McKean and Col Cadwallader are gone with their regiments to the Jersies. 1200 Maryland militia are hourly expected in this city to join the army in the Jersies. Col Miles with 1000 provincial riflemen and with him our friend Major Patton have joined the army in New Jersey. In short Maryland and Pennsylvania are all in motion.

This day an artillery company of militia consisting of 57 men with 2 brass field pieces and every necessary accoutrement marched for the same place.

Mr Wm Livingston of New Jersey is appointed a Provincial Brigadier General.

Our friend Mr Dean is appointed Captn of Marines to one of the frigates here. He desires to be remembered to you.   J. B.

Tr (DLC).
[1] See New Hampshire Delegates to Meshech Weare, June 26, 1776, note 3.
[2] See *JCC*, 5:546–55; and Thomas Jefferson's Notes of Proceedings, July 12–August 1, 1776.
[3] See John Hancock to George Washington, July 1, 1776, note 2.

John Hancock to the New Jersey Convention

Gentlemen,   Philadelphia July 15th. 1776.

The Article of Lead being so essentially necessary, and the Propriety of every Colony being furnished with it so evident, that the Council of Safety of this Colony recommended to the Inhabitants, to spare the Lead Weights from their Windows, and the Lead from their Houses; by which Means they have been furnished with a considerable Quantity, which has been run into Ball, and Part of which, the Council of Safety here have willingly spared, and is now on the Way to the Jerseys. But as under the present Exigency, that Quantity is far short of what is wanted for the Army in New Jersey, and every Method should be used to furnish it, I have it therefore in Charge from Congress, most earnestly to request you, to supply the Flying Camp and Militia, with all the Lead in your Possession, or that you can possibly procure.[1]

The Exigency of our Affairs will not admit the least Delay; and I am convinced, there is no Necessity to use Arguments to induce you to an instant Compliance with this Requisition.

I am to inform you, that as you have not enclosed to Congress Copies of Genl. Washington's and Brigadr. Genl. Livingston's Letters, no Judgment can be formed by Congress concerning the Contents of them, and to request Copies of them to be sent hither.[2]

Measures are taking in Pennsylvania & Maryland, for forming the Flying Camp; and in the mean Time, the associated Militia are marching in great Numbers from Pennsylvania for the Defence of New Jersey. Ammunition has been, and will be supplied by this Congress, for the Defence of New Jersey. With Regard to the Pay of the Militia, I am to acquaint you, that Congress will observe the same Rule of Conduct towards New Jersey, as towards other Colonies.

Four Tons of Powder are on the Way to New Jersey, and a large Number of Muskett Cartridges well balled, will this Day be sent forward.

I have the Honour to be, Gentlemen, your most obed. & very hble Ser.,   John Hancock Presidt

RC (NN). In the hand of Jacob Rush and signed by Hancock.

[1] Sec JCC, 5:558. The convention's response to this request is in Am. Archives, 4th ser. 6:1646. For the Pennsylvania Committee of Safety's May 7, 1776, recommendation about "Lead Weights," see ibid., 5:1227.

[2] Samuel Tucker's July 9 letter to Hancock, complaining that letters from Washington and William Livingston made it appear as if the New Jersey Provincial Congress was being "called upon to make provision for the entire defense of our own shores against the British forces at Staten Island," is in PCC, item 68, fols. 183–84, and Am. Archives, 5th ser. 1:138–39. Washington's offending letter, written on July 6 to Livingston and forwarded by Livingston to the provincial congress, is in Washington, Writings (Fitzpatrick), 5:224–26.

John Hancock to George Washington

Sir,   Philadelphia July 15th. 1776.
In perusing the enclosed Resolves, which I do myself the Honour of transmitting, you will perceive, your Letters of the 11th & 12 Inst. have been received and laid before Congress, and that in Consequence thereof, they have taken such Measures, as are calculated to expedite the raising the Flying Camp, & to furnish them with Articles of the greatest Use and Necessity.[1]

I have wrote to General Mercer, to march the Militia & Flying Camp, to Brunswick, or any other Place in the Jerseys, which he may judge best; provided it does not interfere with any prior Direction from you. All the other enclosed Resolves, I have likewise given Orders to the proper Persons to have executed.

I expect your several Letters, which are now before Congress, will receive a speedy Determination; and that I shall have the Pleasure of forwarding the Result on Tuesday, or Wednesday, at farthest.

I have the Honour to be, with every Sentiment of Esteem, Sir, your most obed. & very hble Sert.   John Hancock Presidt

RC (DLC). In the hand of Jacob Rush and signed by Hancock.

[1] For these resolves, see *JCC,* 5:558–59. Hancock also wrote a letter this day to William Shippen, Jr., informing him of his appointment by Congress as "Surgeon General & Director of the Hospital for the Flying Camp & Militia in New Jersey, with the pay of Four Dollars a Day." PCC, item 12A; *Am. Archives,* 5th ser. 1:346; and *JCC,* 5:562.

Thomas Jefferson to Francis Eppes

Dear Sir   Philadelphia, July 15th, 1776.

Yours of the 3d inst. came to hand to-day.[1] I wish I could be better satisfied on the point of Patty's recovery. I had not heard from her at all for two posts before, and no letter from herself now. I wish it were in my power to return by way of the Forest, as you think it will be impracticable for Mrs. Eppes to travel to the mountains. However, it will be late in August before I can get home, and our Convention will call me down early in October. Till that time, therefore, I must defer the hope of seeing Mrs. Eppes and yourself. Admiral Howe is himself arrived at New York, and two or three vessels, supposed to be of his fleet, were coming in. The whole is expected daily.

Washington's numbers are greatly increased, but we do not know them exactly. I imagine he must have from 30 to 35,000 by this time. The enemy the other day ordered two of their men-of-war to hoist anchor and push by our batteries up the Hudson River. Both wind and tide were very fair. They passed all the batteries with ease, and, as far as is known, without receiving material damage; though there was an incessant fire kept up on them. This experiment of theirs, I suppose, is a prelude to the passage of their whole fleet, and seems to indicate an intention of landing above New York. I imagine General Washington, finding he cannot prevent their going up the river, will prepare to amuse them wherever they shall go.

Our army from Canada is now at Crown Point, but still one half down with the smallpox. You ask about Arnold's behavior at the Cedars. It was this. The scoundrel, Major Butterfield, having surrendered three hundred and ninety men, in a fort with twenty or thirty days' provision, and ammunition enough, to about forty regulars, one hundred Canadians, and five hundred Indians, before he had lost a single man—and Maj. Sherburne, who was coming to the relief of the fort with one hundred men, having, after bravely engaging the enemy an hour and forty minutes, killing twenty of them and losing twelve of his own, been surrounded by them, and taken prisoners also—Gen. Arnold appeared on the opposite side of the river and prepared to attack them. His numbers I know not, but believe they were about equal to the enemy. Capt. Foster, commander of the king's troops, sent over a flag to him, proposing an exchange of prisoners for as many of the king's in our possession, and moreover, informed Arnold that if he should attack, the Indians would put every man of the prisoners to death. Arnold refused, called a council of war, and, it being now in the night, it was determined to attack next morning. A second flag came over; he again refused, though in an excruciating situation, as he saw the enemy were in earnest about killing the prisoners. His men, too, began to be importunate for the recovery of their fellow-soldiers. A third flag came, the men grew more clamorous, and Arnold, now almost raving with rage and compassion, was obliged to consent to the exchange and six days suspension of hostilities, Foster declaring he had not boats to deliver them in less time. However, he did deliver them so much sooner as that before the six days were expired, himself and party had fled out of all reach. Arnold then retired to Montreal. You have long before this heard of Gen. Thompson's defeat. The truth of that matter has never appeared till lately. You will see it in the public papers. No men on earth ever behaved better than ours did. The enemy behaved dastardly. Col. Allen (who was in the engagement) assured me this day, that such was the situation of our men, half way up to the thighs in mud for several hours, that five hundred men of spirit must have taken the whole; yet the enemy were repulsed several times, and our people had time to extricate themselves and come off. It is believed the enemy suffered considerably. The above account of Arnold's affair you may rely on, as I was one of a committee appointed to inquire into the whole of that matter, and have it from those who were in the whole transaction, and were taken prisoners.[2]

My sincere affections to Mrs. Eppes, and adieu,

Th. Jefferson

MS not found; reprinted from Jefferson, *Papers* (Boyd), 1:458–60.

[1] For Eppes' letter of July 3, 1776, see Jefferson, *Papers* (Boyd), 15:576.

[2] Jefferson had been appointed to a committee to consider the prisoner cartel between General Arnold and Capt. George Forster. For Jefferson's notes on Maj. Henry Sherburne's testimony about the Cedars affair and the committee's June 17 report, see ibid., 1:396–404. For the committee's revised report and resolutions approved on July 10, see *JCC*, 5:534–39.

Marine Committee to Nathaniel Shaw, Jr.

Sir   In Marine Committee Philadelphia 15th July 1776
It is necessary that the Cannon, stores &c made prize of and delivered to you should be appraised, for which purpose you are hereby directed to appoint three or more judicious persons to perform this service under Oath, and that you immediately make a return of such appraisement to this Committee.[1]

A proper return will be made to you of the officers and men who have a right to share in such prizes as have been, or may be committed to your care.

I am in behalf of the Marine Committee, Your very hum Sert.
                                                John Hancock Pt.

RC (CtNlHi). In a clerical hand, with closing and signature by Hancock. Addressed: "To Nathaniel Shaw Junr Esq., Agent for Prizes &c, New London, Connecticut."
[1] See Shaw's July 31 letter to Hancock and the enclosed "Invoice of Cannon &c" delivered at New London by Esek Hopkins in Clark, *Naval Documents,* 5:1304–5.

Virginia Delegates to the
Speaker of the Pennsylvania Convention

Sir   Philada. July 15. 1776.
The honorable the convention of Virginia attending to the inconveniencies which may arise from an unsettled jurisdiction in the neighborhood of fort Pitt, have instructed us to propose to your honorable house to agree on some temporary boundary which may serve for preservation of the peace in that territory until an amicable and final determination may be had before arbiters mutually chosen.[1] Such temporary settlement will from it's nature do prejudice to neither party when at any future day a complete information of facts shall enable them to submit the doubt to a just & final decision. We can assure you that the colony of Virginia does not entertain a wish that one inch should be added to theirs from the territory of a sister colony, & we have perfect confidence that the same just sentiment prevails in your house. Parties thus disposed can scarcely meet with difficulty in adjusting either a temporary or a final settlement. The decision, whatever it be, will not annihilate the lands. They will remain to be occupied by ⟨the sons of freedom⟩ Americans, & whether these be counted in numbers of this or that of the United States will be thought a matter of little moment ⟨by an American⟩. We shall be ready to confer on this subject with any gentlemen your house may please to appoint for that purpose[2] & are Sir with every sentiment of respect, Your very humble servts.

FC (DLC). In the hand of Thomas Jefferson. Jefferson, *Papers* (Boyd), 1:465–66.

[1] The June 17 letter of the Virginia Committee of Safety transmitting these instructions to the Virginia delegates is in Jefferson, *Papers* (Boyd), 1:387–89. For the Virginia Convention's June 15 resolution proposing a temporary boundary, see *Am. Archives*, 4th ser. 6:1576. For the comments of the president of the Virginia Committee of Safety, Edmund Pendleton, on this boundary dispute, see Jefferson, *Papers* (Boyd), 1:462–65.

[2] The Pennsylvania Convention did appoint a committee to confer with the Virginia delegates, but the Virginia proposal was rejected and the boundary dispute continued with each state periodically offering counterproposals. See *Am. Archives*, 5th ser. 2:3, 7, 40–42; and Jefferson, *Papers* (Boyd), 1:594–97.

John Adams to Abigail Adams

Philadelphia July 16. 1776

In a Letter from your Uncle Smith, and in another from Mr. Mason which I received by this days Post I am informed that you were about taking the Small Pox,[1] with all the Children. . . .[2] It is not possible for me to describe, nor for you to conceive my Feelings upon this Occasion. Nothing, but the critical State of our Affairs should prevent me from flying to Boston, to your Assistance.

I mentioned your Intention to Mrs. Yard at noon. This Evening our President was here. I was engaged abroad, the whole Evening till it was late. When I came home, I found the inclosed Card from the President.[3] I have not yet had an Opportunity to thank Mr. Hancock for his Politeness, which in this Instance is very obliging, but I shall take the first opportunity of doing it, and of informing him, that your Uncles Kindness of which I shall ever entertain the most gratefull Sentiments, has rendered it unnecessary, as well as improper, for you to accept of his most generous Offer.

I can do no more than wish and pray for your Health, and that of the Children. Never—Never in my whole Life, had I so many Cares upon my Mind at once. I should have been happier, if I had received my Letters, before Mr. Gerry went away this Morning, because I should have written more by him. I rely upon the tender Care of our Friends. Dr. Tufts and your Uncle Quincy, and my Brother will be able to visit you, and give you any Assistance. Our other Friends, I doubt not will give you every Advice, Consolation and Aid in their Power. I am very anxious about supplying you with Money. Spare for nothing, if you can get Friends to lend it you. I will repay with Gratitude as well as Interest, any sum that you may borrow. I shall feel like a Savage to be here, while my whole Family is sick at Boston. But it cannot be avoided. I cannot leave this Place, without more Injury to the public now, than I ever could at any other Time, being in the Midst of scænes of Business, which must not stop for any Thing. . . . Make Mr. Mason, Mr. any Body write to me, by every

Post—don't miss one for any Cause whatever. My dearest Love to you all.

RC (MHi). Adams, *Family Correspondence* (Butterfield), 2:50–51.

[1] Isaac Smith's letter of July 8 to Adams is in Adams, *Family Correspondence* (Butterfield), 2:41–42. For Mason's letter, see John Adams to Jonathan Mason, Jr., July 18, 1776, note 1.

[2] Suspension points in MS, here and below.

[3] Adams enclosed the following letter which he had received from John Hancock this day.

"On a Visit to Mrs. Yard this Eveng. I was inform'd by her that your Lady & Children propos'd to go into Boston, with an intention of Taking the Small Pox by Inoculation, and as the Season is warm, & the present process of Treating that Disorder, requires all the air that can possibly be had, & as any Scituation in Boston is as much Bless'd with a free air as most other, I make a Tender of my house & Garden for their use if you Choose to improve it, & by a Signification of your Consent I will write by this Express to that purport. The fruit in the Garden shall be at their Controal, & a maid Servt. & the others in the House shall afford them every Convenience that appertains to the House. It will give me pleasure to be any way instrumental, however small, in adding to their Convenience." Ibid., p. 51.

Samuel Adams to James Warren

My dear Friend   Philad. July 16, 76
There is no Necessity of my troubling you with a long Epistle at present, for my very worthy Friend and Colleague [1] who kindly takes the Charge of this will fully inform you of the State of Affairs here. He will tell you some things which I have often wishd to communicate to you, but have not thought it prudent to commit to Writing.

Our Declaration of Independance has already been attended with good Effects. It is fortunate beyond our Expectation to have the Voice of every Colony in favor of so important a Question.

I inclose you the Form of a Constitution which the Convention of Virginia have agreed upon for that Colony. It came to my hand yesterday by the Post, and I spare it to you, although I have not had time to peruse it. I suppose there are other Copies in Town. Adieu.

FC (NN).
[1] Elbridge Gerry.

John Alsop to the New York Provincial Congress

Hble. Gentlemen,   Philadelphia, 16th July, 1776.
Yesterday our President read in Congress a resolve of your Honble. Body, dated 9th instant, in which you declare New-York a free and

John Alsop

independent State. I can't help saying that I was much surprized to find it come through that channel. The usual method, hitherto practised, has been for the Convention of each Colony to give their Delegates instructions to act and vote upon all and any important question.

And from the last letter we were favoured with from your body, you told us that you was not competent or authorized to give us instructions on that grand question, nor have you been pleased to answer our letter of the 2d instant, any otherwise than by your said resolve, transmitted to the President. I think we were entitled to an answer.

I am compelled, therefore, to declare that it is against my judgment and inclination. As long as a door was left open for a reconciliation with Great Britain, upon honourable and just terms, I was willing and ready to render my country all the service in my power, and for which purpose I was appointed and sent to this Congress; but as you have, I presume, by that declaration closed the door of reconciliation, I must beg leave to resign my seat as a Delegate from New-York, and that I may be favoured with an answer and my dismission.[1]

I have the honour to be, With esteem, gentlemen, Your most obdt. hble, servt.   John Alsop

Reprinted from *Journals of N.Y. Prov. Cong.*, 1:536.

[1] The New York Convention read Alsop's letter on July 22 and promptly resolved "That the Convention do cheerfully accept of Mr. Alsop's resignation of his seat in the Continental Congress, and that Mr. Alsop be furnished with a copy of this resolution." *Am. Archives,* 5th ser. 1:1428–29. See also *JCC,* 5:560; New York Convention to the New York Delegates, July 22, 1776, in *Am. Archives,* 5th ser. 1:1430–31; and Rick J. Ashton, "The Loyalist Congressmen of New York," *New-York Historical Society Quarterly* 60 (1976): 102–6.

John Hancock to Certain States

Gentlemen,   Philada. July 16th. 1776.

Since I had the Honour of addressing you on the fourth of June, at which Time I transmitted sundry Resolves of Congress, requesting you to call forth your Militia, our Affairs have assumed a much more serious Complexion. If we turn our Attention towards the Northern Department, we behold an Army reduced by Sickness, and obliged to flee before an Enemy of vastly superior Force. If we cast our Eyes to Head Quarters, we see the British Army reinforced under Lord Howe, and ready to strike a Blow, which may be attended with the most fatal Consequences, if not timely resisted. The Situation of our Country at this Season, calls therefore for all the Vigour & Wisdom among us; and if we do not mean to desert her at this alarming

Crisis, it is high Time to rouse every Spark of Virtue, and forgetting all inferiour Considerations, to exert ourselves in a Manner becoming Freemen.

The Intelligence received this day from General Washington, points out the absolute, the indispensible Necessity of sending forward all the Troops that can possibly be collected, to strengthen both the Army in New York, and that on this Side of Canada.[1] I do therefore, once more, in the Name & by the Authority of Congress request & beseech you, as you regard the Liberties of your Country, and the Happiness of Posterity; and as you stand engaged by the most solemn Ties of Honour, to support the Common Cause, to strain every Nerve to send forward your Militia, agreeably to the former Requisitions of Congress. This is a Step of such infinite Moment, that, in all Human Probability, it will be the Salvation of America. And as it is the only effectual Step that can possibly be taken at this Juncture, you will suffer me again, most ardently to entreat your speedy Compliance with it.

In short, the critical Period is arrived, that will seal the Fate, not only of ourselves, but of Posterity. Whether they shall arise the generous Heirs of Freedom, or the dastardly Slaves of imperious Task-Masters, it is in your Power now to determine: and as Freemen, I am sure, you will not hesitate a Moment, about the Choice.

I have the Honour to be, Gentlemen &c,   J. H. Prest.

LB (DNA: PCC, item 12A). Addressed: "Massachusetts Assembly. Connecticut Assembly. Convention of New Jersey."

[1] Washington's letter to Hancock of July 14, describing the arrival at Crown Point of Gen. John Sullivan's smallpox-infested army and the passage up the Hudson of several British "Ships of War and Tenders," is in PCC, item 152, 2:217–24, and Washington, *Writings* (Fitzpatrick), 5:271–76. A brief letter of the 16th from Hancock to Washington, acknowledging receipt of the general's July 14 letter and enclosing certain resolves, is in PCC, item 12A, and *Am. Archives*, 5th ser. 1:367. The resolves in question were probably those directly pertaining to Washington's command that were passed by Congress on this day. See *JCC*, 5:563–66.

John Hancock to the Virginia Council of Safety

Gentlemen,   Philada. July 16th. 1776.

Altho the Council of Safety of this Colony, by a Recommendation to the Inhabitants to spare the Lead Weights from their Windows, & the Lead from their Houses, have collected a considerable Quantity which has been run into Ball, and Part of which is now on the Way to the Jerseys, yet is it by no Means sufficient in our present Exigency. A much greater Quantity is still wanted for the Army in New Jersey, & every Method should be taken to procure it. I have it therefore in Charge from Congress to request you will send by the Return

Waggons, which are now on their Way to your Colony with Powder, as much Lead as you can spare, & that you will order 15 or 20 Tons more of Lead, from the Mines, to this City as soon as possible.[1]

The State of our Affairs will not admit the least Delay; and I am persuaded Arguments are not necessary to induce you to a Compliance with this Requisition with the greatest Dispatch.

I have the Honour to be, Gentlemen, your most obed. & very hble Ser.   J. H. Pres.

LB (DNA: PCC, item 12A).
[1] See *JCC*, 5:559. Hancock sent an almost identical letter this day to Fielding Lewis, superintendent of a small arms factory in Fredericksburg, Va., requesting him "to send by the Waggons, which are now on their Way to your Colony with Powder, all the Lead you can possibly procure at Fredericksburgh." PCC, item 12A; *Am. Archives*, 5th ser. 1:366–67; and *JCC*, 5:558.

Thomas Jefferson to Richard Henry Lee

Dear Sir   Philadelphia July 16. 1776.

We received your letter by post and are much obliged for the enclosures. The queries to the officers shall be answered by this post if we can; otherwise certainly by the next.[1] I suppose it will be best to send the answer to Brigadr. Lewis. Leich's affair shall also be taken care of.[2] Admiral Howe is arrived at New York, and two or three vessels, supposed to be of his fleet, were in sight. The enemy by way of experiment ordered two of their men of war and tenders to hoist anchor and pass up Hudson's river in defiance of our batteries. Wind and tide were fair, and they passed unhurt as far as is known tho' an incessant fire was kept up from our batteries. This experiment indicates I think that they mean to land above New York. I suppose Genl. Washington will make a corresponding alteration in his plan. He is very strong in men, tho' we know not his exact numbers. Our Canadian army is safe at Crown point, but still half down with the small pox. The Convention did nothing yesterday for want of numbers. They expect to meet to day. Dr. Franklin will be president. I am sorry the Convention of Virginia did not accept of my resignation here. The state of Mrs. Jefferson's health obliges me to persist in it. I hope you will be here before the 11th. of August when I propose going: otherwise the colony will be unrepresented. Indeed I wish you would come immediately. The confederation is just brought in and the plan of alliances will be reported to-day.[3] The former is in every interesting point the reverse of what our country would wish. You can never be absent at a time so interesting to your country. I make no doubt it will be long in it's passage through the Committee so that you may be here in

time to attack it in the house from Alpha to Omega. I am Dear Sir
Your friend & servt.   Th. Jefferson

Reprinted from Jefferson, *Papers* (Boyd), 15:577.
  [1] See Virginia Delegates to the Executive of Virginia, July 16, 1776, note 4.
  [2] Probably a reference to Maj. Andrew Leitch's unsuccessful attempt on June 24
to take a Barbadian brig bound with supplies for Lord Dunmore that had run
aground in the Chesapeake. During the encounter Leitch had taken four prisoners
whom he had sent to Gen. Andrew Lewis. See Clark, *Naval Documents,* 5:755–56.
  [3] The "committee appointed to prepare a plan of treaties" did not bring in its
report until July 18. *JCC,* 5:575.

Francis Lightfoot Lee to Richard Henry Lee

Dear Brother,   Philadelphia July 16. 1776
  I have written to you every post, since you left this. If you have
not recd. the Letters, there must still be some villain, in the Post
Office. It is supposed Ld. Howe is arrived, as three ships last Fryday
joined the fleet at N. York, one very large, with St. George's flag at
the masthead, which was saluted by the whole fleet. The rest of his
Myrmidons are not far behind I suppose. Two men of war & their
tenders have run by all our batteries, & got above King's bridge,
without any damage. It always appear'd to me that our Generals
placed more confidence in their batteries than they deserved. It
seems probable, that Howe will Land his Army above Kings bridge,
& cut off all communication with N. York by land, while the fleet
does the same by sea, in which case our Army must starve, or attack
the Enemy in their entrenchments. I fear such an event is not
sufficiently attended to; the defence of N. York seems to engross all
their tho'ts. Col. W. Alleyn arrived yesterday from Crown Point; he
left 6,000 men there, half sick; by their last accts. from St. Johns,
Burgoine had 1000 there, no preparation of boats. It is said the six
nations begin to be troublesome; indeed from all appearances we
shall soon have the whole of the Indians to encounter.
  Genl. Washington has as many men as he wants & least Howe
shoud think fit to march into the Jerseys, we shall soon have 20,000
there to cope with him. But I think it is very improbable, that he
will give up the scheme, of opening a communication with Canada,
by the North River. The 11th of next month Colo. Harrison &
Braxton are no longer delegates, & as Mr. Jefferson is determined to
go home then, we shall be without a representation, unless you join
us. We have not heard when Mr. Wythe intends to be here. I have
now got a very good house, near the State house, in which you may
have choice of good rooms well furnished, except with beds. As we
have but one, it is necessary we shoud know as soon as possible
when to expect you, that we may provide for you. We have this

house certainly till the last of Octr. & a chance for the winter. Our best Love to Chantilly & Stratford, & Respects to all friends in Westmoreland.[1]

Yr. Afft. Bror. & friend,   Francis Lightfoot Lee

RC (NN).
[1] Francis Lightfoot Lee also wrote a letter to Landon Carter this day in which he commented: "It gives me concern to hear that some of your Negroes have joined the Arch Devil, and my friend Mr. Carter's favorite servant too! But Slavery plants a Vice where a Virtue might be expected. Your government I find is at length compleated. God send it may procure internal peace and happiness to the Country." *George D. Smith Autograph Letters* (New York: 898 items, n.d.), item 450.

Thomas Nelson to John Page

Dear Page   Philada July 16th 1776
I was disappointed in not receiving a line from you by yesterdays post, but I suppose your hurry of business in your new department, prevented you taking notice of me.[1] We expected to have heard something from New York yesterday, but I fear the Enemy have taken such possession of the River as to prevent any intelligence being convey'd to us. Two of the Ships of War & two Tenders pass'd our Forts on the North River in defiance of our Batteries. This we imagin'd was done as an experiment. Whether any others of them, or any Transports have follow'd we are not inform'd, not having heard from the General since the 12 Instant at night & then the express cross'd under a strong escort.[2] It is thought that they design to surround our Army & pen them up in the City of N. York, but the General no doubt is aware of this, & will counter plot them, for should such a thing happen, there must be a surrender on our side in a few Months, as they would cut off all supplies. Our Men are in high spirits & wish ardently for an attack that they distinguish themselves from Men fighting for the hire of 4d per day.

I do not think you will have any thing to apprehend in Virginia this Campaign, but from Dunmore & him you may prevent doing any thing except in the predatory way. Could you not then spare a few thousand Militia to come hither to augment the flying Camp that is to be establishd between this Colony & Maryland? They would be of infinite service. I have enclos'd several of Dr Price's excellent Pamplets[3] to you which you will dispose of as they are directed & oblige, Your sincere friend & hbe Sert,

Thos Nelson Jr

RC (PHi).
[1] The Virginia Convention had elected John Page to the governor's council on June 29. *Am. Archives,* 4th ser. 6:1600.

[2] Washington's July 14 letter was read in Congress later this day. *JCC*, 5:563.
[3] Richard Price, *Observations on the Nature of Civil Liberty*.

Robert Treat Paine to Henry Knox

Dear Sr.   Philada July 16th. 1776

The Approach of the Enemy has rendered it necessary to find some other place to cast brass Cannon than yr. Air Furnace; this Colony are about Setting up an Air Furnace for that purpose, but the Congress I believe will employ Mr. Byers if it be found practicable & he will make a reasonable bargain. I should be glad to know if he can Cast brass Cannon in an Air Furnace without Sea Coal. That Article is necessary, I understand, for casting Iron Cannon in an Air Furace & if it be so for casting Brass it will put us to difficulty. I herewith send a Letter to Mr. Byers on this Subject, pray urge him to answer as soon as may be.[1] I think he demands an unreasonable price for his Cannon & I believe the price is not so high in England as you mention, but as they are like to cost so much by the pound, I think they should be made as light as will Answer. Now I observe that Mr. Byers' 6 pounders weigh one hundred & an half more than the English ones which is an exceeding great Odds. I wish to know whether this is accidental or by design fearing they would not be strong enough if made lighter. But I may not trouble you with these matters now your mind is so engaged to entertain your new visitors. I trust you will treat them in a very polite manner & whatever they may say of the Cookery be sure give them their Bellies full. Hoping soon to hear of yr. good Success, I am yr Friend & hble Servt,

R T Paine

P.S. I have wrote Mr. Byers to come to Philada. Please to Seal his Letter & Send it him.

RC (MHi).
[1] Not found, but James Byers' response, dated August 28, 1776, is in the Paine Papers, MHi.

Benjamin Rush to Patrick Henry

My dear friend,   Philada July 16. 1776.

I congratulate you less upon the acct. of your late honourable Appointment than upon the declaration of the freedom & independance of the American colonies.[1] Such inestimable blessings can not be too joyfully received, nor purchased at too high a price. They would be cheaply bought at the loss of all the towns & of every fourth, or even third man in America. I tremble to think of the mischiefs that would have spread thro' this country had we continued our dependance upon G Britain twenty years longer. The contest two years ago found us contaminated with British customs, manners & ideas of government. We begin to be purified from some of them. In particular we dare to speak freely & justly of royal & hereditary power. In a few years we shall vie I hope for wisdom with the Citizens of Athens. But our Virtue will I hope know no bounds. The Conduct of our Militia upon a late Alarm from New York gives me reason to think we may make any thing we please of Americans. Were our officers equal to our men, I believe we might drive a whole Army of Howes & Burgoynes into the Ocean in a few days. They implore their generals every hour for the liberty of attacking our enemies. War, liberty & independance is the common language of them all.

Providence has frowned upon our Arms in Canada. I sometimes think that country has been *earned* by the March of Col. Arnold, & the heroic Achievements & death of the gallant Montgomery, and that the banner of liberty will be planted on some future day by the States of America upon the walls of Quebec. Perhaps this opinion is nothing but the effect of a Veneration bordering upon idolatry for the Services & merit of those illustrious heroes.

The States of America cannot be a Nation without War. They will have Wars in Europe. Canada may be reserved to the Crown of Britain as a nursery of enemies to the States on purpose to keep alive their martial virtue. If this be the case, it becomes us to reconcile ourselves to the Loss of Canada, and to resolve it into the goodness of that being with whom "all partial evil is universal good."

Have you not violated a fundamental principle of liberty in excluding the clergy from your Legislature? I know their danger in a free government but I would rather see them excluded from civil power by custom than by law. They have property, wives & children, & of course are citizens of a community. Why therefore Should they be Abridged of any one priviledge which Other citizens enjoy? Is it not a fact that by investing any men with more, or confining them to fewer priviledges than members of a community enjoy in general we render those men the enemies of that community? Perhaps all the Mischief which the clergy have done in all countries has arisen from the first of the above causes. Will not the clause in your Charter which excludes Clergymen from your Legislature hand down to posterity as well as hold up to the World an idea that you looked upon the Christian religion as well as its Ministers as unfriendly to good government? I wish our governments would treat religion of all kinds, & ministers of all denominations as if no such things or beings existed in the world. They mutually destroy each Other when any Attempts are made by either to support each other.

When you have an idle minute it will give me pleasure to hear that you still remember your old friend, & humble Servant,

B Rush

RC (PPAmP).
[1] For the provenance of this letter, see Lyman H. Butterfield, "Dr. Rush to Governor Henry on the Declaration of Independence and the Virginia Constitution," *American Philosophical Society Proceedings* 3 (June 1951): 250–53.

Virginia Delegates to the Executive of Virginia

[July 16, 1776] [1]

We were informed a few weeks ago that 5000 lb. of lead imported by our colony were landed at Fredsburgh. As it appeared very unlikely it should be wanting in Virginia, and the Flying camp forming [in] the Jerseys, in the face of a powerful enemy, are likely to be in distress for this article, we thought we should be wanting to the public cause, which includes that of our own country, had we hesitated to desire it to be brought here. Had the wants of the camp admitted the delay of an application to you we should most certainly have waited an order from you. But their distress is instantaneous. Even this supply is insufficient. The army in Canada, & the army in N. York will want much lead & there seems to be no certain source of supply unless the mines in Virginia can be rendered such. We are therefore by direction of Congress to beg further that you will be pleased to send them what lead can be spared from Wmsburgh., and moreover order 15 or 20 tons to be brought here immediately from the mines.[2]

We take the liberty of recommending the lead mines to you as an object of vast importance. We think it impossible they can be worked to too great an extent. Considered as perhaps the sole means of supporting the American cause they are inestimable. As an article of commerce to our colony too they will be valuable: & even the waggonage if done either by the colony or individuals belonging to it will carry to it no trifling sums of money.

We inclose you a resolution of Congress on the subject of the forts & garrisons on the Ohio.[3]

Several vacancies having happened in our battalions, we are unable to have them filled for want of a list of the officers stating their seniority. We must beg the favor of you to furnish us with one. We received from Colonel R. H. Lee a resolution of Convention recommending to us to endeavor that the promotions of the officers be according to seniority without regard to regiments or companies.[4] This is the standing rule of promotion. In one instance indeed the Congress have reserved to themselves a right of departing from seniority; that is where a person either out of the line of command, or in an inferior part of it has displayed eminent talents. Most of the general officers have been promoted in this way. Without this reservation the whole continent must have been supplied with general officers from the Eastern colonies where a large army was formed and officered before any other colony had occasion to raise troops at all & a number of experienced, able & valuable officers must have been lost to the public merely from the locality of their situation.

The resolution of our Convention on the subject of salt we shall lay before Congress. The Convention of Pennsylvania did not proceed to business yesterday for want of a quorum. As soon as they do we shall lay before them the proposition from our convention on the differences at Fort Pitt & communicate to you the result.[5] We are Your Excellency's.

FC (DLC). In the hand of Thomas Jefferson. Jefferson, *Papers* (Boyd), 1:460–61.

[1] Although undated, this letter was probably drafted by Thomas Jefferson on July 16 before news of the confirmation of Patrick Henry's election as governor of Virginia had reached Philadelphia. Jefferson's concluding reference to the convening of the Pennsylvania Convention, which met on July 15 and which was also mentioned in his letter to Richard Henry Lee of this date, also supports this conclusion. *Am. Archives*, 5th ser. 2:1.

[2] See *JCC*, 5:558–59. This day Jefferson also drafted a letter for Fielding Lewis of Fredericksburg, Va., requesting him "to stop so many of the powder waggons now on their way to Wmsburgh as may be necessary and return them immediately with this lead, and whatever more you can collect, sending the powder on by other waggons." Jefferson, *Papers* (Boyd), 1:467.

[3] See *JCC*, 5:542. This resolve of July 11, offering to place three western Virginia forts on the Continental establishment, was apparently enclosed with a second letter to Henry this day, in which Jefferson also enclosed John Hancock's letter of this date to the Virginia Council of Safety. See Jefferson, *Papers* (Boyd), 1:466–67.

[4] The Virginia Convention's resolve on the promotion of officers is in *Am. Archives*, 4th ser. 6:1613.

[5] See Virginia Delegates to the Speaker of the Pennsylvania Convention, July 15, 1776.

William Whipple to John Langdon

My Dear Sir   Philadelphia 16th July 1776.

Your favor of 1st inst came duly to hand.[1] There can be no objection to your contracting for guns wherever they are to be had. I find by the backwardness of the furnaces here that they must be got somewhere else. Govr Hopkins has written [2] agreeable to what I wrote last post. However I think it would not be amiss for you to contract if they wont spare you those already made, which they will if they consider the good of the service, as they may make more by the time their ships are ready for them. You may depend the officers will be appointed agreeable to your recommendation; their commissions not being sent need be no hindrance to you in engaging petty officers and men. Provisions I wrote you about last post. I agree with you that these matters have not been properly attended to, but I by no means take any part of the charge of neglect to myself for no poor devil ever begged for alms with more earnestness than I have to get these matters settled and am still determined if possible to have every thing complete before I leave this. Two of the ships were launched here last week viz: the Randolph and Delaware, but when they will get to sea is uncertain as they have no anchors yet.

Independence was proclaimed in the army at New York last Wednesday when the leaden King in the Bowling Green was dismounted and is by this time cast into bullets for the destruction of his tools of Tyranny. May every one of them be properly commissioned. We are daily in expectation of some grand military operations at New York. The Militia are all marching from this Colony. The associates are mostly gone from this City, Cols Dickenson, Cadwallader &c at the head of their regts. No doubt in a very few days 20,000 men if not more will be embodied at New Jersey besides the army at York. This declaration has had a glorious effect—has made these Colonies all alive—all the Colonies forming governments as you'll see by the papers.

I expect there will be some interruption in the communication but hope it won't last long.

In very great haste, yours,   Wm Whipple

[*P.S.*]   Please to send the enclosed paper to the North end. I have sent the play you mention to Mr Brackett.[3]

Tr (DLC).
  [1] Langdon's July 1 letter to Whipple is in Clark, *Naval Documents*, 5:846–47.
  [2] Not found.
  [3] Langdon had asked for "the Pamphlet called the fall of British Tyranny a play." Ibid., p. 847.

John Adams to Joseph Ward

Sir   Philadelphia Wednesday July 17. 1776
    Yesterdays Post brought me your Letter of the 8th inst. with several others containing Intelligence of a Nature very interesting to me.[1] The Prevalence of the Small Pox in Boston is an incident, which I can not but esteem fortunate for the public, altho the Stake I have in it, having all my nearest Connections among the earliest adventurers makes me feel an Anxiety too private and particular, for the situation I am in.[2]
    The Small Pox is really the most formidable Enemy We have to contend with, in the whole Train—and I cannot but rejoice at the

Resolution of my Countrymen to Subdue this Enemy first. It is a great Satisfaction to see that no Dangers dismay, no Difficulties discourage, the good People of America.

You ask when will America take Rank as a Nation? This Question was answered before it was put, but it Seems the answer had not reached Boston. Before now you are satisfied I hope. What would you have next?

Your Troops are all ordered to N. York and Crown Point. The small Pox will Stop all who have taken it, at least for some time. We have not a sufficient Number of Men at New York. I hope our Militia will go. It is a great Grief to me to find by the Returns, that no Massachusetts Militia are yet arrived at New York. I almost wish the Council would order the Regiments from Worcester, Hampshire and Berkshire to march thither.

Rank is not always proportional to Merit, and Promotion seldom keeps Pace with services. The Promotions you mention, are I hope worthy Men: but their Merits and services might perhaps have been sufficiently rewarded with fewer Steps of advancement—or there may be others, who have equally deserved. All that I can Say is that Time and Chance happens to all Men and therefore I hope yours will come sometime or other. Mine I am pretty sure never will. If you come to New York, which I hope you will, you may perhaps have a better Chance.

Our Privateers have the most Skill or the most Bravery, or the best Fortune, of any in America. I hope Captn. Johnson was in a private ship. I dont like to hear that the continental Cruizers have taken so many and the Provincial Cruizers and privateers so few Prizes. Our People may as well fight for themselves as the Continent.

LB (MHi).
    [1] An extract of Ward's July 8 letter to Adams, which is in the Adams Papers, MHi, is in Clark, *Naval Documents*, 5:969.
    [2] Adams also wrote a brief letter this day to his uncle Isaac Smith, Sr., communicating concern over his family's health and the spread of smallpox in Massachusetts. See Adams, *Family Correspondence* (Butterfield), 2:52.

Samuel Adams to James Warren

My dear Sir   Philada July 17 1776
    By this Express the General Assembly will receive the most earnest Recommendation of Congress to raise & send with all possible Speed the 2000 Men requested of them for New York above a Month ago.[1] There never was a more pressing Necessity for their Exertions than at present. Our Army in N Y consists of not more than half the number of those which we have reason to expect will in a very short

Time be ready to attack them. And to this let me add that when
we consider how many disaffected Men there are in that Colony,
it is but little better than an Enemies Country. I am sensible this is
a busy Season of the year, but I beg of you to prevail on the People
to lay aside every private Concern and devote themselves to the
Service of their Country. If we can gain the Advantage of the Enemy
this Campaign we may promise ourselves Success against every Effort
they will be able to make hereafter, But I need not multiply words.
I am sure *your* Mind is fully impressd with the Importance of this
Measure. Adieu my Friend. The Express waits.   S A

FC (NN).
    [1] See John Hancock to Certain States, July 16, 1776. For the response of the
Massachusetts Council to this appeal, which reported that the state was raising
1,500 more men for the northern department, see Richard Derby to John Hancock,
July 23, 1776, in PCC, item 65, 1:97; and *Am. Archives,* 5th ser. 1:550.

John Hancock to the Pennsylvania Convention

Gentlemen,   Philada. July 17th. 1776.
    The Congress, Previous to the Meeting of the Convention of the
State of Pennsylvania, having received Information of such a Nature
as induced them to appoint a Committee who are under an Injunction of Secrecy to make the necessary Enquiry; but as this State is
mostly interested in the Subject of the Enquiry, Congress have
thought proper that the Matter should be made known to a Committee of your Body. I have it therefore in Charge to request that
you will be pleased to appoint a Comee. from your Convention to
be under an Injunction of Secrecy to confer with the Committee
of Congress on this important Matter.
    Having the Honour to be of the Committee of Congress, I should
be glad to be informed of the Names of such Persons as you shall
appoint on the Committee, that a Time & Place may be fixed for
the Conference.[1]
    I have the Honour to be, with Respect, Gentlemen, your most
obed. & very hbl sert.   J. H.

LB (DNA: PCC, item 12A).
    [1] Congress had appointed this committee on July 11 to investigate a report of a
conspiracy "for liberating the prisoners &c in the gaol of Philadelphia." *JCC,*
5:543. No record of any meeting between this committee and a committee of the
Pennsylvania Convention has been found. However, at the request of this congressional committee the convention did agree on July 20 to remove "common
Prisoners" from the new Philadelphia jail and "give up the said new Jail to the
Congress for the use of the State Prisoners." See *JCC,* 5:572, 594; and *Am. Archives,*
5th ser. 2:7.

John Hancock to George Washington

Sir,   Philadelphia July 17th. 1776.

Your Favour of the 14th Inst. was duely received, and immediately laid before Congress.

In obedience to their Commands, I do myself the Honour to forward sundry Resolves.[1]

The Congress being of opinion, that a Quantity of Powder should be distributed thro' the several Counties of New York and New Jersey, I am to request you will give Directions to have it lodged in the Hands of such Persons as may [be] depended upon.

I have delivered Monsr. Kermovan his Commission, and directed him to repair immediately to the Jerseys, and put himself under the Officer who commands the Flying Camp.[2]

You will please to give Orders respecting the appointment of a Sergeant Major, a Quarter Master General, and Paymaster Genl. in each Regiment—and likewise necessary Directions to General Schuyler with Regard to cleansing the Army of the Small Pox.

Mr. Humpton & Mr. Dawson have been Officers in the British army, and I hope will be of Service in ours. They will be ordered to Head Quarters as soon as possible.

Upwards of a Thousand Troops from Maryland are now in this City on their Way to join the Flying Camp in New Jersey. They are an exceeding fine Body of Men, and will begin their March this day.[3]

Agreably to the enclosed Resolves, I have wrote in the most vehement and pressing Manner to the Massachusetts Bay, Connecticut, and New Jersey to forward their Militia—and I do not doubt their Compliance immediately.

With the most fervent, and incessant Wishes, that your Head may be covered in the Day of Battle, and that Success may crown your Arms, I have the Honour to be, Sir, your most obed. & very hble Servt.   John Hancock Presidt

RC (DLC). In the hand of Jacob Rush and signed by Hancock.

[1] For these resolves on military affairs affecting Washington, which were passed by Congress on July 15 and 16, see *JCC*, 5:561, 563–65.

[2] Hancock's July 16 letter to the chevalier de Kermorvan, informing him of his appointment as "an Engineer in the Continental Service, with the Rank of Lieutenant Colonel," is in PCC, item 12A, and *Am. Archives*, 5th ser. 1:367. See also Hancock to the Pennsylvania Committee of Safety, June 28, 1776, note.

[3] Hancock's letter of this date to Col. William Smallwood, the commander of these Maryland soldiers, directing him to "march the Troops from Maryland now in this City, to New York, & there put yourself under the Command of Genl. Washington," is in PCC, item 12A, and *Am. Archives*, 5th ser. 1:388. To Gen. Hugh Mercer, commander of the flying camp in New Jersey, Hancock sent the following brief note this day: "I am reduced to the last Minute, and have only Time to enclose you sundry Resolves of Congress for your Direction, to which

I beg Leave to request your Attention." Ibid. For those "sundry Resolves," of July 16 and 17 pertaining to the flying camp, see *JCC*, 5:565–66, 571.

Caesar Rodney to Thomas Rodney

Sir,   Philadelphia, July the 17th 1776.
I Recd from you a few lines yesterday and am much pleased to hear my harvest is in so good way, hope that this week you will be able to secure it. I am glad the Hay Harvest has engaged your attention—that article will be verry material to us next winter. If it be possible, I will have Betsays shoos done by the time I set out for Newcastle to attend the assembly, where I expect to meet you and the rest of our members. But do assure you it is verry difficult as all most all the tradesmen of every kind have left the City. I have not now a Barber to shave me. In consequence of a bad cold caught on the last week by some means or other unknown to me, and getting verry wet on Sunday in returning from Congress, I have been ever since then confined to my room, but am now so much better as to be able to attend this morning.[1] We have no material news but what you'll find in the papers. Lord Howe's transports with the soldiery are not yet arrived. I am with love to all of you, Yr humble servt.   Caesar Rodney.

MS not found; reprinted from Adrian H. Joline, *Meditations of an Autograph Collector* (New York: Harper and Brothers, 1902), p. 300.
[1] The following sentence was taken from an extract of this letter in *Stan V. Henkels Catalog*, no. 738 (May 8, 1895): item 128.

John Adams to Jonathan Mason, Jr.

My dear Sir.   Philadelphia Thursday July 18. 1776
Your agreable Letter from Boston the 9th July was handed me on Tuesday last by the Post.[1]
The Confusions in America, inseperable from So great a Revolution in affairs, are Sufficient to excite Anxieties in the Minds of young Gentlemen just stepping into Life. Your Concern for the Event of these Commotions, is not to your dishonour. But let it not affect your Mind too much. These Clouds will be dispersed, and the Sky will become more Serene.
I cannot advise you to quit the retired scene, of which you have hitherto appeared to be so fond, and engage in the noisy Business of War. I doubt not you have Honour and Spirit, and abilities sufficient, to make a Figure in the Field: and if the future Circumstances of your Country should make it necessary, I hope you would

not hesitate to buckle on your Armour. But at present I see no Necessity for it. Accomplishments of the civil and political Kind are no less necessary, for the Happiness of Mankind than martial ones. We cannot be all Soldiers, and there will probably be in a very few years a greater Scarcity of Lawyers & Statesmen than of Warriors.

The Circumstances of this Country, from the years 1755 to 1758, during which Period I was a student in Mr Putnams office, were almost as confused as they are now and the Prospect before me, my young Friend, was much more gloomy than yours. I felt an Inclination, exactly similar to yours, for engaging in active martial Life, but I was advised, and upon a Consideration of all Circumstances concluded, to mind my Books. Whether my determination was prudent or not, it is not possible to say, but I never repented it. To attain the real Knowledge, which is necessary for a Lawyer, requires the whole Time and Thoughts of a Man in his youth, and it will do him no good to dissipate his Mind among the confused objects of a Camp. Nocturna versate manu, versate diurna, must be your Motto.

I wish you had told me, particularly, what Lawyers have opened offices in Boston, and what Progress is made in the Practice, and in the Courts of Justice.

I cannot undertake to Advise you, whether you had better go into an office in Boston or not. I rather think that the Practice at present is too inconsiderable to be of much service to you. You will be likely to be obliged to waste much of your Time in running of Errands, and doing trifling drudgery without learning much. Depend upon it, it is of more Importance that you read much, than that you draw many Writts. The Common Writts upon Notes, Bonds and Accounts, are mastered in half an Hour. Common Declarations for Rent, & Ejectment and Trespass, both of assault and Battery and Quare Clausum fregit, are learn'd in very near as short a Time. The more difficult special Declarations, and especially the Refinements of Special Pleadings are never learnd in an office. They are the Result of Experience, and long Habits of Thinking.

If you read Plowdens Commentaries, you will see the Nature of Special Pleadings. In addition to these read Instructor Clericalis— Mallory—Lilly—and look into Rastall and Cooke. Your Time will be better spent upon these Authors than in dancing attendance upon a Lawyers office and his Clients. Many of our most respectable Lawyers never did this att all. Gridly, Pratt, Thatcher, Sewall, Paine never served regularly in any office.

Upon the whole my young Friend, I wish that the State of public affairs would have admitted of my Spending more Time with you. I had no greater Pleasure in this Life, than in assisting young Minds possessed of ambitions to excell, which I very well know to be your Case. Let me intreat you not to be too anxious about Futurity. Mind your Books. Sit down patiently to Plowdens Commentaries, read them through coolly, deliberately, and attentively. Read them in Course. Endeavor to make yourself Master of the Point on which the Case turns. Remark the Reasoning, and the Decision—and tell me a year hence, whether your Time has not been more agreably, and profitably spent than in drawing Writs and running of Errands. I hope to see you eer long. I am obliged to you for this Letter and wish a Continuance of your Correspondence.[2] I am anxious, very anxious, for my dear Mrs Adams, and my Babes. God preserve them. I can do them no kind office, whatever.

LB (MHi).
[1] Mason's July 9 letter is in the Adams Papers, MHi. Mason (1756–1831), Adams' former law clerk, later practiced law in Boston and served in the Massachusetts General Court, 1786–1800, and the United States Senate, 1800–1803. *Bio. Dir. Cong.*
[2] For additional advice on the study of law which Adams sent the following month, see his letter to Mason of August 21, 1776, in Adams, *Works* (Adams), 9:432–33.

Samuel Chase to Horatio Gates

Dear Gates   Philadelphia July 18th. 1776
I wrote to you from this City immediately on my Arrival.[1] I was obliged to return to Maryland on Account of Mrs. Chase's Illness. Every Moment of my Stay there was engrossed by my Attendance on my Lady and our Convention. On yesterday I came to Congress, with Mr. Carroll.
I am extremely concerned for the very disagreable Situation of our affairs with you. I am apprehensive unless some effectual and speedy Measures are taken, we shall lose the Command of the Lakes. While We are Masters of Lake Champlane, the Enemy cannot penetrate into the Colonies. If they become superior I cannot conceive the propriety of erecting fortifications at Crown Point. How can a Garrison there be relieved if the Enemy can prevent Supplies by Water? I took the Liberty of communicating my opinion on these Subjects to General Arnold by a Letter from Saratoga,[2] & if You think the Sentiments of a Gentleman, not of the military, worthy of perusal, General Arnold will shew it to you.
I am very anxious to know the real State of your Army, and to know what You think proper to be done by the Congress.
I am compelled to return to Maryland on 8th of August. Farewell. Your affectionate & obedt. Servt.   Saml. Chase

RC (NHi).
[1] See Chase to Horatio Gates, June 13, 1776.
[2] Writing to Arnold in August, Chase mentioned "my long Letter from Saratoga

of 6th June," but no such letter has been found. See Chase to Benedict Arnold, August 7, 1776.

John Hancock to the Pennsylvania Convention

Gentlemen,   Philada. July 18. 1776.

I have it in Charge from Congress to inform you that they have come to a Resolution of raising a Battalion in the Counties of Westmoreland & Bedford Pennsylvania for the Defence of the Western Parts of that State. I am therefore to request you will immediately recommend proper Persons to Congress for Field Officers of said Battalion.[1] I have the Honour to be, Gentlemen, your most obed. & very hble Sert   J. H. Prest

LB (DNA: PCC, item 12A).

[1] See JCC, 5:589–90. Congress approved the convention's nominees for field officers for this battalion on July 20. JCC, 5:596; and Am. Archives, 5th ser. 2:7.

John Hancock to Philip Schuyler

Sir   Philada. July 18. 1776

In Consequence of the Resolve of Congress respecting the Petition of Capt Benedict, I am most earnestly to Recommend to you to give Attention to the Subject matter of it, & to Desire that the proper payments may be made so far as they appear just & well supported or that the objections to the Adjustment of the Accots. as set forth by the Petitioner, may be explicitly Stated to Congress, to prevent any Prejudice arising to the general Service.[1]

I am with respect Sir, Your very hume Sert.   J H Pt.

LB (DNA: PCC, item 12A).

[1] See JCC, 5:566. Schuyler subsequently informed Hancock: "Captain Benedict's pay was stopped in consequence of an order from the honourable Commissioners of Congress, before whom, it seems, he had been charged with some malpractices in Canada." Am. Archives, 5th ser. 1:856.

John Hancock to George Washington

Sir,   Philada July 18, 1776

Mr Griffin delivered me your letter of the 4th [i.e. 15th] with the packets, which I have laid before Congress.[1] No resolution is taken in consequence thereof, nor has any thing new Occurred since my last, except the Inclos'd Resolves.[2]

I have the honour to be, Sr., your obedt. humble Servt.

John Hancock Presidt.

RC (DLC). In the hand of Charles Thomson and signed by Hancock.

[1] Washington's letter to Hancock of July 15, which he reported "will be handed you by Mr. Griffin," is in PCC, item 152, 2:225–28, and Washington, *Writings* (Fitzpatrick), 5:279–80. Enclosed with this were a circular letter and a declaration by Lord Richard Howe, dated June 20, dealing with the powers of the brothers Howe as peace commissioners. *Am. Archives*, 4th ser. 1:1001–2. Also enclosed were private letters from some of Howe's friends in England to their correspondents in America calculated, in the words of William Ellery, to put "the Character of the Howes in the most amiable point of View, and recommending Reconciliation with G. Britain." William Ellery to Ezra Stiles, July 20, 1776.

[2] Congress decided on July 19 to publish Lord Howe's circular letter and declaration so that "the good people of these United States" could familiarize themselves with the peace terms offered and realize "that the valour alone of their country is to save its liberties." *JCC*, 5:574–75, 592–93. For the "Inclos'd Resolves," see the resolutions on military affairs which were passed by Congress on July 17, in *JCC*, 5:566–72.

Secret Committee Minutes of Proceedings

July 18. 1776

The Come. met. Present Messrs. Morris, Alsop, Hewes, Livingston, Bartlett. The Come. having agreed to pay the full value insurd on the different vessels taken agreable to the letter of their charter-partys, The followg. orders was drawn on the Treasurers for that purpose.[1] In favor of J. & P. Chevalier for 160 dlls. being in full for their ship Two Brothers taken the 26th Decr last. In favor of S. Mifflin Esqr. for 128 dlls in full for his ship Sally [*i.e. Peggy*] taken 8th Decr. last. In favor of King & Harper for 34 Dlls in full for their Brige. Cornelia taken 15th March last. In favor of Elias Boys, Fergus McIlvaine & Robt Brigdes in full for their ship Grace taken 17 March, 53 1/3 dlls.

Messrs. Howel, Chevaliers & McClenachan petitioners to the Come. being calld in, it was agreed—That they make out their respective Accts. of the money actually disbursed by them in consequence of the detention of their vessels wch. will be pd.[2] & in case the vessels delivers their Cargo abroad, the Come. is to allow them such reasonable compensation for the time the vessels were detained in this river as shall be hereafter agreed upon. Mr. Alexander Gillon having delivered in his Acct. by wch. there appears to be 16214 13/27 dlls remaing. in his hands un-expended of the sum advanced him by Contract, Ordered that the Chairmn. write to him for an order, in his favor, for sd. Sum.[3]

MS (MH).

[1] For additional information regarding these accounts, see Secret Committee Minutes of Proceedings, April 9 and June 13, 1776.

[2] On August 31 the committee paid Blair McClenachan $357 1/3 to cover such expenses for his ship *Hope*. Journal of the Secret Committee, fol. 97, MH.

[3] For additional information related to this contract, see Secret Committee Minutes of Proceedings, October 25, 1775, and August 8, 1776.

Samuel Chase to Philip Schuyler

My Dear Sir.   Philadelphia July 19th. 1776
I would before this Time have returned You my Thanks for your polite attention to Me but I was compelled to leave this City immediately after my Arrival and to fly to my dear Mrs. Chase who was then extreamly ill. I have been ever since confined to domestic & public Duty, and only returned to this City last Wednesday, having leave of absence from my Lady, who is something recovered, for these weeks. I shall ever remember the Civilities I received from your worthy Family, and will embrace every opportunity to express the Regard I entertain for You and them.

Our Confederation, and plan of a foreign Treaty engages all our attention. I am afraid our military Operations have been too much neglected.

I have a Letter from General Lee, dated 7th June at Gloster, 60 Miles from Charles Town. He writes, I expect this Night to be in Charles Town. Genl. Clinton is waiting at the bar for a Wind, with 50 Transports. We expect to be in Time & to give him a warm Reception.

Lord Dunmore is driven from Gwynns Island & is now in Mouth of Potomack with 66 Sail of vessells. Our people will endeavor to receive him with proper attention according his Merit.

Lord Howe arrived in the Eagle, the 12th, at Sandy Hook. His fleet sailed before him, were not arrived 16th, but are hourly expected. He & his Brother Genl. Howe are Commissioners. He has sent, with a flagg, a proclamation to pardon, &c. &c.

I am anxious to know the Situation of our affairs with you. On our Return We informed Congress of the abuses & Misconduct, the want of Discipline & the Condition of the Army, & our observations & the Methods to be adopted to remedy in some Measure the Grievances, & to defend the Entrance into these Colonies, if expelled Canada, which we then suspected would happen.

I am sorry to hear our Stand is to be at Crown Point.[1] Reason & observation convince Me the Measure is improper, but the Military are the best Judges & I submit. I gave Myself the Trouble to write to Genl. Arnold, from Saratoga, on this Subject. I hope I have not offended him, nor You by expressing my opinion tho' opposite to either of yours. I think it is the Business of every Man, to think & to offer his Thoughts to the Gentlemen of the Army.

I cannot help intruding a few Questions to your Consideration. Would it not be adviseable to separate the infected with small pox & to remove them some considerable Distance from the Camp? Would it not be prudent to fling the Southern & eastern Troops into different Brigades. Would it not be proper to procure in Time a Number of Men for the Gondolaa's used to the Water? Can Drafts of such Men be made out of the Troops? Ought not a

Number of Men to be immediately exercised to great Guns, & officers appointed to fight the Gondolaas? Dont let the Gentn. who commanded the fire ship be neglected. Ask Colo. Maxwell. Is the Schooner armed?

I beg you would inform Me of State of our Navy for the Lakes, whether the Height opposite Tic[onderoga] is to be neglected—what You want.

I am sorry to find how egregiously You have been represented to the Members of Congress. You have many Enemies. I wrote freely to General Gates, did he communicate to You?

I shall esteem Myself among the Number of your friends, & am your affectionate Servant,   S. Chase

RC (NN).
    [1] Just why Chase assumed "our Stand is to be made at Crown Point" is a mystery, since Congress learned via Washington on July 18 that General Schuyler had decided to abandon Crown Point in favor of making a stand at Ticonderoga. See JCC, 5:575. Washington's letter to Congress and the several enclosures from Schuyler are in PCC, item 152, 2:237–42, and Am. Archives, 5th ser. 1:232–35, 389. Because the decision to abandon Crown Point occasioned great concern among Schuyler's field officers and Washington's staff, and since Chase had only recently returned from an extended trip through the country in question, it is difficult to believe that under such circumstances Chase could have confused Crown Point with Ticonderoga. But in the absence of additional evidence no other conjecture seems plausible. See also Chase's reference to "the propriety of erecting fortifications at Crown Point" in his letter to Horatio Gates of July 18.

John Hancock to the New Jersey Convention

Gentlemen   Philada. July 19th. 1776
    The Congress being informed that there is a large Quantity of Stock on the Sea Coast of your Colony, which are much exposed to the Incursions of the Enemy, and that many of the Proprietors of them, actuated by Motives of Interest, or disaffected to the Cause of their Country, would be glad to dispose of them to the Enemy, I am ordered to forward to you the inclosed Resolution, & earnestly recommend it to you to cause the Stock to be removed back into the Country to a Place of Safety.[1]
    I am Gentlemen, your most obedt. hble Set.   J. H. Prest.

LB (DNA: PCC, item 12A).
    [1] See JCC, 5:571–72. For the convention's action on this resolution, see Am. Archives, 4th ser. 6:1651.

John Hancock to the New Jersey Convention

Gentlemen   Philada. July 19th. 1776.
    I have only time to Acquaint you that a Letter from your Agent

⦿⦿⦿⦿⦿⦿⦿⦿⦿⦿⦿⦿⦿⦿⦿⦿

WEDNESDAY,

⦿⦿⦿⦿⦿⦿⦿⦿⦿⦿⦿⦿⦿⦿⦿⦿

PHILADELPHIA.

In CONGRESS, July 19, 1776.

RESOLVED, That a copy of the circular letters and of the declarations they enclosed from Lord Howe to Mr. W. Franklin, Mr. Penn, Mr. Eden, Lord Dunmore, Mr. Martin and Sir James Wright, late Governors, sent to Amboy by a flag and forwarded to Congress, by General Washington, be published in the several Gazettes, that the good people of these United States may be informed of what nature are the Commissioners and what the terms, with the expectation of which the insidious Court of Britain has endeavoured to amuse and disarm them; and that the few, who still remain suspended by a hope founded either in the justice or moderation of their late King, may now, at length, be convinced that the valour alone of their country is to save its liberties.

Extract from the journals,
CHARLES THOMSON, Secretary.

EAGLE off the coast of the Province of
SIR,   Massachusetts-Bay, June 20, 1776.
Being appointed Commander in Chief of the ships and vessels of his Majesty's fleet employed in North-America, and having the honour to be by his Majesty constituted one of his COMMISSIONERS for restoring peace to his colonies, and for granting *pardons* to such of his subjects therein as shall be *duly solicitous* to benefit by that effect of his gracious indulgence, I embrace this opportunity to inform you of my arrival on the American coast, where my first object will be an early meeting with Gen. Howe, whom his Majesty has been pleased to join with me in the said Commission.

In the mean time, I have judged it expedient to issue the inclosed declaration, in order that all persons may have immediate information of his Majesty's *most gracious intentions.* And I desire you will be pleased forthwith to cause the said Declaration to be promulgated, in such manner, and at such places within the province of New-Jersey, as will render the same of the most public notoriety.

Assured of being favoured with your assistance in every measure for the speedy and effectual restoration of the public tranquility, I am to request you will communicate from time to time, such information as you may think will facilitate the attainment of that important object in the province over which you preside.   I have the honour to be,

With great respect and consideration,

Sir, your most obedient humble servant,

H O W E.

By RICHARD VISCOUNT HOWE of the kingdom of Ireland, one of the KING's COMMISSIONERS for restoring peace to his Majesty's colonies and plantations in North-America, &c. &c. &c.

A DECLARATION.

WHEREAS by an act passed in the last session of parliament to prohibit all trade and intercourse with the colonies of New-Hampshire, Massachusetts-Bay, Rhode-Island, Connecticut, New-York, New-Jersey, Pennsylvania, the Three Lower Counties on Delaware, Maryland, Virginia, North-Carolina, South-Carolina, and Georgia, and for other purposes therein mentioned, it is enacted that " It shall and may be lawful to and for any person or persons, appointed and authorised by his Majesty, to grant a pardon or pardons to any number or description of persons, by proclamation in his Majesty's name, to declare any colony or province, colonies or provinces, or any county, town, port, district, or place, in any colony or province, to be at the peace of his Majesty;" and that, "from and after the issuing of any such proclamation in any of the aforesaid colonies or provinces, or if his Majesty should be graciously pleased to signify the same by his royal proclamation, then from and after the issuing of such proclamation," the said " act, with respect to such colony or province, colonies or provinces, county, town, port, district, or place, shall cease, determine, and be utterly void."

And whereas the King, desirous to deliver all his subjects from the calamities of war, and other *oppressions which they now undergo,* and to restore the said colonies to his protection and peace, as soon as the constitutional authority of government therein may be replaced, hath been graciously pleased, by letters patent, under the great seal, dated the sixth day of May, in the sixteenth year of his Majesty's reign, to nominate and appoint me Richard Viscount Howe, of the kingdom of Ireland, and William Howe, Esq; General of his forces in North-America, and each of us, jointly and severally, to be his Majesty's Commissioner and Commissioners, for granting *his free and general pardons* to all those who, in the tumult and disorder of the times, may have deviated from their just allegiance, and who are willing, by a speedy return to their duty, to reap the benefits of the royal favor: And also for declaring, in his Majesty's name, any colony province, county, town, port, district, or place, to be at the peace of his Majesty, I do, therefore, hereby declare that due consideration shall be had to the meritorious services of all persons who shall aid and assist in restoring the public tranquility in the said colonies, or in any part or parts thereof; that pardons shall be granted, dutiful representations received, and every suitable encouragement given for promoting such measures as shall be conducive to the establishment of legal government and peace, in pursuance of his Majesty's most gracious purposes aforesaid.

Given on board his Majesty's ship the Eagle, off the coast of the province of Massachusetts-Bay, the twentieth day June 1776.   H O W E.

Congress' July 19 Response to Lord Howe's Peace Declaration

to Mr Kinsey was Recd in Congress, in Consequence of which I am Desir'd to forward you the foregoing Resolve,[1] & Inclose you Copies of Lord Howe's Letter & Declaration which Require no Comment. I am to inform you that Congress wish to know by what means that Letter to Mr Kinsey Reach'd his hands, & am to Desire you will Take every method to prevent any Communication with the Enemy from your Colony. This I have in Charge most earnestly to Recommend to you, & beg your immediate Attention to it.[2]

I most sincerely Congratulate you on the Agreeable Intelligence just Rec'd from South Carolina by Express. Have not time to be particular, can only Say that they twice attempted to Land & were Repulsed, their Capital Ships disabled, one Blown up, & in short a total stop put to the Business of the fleet for a long time. The Commodore wounded, one Captain Kill'd, one Capt. lost an Arm, & many officers & men Kill'd on board the Several Ships; General Lee writes our officers & men on our side behav'd as well as any old Troops could, our Loss very trifling, not one officer kill'd & not more than Ten men Kill'd & 22 wounded. Genl. Lee writes he never saw such a fierce incessant fire in all his life.[3]

I hope he who controuls all Events will still Espouse our Cause, & give such success to our Arms in other Quarters as from the Righteousness of our Cause & our Real Reliance on him he shall judge fit.

I am with real Regard, Gentn., Your very hum sert.

John Hancock Presidt

[P.S.] I am vastly hurried. Excuse me, I have not Time to have it Copied.

RC (PPRF).

[1] Hancock wrote this letter immediately below Congress' resolve of July 19 on Lord Howe's circular letters and declarations, which he had copied and certified in his own hand. See JCC, 5:592–93.

[2] Dennis De Berdt, Jr. (ca. 1742–1817), British merchant, was New Jersey's last colonial agent. Michael Kammen, A Rope of Sand: The Colonial Agents, British Politics, and the American Revolution (Ithaca, N.Y.: Cornell University Press, 1968), p. 323. For the convention's response to Hancock's inquiry, see Samuel Tucker to Hancock, July 19, 1776, and enclosure, in Am. Archives, 5th ser. 1:468–69. See also Robert Morris to Joseph Reed, July 21, 1776, note 1.

[3] The "agreeable Intelligence just Rec'd from South Carolina" was news of the June 28 American victory at Sullivan's Island conveyed in Gen. Charles Lee's July 2 letter to Hancock. NYHS Collections 5 (1872): 107–11. Enclosed with Lee's letter was a "Narrative" of this engagement by five deserters from Commodore Peter Parker's squadron. Ibid., pp. 111–13. In regard to this welcome news, Hancock this day wrote the following brief note to John Dickinson, then in Elizabethtown, N.J., with his battalion of Pennsylvania militia: "I congratulate you on the Success of our Arms in So. Carolina. The particulars as far as Time would admit I have sent to Genl Mercer who will inform [you.] God Bless you." R. R. Logan Collection, PPL.

John Hancock to George Washington

Sir,   Philadelphia July 19th. 1776.
My Earnestness to convey to you as soon as possible, the Intelligence this Moment received from South Carolina, on which I most sincerely congratulate you, I am confident, will apologize for my not adding more, than to tell you, that enclosed you will find the Copy of General Lee's Letter, and the Account from the Deserters who escaped after the Action. I am loth to hinder the Express one Moment. He is ready; and I will only say, that the enclosed Resolves of Congress were this Day Passed, & to which I Beg Leave to refer you.[1] I will write General Schuyler tomorrow.

You will please not to print the Letter &c received from Genl. Lee as by tomorrow's Post, I shall write you again, and forward the Account printed for the public Information.

I have the honour to be, with great Regard, Sir, your most obed. & very hble Sert.   John Hancock Presidt

[P.S.] I cannot detain the Express to give you the particulars of Gov. Rutledges Letter but will print it with the other parts submitted to me by Congress & forward you by to morrow's post.[2]

God Bless you my Dr. Sir, may you ever be under the Divine protection, & see an happy Issue to your noble Exertions. Yrs.

                                                      J H

RC (DLC). In the hand of Jacob Rush, with signature and postscript by Hancock.
   [1] These resolves dealt with the signing of the Declaration of Independence, affairs in General Schuyler's army, British peace terms, and other matters more directly related to Washington's command. JCC, 5:590–93.
   [2] With this letter Hancock also enclosed the following note from Edward Rutledge and a brief extract of a letter from his brother Hugh that Rutledge had transcribed for Hancock: "I send you a Letter from my Brother Hugh. It relates in general to the Action. You may have such parts published as you think fit." The note and the extract, both undated, are in Washington Papers, DLC.

Secret Committee Minutes of Proceedings

                                                July 19. 1776.
   The Come. met. Present Messrs. Morris, Alsop, Hewes, Lewis, Bartlett, Livingston. The Come. agreed that Mr. Morris purchase a Cargo of Tobo. to be shipped on board a vessel belonging to the Continent, now lying at Egg Harbour. Order on the Treasurers, favor J. Hannum for 623 1/3 dlls, being amount of 55 stand Arms delivered the Delaware battalion in continental service.

MS (MH).

Richard Stockton to Thomas Jefferson

Dear Sir   Trenton July 19th. 1776

Upon my arrival at this place I waited upon the New Jersey Convention, and proposed to them their agreeing to furnish 2000 Men for the increase of the flying Camp: they alledged the reasons against the measure which I expected, to wit, their having furnished their full proportion. However, upon my urging the importance of the measure, I was so happy as to be assured that they would, without any regard to their quotas, endeavour to furnish the 2000 Men, and that they should immediately take the field. They are under the necessity nevertheless of furnishing them from the Militia, which must have a rotation; but their Militia are well disciplined, and the Convention will be careful that this number of 2000 shall be continually in the feild as part of the flying Camp, untill the first of December.[1]

The Convention will forward this immediately by express. With great respect, I am Dr. Sir, Your most obedt. hb[le. servt.,]

Richd. Stockton

RC (DLC). Jefferson, *Papers* (Boyd), 1:467–68.

[1] Jefferson and Stockton were both members of a committee appointed on July 15 "to consider the propriety and means of augmenting the flying camp." On July 16 Congress had passed a resolve calling upon New Jersey to replace 2,000 soldiers in the flying camp, whom Washington had been authorized to call to his assistance, with an equal number of state militia. *JCC*, 5:562, 565–66. For the New Jersey Convention's July 18 ordinance complying with this resolution, see *Am. Archives*, 4th ser. 6:1647–49.

John Adams to Abigail Adams

Philadelphia July 20. 1776

I cannot omit the Opportunity of writing you a Line, by this Post. This Letter will I suppose, find you, in some degree or other, under the Influence of the Small Pox. The Air is of very great Importance. I dont know your Phisician, but I hope he wont deprive you of Air, more than is necessary.

We had Yesterday, an express from General Lee, in Charlestown, South Carolina, with an Account of a brilliant little Action between the Armament under Clinton, and Cornwallis, and a Battery on Sullivans Island. Which terminated very fortunately for America. I will endeavour to inclose, with this a printed Account of it.[1] It has given Us good Spirits here and will have an happy Effect, upon our Armies at New York and Ticonderoga. Surely our northern Soldiers will not suffer themselves to be outdone by their Brethren so nearly under the Sun. I dont yet hear of any Massachusetts Men, at New York. Our People must not flinch, at this critical Moment, when their Country is in more danger, than it ever will be again perhaps. What will they say, if the Howes should prevail against our Forces, at so important a Post as New York for Want of a few Thousand Men from the Massachusetts?

I will likewise send you, by this Post, Lord Howes Letter and Proclamation, which has let the Cat out of the Bag.[2] These Tricks deceive no longer. Gentlemen here, who either were or pretended to be deceived heretofore, now see or pretend to see, through such Artifices. I apprehend, his Lordship is afraid of being attacked upon Staten Island, and is throwing out his Barrells to amuse Leviathan, untill his Reinforcement shall arrive.[3]

RC (MHi). Adams, *Family Correspondence* (Butterfield), 2:52–53.

[1] After Gen. Charles Lee's letter of July 2 was read in Congress on July 19, Congress ordered its publication and resolved "that the thanks of the United States of America be given to Major General Lee, Colonel William Moultrie, Colonel William Thompson, and the officers and soldiers under their command." *JCC*, 5:593.

[2] For further information on the reception in Congress of Lord Howe's circular letter and declaration, see John Hancock to George Washington, July 18, 1776.

[3] This day Adams also wrote a second letter to Abigail, complaining about her failure to write recently, a matter he also discussed in his letter to Cotton Tufts this date. See Adams, *Family Correspondence* (Butterfield), 2:53–54.

John Adams to Cotton Tufts

Dear Sir   Philadelphia July 20. 1776. Saturday

Yours of July 5th never reached me, till this Morning. I greatly regret its delay. But that it might answer its End, without further Loss of Time, I waited on my Friend Dr. Rush, an eminent Phisician of this City, and a worthy Friend of mine, who with a Politeness and Benevolence, becoming his Character, promised to furnish me with his Sentiments, concerning Inocculation, so that I may forward them to you by the next Post, and I have obtained his Leave for you to publish them, in Print, if you please. He practices with great Success. Several of our Members, have been under his Hands and come out, almost without an Alteration of Countenance.

You say you got leave to lodge yours in Mrs. Adams's Letter. But no Letter from her accompanied it, which has distressed me much, both because I was very impatient for a Letter from her, and because it creates a Jealousy of some unfair Practice in the Post Office. . . .[1] I observe however upon the back of your Letter the Words "to be left at the Post office" in her Hand Writing, which makes it not improbable that she might send it without a Line from herself.

It is a long Time, since I heard from her or indeed any Thing concerning her only that she was determined to have the Distemper, with all my Children. How do you think I feel? supposing that my Wife and Children are all sick of the small Pox, myself unable to see them, or hear from them. And all this in Addition to several other Cares, public and private, which alone would be rather troublesome?

However, I will not be dejected. Hope springs eternal in my Breast, and keeps me up, above all Difficulties, hitherto.

I am, sincerely Yours.

LB (MHi). Adams, *Family Correspondence* (Butterfield), 2:54–55.

[1] Suspension points in MS.

Samuel Adams to Samuel Cooper

My dear sir,   Philade July 20 1776

I have the Pleasure of informing you, that the Continental Troops under the Command of Major Genl Lee, have tryumphd over the British Forces in South Carolina, the particulars of which you have in the inclosd Paper.[1] I trust this Blow has given so great a Check to the Power of the Enemy as to prevent their doing us any material Injury in that part of America. We look towards New York, and earnestly pray that God would order a decisive Event in our Favor there. You must have earlier Intelligence from time to time of the Circumstances of our Affairs in that Department than you can have from this place. Yesterday Circular Letters with inclosd Declarations from Lord Howe to the late Governors of New Jersey & the Colonies Southward as far as Georgia, were laid before Congress. As they were orderd to be publishd, I have the opportunity of transmitting a printed Copy of them for your Amusement.[2] There were also Letters from London to private Persons probably procured if not dictated by the British Ministry and written with a manifest Intention to form a Party here in favor of his Lordship, to induce People to believe that he is a cordial Friend to America, and that he is empowered to offer Terms of Accommodation acceptable to the Colonists. But it is now too late for that insidious Court to play such Tricks with any reasonable Hopes of Success. The American States have declard themselves no longer the Subjects of the British King. But if they had remaind such, the Budget is now opened to the World, and the People see with their own Eyes, with how much *Magnanimity* the Prince offers them Pardon on Condition that they will submit to be his abject Slaves.

I was informd in a Letter I recd from London last March, that

this very Nobleman declind to accept the Commission until he
should be vested with Authority to offer to us honorable Terms—
that he made a Merit of it—And yet he now comes with Terms
disgraceful to human Nature. If he is a good kind of Man, as these
Letters import, I am mistaken if he is not weak & ductile. He has
always voted, as I am told, in favor of the Kings Measures in
Parliament, and at the same time professd himself a Friend to
the Liberties of America! He seems to me, either never to have
had any good Principles at all, or not to have had Presence of
Mind openly and uniformly to avow them. I have an Anecdote
which I will communicate to you at another Time. At present I
have not Leisure. Pray let me have a Letter from you soon. You
cannot do me a greater Act of Kindness or more substantially
serve me than by writing often. I am affectionately, Your Friend,
                                                                    S A

[*P.S.*] Will you be kind enough to let my Family know that I am
in health.

I wish you wd present my most respectful Compts to my very
venerable Friend Dr C—y.³ I hope the worthy old Gentleman is
yet in Health & Spirits.

FC (NN).
    ¹ Probably the broadside printed this day containing extracts of two letters de-
scribing the attack on Sullivan's Island, a photocopy of which is in Clark, *Naval
Documents*, 5:1161.
    ² See John Hancock to George Washington, July 18, 1776.
    ³ Undoubtedly Charles Chauncy.

Board of War to George Washington

Sir   War Office July 20th. 1776
    I have it in Direction from the Board of War to request your
Excellency would give them your Advice on the enclosed Application from Mr William Goddard whom as well as every Person
qualified to fill the several Stations in the Army they would wish
to provide for consistent with Regularity & the Good of the Service. You will perceive that Mr Goddard applies for a Lieut
Colonelcy which depends on the Removal of several Officers into
superior Stations & in his Opinion these removals should be made
according to the Precedence of the Officers considered with Relation to the whole Army. Whether Vacancies should be filled
colonially or *continentally* is a Matter which has not yet been
settled & about which there are various Opinions; & whether, in
the particular Cases pointed out by Mr Goddard, it is expedient
to make the Arrangements mentioned in his Letter to the Board,

is a Matter which without your Excellency's Assistance they can form no Judgment. One of the Regts. mentioned by Mr Goddard is a Massachusetts Regt., the others are of Connecticut. It has been mention'd to Mr. G. that an Objection will arise from the Officers of Parsons's over whom he is desirous to be placed, that he, not having been in the Army, before, should be immediately created a Lieut. Col., in Preference to the Officer who would be entitled to the rise. He says in Answer to this that it is perfectly agreable to the Corps that it should be so; but of this you will be so good as to make the necessary Enquiries. He mentions also a Regt. of Artificers, the Field officers of which are not completed to their Number, commanded by Col. Parke. As the Board do not wish to serve Mr Goddard at the risque of creating Uneasiness among the Officers, they have troubled you with the Matter that you may be pleased to give them the proper Information.[1]

It is the Desire of the Board to form a regular List of the Army to avoid Inconveniencies arising from Promotions of Persons not entitled to it from their Rank in the Army & therefore they would be happy if you could spare the Time from your more important Engagements to attend to the requests made in their first Letter to you on the Subject of their Appointment.[2]

I have the Honour to be, your Excellency's most obedt, & most hble Servt.   Richard Peters, Secy. Bd. War & Ordinance

RC (DLC).
[1] In regard to this application, Washington wrote the board on July 29 that Goddard's "Introduction . . . into the Army as Lieut: Colonel would be attended with endless confusion." Washington, *Writings* (Fitzpatrick), 5:350. Goddard's petition to Congress, which was read on June 24 and then referred to the board, is in *Am. Archives*, 4th ser. 6:1012–13.
[2] On July 29 Washington informed that board that in compliance with a June 27 resolve, he had already submitted a list of Continental officers to Congress. Washington, *Writings* (Fitzpatrick), 5:347–48, 351. See also *JCC*, 5:486.

Charles Carroll of Carrollton to Charles Carroll, Sr.

Dr Papa,   Saturday 20th July 1776 Pha.
I arrived here last Tuesday evening.[1] Considering the Season I had pleasant weather. The next day I sent Molly's letter to Mrs. Maxfield. I met her the day before yesterday in the streets; she told me She did not believe she could procure the things Molly wrote to her for. The cotton she will give to a good weaver at the Bettering house; She admired the finess of the thread. Newton the shoe maker I have not yet seen; he has promised to call on me.
I am appointed one of the War office.[2] We meet at 8 in the

morning & at 7 in the Evening. The house meets at 9 and generally sits till three. Judge now what time I have to myself. Mr. Morris told me he had got a chap for my bill of Ex[change] at 90 per Cent but I have not yet seen him. I expected he would call on me yesterday evening.

As to news from S. Carolina I refer you to the newspaper of this day, vizt. Humphrey's, which we take & therefore I send it not inclosed.[3] Our army is driven out of Canada. It consists of 6000 men, whereof 3000 are sick & sent off to Fort George on Lake George. The other 3000 are fortifying a hill on the east side of Lake Champlain opposite to Ticonderoga: a most advantageous post. They have left Crown Point by the unanimous consent & determination of the General officers. I have seen Lt. Col. Wm. Allen lately from Canada, who distinguished himself at the attack at 3 Rivers: he confirms me in the opinion I had entertained of the want of conduct in the enemy: he says had they acted with spirit, prudence, & activity not one of the 1500 men had returned to the Sorel.

You will see by Humphrey's paper what the long expected Commissioners are come to. Howe brings a declaration offering pardon to those who will lay down their arms & return to their duty. This seems a preliminary condition. It is treated with contempt & indignation by every good & honest American. I believe every man's eyes must now be open. The blindest & most infatuated must see, & I think, detest the perfidy & Tyranny of the British Court, Parlt. & Nation. It is remarkable that even these harsh terms of Submission & pardon have not been offered to the N. England Govts. They, I suppose, must expect no mercy. We heared the 16th from G. Washington. I am informed by Mr. Griffin very lately from N. York that our army is in great spirits. The enemy I fancy will attempt to pass the highlands with some of their Ships. If they attempt it, I believe they will succeed, if the defences are in no better condition than when we Saw them last. Lord Howe's fleet is not yet arrived. He himself has had nine weeks passage. He sailed before the fleet. Our battalion, which is now here & is to march to N. Y. tomorrow to be under the immediate command of Gen. Washington, is much admired, and such is the spirit of the officers & men that I have the most Sanguine expectation they will signalise themselves if they should have an opportunity. The militia of this Province is zealous. So far from wanting incitements to march, the men can hardly be kept at home, and Congress have been obliged to give express orders not to suffer Journeymen employed at the paper & powder mills to march. Towards the end of the month I expect we shall have on the Jersey shore opposite to N. Y. near 20 Thousand men. Mr. Chase desires his complts to all the family. My love to Molly, little Poll, & Mrs. Darnall. Remember me to all friends. I am, yr. most affectionate Son,   Ch. Carroll of Carrollton

RC (MdHi).
[1] Carroll had written to his father on July 5 explaining his plans for attending Congress. "Contrary to my expectation I am appointed a Deputy to Congress, and much against my inclination I find myself obliged to set off for Philadelphia in a week at farthest. Mr. Johnson cant go, his wife is nigh her time. Mrs. Chase is too ill to permit Chase to go. Mr. Tilghman is prevented by something or other. So I am reduced to the necessity of being there very soon as we have now no Representation, Mr. Rogers being left out of the appointment." Charles Carroll Papers, MdHi.
[2] Carroll had been added to the Board of War on July 18. *JCC*, 5:575.
[3] A reference to the *Pennsylvania Ledger: or the Virginia, Maryland, Pennsylvania, & New Jersey Weekly Advertiser,* printed by James Humphreys, Jr.

William Ellery to Ezra Stiles?

[July 20, 1776] [1]

Ld. Howe is arrived in the Eagle Man o'War. The Reinforcmt is not arrived & I hope will never arrive. His Ldship sent a Flag o' truce a few days ago with Letters to Gen. Washington directed "to George Washington Esq." which were not received because his proper Title was not given him: since that some others have been sent to him with a similar Superscription & were for the same Reason not received. After this a flag was sent to Amboy with Letters to all the late Governors So. of N. York inclosg written Declarations containing his & his Brother's (Genl Howe) appointmt as Commissioners to receive the Submission of the Colonies or private Persons & grant Pardons agreeable to the late act of the Brit. Parliament, and a number of Letters principally from *Friends* in London to *Friends* here placing the Character of the Howes in the most amiable point of View, & recommending Reconciliation with G. Britain. These Letters were all sent by the commanding Officer at Amboy to G. Washington, & were transmitted by him to Congress, and were opened & read, that part of them, I mean which related to our Affairs. Among the Letters were some to Dr Franklin, one to the Farmer, and one to Mr Stockton. Dr Franklin was not in Congress when the Letters were bro't in, but was sent for. When he entered, his Letters were delivered to him sealed. He opened them, looked over them, and handed them to the President desiring him to read them. They were accordingly read to Congress & contained much the same Sentiments with those to *Friends,* as did that to Mr Stockton, who is a Member of Congress, and who was treated and behaved in the same manner that Dr Franklin did. As the *Farmer* is in the Jersey at the Head of his Battalion, his Letter is kept sealed by the President until he shall return & receive it in Congress. The Letters

to the late Governors & the Declarations are ordered to be printed
to let the People see upon what Terms Reconciliation is proposed
to them: Odi Danaös, etiam Dona ferentes: but when what some
People, Tories, may call the Olive-plant is handed to us at the point
of the Bayonet, or is hurled to us from the Mouths of Canon, if
possible I should more than hate it. The Truth is the Door is shut, &
it would now be in vain, to talk of any sort of Alliance with Britain
but a Commercial One. We have been driven into a Declara of
Independency & must forget our former Love for our British
Brethren. The Sword must Determine our Quarrel. Our Repulse
from Canada is disagreeable, but we must expect repeated Defeats.
The *Road to Liberty, like the Road to Heaven is strewed with
Thorns. Virtue lives in Exertion.* But thank Providence, altho' our
Northern Army hath been unsuccessful, our Southern Forces under
Gen. Lee have been successful. A Letter which Congress this day
received by Express from him dated at Charlesto[n] July 2d gives
us a very agreeable acco[unt] of a severe Repulse given to the fleet
under Capt Parker by our fort on Sullivans Island &c.

MS not found; reprinted from Ezra Stiles, *The Literary Diary of Ezra Stiles . . .*,
ed. Franklin B. Dexter, 3 vols. (New York: C. Scribner's Son's, 1901), 2:31–32, where
Stiles describes it as "A Letter from Mr Ellery in Congress dated Philada 20th
Inst. Extract."
[1] Ezra Stiles (1727–95), Congregational clergyman and scholar of wide-ranging
interests, pastor of the Second Congregational Church, Newport, R.I., 1755–76, and
president of Yale, 1778–95, was living in Dighton, Mass., at this time. *DAB*. It is
possible that Ellery actually wrote this letter to his son-in-law, William Channing,
and that Stiles merely copied part of it for his own use, for Stiles noted in his
diary on July 26: "This Eveng Mr. Channing received a Letter from his Father
Ellery in the Gen. Congress dated at Philada 20th July, with a Pensylva Ledger
20 July. We have a Confirma[tion] of the Success of our Forces at Charlesto[n] So
Carolina in a great Naval action which happened there on Friday 28th June last."
Stiles, *Literary Diary*, 2:31.

Benjamin Franklin to Lord Howe

My Lord,   Philada. July 20th. 1776.[1]
    I received safe the Letters your Lordship so kindly forwarded to
me, and beg you to accept my Thanks.
    The Official Dispatches to which you refer me,[2] contain nothing
more than what we had seen in the Act of Parliament, viz. Offers
of Pardon upon Submission; which I was sorry to find, as it must
give your Lordship Pain to be sent so far on so hopeless a Business.
    Directing Pardons to be offered the Colonies, who are the very
Parties injured, expresses indeed that Opinion of our Ignorance,
Baseness, & Insensibility which your uninform'd and proud Nation
has long been pleased to entertain of us; but it can have no other

Effect than that of increasing our Resentment. It is impossible we should think of Submission to a Government, that has with the most wanton Barbarity and Cruelty, burnt our defenceless Towns in the midst of Winter, excited the Savages to massacre our Farmers, and our Slaves to murder their Masters, and is even now bringing foreign Mercenaries to deluge our Settlements with Blood. These atrocious Injuries have extinguished every remaining Spark of Affection for that Parent Country we once held so dear. But were it possible for *us* to forget and forgive them, it is not possible for *you* (I mean the British Nation) to forgive the People you have so heavily injured; you can never confide again in those as Fellow Subjects, & permit them to enjoy equal Freedom, to whom you know you have given such just Cause of lasting Enmity. And this must impel you, where we again under your Government, to endeavour the breaking our Spirit by the severest Tyranny, & obstructing by every means in your Power our growing Strength and Prosperity.

But your Lordship mentions "the Kings paternal Solicitude for promoting the Establishment of lasting *Peace* and Union with the Colonies." If by *Peace* is here meant, a Peace to be entered into between Britain and America as distinct States now at War, and his Majesty has given your Lordship Powers to treat with us of such a Peace, I may venture to say, tho' without Authority, that I think a Treaty for that purpose not yet quite impracticable, before we enter into Foreign Alliances. But I am persuaded you have no such Powers. Your Nation, tho' by punishing those American Governors who have created & fomented the Discord, rebuilding our burnt Towns, & repairing as far as possible the Mischiefs done us, She might yet recover a great Share of our Regard & the greatest part of our growing Commerce, with all the Advantage of that additional Strength to be derived from a Friendship with us; I know too well her abounding Pride and deficient Wisdom, to believe she will ever take such Salutary Measures. Her Fondness for Conquest as a Warlike Nation, her Lust of Dominion as an Ambitious one, and her Thirst for a gainful Monopoly as a Commercial one (none of them legitimate Causes of War) will all join to hide from her Eyes every View of her true Interests; and continually goad her on in these ruinous distant Expeditions, so destructive both of Lives and Treasure, that must prove as pernicious to her in the End as the Croisades formerly were to most of the Nations of Europe.

I have not the Vanity, my Lord, to think of intimidating by thus predicting the Effects of this War; for I know it will in England have the Fate of all my former Predictions, not to be believed till the Event shall verify it.

Long did I endeavour with unfeigned and unwearied Zeal, to preserve from breaking, that fine & noble China Vase the British Empire: for I knew that being once broken, the separate Parts could not retain even their Share of the Strength or Value that existed in the Whole, and that a perfect Re-Union of those Parts could scarce even be hoped for. Your Lordship may possibly remember the Tears of Joy that wet my Cheek, when, at your good Sister's in London, you once gave me Expectations that a Reconciliation might soon take place. I had the Misfortune to find those Expectations disappointed, & to be treated as the Cause of the Mischief I was labouring to prevent. My Consolation under that groundless and malevolent Treatment was, that I retained the Friendship of many Wise & Good Men in that Country, and among the rest some I have in the Regard of Lord Howe.

The well founded Esteem, and permit me to say Affection, which I shall always have for your Lordship; makes it painful to me to see you engag'd in conducting a War, the great Ground of which, as expressed in your Letter, is, "the Necessity of preventing the American Trade from passing into foreign Channels." To me it seems that neither the obtaining or retaining of any Trade, how valuable soever, is an Object for which Men may justly Spill each others Blood, that the true and sure means of extending and securing Commerce is the goodness and cheapness of Commodities, & that the profits of no Trade can ever be equal to the Expence of compelling it, and of holding it, by Fleets and Armies. I consider this War against us therefore, as both unjust, and unwise; and I am persuaded cool dispassionate Posterity will condemn to Infamy those who advised it; and that even Success will not save from some degree of Dishonour, those who voluntarily engag'd to conduct it. I know your great Motive in coming hither was the Hope of being instrumental in a Reconciliation; and I believe when you find *that* impossible on any Terms given you to propose, you will relinquish so odious a Command, and return to a more honourable private Station.

With the greatest and most sincere Respect, I have the honour to be; My Lord, Your Lordships most obedient humble Servt.

B. Franklin

Tr (CSmH).

[1] Although one of Franklin's editors printed this document (from a copy in the British Museum) under the date July 30, it is clearly dated July 20. Franklin, *Writings* (Smyth), 6:458–62. Franklin undoubtedly wrote it immediately after Congress formally resolved, this date, "That Dr. Franklin may, if he thinks proper, send an answer to the letter he received from Lord Howe." *JCC*, 5:597.

[2] Richard Lord Howe (1726–99), commander of the British fleet in America and joint commissioner (with his brother Gen. William Howe) to negotiate peace with the colonies, had arrived at Staten Island on July 12. En route to New York from Halifax, he had prepared a series of letters announcing his peace commission— ostensibly addressed to several of the colonial governors and dated "Eagle, off the Coast of the Province of Massachusetts-Bay, June 20th, 1776"—but he did not attempt to post them until the day after anchoring at Staten Island. Those letters, together with one to Franklin and "sundry letters to several private persons," were taken to Washington's headquarters and then forwarded to Congress, which on July 18 immediately referred them to a committee.

"The Official Dispatches to which you refer me" consisted of the letters that were referred to committee and subsequently published—"that the good people of these United States may be informed of what nature are the commissioners, and what the terms" are now offered. Howe's letter to Franklin, dated June 20 but bearing a postscript "Off Sandy Hook, 12th of July," is in Franklin, *Writings* (Smyth), 6:458. For Congress' response to the various issues arising from Howe's conduct, see *JCC*, 5:567, 574–75, 592–3, 597. For a careful assessment of Lord Howe's mission to America, see Ira D. Gruber, *The Howe Brothers and the American Revolution* (New York: Atheneum, 1972), pp. 89–126.

John Hancock to Samuel Cooper

Dear Sir,   Philada. 20 July 1776

My constant Attention to the Business of my Departmt. both Day & Night prevents me the pleasing Satisfaction of duly attending to my Friends, & under these Circumstances I trust I shall stand Excus'd for not writing oftner, they however are very near my heart, & to whom I wish every Good.

I have only Time to Inclose you this Morning's paper, to which Refer you for every thing stirring here. I most sincerely Congratulate you on the Success of our Arms in South Carolina, may the same Almighty Being who has so interpos'd hitherto in our fav[or] still protect & Defend us, & may our future Conduct be such as to see his further Salvation.

I Beg my Respects [to] your good Lady & Family, in which Mrs. Hancock Joines me, & to yor Brother & Lady & Family, & indeed to all Friends.

I am in great haste, with every wish in your fav., Dr Sir, Your very hum set,   John Hancock

RC (CSmH). Addressed: "To The Revd. Docr Samuel Cooper In Boston."

John Hancock to George Washington

Sir   Congress Chamber, 3 oClock AM, 20 July 1776

I have only Time to inform you that this moment your favr. of 19th is come to hand.[1] Inclos'd is this morning's paper, to which beg to Refer you.

My best wishes attend you & am Your most obedt Svt,
John Hancock Prest.

RC (DLC).
[1] Washington's July 19 letter to Hancock is in PCC, item 152, 2:243–48, and Washington, *Writings* (Fitzpatrick), 5:304–7.

Edward Rutledge to John Jay

My dear Jay   Philada. July 20th. 1776.

I am much obliged to you for your friendly Letter of the 6th which did not come to Hand until a few Days ago, and I have been so much engaged since that I really had no time to acknowledge the Receipt of it.[1] But I can no longer delay it, when I have it in my Power to communicate a piece of Intelligence which I am sure must afford you (who are interested in the Happiness of my Countrymen) the highest Satisfaction. By Express which arrived yesterday we learn that the British Fleet has been repulsed with very considerable Loss. Two 50 Gun Ships have received so much Damage that it is thought they will never be able to go to Sea again—another the Actdon [Actaeon] of 28 blown up, the remainder considerably injured—The Captain of the Experiment kill'd, the Captain of the Bristol lost his Arm—Sir Peter Parker wounded—104 Seamen & inferior Officers kill'd & about 64 wounded, several of whom have since died of the wounds. The Loss of our side is—12 kill'd & 24 wounded, all privates. The Battle lasted near 12 Hours during the whole of which time Genl. Lee says our Men were as cool & as determined as ever he saw Men in his Life. This is the more to be wonder'd at when I tell you, that their Number was but 500 and that but one of that Number had ever seen a battle. At the time that the Ships lay before the Fort, Genl. Clynton attempted to land about 2000 of his Forces at another part of the Island. They were in 35 Flat Bottom Boats, but they were twice repulsed by Colonel Thompson of our Rangers, commanding 300 Men with considerable Loss on their Side, but none on ours.

It is thought that they would make another Attack with their Land Forces, but Lee says they may do in that as they please. He is confident we shall repulse them as often as they attack with as much Honour to ourselves as we have done already. Remember me to Morris. I am in very great Haste. Shall answer some Queries in your Letter in a day or two.[2]

God bless you, My dear Friend. I am, sincerely & affectionately yours,   E. Rutledge

RC (NNC). Addressed: "John Jay Esquire, at the Congress at New York."

[1] For Jay's letter, see Rutledge to Jay, June 29, 1776, note 2.

[2] This day Rutledge also wrote a letter to Robert R. Livingston, from which only the following extract has been found:

"I should have answer'd my Friend's obliging favour sooner, had I not thought that he would chearfully escuse me until I had call'd the Attention of the House effectually to the Suport of his Country. I trust this is in some Measure now done. We have sent off Express to the Eastern States and to Maryland with my strong requests and in order to *compel* the Jerseys to afford a further assistance we have directed (not permitted) General Washington to call into your City from the Flying Camp 2000 men, judging I should suppose truly that the People of that Colony would not suffer their Country to be over run, but when convinced that they must contribute to the Common Cause, they would do it at once. You will receive by this Conveyance what to me & to all who love me has & will be a most pleasing piece of Intelligence—I mean an Account of a very complete Defeat of the British Navy in So. Carolina. On the 28th of June the Experiment of 50 the Bristol of 50, the Solbay, Syria, Actoon [*Actaeon*] & Action [*Active*] of 28 each, the Friendship of 26, the Sphynx of 20 & the Thunder Bomb drew up in Line of Battle before our Fort at Sulivan's Island about 5 miles from & in full sight of the Town—to divert the attention of the People the Bomb began to throw her shells until the Ships could be brought to bear on the Fort, at the same time they attempted to land a Body of about 2000 men from 35 Flat Bottom Boats on a distant part of the Island judging that we had so many out of the Fort—but in that they were wrong, as indeed in almost every thing else, for we had abt. 3000 men posted there with 2 Field pieces & an 18 poundr under the Command of Col. Thompson of the Rangers who twice repulsed their whole Force with Loss on their Side, but none on his own.

"The Fleet during the whole of this time indeed from 11 o'clock A.M. until 10 at Night kept up a most furious Fire on the Fort but were at last gallantly repulsed, with a mere handful of Men, a force which to one so little skill'd in war as I am, would have appear'd totally inadequate for the purpose—We had but 800 Men in the Fort & could bring but 12 Guns to bear upon the Fleet. The Loss as to Men on our part was inconsiderable as to No. & Character (other than being as brave as they could be—there were but 12 kill'd & 24 wounded, not an officer beyond a Serg; the least part,—Genles Lee & Howe says they behaved to a share with as much coolness & courage as they ever saw—& what makes it more singular is, that but one of the whole Number had ever been in Action. The Bristol lost her Mizen Mast the 1st shot, her main and fore mast her Hall Yard etc vastly damaged—the Capt. of the Commodore lost his Arm, the Commodore was wounded in the thigh and knee and had his Breeches torn off 44 Men kill'd 30 wounded 20 of whom are since dead—the Experiment's Capt. kill'd togr. with 57, others & 30 wounded—the Ship vastly hurt, several of her Parts brok into one or it is the general opinion that neither of the above Vessels will ever get to Sea again— Uncertain what the others lost—The Actoon got aground & was set on fire by her own people but did not blow up before a Mr. Milligan a Marine officer had boarded her brought off her Colours her ships Bell, Sails, Stores, etc. The Thunder Bomb shatter'd her Bed in the Firing so much that she must go into Dock to refit before she will be able to cut—this my dear Friend is as much as I can relate of a Defense which must redound to the Honour of our valiant Countrymen. I think it will have most happy Consequences, not to that Colony alone, but to all America, it will fill her with a Spirit of Emulation & go far I hope towards over throwing opposition." Samuel T. Freeman & Co. Catalog, *The Frederick S. Peck Collection of American Historical Autographs* (February 17, 1947), pp. 30–31.

James Wilson to John Montgomery and Jasper Yeates

Gentlemen   Philada. July 20th. 1776

Doctor Franklin and I have been favoured with your Letter of the 14th instant. At his Request I write this Answer for him and myself. I believe the Congress have no particular Views which they would wish to accomplish at the ensuing Treaty.[1] Their Intention and their earnest Desire is that Peace and Friendship may be preserved and cultivated between the United States and the Indian Tribes. Presents are the most prevailing Arguments that can be used with the Savages for this Purpose. Mr Morgan has purchased a considerable Quantity of Goods. Mr Butler has provided a few more. All will be at your Service. I am informed that Messrs Gratz have a small Assortment at Pittsburgh. Your Presents, if dificient, may be supplied from it. I have sent you three thousand Dollars. If this Sum should prove to be too small, your Credit with the Congress will, I am sure, be good enough for a larger. I congratulate you on the News from South Carolina; and refer you to Major Butler and Mr Boyd for Particulars.

Inclosed are some Resolutions of Congress which will shew you what is intended to be done on the Frontiers of Pennsylvania.[2] One of them is particularly directed to the Commissioners of Indian Affairs in the Middle Department. I know you will make the strictest and speediest Enquiry concerning its Objects.

Please to remember me to all my good Acquaintances in Westmoreland. I am, Gentlemen, Your very humble Servant,

James Wilson

RC (InU). Addressed: "Jasper Yeates and John Montgomery Esqrs., Commissioners for Indian Affairs, Pittsburgh."

[1] See Benjamin Franklin and James Wilson to Jasper Yeates, July 4, 1776.

[2] Probably resolutions of July 11, 15, 18, and 20 on frontier defense and the recruitment of a new battalion in Westmoreland and Bedford Counties. See JCC, 5:541–42, 562, 589–90, 596.

John Adams to Jonathan Dickinson Sergeant

Dear sir.   Philadelphia July 21. 1776

Your Favour of the 19th from Trenton, reached me, yesterday.[1] It is very true that We were Somewhat alarmed at the last Clause in your Constitution. It is a pity that the Idea, of returning under the Yoke, was held up, in so good a System, because it gives Something to Say, to a very unworthy Party.

I hope you will assume the Style of the Common Wealth of New Jersey, as Soon as your new government is compleated. Virginia has done it—and it is the most consistent Style.

It is a great Pleasure to learn that you have formally ratified Independency, and that your Unanimity and Firmness increase. This will be the Case every where as the War approaches nearer. An Enemies Army brings a great Heat with it, and warms all before it. Nothing makes and Spreads Patriotism so fast.

Your ordinance against Treasons will make Whiggs by the thousand. Nine tenths of the Toryism in America, has arisen from sheer Cowardice, and avarice. But when Persons come to see their is

greater danger to their Persons and Property from Toryism than
Whiggism, the same Avarice and Pusillanimity will make them
Whiggs. A Treason Law is in Politicks like the Article for Shooting
upon the Spot, a Soldier who shall turn his back. It turns a Mans
Cowardice and Timidity into Heroism, because it places greater
danger behind his back than before his Face.

While you are attending to military Matters, dont forget Salt
Petre, Sulphur, Powder, Flints, Lead, Cannon, Mortars.

It grieves me to hear that your People have a Prejudice against
liberal Education. There is a Spice of this every where. But Liberty
has no Enemy more dangerous than such a Prejudice. It is your
Business, my Friend, as a Statesman to soften and eradicate this
Prejudice. The surest Mode of doing it is to perswade Gentlemen of
Education to lay aside Some of their Airs, of Scorn, Vanity and
Pride, which it is a certain Truth that they Sometimes indulge
themselves in. Gentlemen cannot expect the Confidence of the common People if they treat them ill, or refuse hautily to comply with
some of their favorite Notions which may often be most obligingly
done, without the least deviation from Honour or Virtue.

Your Delegates behave very well: but I wish for you among them.
I think however, that you judged wisely in continuing in Convention
—where I believe you have been able to do more good, than you
could have done here.

I should be obliged to you for a Line now and then. Mr. S. Adams
recd. your Letter from Bristol.[2] You will See the new Delegates for
Pensilvania. What is the Cause, that Mr Dickinson never can maintain his Popularity for more than two or three years together, as they
tell me has ever been the Case! He may have a good Heart, and
certainly is very ready with his Pen, and has a great deal of Learning,
but his Head is not very long, nor clear. I am

LB (MHi).

[1] Sergeant sent Adams news of the latest political developments in New Jersey
in his July 19 letter.

"I am told You are alarmed at Philada. with the last clause in our charter. That
& another respecting Judges was hard fought; especially that of *Reconciliation*,
upon a Motion to defer printing the Copy 'till it could be reconsidered.

"However we have formally ratified *Independency* & assumed the Stile of *the
Convention of the State of New Jersey*—this very unanimously, & the Votes go
down by this Express to the printer.

"We are mending very fast here. East Jersey were always firm; West Jersey will
now move with Vigour. The Tories in some parts disturbed us, but they have
hurt us more by impeding the Business of the Convention & harassing with an
Infinity of Hearings. But for this we have provided a Remedy by our Ordinance
for trying Treasons, Seditions & Counterfeitings. And now we shall apply our
chief Attention to Military Matters, for which End we remove to Brunswick on
Monday, after delaying it too long." Adams Papers, MHi.

[2] See Abraham Clark to Elias Dayton, July 4, 1776, note.

Elbridge Gerry to John Adams and Samuel Adams

Dear sirs   Kings Bridge July 21. 1776

I have been fully employed since Thursday Noon in obtaining some Knowledge of the State of the Army & conferring with the different Corps of officers from the General to the Field officers & have the pleasure to inform You that they appear to be in high Spirits for Action & agree in Sentiments that the Men are as firm & determined as they wish them to be, having in View, since the Declaration of Independence an object that they are ready to contend for, an object that they will chearfully pursue at the Risque of Life & every valuable Enjoyment.

The Army including officers & the Sick are about 18000 strong, & these are posted at Paulis Hook, Governors Island which is about half a Mile from the Battery near the Bowling Green, Long Island, New York City, & this post; at which places they have thrown up a great Number of Works some of which exceed any I ever have seen & appear to be well calculated for Defence. In short our Men are so expert at the Shovel & Haw that they light on every advantageous Spot & in a Day or two produce a Fortification that a few years ago would have been considered by our Assemblies as a great Undertaking for a Colony & cost it more for the Time spent in considering the Measure than it now Costs the Continent to compleat the Work. It is however necessary that the remaining seven thousand Men should come in & the Harvest being nearly over I hope it will soon be the Case. It is a happy Circumstance that in the Jersies, this Colony & the eastern Ones the Women & Children are endeavouring to supply the places of the Men who are called to defend the country, & with a Zeal little short of Enthusiasm are exerting themselves in the Field to gather the Harvest & perform the Business which they have heretofore been mostly Strangers to. Surely whilst such a Spirit remains there can be but little Danger of loosing our Cause. Stores of every Kind are plenty here excepting Flints, & I shall endeavour to send some from the Massachusetts Bay.

I most heartily Congratulate You on the Success of our Arms at the Southward; the News reached New York yesterday & was highly relished by the Camp. I wish Mr. Howe could be prevailed on to make his attack with the Troops he now has; I think he would not find it necessary to be at any further Expense on *their* Account.

You will undoubtedly be informed by the General with the Substance of the Intercourse between him & General Howes Adjt General by Flag of Truce. It seems that Lord Howe is sorry that he did not arrive a Day or two before & thinks he could have prevented the Declaration of Independence. General Howe is desirous of keeping open a Communication with our General & thinks he has made the *first Advances to an Accomodation*. I suppose he would be glad to amuse him daily, as his officers who are our prisoners have attempted to amuse Congress, that his Attention to more important Objects may be diverted. He proposed to exchange Master Lovell for Major Skeene, but the General referred him to Congress as the offer originated from thence, And being refused by him must now be confirmed by the same Body.[1]

I think Things are in a good Way in this Government. The Convention have resolved to raise 6000 Men for the Defence of the Highlands & places adjacent at their own Expence & have applyed to Genl Washington for the Loan of £20000 for this purpose. The military Chest being low the General could not oblige them, but to promote the Measure has lent them 20000 Dollars.

The important objects of Congress appear to be few & if conducted with Spirit must soon make the united States most formidable to their Enemies.

In the first place the northern Army must be assisted & in order thereto Schuyler recalled as the good of the Service requires it. I am well informed that the officers & soldiers in that Army are dissatisfied at his having the Command & never will have Confidence untill he is removed. The N England Colonies are warm for the Measure & the officers in general in this Department. This You may depend on, that Matters never will go well untill this evil Genius is removed. Why is the honest Wooster *censured* & tried & finally found faultless & Schuyler unimpeached amidst many Misdemeanors. He is exceedingly attached to the present Deputy Commissary Livingston & between them I wish the Continent may not be unnecessarily drained of large Sums of Money. I have seen a Receipt of Mr L of £24000 for 4000 bls. pork purchased last April when pork was £4 per barell. He gave his Receipt in June promising to return the pork when called for or to pay the market price at the Time demanded. The Demand was not made until July & thus has he thrown away or given to his Relative Livingston in one article £8000.[2] The Quarter Master General was lately applyed to by Schuyler for Cloathing for the naked Men that were taken prisoner at the Cedars & he gave him an order for the Cloathing on a Man that lives within three Doors of his House who had before offered him (Schuyler) the Cloathing 50 per Cent Cheaper as I am credibly informed than it could be obtained in New York; this he refused & the Men were suffering whilst he was taking this extraordinary Step. He certainly acted a weak or wicked part in giveing Notice of his Intention to Sir John Johnson to take him & thus loosing the oppertunity of securing this dangerous Enemy to America. He has been uniformly obliging to officers of the Enemy & morose & insolent to our officers & Men. He has been constantly attached to the proprietary Interest in the middle Colonies & kept in his place by their Influence in Congress, but if he is not to be removed the Army must continue retreating & I expect in a short Time that they will be in good Quarters in the City of Philadelphia. It gives me Pain to say anything on this head to my Friends, but if he can be sent to Boston, recalled to answer any Charges that may be brot against him, or otherwise removed, I know it will give them pleasure & certain it is that there is a prospect of Serving the Cause. The Army must be cleansed of the small pox & Cloathing sent for this purpose; if the Quarter Master were directed to send 1000 Suits, I think it would be done.

I have conferred with the General upon the Necessity of giving Bounties to reinlist our Men for the next Campaign. He is very attentive to it & is convinced that the present offer of ten Dollars is ineffectual. He thinks that 5000 Men may be obtained, & if 20 Dollars is afterwards offered perhaps 5000 more may inlist for 3 years; but is convinced that nothing less than 20 Dollars & 100 Acres of Land will obtain the Number wanted, & if the Number first mentioned should inlist without Land he thinks it would be a source of constant uneasiness if Land should be afterwards given unless they also should have it. Upon the whole the Generals Sentiments fully coincide with those of many Gentlemen who were for a generous Bounty, that It will be the most prudent, politic & cheapest Method to make a generous offer at first & never to deviate from it, rather than for Congress to bid on itself & prevent Men from inlisting for one Bounty by giving them Hopes that a greater will be hereafter offered. If this Matter is left as it was the last Year We shall run a Risque that may be ruinous & it is now the eleventh Hour; indeed there is a difficulty in Congress coming at the Land wch I mentioned to the General. He thinks it may be easily removed & has promised his Sentiments in writing against my Return. I think it ought not however to be omitted a Moment longer.

A third Thing is Cloathing which I find will be greatly wanted in the Army. In addition to what has been done I wish the Assemblies & Conventions could be immediately called on for an Estimate of the Cloathing that Congress may depend on their manufacturing or purchasing for the Army; this would be acting understandably & I think it would be a fresh Stimulus to the Assemblies and a Hint that the Measure is important. Pray carry in a short Resolve & the Business is done in a second. If the paymaster of the Regiments were directed to procure Frocks of Oznabrigs which is plenty in Philadelphia the soldiers would have their Cloathing & pay for them out of their Wages.

The fourth Thing is an Augmentation of the Army at New York. By undoubted Intelligence it is the Intent of the Enemy to aim at taking a Ridge abt. 12 Miles from Kings Bridge which runs from River to River & thus endeavour to cut off the Communication between the Camp & the Eastern Colonies. General Mifflin is of opinion that 5000 Men added to the 25000 already ordered here will enable the General to possess himself of this Ridge & I am certain that not a Man less will answer the purpose. It is not worth while to starve the Campaign for such an inconsiderable Number, & I am for bringing them from the N. E. Colonies & letting the Army know that We expect them to beat these Fellows at all Events. I cannot see the Necessity of keeping two Regiments at Rhode Island & am for ordering one of them to this place.

The Augmentation of the flying Camp, plan of foreign Treaty, Manufactory of Flints, Resolve for obtaining the Lead on Houses thro' out the Continent, & Loan office Resolves I conclude are nearly finished, at least that they are vigorously pursued. Would it not be a good Measure to propose to the French Court to supply wth. Grain their Army in the West Indies & to impower them to empoly suitable persons in the States for that purpose, who shall be supplyed by Congress wth Money & ship it on their own Vessels; whilst they are to make Returns by allowing Us a Factor in their Kingdom to purchase Arms or other military stores to a certain amount who is to be furnished by their Court with Money for that purpose. This would be a speedy Way of coming at Arms & Ammunition & open a Channel for a Breach with Britain. I have not yet received a Copy of the Confederation.

Pray subscribe for me the Declaration of Independence if the same is to be signed as proposed. I think We ought to have the privilege when necessarily absent of voting and signing by proxy.

Monday Morn
I have seen some Members of the York Convention & am to dine at White Plains this day. I have a plan in View for obtaining in a short Time a Number of brass Cannon & Howitzers that I think will be adopted by the Convention & will be very useful.[3] It will be put on Foot by the Members I have seen & may supply Us with an Article that we have not been able to procure & wch is exceedingly necessary.

A Mr Wybert recommended as an Engineer by the War office if I rightly remember, is a very useful Man & does great Service here. He mentions a Monseiur De Saint Martin as an able Officer of Artillery which General Mifflin tells me is exceedingly Wanted. Pray appoint him to a Captaincy which will do to begin with & send him to the Camp here. Mifflin is very desirous of its being done speedily.[4]

I think it Time to conclude *in Haste* & remain sirs, your assured Friend & very huml sert.   Elbridge Gerry

P.S. Mons. Martin lives with a Mr. Duchemen in Philadelphia.

RC (NN).
[1] On July 24 Congress resolved "That General Washington be empowered to

agree to the exchange of Governor Skene for Mr. Lovell." *JCC,* 5:607. For further information on the exchange of James Lovell, see John Hancock to George Washington, January 6, 1776, note 1.

[2] For additional information on efforts to obtain Walter Livingston's removal from his commissary position, see Elbridge Gerry to Joseph Trumbull, September 12, 1776, note 2.

[3] Gerry also wrote to Gen. Henry Knox describing the need for brass cannons and howitzers and urging him to arrange for their production. Gerry to Knox, July 23, 1776, Knox Papers, MHi.

[4] Monsieur St. Martin was appointed an engineer with the rank of lieutenant colonel and ordered to New York on July 23. *JCC,* 5:602.

John Hancock to John Haslett

Sir   Philada. Sunday Morng 21st July 1776

In Consequence of a Resolution of Congress pass'd yesterday Eveng. I am to Direct you immediately & without loss of time after the Recepit of this to March with the Troops under your Command to Philadelphia, there to do duty until the further order of Congress. If the Company order'd to Lewistown be still there, you are not to include that Company in your Marching orders for Philada. On your Arrival here you will Station your Troops in the Barracks.[1]

I am with much Respect, Sir, Your most obedt Servt,

J H Pt.

LB (DNA: PCC, item 12A). Addressed: "To Coll. Haslett, Or Officer Commandg the Battalion of Continental Troops in Delaware Governmt."
[1] See *JCC,* 5:596.

Robert Morris to Joseph Reed

Dear sir   From the Hills of Schuylkill July 21st. 1776

I received your obliging letter of the 18th yesterday in Congress, and shou'd have been tempted to have laid the enclosure immediately before the House, had not a letter from the same person on the same Subject & in a similar stile addressed to J. Kinsey Esqr. of New Jersey been read in Congress the day before.[1] The Temper of the House was plain and you may judge what it was, when I tell you the only enquiry that letter produced was how it got to Mr. Kinseys hands.

I am sorry to say there are some amongst us that cannot bear the thought of reconciliation on any terms.[2] To these men all propositions of the kind sound like high Treason against the States and I really believe they wou'd sooner punish a Man for this Crime than for bearing arms against us.

I cannot help Condemning this disposition as it must be founded in keen resentment or on interested Views where we ought to have the Interest of our Country and the Good of Mankind to Act as the main Spring in all our Public Conduct. I think with you that if the Commissioners have any propositions to make they ought to be heard. Shou'd they disclose powers different from what we immagine them to be Vested with, and an inclination to imploy those powers favourably for America, it is our duty to attend to such offers, weigh well the Consequences of every determination we come to and in short to lay aside all prejudices, resentments and sanguine Notions of our own Strength in order that reason may influence and Wisdom guide our Concils. If the admiral & General are really desirous of a Conference I think & hope they will address our General properly. This may be expected if they have powers beyond granting pardons. If they have not it is Idle for them to solicit any intercourse as no good can possibly arise to them or their Cause from it, but on our parts I think good Policy requires that we shou'd hear all they have to say. I am not for making any Sacrifice of Dignity, but still I woud hear them if possible, because if they can offer Peace on admissible terms I believe the great majority of America wou'd still be for accepting it. If they can only offer *Pardons* & that is fully ascertained it will firmly Unite all America in their exertions to support the Independency they have declared and it must be obvious to every body that our *United Efforts* will be absolutely necessary. This being the case why should we fear to Treat of Peace or to hear the Commissioners on that Subject. If they can offer terms that are advantageous & honorable for this Country, let us meet them. If they cannot We are not in a situation or temper to ask or receive pardons & all who dont mean to stoop to this Ignominious submission will consequently take up their Arms with a determination to Conquer or die. If they offer or desire a Conference & we reject it, those who are already dissatisfyed will become more so and others will follow their example & we may expect daily greater disunion & defection in every part of these States. At least such are my apprehensions on this Subject. I have uniformly Voted against & opposed the declaration of Independance because in my poor oppinion it was an improper time and will neither promote the interest or redound to the honor of America, for it has caused division when we wanted Union, and will be ascribed to very different principles than those which ought to give rise to such an Important measure. I did expect my Conduct in this great Question woud have procured my dismission from the great Council but find myself disapointed for the Convention have thought proper to return me in the New Delegation, and altho my interest & inclination prompt me to decline the Service yet I cannot depart from one point that first induced me to enter in the Public

Line.[3] I mean an oppinion that it is the duty of every Individual to Act his part in whatever Station his Country may Call him to, in times of difficulty, danger & distress. Whilst I think this a duty I must submit, altho the Councils of America have taken a different course from my Judgements & wishes. I think an individual that declines the Service of his Country because its Councils are not conformable to his Ideas, makes but a bad Subject; a good one will follow if he cannot lead.

Untill the good News from Carolina raised our Spirits, they were constantly depressed by every Account We received from the Northern Army. Such scenes of mismanagement, misconduct and Ill success as have been exhibited in that quarter ever since the loss of the Brave Montgomery have no paralel. There is a Committee of Congress appointed to inquire into the Causes of our Ill Success in Canada. Probably it may be no difficulty to ascertain the cause in a general point of light, but it may not be easy to saddle individuals with their just share of reproach for it seems to me that every officer & other person that has been connected with our operations in that Country have on their return given different & contradictory Accounts, some blaming one party, some another, but all Complaining of mismanagement in every department.

I don't know Genl. Schuyler personally but he holds an able pen and his clear intelligent manner of writing, with an apparent Anxiety expressed in all his letters for the good of the Service had gained my entire Confidence and I cannot help feeling a reluctance to receive unfavourable impressions, yet if that Man is sacrificing the interest of America to his ambition or avarice he must be a Wretch indeed. I hope this will not prove to be his Case, but at any rate as he is more of a Commissary & Quarter Master than a General, it may probably be best to shift his Station that Gates may be left at liberty to put our affairs at the Lakes in the best posture that can be.

I hope you are or will be properly Strengthened and Supported at New York. For my own part I dont like your situation there, but think you had better give up that City to the Enemy than let them get behind & pen you in there, as they were cooped in Boston last year. However, I dont pretend to any Judgement in this matter nor to have Considered the Subject. My Confidence in the abilities of Genl. Washington is entire. His Life is the most Valuable in America & whenever an engagement happens I sincerely hope he will think how much depends on it and guard it accordingly. The Public papers will Anounce to you the New appointments & Changes here, and as I have not much unemployed time I am always ready to spare the use of my pen. This being Sunday morning & in the Country I have spun out this letter to a length not common with me nowadays.

I beg my Compts to the Genl. I dined in Company with Mrs. Washington yesterday at Colo Harrisons & expect her here at dinner to day. Remember me to Genl. Mifflin, Col Shee & Moylan and believe me to be very Sincerely, sir, Your obedt hble servt.

Robt Morris

P.S. I will lay the London Letter before Congress tomorrow.

RC (NHi).
[1] Both Reed's letter to Morris of July 18 and the enclosure (a letter to Reed from his brother-in-law, Dennis DeBerdt, dated London, May 3, 1776) are in *Am. Archives,* 5th ser. 1:372–73, 415–16. DeBerdt's letter to James Kinsey apparently has not survived. For additional information on the issue raised by DeBerdt's letters, which pertained to the arrival in America of Lord Howe as peace commissioner with credentials authorizing him to open negotiations for seeking a reconciliation, see John Hancock's second letter to the New Jersey Convention, July 19; and Benjamin Franklin to Lord Howe, July 20, 1776.
[2] In response to the recommendations of a committee appointed to study Lord Howe's various letters and declarations announcing his arrival, Congress had resolved on July 19 to publish such documents in order to warn Americans against the efforts of "the insidious court of Britain . . . to amuse and disarm them." *JCC,* 5:592–93.
[3] Morris had just been reelected a delegate to Congress by the Pennsylvania Convention the previous day. *Am. Archives,* 5th ser. 2:6.

Josiah Bartlett to John Langdon

My Friend, Philadelphia July 22d 1776

By yours of the 6th inst I rec'd your genteel but just reprimand for not answering your letters and shall in future endeavor to give you the trouble of a line at least, every week without further excuse or ceremony.

By the enclosed paper you will see the account of General Clinton and Sir Peter Parker's defeat in South Carolina. The Virginians have likewise drove Lord Dunmore from Gwin's Island with loss. These are agreeable events after our repeated crosses in Canada. Some of our Southern brethren seem much elated with their success; by all accounts the troops there behaved with incomparable bravery. I am sorry I can't say the same of our troops in Canada. Some of the Southern gentlemen say America must be saved by the Southern not the Northern troops. However I hope it will yet appear that the New England Troops are not behind any of the Continent in point of bravery. The papers will inform you of the march of the militia of this State to New Jersey. Three regts are ordered from Virginia to the Jersies. I hope soon there will be an army there of 15 or 20000 men besides those at New York. We must at all events prevent their getting possession of New York and Hudson's River which I believe is their principal view and by that way open a communication with Canada.

Lord Howe's proclamation has now convinced every body that no offers are to be made us but absolute submission. I think it very happy for America that Britain has insisted on those terms for had she proposed a Treaty and offered some concessions there would have been danger of divisions or at least of our not acting with unanimity and spirit as I think will now be the case.

The convention here have taken on them the govt of this Colony and have appointed delegates for Congress, men who will forward and not hinder spirited measures. In short there is a far greater harmony in carrying on spirited measures in Congress than heretofore. The conventions of even Maryland and New York seem now to be in earnest.

The confederation is now before a Committee of the whole. By reason of so much other business it goes on but slow; when it is laid before our Legislature brother Whipple expects to be at home and can inform them of some things they may want to be informed of concerning it. Our Court I hear is to set again the first of September.

With sincerity I am your friend,   Josiah Bartlett

P.S. I have omitted enclosing this day's paper as brother Whipple has sent one to you in his letter.[1]

Tr (DLC).
[1] William Whipple to John Langdon, this date.

Benjamin Franklin to George Washington

Sir   Philada. July 22. 1776.

The Bearer, Mr. Joseph Belton, some time since petitioned the Congress for Encouragement to destroy the Enemy's ships of War by some Contrivances of his Invention.[1] They came to no Resolution on his Petition; and, as they appear to have no great Opinion of such Proposals, it is not easy, in the Multiplicity of Business before them, to get them to bestow any part of their Attention on his Request. He is now desirous of trying his Hand on the Ships that are gone up the North River; and, as he proposes to work intirely at his own Expence, and only desires your Countenance and Permission, I could not refuse his desire of a Line of Introduction to you, the Trouble of which I beg you to excuse. As he appears to be a very ingenious Man, I hope his Project may be attended with Success.

With the sincerest Esteem and Respect, I have the Honour to be, Your Excellency's most obedient and most humble Servant,

                                              B. Franklin.

RC (Kunstsammlungen der Veste Coburg, Coburg, Germany).
[1] Although little information survives pertaining to Belton's proposals for build-

ing an underwater "Machine" to attack British ships, see *Pa. Archives,* 1st ser. 4:650–52, 654, for proposals he had made to the Pennsylvania Committee of Safety in September 1775. The result of Belton's application to Washington is not known. It appears that the timing of the proposal was unfortunate for Belton because David Bushnell, with a submarine that had been tested, was already preparing such an attack. For an account of the unsuccessful attempt, on September 6, 1776, by Bushnell's submarine *Turtle* to afix a mine to the hull of Lord Howe's flagship *Eagle,* see Frederick Wagner, *Submarine Fighter of the American Revolution, the Story of David Bushnell* (New York: Dodd, Mead & Co., 1963), pp. 50–65. See also Clark, *Naval Documents,* 6:1499–1511.

John Hancock to Samuel Griffin

Sir,   Philadelphia July 22d. 1776.

The Congress, in Consideration of your Merit, and uniform Attachment to the Liberties of the American States, have been pleased to appoint you, Deputy Adjutant Genl. to the Flying-Camp, with the Rank of Colonel.[1]

I enclose your Commission with the greatest Pleasure; being fully persuaded, your Abilities, and Attention, will enable you to discharge the Duties of your Department with Reputation to yourself, & Advantage to your Country.

As it is necessary this important Department should be immediately filled, you will please to repair, for that Purpose, to the Flying Camp, as soon as possible, and put yourself under the Direction of the Commanding Officer in that Quarter.

I Am, Sr., your most Obedt. & very Hble Servt.

John Hancock Prest.

RC (InU). In a clerical hand and signed by Hancock. Addressed: "Colo. Griffen, Depy. Adjt. Genll. to the Flying Camp."
[1] See *JCC,* 5:592.

John Hancock to Charles Lee

Sir,   Philada. July 22d. 1776.

Your Favour of the 2d Inst. containing the very agreeable Intelligence of the Success of the American Army under your Command, I had the Honour of receiving, and immediately laid the same before Congress.[1]

It affords me the greatest Pleasure to convey to you, by their Order, the most valuable Tribute which a free People can ever bestow, or a generous Mind wish to receive, the just Tribute of Gratitude for rendering important Services to an oppressed Country.

The same enlarged Mind, and distinguished Ardor in the Cause of Freedom, that taught you to despise the Prejudices which have enslaved the Bulk of Mankind, when you nobly undertook the Defence of American Liberty, will entitle you to receive from Posterity the Fame due to such exalted & disinterested Conduct.

That a Handful of Men, without the Advantage of military Experience, animated only with the sacred Love of Liberty, should repulse a powerful Fleet & Army, are Circumstances that must excite Gratitude & Wonder in the Friends of America, & prove a Source of the most mortifying Disappointment to our Enemies.

Accept therefore, Sir, the Thanks of the independent States of America, unanimously declared by their Delegates to be due to you, and the brave Officers & Troops under your Command, who repulsed with so much Valour the Attack that was made on the State of South Carolina on the 28th of June by the Fleet, & Army of his Britannic Majesty; and be pleased to communicate to them this distinguished Mark of the Approbation of their Country.[2]

I have the Honour to be, with great Respect, Sir, your most obed. & very hble Servt.   J. H. Prest.

LB (DNA: PCC, item 12A).
[1] On July 19 Congress had received General Lee's July 2 letter to Hancock and enclosure describing the American victory over Commodore Peter Parker and Gen. Henry Clinton at Sullivan's Island on June 28. See *JCC*, 5:593–94; and *NYHS Collections* 5 (1872): 107–13.
[2] This day Hancock also sent letters of thanks and congratulations to South Carolina Cols. William Moultrie and William Thompson for the distinguished roles they had played in repelling the British attack on Sullivan's Island. See PCC, item 12A; and *Am. Archives*, 5th ser. 1:494.

John Hancock to Andrew Lewis

Sir,   Philada. July 22d. 1776.
As it is impossible to ascertain the Strength of our Enemies, or the Force destined for the Attack of New York, it is incumbent on Us to be prepared to defend ourselves agt. any Number of Troops, that may be ordered agt. that Place. For this Purpose the Congress have judged it necessary to augment the Flying Camp. I have it therefore in Command to direct, that, immediately on the Receipt of this, you order two Battalions of the Continental Troops in the State of Virginia to march with all possible Dispatch to the Flying Camp in New Jersey under the Command of Genl. Mercer.[1]

The State of Our Affairs, & the hourly Expectation of the Arrival of the Foreign Troops, render it absolutely necessary, that the Troops should be sent forward with the greatest Expedition.

I am further to direct, that you forward to South Carolina the whole five Tons of Powder which were sent to you for the Use of Virginia, & South Carolina.[2]

Should the Governor & Council of Virginia have Reason to apprehend an Invasion of that State, and in Consequence thereof, call forth two Battalions of Minute Men or Militia, the Congress have agreed, that they shall, while in Service, be in Continental Pay. I shall write by the present Conveyance to the Govr. and Council to inform them of this Resolution.[3]

I have the Honour to be, Sir, your most obed. & very hble Ser.

J. H. Prest.

LB (DNA: PCC, item 12A).

[1] See *JCC*, 5:597–98. Andrew Lewis (1720–81), member of the Virginia House of Burgesses and the Virginia Convention and an officer in the French and Indian and Lord Dunmore's Wars, had been appointed a brigadier general in the Continental Army on May 1, 1776. Lewis resigned his Continental commission in April 1777 but continued to serve until his death as a Virginia militia officer and a member of the Virginia Executive Council. *DAB*; and *JCC*, 4:181. See also Lewis to Hancock, August 3, 1776, in *Am. Archives*, 5th ser. 1:736.

[2] See *JCC*, 5:595.

[3] Hancock's letter of this date to Virginia Governor Patrick Henry, informing him that two battalions of Virginia Continental troops had been ordered to New Jersey, is in PCC, item 12A, and *Am. Archives*, 5th ser. 1:494. "Should you have Reason to apprehend an Invasion," Hancock informed Henry, "and in Consequence thereof, call forth an equal Number of Minute Men, or Militia, the Congress have resolved, that while in Service, they shall be in Continental Pay." For Virginia's reaction to this arrangement, see John Page to Hancock, August 3, 1776, in *Am. Archives*, 5th ser. 1:736.

John Hancock to the New Jersey Convention

Gentlemen,   Philada. July 22d. 1776.

The Congress, taking into Consideration the Strength of our Enemies, and the Force destined for the Attack of New York, have come to a Resolution to increase the Flying Camp. For this Purpose, I have it in Charge to request, you will immediately augment your Quota for the Flying Camp, with three Battalions of Militia, in Addition to those formerly desired by Congress, and send them with all possible Dispatch to join the Flying Camp.[1]

The Battalions are to be officered, payed, and provided, agreeable to former Resolutions of Congress for establishing said Camp.

I have the Honour to be, Gentlemen, your most obed. & very hble Ser.

J. H. Prest.

LB (DNA: PCC, item 12A).

[1] See *JCC*, 5:598. Hancock sent a similar letter this day to the Pennsylvania Convention, calling upon Pennsylvania to raise four battalions for the flying camp. PCC, item 12A; and *Am. Archives*, 5th ser. 1:495. For the response of both conventions to these resolutions, see *Am. Archives*, 4th ser. 6:1653, 5th ser. 2:7–8.

Samuel Huntington to Joseph Trumbull

Dear Sir   Philadelphia 22d July 1776
   This will be handed you by Mr Thomas Bedwell the person who
has Contracted to manufacture Sulphur at Middletown. He is now
on his way for that place, & expects a small box or two containing
necessary articles for carrying on his business will soon be Sent forward by Land from hence to New York. I am to desire you in his
behalf to point him to Some Suitable person who will receive those
boxes at N York & Immediately forward them to New Haven, or
Middletown by water if it may be done with safety; it being of
Importance to the public they should be forwarded as soon as
possible. Mr Bedwell being a perfect Stranger at York & the peculiar
Situation of that place at present is my only excuse for giving you
this trouble in the multiplicity of your business.
   Give me leave to Congratulate you on the Success of American
arms at S. Carolina & be so kind as to advise me of any material
Occurrences as often as is convenient. Be assured I am with Esteem
& Consideration, your Humble Servant,   Saml Huntington

   RC (CtHi).

Maryland Delegates to the Maryland Council

Gentlemen,   Philad. 22 July 1776
   The five thousand Dollars granted by Congress for raising the four
German Companies in our Province have been paid into our Hands
and retained by us for the Purpose of exchanging it for our Maryland
Convention Money and by this means to give our Currency Credit &
Circulation here.[1] Had we not taken this Measure our Emissions
would have been useless here & the Commercial Connection between
this & our Province would have been greatly if not totally obstructed.
[We] had exchanged the whole Sum with the merchants & Shop-
keepers and we have advanced as per Account enclosed. Mr. Hughes
having obtd. a large Sum of Continental Money he exchanged
with us as far as we had our Convention Currency in our Hands.[2]
This gives us a fresh fund to keep up the Credit of our Money here.
Youll be pleased to advise us whether this Measure of ours meets
with your approbation. If not we will remit the whole immediately
to you.
   Capt. Stricker being appointed Lt. Col. of the German Battalion
and being desirous to proceed immediately to Frederick County to
forward with all Expedition the raising of the Companies, we
thought proper to advance him 1520 Dollars of the Sum appropriated for that Purpose; and we also have taken the Liberty of ad-

vancing Col. Ware £15.0.0 and Major Gist £67.10, which Sums they request you will charge to their account.

We are Gentlemen, yr. Obedt. hble Servts.

T. Stone

Wm. Paca

[*P.S.*] The 2500 Dollars mentioned by T.S. in his letter to D. of J. was a mistake.[3]   T.S.

RC (MdAA). Written and signed by Paca, with postscript and signature by Stone.

[1] See *JCC,* 5:487–88.

[2] For the activities of Samuel Hughes, who was in Philadelphia to obtain a contract for casting cannon, see *Md. Archives,* 12:29, 40; and *JCC,* 5:593, 599. See also Joseph Hewes to Samuel Purviance, July 23, 1776, note 1.

[3] No letter from Thomas Stone to Daniel of St. Thomas Jenifer mentioning $2,500 has been found.

William Whipple to John Langdon

Dear Sir,   Philadelphia 22d July 1776

I have your favor of the 6th inst. In answer to the part of it respecting the Commissions I can only say, I am perpetually dunning the President to send them.[1] If any alteration in the wages of the Commission officers they will be higher, so there can be no difficulty with them. If any are lower'd it will be the Mates, Midshipmen, Coopers, Sailmakers and some other of the petty Officers & Perhaps Boatswain, Carpenter & Gunner. If the three last are alter'd it will [*be*] but a trifle say one doller. The number of men I sent you some time ago, 80 seamen, 80 Landmen & 80 or 90 Marines, but its my Opinion if a greater proportion of Seamen are enter'd & less landmen there can be no harm done. If the officers have boys no doubt they must be on the Roll. It cannot be a question whether the men are to have Hammocks, to be sure they must, the men to be enter'd for a Year & as much longer as you can get them. If you can get Arms the sooner the better. The Agent will have a Commission for the Business he does, therefore I suppose will employ what Clerks he thinks necessary.

I always thought you had ample Powers to fit the Ship for sea, & I believe its so understood by the Committee. Its impossible to get the exact dimentions of the Guns as there are but few made here & its altogeather uncertain whether these can be sent to you. The furnices here have met with many accidents, & I am of opinion your guns must come from Providence or some other furnice Eastward.

I shall not have the Pleasure of seeing you so soon as I hoped as some very important matters are now on the Tapis which I want to hear debated. Besides I wod fain have the Marine matters settled before I leave this. I therefore think it will be the latter end of August before I shall be able to injoy that Satisfaction, which have flatter'd myself wod be much earlier.

How goes on the Cor——p? [2] Have you well consider'd the matter? I wod just beg leave to remind you of an observation of one of the first Philosophers of age, that a man who thinks of Marying a woman twenty years younger then himself, ought to consider who is to be her Husband twenty years hence. I hope you won't think by this hint that I have any objection to the connection, so far from it that you may be assur'd my Dear Sir that whatever contributes to your Happiness will be an addition to mine.

I am in pain for the frontier settlements in our Colony, not that I think there is any real immediate danger but I know the People must be alarm'd. I think there shod be scouting parties immediately placed on the frontiers. I wish may have directions to make application to Congress for that purpose. Our late Successes at the Southward is almost a Ballance for our misfortunes in Canada consider'd Continentaly. Must refer you to the [3] papers for News. I hope the bravery of the Carolinians will inspire the Yankees with new courage and not let it be said that they have transferred the whole of that virtue to their Southern brethren.

This Colony and New Jersey are all alive. The associates are all gone from this City. Men of fortune don't think themselves too good to march in the character of private soldiers and I hope wont be ashamed to face the enemy. Col. Dickinson and all the other Colonels have marched with their battalions. In short the declaration of Independence has done wonders.

I have Mr Hancock's promise that the Commission and blank warrants shall go off in a day or two by express. The Gentlemen are appointed agreeable to your recommendations. There can be no difficulty in their acting, tho' they have not their commissions, as they will soon have them. [4]

I am much obliged to you for mustering the regiment. It would give me great pleasure to see them in as good order as the battalions of this City but that is next to impossible owing to their being so much scattered and the want of uniforms. However we must do the best we can with them.

I am with great respect yours,   Wm Whipple

[P.S.] The order the officers stand appointed.

Peter Shores 1st Lt.	George Jerry Osborne Capt Marines
John Wheelwright 2nd Lt.	Stephen Meads 1st Lt.
Josiah Shackford 3rd Lt.	Nath Thwing 2d

Warrants will be filled up with the names you sent.

RC (Capt. J. G. M. Stone, Annapolis, Md., 1973); Tr (DLC).

[1] Langdon's July 6 letter to Whipple is in Clark, *Naval Documents*, 5:943–45.

[2] That is, Langdon's courtship with Elizabeth Sherburne, whom he married in February 1777. Lawrence S. Mayo, *John Langdon of New Hampshire* (Concord, N.H.: Rumford Press, 1937), pp. 140–41.

[3] Remainder of letter taken from Tr.

[4] The officers for the frigate *Raleigh* were appointed on July 22, 1776. *JCC*, 5:601.

John Adams to Abigail Adams

July 23, 1776

This Mornings Post brought me yours of July 13 and 14 and has relieved me from an huge Load of Anxiety. Am happy to hear that you are so comfortably situated, have so much agreable Company, and such fine Accommodations. I would very joyfully agree to have the small Pox, over again, for the Sake of the Company.

Since the Letters of July 3d and 4th which you say you have received, I have written to you of the following dates. Two Letters July 7. July 10. 11. 15. 16. Two Letters of July 20th. This Morning I inclosed a Letter from Dr. Rush to me, containing Directions for managing Patients under Inocculation for the small Pox.[1] Rush has as much success as any without Exception.

You will find several dull Hours, and the Children will fatigue you. But if you had sent me a Present [2] of an hundred Guineas, it would not have pleased me so much as to hear that Nurse is there. You cant be low spirited, while she is there, and you cant possibly suffer for Want of Care. But I am somewhat afraid you have not Nurses and Servants enough in the House for so large an Hospital.

I dont know how I can better entertain you, than by giving you some Idea of the Character of this Dr. Rush. He is a Native of this Place, a Gentleman of an ingenious Turn of Mind, and of elegant Accomplishments. He has travelled in England, where he was acquainted with Mrs. Maccaulay, with whom he corresponded while there, and since his Return. He wrote an elegant, flowing Letter to her, while he was in England, concerning a Plan of a Republic which she wrote and addressed to Pascal Paoli. He afterwards travelled in France, and contracted a Friendship there with M. Dubourg, with whom he has corresponded ever since. He has published several Things upon Philosophy, Medicine, and Politicks, in this City. He is a Lecturer in the Colledge here, in some Branch of Physick or surgery, and is a Member of the American Philosophical Society. He has been sometime a Member of the City Committee and was last Week appointed a Delegate in Congress for this Place, in the Room of one, who was left out. He married last Winter, a young Lady, daughter of Mr. Stockton of New Jersey, one of the Judges of the Supream Court of that Government, and lately appointed a delegate in this Congress. This Gentleman is said to be a staunch American, I suppose, truly.

Dr. Cooper has promised me, to visit you, and contribute all in his Power to amuse you and make your Stay agreable. I love him the more for this Kindness. I loved him much before.

Dont give yourself the least Pain about an incurable Lameness. Sell or give away the Creature, to a good Master; or keep her for the good she has done, and let her enjoy Life, in Ease for the future. How shall I get home? I feel every generous Passion and every kind sentiment, rushing for Utterance, while I subscribe myself yours.

RC (MHi). Adams, *Family Correspondence* (Butterfield), 2:59–60.

[1] Abigail apparently gave Benjamin Rush's letter to Cotton Tufts, but it is not now extant. See Tufts to Adams, August 6, 1776, in Adams, *Family Correspondence* (Butterfield), 2:81.

[2] The following four words, omitted in the RC, were taken from the letterbook copy in the Adams Papers, MHi.

Samuel Adams to Samuel P. Savage

My dear Friend   Philad July 23 1776

I must plead the Want of Leisure as an Apology for not acknowledging your very obliging Letter which came to my hand several Months ago. I assure you there is no one with whom I would chuse to keep up an epistolary Correspondence, rather than with you.[1] The long Acquaintance I have had with you, and the unsuspected Sincerity of your Friendship, are strong Inducements to me to write to you very frequently—but I cannot give you any Reason to expect it. I would therefore beg you to favor me with your Letters as often as your Leisure will allow. I shall receive them gratefully. You have before this time heard of the Success of the Continental Arms in South Carolina. This happy Event has, I hope, given such a Check to the Power of the Enemy as to prevent their doing us any material Injury in that part of America. I do not say any thing of our Affairs in Canada—the Subject is too mortifying. We must at all times submit to the Determinations of Providence "whose ways are ever gracious, ever just." We now look towards N York. May Heaven prosper our Arms there! The Express which brought the Carolina News, will return in a few days. I shall take that oppy to forward your Letter to your Son. He was in health last Spring as one of the gentlemen of that Colony informs me. The Post is this Moment going. Present my friendly regards to Mrs Savage &c & be assured that I am affectionately your Friend

RC (MHi). In Adams' hand, though not signed.

[1] Samuel P. Savage (1718–97), resident of Weston, Mass., and a merchant in Boston, was appointed to the Massachusetts Board of War in 1776. *Columbian Centinel* (Boston), December 13, 1797.

Charles Carroll of Carrollton to Charles Carroll, Sr.

Dr Papa,   23d July 1776

I have just wrote a letter to Deards containing all the news now stirring. I have desired him to communicate that letter to you.[1] I have sold yr. bill of Ex[chang]e at 90 per Cent. Mr. Morris is to receive the cash for me. We are busily engaged and in very interesting matters which I am not at liberty to mention. I have not seen Mrs. Maxfield since my last letter & therefore know not whether she has executed Molly's commissions. Some of them I believe she will not have it in her power to execute.

I hold my resolution of being at our Convention provided I am chosen of it. If I should be left out, I shall remain here till I am superseded, or a new deputation made out.

All intelligence or communication with Europe is become extreamly difficult. I flatter myself the enemy's reinforcements will not be here before the last of this month, perhaps not till the middle of August. By that time we shall have a fine army to oppose to them, provided the small pox can be kept out of our camps.

In Congress 11. O'clock

Post just arrived from N. Y. Nothing new except that Col. Paterson Adj. Gen. of Gen. Howe's army has had an interview with Gen. Washington proposing a conference. It terminated in nothing. Paterson said G. Howe & Ld. Howe had great powers. Washington replied these powers were only to pardon—that in defending our just rights we conceived we had not offended. The interview was conducted with great civility & Paterson returned.

A desperate Design of the Tories at Albany has been discovered. 3 persons, one a ringleader, are confined. The particulars of this conspiracy are not yet known. Gen. Washington writes that 10 vessels are off the Hook supposed to be part of Ld. Howe's first division.

Wishing you a long enjoy[men]t of health I remain, Yr. Affectionate Son,   C. C. of Carrollton

RC (MdHi).
[1] Not found.

Joseph Hewes to Samuel Purviance, Jr.

Dear Sir   Philadelphia 23d July 1776

I received your favour per Mr. Hughes and immediately went with him to a member of Committee for the Cannon Contracts, they have agreed with him for a large quantity of Cannon.[1] My ill state of health has prevented me from attending much to business lately and has obliged me for some time past to make an excursion or two into the Country. I propose to return to North Carolina shortly where I mean to retire from public business for a month or two. I have laid your accounts before the marine Committee and shall see that they are properly setled. I have not seen the person in whose favour you drew, and your Brother is not in Town. To whom must the money be paid? I do not hear of any person that has been recommended as Lieutenant for the Ship you are building, nor have I as yet received your recommendations. Please to send me the Names of Three Gentlemen in the order that you & Capt. Nicholson would wish them to stand. I have mentioned Doctor Budd to the Committee. He is not yet appointed. I have no doubt but he will be, at the same time the Lieutenants are appointed.[2] I am with much respect, Dr Sir, your mo. Obed hum Sert,   Joseph Hewes

RC (MdHi).

[1] On the previous day Samuel Hughes had written to Purviance: "I have contracted with Congress for 1000 tons of Cannon at £36.10.0 to be delivered again the 1st January 1778." Clark, *Naval Documents,* 5:1182.

[2] On this point, see also the extract from Purviance's July 27 letter to Hewes, ibid., pp. 1246–47.

Francis Hopkinson to Samuel Tucker?

Sir,[1]   Philada. 23d July 1776

I beg leave to submit to the Consideration of your House the Propriety of passing an Ordinance for the Regulation of *Elections* in our Province. What I have principally in View is the collecting of Votes by *Ballot* only, and providing effectual Means for the Prevention of Fraud in Elections. This is undoubtedly the most equitable way of ascertaining the Choice of the People, and I am confident would be very acceptable to our Constituents. Elections are now of greater Importance, if possible, than heretofore; because by your late excellent Constitution the Source of all Government originates with the People at large. I thought it my Duty to suggest this Hint & hope it will be deemed worthy the attention of the House.

I have further to request that the House would be so good as to furnish their Delegates with printed Copies of your new Constitution, & with such other Ordinances & Regulations as you may pass from Time to Time. We should likewise be glad of a Copy of that part of your Minutes which ascertains what Number of Delegates shall represent the Province in Congress. I am told you have made one Delegate sufficient for this Purpose; but as I have no good Authority for this opinion & was the other Day the only member from Jersey attending in Congress, I was in great Doubt as to the Propriety of giving my vote.[2]

With great Respect to the Honble Convention, I am sir, Your very humble servant,   Fras. Hopkinson

RC (MeHi).

[1] The contents of this letter demonstrate conclusively that Hopkinson wrote it to a member of the New Jersey Provincial Congress; and Samuel Tucker, as president of this body, would appear to have been the most likely intended recipient.

[2] On June 22, 1776, the New Jersey Provincial Congress had declared that any one of New Jersey's five delegates in Congress "shall have power to vote." *Am. Archives,* 4th ser. 6:1628.

Thomas Jefferson to Francis Eppes

Dear Sir   Philadelphia, July 23, 1776.

We have nothing new here now but from the southward. The successes there I hope will prove valuable here, by giving new spirit to our people. The ill successes in Canada had depressed the minds of many; when we shall hear the last of them I know not; everybody had supposed Crown Point would be a certain stand for them, but they have retreated from that to Ticonderoga, against everything which in my eye wears the shape of reason. When I wrote you last, we were deceived in General Washington's numbers. By a return which came to hand a day or two after, he then had but 15,000 effective men. His reinforcements have come in pretty well since. The flying camp in the Jerseys under General Mercer begins to form, but not as fast as exigencies require. The Congress have, therefore, been obliged to send for two of our battalions from Virginia.[1] I hope that country is perfectly safe now; and if it is, it seemed hardly right that she should not contribute a man to an army of 40,000, and an army too on which was to depend the decision of all our rights. Lord Howe's fleet has not yet arrived. The first division sailed five days before he did, but report says it was scattered by a storm. This seems probable, as Lord Howe had a long passage. The two other divisions were not sailed when he came away. I do not expect his army will be here and fit for action till the middle or last of August; in the meantime, if Mercer's camp could be formed with the expedition it merits, it might be possible to attack the present force from the Jersey side of Staten Island, and get rid of that beforehand; the militia go in freely, considering they leave their harvest to rot in the field.

I have received no letter this week, which lays me under great anxiety. I shall leave this place about the 11th of next month. Give my love to Mrs. Eppes, and tell her that when both you and Patty fail to write to me, I think I shall not be unreasonable in insisting she shall. I am, dear sir, Yours affectionately,

Th. Jefferson

MS not found; reprinted from Jefferson, *Papers* (Boyd), 1:472–73.
[1] See John Hancock to Andrew Lewis, July 22, 1776.

Francis Lewis to Jonathan Trumbull, Jr.

Dear Sir, Phila 23d July 1776

By Order of Congress I am directed to transmit you the inclosed four drafts upon Persons in Albany for Nineteen Hundred & One pounds twelve Shillings & 3d New York Currancy. When honoured please to furnish me with a Certificate of your receiveing the amount that I may be enabled to receive the money here, and you'l please to Account with Congress for the same. I am respectfully, Sir Your very Humble Servt. Frans Lewis

[*P.S.*] Inclosed you have Letters of advice.

RC (CtHi).

Maryland Delegates to
the Maryland Council of Safety

Gentlemen Philadelphia July 23rd 1776

Yesterdays Post brought Us your Letter of the 19th Inst.[1] The Copies of the Letters from Colonels Barnes and Jordan You omitted to enclose.[2] We hope the Necessity of recalling the Captains Thomas and Hindman will soon be removed, and that they will be permitted to march to the flying Camp as soon as possible. It is of the last Consequence to collect a sufficient force to oppose the British Army which may be hourly expected at Staten Island. General Washington has not above 15,000 Troops. Two Battalions of the Virginia Regulars are ordered to N York. Four Battalions in this province and two more in New Jersey are ordered to reinforce the flying Camp.

We agree with You that it will be useless to send Men without arms. We have had no opportunity to consult Congress relative to the Subsistance of the Men during the Time they are collecting. We doubt not the Expence will be continental. If they should be employed on your Works it would contribute to their Health, & defray the Expence of provisions.

A Man who professes to be an Adept in the Refining Sulphur has applied to Us & enclosed are his Terms. We are ignorant whether any Quantity of Sulphur has been discovered in our Colony, & do not know whether You want such a Man.

We have no Intelligence from N. York since the 19th. Lord Howes fleet not then arrived.

We shall be obliged by the Communication of any Intelligence worthy of Notice, and at all Times ready to obey your Commands.[3]

We are, Gentlemen, with Respect, Your Most obedt. Servants,

Saml. Chase

T. Stone

RC (MdAA). Written by Chase and signed by Chase and Stone.

[1] See *Md. Archives,* 12:80–81.

[2] The council remedied this oversight when it enclosed the letters from Richard Barnes and Jeremiah Jordan in its next letter to the Maryland delegates on July 26. Ibid., p. 119.

[3] The following day Stone sent a letter to the council explaining the details of a shipment of powder and arms for Maryland which he had just arranged. Ibid., p. 110.

Benjamin Rush to Charles Lee

Dear General,   Phila July 23d 1776.

It would take a Volume to tell you how many clever things were said of you, and the brave Troops under your command after hearing of your late victory.[1] It has given a wonderful turn to our affairs—The loss of Canada had sunk the spirits of many people who now begin to think our cause is not desperate, & that we shall yet triumph over our enemies.

The declaration of independence has produced a new æra in this part of America. The Militia of Pennsylvania seem to be actuated with a spirit more than Roman. Near 2000 citizens of Philada have lately marched towards New-York in order to prevent an incursion being made by our enemies upon the state of New-Jersey—The cry of them all is for BATTLE. I think Mr Howe will not be able to get a footing in New-York, and that he will end the present or begin the next compaign in Canada, or in some one of the Southern Colonies —the only places in which America is vulnerable. We depend upon Gates in the North, & *you* oblige us to hope for great things from the South.

The tories are quiet—but very surly. Lord Howes proclamation leaves them not a single filament of their cobweb doctrine of reconciliation.[2] The spirit of liberty reigns triumphant in Pennsylvania. The Proprietary gentry have retired to their Country Seats, and honest men have taken the Seats they abused so much in the government of our State.

The papers will inform you that I have been thrust into Congress.[3] I find there is a great deal of difference between sporting a sentiment in a Letter or over a glass of wine upon politicks, & discharging properly the duty of a Senator. I feel myself unequal to every part of my new Situation except where plain integrity is required.

My former letters to you may pass hereafter for a leaf of the Sybills. They are full of predictions, and what is still more uncommon—some of them have proved true. I shall go on—and add that I think the Declaration of independence will produce union and new exertions in England in the same ratio that they have done in this country. The present Campaign I believe is only designed to train us for the Duties of next Summer. What do you think of the States of America being divided between two or three foreign States & of seeing the Armies of two or three of the most powerful Nations in Europe upon our Coasts?

Adieu, Yours Sincerely,   B. Rush.

P.S. I sent a copy of that part of your letter in which you commend Mr Morris so highly to his father.[4] My Complts to the gallant youth.

MS not found; reprinted from *NYHS Collections* 5 (1872): 161–63. Addressed: "Major General Lee, Charlestown, So. Carolina."

[1] Lee's letter to Rush of June 29 reporting the repulse of the British attack on the fort on Sullivan's Island guarding Charleston is in *NYHS Collections* 5 (1872): 94–96.

[2] For Lord Howe's proclamation, see *Am. Archives,* 5th ser. 1:1466–67.

[3] Rush had been elected to Congress by the Pennsylvania Convention on July 20. See *JCC,* 5:596.

[4] On July 22 Rush wrote the following brief letter to Lewis Morris. The complimentary passage pertaining to Morris' son—Lewis, Jr. (*ca.* 1750–1824), General Lee's aide-de-camp—was taken from Lee's letter to Rush of June 29. The confused reference to "your son Jacob" is an unaccountable error on the part of Rush. "I have just received a Letter from Gen Lee in which after giving a particular acct. of the late gallant behaviour of our troops at South Carolina, he begs me to inform you that your son Jacob shared largely in the honor of that important victory. His words are 'Congratulate Lewis Morris in my name for having such a son. Amongst other becoming qualities, he is a full inch taller in the midst of a hot cannonade than at other times. Upon my soul he is a fine boy, as is my other aid de camp Byrd [Francis Otway Byrd]. I believe they will go down to Tartarus for the three headed dog of darkness, if I order them.'" Frederick R. Kirkland, ed., *Letters on the American Revolution in the Library at "Karolfred,"* 2 vols. (Philadelphia: Privately printed, 1941–52), 2:23.

Benjamin Rush to Julia Rush

My dearest Jewel,   Tuesday night [July 23, 1776] [1]

I am happy in finding that my appointment in Congress gives you so much pleasure. I believe it has operated in the manner You expected upon some of my *Old* friends. I spoke for the first time this day,[2] About ten minutes upon a question that proved successful. I felt that I was not thundering like Cato in the Uttica of our committee of inspection. The Audience is truly respectable. Dr. Franklin alone is eno to confound with his presence a thousand such men as myself. I hope however in a little time to experience the same freedom & confidence in speaking that I Observe in other members. I find even our illustrious body is marked with features of human nature. We can talk nonsense now & then as well as our neighbours. This reconciles me to myself.

I wish you would return with your Papa the latter end of this, or the beginning of next week. I cannot support the burden of public & private business which now lays upon my Shoulders without you. You Shall go to Morven Again with your Papa when he goes to take charge of the governmt. of New Jersey an event which all parties say is inevitable. Think my love how long our house must be left without a head in my necessary attendance upon Congress. Wm fell asleep as usual this evening—Betsey walked out—& I was Obliged to wait near an hour before I could go out to visit a patient—and at last got one of the neighbours to watch the door. My business suffers from the want of you. My prentices are young & Betsey too much out of the way to give answers. Do come home as soon as possible, or I tremble at the consequences. I languish for want of company. All our neighbours & friends you know are in the country or the camp. I shall execute all your commissions. God bless you! How I long to tell you how much I love you.

I shall have a regiment of prentices, having had an application this day from a lad in the Jerseys—but the Jews house in the alley will make an excellent barrack for them. I am pleased with taking Johney Pintard into the house. I suppose you told him the fee was 100 guineas. This Sum with what we have by us, & what I expect soon to receive will enable us to realize our money in a house or a plantation. It is impossible now to put money out to interest. Heaven requires only the heart. I was *willing* to be poor, that my country might be free. The latter I hope will be granted, and contrary even to my wishes I find I am growing rich. My Attendance in Congress does not hurt my business having as much to do as ever. My wages in Congress are 20/ per day. Good night my charming Girl. I shall close my letter in the morning.

Wednesday morning. Have just read in the paper a list of the committee of Safety. A majority of them are *good* men. Cannon & Matlack are among them!!!

Much love to every body. Mama must part with you. The condition of this Obligation remember is that you are to pay another visit for a week, or two next month. Yours my dearest,

B Rush

P.S. No letter from James since he went away.

RC (CtY). Addressed: "Mrs. Rush, at Morven, Princetown." Mrs. Rush was at this time at the home of her father, New Jersey delegate Richard Stockton.

[1] The date of this letter has been established from Rush's comment in his "Wednesday morning" postscript that he had "just read in the paper a list of the committee of Safety." The newly elected members of the Pennsylvania Council of Safety were listed in the *Pennsylvania Journal; and the Weekly Advertiser* on July 24. See also Benjamin Rush, *Letters of Benjamin Rush,* ed. Lyman H. Butterfield, 2 vols. (Princeton: Published for the American Philosophical Society by Princeton University Press, 1951), 1:105–8.

[2] The previous day Rush had also written a letter to his wife. The following extract from that letter, which was described as a three-page autograph letter signed, dated Philadelphia, July 22, 1776, was printed when the letter was offered for sale in 1946. "I took my Seat this day in Congress—But I believe with very different emotions from what are generally experienced upon such occasions. The difficulties & precarious tenure of my trust—my want of knowledge in many subjects upon which I must speak, or vote, & lastly the envy & slander to which my new situation now exposes me all crowded upon my imagination, and sunk my Spirits so much that I found but upon the threshold of my entering upon public life that the road to happiness is not thro' ambition or popular favor." *The Collector* 59 (July–August, 1946), item J1546. Rush also dated his signature on the secrecy resolution "22 July 1776." See facsimile opposite p. 1916, *Am. Archives,* 4th ser. vol. 3.

Secret Committee to Nathaniel Shaw, Jr.

Sir   Philadelphia 23rd July 1776

Some time ago we agreed with Mr Christopher Champlain of Rhode Island to Charter a Ship of his called the Peggy now lying at Norwich in your Province, provided a Suitable Cargo could be procured for her There.[1]

As we wish you to act as our Agent in this business, we request you will inform us of the different articles of your Produce together with the Prices, and what you would recommend to load said Vessell with at this time or in one or two Months hence for the European Market. As soon as we receive your Answer we shall direct you how to proceed in the Purchase, and will send you the terms on which we agreed to Charter the Vessell.[2]

We are sir, Your hble servts.

By order, Robt Morris, Chair Man of the Secret Comme.

RC (CtNlHi). In a clerical hand and signed by Robert Morris.

[1] Christopher Champlin's June 28 petition to Congress, outlining the misfortunes of the *Peggy* since July 1775 and requesting relief, is in Clark, *Naval Documents,* 5:790–92.

[2] This day Robert Morris also wrote a brief note on behalf of the Secret Committee to Paymaster General William Palfrey acknowledging receipt "per the hands of Mr. Griffin a bag of Gold contg one hundred and seventy four pounds lawfull Money forwarded to him [*Palfrey*] by Messrs. Clarke & Nightingale of Rhode Island for Accot. of the Secret Committee." William Palfrey Papers, MH.

William Whipple to Joshua Brackett

My Dear Sir,   Philadelphia 23d July 1776

I receiv'd your favor of the 9th instant & shall forward the papers you desire so soon as I can obtain them. A Resolution for confiscating West India Property, has been some time prepar'd, but Congress has been so extreamly engag'd they have not yet pass'd it.[1]

What is Mr. Kings reason for not accepting his appointment? Is it that he is doubtful? If that is the case I think it a pity he shod ever be noticed hereafter. Its high time that every one declar'd on one side or the other. He that is unwilling to take an active part with us ought to be look'd upon as an Enemy & treated accordingly.[2]

I congratulate you on the Success of our Arms at Carolina & Verginia; for the particulars of which must refer you to the news papers which I enclose to Mr Langdon. Lord Dunmore has now no place to lay his head, but is continualy ferreted about Chesapeak Bay. Its probable Lord Howe has sent some assistance to the pirates at South Carolina, but they will be too late to do us any mischief in that quarter.

Our army on the Lakes are still in a very unhappy scituation. I think there shod be some Scouting parties on our frontiers. I very much wonder that was not ordered, before the Court adjourn'd; tho I dont think that there is so much danger as to oblige the people to quit their farms: yet there ought to be a guard. The army at New-York are I believe well prepared for the Enemy. Lord Howe will meet a very warm reception if he thinks proper to make an attack. He has sent two flaggs ashore at York, with Letters directed to Geo. Washington Esqr; but the Genl. refus'd to receive them, they not being properly address'd: which conduct is highly approv'd by Congress.[3] However, his Lordship sent a number of Letters ashore at New Jersey. The Circular letters to the Govrs. you'll see a specimen of in the paper above refer'd to. He also wrote a friendly letter to Dr. Franklin, to which the Good old Docr. has made a very suitable reply. Matters go on much better since we have got rid of that fantom reconciliation; but we have still much to do. I hope due circumspection will be observ'd in each of the United States and that every one who has a hand in this *Glorious* Revolution, will consider that the Happiness of future Generations, as well as the present, depend on their doings. It is our own fault if future Generations do not Call us Blessed.

I intended to have wrote My Bror. by this post but shall not have time, must therefore defer it till the next, as also an answer to Mrs. B. very highly Esteem'd favor. I may possibly get home in August but can't possitively say what time in that month but am inclin'd to think it will be the later end. Adieu. Yours affectely,

                                                    Wm. Whipple

RC (MHi).
    [1] This resolution was passed the next day. *JCC,* 5:606.
    [2] George King, Portsmouth, N.H., merchant, had refused to accept an appoint-
ment as justice of the Inferiour Court of Common Pleas for Rockingham County,
and he was replaced by Samuel Penhallow. *N.H. State Papers,* 8:110, 194–95, 500.
    [3] See *JCC,* 5:567; and John Hancock to George Washington, July 18, 1776, note 1.

John Adams to Nathaniel Barber, Jr.

Sir   Philadelphia July 24. 1776
    Your Letter of the 15th instant came duely to Hand by yesterdays
Post.[1] I shall be happy to render you any Service in my Power. But I
conceive the most regular Method will be for you to make application to General Ward, and request him to make a Representation of
your affair to Congress, either directly, or through General Washington. In this Mode, I conceive there will be no difficulty in
obtaining Captains Pay for yourself and fifteen dollars per Month
for the two Conductors under you.
    If I were to move in Congress, or in the Board of War, for these
Establishments, for Want of Sufficient Information of the Nature
and Duties of your office, I should not be so likely to succeed, as if
the Proposition comes from the Commander in Chief in your department.
    I am, your humble Servant

LB (MHi). Addressed: "To Nathaniel Barber Junr, Conductor of Military Stores,
Boston."
    [1] Nathaniel Barber, Jr. (1728–87), was commissary of military stores at Boston
until 1781 and later state naval officer. *Massachusetts Centinel* (Boston), October
20, 1787; and *JCC,* 19:232. His July 15 letter to Adams is in the Adams Papers,
MHi.

John Adams to James Warren

My dear Sir   Philadelphia July 24. 1776
    Yours of the 10th instant, came by Yesterdays Post.[1] This I
Suppose will find you, at Boston, growing well of the Small Pox.
This Distemper is the King of Terrors to America this Year. We shall
Suffer as much by it, as We did last Year by the Scarcity of Powder.
And therefore I could wish, that the whole People was innoculated.
It gives me great Pleasure to learn, that Such Numbers have removed
to Boston, for the Sake of going through it, and that Innoculation is
permitted in every Town. The plentifull Use of Mercury is a Dis-
couragement to many: But you will see by a Letter from Dr Rush
which I lately inclosed to my Partner, that Mercury is by him wholly

laid aside. He practices with as much success and Reputation as any Man.[2]

I am much grieved and a little vexed at your Refusal of a Seat on a certain Bench. Is another appointed? Who is it?

Before now you have the Result of our Proceedings the Beginning of this Month. A Confederation will follow very soon and other mighty Matters.

Our Force is not Sufficient at New York. Have Suffered much Pain, in looking over the Returns, to see no Massachusetts Militia at N. York. Send them along, for the Lands sake. Let Us drubb Howe, and then We shall do very well. Much depends upon that. I am not much concerned, about Burgoine. He will not get over the Lakes this year. If he does he will be worse off.

I rejoice at the Spread of the Small Pox, on another Account. Having had the Small Pox was the Merit which originally recommended me to this lofty Station. This Merit is now likely to be common enough, and I shall Stand a Chance to be relieved. Let some others come here, and see the Beauties and Sublimities of a Continental Congress. I will stay no longer. A Ride to Philadelphia, after the Small Pox, will contribute prodigiously to the Restoration of your Health.[3]

I am &c

RC (MHi). In Adams' hand, though not signed.
[1] Warren's July 10 letter to Adams is in the *Warren-Adams Letters*, 1:258–60.
[2] See Adams to Abigail Adams, July 23, 1776, note 1.
[3] This day Adams also wrote a brief letter to Thomas Cushing, Suffolk County probate judge, declining Cushing's request to serve as the executor of the will of Josiah Quincy, Jr. Both Cushing's July 15 letter to Adams and the letterbook copy of Adams' response are in the Adams Papers, MHi.

John Hancock to Philip Schuyler

Sir,   Philada. July 24th. 1776.

The enclosed Resolves, which I do myself the Honour of transmitting, are so explicit, that I need only refer your Attention to them.

The Congress are extremely concerned to find there should be a Necessity of recommending Harmony to the officers and Troops of different States under your Command. At a Time like this, when the greatest Confidence is so essentially required, Nothing can show greater Weakness or Wickedness than to throw provincial Reflections on one another, which must have a direct Tendency to impede the public Service, and to weaken the Union of the American States. I am therefore to request, you will discountinance and suppress, by every Means in your Power, such ungenerous & base Practices, and promote Discipline, Order, and Zeal in the Army as much as possible.[1]

The Commissioners appointed to audit the Accounts of the Army in the Northern Department, have been with me. They are preparing to set out immediately, and I expect, will be in New York in a few Days.[2]

The Congress having empowered the Commander in Chief in each Department to negotiate an Exchange of Prisoners, you will please to conduct the Business agreably to the enclosed System.[3]

In Consequence of a Flag from Lord Howe with a Letter directed to George Washington Esqr which he declined receiving as an improper Direction considering his Rank & Station, the Congress came to a Resolution, not only expressing their approbation of his Conduct, but ordering for the future, that no Commander in Chief, or other the Commanders of the American Army, should receive any Letters from the Enemy, but such as are directed to them in the Characters they sustain.[4]

You will please to enquire into the Complaints of the Soldiers as soon as possible; and give strict Orders, that the Goods furnished them, shall not be charged at a higher Price, than the first Cost of them, and an Allowance of 5 per Cent for Charges.

I have the Honour to be, with every Sentiment of Esteem & Respect, Sir, your most obed. & very hble Sert.   J. H. Prest.

LB (DNA: PCC, item 12A). Addressed: "Genl. Schuyler, Albany—or elsewhere."

[1] Congress passed this resolve "recommending Harmony" on July 19 after learning of the opposition among many of General Schuyler's officers—especially those from New England—to the July 7 decision of a council of war of the northern army to abandon Crown Point and pull back to Ticonderoga, but this was only the latest in a long series of disputes between officers and soldiers from different states under Schuyler's command. See JCC, 5:575, 591; Am. Archives, 5th ser. 1:232–35, 650–51; and Washington, Writings (Fitzpatrick), 5:289–97, 302–7. See also Jonathan G. Rossie, The Politics of Command in the American Revolution (Syracuse: Syracuse University Press, 1975), chaps. 4 and 7. For an account of Schuyler's deficiencies from the perspective of a Massachusetts delegate, see Elbridge Gerry to John Adams and Samuel Adams, July 21, 1776. Hancock also sent Schuyler another July 19 resolve about curbing the exorbitant costs of supplies for his men as well as a resolve of an earlier date "prohibiting any officer from holding more offices than one."

[2] See JCC, 5:564–65.
[3] See JCC, 5:599.
[4] See JCC, 5:567.

John Hancock to the Governor of South Carolina and the Convention of Georgia

Sir,   Philada. July 24th. 1776.

The Congress being of opinion, that the Service of the United

States will be promoted by taking into Pay a Number of Troops, in the State of South Carolina, who are to act either as Infantry or light Horse, as Occasion may require, have come to the enclosed Resolves, which I do myself the Honour of transmitting in Obedience to their Commands.[1]

In Consideration that these Troops will go thro' more than ordinary Duty, and be put to greater Expence than others, the Congress have augmented their Pay in Proportion.

I have delivered blank Commissions to the Delegates of your State. With most hearty & sincere Wishes for your Health and Happiness and the Prosperity of the State over which you preside, I have the Honour to be, with great Respect, Sir, your most obedt. & very hble Sert.   J. H. Prest.

LB (DNA: PCC, item 12A). Addressed: "To Govr. Rutledge of South Carolina. To the Convention of Georgia."

[1] For Congress' resolutions of this date about "rangers" in South Carolina and Georgia, see *JCC*, 5:606–7. In his July 2 letter to Hancock, which was read in Congress on July 19, Gen. Charles Lee had stated: "Indeed, Sir, without a strong Corps of cavalry I do not see how it is possible to protect these Southern Colonies, and with one thousand good cavalry, I think I cou'd ensure their protection." *NYHS Collections* 5 (1872): 109.

John Hancock to George Washington

Sir,   Philadelphia July 24th. 1776.

I do myself the Honour to enclose sundry Resolves, to which I must entreat your Attention.[1]

The Congress, you will there find, reposeing the most entire Confidence in your Judgment, have left the Disposition of the Troops at New York, the Flying Camp, and Tyonderoga, wholly with you; being fully assured, you will make such an Arrangement, as in your Opinion, will conduce most to the Public Good.[2]

The Commissioners appointed to audit the Accounts of the Army in the York Department have been with me. They are preparing to set out, as soon as possible; and I expect will be at New York in a few Days.[3]

You will observe the Congress have empowered the Commander in Chief in each Department, to negotiate an Exchange of Prisoners; which you will please to conduct agreeably to the enclosed System.

I have wrote to Genl. Schuyler, and forwarded a Copy of the enclosed Resolves.

I have the Honour to be, with the highest Esteem & Respect, Sir, your most obed. & very hble Servt.[4]   John Hancock Presidt

RC (DLC). In the hand of Jacob Rush and signed by Hancock.

¹ For these resolves, dealing with a variety of military matters relating to Washington's and Schuyler's commands and passed by Congress on July 16, 17, 19, 22, 23, and 24, see *JCC*, 5:564–65, 567, 591, 599, 602, 605–7.

² See *JCC*, 5:602; and Washington, *Writings* (Fitzpatrick), 5:304–6.

³ See *JCC*, 5:564–65; and Washington, *Writings* (Fitzpatrick), 5:253–54.

⁴ Hancock also wrote the following letter this date to Paymaster General William Palfrey:

"I beg the Favour of you to take Charge of the two small Packets sent herewith—one to Captain Graydon, the other to his Brother, and see them safely delivered.

"Tomorrow I shall write you fully, having the Authority of Congress to send a Flag to Staten Island for the Demand of some Money, & shall desire you to go. I shall write the General also.

"Hurry. I can't add. Yours, J. Hancock." William Palfrey Papers, MH. See also John Hancock to George Washington, July 29, 1776, note 2.

Joseph Hewes to Samuel Johnston

Dear Sir,   Philada. 24th July 1776

I have not seen Mr. Gibson since I received your favour of the 29th of June. When I do, I shall pay him agreeable to your request.

The manager of the Linnen Manufactory in this City informs me that it is his opinion that small Manufactories set up by private persons in their own Families would be much more profitable both to the adventurers and to the Community in general than large ones established by the public or by Companies. He seems to be a sensible fellow and well acquainted with the business and I think his observations are very just. The more I converse with him on the Subject the less inclination I feel to be concerned in any thing of the kind. So many people in these Colonies are going into it, that I despair of geting a Weaver for you on any Terms. Those that are good for any thing are chiefly engaged, and the army & navy pick up all the rascally Artificers of every kind.

Lord Howe is arived with four or five Men of War but no Troops. A large Fleet is hourly expected having on board some say 20 others 30 thousand Men. His Lordship it is said expresses a great desire to promote a reconciliation. He has sent at three different times a boat with a Flag and a Letter to Genl Washington but the Letter being directed to Geo Washington Esqr. was not received tho much pressed by the officer in whose charge it was sent. The officer who was a Col. and adjutant general that went on shore with the last boat had an interview with Genl Washington. The conversation was chiefly about prisoners. In the close of it he produced a Letter which he said was from Lord Howe but being directed as before was refused. What powers his Lordship may have is not known but from all circumstances that have yet appeared they extend no farther than to receive submissions and grant Pardons. As the people of the united Colonies are only defending their Just rights and Liberties and have committed no Offence they have nothing to ask pardon for, consequently cannot negotiate with his Lordship. No Late accounts from England or France. My Compliments to your Family.

I Am with much respect, Dear Sir, your mo. Obed Servt,

Joseph Hewes

N.B. Mr. Hooper came to Town last evening. I have not yet seen him.

RC (PHi).

Benjamin Rush to Benjamin Franklin

Wednesday, 3 oClock [July 24–August 7? 1776] [1]

Dr. Rush begs leave to inform Dr. Franklin that the members of the Canadian Committee will wait upon him this afternoon at 6 oClock at his own house.

RC (PPAmP). In the hand of Benjamin Rush.

[1] This undated note was obviously written after the appointment of "the committee on sundry Canadian petitioners" and before the submission of its report on August 10, 1776. The date the committee was appointed is not known, because the entry in Secretary Thomson's manuscript journal pertaining to its appointment was erased and amended after it was originally written. That entry appears under the date July 17, the day a petition from "Jean Baptiste de Vidal, of Canada," was presented to Congress and referred to committee, but examination of Thomson's manuscript reveals that Congress subsequently redirected Vidal's petition from the committee originally indicated to a new "committee of five." Since Rush did not attend Congress until July 22 and since the names of the committee members were later written into the journal with a different pen and a slightly bolder stroke than the rest of the July 17 entry, it seems clear that the committee was appointed no earlier than the 22d. Therefore this note must have been written on July 24, 31, or August 7, one of three Wednesdays that fell between Rush's appointment to the committee and the submission of its report to Congress. See *JCC*, 5:572, 645–46; and PCC, item 1, 3:143.

Although Rush's note contains no information on the subjects discussed by the committee with Franklin, it does provide a glimpse into the manner in which committees of Congress conducted business after hours and a reminder that the journals must occasionally be studied with care to resolve apparent anomalies that survive in the printed texts.

Willing, Morris & Co. to William Bingham

Sir   Philada. July 24th. 1776

We were much Concerned to find you were so long detained at Cape May, but as you did at last escape clear of the Men of Warr on this Coast, we hope you will arrive safe at Your destined Port and there be able to execute your Commission so as to be very satisfactory to all Concerned. We are told Mr. La Maitre arrived safe at Martinico but have no Certainty of it. Sorry we are that Mr. Merediths Sloop fell into the Enemys hands, for its not only a Considerable loss but disapoints you & the Publick. The Brigt this goes by will we hope have better luck and make up for the loss and disapointment of the other, but we feared to put any Goods onboard on our own Account as the Coast now swarms with Men of Warr.

We hope however that you may send us back some Goods by the Reprisal on the footing proposed in our former letter, and you may depend on our attention in the sale & remittances for them. We send you by this Conveyance the News Papers by which you'l see the Changes in our Public Bodys. The Writer of this is again returned one of the Delegates in Congress. Colo. Harrison & Colo Braxton are out which we are extreamly sorry for.[1]

The enclosed declaration Speaks for itself. I don't know whether you will have a letter from the Committee by this Conveyance or not. Shou'd Mr Bealle be arrived in the West Indies when this gets to hand tell him We think Occracock Inlet in North Carolina is at this time the safest place along the Coast. We are sir, your obedt hble servts,   Willing, Morris & Co.

RC (DLC). In the hand of Robert Morris. Addressed: "To Mr William Bingham in Martinico."

[1] Robert Morris was reelected a delegate to Congress by the Pennsylvania Convention on July 20. *Am. Archives*, 5th ser. 2:6. Benjamin Harrison and Carter Braxton were not among the five delegates elected by the Virginia Convention on June 20, although Harrison was subsequently named on October 10, 1776, to replace Thomas Jefferson. Ibid., 4th ser. 6:1582; and *Journal of the House of Delegates of Virginia, 1776* (Williamsburg: Alexander Purdie, 1777), p. 8.

John Adams' Notes of Debate

July 25. 1776.[1]

Art. 14. of the Confederation.[2]

Terms in this Article, equivocal and indefinite.

Jefferson. The Limits of the Southern Colonies are fixed. . . .[3] Moves an Amendment, that all Purchases of Lands, not within the Boundaries of any Colony shall be made by Congress, of the Indians in a great Council. Sherman seconds the Motion. . . .

Chase. The Intention of this Article is very obvious, and plain. The Article appears to me to be right, and the Amendment wrong. It is the Intention of some Gentlemen to limit the Boundaries of particular States. No colony has a Right to go to the S[outh] Sea.

They never had—they cant have. It would not be safe to the rest. It would be destructive to her Sisters, and to herself.

Art. 16 [*i.e.* 15]. . . .[4]

Jefferson. What are reasonable Limits? What Security have We that the Congress will not curtail the present Settlements of the States. I have no doubt, that the Colonies will limit themselves.

Wilson. Every Gentleman has heard much of Claims to the South Sea. They are extravagant. The Grants were made upon Mistakes. They were ignorant of the Geography. They thought the S. Sea within 100 Miles of the Atlantic Ocean. It was not conceived that they extended 3000 Miles. Ld. Cambden considers the Claims to the South Sea, as what never can be reduced to Practice. Pensilvania has no Right to interfere in those claims. But she has a Right to say, that she will not confederate unless those Claims are cut off. I wish the Colonies themselves would cutt off those Claims. . . .

Art. 16.

Chase moves for the Word deputies, instead of Delegates, because the Members of the Maryland Convention are called Delegates, and he would have a Distinction. Answer. In other Colonies the Reverse is true. The Members of the House are called deputies. Jefferson objects to the first of November. Dr. Hall moves for May, for the time to meet. Jefferson thinks that Congress will have a short Meeting in the Fall and another in the Spring. Hayward thinks the Spring the best Time. Wilson thinks the fall—and November better than October, because September is a busy Month, every where. Dr. Hall. Septr. and Octr. the most sickly and mortal Months in the Year. The Season is forwarder in Georgia in April, than here in May. Hopkinson moves that the Power of recalling Delegates be reserved to the State not to the Assembly, because that may be changed.

Art. 17.

Each Colony shall have one vote.

MS (MHi). Adams, *Diary* (Butterfield), 2:241–42.

[1] The committee to prepare the form of a confederation presented its draft articles to Congress on July 12, but apparently these were not debated in the committee of the whole until July 22. Congress then debated them intermittently until August 20, when a revised version was ordered to be printed for further consideration. Adams' Notes of Debates for July 25, 26, and 30 and August 1 and 2, together with Thomas Jefferson's Notes of Proceedings, July 12–August 1, and Benjamin Rush's Notes for a Speech in Congress, August 1, 1776, provide the most detailed information available on these debates in the committee of the whole. See also *JCC*, 5:546–56, 600, 674–89.

[2] The article numbers correspond with those in the draft presented to Congress on July 12. *JCC*, 5:546–56.

[3] Suspension points in MS, here and below.

[4] Article 15 dealt with the states' boundaries and Article 16 with the appointment of delegates to Congress. *JCC*, 5:549–50.

John Adams to John Avery

Sir   Philadelphia July 25. 1776

I find myself under a Necessity of applying to the Honourable the general Court for Leave to return home.[1] I have attended here, so long and so constantly, that I feel myself necessitated to ask this Favour, on Account of my Health, as well as on many other Accounts.

I beg Leave to propose to the Honourable Court an Alteration in their Plan of Delegation in Congress, which, it appears to me, would be more agreable to the Health, and Convenience of the Members and much more conducive to the public Good, than the present.[2] No Gentleman can possibly attend to an incessant Round of thinking, Speaking, and writing, upon the most intricate, as well as important Concerns of human Society, from one End of the Year to another, without Injury both to his mental and bodily Strength. I would therefore humbly propose, that the Honourable Court would be pleased to appoint Nine Members to attend in Congress, Three or five at a Time. In this Case, four, or Six, might be at home, at a Time, and every Member might be relieved, once in three or four Months. In this Way, you would always have Members in Congress who would have in their Minds, a compleat Chain of the Proceedings here as well as in the General Court, both Kinds of which Knowledge are necessary for a proper Conduct here. In this Way, the Lives and Health, and indeed the sound Minds of the Delegates here, would be in less Danger than they are at present, and in my humble opinion the public Business would be much better done.

This Proposal, however, is only Submitted to the Consideration of that Honourable Body, whose Sole Right it is to judge of it. For myself, I must intreat the General Court to give me Leave to resign, and immediately to appoint some other Gentleman in my Room. The Consideration of my own Health, and the Circumstances of my Family and private Affairs would have little Weight with me, if the Sacrifice of these was necessary for the Public: But it is not, because those Parts of the Business of Congress, for which (if for any) I have my Qualifications, being now nearly compleated, and the Business that remains, being chiefly military and commercial, of which I know very little, there are Multitudes of Gentlemen in the Province, much fitter for the public Service here than I am.

With great Respect to the General Court, I am, sir, your most obedient servant,   John Adams.

RC (M–Ar). Addressed: "The Deputy Secretary."

[1] Adams did not leave for home until October 13, 1776; and he remained a member of Congress until his appointment as a commissioner to France on November 28, 1777. Adams, *Diary* (Butterfield), 2:251; *JCC*, 9:946–47.

[2] Adams' plan to rearrange the Massachusetts delegation in Congress arrived in Boston during the general court's August adjournment. When the court returned

on August 26, it was read in the council and referred to the house of representatives for their consideration. In a message to the council the house made this comment on Adams' plan: "The House will consider of his request with a proper degree of tenderness for his person And if Any other mode of delegation in Congress can be devised for the ease and benefit of those respectable persons attending that duty consistant with the public service the House will very readily adopt it." There the question rested. Journal of the Massachusetts Council, August 26 and September 6, 1776. Early State Records microfilm, DLC.

John Hancock to John Bradford

Sir   Philadelphia July 25th 1776

Your letters to 15th Inst. inclusive, I have duly receiv'd.[1] Matters of very great moment, in which the Interest of the United States is involv'd, having been for sometime under the Consideration of Congress, have prevented my regularly Replying to your Letters, and forwarding your Commission. I am greatly surpriz'd at what you relate of the Conduct of the late Agents, and at their insisting on Acting, untill your Commission should arrive; Sir, the very moment you recd my first letter under the Sanction of Congress, informing you of your Appointment as Agent, that very moment they were Superceeded, and were Accountable to you for all monies then in their hands belonging to the United States, in Consequence of any Captures, and Sales of Continental Property. However as I am always dispos'd to Accommodate matters, and to put things on a stable footing, I now enclose your Commission, and now not only Authorise, but Direct, you to call upon the Gentlemen, who have hitherto Acted as Agents, to render their Acco[u]nts to you, and to pay what monies they may have in their hands belonging to the Public to you, and to cease all further proceedings in that Department, the sd. Accts. with the vouchers to be Transmitted to me, to be laid before the Marine Committee, for their Examination and Approbation, you to render an Accott. of such monies recd, and to be accountable therefor. And the former Agents are hereby directed immediately on your Application to Render their Accotts. and pay the monies they may have in their hands to you; I wish to settle this matter as early as possible, for altho' their Conduct is highly Reprehensible yet I would gladly pass it over without a public mention, but with respect to the Arms, order'd by Congress to be sent to Genl. Washington, and which Mr. Glover mentions he without Consulting you had dispos'd of among the Troops, in his Brothers Regiment, I must insist that you immediately carry that Resolution into Execution,[2] and that the Arms be forwarded to the Genl. as at first order'd by Congress, it being my Duty to see every Resolve of Congress executed, [. . .][3] now in the hands of the former Agents, you will have sufficient to answer present demands, and to pay for the Vessell bought by order of Mr. Morris, if a deficiency yet should happen you must draw on me.

You will please keep me duly advis'd of all matters.

I inclose, you the papers to which I refer you. Do give me all the news.

I wish you and Family well, and happy, and am with Sentiments of Esteem, Sir Your very Hume Servt.

John Hancock Presidt.

MS not found; reprinted from Burnett, *Letters,* 2:25–26, where it is described as: "Copied from the original, then in possession of Mr. Charles E. Goodspeed of Boston."

[1] For letters of May 15, June 17 and 20, and July 1 and 11 from John Bradford, Continental prize agent in Massachusetts, to Hancock, see Clark, *Naval Documents,* 5:102, 575–76, 635–36, 849–50, 1025–26.

[2] For the disputes between Bradford and Jonathan Glover, who had been appointed by Washington in October 1775 as prize agent for Marblehead, Mass., and the surrounding area, see Bradford to Hancock, July 1, and Glover to Washington, July 20, 1776, ibid., pp. 849–50, 1152–53.

[3] At this point in the MS Burnett noted: "about 60 words torn out here."

Francis Lewis to William Palfrey

Dear Sir,   Phila. 25th July 1776

I am directed by Congress to transmit you the inclosed two Bills vizt Townsend & Griffin on Murray, Sansom & Co. for one hundred pounds Sterling each, accepted for payment of Two hundred pounds New York Currency each, which I am informed will be immediately honoured. When paid, please to furnish me with a Certificate thereof that I may be enabled to receive that sum here. This money is to be applyed to the Public Service.[1]

I have the honor to subscribe myself sincerely, your very Humble Servt,   Frans Lewis

RC (MH).

[1] Paymaster General Palfrey wrote Lewis on July 31: "I have presented to Messrs. Murry & Sansom the two drafts for £100 sterling each, for which I received one thousand dollars in payment; which sum I shall apply to the publick service, and credit to the United States of America accordingly." *Am. Archives,* 5th ser. 1:696.

Robert Morris to Horatio Gates

Dear sir   Philada July 25th. 1776

I ought to have wrote you a fortnight ago that Mrs. Gates with your Son Bob had gone for Virginia after about a Weeks stay with us during which you had the misfortune to loose a horse. I believe he had been too hard drove. At least Bob thought that was the cause of his Death altho' the Servant wou'd not allow it. Mrs. Gates bought another from Mr. Hancock for which I am to pay him forty pounds & shall charge it to your Account. Mrs. Gates did not take the Money she wanted at home but is to draw on me for it.

I hope you will be able to put our affairs at the Lakes on a more respectable footing than they have ever been since the days of poor Montgomery; certainly there has been great mismanagement in that department and I find some People attributing this to a Source I never shoud have suspected. Is it possible that a man who writes so well & expresses such anxiety for the Cause of his Country as Genl. S——r does, I say is it possible that he can be sacrificing the Interest of that Country to his Ambition or Avarice. I sincerely hope it is not so but such insinuations are dropped.

I beg leave to recommend Major Wood to your Patronage. Youl find him a bold intrepid officer & as Lt Colo Allen has resigned I shall push for the Major to have that Vacancy.[1]

You'l be pleased with Lee's Success at Carolina. The Enemy were mauled greatly & I think the repulse disgraces them, consequently reflects great honor on our People.

You are no doubt well informed of what passes at New York & as I have full employment for my whole time I shall only assure you of the esteem & regard with which I am Dr sir, Your affectionate, hble Servant, Robt Morris

RC (NHi).
[1] Joseph Wood was appointed lieutenant colonel of the second Pennsylvania battalion in the place of William Allen on July 29, 1776. JCC, 5:615.

South Carolina Delegates to John Rutledge

Sir, Philadelphia, 25 July, 1776

Immediately upon the receipt of your letter, we applied to Congress for permission to order the East India tea now in your stores to be sold and to direct the produce thereof to be carried into the Colony Treasury to be appropriated in such manner as your Assembly should judge right.[1]

In consequence of this application, a debate of some length ensued, in which the House indicated a strong inclination to lay their hands upon the profits which should arise from the sale, either for the use of the Continent at large, or to be carried into a fund to reimburse those Colonies whose property should be seized in England. There appeared neither reason nor justice in these measures, and we endeavoured to obviate the objections which were made to the application and to answer the arguments which had been advanced against it.

We observed that this property should be looked upon as belonging to the King of Great Britain and not to the East India Company, as the latter had been divested of it, both by the seizure which the Custom House officers had made of it and by the indemnification of the Parliament, that the Congress had therefore no more right to apply this tea to the use of the Continent at large than they had to dispose of the cannon in our forts or the Crown lands within the limits of the Colony. But that, if it was the East India Company's property, they had occasioned such an expence to the State of Carolina as to justify them fully in the seizures. That it would be repugnant to the principles of justice to insist that this tea should be sold for the benefit of those whose property had been, or might be, seized in England in exclusion of those whose property had been seized in America, and that it would be impracticable to bring every species of loss into one common account.

That the seizure of property had been a common misfortune of which, as well as of public expences, we have had our full proportion, and that therefore it would be injurious to our State not to be permitted to make use of the advantage in this instance which the possession of the tea had given. It was confessed that we had a right to sell it if we chose and apply the profits as we pleased, but as we had asked the opinion of the House upon the subject, we should now be governed by the disposition which they should think proper to make, and that they should take time to consider of it. The Delegates, being by this time fully convinced that there were many in the House who wished to dispose of it in a manner injurious to the interest and the right of our State, agreed to withdraw the motion for which they obtained the leave of Congress, and we now, with one voice, advise you to recommend to your Assembly immediately to sell the same and apply the profits thereof to Colonial purposes. Indeed we were not a little surprized at your requesting us to lay the same before Congress, and we hope that you will determine for yourselves in future in all causes where the concern is of a Provincial and not of a Continental nature.

We are, with regard, your Excellency's most obedient humble servants,

Thomas Lynch	Arthur Middleton
Edward Rutledge	Thomas Heyward, Junior
	Thomas Lynch, Junior

MS not found; reprinted from William E. Hemphill et al., eds., *Journals of the General Assembly and House of Representatives, 1776–1780* (Columbia: University of South Carolina Press, 1970), pp. 79–80.

[1] For further references to the subject of this letter, see Richard Smith's Diary, January 12, 1776, note 2.

James Wilson to Jasper Yeates
and John Montgomery

Dear Gentlemen   Philada 25th July 1776
Major Butler waits while I write you a few Lines. His Brother
Captain Butler has a Quantity of Indian Goods at Pittsburgh. The
whole of them, or whatever Part you wish to have, will be disposed
of to you. No particular Sum was fixed by Congress as a Reward
for Major Butler's Services while he was employed in the Indian
Department. You will have an Opportunity of being informed what
his Services were. Please to write me what you think will be a
proper Compensation for them. I refer you to Mr Butler for news.
I shall have an Opportunity of writing to you more fully in a few
Days by Mr Anderson. I am, Gentlemen, yours very sincerely,
                                                    James Wilson

RC (NN). Addressed: "Jasper Yeates and John Montgomery Esqrs, Commissioners
for Indian Affairs in the Middle Department."

John Adams' Notes of Debate

July. 26. [1776]
Rutledge and Linch oppose giving the Power of regulating the
Trade and managing all Affairs of the Indians, to Congress.[1] The
Trade is profitable they say.
Gwinnett is in favour of Congress having such Power.
Braxton is for excepting such Indians as are tributary to any
State. Several Nations are tributary to Virginia.
Jefferson explains it to mean the Indians who live in the Colony.
These are Subject to the Laws in some degree.
Wilson. We have no Right over the Indians, whether within or
without the real or pretended Limits of any Colony. They will not
allow themselves to be classed according to the Bounds of Colonies.
Grants made 3000 miles to the Eastward have no Validity with the
Indians. The Trade of Pensilvania has been more considerable with
the Indians than that of the neighbouring Colonies.
Walton. The Indian Trade is of no essential service to any Colony.
It must be a Monopoly. If it is free it produces Jealousies and
Animosities, and Wars. Carolina very passionately considers this
Trade as contributory to her Grandeur and Dignity. Deerskins are a
great Part of the Trade. A great difference between S. Carolina and
Georgia. Carolina is in no danger from the Indians at present.
Georgia is a frontier and Barrier to Car. G. must be overrun and
extirpated before Car. can be hurt. G. is not equal to the Expence
of giving the Donations to the Indians, which will be necessary to

keep them at Peace. The Emoluments of the Trade are not a Compensation for the Expence of donations.

Rutledge differs from Walton in a Variety of Points. We must look forward with extensive Views. Carolina has been run to an amazing expence to defend themselves vs. Indians. In 1760 &c. fifty thousand Guineas were spent. We have now as many Men on the frontiers, as in Charlestown. We have Forts in the Indian Countries. We are connected with them by Treaties.

Lynch. Congress may regulate the Trade, if they will indemnify Car. vs. the Expence of keeping Peace with the Indians, or defending Us vs. them.

Witherspoon. Here are two adjacent Provinces, situated alike with respect to the Indians, differing totally in their Sentiments of their Interests.

Chase. S. Carolina claims to the S. Sea. So does North, Virginia, and Massachusetts Bay. S. Carolina says they have a Right to regulate the Trade with the Indians. If so 4 Colonies have all the Power of regulating Trade with the Indians. S.C. alone could not stand alone vs. the Indian Nations.

Sherman moves that Congress may have a Superintending Power, to prevent Injustice to the Indians or Colonies.

Willson. No lasting Peace will be with the Indians, unless made by some one Body. No such language as this ought to be held to the Indians. We are stronger, We are better. We treat you better than another Colony. No Power ought to treat, with the Indians, but the united States. Indians know the striking Benefits of Confederation— they have an Example of it in the Union of the Six nations. The Idea of the Union of the Colonies struck them forcibly last Year. None should trade with Indians without a Licence from Congress. A perpetual War would be unavoidable, if every Body was allowed to trade with them.

Stone. This Expedient is worse than either of the alternatives. What is the meaning of this Superintendency? Colonies will claim the Right first. Congress cant interpose untill the Evil has happened. Disputes will arise when Congress shall interpose.

MS (MHi). Adams, *Diary* (Butterfield), 2:243–44.

[1] Debate this day in the committee of the whole centered on the clause in article 18 of the July 12 draft articles of confederation granting Congress exclusive rights for "Regulating the Trade, and managing all Affairs with the Indians." *JCC*, 5:550.

John Adams to James Warren

Dear Sir   Philadelphia July 26. 1776

My Health has lasted much longer, than I expected but at last it fails. The Increasing Heat of the Weather added to incessant application to Business, without any Intermissions of Exercise, has relaxed me to such a degree that a few Weeks more would totally incapacitate me for any Thing. I must therefore return home.

There will be no difficulty in finding Men Suitable to send here.[1] For my own Part, as General Ward has so resigned his Command in the Army, I Sincerely wish you would send him here. The Journey would contribute much to the Restoration of his Health, after the small Pox, and his knowledge in the Army and of military Matters is very much wanted here at present.

Send Dana along for another, and come yourself by all Means. I should have mentioned you, in the first Place. Will Lowell do? or Sewall? You will want four or five new ones.

Major Hawley must be excused no longer. He may have the small Pox here without keeping House an Hour, and without absence from Congress four days. It would be vastly for his Health to have it.

Send Palmer, or Lincoln, or Cushing if you will. Somebody you must send. Why will not Mr Bowdoin or Dr Winthrop take a Ride?

RC (MHi). In Adams' hand, though not signed.

[1] For Adams' plan for the new Massachusetts delegation to Congress, see Adams to John Avery, July 25, 1776.

John Dickinson to James Wilson

Dear sir,   Elizabeth Town July 26th 1776

I have lately recd. a Letter from my Friend General Lee, in which he expresses his Anxiety to have something secured to him in Consequence of the Resolution of Congress at the Time of his entring into our service.[1]

It is not to be expected that he can produce proofs of his Estate being confiscated in England—but it is very probable, that Administration will entirely prevent his receiving any Benefit from it. His Bills have actually been protested, and I believe solely on Account of the part he has taken.

He has purchas'd an Estate in Virginia, which is mortgag'd to Mr. R. Morris for the purchase Money, about 5 or 6 thousand Pounds. This sum at least and a thousand Pounds more, to carry on some Improvements, the General is desirous of having advanc'd. His Request is so very reasonable, that I hope Congress will immediately grant it, without waiting for a direct application from him—which, I think, he ought not to be compell'd to make. If he ever recovers his Estate, this Money will only be lent to him by the Continent. If his Estate is lost, the Continent ought to indemnify him. I do most earnestly beg of You to advocate his Cause, and to speak to as many of your Friends in Congress as You conveniently can, on the Subject. I should be exceedingly sorry if Congress should not act on the

Occasion in such a Manner as to give the General entire Content, and also to do him Honor. His Services deserve such a Behaviour towards him. I have recd. a Letter from Mr. John Rutledge, in which he mentions his indefatigable Industry in our Cause.

I am, sir, your very hble Servt.   John Dickinson

RC (PCarlD).
¹ Lee's letter to Dickinson of July 3 is in the Robert R. Logan Collection, PPL. For Congress' commitment to "indemnify General Lee for any loss of property which he may sustain by entering into their service," see their resolution of June 19, 1775, *JCC*, 2:98–99. A discussion of this issue can be found in John R. Alden, *General Charles Lee, Traitor or Patriot?* (Baton Rouge: Louisiana State University Press, 1951), pp. 76–79. A letter from Lee to Robert Morris of July 2, 1776, discussing the very point Dickinson explains in this letter to Wilson, is in *NYHS Collections* 5 (1872): 117–19.

Dickinson wrote a letter to Lee dated "Elizabeth Town in Jersey, July 25th 1776," explaining that because of his opposition to Independence he was no longer in Congress and therefore deprived "of the little power I once possest." Nevertheless, he explained—undoubtedly referring to this letter to Wilson—"I have wrote on the subject to a particular friend of mine, who is a Delegate and a man of abilities, which I am convinced he will exert in your Cause." Ibid., pp. 166–68.

The issue came before Congress at this time because of a "proposal" from John Rutledge to reimburse Lee for his property confiscated in Britain, undoubtedly because the South Carolina president was sensitive to Lee's contributions in the recent defense of Sullivan's Island. For Congress' response to Rutledge's proposal, which led to a resolve of October 7, 1776, to advance Lee $30,000, see *JCC*, 5:608, 741–42, 851; and Alden, *Charles Lee*, pp. 138–39.

Evidence that Samuel Adams was among those who backed the proposal is contained in John Rutledge's letter to Charles Lee of August 20, 1776, in which Rutledge quoted the following extract from a July 25 letter he had received from Adams. "Your Proposal with regard to Gen. Lee coincides with my Inclination and Judgment. There is no one, more heartily disposed to gratify that Gentleman's Wishes than I am & I think to omit it in this Instance wd be hardly just. It has been moved in Congress & I have reason to believe the matter will be speedily compleated to your satisfaction." *NYHS Collections* 5 (1872): 237.

John Hancock to George Washington

Sir   Friday 26 July [1776] 4 oClock P M

Congress being Adjourn'd, I have to Acknowledge the Rect. of yor favr. of 25th, this moment come to hand.¹ The Subject of it is so just that I will venture to Say that it will be Complied with in it's fullest lattitude.

The Preamble to the Resolution for Confiscating the Property of the Subjects of the King of Great Brittain, havg. been this day Expung'd, & the Resolution alter'd, agreeable to the one now Inclos'd you, I am to Request you will please to Erase that from the Resolves I inclos'd you a few days past, & Substitute the one I now transmitt in its place.²

With every wish in yor favr. & every Sentimt. of Esteem, I am, Sir, Your very hum servt,   John Hancock Presidt.

[*P.S.*] Brigadier Gen. Sullivan this Day Sent me a Letter of Resignation, which is order'd to lie on the Table untill Monday. I have not Seen him.[3]

RC (NjHi).
[1] Washington's July 25 letter to Hancock, requesting an increase in the number of his aides-de-camp, is in PCC, item 152, 2:297–300, and Washington, *Writings* (Fitzpatrick), 5:337–38. Congress responded to this request on July 29 by authorizing Washington to employ an additional aide-de-camp. *JCC,* 5:613. A facsimile of Hancock's July 29 letter informing Washington of Congress' action is in Washington, *Writings* (Fitzpatrick), opposite 5:337.
[2] See *JCC,* 5:605–6.
[3] Sullivan, who was miffed by Congress' decision to appoint Horatio Gates instead of himself as commander of the American army in Canada, withdrew his resignation on July 29 after Hancock explained "the Reasons of Congress promoting Genl. Gates over him." See *JCC,* 5:612–13; and Hancock to Washington, July 31, 1776. Sullivan's letter of resignation has not been found, but for an explanation of his decision to resign, see his July 6 letter to General Schuyler in *Am. Archives,* 5th ser. 1:235.

Secret Committee to Thomas Mumford

Sir   Philada. July 26th 1776
It is probable the dispute about the Powder may be settled before this reaches you. If not we hope the enclosed letter will put the matter right & procure the delivery of the Powder to you or Your order, and We request you will apply to Govr. Trumbull for an Account of the Powder lent by your Colony to Genl. Washington when before Boston. We dont know exactly the quantity but believe it was about four Tons. The Governor or some officer of your Government have a receipt or Certificate either from the General or Commissary which you'l please to take up, paying the Powder and transmit the same to us with a receipt for the Powder you so repay.
We shall be glad to hear of your further Success in the way of Importation, and to know what price you obtain for the Salt & remain, Sir, Your obedt servants. By order of the Secret Committee,
Robt Morris, Chair Man

RC (NjR: Elsie O. and Philip D. Sang deposit, 1972). Written and signed by Robert Morris.

John Adams to Abigail Adams

Philadelphia July 27. 1776
Disappointed again. The Post brought me no Letter from you, which I dont wonder at much, nor any Intelligence concerning you, which surprizes me, a good deal. . . .[1] I hang upon Tenterhooks.

Fifteen days since, you were all inocculated, and I have not yet learned how you have fared. But I will suppose you all better and out of Danger. Why should I torture myself when I cant relieve you?

It makes me happy to hear that the Spirit of Inocculation prevails so generally. I could wish it, more universal. The small Pox has done Us more harm than British Armies, Canadians, Indians, Negroes, Hannoverians, Hessians, and all the rest. We must conquer this formidable Enemy without Hesitation or delay.

Sullivan is here, and in a Miff, at the Promotion of Gates, has asked Leave to resign his Commission.[2] I am sorry for this inconsiderate Step. It will hurt him more than the Cause. It is conjectured at New York, I am told, that he expects to be first Man in New Hampshire. If this is really his Motive, he ought to be ashamed of it, and I hope he will be dissappointed. The Ladies have not half the Zeal for Precedence, that We find every day among the Gentlemen.

The Judge Advocate[3] came in this Evening, in fine Health and gay Spirits. The Army is the Place for Health—the Congress the Place of Sickness. God bless you all.

Adieu.

RC (MHi). Adams, *Family Correspondence* (Butterfield), 2:63.
[1] Suspension points in MS.
[2] See John Hancock to George Washington, July 26, 1776, note 3.
[3] William Tudor.

John Adams to James Warren

Dear Sir   Philadelphia July 27. 1776

I have directed a Packett to you, by this days Post, and shall only add a few Words by Fessenden. I assure you the Necessity of your sending along fresh delegates here, is not chimerical. Paine has been very ill for this whole Week and remains in a bad way.[1] He has not been able to attend Congress, for several days, and if I was to judge by his Eye, his Skin, and his Cough, I should conclude he never would be fit to do duty there again, without a long Intermission, and a Course of Air, Exercise, Diet, and Medicine. In this I may be mistaken. The Secretary,[2] between you and me, is compleatly worn out. I wish he had gone home Six months ago, and rested himself. Then, he might have done it, without any Disadvantage. But in plain English he has been so long here, and his Strength, Spirit and Abilities so exhausted, that an hundred such delegates here would not be worth a Shilling. My Case is worse. My Face is grown pale, my Eyes weak and inflamed, my Nerves tremulous, and my Mind weak as Water. Fevourous Heats by Day and Sweats by Night are returned upon me, which is an infallible Symptom with me that it is Time to throw off all Care, for a Time, and take a little Rest. I have several Times with the Blessing of God, saved my Life in this Way, and am now determined to attempt it once more.

You must be very Speedy in appointing other Delegates, or you will not be represented here. Go home I will, if I leave the Massachusetts without a Member here. You know my Resolutions in these Matters are not easily altered. I know better than any Body what my Constitution will bear, and what it will not, and you may depend upon it, I have already tempted it, beyond Prudence, and Safety. A few Months Rest and Relaxation will remit me. But this is absolutely necessary for that End. I have sent a Resignation to the General Court and am determined to take six Months rest at least. I wish to be released from Philadelphia forever. But in Case the General Court should wish otherwise, which I hope they will not, I dont mean Surlily to refuse them. If you appoint Such a Number, that We can have a Respit, once in Six Months at furthest, or once in three if that is more convenient, I should be willing to take another Trick or two. But I will never again undertake upon any other Terms, unless I should undertake for a Year, and bring my Wife and four Children with me, as many other Gentlemen here have done, which, as I know it would be infinitely more agreable, and more for the Benefit of my Children, so in my sincere opinion, it would be cheaper for the Province, because I am sure I could bring my whole Family here, and maintain it, as cheap as I can live here Single at Board with a servant and two Horses. I am &c.

RC (MHi). In Adams' hand, though not signed.
   [1] Paine had recorded the start of his sickness on July 19: "Taken very ill with a fever." Robert Treat Paine's diary, July 19, 1776, MHi.
   [2] Samuel Adams.

Samuel Adams to Benjamin Kent

My dear friend   Philad July 27 1776
   I must beg you to impute to the true Reason my not having yet acknowledgd & answerd your very obliging Letter of the 24 May [1]— The *Want of Leisure* often prevents my indulging the natural Inclination of my Mind to converse with my distant Friends by familiar Epistles; for however unequal I feel my Self to the Station in which our Country has placed me here, I am indispensibly obligd to attend the Duties of it with Diligence.

   It has been difficult for a Number of persons sent from all parts of so extensive a Territory and representing Colonies (or as I must now call them *States*) which in many Respects have had different Interests & Views, to unite in Measures materially to affect them all.

Hence our Determinations have been necessarily slow. We have however gone on from Step to Step, till at length we are arrivd to perfection, as you have heard, in a Declaration of Independence. Was there ever a Resolution brot about, especially so important as this, without great internal Tumults & violent Convulsions! The Delegates of every Colony in Congress have given their Voices in favor of the great Question, & the People I am told, recognize the Resolution as though it was a Decree promulgated from Heaven. I have thot that if this decisive Measure had been taken six months earlier, it would have given Vigor to our Nothern Army & a different Issue to our military exertions in Canada. But probably I was mistaken. The Colonies were not then all ripe for so momentous a Change. It was necessary that they shd be united, & it required time & patience to remove old prejudices, to instruct the unenlightened, convince the doubting and fortify the timid. Perhaps if our Friends had considerd how much was to be previously done they wd not have been, as you tell me some of them were "impatient under our Delay."

New Govts are now erecting in the several American States under the Authority of the people. Monarchy seems to be generally exploded—and it is not a little surprising to me, that the Aristocratick Spirit which appeard to have taken deep Root in some of them, now gives place to that of Democracy. You justly observe that "the Soul or Spirit of Democracy is *Virtue.*" No State can long preserve its liberty "where Virtue is not supremely honord." I flatter my self you are mistaken in thinking ours is so very deficient, and I do assure you, I find relief in supposing your Colouring is too high. But if I deceive my self in this most essential point I conjure you and every Man of Influence by Example and by all Means to stem the Torrent of Vice, which, as a celebrated Author tells us, "prevailing would destroy, not only a Kingdom or an Empire, but the whole moral Dominion of the Almighty throughout the Infinitude of Space." I have Time only to add that I am very affectionately yours,

                                                                S A

FC (NN).
[1] Kent's letter is in the Samuel Adams Papers, NN.

Charles Carroll of Carrollton
to Charles Carroll, Sr.

Dr. Papa,   Pha. 27th July 1776.
    The vessels mentioned in my last dated in Congress landed Some highlanders: we know not how many. The enemy's fleet has had a

long voyage & I hope the men in the 1st division at least will arrive in a sickly State: I begin to flatter myself the enemy's whole force will not arrive before the latter end of next month, by that time Gen. Washington will have collected a strength sufficient to defy their utmost efforts: he has at present but 15 thousand exclusive of the forces on the Jersey Shore.

The enemy's vessels which passed N. York have not yet attempted the highlands. We have not lately heared from Canada. One army is fortifying an advantageous post opposite Tionderoga. I have not yet had a letter from you, only two from Mr. Deards.

Dunmore gives us no uneasiness. If we can confine Howe all will be well.

I find this city very hot. If I am chosen of the Convention I shall return to Maryd. the 9th of next month by Elkridge—if not I shall remain here till I am superseded. My love to the 2 Mollies & Mrs. Darnall. God grant you a continuance of yr. health & spirit. I am, yr. aff. Son,   Ch. Carroll of Carrollton

P.S. Mr. Chase desires his complts to the family. Newton the shoe maker is gone to the flying camp: so no shoes for the ladies.

RC (MdHi).

John Hancock to Joseph Trumbull

Sir   Philadelphia 27 July 1776
Inclos'd you have a Resolution of Congress for the Supply of Provisions to the Frigates in the Eastern Departmt. out of the Stock of Provis[ion]s in that Quarter, & am to Request you will by the next Post issue your orders to your Deputy there to furnish such Quantities as shall be applied for by Mr Cushing & others who have the Care of the Ships.[1]

I have paid all your Bills that have been presented; Money will soon be sent to the paymaster.

I wish you happy & am, Sir, Your very hum Servt,
                                       J H Pt.

LB (DNA: PCC, item 12A). Addressed: "To Joseph Trumbull Eqr., Commissary Genl. New York."

[1] For the enclosed resolution, which was passed by Congress on May 25, see *JCC,* 4:393–94. The passage of this resolution was apparently prompted by a May 8 letter to Trumbull from Charles Miller, his deputy in Boston, which was read in Congress on May 23. PCC, item 78, 15:37–38; *Am. Archives,* 4th ser. 5:1238; and *JCC,* 4:384. Trumbull's reply to this letter from Hancock, dated July 29, is in PCC, item 78, 22:77–78, and *Am. Archives,* 5th ser. 1:643.

Maryland Delegates to
the Maryland Council of Safety

Gent,   Pha. 27th July 1776.

Colonel Smallwood apprehending that his battalion would be in want of many necessaries at the Camp applied to us for a Sum of money and we advanced him 1335 dollars for which he is to be accountable to the Convention of Maryd. We hope this advance will meet with their & your approbation, as not much can be expected from Soldiers badly provided; and such is the discretion & oeconomy of Colonel Smallwood that we are persuaded he will make a very judicious application of this money.

The Congress has allowed a regimental paymaster to each battalion in the flying Camp, the appointment of which officer is left to the Several States from which those battalions come. In the Recess of our Convention the appointment is on you, & we beg you will appoint one as soon as may be. Colonel Smallwood recommended to us for this place Mr. Christopher Richmond. We mention this circumstance, because we know the appointment of Mr. Richmond will be very agreeable to the Colonel.[1]

There are now lodged in Mr. Stone's house 50 odd muskets lately imported for the use of our State: they want repairing & cleaning. We submit it to you whether we shall not best keep these Muskets here to arm in a part one of our militia companies passing thro' this city on its way to the flying Camp: this will save the expence & trouble of sending them to Maryd.

We are informed that there are large quantities of flint stones at the landings on Wye & Choptank rivers. These were brought by the ships as ballast & thrown out on the banks. The Congress has desired us to write to you on the subject & to procure some person, who understands flints, to look after them & report to Congress whether they are good or not.

We have nothing new from N. York. The post is not yet come in. We heared from Gen. Washington yesterday. All was quiet. The 10 vessels mentioned in the papers appearing in the offing at N. York brought over highlanders. How many we know not. As the harvest is now over We imagine the Militia will come in fast to compose the flying camp & we hope the Maryd. Militia will march with all possible expedition. We are with regard, Gentlemen, yr. most hum. Servants,

Saml. Chase

Ch. Carroll of Carrollton

RC (MdAA). Written by Carroll and signed by Carroll and Chase.

[1] The Maryland Council appointed Christopher Richmond paymaster to Col. William Smallwood's battalion on August 2. Md. Archives, 12:159, 161.

Robert Treat Paine to Henry Knox

Dear Sr,   Philada. July 27. 1776.

I was sorry Mr. Byers left N York before he had finished your business. He has been longer here than was intended, & very unhappily when he came I was so sick of a fever that nothing but the nature of his business induced me to see him, & in short I have not been able to settle the plan of another Air Furnace in the manner proposed. I got some of the Committee to my Room & all that could be agreed upon was that Mr. Byers Should Work up your Mettal first & then purchase all the mettal he could in N York & make six pounders. I wish it was determined whether the *Congress* mortar is serviceable as a Mortar, if not I think it had better be cast into Cannon. I have desired Mr. Byers as he returns to take the pattern of the Pensyl 6 lb & 12 lb now in the Jerseys. Handsomer Guns I never saw, the former of wch. weighs 4.2. &c the other 8.0.9. As soon as I recover a little Strength I hope to devise some Method of having this business enlarged. I wish the Iron Cannon that lay at Kings bridge were put into some use, they are as good as any guns to be stationary & defend lines to Vast advantage, if mounted only on Ship Carriages. I would suggest to you the advantage of having vast quantity of chain & barr shott & other Contrivances to cut Rigging especially at the Forts in the Highlands. We have Contracted with a man to cast 18, 24, & 32 pounders, he has succeeded so well in long 18 pounders that we hope he will answer our desires in the rest.

Yrs &c,   RTP

FC (MHi).

Joseph Hewes to Samuel Johnston

Dear Sir   Philadelphia 28th July 1776

Since my last by Mr. Wyatt I have seen Mr Gibson and should have paid him but looking over the Account I found you had not mentioned what currency it was, and as Mr. Gibsons Books are in the Country where his Family resides the matter is suspended till he examines the Acct. with his Books. I wish you had said whether it is Proc. or currency of this Province.

Much of our time is taken up in forming and debating a Confederation for the united States, what we shall make of it God only knows, I am inclined to think we shall never modell it so as to be agreed to by all the Colonies. A plan for foreign Alliances is also formed and I expect will be the subject of much debate before it is agreed to. These two Capital points ought to have been setled before our declaration of Independance went forth to the world, this was my opinion long ago and every days experience serves to confirm me in that opinion. I think it probable that we may Split on these great points. If so our mighty Colossus falls to pieces when (as our old friend Mr Gordon used to say) we shall be in a whimsical Situation.

I have enclosed to R Smith a news paper which contains a state of what passed at the interview between Genl. Washington and the Adjutant General of Howes Army. We have no news from any quarter.

I am with best Compliments to your family, Dear Sir, Your mo. Obed Serv,   Joseph Hewes

RC (NN).

John Adams to Abigail Adams

Philadelphia July 29. 1776

How are you all this Morning? Sick, weak, faint, in Pain; or pretty well recovered? By this Time, you are well acquainted with the Small Pox. Pray how do you like it?

We have no News. It is very hard that half a dozen or half a Score Armies cant supply Us, with News. We have a Famine, a perfect Dearth of this necessary Article.

I am at this present Writing perplexed and plagued with two knotty Problems in Politicks. You love to pick a political Bone, so I will even throw it to you.

If a Confederation should take Place, one great Question is how We shall vote. Whether each Colony shall count one? or whether each shall have a Weight in Proportion to its Numbers, or Wealth, or Exports and Imports, or a compound Ratio of all? [1]

Another is whether Congress shall have Authority to limit the Dimensions of each Colony, to prevent those which claim, by Charter, or Proclamation, or Commission to the South Sea, from growing too great and powerfull, so as to be dangerous to the rest. [2]

Shall I write you a Sheet upon each of these Questions. When you are well enough to read, and I can find Leisure enough to write, perhaps I may.

Gerry carried with him a Cannister for you. But he is an old Batchelor, and what is worse a Politician, and what is worse still a kind of Soldier, so that I suppose he will have so much Curiosity to see Armies and Fortifications and Assemblies, that you will loose many a fine Breakfast at a Time when you want them most.

Tell Betcy that this same Gerry is such another, as herself, Sex excepted. How is my Brother and Friend Cranch. How is his other Self, and their little Selves. And ours. Dont be in the Dumps, above all Things. I am hard put to it, to keep out of them, when I look at home. But I will be gay, if I can.

Adieu.

RC (MHi). Adams, *Family Correspondence* (Butterfield), 2:68–69.

[1] For some of the discussion in Congress on the question of voting rights in Congress, see Adams' Notes of Debates, July 30 and August 1, 1776.

[2] Some of the debates over the territorial claims and limits of the provinces are recorded in Adams' Notes of Debates, July 25 and August 2, 1776.

Josiah Bartlett to John Langdon

My Friend   Philadelphia July 29 1776

Yours of the 15th inst is now before me and with you I lament the selfish disposition that is but too prevalent among almost all orders and degrees of men. Even the Senate and Army are not entirely free; however we must not expect perfection in human nature but must endeavor to correct it in ourselves and to point it out and oppose it in others. The retreat of our army to Ticonderoga has no doubt alarmed the western parts of our *State*. Though I think there will be no great danger at present as there is a very powerful army there who are now getting well of the small pox and will be soon ready for action besides the numerous militia who are marching to join that army. Our friend General Sullivan is disgusted at the appointment of General Gates to be a Major General and being sent to the Northern Army; by permission of the Generals Schuyler and Washington he (G. Sullivan) has left the army and is now here and has petitioned Congress for leave to resign his Commission. What will be done in the case, I cant say but hope it will be settled without his dismission.[1]

Brother Whipple is here yet and will not set out for home till the confederation is settled which may possibly take a week or ten day's time as there is a great deal of other business to be done in the mean time and the Sentiments of the members of Congress very different on many of the articles. I should be glad he might hear the whole of the debates here and be present in our Colony when it is laid before our Legislature for their concurrence to answer any questions and remarks that may be made upon it. It is a matter of the greatest importance, but the interests and opinions of the several members are so various that I see it will not be settled agreeable to my mind.

It is a very still time as to news here; the fleet and armies at New York and Staten Island remain in *statu quo*—the army in the Jersies is encreasing very fast, so that there will soon be a powerful body of men there.

July 31st. I can now inform you that the affair with General Sullivan is settled and he is to return to New York to be employed by General Washington in that department; so hope you will not make many words about it.[2]

I am Sir, your friend and most obedient humble servant,

Josiah Bartlett

P.S. By the enclosed you will see the Resolves passed by Congress and sent to General Howe and Burgoyne in consequence of the affair at the Cedars.[3] By letters yesterday from Virginia we are informed that Dunnmore with his fleet are gone up Potomack River, has burnt some houses near the shores and has endeavored to burn more but was hindered—that the Virginians had taken a tender with one of the most infamous Tories in the Province on board—the number of men and guns I have forgot. They have also taken a vessel from Dunmore with linens &c said to be worth 20,000 pounds sterling.

Tr (DLC).
   [1] See John Hancock to George Washington, July 26, 1776, note 3.
   [2] An entry in the journals noting the reception of a July 29 letter from John Sullivan "desiring to recall his petition for leave to resign his commission" was crossed out. *JCC*, 5:613. See also John Hancock to George Washington, July 31, 1776.
   [3] Undoubtedly the published report of the committee of Congress "to whom the cartel, between Brigadier General Arnold and Captain Foster, with the several papers thereto relating, were recommitted." *JCC*, 5:533–39, 601.

Charles Carroll of Carrollton to Charles Carroll, Sr.

Dr. Papa,   29th July 1776.

I have recd. yr. letters of the 21 & 25th instant. I have ansd. already yr. queres respecting the Canada army in my former letters. Burgoyne will not be able for want of a naval force to cross the lake till towards the latter end of August or middle of Sept. In short time I hope we shall have our army on that frontier recruited & well provided, a naval force on lake Champlain sufficient to check, if not defeat, the enemy. The sick are removed to fort George on Lake George as I wrote you before. Washington has only 15 thousand—under Mercer are 3 thousand: but as the harvest is over the Militia will pour in fast. If our troops arrive slowly, the enemy's arrive still slower. I much question their having 16 thousand men at Staten Island before the last of next month or middle of Septr. The 1st division of Ld. Howe's reinforcements or part of that division I fancy is arrived at N. Y. as Washington writes. A report prevailed that 8 vessels were seen in the offing. These vessels must have had

12 or 13 weeks passage & consequently the troops must have suffered much.

The information D.C.[1] gave you about gentlemen being sent to France on the day Independence was declared is not true: at least I have heared nothing of it.

I now answer yours of the 25th. I had bought the Phamphlet you wrote for before I recd. your letter. I shall bring it with me—it is very sensible & well written. I am exceedingly sorry for Mr. Wm. Brent's loss: never was a war between civilized nations carried on in so destructive a manner.

I desire my love to Molly, Mrs. Darnall & little Poll. I understand the Hammonds are making interest agt. me because I voted agt. instructions which I deemed to be dishonest, & which I was convinced were not agreeable to the sense of a Majority of my Constituents unless I could suppose *that* Majority dishonest.[2] They were rather the instructions of the Hammonds & [a] few who were surprised into them without reflecting on the private injustice of them & public pernicious tendency. Had the resolve passed the Convention for stopping public interest (which was one of the instructions) it would have subverted public credit & struck at our paper money. This is too obvious to insist on. I voted for a more reasonable resolve relating to private interest, which you will find in the votes & proceedings.

I hear the Barrister[3] will go for our county. I hope Mr Johnson is secure of a seat. Chase I know is—& I know these two men have the will & power to be useful. Nothing can be alledged agt. Paca, he has of late attended diligently the Congress. I hope he will be chosen also. As to myself, if they can find a better Representative, they have my free consent to chuse him. I shall never court popular favour but always endeavour to deserve it.

Every thing remains quiet at N. Y. We recd. a letter this day from Washington dated 27th. The enemy's Ships, which passed N. York have not yet attempted to go thro' the high lands: they have committed some depredations.

If the enemy should not soon receive a large reinforcement, & our militia should come in fast now the harvest is over, I am inclined to think an attempt will be made to dislodge the enemy from Staten Island. The silly declaration of Ld. Howe has, or will soon unite all parties, & make all Americans Independents. I shall not close this letter till tomorrow after the arrival of the N. York which will be about 11 o'clock.

11 o'clock in Congress

The post is not yet come: a letter from Gen. Mercer, who commands the flying camp at Amboy, dated the 28th instant was read just now, it contains nothing new, from whence I presume the enemy remains quiet on Staten Island. Colo. Smallwood's battalion is stationed at Elizabethtown.

I have seen the Pena. Convention's determination respecting religious toleration: they have established it on the broadest basis & admit all persons into offices of trust & profit taking a civil test or oath of fidelity to the govt. I have desired Mr. Mead to buy the Hackles & pipes ordered in your last & an umbrella for Molly which I shall bring with me. Wishing you health & a long continuance of it I remain, Yr. most affectionate Son,

Ch. Carroll of Carrollton

P.S. Give my complts to all friends.

RC (MdHi).
   [1] Probably Daniel Carroll.
   [2] For discussions of the political activities of Matthias and Rezin Hammond against the Carroll party in Maryland during the elections for deputies to the Maryland Convention that convened at Annapolis on August 15 to create a new state government, see Ronald Hoffman, *A Spirit of Dissension: Economics, Politics, and the Revolution in Maryland* (Baltimore: Johns Hopkins University Press, 1973), pp. 170–77; and David C. Skaggs, *Roots of Maryland Democracy, 1753–1776* (Westport, Conn.: Greenwood Press, Inc., 1973), pp. 187–90.
   [3] Charles Carroll, Barrister, who was one of the four delegates to the Maryland Convention elected from Anne Arundel County on August 1.

John Hancock to George Washington

Sir   Philada. July 29th. 1776
   I have been honour'd with your favrs. of 22d, 25th & 27th Inst.[1] I hope by to morrow's Post to Transmitt you Answers to the whole of your Letters which are yet unanswer'd. The exceeding warm Season, & the constant Attention of Congress to Business the last week, induc'd Congress to Adjourn from Friday Eveng. to this morning. I shall directly lay yr Letters before them, & request their immediate Attention to them.

   Congress having Indulg'd me to make a Demand of Money from Mr Brimer who I Judge to be with Mr Howe on Staten Island, I have Sent the Bill to Mr Palfrey & desir'd him to apply to you, & I Request you will please to suffer him to Conduct this matter for me.[2]

   I have the honor to be with much Esteem, Sir, Your very huml servt,   John Hancock Presidt

RC (DLC).
   [1] These letters are in PCC, item 152, 2:265–68, 271–74, 297–300, and Washington, *Writings* (Fitzpatrick), 5:320–25, 337–38, 342–44.
   [2] There is no mention of this matter in the journals. In regard to it, however, Hancock wrote the following letter to Paymaster General William Palfrey on this date:

"I have only time to tell you that Congress have indulg'd me in makg a Demand of the Money for the Inclos'd Bill, do Conduct it for me, apply to the Genl., I have wrote him. If you get the Money Transmit the hard Cash here as it is wanted here.

"Do the best you can, I have paid all your Bills.

"Remember me to all friends. I am, Yours sincerely, John Hancock." William Palfrey Papers, MH.

This letter bears the following endorsement: "From the Honble John Hancock, inclosing Bill of Exchange on Brymer July 29. 1776. The Bill was return'd to Mr Hancock Jany 177[8?]." See also Washington, *Writings* (Fitzpatrick), 5:353.

Thomas Jefferson to Richard Henry Lee

Dear Sir   Philadelphia July 29. 1776.

I inclose you Dr. Price's pamphlet.[1] I should have done so sooner but understood your brother was sending many to Virginia and not doubting one would be to you, I laid by the one I had purchased for that purpose. Little new here. Our camps recruit slowly, amazing slowly. God knows in what it will end. The finger of providence has as yet saved us by retarding the arrival of Ld. Howe's recruits. Our army from Canada is now at Tyonderoga, but in a shattered condition. General Sullivan left it and came here to resign on Gates's appointment. His letter of resignation was put in on Friday. It was referred to this morning that a proper rap of the knuckles might be prepared, but on the advice of his friends he asked leave to withdraw it and repair to his duty.[2] The minutiae of the Confederation have hitherto engaged us; the great points of representation, boundaries, taxation &c. being left open. For god's sake, for your country's sake, and for my sake, come. I receive by every post such accounts of the state of Mrs. Jefferson's health, that it will be impossible for me to disappoint her expectation of seeing me at the time I have promised, which supposed my leaving this place on the 11th of next month. The plan of ——— is yet untouched. After being read it was privately printed for the consideration of the members and will come on when we shall have got through the Confederation.[3] I am Dr. Sir,

[*P.S.*] I pray you to come. I am under a sacred obligation to go home.

RC (ViHi). Jefferson, *Papers* (Boyd), 1:477–78.

[1] For Richard Henry Lee's letter of July 21, in which he requested a copy of Richard Price's *Observations on the Nature of Civil Liberty*, see Jefferson, *Papers* (Boyd), 1:471.

[2] For a resolution on the Sullivan case, which Jefferson drafted but never presented to Congress, see ibid., 1:478–79. See also John Hancock's letters to George Washington of July 26 and 31, 1776.

[3] A plan of foreign treaties, which had been reported on July 18, was not taken up in Congress until August 22. See *JCC*, 5:575–89, 696, 709–10, 718.

Charles Thomson to John Dickinson

Dear Sir,   Summerville July 29. 1776

I had not time to write, when the news arrived of our success at Charlestown; but I took care to have forwarded to you some letters that came by the express, which I imagined gave you a circumstantial account of the matter. Is it not amazing that in so furious & long a cannonading our loss was so small. Surely there is a God, who judges of the righteousness of our cause & covers our heads in the day of battle, and I hope He will cover yours & protect you in the day of danger & restore you to your friends who love and esteem you; though the tide of popularity is just now in the ebb. But of this you have, in the course of your life, experienced several ebbs & flows, & therefore I trust there is no occasion to remind you of Horace's advice "Aquam memento rebus in arduis servare mentum."

How do you bear the fatigues of a camp? Is your health confirmed? Are your men in good spirits? Are they reconciled to discipline and subordination? Are your sentries vigilant, your guards prompt, & your army alert & ready "with hearts resolved and hands prepared, the blessings they enjoy to guard."

I received your note concerning Colonel Miles, and spoke to our Cumberland friend,[1] that he might bring it on, but to my surprize I found him resolved to oppose it, at least till a friend of his was promoted. I therefore left him without pressing him & applied to Mr Morris, who had before moved in Col M's behalf. He took your note & promised he would prepare the members & embrace the first opportunity of bringing it on. The New Hampshire brigadier came to town on Thursday.[2] He has left the army in disgust, thinking his honour hurt by the promotion of Gates: And on Friday applied for leave to resign. I fancy it will be granted not much to his satisfaction. What shall we say of this phantom *honour,* the soldier's deity & object of worship. I would not have a soldier devoid of it: But I think it a plant better suited for the gardens of monarchy; than those of a republic. Our minds are too much depraved with monarchical principles. For my part I am inclined to think it a weed, and am therefore ready to order it to be thrown over the fence, provided I could have enough of amor patria to plant in its stead.

What a rambling letter is this you will say. The reason is because I have nothing particular to write about. However I can make up for the want of a subject by telling you what will give you more pleasure than any thing else. I can inform you, that Mrs. D & Sally are well. They were here yesterday with Aunt Betty. The wars between the Houses of Summerville & Duchess Hall deprive me of the pleasure of seeing them as often as I wish.

I should have informed you before that the general transmitted to Congress some letters which were sent by a flag to Amboy.[3] The public letters to the late governors were sent under a flying seal, inclosing a proclamation. These you must have seen as they were published. Along with them came a number of private letters, some directed to members of Congress, others for gentlemen of the town. It was agreed that the letters of the former should be delivered in Congress, & that the latter should be opened. They were all written with a view to be seen & examined by his Lordship or his secretary & therefore you may easily judge of their contents. One from Doctr. F. of London to yr f[rien]d Jas. P——n,[4] after launching out in praises of his Lordship's good disposition &c, desires J.P. to go to him & "boldy demand protection for himself & all *honest* men." They have been all sent to the persons to whom directed; except one for yourself which could not be sent nor opened agreeable to the order taken. Your friends pressed to have it opened as you could not attend, & they were sure it contained nothing you would wish to conceal. I could just observe that the members who had letters, after opening them, delivered them at the table & desired they might be read which was done. I think it would be proper to write a line to the president who has yours directing it to be opened & sent to you.[5] Your friends at Summerville desire to be remembered to you. If their prayers & good wishes will be of any avail I believe you will experience the good effects, for they are fervent for you.

I shall leave this open till I go to town, that I may add to it if there is any thing new.

I do not find there is any thing new. Mr Flower's commission will be sent by to morrow's post.

I am, your affectionate, Chas Thomson

RC (PPL).
[1] James Wilson.
[2] A reference to Gen. John Sullivan. A few days later Thomson wrote a brief note to Dickinson, primarily to explain that his letter of July 29 might have "miscarried" because it had not been properly addressed, in which he added the following information on Sullivan. "I mentioned to you that brigr. S. had applied for leave to resign. But upon finding there was a possibility of obtaining that favour, like a good Aberdeen's man, he took back his words again and matters remain in statu quo." Thomson to Dickinson, August 2, 1776, Robert R. Logan Collection, PHi.
[3] The letters sent ashore by Lord Howe on July 13, the day after he arrived at Staten Island.
[4] Probably a letter from Dr. John Fothergill to James Pemberton.
[5] In his response to Thomson of August 7, Dickinson explained as follows: "I wrote above a week ago to Mr. Hancock, desiring Congress to open my English Letter, and to send it to Me. I also enclos'd two Letters, one for Genl. Lee & another for Mr. John Rutledge. I have never recd. a Line from Mr. Hancock since. Do '*flap*' him. I wrote also to Mr. Robt. Morris on some public affairs. Pray jog him." Charles Thomson Papers, DLC.

Dickinson's letter to Hancock nevertheless apparently failed to elicit a response, because on September 5 he drafted another on the same subject. "I understand that the Congress about two months ago directed my English Letter to be sent to Me. If You have not any farther occasion for it, I should be glad to receive it; If You have, You are wellcome to take a Copy, and to keep that or the Original, if such is your Pleasure." Dickinson to John Hancock, September 5, 1776, Robert R. Logan Collection, PHi.

William Whipple to Joshua Brackett

My Dear Sir,   Philadelphia, 29th July, 1776.
It gives me pleasure to find that any part of my conduct meets your approbation. While I act in a public character, I shall ever consider myself so far a servant of the public as to obey whatever instructions I may receive from my constituents, provided they do not militate with the dictates of my own conscience. If they should, it would then be my duty to resign. Our General Court, no doubt, makes some wild steerage; and, considering all circumstances, it is not to be wondered at. However, if the virtuous few will exercise patience and perseverance, I make no doubt we shall have matters settled on the true principles of liberty. Perhaps it may take some time to do this great work. I call it a great work; for, in my opinion, it is more difficult to reduce a society of men, who have drunk deep of waters of corruption, to the true principles of virtue, than to bring a society from the state of nature to the same meridian. Prudence and moderation, with a proper spirit, seasonably applied, will do great things; and, notwithstanding all the difficulties that now appear, I hope to see New Hampshire, in a few years, one of the happiest branches of the Great Republic. But this business can't be completed without some exertions; and it is the duty of every one to exert himself on this occasion. Every private consideration ought to give place to the public good. It would certainly give me more pleasure to hear that my great-grandfather had been instrumental in establishing a form of government that would entail happiness on future generations, than to hear he had left a great estate. But as I know you are nearly of my opinion on these matters, and as I have not time to enlarge, must bid you adieu.
                                                     W. Whipple.

[P.S.] I intend to set out about the 10th of next month.[1] Must refer you to the papers for news.

MS not found; reprinted from *Proceedings of the Massachusetts Historical Society* 5 (April 1860): 6.
   [1] Whipple left Philadelphia on August 12, 1776. See Josiah Bartlett to John Langdon, August 11, 1776.

William Whipple to Joseph Whipple

My Dear Brother   Philadelphia 29th July 1776
   I receiv'd Yours of the 3d inst. Am really in pain for you; Tho I
do not think there is any immediate danger it must give you great
anxiety to see the country above you deserted by its inhabitants. I
hope some Methods will be taken to quiet their minds. A few
Companies properly station'd wod effectually secure you against any
small parties of Indian that may be sent to our Frontiers & there is
no danger of any large bodies marching thro' that Country, as the
army must have more important objects in view. I find the enemies
army has increas'd amazingly in immagination. There certainly was
no more than 4 thousand sail'd with Burgoyne & the same number
to follow him, no advice of the latters having left England. We have
no certain accots. of the strength of the Enemy in Canada but by
the best information have not the least reason to think they have
more than five thousand, or at the extent six. Our army has suffer'd
extreamly by the Small pox. They are now at Tyconderoga & not
more than 3000 strong more than half being sick. However they are
now geting better, but the most we can expect this Campaign is to
prevent the Enemy from geting possession of the Lakes which I hope
we shall effect. I do most Heartily Lament the repeted & unaccountable Misfortunes, our army have meet with in Canada. I wish
we may be able to get at the Bottom of them, a full investigation of
the Causes will enable us in some measure to avoid the like in
future.[1] Our army at York are about 20,000 in high Spirits & the
Flying Camp now Station'd in New Jersey consists of about 15,000
to be augmented 5,000. They (the Enemy) have not Yet begun their
Operations, but I hope it won't be long before our army will give a
good accot. of them. Its uncertain as to their numbers but its
suppos'd not more than 8 or 10 thousand Land Forces but more
expected. Genl Lee has been successful in repulsing the Enemy at
South Carolina. In Verginia we have also succeeded against Lord
Dunmore so far as to drive him from his entrenchments & oblige
him to embark since which he has not been able to land. If we can
keep him on board his vessels, disease will do his business as effec-
tualy as the Sword. The People in this Country are in high Spirits.
Gentn. of the first Fortunes take up their Musketts and March. No
late accots from abroad; its probable our Letters have fallen into
the hands of the Enemy. I agree with you that we are too late in all
our movements. [How]ever these delays answer one good purpose,
they certainly tend to produce unanimity, which is a desireable
object in perfecting the Revolution. Congress were unanimous in the
Declaration of independency which wod not have been three weeks
sooner. Things go on much smoother now, then before that important Question was determin'd. I think to set out for home about

the 10th next month & wish may be able to carry some agreeable news with me. Perhaps I may be passing through York at the time of action. I shod like it exceedingly, Provided our arms are successfull but I must confess it wod be no very agreeable sight otherwise, not that I shod have the least objection to take my Chance. I do most heartily wish I had gone into the Army the last Campaign, in that case by this time I might have been a tolerable Soldier.

Your apprehentions of Britains forming an alliance with France, I hope is without foundation, the latter knows her own interest too well, it wod be vastly more for her intrest to have a Commercial alliance with the American States which I flatter myself will take place e'er long. There is great reason to believe France will Commence Hostilities against Britain very soon perhaps before the commencement of another year. If so there will be no danger from that Quarter. In short I am under no apprehentions but America will support her Independency & an alliance with her will most certainly be a desirable object to every state in Europe who have any connections in America. If we have Wisdom & Vertue Enough to regulate our internal Police we may be a happy People. Its our own faults if we [are] not the happiest People on Earth. If I live to see that happy day I shall arrive to the Summit of all my wishes. By the length of this letter you wod not suppose me in a hurry but I am so much hurried that I cannot read what I have wrote, must therefore beg you'll correct any inaccuracies. Your very Affect. Bror,

W. Whipple

RC (MH).
[1] Whipple was a member of the committee "to enquire into the causes of the miscarriages in Canada." Its reports were discussed in Congress over the course of several weeks and produced sundry related resolutions, but apparently no final report was adopted. *JCC*, 5:592, 617–21, 623, 629, 633, 644–45, 741, 852–53. Whipple may have taken extensive notes during the committee's investigation, as did Thomas Jefferson and Robert Treat Paine, but only his notes for July 30, when the committee apparently questioned New Hampshire's Gen. John Sullivan, who had arrived in Philadelphia on July 25, have been found. Whipple probably considered these notes a part of the committee's papers and turned them over to Secretary Thomson. They are somewhat misplaced among various "miscellaneous papers" in PCC, item 58, fols. 383–86. See also John Hancock to George Washington, June 21, 1776, note 1.

John Witherspoon to David Witherspoon

Dr David [1]   Philadelphia July 29. 1776
Though I wrote You by a Waggon at some Length lately by which I sent Mr Smith a good Many Books & Sundry News papers &

pamphlets I embrace this opportunity of Mr Mayo to write you again. Remember what I told You long ago about black Lines for writing Your Letters. The Lines of them are often very irregular. Be accurate in whatever you do. It gives me great pleasure to hear from every quarter that the School is increasing & I hope to hear that You are exerting Yourself for your own Improvement & to be useful in your station. You will hear that our Northern Army have retreated as far as Ticonderoga. I had a Letter from Your Brother James lately in which he tells me he & Mr Whitelaw with another went over through the Woods for Intelligence & when they came to St. Johns found it in the Enemys hands, were in great Danger of being taken & obliged to return through the Woods with but one Bisket a piece to maintain them for two or three Days. The People in Rygate have left the Town & come to Newberry where they are making a fort to protect their Women & Children from the Indians. Mr. Mayo will no doubt tell you all the news of this Country so that I shall not need to repeat them. Our College is broke up for 3 Weeks.

Pray write me as often as You please by the post for I dont think the Letters are often broken open now & be particular as to Your own Situation & what Studies You are applying to. Improve & perfect Your French which you may easily do now. Your Brother John is at New York in the general Hospital & well pleased with his Situation. I have not been at Princeton these 10 Days, but our friends there are well. Fanny & I Still propose a Journey to You in October though as to our choice must be some uncertainty on Acct of the Congress. I will now Send You a Copy or two of my Sermon Complete & could send a good Many for sale if Mr Mayo could carry them along.[2] I will advise him also to take News papers for Your Entertainment.

As the Distance between us is so great I must not omit my dear Child to put You in Mind to walk with fear of God. Give Your Self much to the Exercise of Prayer & if you desire to improve & persevere in that Duty You must be punctual as to the times of it. Irregular people do nothing to purpose either in that or any other Respect.

I am Dr David, Your affec Father,   Jno Witherspoon

FC (NjHi).

[1] David Witherspoon (1760–1801), Witherspoon's second youngest living son, was currently a teacher at Hampden-Sidney Academy in Virginia. In 1777 he became lieutenant of a company of Hampden-Sidney student volunteers and in 1780 secretary to Samuel Huntington, then president of Congress. Varnum Lansing Collins, *President Witherspoon: A Biography*, 2 vols. (Princeton: Princeton University Press, 1925), 1:25n.19, 193n.37.

[2] John Witherspoon, *The Dominion of Providence over the Passions of Man. A Sermon Preached at Princeton on the 17th of May 1776. Being the General Fast Appointed by the Congress Through the United Colonies* (Philadelphia: R. Aitken, 1776).

John Adams' Notes of Debate

July 30. 1776.

Dr. Franklin. Let the smaller Colonies give equal Money and Men, and then have an equal Vote. But if they have an equal Vote, without bearing equal Burthens, a Confederation upon such iniquitous Principles, will never last long.[1]

Dr. Witherspoon. We all agree that there must and shall be a Confederation, for this War. It will diminish the Glory of our Object, and depreciate our Hope. It will damp the Ardor of the People. The greatest danger We have is of Disunion among ourselves. Is it not plausible, that the small States will be oppressed by the great ones. The Spartans and Helotes—the Romans and their Dependents.

Every Colony is a distinct Person. States of Holland.[2]

Clark. We must apply for Pardons, if We dont confederate. . . .[3]

Wilson. . . . We should settle upon some Plan of Representation.[4]

Chase. Moves that the Word, White, should be inserted in the 11. Article. The Negroes are wealth. Numbers are not a certain Rule of wealth. It is the best Rule We can lay down. Negroes a Species of Property—personal Estate. If Negroes are taken into the Computation of Numbers, to ascertain Wealth, they ought to be in settling the Representation. The Massachusetts Fisheries, and Navigation ought to be taken into Consideration. The young and old Negroes are a Burthen to their owners. The Eastern Colonies have a great Advantage, in Trade. This will give them a Superiority. We shall be governed by our Interests, and ought to be. If I am satisfied, in the Rule of levying and appropriating Money, I am willing the small Colonies may have a Vote.

Wilson. If the War continues 2 Years, each Soul will have 40 dollars to pay of the public debt. It will be the greatest Encouragement to continue Slave keeping, and to increase them, that can be to exempt them from the Numbers which are to vote and pay. . . . Slaves are Taxables in the Southern Colonies. It will be partial and unequal. Some Colonies have as many black as white. . . . These will not pay more than half what they ought. Slaves prevent freemen cultivating a Country. It is attended with many Inconveniences.

Lynch. If it is debated, whether their Slaves are their Property, there is an End of the Confederation. Our Slaves being our Property, why should they be taxed more than the Land, Sheep, Cattle, Horses, &c. Freemen cannot be got, to work in our Colonies. It is not in the Ability, or Inclination of freemen to do the Work that the Negroes do. Carolina has taxed their Negroes. So have other Colonies, their Lands.

Dr. Franklin. Slaves rather weaken than strengthen the State, and there is therefore some difference between them and Sheep. Sheep will never make any Insurrections.

Rutledge. . . . I shall be happy to get rid of the idea of Slavery. The Slaves do not signify Property. The old and young cannot work. The Property of some Colonies are to be taxed, in others not. The Eastern Colonies will become the Carriers for the Southern. They will obtain Wealth for which they will not be taxed.

MS (MHi). Adams, *Diary* (Butterfield), 2:245–46.

¹ Article 17, giving each state one vote in Congress, was the subject under consideration in this day's debates on the articles of confederation in the committee of the whole.

² See Josiah Bartlett's Notes on a Plan of Confederation, June 12–July 12, 1776, for references to representation in the Dutch Republic. See also John Witherspoon's Speech in Congress, this date.

³ Suspension points in MS, here and below.

⁴ A blank in MS indicates a shift in the discussion to article 11, governing proportional contributions to the support of a federal government. *JCC*, 5:548.

John Adams to Abigail Adams

Philadelphia July 30. 1776 Tuesday

This is one of my fortunate days. The Post brought me, a Letter from you and another from my Friend and Brother.[1]

The particular Account you give me of the Condition of each of the Children is very obliging. I hope the next Post will inform me, that you are all, in a fine Way of Recovery. You say I must tell you of my Health and Situation. As to the latter, my Situation is as far removed from Danger, I suppose, as yours. I never had an Idea of Danger here, nor a single Sensation of Fear. Delaware River is so well fortified with Gallies, fixed and floating Batteries, Chevaux de Frizes, Ships of War, Fire Ships, and Fire Rafts, that I have no Suspicions of an Enemy from Sea, although vast Numbers of People have removed out of this City, into the Country, for fear of one.

By Land, an Enemy must march an hundred Miles, to get here, and they must pass through Woods, Difiles, and Morasses, besides crossing Rivers, which would take them a long time to accomplish, if We had not a single Man to oppose them. But we have a powerfull Army at New York, and New Jersey, watching their Motions, who will give Us a good Account of their Motions, I presume, whenever they shall think fit to stir. My Health has lasted longer than I expected, but with Intermissions of Disorder as usual, and at

length, I fear, is departing. Increase of Heat in the Weather, and of
Perplexity in Business, if that is possible, have become too much for
me. These Circumstances, added to my Concern, for those other
Parts of myself in Boston, would certainly have carried me there before now, if I could have got there: But I have no servant, nor
Horse. I am now determined to go home: but the precise Time, I
cannot fix. I know not how to go. I have been deliberating whether
to go by the stage to New York, and trust to the Chapter of Accidents to get from thence to Boston; or whether to hire, or purchase
an Horse here, or whether to get along some other Way, with Coll.
Whipple, or Mr. S. Adams. But am still undetermined. If I knew
that Bass was at Leisure, and if I knew where you could get Horses,
I should request you to send him here, to bring me home. But I
dont know what to say. If he should come, he must keep a good look
out, and make a strict Enquiry all along the Road, for me, least he
should miss me, least I should pass by him on my Way home. After
all, I cannot reconcile myself to the Thoughts of staying here so
long as will be necessary for a servant and Horses to come for me. I
must get along as well as I can by the Stage or by procuring a Horse
here.

The Conspiracy, at New York, betrayed the Ignorance, Folly,
Timidity and Impotence of the Conspirators, at the same Time,
that it disclosed the Turpitude of their Hearts. They had no Plan.
They corrupted one another, and engaged to Act, when the Plan
should be formed. This they left for an After Consideration. The
Tory Interest in America, is extreamly feeble.

Your Successes by Sea, give me great Pleasure, and so did the
heartfelt Rejoicings at the Proclamation of Freedom. Mr. Bowdoins
Sentiment did him Honour.

Adieu.

RC (MHi). Adams, *Family Correspondence* (Butterfield), 2:70–72.
    [1] Abigail's letter of July 21 and Richard Cranch's of July 22 are in Adams, *Family
Correspondence* (Butterfield), 2:55–58.

Samuel Chase to Richard Henry Lee

My Dear Sir,   Philadelphia July 30th. 1776
    Your Letter of the 14 Inst. followed Me to this City, and your
other favour of the 21st was delivered by yesterdays Post.

I hurried to Congress to give my little assistance to the framing a
Confederacy and a plan for a foreign alliance, both of them Subjects of the utmost Importance, and which in my Judgment demand immediate Dispatch. The Confederacy has engaged our close

Attention for a Week. Three great Difficulties occur. Representation, The Mode of Voting, and the Claims to the South Sea. The whole might in my opinion be settled if Candor, Justice and the real Interests of America were attended to. We do not all see the Importance nay the Necessity of a Confederacy. We shall remain weak, and distracted and divided in our Councils, our Strength will decrease, we shall be open to all the arts of the insidious Court of Britain, and no foreign Court will attend to our applications for Assistance, before We are confederated. What Contract will a foreign State make with Us, when We cannot agree among Ourselves?

Our Army at Tionderoga consists of 6,000 of which 3,000 are in the Hospital from the Small Pox and other Camp Disorders. Our Army at N York contains 14,000, of which only 10,000 are effective. Our Flying Camp in the Jerseys has but between 3 & 4000 Troops.

No News from Gen. Washington. He writes 27th that 8 Sail, supposed to be part of Lord Howes fleet, arrived at the Hook that Day.

I shall always be glad to hear from you, and am with great Esteem, Your Affectionate Friend, And Obedt. Servant,

Saml. Chase

RC (PPAmP).

Samuel Chase to the Maryland Council of Safety

Gentlemen, Philadelphia July 30th. 1776

I this Moment received the enclosed Letter from Colonel Stricker, and send it to you for your orders to him.[1]

If you think proper to grant him the Liberty of enlisting into the German Battalion from the Companies raising for the flying Camp, it might promote the Service, as the former are enlisted for three Years, & the latter only 'till December. I am sensible Difficulties will occur.

Arms and blankets are as necessary as Men, but an Account should be transmitted to your Board.

Unless you give orders as to the Quantity and Mode of Subsistance, I am afraid great Extravagance will happen.

No News from New York except that 8 Sail, supposed part of Lord Howes fleet, arrived at the Hook the 27th.

I am, Gentlemen, with Respect, Your obedt. Servt.

Saml. Chase

RC (MdAA).
[1] Lt. Col. George Stricker's July 25 letter to Chase is in *Md. Archives*, 12:116.

Committee of Secret Correspondence
to John Bradford

Sir: Philadelphia, July 30, 1776
   We take the liberty to enclose herewith some dispatches for
Messrs Samuel and J.H. Delap, merchants in Bordeaux, which you
will please deliver into Captain Cleveland's own hands, with a strict
charge to take the utmost care of them, and follow the orders also
enclosed herein, directed to him, which you will please deliver, and
enjoin his punctual obedience on which will depend his future
employment and advancement in the public service.
   Mr. Morris informs us of the alacrity with which you have executed his commissions in the purchase of the brigantine Dispatch;
and if anything further of this kind offers, the Committee will
claim the liberty of troubling you again, being very respectfully,
Sir, Your obedt servts,

                                          Benjamin Franklin
                                          Benjamin Harrison
                                          Robert Morris

P.S. You will oblige me by putting up a Collection of the Public
News Papers directed to Messers Samuel & J.H. Delap, Merchants
in Bordeaux, and send them by Captain Cleveland.[1]

Tr (CtY). Endorsed: "Mr. Morris, July 30th With Mr. Franklin's Letter." Another
Tr, at ViWC, contains the following notation: "The above postscript in the autograph of Robert Morris." An FC of this letter, in the hand of Robert Morris, is in
PCC, item 37.
   [1] See also Robert Morris to John Bradford, this date.

Committee of Secret Correspondence
to Stephen Cleveland

Sir,   Philadelphia July 30th. 1776
   We have been regularly informed by John Bradford Esqr. of his
purchasing, Loading & fitting the Brigt. Dispatch in Consequence of
our Orders,[1] and we approve of his having appointed you to the
Command of that Brigt. in the Continental Service as he gives you
an extreme good Character of which we hope & expect to find you
very deserving. The Honble Continental Congress of which we are
Members Authorized us as a Committee to purchase the Brigt. and
to order her on such Voyage as woud best answer certain purposes
to the States of America.
   You will receive this by the Hands of John Philip Merkle Esqr,[2]

and are to be governed by the following Instructions during the present Voyage or untill you receive others from Congress or from this or some other Committee of Congress. Mr Bradford will require bills of Loading from you for the entire Cargo on board the Dispatch Consigned to the above mentioned John Philip Merkle Esqr (who is to go passenger in the Brigt.) At her discharging Port in Europe, such bills of Loading you are to sign, receive Mr Merkle on bd., assist him in providing Sea Stores and then proceed with the utmost dilligence for the Coast of France avoiding most carefully all Vessells at Sea, and put into the first convenient Port you can make in that Kingdom; Nantes or Bourdeaux may perhaps be the safest, and you must there deliver to Mr. Merkle any part of the Cargo he may find it convenient to sell or the whole if he chuses it. We inclose to Mr Bradford by this Conveyance a Packet directed to Messrs. Sam. & J. H. Delap, Merchts. in Bourdeaux. Mr Bradford will deliver that Packet to you and we require your utmost Care of it, shoud you have the Misfortune to be taken you must throw it overboard slung with a weight that will sink it, for on no Account must this fall in the Hands of our Enemies. On the contrary if you get safe into Bourdeaux deliver it yourself to Messrs. Sam. & J. H. Delap, Merchts. there. If you go into any other Port forward it to them by Post or special Messenger as you may be advised is safest & best. You must also advise these Gentlemen what other ports or places Mr. Merkle intends to order you for, and desire them to write you a few lines telling you how to direct letters to Silas Deane Esqr. so that they will certainly fall into his Hands. We expect Mr Merkle will direct you to proceed from France to Amsterdam, and you must obey his Orders delivering to him the rest of the Cargo at any Port or Ports he may desire. He is not to pay any freight but will supply you with all things necessary for the Brigt. & Money to pay Charges. For all you receive in Money, Stores, Outfitt &c you'll grant him proper Receipts and when you have discharged entirely the present Cargo, you are to receive from him all such Goods, Wares, Merchandize, Arms & Ammunition as he may think proper to ship granting him bills of Loading for what he puts on board. We also give you liberty to Arm the Brigt. in the most compleat Manner with as many four Pounder Cannon, Swivells, Blunderbusses, Musquets, Cutlasses &c. as may be proper for such a Vessell. You may also ship as many good Seamen as you can conveniently accommodate obtaining them on the best Terms in your power. Lay in a suitable Stock of Provisions, a sufficient quantity of Ammunition &c, the Cost & Charges of all which Mr Merkle will defray taking your Receipts.

Whilst this business is transacting you will write immediately after your Arrival at the Port where it is to be done to Messrs. Sam. & J H Delap of Bourdeaux & also to Silas Deane Esqr. if you obtain

from them in time his Address. Tell them how to direct letters to
you and when you expect to sail, and we expect you will receive
back from them letters & Packets for us. If you do the utmost Care
must be taken of them. Dont let them be seen by any person whatever, sling them with a wt. ready for sinking and if taken be sure to
let them go overboard in time, but we hope you will have better
fortune & bring them safe.

When your Vessell is completely fitted, the Cargo on board & you
have received your dispatches from Mr Merkle, you are then to put
out to Sea and make the best of your Way back to America.

We think it best not to fix on any particular Port for you to aim
at, but leave you at liberty to push into the first safe Harbour you
can make in any of the United States of America, and on your
Arrival apply to the Continental Agent if there be one at or near
that place, if not to the Persons in Authority there, desiring their
Advice & Assistance to forward with the utmost Expedition to us all
the letters, Packets &c. you bring. You will also write us the State &
Condition of your Vessell and we shall return Orders for your further proceedings. We send you herewith a Commission, a Book of
Regulations respecting Captures &c. and a List of the Continental
Agents for your Government if you shod. take any prizes, but you
are to remember Prizes are not your Object. We wish you to make
an Expeditious & safe Voyage and for this reason desire you will
make all possible dispatch both at Sea & in Port. We expect you will
be careful of the Brigt. her Stores & Materials, allow your people
plenty of good Provisions but suffer no Waste, and be as frugal as is
consistent with true Oeconomy in your Expences & Charges. These
things duely observed will recommend you to the Governing Powers
in America, and in time your utmost ambition may be gratifyed
provided Merit leads the way to Promotion.

If any American Masters or Mates of Ships or Seamen want passages you may accommodate them free of any Charge or Expence.
Probably Mr Merkle may find it proper to make your Vessell a
French or Dutch Bottom and clear you out for the West Indies, in
such case you will do what is needful on your part to answer his
Views, and we hope you will be attentive to accommodate & please
him during this Voyage.

We are Sir, Your hble Servants,   B Franklin

                                             Benj Harrison

                                             Robt Morris

RC (PPAmP). In a clerical hand and signed by Franklin, Harrison, and Morris.
Addressed by Morris: "To Capt Stephen Cleveland, of the Brigt Dispatch."
   [1] See Robert Morris to John Bradford, May 8, 1776; and Bradford's letters to
Morris of May 30 and July 14, 1776, in Clark, *Naval Documents*, 5:304–5, 1071.
See also Robert Morris to John Bradford, this date.

The brig *Dispatch*, which Bradford had purchased and fitted out in Massachusetts, was formerly the *Little Hannah*, which Capt. John Manley had captured in December 1775. The brig *Dispatch* that sailed under Capt. Peter Parker from Philadelphia in mid-July had been captured on July 22 by H.M.S. *Orpheus* cruising off Cape Henlopen. See Committee of Secret Correspondence to Peter Parker, July 10, 1776; and Clark, *Naval Documents*, 5:267n, 1183n.

[2] See Secret Committee Minutes of Proceedings, June 27, 1776, note 1.

Committee of Secret Correspondence to Samuel and J. H. Delap

Gentn.   Philada. July 30th. 1776

We must frequently give you the trouble to receive & forward our dispatches to Silas Deane Esqr. As you will be possessed of his address, & from the Nature of his business which requires him to move from place to place we cannot, you will therefore hold us excusable and he will pay any charge that arises by postage or otherways. We send this by Capt Stephen Cleveland of the Brigt Dispatch which will put into some Port in France. If it shou'd happen to be yours he will deliver these dispatches himself; if any other he will forward them by Post or special messenger as may be thought best by those he Consults.

A Jno Philip Merkle Esqr. goes passenger and to him this Vessell & Cargo is addressed. If they call at Bordeaux we beg to recommend Mr Merkle to your attention. We have desird Capt Cleveland to inform you either in person or by letter where he is to land his Cargo, when he expects to Sail from thence, & how you can direct to him with a certainty of your letters reaching his hands. We also desired him to ask of you Mr Deanes address for as we have a good oppinion of this proving safe Conveyance we wish to hear from you & Mr Deane by Capt Cleveland who will take particular care of the letters, and you will gratify us very much by transmitting us all the Public News, News Papers, Commercial intelligence &c that you think can be any ways usefull. We are, sirs, Yours &c.

FC (DNA: PCC, item 37). In the hand of Robert Morris.

John Hancock to Thomas Cushing

Dear Sir,   Philadelphia 30th July 1776

I Rec'd your Letters by the last Post;[1] The Business of my Department increases so much that I cannot think of Continuing to Act in the Marine Committee, but before I quit it I should wish to Close my Cash Accott. & to Leave every thing as clear as possible.[1] I must therefore desire you will immediately forward me your Accott. of the Money Rec'd, & the Expenditure. I mean not now to go to Particulars, but the general State of the Accott. that I may Close the Money Concerns with the Come. & deliver the papers to my Successor in that Departmt. This I wish to have done as soon as possible, for I have Determin'd to move my Family to Boston the Beginning of September, and propose being there my self in all that month. You will order the two Frigates to be got ready for the Sea, I mean to be furnish'd with every necessary that is to be had with you. Cannon are Casting, but when we shall have a sufficiency I know not. I have Sent the Commissary General an order for the Delivery of what Provisions are necessary for the Frigates, and I shall by next Post send you the same order to Receive them of the Deputy Commissary in our Colony. I cannot furnish the Captains of the Frigates with their Commissions yet, Congress having Resolved that no Commissions issue untill the Rank of the thirteen Capts. is Settled. I intend to morrow to move in Congress that Settlement, and then will forward their Commissions & every thing relative to the Ships.

I enclose you a News paper to wch. Refer you for every thing stirring here. What are you all doing? We seldom hear any thing from our Colony, I could wish you would write some particulars of Matters with you. I Remember about Six Months ago I Requested you to send me Copies of some Letters, that is not yet done, but it's no matter now, I shall be with you in Septr. I hope.

Remember to all such as are Real Friends; Complimts. to your Family.

I am Your very hum servt,   John Hancock

[*P.S.*] No Recommendation of officers of the Marine Companies, I will have some appointed soon, you certainly forget.

RC (MHi).
   [1] Probably either Cushing's July 18 or July 22 letter to Hancock, extracts from both of which are in Clark, *Naval Documents,* 5:1123, 1178.
   [2] Hancock's failure to carry out this resolution eventually led to a stinging criticism of his work in the committee by Josiah Bartlett, who argued that the president of Congress was too busy to give proper attention to matters coming before the Marine Committee. See Josiah Bartlett to John Langdon, October 7, 1776.

John Hancock to Samuel Morris

Sir,   Philada. July 30th. 1776
   In Consequence of an Application from Genl. Mercer for six light Horse to be sent to him at the Flying Camp in New Jersey as soon as possible, I am to request by order of Congress you will

give the necessary Orders to Mr Randolph, and the Party who are engaged with him on that Service, to repair to the Flying Camp immediately. You will please to lose no Time in complying with this Requisition.[1]

I am, Sir, your most obed. & very hble Ser.   J.H. Prest.

LB (DNA: PCC, item 12A). Addressed: "Capt. Saml. Morris, Commanding the light Horse. Philada."
[1] See JCC, 5:616.

John Hancock to the North Carolina Council of Safety

Sir   Philadelphia July 30th. 1776.

The Congress having received Information from the State of South Carolina that the Cherokees had committed Hostilities against the Inhabitants thereof, and that the President of that State had thought proper to carry the war immediately into the Heart of the Enemy's Country; I am directed by the Congress to inform you of their Request that you will afford all necessary Assistance to & co-operate with the State of South-Carolina in carrying on with Vigor the intended Expedition, that Justice may be done for Injuries sustained, and Peace be established with the Savages in that Country.[1]

I have the Honour to be, sir, most respectively, your very obedt Servt.   John Hancock Presidt.

RC (Nc-Ar). Written by Edward Rutledge and signed by Hancock. Addressed: "To The President of the Council of Safety of the State of North Carolina."
[1] See JCC, 5:616–17. Hancock was under instructions from Congress to write similar letters to the governor and council of Virginia and the president of Georgia. JCC, 5:617. For a recent account of the Cherokee War of 1776, see James H. O'Donnell III, Southern Indians in the American Revolution (Knoxville: University of Tennessee Press, 1973), chap. 2.

John Hancock to George Washington

Sir,   Philadelphia July 30th. 1776

I do myself the Pleasure to enclose, at this Time, sundry Resolves of Congress, relating principally to new Appointments and Promotions in the Army.[1]

The Return of Col. Elmores Regimt. (which you will please to give Orders to join you) I now transmit, together with blank Commissions, to be filled up with the Names of such Officers as appear with their respective Companies in the Regiment.

I shall deliver Commissions agreeably to the enclosed Resolves, as soon as possible; and order the Gentlemen to repair to their respective Departments.

The Regiment raised in Connecticut under Col. Ward, you will order where-ever the Service, in your Judgement, shall require it.

I have the Honour to be, with Sentiments of the highest Esteem, Sr, your most obed. and very hble Sert.

John Hancock Presidt.

[*P.S.*] I return you the Letter for Mrs. French.[2]

Your favr. of 29th this moment came to hand.[3]

I shall Send the Blank Commissions this Eveng. by Fessenden.

Several Resolutions are pass'd in Consequence of yor. Letters, I will Send by Fessenden & not longer detain the Post.

500,000 Dolls. will be on the way to you to morrow. 60,000 also to the Flying Camp.[4]

RC (DLC). In the hand of Jacob Rush, with signature and postscript by Hancock.

[1] For these resolutions, which were passed by Congress on July 29, see *JCC*, 5:614–15. Hancock also wrote another letter to Washington this date, informing him of the appointment of "Monsr St. Martin . . . a Gentleman conversant in the Engineering Branch" as an engineer in the Continental Army with the rank of lieutenant colonel. PCC, item 12A; and *Am. Archives*, 5th ser. 1:669. Congress made this appointment on July 23. *JCC*, 5:602.

[2] For this reference to British prisoner Christopher French's letter to his wife, see Washington, *Writings* (Fitzpatrick), 5:342.

[3] This letter is in PCC, item 152, 2:309–12, and Washington, *Writings* (Fitzpatrick), 5:346–47.

[4] See *JCC*, 5:620.

Thomas Jefferson to John Page

Dear Page   Philadelphia, July 30. 1776.

On receipt of your letter we enquired into the probability of getting your seal done here.[1] We find a drawer [2] and an engraver here both of whom we have reason to believe are excellent in their way. They did great seals for Jamaica and Barbadoes both of which are said to have been well done, and a seal for the Philosophical society here which we are told is excellent. But they are expensive, and will require two months to complete it. The drawing the figures for the engraver will cost about 50 dollars, and the engraving will be still more. Nevertheless as it would be long before we could consult you and receive an answer, as we think you have no such hands, and the expence is never to be incurred a second time we shall order it to be done. I like the device of the first side of the seal much. The second I think is too much crouded, nor is the design so striking. But for god's sake what is the 'Deus nobis haec *otia* fecit.'

It puzzles every body here; if my country really enjoys that *otium*, it is singular, as every other colony seems to be hard struggling. I think it was agreed on before Dunmore's flight from Gwyn's island so that it can hardly be referred to the temporary *holiday* that has given you. This device is too aenigmatical, since if it puzzles now, it will be absolutely insoluble fifty years hence.

I would not advise that the French gentlemen should come here. We have so many of that country, and have been so much imposed on, that the Congress begins to be sore on that head. Besides there is no prospect of raising horse this way. But if you approve of the Chevalier de St. Aubin, why not appoint him yourselves, as your troops of horse are Colonial not Continental?[3]

The 8th battalion will no doubt be taken into Continental pay from the date you mention. So also will be the two written for lately to come to the Jersies. The 7th should have been moved in Congress long e'er now, but the muster roll sent us by Mr. Yates was so miserably defective that it would not have been received, and would have exposed him. We therefore desired him to send one more full, still giving it the same date, and I inclosed him a proper form. If he is diligent we may receive it by next post.[4]

The answer to your public letter we have addressed to the governor.[5]

There is nothing new here. Washington's and Mercer's camps recruit with amazing slowness. Had they been reinforced more readily something might have been attempted on Staten island. The enemy there are not more than 8, or 10,000 strong. Ld. Howe has recd. none of his fleet, unless some Highlanders (about 8, or 10 vessels) were of it. Our army at Tyonderoga is getting out of the small pox. We have about 150 carpenters I suppose got there by now. I hope they will out-build the enemy, so as to keep our force on the lake superior to theirs. There is a mystery in the dereliction of Crown-point. The general officers were unanimous in preferring Tyonderoga, and the Feild officers against it. The latter have assigned reasons in their remonstrance which appear unanswerable, yet every one acquainted with the ground pronounce the measure right without answering these reasons.

Having declined serving here the next year, I shall be with you at the first session of our assembly. I purpose to leave this place the 11th of August, having so advised Mrs. Jefferson by last post, and every letter brings me such an account of the state of her health, that it is with great pain I can stay here till then. But Braxton purposing to leave us the day after tomorrow,[6] the colony would be unrepresented were I to go. Before the 11th I hope to see Colo. Lee and Mr Wythe here, tho' the stay of the latter will I hope be short, as he must not be spared from the important department of the law. Adieu, Adieu.

Reprinted from Jefferson, *Papers* (Boyd), 1:482–84.

[1] For John Page's July 20 letter to Jefferson, see Jefferson, *Papers* (Boyd), 1:468–70.

[2] Pierre Eugène DuSimitière. For a discussion of the Virginia seal, see ibid., pp. 483–84, 510–11.

[3] On August 23 the Virginia Council approved St. Aubin's appointment as a cadet to assist in training Capt. Theodorick Bland's company of Virginia cavalry. *Journals of the Council of the State of Virginia*, ed. H. R. McIlwaine, 3 vols. (Richmond: Virginia State Library, 1931–52), 1:130.

[4] For the August 13 resolution of Congress taking the Seventh and Eighth Virginia battalions into Continental pay, see *JCC*, 5:649.

[5] Not found.

[6] The Virginia delegates' account with Willing, Morris & Co., March 16–July 26, 1776, which included a July 26 disbursement of £ 375.14.10 1/2 "to Carter Braxton Esqr. for Balla. of his acct.," is in Robert Morris Papers, DLC. Although Braxton was winding up his affairs in Philadelphia, he remained long enough to sign the engrossed copy of the Declaration of Independence on August 2.

Robert Morris to John Bradford

Sir,   Philadelphia July 30th, 1776.

You will receive this by the Hands of John Philip Merkle Esq'r whom I beg leave to Introduce to your Attention. This Gentleman is to take passage in the Brig't Dispatch, Captain Cleveland, which you have bought, fitted & loaded by my Orders.[1]

You will please to take Capt. Cleveland's bills of Loading for the entire Cargo on board the Dispatch, Consigned to the said John Philip Merkle Esq'r at her discharging Port in Europe Freight Free. One of those bills with a regular Invoice of said Cargo you'll deliver to Mr. Merkle and immediately send off the said Brig't directing the Captain to obey the Instructions he will receive from a Committee of Congress by the Hands of Mr. Merkle. This Gent'n must not pay any thing for his passage, nor shoud any other Passengers go in the Brig't unless by your desire being such persons as you can depend on their attachment to our Cause and whom you desire to oblige. The Captain no doubt will assist Mr. Merkle in supplying Sea Stores, and he must treat him with all the Respect & Attention he can. A hint from you to that Effect will no doubt have it's Force.

If the Master, Mates, & Seamen want more Money advanced them in Consequence of their long detention be pleased to comply therewith in a reasonable degree. You will no doubt be enabled to pay for this Vessel & Cargo out of the Continental Prize Money but in order to keep all Accounts regular, you'll please to transmit me an Account of the Cost & Outfit of the Brig't in one Account and draw one bill on me for the exact Amount. You'll send the Invoice with the Cost & Charges of the Cargo separate, and draw another bill on me for that exact Amount. The Money for payment of both has been ready from the Moment I gave the Orders and much Uneasiness it has given me to think you shoud suffer Inconvenience for the Want of it, we must avoid such things in future.

I know nothing of the Fish Col. Gerry spoke to you about, but as Mr. Gerry of the Congress is now gone Home and it must have been bought by his Order I presume he will do the needful therein. Pray present my Comp'ts to him and accept the same yourself as I am very truly, Sir, Your Obed't hble Servant,

Rob't Morris

Tr (ViWC). Addressed: "John Bradford Esq'r, Continental Agent for Prizes etc, Boston." Transcriber's notation: "Address in Robert Morris' autograph."
[1] See Committee of Secret Correspondence to Stephen Cleveland, this date.

North Carolina Delegates to the North Carolina Council of Safety

Dear Sir,   Philadelphia July 29 [i.e. 30] 1776[1]

This morning in Consequence of a letter from Governour Rutlege informing the Congress that the Cherokee nation had begun Hostilities, a Resolve has passed recommending to the Provinces of Virginia, North Carolina and Georgia to assist and cooperate with South Carolina in carrying on a War with all possible vigor against those savages. This however is by no means intended to alter the plan of military operations which you have begun or to draw off the Strength of our back Country to a distant part merely for the sake of acting in the same place with the South Carolinians, if the Opposition can be made as effectually in any manner devised by yourselves and from a part of your province from whence hostilities may successfully be carried into the bosom of the Cherokee Country. In fact nothing is meant but to subdue the Cherokees.

We intended to have wrote you the other day by Capt Tool but his precipitate departure prevented it. Nothing very material has occured since he left this—what before you will find by having recourse to the newspapers which by him We inclosed to your Council of Safety. General Washington is at New York with a large army—Gen Howe on Staten Island with about 10,000 men and expecting every day reinforcements. Some slight skirmishes have happened but nothing decisive. We expect soon to hear that the Armies are in contact & then We shall write you again.

We have taken advantage of a moments leisure from the Business of New York to call the Attention of the Congress to the State of North Carolina. This Evening they meet & from the disposition of the congress We flatter ourselves the very reasonable requisitions signified in your Letter & some other matters which have occurred to us since as necessary for the safety of our Colony will be duely attended to.[2]

Pray make our best respects to your honourable Board & believe us to be, with great Regard Your most Obedt Hum Serts,

Wm Hooper

Joseph Hewes

John Penn

RC (Nc-Ar). Written by Hooper and signed by Hooper, Hewes, and Penn.
[1] Since the resolves mentioned in the first paragraph were passed by Congress on July 30, this letter must have been dated July 29 by mistake. JCC, 5:616–17.
[2] Letters from the North Carolina Council of Safety to Hancock, June 24, and to the North Carolina delegates, June 24 and July 7, setting forth the state's military requirements, are in N.C. Colonial Records, 11:299–302, 308–9. The letter to Hancock was presented to Congress on July 24. PCC, item 72, fols. 17–20; and JCC, 5:608. On July 30 Congress appointed a committee to consider the condition of North Carolina, and, on the basis of the committee's report, adopted several resolves pertaining to the state's defense on the following day. JCC, 5:617, 623–24. See also the resolves passed on August 6 and 12 concerning military supplies for North Carolina. JCC, 5:633, 647.

Benjamin Rush to Walter Jones

Dr Walter,[1]   Philada. July 30. 1776.

Col. Lee has just now whisperd to me that he had given you reason to expect a long letter from me. I have stole a few minutes from the congress into a committee room to drop you a few lines, not to inform you of any news, but to convince you that in my political as well as medical line I am still your friend.

What shall I say of the august assembly of our States? It is a wide field for speculation. Here we behold the strengths and weakness of the human Understanding and the extent of human virtue & folly. Time will meliorate us. A few more misfortunes will teach us wisdom & humility, and inspire us with true benevolence. The republican soil is broke up—but we have still many monarchical & aristocratical weeds to pluck up from it. The history of the Congress that will sit in the year 1780 will be the history of the Dignity of human nature. We have knocked up the substance of royalty but now & then we worship the shadow. O' liberty—liberty—I have worshipped thee as a substance, and have found thee so. The influence of the declaration of independance upon the senate & the field is inconceivable. The militia of our state pant for nothing more than to avenge the blood of our brave countrymen upon our enemies on Staten Island.

Adieu my dear sir. *Continue* to enlighten your fellow citizens in the doctrine of a free government. Make them wise & virtuous, and they will be happy. Yours sincerely,   B Rush

RC (DLC). Addressed: "Dr. Walter Jones, Physician, Richmond, Virginia."
[1] Walter Jones (1745–1815) had been Rush's friend since 1766 during their student days at Edinburgh, where both men received their medical degrees. He returned to his native Virginia to practice medicine but eventually accepted an active public role and held several elective offices, 1785–1811. When Jones was elected "physician general of the hospital in the middle department" in April 1777, he declined the appointment and Rush was elected to the position in his stead. *JCC*, 7:253, 8:490, 518; and *Bio. Dir. Cong.*

Thomas Stone to the Maryland Council of Safety

Gent.   Phila. July. 30. 1776.
We shall endeavour to procure the Instruments desired by yours of the 25th but they are not easily procured,[1] the Demand for the Continental Army being great and many of the Cutlers of this City having gone to Jersey with the Militia. The Powder and Arms were sent some days ago to Annapolis which we hope will be attended with no Inconvenience.[2] We have not the least Doubt but every thing in your Power will be done in the best Manner for the publick Service and the preservation of every part of the united States. Maryland to be sure must be a principal Object of your Attention, and we hope considering the Spirit and Alacrity which all ranks of men have shewn when our Province required their Service, that our Coast will be secured against the Dangers of Dunmore and his rascally Gang of Pirates. We have Nothing lately from Ticonderoga. The Enemy do not stir from Staten Island. 8 Ships arrived there a few days ago but whether they brought Soldiers or not we have not heard. Genl Washington has now a considerable Strength at N. York, but there are only 3000 Men in Jersey, where there ought to be at least 10,000. Col. Smallwood is at N. York. We have no Doubt but the Subsistance Money will be readily paid. And we wish every Necessary which can be had may be furnished the Militia before they march. Money will be advanced to them here if they need it. Hunting Shirts will be a convenient & good uniform if they can be had. We shall at all Times give you the earliest Information of all important Occurrencies and shall with pleasure execute your Commands, and have the Honour to be, Yr most obt Sert.,
                                                T. Stone
[*P.S.*] My Brothers are engaged in other Business, and the Post is going so that their signatures must be dispensed with. T. S.

RC (MdAA).
   [1] A reference to the council's letter of July 26 to the Maryland delegates. See *Md. Archives*, 12:119–20.
   [2] See Maryland Delegates to the Maryland Council of Safety, July 23, 1776, note 3.

John Witherspoon's Speech in Congress

[July 30, 1776] [1]

The absolute necessity of union to the vigour and success of those measures on which we are already entered, is felt and confessed by every one of us, without exception; so far, indeed, that those who have expressed their fears or suspicions of the existing confederacy proving abortive, have yet agreed in saying that there must and shall be a confederacy for the purposes of, and till the finishing of this war. So far it is well; and so far it is pleasing to hear them express their sentiments. But I intreat gentlemen calmly to consider how far the giving up all hopes of a lasting confederacy among these states, for their future security and improvement, will have an effect upon the stability and efficacy of even the temporary confederacy, which all acknowledge to be necessary? I am fully persuaded, that when it ceases to be generally known, that the delegates of the provinces consider a lasting union as impracticable, it will greatly derange the minds of the people, and weaken their hands in defence of their country, which they have now undertaken with so much alacrity and spirit. I confess it would to me greatly diminish the glory and importance of the struggle, whether considered as for the rights of mankind in general, or for the prosperity and happiness of this continent in future times.

It would quite depreciate the object of hope, as well as place it at a greater distance. For what would it signify to risk our possessions and shed our blood to set ourselves free from the encroachments and oppression of Great Britain—with a certainty, as soon as peace was settled with them of a more lasting war, a more unnatural, more bloody, and much more hopeless war, among the colonies themselves? Some of us consider ourselves as acting for posterity at present, having little expectation of living to see all things fully settled, and the good consequences of liberty taking effect. But how much more uncertain the hope of seeing the internal contests of the colonies settled upon a lasting and equitable footing?

One of the greatest dangers I have always considered the colonies as exposed to at present, is treachery among themselves, augmented by bribery and corruption from our enemies. But what force would be added to the arguments of seducers, if they could say with truth, that it was of no consequence whether we succeeded against Great Britain or not; for we must, in the end, be subjected, the greatest part of us, to the power of one or more of the strongest or largest of the American states? And here I would apply the argument which we have so often used against Great Britain—that in all history we see that the slaves of freemen, and the subject states of republics, have been of all others the most grievously oppressed. I do not think the records of time can produce an instance of slaves treated with so much barbarity as the Helotes by the Lacedemonians, who were the most illustrious champions for liberty in all Greece; or of provinces more plundered and spoiled than the states conquered by the Romans, for one hundred years before Caesar's dictatorship. The reason is plain; there are many great men in free states. There were many consular gentlemen in that great republic, who all considered themselves as greater than kings, and must have kingly fortunes, which they had no other way of acquiring but by governments of provinces, which lasted generally but one year, and seldom more than two.

In what I have already said, or may say, or any cases I may state, I hope every gentleman will do me the justice to believe, that I have not the most distant view to particular persons or societies, and mean only to reason from the usual course of things, and the prejudices inseparable from men as such. And can we help saying, that there will be a much greater degrce, not only of the corruption of particular persons, but the defection of particular provinces from the present confederacy, if they consider our success itself as only a prelude to a contest of a more dreadful nature, and indeed much more properly a civil war than that which now often obtains the name? Must not small colonies in particular be in danger of saying, we must secure ourselves? If the colonies are independent states, separate and disunited, after this war, we may be sure of coming off by the worse. We are in no condition to contend with several of them. Our trade in general, and our trade with them, must be upon such terms as they shall be pleased to prescribe. What will be the consequence of this? Will they not be ready to prefer putting themselves under the protection of Great Britain, France or Holland, rather than submit to the tyranny of their neighbours, who were lately their equals? Nor would it be at all impossible, that they should enter into such rash engagements as would prove their own destruction, from a mixture of apprehended necessity and real resentment.

Perhaps it may be thought that breaking off this confederacy, and leaving it unfinished after we have entered upon it, will be only postponing the duty to some future period? Alas, nothing can exceed the absurdity of that supposition. Does not all history cry out, that a common danger is the great and only effectual means of settling difficulties, and composing differences. Have we not experienced its efficacy in producing such a degree of union through these colonies, as nobody would have prophesied, and hardly any would have expected?

If therefore, at present, when the danger is yet imminent, when it is so far from being over, that it is but coming to its height, we shall find it impossible to agree upon the terms of this confederacy, what madness is it to suppose that there ever will be a time, or that circumstances will so change, as to make it even probable, that it will be done at an after season? Will not the very same difficulties that are in our way, be in the way of those who shall come after us? Is it possible that they should be ignorant of them, or inattentive to them? Will they not have the same jealousies of each other, the same attachment to local prejudices, and particular interest? So certain is this, that I look upon it as on the repentance of a sinner— Every day's delay, though it adds to the necessity, yet augments the difficulty, and takes from the inclination.

There is one thing that has been thrown out, by which some seem to persuade themselves of, and others to be more indifferent about the success of a confederacy—that from the nature of men, it is to be expected, that a time must come when it will be dissolved and broken in pieces. I am none of those who either deny or conceal the depravity of human nature, till it is purified by the light of truth, and renewed by the Spirit of the living God. Yet I apprehend there is no force in that reasoning at all. Shall we establish nothing good, because we know it cannot be eternal? Shall we live without government, because every constitution has its old age, and its period? Because we know that we shall die, shall we take no pains to preserve or lengthen out life? Far from it, Sir: it only requires the more watchful attention, to settle government upon the best principles, and in the wisest manner, that it may last as long as the nature of things will admit.

But I beg leave to say something more, though with some risk that it will be thought visionary and romantic. I do expect, Mr President, a progress, as in every other human art, so in the order and perfection of human society, greater than we have yet seen; and why should we be wanting to ourselves in urging it forward? It is certain, I think, that human science and religion have kept company together, and greatly assisted each other's progress in the world. I do not say that intellectual and moral qualities are in the same proportion in particular persons; but they have a great and friendly influence upon one another, in societies and larger bodies.

There have been great improvements, not only in human knowledge, but in human nature; the progess of which can be easily traced in history. Every body is able to look back to the time in Europe, when the liberal sentiments that now prevail upon the rights of conscience, would have been looked upon as absurd. It is but little above two hundred years since that enlarged system called the balance of power, took place; and I maintain, that it is a greater step from the former disunited and hostile situation of kingdoms and states, to their present condition, than it would be from their present condition to a state of more perfect and lasting union. It is not impossible, that in future times all the states on one quarter of the globe, may see it proper by some plan of union, to perpetuate security and peace; and sure I am, a well planned confederacy among the states of America, may hand down the blessings of peace and public order to many generations. The union of the seven provinces of the Low Countries, has never yet been broken; and they are of very different degrees of strength and wealth. Neither have the Cantons of Switzerland ever broken among themselves, though there are some of them protestants, and some of them papists, by public establishment. Not only so, but these confederates are seldom engaged in a war with other nations. Wars are generally between monarchs, or single states that are large. A confederation of itself keeps war at a distance from the bodies of which it is composed.

For all these reasons, Sir, I humbly apprehend, that every argument from honour, interest, safety and necessity, conspire in pressing us to a confederacy; and if it be seriously attempted, I hope, by the blessing of God upon our endeavours, it will be happily accomplished.

MS not found; reprinted from John Witherspoon, *The Works of John Witherspoon . . .*, 9 vols. (Edinburgh: J. Ogle, 1815), 9:135–41, where it appears under the heading: "Part of a Speech in Congress, upon the Confederation."

[1] Thomas Jefferson's Notes of Proceedings in Congress, July 12–August 1, and John Adams' Notes of Debates, July 30, 1776, strongly suggest that this is the speech Witherspoon delivered in Congress on the 30th. Edmund C. Burnett assigned the date November 25, 1778, to this speech, but in doing so he admitted that "It is not known when this speech was made" and that it "might have been appropriate at almost any time when the Confederation was under discussion." Burnett, *Letters*, 3:508n.2. In addition to the summaries of Witherspoon's remarks by Adams and Jefferson, there is also internal evidence justifying an earlier date for this document. Witherspoon's frequent use of the term "colonies" is suggestive of a period not long after independence had been declared, and his reference to the general situation then facing Congress as one of "danger . . . yet imminent . . . coming to its height" seems more appropriate to the summer of 1776 than the fall of 1778.

John Hancock to Benjamin Flower

Sir,   Philada. July 31t. 1776.

The enclosed Commission of Commissary of military Stores for the Flying Camp has been ready for you ever since the Date of it.[1]

I should have forwarded it sooner, if I had known where to have sent it. It was not till yesterday that I heard you were with Col. Dickinson at the Flying Camp.

I am, Sir, your most hble Ser.   J.H. Prest

LB (DNA: PCC, item 12A).

¹ Congress had appointed Flower "commissary of military stores" for the flying camp in New Jersey on July 16. *JCC*, 5:566. A July 10 petition to Congress from Flower, a lieutenant in the First Battalion of Pennsylvania Associators, soliciting this appointment, is in PCC, item 42, 3:5, and *Am. Archives*, 5th ser. 1:156.

John Hancock to Hugh Mercer

Sir,   Philada. July 31t. 1776

I do myself the Honour of transmitting the enclosed Resolves; by which you will perceive that your application to Congress relative to building Boats for the Use of the Flying Camp is referred to Genl. Washington, to whom I have written on the Subject by this Conveyance to give such Directions as he shall judge necessary.

I have also wrote to the Council of Safety of Pennsylvania to forward to you immediately ten six Pounders & an equal Number of four Pounders.

The Congress have allowed you a Secretary as long as you shall continue to act in a seperate Command.

The sixty Thousand Dollars for the Use of the Flying Camp will be sent as soon as possible.¹ I have the Honour to be, with great Respect, Sir, your most obedt. & very hble Servt. J.H. Prest.

P.S. The Appointmt. of a Brigade Major resting entirely with yourself, you are authorized to nominate one as soon as ever you shall think proper.

LB (DNA: PCC, item 12A).

¹ For these resolves, see *JCC*, 5:620–21. Congress passed them in response to Mercer's July 20 and 26 letters to Hancock. PCC, item 159, fols. 145–47, 153–54; and *Am. Archives*, 5th ser. 1:469–70, 599–600.

John Hancock to the Pennsylvania Council of Safety

Gentlemen,   Philadelphia July 31t. 1776.

The Service at the Flying Camp requiring some Pieces of Artillery, I have it in Charge from Congress to request you will immediately send to Genl. Mercer ten six Pounders and an equal Number of four Pounders. If you cannot furnish them out of the

Stores of the State of Pennsylvania, I am to request, you will procure them with all possible Dispatch, and forward them to Amboy in New Jersey. Whatever Number you can spare, you will please to forward immediately, and procure the Remainder as soon as possible.[1] Your Ardor and Zeal in the Cause of your Country, will, I am persuaded, supercede the Necessity of Arguments to induce You to an immediate Compliance with this Requisition.

I have the Honour to be, with Respect, Gentlemen, your most obed. & very hble Sert.   John Hancock Presidt

RC (PHi). In the hand of Jacob Rush and signed by Hancock.
[1] See *JCC*, 5:621. This resolve was prompted by Gen. Hugh Mercer's July 26 letter to Hancock, which was read in Congress on July 29. *Am. Archives*, 5th ser. 1:599–600; and *JCC*, 5:613. For the Pennsylvania Council's response to Hancock's letter, see *Am. Archives*, 5th ser. 1:1303.

John Hancock to George Washington

Sir,   Philadelphia July 31t. 1776.
The enclosed Resolves, which I do myself the Honour of transmitting, are so explicit, that I need only refer your Attention to them.[1]

You will please to give such Orders, with Regard to building Boats for the Service of the Flying Camp, as you shall judge necessary. A Copy of Genl. Mercer's Letter to Congress on this Subject, you have enclosed.[2]

I have wrote to the Council of Safety of this State to forward to Genl. Mercer ten six Pounders, and an equal Number of four Pounders, with the greatest Expedition.

Your Favour of the 29th came safe to Hand, and was immediately laid before Congress. I have forwarded to Generals Schuyler and Mercer a Copy of the inclosed Resolves, as far as they relate to their respective Departments.[3]

I have the Honour to be, with Sentiments of the greatest Respect & Esteem, Sir, your most obed. & very hble Servt.
                                        John Hancock Presidt.

P.S. Upon conversing with Genl. Sullivan, and stating to him the Reasons of Congress promoting Genl. Gates over him, he desired Me to move for leave to withdraw his Application to resign—in which the Congress have acquiesced.[4] He has now Orders to repair to New York, where you will please to assign him such Post of Duty as you shall think proper.[5]

RC (DLC). In the hand of Jacob Rush and signed by Hancock.
[1] These resolves, which were passed by Congress on July 30 and 31, dealt with

the congressional investigation of the American invasion of Canada, Indian affairs in the middle department, the flying camp in New Jersey, the defense of North Carolina, the Massachusetts militia, and gunpowder for Washington's army. *JCC*, 5:617–24.

[2] See Hugh Mercer to Hancock, July 20, 1776, in *Am. Archives*, 5th ser. 1:469–70.

[3] Hancock's letter of this date to Schuyler, apparently enclosing resolves of July 30 and 31 on the Canadian expedition investigation and a resolve of July 30 about Schuyler's handling of Indian affairs, is in PCC, item 12A, and *Am. Archives*, 5th ser. 1:691. See also *JCC*, 5:617–21, 623. Another letter of this date from Hancock to Commissary General Joseph Trumbull, explaining a July 31 resolve respecting rations for the Massachusetts militia, is in PCC, item 12A, and *Am. Archives*, 5th ser. 1:691. See also *JCC*, 5:623.

[4] For further information about Sullivan's threatened resignation, see Hancock to Washington, July 26, 1776, note 3.

[5] Hancock added some recent naval intelligence to the cover of this letter before sending it off to Washington. The cover itself was discarded after reaching Washington but not before a clerk had apparently summarized Hancock's remarks on the back of the letter as follows: "Con[tinenta]l Ship arrivd at Chester with 366 pigs of Lead—54 Boxes Musqt Ball, 1000 Stand of Arms with Bayonetts, 1 Bar Flints, 193 Whole Barls powdr. Indorsed on cover of Letter by J. H. Esq. Also a Priv[atee]r had brought in a West India[man] bound to London havg on board besides produce, 1100 Joans., 700 Guins. &c." See also Washington, *Writings* (Fitzpatrick), 5:370.

Francis Hopkinson to Samuel Stringer Coale

Dear Brother,[1]   Philada. 31st July 1776

I much fear you have not received a Letter I wrote two or three weeks ago to my Sister with a Postscript to yourself,[2] which I sent by a Gentleman who carried Letters also from my Mother & the rest of the Family. New Jersey hath thought proper to honour me with a Part of their Delegation in Congress, so that for the Present I have taken up my abode with my Mother in order to attend that venerable Body. The Service is indeed very severe, as we have a vast deal of Business of the first Importance to go thro: but if my poor Abilities can be of the least Service to my Country in this her Day of Trial I shall not complain of the Hardship of the Task.

I have the greatest Pleasure in hearing of your Wellfare & of the happy Increase of your Family. I sincerely pray God to continue & enlarge your Satisfaction without Allay. We all look forward with Impatience to September, when we hope to meet once more in a Family Way. If my Brother Thomas will be of the Party our Union will be compleat. Your Edward must supply the Place of my darling Jimmy. Excuse me for mentioning that Idol of my Soul. I endeavour to forget him continually, but that very Endeavour brings him to Mind & opens my wounds afresh. But no more of this.

I returned yesterday from a short Visit to Borden Town & have brought with me Mrs. Hopkinson & Mrs. Morgan, who is now one of my Family. The Dr is at New York in the Service of his Country.

We expect every Day to hear of some important Event from that Quarter. We are very anxious but have lively Hopes of Success. Our Troops are hearty, eager for Action & full of Spirits—animated I verily believe by the true Spirit of Patriotism. When men of Fortune turn common Soldiers to fight for their Liberties against [the] Hand of Oppression, Success I b[elieve] must attend their bravest Efforts [and] the mercenary Tools of Tyrannic Power must shrink from before them.

Nancy joins me in hearty Love to you & yours, to our Sister Jane & Brother Thomas. It is not long since I wrote to Jenny, notwithstanding her loud Complaints. Remember me to your Brother. With Compt. to your good Family, I am ever, Your affectionate,

F. Hopkinson

RC (PHi).
¹ Dr. Samuel Stringer Coale, a graduate of the Philadelphia Medical College who was residing in Baltimore, was married to Hopkinson's sister, Ann. George E. Hastings, *The Life and Works of Francis Hopkinson* (Chicago: University of Chicago Press, 1926), p.214n.2.
² Not found.

Samuel Huntington to Jabez Huntington

Sir   Philadelphia 31st July 1776

I am favour'd with yours of the 17th Instant; it gave me pleasure to hear from you, & the welfare of my famaly Communicated by your Letter which was the first Intelligence from them Since I left home. The hint you give of War being proclaim'd between Spain & Portugal is News of Importance tho perhaps the Information you have receiv'd is premature yet I observe a Scetch of the Same Import in the News paper via Boston Since I receiv'd yours.

You will doubless before this comes to hand receive accounts of the Success of American Arms at South Carolina and at Gwin's Island in Virginia. Have nothing further of moment to communicate.

The Congress are crouded with business & the Heat at this Season in this City is much more Tedious than I ever experienced in Connecticut.

I am thro a kind Providence in usual health, & only add I am with Esteem, Your Humble Servt,   Saml Huntington

P.S.
N.B. Col. Williams is arriv'd.

RC (CtHi). Jabez Huntington drafted his August 15 reply to this letter on the verso.

Robert Treat Paine's Diary

[July 31, 1776]

Exceedingly sultry.

I went to Congress.[1]

This Month has been very hott but frequently refreshed wth Showers.

MS (MHi).

[1] Paine had just recovered from a severe illness that had plagued him since July 19. See also John Adams to James Warren, July 27, 1776, note 1.

John Adams' Notes of Debates

Aug. 1. 1776.

Hooper.[1] N.C. is a striking Exception to the general Rule that was laid down Yesterday, that the Riches of a Country are in Proportion to the Numbers of Inhabitants. A Gentleman of 3 or 400 Negroes, dont raise more corn than feeds them. A Labourer cant be hired for less than £24 a Year in Mass. Bay. The neat profit of a Negro is not more than 5 or 6£ per Annum. I wish to see the day that Slaves are not necessary. Whites and Negroes cannot work together. Negroes are Goods and Chattells, are Property. A Negro works under the Impulse of fear—has no Care of his Masters Interest.[2]

17. Art.

Dr. Franklin moves that Votes should be in Proportion to Numbers.

Mr. Middleton moves that the Vote should be according to what they pay.

Sherman thinks We ought not to vote according to Numbers. We are rep[resentative]s of States not Individuals. States of Holland. The Consent of every one is necessary. 3 Colonies would govern the whole but would not have a Majority of Strength to carry those Votes into Execution.

The Vote should be taken two Ways. Call the Colonies and call the Individuals, and have a Majority of both.

Dr. Rush. Abbe Reynauld has attributed the Ruin of the united Provinces to 3 Causes. The principal one is that the Consent of every State is necessary. The other that the Members are obliged to consult their Constituents upon all Occasions.

We loose an equal Representation. We represent the People. It will tend to keep up colonial Distinctions. We are now a new Nation. Our Trade, Language, Customs, Manners dont differ more than they do in G. Britain.

The more a Man aims at serving America the more he serves his Colony.

It will promote Factions in Congress and in the States.

It will prevent the Growth of Freedom in America. We shall be loth to admit new Colonies into the Confederation. If We vote by Numbers Liberty will be always safe. Mass. is contiguous to 2 small Colonies, R.[I.] and N. H. Pen. is near N. J. and D. Virginia is between Maryland and N. Carolina.

We have been to[o] free with the Word Independence. We are dependent on each other—not totally independent States.

Montesquieu pronounced the Confederation of Licea the best that ever was made. The Cities had different Weights in the Scale.

China is not larger than one of our Colonies. How populous.

It is said that the small Colonies deposit their All. This is deceiving Us with a Word.

I would not have it understood, that I am pleading the Cause of Pensilvania. When I entered that door, I considered myself a Citizen of America.[3]

Dr. Witherspoon. Representation in England is unequal. Must I have 3 Votes in a County because I have 3 times as much Money as my Neighbour. Congress are to determine the Limits of Colonies.

G[overnor] Hopkins. A momentous Question. Many difficulties on each Side. 4 larger, 5 lesser, 4 stand indifferent. V.M.P.M. make more than half the People. 4 may alw[4]

C., N.Y., 2 Carolinas, not concerned at all. The dissinterested Coolness of these Colonies ought to determine. I can easily feel the Reasoning of the larger Colonies. Pleasing Theories always gave Way to the Prejudices, Passions, and Interests of Mankind.

The Germanic Confederation. The K. of Prussia has an equal Vote. The Helvetic Confederacy. It cant be expected that 9 Colonies will give Way to be governed by 4. The Safety of the whole depends upon the distinctions of Colonies.

Dr. Franklin. I hear many ingenious Arguments to perswade Us that an unequal Representation is a very good Thing. If We had been born and bred under an unequal Representation We might bear it. But to sett out with an unequal Representation is unreasonable.

It is said the great Colonies will swallow up the less. Scotland said the same Thing at the Union.

Dr. Witherspoon. Rises to explain a few Circumstances relating to Scotland. That was an incorporating Union, not a federal. The Nobility and Gentry resort to England.

In determining all Questions, each State shall have a Weight in Proportion to what it contributes to the public Expences of the united States.

MS (MHi). Adams, *Diary* (Butterfield), 2:246–48.

¹ This is a continuation of the debate of July 30 on article 11 of the articles of confederation. See Adams' Notes of Debates, July 30, 1776.

² One-half of a blank page follows in the MS. Adams' notes resume with a discussion of article 17, which was also debated on the previous day. Ibid.

³ For a more complete version of Rush's remarks, see Benjamin Rush's Notes for a Speech in Congress, this date.

⁴ Thus in MS.

Samuel Adams' Notes on
Military Operations in Canada

[August 1, 1776]¹

Last Spring there were 10 Battalions amounting to 6400 Men sent from N York. There were at the same time in Canada two Batta[lions] of Pennsylvania—three from N England—One or two from. Jersey, all of them strong amounting to 4000 more—making in all upwards. of 10,000 strong. There are now (Augt 1) 3000 sick & about as many well. Suppose 1000 in the Hands of the Enemy—1000 dead—where are the 2000? No order, Subordination or Harmony. Officers as well as Men of different Colonies quarrelling with each other. This State of things inducd the Genl Officers in Council of War to retreat to Tyconderoga—to occupy a Post on the East Side the Lake—very advantageous—commands the Entrance of Lakes Champlain & George—inaccessible but in 2 places where they propose Roads—the rest surrounded by Rocks & Precipices—Supplys easily had from Skeensborough at the head of Lake Champlain. Hence they may easily retreat into the Country —which without a naval Superority on the Lakes they must do unless soon reinforcd. Our Naval Force, a Schooner of 12 Carriage Guns, a sloop of 8, 2 small Schooners of 4 or 6 & 3 Gondolas—the large Schooner in good sailing Order, about to take a Trip down the Lake for Discovery. The Sloop an unmannageable thing—the 2 Schooners not armd—the Gondolas not armd. The Enemy at St Johns repairing the Works. No doubt every thing ready to their hand—building three Schooners & 2 Sloops—Rigging no doubt made & Guns mounted. Gates orderd to command in Canada & Schuyler in N York! G probably discontented finding himself thus limitted, & a wretched Spectator of the ruin of the Army without Power even to attempt to save it. Small Pox—imprudent runing into Inoculation. Troops clamord for Want of Cloathing, Provision & Wages—whose Fault? The Enemies Force at the Cedars very inconsiderable—not more than 37 regulars & 2 or 3 hundred Indians— the latter loth to go—mostly tarried at Oswego lake. Had our Men behaved well the Defeat could not have happend. Why they were thus neglected & left without Supplys & Wages ought strictly to be enquired into.

MS (NN). In the hand of Samuel Adams.

[1] After the precipitous retreat of the American army in Canada, Congress appointed a committee on June 24 "to enquire into the cause of the miscarriages in Canada." Although Samuel Adams was not on this committee—Robert Treat Paine represented Massachusetts—he undoubtedly paid close attention to the testimony taken by it and to its reports to Congress. These notes do not appear to be based on actual testimony before the committee, and no evidence survives to indicate the purpose for which they were made, but Adams may have written them in anticipation of returning to Massachusetts later in the month and reporting to the state legislature. See JCC, 5:474, 592, 617–20, 623; and John Hancock to George Washington, June 21, 1776, note 1.

Charles Carroll of Carrollton to Charles Carroll, Sr.

Dr. Papa,   Pha. 1st Aug. 1776.

I have the pleasure to inform you that a vessel is arrived at Chester (17 miles from this) with 1000 stand of arms, 10 Tons of gunpowder & 40 Tons of lead. This cargo she took in on account of the continent at Marseilles, which place she left some time in June as she brings letters dated from Marseilles the 6th & 8th of that month. These letters mention that the court of France is disposed to protect the Colonies & that the question asked by that court of persons applying for permits to export arms & ammunition is *are you empowered by Congress.*"

The person who shipped off these above arms & powder was obliged to take a trip to Paris to get leave to export them, which was given immediately on its being known they were intended for the Congress. The Court of Spain will follow the System of France, and that power is certainly preparing for war. So is Spain. It was reported, says our correspondent, that the foreign mercenaries were stopped in England; that ministry being jealous of the armaments of France. This he mentions only as a report & therefore can not much be depended on. The above facts are certain: I much question the truth of the report as within these ten days 20 transports have come within the Hook: we know not what number of troops they have brought or indeed whether they have brought any.

We are making preparations to burn the enemy's ships at N. York: God send our attempt may succeed. Nothing new from Canada. Schuyler is at Indian Treaty up the Mohawk now. It is said the Six Nations are impressed with a high idea of our strength owing to the report of some Indians who left Ph[iladelphi]a about 2 months ago.

We are engaged in very important business. I am in hopes justice & true policy will at last prevail over distinct & separate interests. If it should not, I will predict that a confederation formed on partial & interested views will not be lasting.

I was disappointed in not receiving a letter from you by this day's post. My love to Molly, little Poll & Mrs Darnall. I hope to be with you the 11th instant. This place is insupportably hot. As there will not be a representation, even if I should not be chosen into Convention I shall return home. Mr. Chase desires to be remembered to all the family. Wishing a long enjoy[men]t of yr. health I remain, yr. affectionate Son,

Ch Carroll of Carrollton

RC (MdHi).

Abraham Clark to James Caldwell

Dear Sir,[1]   Philaa. August 1t. 1776.
Your favour of the 24th Ulto. & of Mr. Daytons of the 25th I this day had the Pleasure of receiving. The frequent miscarriage of Letters sent your way makes me more indolent in the Writing way than I should otherwise be.

The State of the British Army on Staten Island is uncertain. They at first amounted to between 8 to 10 thousand, but Vessels are daily Arriving. 2000 highlanders got there some days past, & since that 15 or 16 Vessells came in at a Time, but as the Forces Occupy All parts of the Island it is difficult for us to know their Strength, but I am Persuaded they will soon be 20,000 Strong. A flying Camp is forming in the Jerseys from Amboy to Eliza. Town Point, when full it is to consist of About 16 Thousand, but at Present there is not I believe 5 thousand, tho' they Are gathering fast. They have fortifications at all the Principal passes on the Island, as we have on the Jersey Shore. I can't learn there is any design to Attack the Forces on the Island, they have become too Numerous. I expect we shall have Serious work with them soon. Such a Numerous force as they have or soon will have will induce them to make a push soon. We have 8 field pieces belonging to the Jerseys and 6 brass field pieces carried by the Phila. battalio[ns], and 10 More went yesterday or this morning from this City but not mounted, the Carriages are to make. Phila. is almost Striped of Inhabitants, all the City battalions are in the Jerseys. The Country battalions are now on their March, every day comeing into this Town on their way.

Our Congress have now under Consideration a Confederation of the States. Two Articles give great trouble, the one for fixing the Quotas of the States towards the Public expence—and the other whether Each state shall have a Single Vote or in proportion to the Sums they raise or the num[be]r of Inhabitants they contain. I assure you the difficulties attending these Points at Times appear very Alarming. Nothing but Present danger will ever make us all Agree, and I sometimes even fear that will be insufficient.

I this day saw a Letter from a Mercht. in France dated June 6th informing of the Friendly disposition of the French to us, but I find by it what I always Supposed that they were seeking their own Interest only.[2] They have Opened all their Ports to us—and tho' by reason of great preperations for War in France they Prohibit the exportation of Arms & Ammunition yet upon Application to Court by some of their Merchants, they allow that previlidge to us, a Vessel having just Arrived in Chester from thence with 1000 Stand of Arms & Ten Tons of Powder. I now hear She is come up to town.

I Notice what you say About the want of Cash. The Post that brought your Letter, brought one from Genl. Schuyler directed to Genl. Washington & by him sent forward, making the same Complaint, which was referred to the board of War.[3] Your wants in that respect I hope will soon be Supplied; There hath been no complaint on that head from your Quarter before that I have heard of. Money is not such a trifling Article with the "States General" as to make them thoughtless about it, tho' in some quarters the value of it seems trifling, as it is no uncommon case to order five hundred thousand [dollars] sent of[f] at a Time notwithstanding "our daily feasting in the City."

As to your Regts. inlisting for 3 years upon Condition of leaving that Country before Winter, I must Observe your Campain is but beginning, and the issue very uncertain, it is impossible to foresee the State of Affairs with you next fall. Necessity may require your comeing away by that Time, and may also require your Staying there—but this you may rest Assured of, that any service within my Scanty powers, in what you desire, so far as the Public service will admit, you may most assuredly rely upon, but at present I think it a Subject improper to mention in public but shall nevertheless, communicate the matter to particular friends, as opportunity offers.

Colo. Dayton mentions his being uninformed of the State of his family in these troublesom Times. Both Mrs. Caldwell & Mrs. Dayton have provided themselves Asylums back in the Country. Mrs. Dayton hath removed her Valuable effects, & stands ready to take her self away if the Enemy land in Jersey. I have frequently given this information and am Surprized it had not reached you both. I need not write to Mr. Dayton now, this Letter as all my others I design for both of you. I am Dear Sir, your & Colo. Daytons Sincere & Affectionate Friend & Humble Servt.,   Abra. Clark

P.S. Doctor Witherspoon send[s] you his Compli[ments].

RC (MH).
    [1] James Caldwell (1734–81), a graduate of the College of New Jersey and pastor of the First Presbyterian Church in Elizabethtown, was serving as chaplain to the Third New Jersey Battalion, commanded by Col. Elias Dayton. Clark and Dayton were both members of Caldwell's church. Rev. Nicholas Murray, "A Memoir of the Rev. James Caldwell of Elizabethtown," *Proceedings of the New Jersey Historical Society* 3 (1848–49): 77–89.
    [2] Clark is almost certainly referring to a June 6 letter from Estienne Cathalan, a Marseilles merchant, to Willing, Morris & Co. See Clark, *Naval Documents*, 6:406–8, 827.
    [3] Schuyler's July 24 letter to Washington, stating that he had only received $200,000 of the $500,000 Congress had agreed to send his army on May 22, is in *Am. Archives*, 5th ser. 1:559–63. On August 2, in response to Schuyler's complaint, Congress ordered $200,000 to be sent to his army. An additional $500,000 was appropriated for the same purpose on August 15. *JCC*, 5:627, 659. See also *JCC*, 4:378; and Washington, *Writings* (Fitzpatrick), 5:354, 360.

William Hooper to Joseph Trumbull

Dear Sir   Philadelphia Augt 1. 1776
    I beg yr Care of the Inclosed, pray hand it to Major Frazier & prevail upon him to write me immediately and in a very particular manner. I hope to hear from you, perhaps the Subject has come within your knowledge.[1] Your vicinity to this will furnish you frequent Oppertunities to write me, pray embrace them as they occur & oblige, your's truly,   Wm Hooper

[*P.S.*] Remember me to my friends in Camp
    Pray seal the inclosed.

RC (CtHi). Addressed: "To Joseph Trumbull Esquire, Commissary General in New York."
    [1] Hooper's enclosure for Major Frazier has not been found, and "the Subject" of it remains unknown.

Benjamin Rush's Notes for a Speech in Congress

[August 1, 1776][1]
Question of great importance
    The Abbe Reynall, an author who predicted so exactly all the circumstances of the present contr[overs]y 7 years ago, informs us that the liberties of the 7 United Provinces were lost from the foll[owin]g causes.[2]

1. Perfect unan[imit]y being required in their counsels.

2. Each province & city being unable to assent to anything 'till it had cons[ulte]d its Constituents.

3. Each province having an equal Vote.

From the experience we have had of the effects of the second of these causes—much weight in the last. We have lived to see several colonies well nigh ruind—nay more—the union of the whole well nigh dissolved—by the fatal operation of instructions, & I apprehend many of us will live to see greater evils to indiv[idua]l states, & to the whole if each state is all[owe]d a seperate Vote.

I am not able to point out all the mischiefs &c. In every case of doubtful issue it becomes us to imitate the mariner who has lost sight of the sun—keep eye steadily fixed upon his compass—thus we should keep our eyes steadily fixed on the principles of reason & rules of justice.

Shall attempt to point out the misch[ief] of this mode of vot[ing].

1. [dist?]. Equal repres[entation] the found[ation] of liberty. To face the effects of unequal repres[entation] would be to point out the principal cause of the downfall of liberty in most of the free States of the world.

The members of the congress it is true are app[ointe]d by States, but repres[ent] the people—& no State hath a right to alienate the priviledge of equal rep[resentation]n: it belongs solely [to] the people. The Objects before us are the people's rights, not the rights of States. Every man in America stands related to two legislative bodies—he deposits his prop[ert]y, liberty & life with his own State, but his trade [and] Arms, the means of enriching & defending himself & his honor, he deposits with the congress.

If entitled to equal rep[resentation] in the first case, why not in the second?[3]

I add further—that the people of America have been accustomed to view the Congress without the intervent[ion] of the states to which they belonged. And no wonder—the constitution & leaders of their states betrayed them—they looked up [to] the congress & it saved them. [. . .] I apprehend will the case [. . .] if time.

2. Evil—keeps up colony distinctions—we are now One people— a new nation—our Interests, language & trade not more divided than they are among the people in Britain who with a Better form of gov[ernment] might have been happy & free under one complete System of Laws forever. Strange if we cannot, who are bound only by a few, & those chiefly in the time of war.[4]

But I go further—our variety of interests is an Advantage to us— had our produce or manufactures between the same in our colony, more reason for jealousy—but the variety of both in every State points out that heaven intended us for one people.

Colony distinctions should be lost here. The more any man forgets the State which gave his birth, or which he represents, the better member of congress, & as in private life the more a man promotes the happiness of his neighb[ors], the more *finally* his own. So the more a man aims to promote the honor & happiness of the whole continent, the more certainly his own state. Every Act of the Conf[ederatio]n is general—all tend to the advancement of the whole.

3. Promote faction—a majority of the people, not states, will determine questions out of doors, and wherever we go contrary to their sentiments they will resent it—perhaps with arms. Already the States & people have divided upon the subject of independence. Bad consequences from it perc[eive]d—perhaps not fully known. Perhaps they will be known & felt in the course of the present war.

4. By this mode of representation we check the progress of freedom in this country. We shall soon experience such inconv[eniencie]s from voting by colonies that we will not readily admit small colonies into the confederation. But if they vote by numbers congress may judge when to admit colonies just as legislatures judge when to admit counties. If we do, whole system of confed[eratio]n be altered.

Sir I am alarmed at the consequences of the mode of voting proposed in this article. If we vote by numbers I maintain that we cannot deposit too much of our liberty & safety in the hands of the congress. They cannot be put out to better interest any where. Here colony factions may be destroyed—here the Aristocratic will cease to pant for a title—or to complain of the inequality of mankind. But if we vote by colonies I maintain that we cannot deposit too little in the hands of the congress. The Scheme is big with ruin, not only to one but to all the colonies.

But Sir, providence has held up a testim[on]y against this manner of voting. If ever colonies should think of having seperate interests, it must be those that are contiguous to each other. Now Sir let us examine the rel[ationshi]p which the several colonies have to each other. M. Bay lies contiguous to Rh. Island & New Hamshire—Pens[ylvania] to New Jersey & the *lower Counties*—N. Carolina to South Carolina & Georgia. If they vote by Colonies, think of the weight any one of these three large martial colonies will derive from their neighbours—but if by numbers they can derive no advantage from them that will not be ballanced by the members who will Vote in the other large colonies that are remote from it.

Sir, some of the colonies have lost sight of their true situation by being too familiar with the word *independance.* When confed[erate]d Sir, they are independant *states,* but in their seperate capacity, as they are *dependant* states, They cannot exist without each other. ⟨*Still however they are* free *and*⟩ Our weakness, & strength of enemies, &c require it. Their dependance differs from former dependance on the crown of &c, in their still retaining their freedom.

The congress interferes with no internal legislature, & each colony has a voice in proportion to the services it renders the states.

I have heard it said, that if we vote by Colonies 3 can bind the whole. If this the case, these three colonies are so seperated [*they*] can have no interest but within the interest of the whole. But if by Colonies don't the minority of people bind majority?⁵

By one article, 7 Colonies are to assess proport[ion] of taxes [for] each colony. Is there no danger from this to the large colonies? Is [*it*] not Subjecting them to the very evil We fled from G.B. to avoid —taxation without *representation?*

They say small colonies will plunge them into a war &c—no—here let 3/4 or 4/5 Determine.

Appeal once more to history to determine the question. Montes-quieu pronounces the Confed[eratio]n of *Lycia* the best in the world. 25 cities,⁶ large ones 3 votes, second size 2, small ones one. Strabo says the happiest & freest people in the world.⁷

But suppose 9 now include a majority—will this always be the case? May not some one from excell[enc]y of laws, soil, climate, become more popul[ous] than Whole? But, again suppose only 8 concur—shall we have no peace, alliances, money, &c? Or shall we [bribe?], persuade &c the 9th colony, or dissolve without doing any thing?

They say small Colonies deposit their *all.* Suppose we admit 8 or 10 Colonies with 5000 or 10000 inhabitants each. They deposit all too, but would the smallest colony among us be *now* willing to give each of them a Vote equal with itself? I believe not. But Sir—We are deceived here with a word. To suppose that a colony deposits *all* its liberty in the Congress is to give it one life—to make it as one man. This Idea is a most dangerous one. It is to contract millions to a span. It is to give a colony a single [. . .], & whether it is, intended or no, it is to invest the Congress with the power of a Caligula.

I might mention the advantages of voting by numbers. If any exclusive advantages from it will induce Colonies to cultivate the arts of population—to reform, & perfect their gov[ernmen]ts, to destroy religious establish[men]ts & to keep down arb[itrar]y power of every kind.

I am not plead[in]g the Cause of Pensylvania. In half a century she may be and probably will be as near the smallest as she now is the greatest states. New Hamshire & Georgia will probably receive most benefit from it if any exclusive Advantages from repres[entatio]n by numbers. No Sir—I am pleading the cause of the Continent—of mankind—of posterity.

I shall not say I will not sign the confed[erac]y if we vote by num-bers—but I will say that every man who does, signs the death warrant of the liberties of America.

Propose a plan—every 5000 a member; when the congress amounts to above 100, encrease the proportion of people who are to send a member.

This is not the most perfect that can be wished; is certainly much better than the worst that can be contrived.

MS (PPL). In the hand of Benjamin Rush. Endorsed: "Notes of Speeches delivered in Convention in 1776, in Congress in 1776 & in Convention of Pennsya 1776."

[1] It is clear from the notes of debates of both John Adams and Thomas Jefferson, this date, that Rush delivered this speech on August 1, 1776.

[2] The abbé Raynal (Guillaume Thomas François) discussed the government of the Dutch Republic in book 19 of his *Histoire philosophique et politique des établissemens et du commerce des Européens dans les deux Indes.* See *Philosophical and Political History of the Settlements and Trade of the Europeans in the East and West Indies,* trans. J. O. Justamond, 6 vols. (London: J. Mundell & Co., 1798; reprint ed., New York: Negro Universities Press, 1969), 6:265–68.

[3] At this point, Rush attached a small sheet of paper to his notes with sealing wax, masking over the following passage, which he probably ignored when he delivered his speech. "One right excepted which belong [to] States—boundaries— this perhaps by colony Voting. The rest are all the rights of individuals—no state can alienate them."

[4] Here Rush attached a second insert, containing the next paragraph, which overlays the following lined out passage. "Let us remember our number [is] small— 300000 [3000000?] of people a small nation."

[5] Rush interlined four words between this paragraph and the next: "in 9 binding 13."

[6] According to Montesquieu, who cited book 14 of Strabo's *Geography,* the Lycian Confederation consisted of 23 cities. Montesquieu, *The Spirit of Laws,* bk. 9, chap. 3.

[7] Here Rush attached a third insert, containing the next two paragraphs, which overlay the following passage. "Our Confederation will partake of the infirmities of men. But let it be slight disordered. Dont let us [. . .] it that will 'grow with its growth, strengthen with its strength'—& finally ending its ruin." The biological metaphor Rush developed here undoubtedly rests upon his reading of Alexander Pope. "The young disease, that must subdue at length, Grows with his growth, and strengthens with his strength." *Essay on Man* 2.135.

Secret Committee to George Washington

Sir   In Secret Committee. Philada August 1st. 1776

We have the honor to transmit you five Tons of Musquet Powder by the bearer hereof agreable to an order of Congress passed yesterday [1] and as our Stock here is not considerable We beg to remind you that three Powder Mills are now employed in making Continental Powder near New York, Vizt. Mr. Livingston & Mr. Wisners Mills in N York Government and Colo Fords in the Jerseys from whence this supply might have been drawn and when more is wanted it will be found there.

By order of the Secret Committee, I have the honor to be Your Excellencys Most obedt. hble servt.

Robt Morris, Chair Man

RC (Cabell Gwathmey, Berkeley, Calif., 1950). Written and signed by Robert Morris.

  [1] See *JCC*, 5:623.

John Adams' Notes of Debates

Aug. 2d. [1776]

Limiting the Bounds of States which by Charter &c. extend to the South Sea.[1]

Sherman thinks the Bounds ought to be settled. A Majority of States have no Claim to the South Sea. Moves this Amendment, to be subsituted in Place of this Clause and also instead of the 15th Article.

No Lands to be seperated from any State, which are already settled, or become private Property.

Chase denys that any Colony has a Right, to go to the South Sea. . . .[2]

Harrison. How came Maryland by its Land? but by its Charter: By its Charter Virginia owns to the South Sea. Gentlemen shall not pare away the Colony of Virginia. R. Island has more Generosity, than to wish the Massachusetts pared away. Delaware does not wish to pare away Pensilvania.

Huntington. Admit there is danger, from Virginia, does it follow that Congress has a Right to limit her Bounds? The Consequence is not to enter into Confederation. But as to the Question of Right, We all unite against mutilating Charters. I cant agree to the Principle. We are a Spectacle to all Europe. I am not so much alarmed at the Danger, from Virginia, as some are. My fears are not alarmed. They have acted as noble a Part as any. I doubt not the Wisdom of Virginia will limit themselves. A Mans Right does not cease to be a Right because it is large. The Q[uestion] of Right must be determined by the Principles of the common Law.

Stone. This Argument is taken up upon very wrong Ground. It is considered as if We were voting away the Territory of particular Colonies, and Gentlemen work themselves up into Warmth, upon that Supposition. Suppose Virginia should. The small Colonies have a Right to Happiness and Security. They would have no Safety if the great Colonies were not limited. We shall grant Lands in small Quantities, without Rent, or Tribute, or purchase Money. It is said that Virginia is attacked on every Side. Is it meant that Virginia shall sell the Lands for their own Emolument?

All the Colonies have defended these Lands vs. the K. of G.B., and at the Expence of all. Does Virginia intend to establish Quitrents?

I dont mean that the united States shall sell them to get Money by them.

Jefferson. I protest vs. the Right of Congress to decide, upon the

Right of Virginia. Virginia has released all Claims to the Lands settled by Maryland &c.

MS (MHi). Adams, *Diary* (Butterfield), 2:249–50.
   [1] This phrase paraphrases a clause in article 18 of the Articles of Confederation, giving Congress the power to limit state boundaries, which had previously been debated in the committee of the whole on July 25. See *JCC*, 5:550–51; and Adams' Notes of Debates, July 25, 1776.
   [2] Suspension points in MS.

John Adams to Richard Cranch

My dear Sir   Aug. 2. 1776
   I received your Favour of 22 July, by last Tuesdays post.[1] I thank you for the Trouble you have taken to inform me of the Circumstances of your Family and my own. It gives me great Joy to think your Symptoms were so favourable. I had a Letter, from my best Friend by the same Conveyance, which gave me more Pleasure than many Times its Weight in Gold would have done.
   You mention the Exultation at a Declaration of Independence. Is not the Change We have seen astonishing? Would any Man, two Years ago have believed it possible, to accomplish such an Alteration in the Prejudices, Passions, Sentiments, and Principles of these thirteen little States as to make every one of them completely republican, and to make them own it? Idolatry to Monarchs, and servility to Aristocratical Pride, was never so totally eradicated, from so many Minds in so short a Time.
   I thank you for your Account of the Prizes taken, by our little Fleet. We may judge by a little what a great deal Means. I hope We shall have more Power at sea, before long.
   I wish it was in my Power to serve the Interest of Mr. N.C.[2] both for his Merit, services and sufferings. But I dont see, how it will be possible for me to do it. The Appointment of all subordinate Officers in the Quarter Masters and Commissaries Departments is left to the Principals. Promotions of Persons from the Staff Offices, into the Line, gives Disgust, and creates Confusion, if Mr. C's Inclination should lead him to military Preferment. In short there is not the least Probability, that I can see, that any Opportunity will turn Up, in which it will be possible for me to serve him, but if it should I will most chearfully embrace it. I shall inclose to my other self, some News papers. Barry has taken another Tender. Another Prize is taken and carried into Egg Harbour, and a Vessell has arrived here with a rich Cargo of Arms, Ammunition, Flints and Lead, and dry Goods from Marseilles. She brings no bad News from France.

Remember me, to the whole Hospital, and all other Friends. Adieu.

RC (MHi). Adams, *Family Correspondence* (Butterfield), 2:73–74.
[1] Cranch's July 22 letter is in Adams, *Family Correspondence* (Butterfield), 2:57–58.
[2] Despite the reservations he expressed here, Adams did subsequently recommend Nathaniel Cranch to Thomas Mifflin, the former quartermaster general. See Adams to Mifflin, August 15, 1776. See also Adams, *Family Correspondence* (Butterfield), 3:328–29n.5.

Abraham Clark to James Caldwell

Sir,   Phila. Augt. 2d. 1776
The Ship I mentioned to have come up yesterday I hear hath a large quantity of Blankets. A Prize a few days ago was brought into Egg Harbour with 1067 half Jos & 600 Guineas on board besides other Valuable Articles. Several Valuable Prizes have lately been carried in to the Eastward which you will see in the Papers. You will excuse me if I neglect to Address you by your New Indian Name. I can neither Spell or pronounce it. Colo. Daytons if possible is yet harder to come at. I hope Colo. Dayton will not Ask a Dismission from his Station as every department here is filled up at present. Mrs. Caldwell expects your return upon hearing the Kings Troops are so near us. I not only fear for New Jersey, but the Army at N. York. If the British Army should Land above them they could neither retreat or get Supplies. We have only to rely upon the Almighty, but that reliance is scarcely to be seen. At my coming to Congress, I moved for a Chaplain to Attend Prayers every morning which was carried—and some of my Starch breathren will scarcely forgive me for Naming Mr Duche. This I did knowing without such a one many would not Attend. He hath Composed a form of Prayer Unexceptionable to all parties.[1] Dr. Sir, Adieu.

                                                    Abra. Clark

RC (MH). Addressed: "To The Revd. James Caldwell, Chaplain of the Army at Fort Stanwix."
[1] See John Hancock to Jacob Duché, July 9, 1776.

John Hancock to George Washington

Sir,   Philadelphia 2d August 1776 [1]
I am particularly instructed by Congress to Answer that part of your Letter of 29th Ulto. directed to the Board of War, which Relates to the filling up Vacancies in the Army. The Congress are

Concern'd to find that an opinion is entertain'd that greater Confidence has been plac'd in, & larger powers given to other Commanders in that respect, than to yourself. They have in no instance, except in the late Appointment of General Gates to the Command in Canada, parted with the power of filling up Vacancies. The great Confusion & many Disorders prevalent in that Army & its Distance, induc'd Congress to lodge such a power in that General for the limited space of three months, & only during his Continuance in Canada. Should Congress ever empower its Generals to fill up the Vacancies in the Army, they know of no one in whom they would so soon Repose a Trust of such Importance as in yourself; but future Generals may make a bad use of it. The Danger of the Precedent, not any suspicion of their present Commander in Chief, prompts them to Retain a power, that, by you, Sir, might be exercised with the greatest public Advantage.[2]

I do myself the Honour to enclose sundry Resolves, and to request your Attention to them.[3] They relate, principally, as you will perceive to some new Regulations with Regard to Paymasters, Commissaries and Quarter Masters in the American Army and are intended to prevent Confusion and Disorder in those several Departments.

The Congress approve of your employing in the Service of the States the Stockbridge Indians, if you think proper.

The enclosed Resolve for taking into the Pay of the States such of the Seamen as may fall into our Hands on Board of Prizes, will, I trust, be attended with the good Effects Congress had in View when they passed it.

I have the Honour to be, with perfect Respect & Esteem, Sir, your most obedt. & very hble Servt.

John Hancock Presidt

[*P.S.*] Your favr. of 5 Inst., just Came to hand, will be Replied to by to morrow's post.[4]

RC (DLC). First paragraph in a clerical hand, remaining paragraphs in the hand of Jacob Rush, with signature and postscript by Hancock.

[1] Although clearly dated August 2, this letter was actually composed in at least three different parts on August 1, 2, and 5. The first paragraph was drafted by the Board of War on August 1. *JCC*, 5:625. The next two paragraphs were composed on August 2, when the resolves referred to therein were passed, while the two succeeding paragaphs must have been written on August 5, the day Congress passed the resolve on seamen. It is also possible that Hancock added the postscript on August 6, for that is when Congress read Washington's August 5 letter. *JCC*, 5:627–28, 630–31, 633.

[2] On this point, see *JCC*, 5:448; and Washington, *Writings* (Fitzpatrick), 5:347–51.

[3] For these "sundry Resolves," which were passed by Congress on August 2 and 5, see *JCC*, 5:627–28, 630–31. See also Washington, *Writings* (Fitzpatrick), 5:355–56.

[4] This letter is in PCC, item 152, 2:329–32, and Washington, *Writings* (Fitzpatrick), 5:370–72.

North Carolina Delegates to
the North Carolina Council of Safety

Honoured Sir,   Philadelphia August 2 1776
    Permit us, thro' you, to address the honourable body in which
you preside, and inform them that we were favoured with their two
last letters by Mr Hooper, and have seized the earliest, and most
probable method to carry the contents of them into execution.[1] We
have stated to the continental congress, with all the energy we are
capable of, the present distressed and necessitous State of our Province, and the means which may tend most effectually to relieve it.
We have been as fortunate as your most Sanguine expectations, and
the inclosed Resolve will convince you, that North Carolina bears
no inconsiderable weight in the favour of the Continental Congress.[2] The readiness which they discover upon all occasions to comply with the just requisitions of our State, evince that they entertain
a grateful sense of our patriotick exertions, & wish to furnish to us
every inducement to persist in a conduct from which we have to
expect liberty, peace, and happiness.
    In Addition to the several Articles which you recommended to our
care, We have bestowed our Thoughts upon the Subject of pro-
curring Cloaths for our Troops. Men as prompt as they are, to
encounter every difficulty and danger, deserve every comfort and
convenience that from the present pittance of Stores can be procured
for them in this part of the Continent. The Soldiers raised here,
not from any advantages which they derived from nature in point of
appearance, but from being decently clad, and covered from the
Inclemency of the Sun & Rain, shew themselves to great advantage,
& rival regular Troops in decency and cleanliness, whilst our's with
scarce a shirt to their Backs, feel forcibly the effects of poverty, they
become dispirited from Neglect & feel an indifference to a Service
which so sparingly recompences the exertions of those who fight for
it, and brave every [danger?] to protect the liberties of their Country.
Aware of the difficulty of procuring Cloathing in Carolina, We have
prevailed upon the Congress to send a supply from this, & by their
direction have this day employed one of the continental Commissaries to have *made up* for them, as many *Cloth Short Coats,
Breeches, Stockings, Shoes, & Shirts* as may tend to relieve their
urgent wants & prepare them to meet the Weather when it becomes
less favourable to their present destitute situation.[3] It will take some
time to collect the materials & have them made up for use, but be
assured nothing shall be wanting to urge to completion this necessary
business, & to forward the Articles as soon as they are in readiness.
We shall not omit to send Hats, if besides these you should think

proper to order Canteens, Cartouch boxes or any other military Appendage (Arms excepted), We shall pay a punctual Obedience to such orders, Arms not being to be procured.

The 4 Tons of Gunpowder mentioned in the resolve inclosed will be forwarded as soon as Waggons and Horses can be purchased; in this we have made some advances & we hope in a few days to have the necessary Article in motion.

The field pieces cannot at present be had, no pains have been spared to procure such as would answer our purpose but we have not been able in the publick Stores or in private hands to find any. We must wait the contingency of the arrival of Vessels with Stores & it will be among the first Objects to minister in this respect to the defence of North Carolina.

Battering Cannon cannot for some time be sent to you, Few are made but in Maryland & these only At one Work, few Mechanicks can be found that are acquainted with the process, & like all new undertakings it goes on slowly and its first efforts often prove unsuccessfull. The Works at Maryland and elsewhere are under contract to the Continent for what they make & you will of course come in for a share of what the Attempts produce. With plenty of Iron in our province, and the ground Work of a foundery at deep river could we possibly procure an able Operator to carry on the manufactury of Guns, it would be an Object well worthy publick Attention, & merit almost any expence that might attend the carrying so useful a design into execution. It would put us out of dependance upon others & furnish a necessary & profitable Article for the supply of our Neighbours.

We have consulted Doctor Franklin and others upon the Subject of Salt pans, he has promised us his Assistance in preparing the plans, and directing the mode of making the pans. As soon as an Operator can be found who will undertake them, We shall set him at Work. Just now all Manufacturies are at a stand here. The large draughts that have been made from this City for the defence of the Jersies & New York have scarce left enough behind to supply the necessary demands of cloathing for the Inhabitants. We shall find great difficulty to hire Men to drive our Waggons. The exertions of this City are beyond Comprehension, and all Ranks have rushed to New York as to the field where they soon expect to gather the fruits of their bravery, and secure liberty to these united States. May Heaven crown them with Success.

The Books which you ordered[4] with some small alteration which we thought it prudent to make by adding a few others which have some reputation in the military way and a few Pamphlets the design of which will appear from the preface not inapplicable to our province *altogether* with *Catridge* & writing paper will accompany or follow Soon after the Gunpowder.

We beg leave to press upon you as a matter of the most serious concern the manufactures of Salt petre, Common Salt & Gunpowder. Should Britain spread her immense Navy along our Coasts our Supplies from abroad are at an end; upon ourselves must we rely, and should we fall short in our Attempts, the consequences are too alarming to predict & must be obvious to every one. The people here and at the Eastward have found it necessary to be at great expence in the commencement of these manufacturies but the Success has amply compensated them, & they will soon defy the endeavours of Britain to withhold their necessary supplies. You best know the policy of fitting out and loading one or more vessels for the purpose of procuring Salt for the present exigency. When the people feel the total want of that Article we fear it may drive them to some desperate resolutions.

We hear with extreme concern that the Currency of N Carolina has been counterfeited & the deceit so well executed as to endanger the property of the best Judges of our money. We humbly beg leave to hint that one expedient & one only can relieve us, the calling in all the circulating Currency of the Colony and emitting bills in lieu of it. This will put the old & new on a footing & prevent from a Comparison of the new with the old any discrimination being made (as by wicked men it at present is) in favor of the latter. Should you think with us & be confident that the Convention when it sets will adopt this expedient will it not be prudent to order the Bills to be *struck here* (rather printed) as the Continental bills are, and on paper of the same kind. This will secure it from fraud after this, as far as human Invention can disappoint the ingenuity of Villains. Should this be resolved upon the sooner it is accomplished the better. If any great Quantity of the base Currency gets into Circulation and should reach the Soldiery the unavoidable consequences will be clamor, mutiny and desertion.

By Capt Tort we inclosed you the late Newspapers. We now send those which are subsequent to which we refer you for any news which is stirring here In hopes to hear from you by the first Opportunity. We offer our most respectful Compliments to the Gentlemen of your Honourable Board & Subscribe ourselves, with great respect, Sir, Your most Obedt. Humble Servts.

> Will Hooper
>
> Joseph Hewes
>
> John Penn

P.S. The Drums, Colours & fifes will be sent as soon as the men return from the Army whose business it is to make them. We hope this will be in a few days.

RC (Nc–Ar). Written by Penn and signed by Penn, Hewes, and Hooper.

¹ Cornelius Harnett was president of the council of safety. For the council's "two last letters" to the North Carolina delegates, which were carried by William Hooper, who arrived in Philadelphia on July 23, see North Carolina Delegates to the North Carolina Council of Safety, July 30, 1776, note 2.

² For the resolve on sending "four tons of gunpowder and six four pounders" to North Carolina, which was passed by Congress on July 31, see *JCC*, 5:623.

³ See ibid.

⁴ See North Carolina Council of Safety to the North Carolina Delegates, July 7, 1776, in *N.C. Colonial Records*, 11:308–9.

John Adams to Abigail Adams

Aug. 3. 1776

The Post was later than usual to day, so that I had not yours of July 24 till this Evening. You have made me very happy, by the particular and favourable Account you give me of all the Family. But I dont understand how there are so many who have no Eruptions, and no Symptoms. The Inflammation in the Arm might do, but without these, there is no small Pox.

I will lay a Wager, that your whole Hospital have not had so much small Pox, as Mrs. Katy Quincy. Upon my Word she has had an Abundance of it, but is finely recovered, looks as fresh as a Rose, but pitted all over, as thick as ever you saw any one. I this Evening presented your Compliments and Thanks to Mr. Hancock for his polite offer of his House, and likewise your Compliments to his Lady and Mrs. Katy.

Aug. 4. Went this Morning to the Baptist Meeting, in Hopes of hearing Mr. Stillman, but was dissappointed. He was there, but another Gentleman preached. His Action was violent to a degree bordering on fury. His Gestures, unnatural, and distorted. Not the least Idea of Grace in his Motions, or Elegance in his Style. His Voice was vociferous and boisterous, and his Composition almost wholly destitute of Ingenuity. I wonder extreamly at the Fondness of our People for schollars educated at the Southward and for southern Preachers. There is no one Thing, in which We excell them more, than in our University, our schollars, and Preachers. Particular Gentlemen here, who have improved upon their Education by Travel, shine. But in general, old Massachusetts outshines her younger sisters, still. In several Particulars, they have more Wit, than We. They have Societies; the philosophical Society particularly, which excites a scientific Emulation, and propagates their Fame. If ever I get through this Scene of Politicks and War, I will spend the Remainder of my days, in endeavouring to instruct my Countrymen in the Art of making the most of their Abilities and Virtues, an Art, which they have hitherto, too much neglected. A philosophical society shall be established at Boston, if I have Wit and Address enough to accomplish it, sometime or other. Pray set Brother Cranch's Philosophical Head to plodding upon this Project. Many of his Lucubrations would have been published and preserved, for the Benefit of Mankind, and for his Honour, if such a Clubb had existed.

My Countrymen want Art and Address. They want Knowledge of the World. They want the exteriour and superficial Accomplishments of Gentlemen, upon which the World has set so high a Value. In solid Abilities and real Virtues, they vastly excell in general, any People upon this Continent. Our N. England People are Aukward and bashfull; yet they are pert, ostentatious and vain, a Mixture which excites Ridicule and gives Disgust. They have not the faculty of shewing themselves to the best Advantage, nor the Art of concealing this faculty. An Art and Faculty which some People possess in the highest degree. Our Deficiencies in these Respects, are owing wholly to the little Intercourse We have with strangers, and to our Inexperience in the World. These Imperfections must be remedied, for New England must produce the Heroes, the statesmen, the Philosophers, or America will make no great Figure for some Time.

Our Army is rather sickly at N. York, and We live in daily Expectation of hearing of some great Event. May God almighty grant it may be prosperous for America. Hope is an Anchor and a Cordial. Disappointment however will not disconcert me.

If you will come to Philadelphia in September, I will stay, as long as you please. I should be as proud and happy as a Bridegroom. Yours.

RC (MHi). Adams, *Family Correspondence* (Butterfield), 2:75–76.

John Adams to William Heath

Dear Sir   Philadelphia Aug. 3. 1776

Yours of the 20th Ult. is before me.[1] I am much obliged to you for it, and most heartily wish for a more free and intimate Communication of Sentiments, upon the State both of our Councils and Arms. I should be happy, in a few Hours Conversation, but as this cannot be, I must be content with a Letter.

We have now a Nation to protect and defend; and I can easily see the Propriety of the observation you quote from the Prussian Hero, that the Prosperity of a State depends upon the Discipline of its Army. This Discipline reared the Roman Empire and the British: and the American will Stand or fall, in my opinion, according as it adheres to or deviates from the Same Discipline.

If there is not Wisdom and Vigour enough in the civil Government to Support the military officers, in introducing and establishing Such a Discipline, it must be owing to the Advantages of Soil and Climate, and our extream Distance from our Enemies, not to our own Strength, Virtue, or Wisdom, if We do not fail.

The Army must be well officered, Armed, disciplined, fed, cloathed, covered, and paid. In these Respects We do as well as We can. Time, I hope, will assist Us, and every officer of the Army, would do well to suggest to his Friends and Correspondents in Congress, and in the Legislatures of the Several States, every defect, and every Improvement in those Particulars, which occurs to him. I am in more Anxiety for Cloaths and Tents than any Thing, because the Health as well as Discipline of the Army, depend much upon them.

We shall never do well, untill We get a regular Army, and this will never be, untill Men are inlisted for a longer Duration, and that will never be effected untill We are more generous in our Encouragement to Men. But I am convinced that Time alone, will persuade Us to this Measure: and in the mean Time We shall, very indiscreetly waste a much greater Expence than would be necessary for this great Purpose in temporary Calls upon Militia, besides risquing the Loss of many Lives, and much Reputation.

Congress has not determined to have no Regard to the Line of Succession in Promotions, but only that this Line shall not be an invariable Rule. Cæteris paribus, the Line will be pursued. But they mean to reserve a Right of distinguishing extraordinary Merit, or Demerit. This Rule may be abused. But is it not necessary? All good Things are liable to abuse. I am afraid, nay I know it will be abused, in particular Instances. But if We make the succession an invariable Rule, will not the Abuse be greater?

Is it not common in the British Army, to promote junior officers, over the Heads of their Superiours? Nay even officers in the same Regiment and on the same Command? I have been told of several Instances. This however is wrong.

Your opinions of Men and Things, I wish I knew in more detail, because I have a good opinion of your Judgment of both, and I fear, situated as I am, many Things relating to both may not have come to my Knowledge, that I ought to know. As the first officer in the Massachusetts Service, you have in some sort the Patronage of all the officers of that State. I hope you will recommend the best Men for promotion.

I confess myself very ignorant of the military Characters from that State.

By some Expressions in the Close of your Letter, I conclude you were not perfectly Satisfyed with a late Promotion. Be assured, Sir, if that was raising a junior officer, over the Head of any Superiour, it was not considered in that light by the Gentlemen who did it. The

Person promoted was thought to be the oldest Brigadier, and intituled to Advancement by the Line of Succession. And it is my
opinion he would have been made a Major General much sooner
if his Experience had not been thought indispensible in the Adjutant
Generals Department.[2] I am, Sir, with great Respect, your affectionate Servant,   John Adams

RC (MHi).
  [1] Heath's July 20 letter to Adams is in the Adams Papers, MHi, and *Collections
of the Massachusetts Historical Society*, 7th ser. 4 (1904): 11–13.
  [2] A reference to Horatio Gates. Heath was promoted to major general on August
9, 1776. *JCC*, 5:641.

John Adams to Daniel Hitchcock

Sir   Philadelphia August 3. 1776
Your obliging Favour of the 22 Ult. came duely to Hand,[1] and I
thank you for it. A free Correspondence between the Members of
Congress and the officers of the Army will probably be attended
with Advantages to the public by improving both the Councils and
Arms of America.
    The Burthen of contracting for Cloaths, Arms, and accoutrements
for the Regiments ought not to lie upon the collonells. A Pay
master for each Regiment has been ordered by Congress, and if this
officer is not enough, if a Representation was made of it, another
would be appointed. But I suppose a Pay master would answer all
the Purposes. If not be so good as to point out to me, what other
Regulation is needfull.
    There is some ground for your observation that Officers are ad-
vanced faster to Posts of Honour, to the Southward than Northward.
But I cannot think that the Instance you have mentioned, is a
Proof of it, or that in that Case the Promotions were exceptionable.
You say that every one who was Coll there last year, has been this
year made a General. This in two illustrious Instances, Henry &
Gadsden, did not hold. But in the other Cases it was not Wrong.
Mercer, Lewis, More, and How were not only Men of Fortune, and
Figure, in their Countries and in civil Imployments, but they were
all veteran Soldiers, and had been Collonells in a former War. It is
true, their Provincial Legislatures had made them only Collonells
last year, and the Reason was because they only raised Regiments,
not Brigades. But as soon as those Colonies came to raise Brigades,
it was but reasonable these officers should be appointed Brigadiers.
These officers stood in the Light of Thomas, Fry, Whitcomb, Putnam, &c &c with this difference, that the Gentlemen themselves were
Superiour in Point of Property and Education. Besides, it has been

our constant Endeavour, that each State should have a reasonable Number of General officers in Proportion to the Number of Troops they raise. It should be considered that We have constituents to satisfy as well as the Army, and Colonies to rank as well as Collonells and Generals. Massachusetts has most Cause of Complaint upon this Head. That there have not been many Promotions of Collonells to the Northward, is true. But how can it be avoided. If I were left to myself, to my Judgment and Inclination, I should not hesitate a Moment. But We must not deviate from the Line of Succession. If We do, We are threatened with Disgust and Resignations. And how can We follow the Line? Wooster, Heath and Spencer ought to be made Major Generals, But is this the opinion of the Army?

Reed, Nixon, Prescott and others, the oldest Collonells, and veteran soldiers and undoubtedly brave officers. But there is not one Gentleman in this Congress, I believe who knows the Face of any one of them except the last, or that ever received a letter from any one of them. What are their Educations, their Abilities, their Knowledge of the World, their Sentiments? Have they that Authority and Command, which a General Officer ought to have, and which is so essential to the Discipline of an Army, upon which according to the K. of Prussia the entire Prosperity of every State depends.

My own opinion is, that it is safest to promote those officers in Succession, but I fear it will never be done. It never will unless the General recommends it, and I dont believe he will do it. Besides the Colonies must and will have their Shares of Generals, except the Massachusetts.

Such is the Nature of Mankind in Society, especially in Armies, that I believe it is best to pursue the Line of Succession in Promotions excepting extraordinary Cases of Merit and Demerit. But if it would not occasion Confusion, I think a General Officer ought to be a Man of Letters, Taste and Sense, and therefore Parsons, Varnum, Hitchcock, and others of the like Character would certainly have my Vote. But then you know that old officers would tare up the ground, if such Youths, and inexperienced People, as they would express themselves were put over their Heads.[2]

I have written with great Freedom, in Confidence that no ill use will be made of it. I wish your Sentiments upon these subjects with the Same Candor.

The affair of the Bounty, has given me Uneasiness enough to no Purpose.[3] I see We shall never get a regular, permanent Army, but must go on patching up an Army every 3 Months, with fresh Militia, at double the Expence. Reason and Experience are sometimes lost upon the wisest and the best of Men.

LB (MHi). Addressed: "Coll Daniel Hitchcock, Camp in Long Island."
[1] The July 22 letter from Daniel Hitchcock (d. 1777), commander of the Eleventh Continental Regiment, is in the Adams Papers, MHi.

[2] On August 9 Congress appointed four major generals—William Heath, Joseph Spencer, John Sullivan, and Nathanael Greene—and six brigadier generals—James Read, John Nixon, Arthur St. Clair, Alexander McDougall, Samuel H. Parsons, and James Clinton. *JCC,* 5:641.

[3] In his July 22 letter Hitchcock had complained that the ten dollar bounty voted by Congress on June 26 for "every non-commissioned officer and soldier, who will inlist to serve for the term of three years" would not be sufficient to induce men from New England to enlist. See *JCC,* 5:483.

John Adams to Samuel H. Parsons

Dear Sir   Philadelphia August 3. 1776

Your Favour of 24 Ult. is before me.[1] Your observations concerning the Encouragement We ought to give to soldiers to inlist, I think, are just; but a Wisdom Superiour to mine determined otherwise, and therefore I must take it for granted, that it is Superiour Wisdom to live from Hand to Mouth, to trust to temporary Expedients, and to depend upon fresh Reinforcements of raw Militia every 3 Months instead of a regular, well disciplined Army.

The Rule of Promotions is still unsettled, and I believe will continue so. The Time will soon arrive, when every state will appoint its own officers, and fill all Vacancies, under the Generals. For my own Part I have sometimes thought the best Rule would be to make the Promotion of Captains and Subalterns Regimental, and of Field officers Colonial. To make it continental is impracticable. The Case of Coll Tyler and Coll Durkee, will be considered by the Board of War, this Evening.[2] How they will determine, I know not. It will be determined with Integrity, I am very sure, I hope with Judgment, and in a Manner that will give Satisfaction. But this I am fully convinced of, that every Promotion, almost without Exception, that ever will be made, let it be done with ever so much Skill and Integrity and let us observe what Rule We may, will give Discontent, open or secret, to somebody, or other. There is no Possibility of giving universal Satisfaction to great Numbers of Men.

Your Memorial has been duely attended to, and is under the Consideration of a Committee.[3] It is a difficult Case. I am, with Respect, and Esteem, your most obedient servant.

John Adams

RC (NjR: Elsie O. and Philip D. Sang photostat, 1972).

[1] Parsons' July 24 letter to Adams is in the Adams Papers, MHi.

[2] John Tyler and John Durkee were promoted to colonel on August 10. *JCC,* 5:644.

[3] Parsons' memorial asked for the arrest of Bazil Bouderot, a Canadian prisoner, for the murder of Parsons' brother. It was read in Congress on July 25 and committed to a committee of which Adams was a member. On August 21 Congress ordered that Bouderot be imprisoned in Massachusetts until his trial or removal to Nova Scotia. See *JCC,* 5:609, 692–93; and Adams, *Diary* (Butterfield), 3:407–8n.1.

Samuel Adams to Joseph Trumbull

My dear Sir   Philada Augt 3 1776

Our Friend Coll W. (not Mr Lewis) brought and deliverd to us your Letter of the 25th of July directed to Mr J A and my self.[1] The Inclosures clearly show the deplorable State of our Affairs in the Northern Department, and it is easy to trace the Source of them. I am fully of opinion that *one Man* must be removd to some other Department to put an End to our Misfortunes there; This has been attempted and urgd, but has hitherto been impracticable. A little Time may perhaps unravel Mysteries and convince Gentlemen that they have been under certain Prejudices to which the wisest Men are lyable. It appears to me very extraordinary that Mr L should insist upon acting after being apprizd of the Resolve of Congress,[2] and it is still more surprizing that he is supported by————[3] in this Conduct. I am very sure that our Affairs must suffer greatly if he is allowd to persist in so doing. You are the best Judge of the Part proper for you to take on this Occasion in your own Department; but as your own Reputation in your office as well as the publick Service is at Stake would it be amiss for you to state the Matter to the General. By this Means it might come before Congress. I shall certainly do all in my Power to have the Evils you mention corrected. I have communicated your Letter to Several Gentlemen who will joyn with me in every practicable Method for this Purpose. Congress have this day passed several Resolutions which I hope will be attended with a good Effect.[4] Pay Master and Deputy Pay Master are to make weekly Returns to Congress of the State of the military Chests under their Direction. *Jonathan Trumbull* Esqr Pay Master in the Northern Department is to transmit to Congress as soon as possible an Account of all the Monies which have passed through his hands. Commissaries General & Deputies in the several Departments are to transmit to Congress weekly Accounts of Monies they receive of Pay Masters or their Deputies. Quarter Masters and Deputy Quarter Masters are to do the same. Commissary General, Quarter Mr Genl and their Deputies are to make Monthly Returns at least of Stores in their Possession and the Distribution of them; and the Commanding Officers in each Department are to make monthly Returns to Congress of the Drafts they make on the respective Pay Masters. These Resolutions perhaps may not please *every Body*, but if they are duly executed they may detect Mistakes, or *Frauds* if any should happen. As to what has passd in Canada & near it, some Person has in my opinion been most egregiously to blame, and, to use a homely Proverb, the Saddle has been laid, or attempted to be laid on the wrong horse. I hope by strict Scrutiny the Causes will be found out and the guilty Man be made to suffer. My Regards to General Mifflin & all Friends. I am very respectfully, Yours,

S A

[*P.S.*] Since writing the foregoing I have turnd to the printed Journals of Congress and find that on the 17 July 1775 Walter Livingston Esqr was appointed "Commissary of Stores & Provisions for the New York Department during the *present* Campaign." Upon what Grounds then does he speak of himself as vested by Congress with full Powers to act *till revoked*. The last Campaign which limitted his power to act, is finishd. Under what Pretence can he be supported by his Patron, especially since by the Resolution of Congress of the 9th July last, you have "full Power to supply both Armies, that upon the Lakes as well as that at New York, and also to appoint and employ such Persons under you and to remove any Deputy Commissary as you shall think proper and expedient," and for this express Reason "it being absolutely necessary that the Supply of *both* Armies should be under *one* Direction." Has not General S[chuyler] seen this Resolution? Or, if he has seen it, Does he judge that the supply of the two Armies should be under different Directions, and undertake to order the Matter accordingly. If the Persons whom you send to act under you in the Northern Army, are confined & limited by *any* other Person after they arrive there, unless by order of Congress, and without giving you Notice in Case such order should be made, We must expect a Repetition of the most mortifying Disappointments. Upon my Word, I think it your Duty to remonstrate this either to the Commander in Chiefe or the Congress. The former I should suppose you wd prefer. Adieu,

S A

RC (Ct).

[1] Trumbull's July 25th letter, which is in the Samuel Adams Papers, NN, probably had been delivered by William Williams, who arrived in Philadelphia as a delegate to Congress at the end of July.

[2] For additional information on Trumbull's dispute with Walter Livingston and the latter's resignation in September, see Elbridge Gerry to Joseph Trumbull, September 12, 1776. See also Roger Sherman's Memorandum of a Conversation, November 13, 1775, note 1.

[3] Undoubtedly Philip Schuyler.

[4] Adams is referring to the resolves passed by Congress on August 2. *JCC,* 5:627–28.

Caesar Rodney to Thomas Rodney

Sir   Philada. August the 3d 1776

I Recd yours of the 30th of July and Shall endeavour to Answer it. Captn. Gordon might have had the place you mentioned But on talking with me Very prudently declined it. The History of your Maneuvers, procession &c please me and the more so, as I had heard of the Choice without knowing the principal on which it was made.

With respect to the return made me by the field officers, They have neglected to send me the dates of their Commissions or appointments in the Militia. I have therefore wrote to them[1] to return me the dates before Commissions Can be made out. As to the Subalterns, there being placed with an Older or Younger Captain does not affect their Rank as that will be preserved by the Commission made out for them, and as that Will be the Case it is better they Should be fixed in Such Companies as best please them. I Showed Captain Gordon the return made me by the Field-Officers Showing the order in which they Chose to be placed with respect to the Companies, Which Mr. Gordon Said was agreable to their desire so far as he had knowledge in it. That he was shure it was right as to Caldwell's Company.

With Respect to the Choice of a Convention, I would Submit it to you and Your friends Whether (when you have fixed on Such Ticket as meets with your approbation) it would not be best to persue and Endeavour to impress the Utility of Such Choice being made by the people (Especially at a time when the Establishing their Rights and priviledges as freemen depends on Such Choice) Upon Your former plan, I mean of true Whiggism, True patriotism. This plan if persued with diligence and such Cool argument & reasoning as the Cause will point out & justify, I think Must Carry with it Persuation and Conviction. It Certainly will with all such as are not Governed by a party Spirit. If any person or persons be proposed in oposition to your ticket who have heretofore been unfriendly to the Cause, point out to the people their former Conduct, and Submit to them the propriety of trusting to Such men, at Such an Important Crisis. Your Scheme ought to hold out to the people more of the Patriot than of party-man. I will again Submit as before, Whether the Enquiry & Examination proposed to be had before the Committee will not tend so to irritate As to occasion many people by taking Sides in that matter To loose sight of the Cause, their true interest, for if they are lead to believe that you and Your friends are Governed more by party Sperit than by the true Interest of America, they Will hold you in the Light of all other party-men and deal with you Accordingly. You say the Committee are about to make this Enquiry. Are there a Sufficient Number of Patriots in that Committe to answer Your Expectation? Are there a Considerable Majority of them that Wish the Enquiry should be had? Will they (if matters turn out as you Expect) publish their opinions to the County So that the friends to Liberty may benefit by it? It is an Enquiry that ought to have been made but it is an Enquiry that ought to be made by men of Understanding only. Do Such make a Majority of the Committee tho good men? By What authority do they take it up? Are not many of the members principals in the matter of Enquiry? All these things I Submit to the Good Sense and prudence of You and Your friends. Tho you Seem to have ditermined on the measure (by Your Letter) before my opinion was Asked. In Short it is difficult for me to give an opinion in this Case as I am a stranger to the present Complection of the Committee. However as this Convention is undoubtedly the most important assembly that Ever was Chose in that Government, would advise the Avoiding Every kind of Violence, and on the other hand the utmost diligence and persuation to procure as many friends to Liberty on the return as possible. By this means Men who have been known to be heretofore unfriendly to Liberty (if properly pointed out) Cannot prevail. The people when uninitiated Generally hearken to reason and make prudent Choices. But you may be able to let me know more about these things by the next Post.[2]

Yesterday Came to town a Ship belonging to the Congress from France with Ten Tunns of Powder, about forty Tunns of Lead, one thousand Stand of Arms &c &c. And the Same day an Armed Veshell taken by Captain Barry at Sea. I have put your thread in the hands of a Weaver. I am with love to all, Yours &c.

                                                          Caesar Rodney

RC (MeHi).
  [1] Not found.
  [2] See Thomas Rodney to Caesar Rodney, August 5, 1776, in Rodney, *Letters* (Ryden), pp. 101–2. For a discussion of the inquiry into the "insurrection" of June 9 and its effects on the election in Delaware, see William Baskerville Hamilton, *Thomas Rodney: Revolutionary and Builder of the West* (Durham, N.C.: Duke University Press, 1953), pp. 23–24.

Caesar Rodney to Thomas Rodney

Sir   Philada. August 3d 1776
  Since I finished my other Letter have been up at Congress where We Recd Inteligence by letter from Captn Weeks[1] in the Congress Ship the Reprisal that he has at Sea on the 13th of July taken two prizes, a Ship and a Schooner bound for Liverpool Loaded with Cotton, Sugar, Rum &c. The Letters Came by the Prize Schooner which arrived in an Inlet near Egg Harbour, and the Ship Prize has been Seen off the Capes of Delaware and Supposed by this time got in. This days Post is not Yet Come in from New-York. It is past his Usual time of Coming, and therefore Imagined there will be Something Important which delayed him. I wish it may be Good. The Delaware Came to Town this Morning, and there passed an Order of Congress Yesterday Morning for Captain Darby and his Company now at Lewis To Come up and join the Battalion, or at least to follow them, for as the Congress have now Got Arms I imagine they will not Stay long here.[2] Let not the Contents of my other letter be Seen by any Unless a friend in Whom you Can Confide. I believe I Shall never be Able to get that scoundrel to make Betsey's & Sally's

Shooses. I have not time to say any thing about my plantation affairs, but hope you will have an Eye to them, that they may not suffer. I have (without the least Expectation of being gratified) a Strong desire to be at Home once more. I am &c,   Caesar Rodney

RC (PHi).

[1] Lambert Wickes. See Clark, *Naval Documents*, 5:1030, 1069.

[2] This day John Hancock wrote to "the Officer commanding the Battalion of Continental Troops now in this city, Colonel Hasletts Battalion," and directed him "to order the company of your battalion posted at Lewis Town as soon as possible to march to Philada, and join their battalion now stationed at the barracks in this city." PCC, item 12A; and *Am. Archives*, 5th ser. 1:739.

John Adams to Nathanael Greene

Dear Sir   Philadelphia August 4. 1776

Your Favour of the 14 of July is before me.[1] I am happy to find your Sentiments concerning the Rewards of the Army, and the Promotion of officers so nearly agreable to mine. I wish the general sense here was more nearly agreable to them. Time I hope will introduce a proper sense of Justice in those Cases where it may for Want of Knowledge and Experience be wanting.

The New England Collonells, you observe, are jealous, that Southern officers are treated with more attention than they, because Several of the Southern Collonells have been made Generals, but not one of them.

Thompson was somehow or other, the first Coll upon the Establishment and so intituled to Promotion, by succession, and it was also supposed by ability and Merit. This ought not therefore to give offence. Mercer, Lewis, Howe, More were old veteran officers, and stood in the Light of Putnam, Thomas, Fry, Whitcomb &c among the New England officers. Added to this, We have endeavoured to give Colonies General Officers in some Proportion to their Troops—and Colonies have nice feelings about Rank as well as Collonells. So that I dont think, our Coll's have just Cause to complain of these Promotions. Lord Sterling was a Person so distinguished by Fortune, Family, and the Rank and Employments he had held in civil Life, added to his Experience in military life, that it was thought no great Uneasiness would be occasioned by his advancement. Mifflin was a Gentleman of Family and Fortune in his Country, of the best Education and Abilities, of great Knowledge of the World, and remarkable Activity. Besides this, the Rank he had held as a Member of the Legislature of this Province, and a Member of Congress, and his great Merit in the civil Department, in Subduing the Quaker and Proprietarian Interests added to the Tory Interests of this Province to the American System of Union, and especially his activity and Success in infusing into this Province a martial Spirit and ambition which it never felt before, were thought Sufficient Causes for his Advancement.

Besides all this, my dear sir, there is a political Motive. Military Characters in the southern Colonies, are few. They have never known much of war and it is not easy to make a People Warlike who have never been so. All the Encouragement, and every Incentive therefore, which can be given with justice ought to be given, in order to excite an Ambition among them, for military Honours.

But after all, my dear Sir, I wish I could have a few Hours free Conversation with you upon this important Subject. A General officer ought to be a Gentleman of Letters, and general Knowledge, a Man of Address and Knowledge of the World. He should carry with him Authority and Command. There are among the New England officers, Gentlemen who are equal to all this—Parsons, Hitchcock, Varnum, and others younger than they and inferiour to them too in command. But these are a great Way down, in the List of Collonells, and to promote them over the Heads of so many veterans, would throw all into confusion. Read, Nixon, and Prescott are the oldest Collonells. They are allowed to be experienced officers and brave Men. But I believe there is not one Member of Congress who knows the face of either of them—and what their accomplishments are, I know not. I really wish you would give me your Advice freely upon these Subjects in Confidence. It is not every Piece of Wood that will do to make a Mercury, and Bravery alone, is not a Sufficient Qualification for a General officer. Name me a New England Coll of whose real Qualifications, I can speak with Confidence, who is intituled to Promotion by succession and If I do not get him made a General Officer, I will join the N. E. Collonells in their Jealousy and outclamour the loudest of them.[2] There is a real difficulty, attending this Subject, which I know not how to get over. Pray help me. I believe there would be no difficulty in obtaining Advancement for some of the N. E. Colls here. But by promoting them over the Heads of so many, there would be a Difficulty in the Army, for Massachusetts will fare the worst.

LB (MHi).
[1] Greene's July 14 letter is in the Adams Papers, MHi.
[2] For the six colonels elected brigadier generals on August 9, see JCC, 5:641.

Josiah Bartlett to John Langdon

Sir   Philadelphia August 5th 1776.

Since my last, a vessel fitted out by the Secret Committee has arrived here from Marseilles in France which place she left the 8th of June. She has brought for the use of the American States 1000 good muskets, about ten tons of powder and about 40 tons of lead &c &c. A small privateer from this City called the Congress has taken a vessel bound from the West Indies to Halifax and sent her safe into port. Beside a cargo of West India goods, there was found on board her 1078 Joes, 672 guineas and some other gold coin. Capt Barry in the Lexington, one of the Continental vessels, has taken and sent in here a privateer of six carriage guns commanded by another of them infamous Goodrichs of Virginia. Capt Weeks in the Reprisal another Continental vessel has taken and sent in a sloop bound from the West Indies to Liverpool. He has also taken a ship from Grenada to London which is not yet arrived—both loaded with West India goods.[1]

Since the Declaration of Independence your friend John Alsop has wrote to the Convention of New York to resign his seat in Congress and made some reflections on the Convention for their agreeing so unanimously to that declaration.[2] The Convention in return voted cheerfully and unanimously to accept of his resignation with some severe and cutting reflections on him for his conduct, which were all sent to Congress. I believe his boarding with our friend Wharton has been no advantage to him—possibly he was obliged to resign his seat as a previous condition to his taking full possession of the lady. As I had no letter from you last post (for I look on the cover to Col Whipple's letters to be nothing) I hope you will consider this as bringing you one letter in debt or at least that it be put to my credit to make up former deficiencies, which will be but justice to, Your most obedient   Josiah Bartlett

P.S. August 6. Yesterday arrived here two prizes taken by Capt Weeks—one the ship before mentioned, having on board it is said 500 hogsheads of sugar—the other a brig bound from the West Indies to Ireland taken since the ship and sloop—the particulars of her cargo I have not heard. This is the best way of supplying ourselves with necessaries since Britain will not suffer us to procure them by trade and I expect another year we shall be well supplied this way. Yours &c,   J. B.

Tr (DLC).
  [1] For Capt. Lambert Wickes' letters of July 11 and 13, 1776, see Clark, *Naval Documents*, 5:1030, 1069.
  [2] See John Alsop to the New York Provincial Congress, July 16, 1776.

Thomas Jefferson to John Page

Dear Page   Philadelphia Aug. 5. 1776.
  I am sorry to hear that the Indians have commenced war, but greatly pleased you have been so decisive on that head.[1] Nothing

will reduce those wretches so soon as pushing the war into the heart of their country. But I would not stop there. I would never cease pursuing them while one of them remained on this side the Misisippi. So unprovoked an attack and so treacherous a one should never be forgiven while one of them remains near enough to do us injury. The Congress having had reason to suspect the Six nations intended war, instructed their commissioners to declare to them peremptorily that if they chose to go to war with us, they should be at liberty to remove their families out of our settlements, but to remember that they should not only never more return to their dwellings on any terms but that we would never cease pursuing them with war while one remained on the face of the earth: and moreover, to avoid equivocation, to let them know they must recall their young men from Canada, or we should consider them as acting against us nationally. This decisive declaration produced an equally decisive act on their part: they have recalled their young men, and are stirring themselves with anxiety to keep their people in quiet, so that the storm we apprehended to be brewing there it is hoped is blown over. Colo. Lee being unable to attend here till the 20th inst. I am under the painful necessity of putting off my departure, notwithstanding the unfavorable situation of Mrs. Jefferson's health. We have had hopes till to day of receiving an authentication of the next year's delegation, but are disappointed. I know not who should have sent it, the Governor, or President of Convention: but certainly some body should have done it. What will be the consequence I know not. We cannot be admitted to take our seat on any precedent or the spirit of any precedent yet set. According to the standing rules not only an authentic copy will be required, but it must be entered in the journals verbatim that it may there appear we have right to sit. This seems the more necessary as the quorum is then to be reduced. Some of the newspapers indeed mention that on such a day such and such gentlemen were appointed to serve for the next year, but could newspaper evidence be received, they would not furnish the form of the appointment, nor yet what quorum is to be admitted.[2] Ld. Howe is recruiting fast. Forty odd ships arrived the other day, and others at other times. It is questionable whether our recruits come in so speedily as his. Several valuable West Indian men have been taken and brought in lately, and the spirit of privateering is gaining ground fast. No news from Tionderoga. I inclose you (to amuse your curiosity) the form of the prayer substituted in the room of the prayer for the king by Mr. Duché chaplain to the Congress. I think by making it so general as to take in Conventions, assemblies &c. it might be used instead of that for the parliament. Adieu.

RC (InU). Jefferson, *Papers* (Boyd), 1:485–87.
[1] An account of the July 20 engagement between the Fincastle militia and some

Creeks and Cherokees near "the Great Island of Holstein" is in *Am. Archives,* 5th ser. 1:464.

² Although the terms of the Virginia delegates expired on August 11, the credentials of the new delegation, which reduced the quorum requirement to three, were not presented to Congress until August 28. *JCC,* 5:712.

William Whipple to Joshua Brackett

Dear Sir,   Philadelphia 5th Augt 1776

It gives me Pleasure to hear that the Declaration is so acceptable in N. Hampshire. Pray did the Sherriff read it with a good Grace? I hope by this time he is wean'd from his Tyranic Connections, & approves of a System of Politicks founded on the true Principles of Liberty.

I am glad to hear of the Prizes taken, Northward. We also take some this way. A tender of 8 Guns arriv'd here last week taken by the Brig Lexington, also a Schooner from Granada Bound to Hallifax taken by the Reprisal, who also took a ship Bound from Granada, for London, which is not yet arriv'd. A Brig from Nevis bound for Hallifax with a considerable sum of money was sent into Egg Harbour a few days since by a Privateer belonging to this place. A ship fitted out by Congress last Winter arriv'd here on Thursday last from Mercelles [Marseilles] with abot 40 Tons Lead, 1000 Musketts, 10 Tons Powder, 1 bbl. Flints. We have had no certain intelligence from the Southward lately, but its reported that Sir Peter Parker died of his wound receiv'd at the attack on Sullivans Island.

I shall set out in a few days, & shall be happy if I shall have it in my Power to carry you any good news. In the Mean time I am, very Sincerely Yours,   W Whipple

[*P.S.*] I have just heard that the ship before mentioned as taken by the Reprisal is arriv'd in the River, also a Brig from the West Indies for Ireland taken by the same ship.

RC (MHi).

John Adams to Abigail Adams

Philadelphia August 6. 1776

Yours of 29 July came by this days Post, and made me very happy. Nabby, Charles, and Tommy will have the small Pox, well, I dont doubt. Tell John he is a very lucky young Gentleman, to have it so much better, than his Mamma, his sister, and Brothers.

Mr. S[amuel] A[dams] will set out for Boston, on Monday, the

12 of August. I shall write by him. But I will not neglect Writing a few Lines by the Post. I have written a Resignation of my Place here, to the General Court, sometime ago,[1] but it seems, they were adjourned, and therefore will not be able to consider the Matter, untill the 28 of this Month, when they will send some other Person here in my Stead. How I am to get home I dont know. When I see how Mr. A. goes, I will write you more particularly upon the subject. Whether to hire a Horse here, or to have a Man and two Horses come for me, I am not determined, must leave all undetermined at present. I want the Exercise of a Journey so much, that I must return soon. The General Court will appoint some one to relieve me, the first Thing they do, after they come together. I shall take it for granted, that they will sett off, accordingly. My Health is so infirm that I can stay no longer.

We are in daily Expectation of some decisive Stroke at N. York. Dunmore has fled from Cheasapeak, and Clinton from Charlestown, and both have joined How, at Staten Island.[2]

RC (MHi). LB (MHi). Endorsed: "Sent by Post Aug. 10. 1776. with several News-papers." Adams, *Family Correspondence* (Butterfield), 2:80–81.

[1] See John Adams to John Avery, July 25, 1776, note 1.

[2] Adams probably added this last paragraph after General Washington's August 7 letter to Congress containing this information had been received. See John Hancock to George Washington, August 8, 1776.

Board of War to the Maryland Convention or Committee of Safety

Gentlemen,   War office 6th Augst 1776 Philada.

By a Resolve of Congress on the subject of Prisoners it is determined "that a List of the Prisoners in each Colony be made out by the Comittees of the Counties, Towns or Districts where they reside and transmitted to the Assembly, Convention or Council or Comittee of Safety of such Colony respectively, who shall send a Copy thereof to Congress." [1] The Board of War who have by Direction of Congress, the Care of all Prisoners, are much Obstructed in that Business by the Resolution before quoted not having been Complied with, I am therefore to press you by all Means to prevail on the several Comittees in your State to enable you immediately to transmitt an accurate List of all Prisoners of War now in your State to the Board that this matter which has heretofore been in Confusion may be reduced to proper Order.

I have the Honour to be, your most obedt humble Servt,

Richard Peters Secy

P. S. Please to send also a List of all Officers, their Ranks and Dates

of Comissions of any Continental Troops raised in your State and
the Time for which they were enlisted.

RC (MdAA). In a clerical hand and signed by Peters. Addressed: "Honble Convention or Committee of Safety of the State of Maryland at Annapolis. Free.
E. Rutledge." Texts of this letter in M–Ar and *N. C. Colonial Records,* 10:726,
indicate that it was a circular letter to all the states.
[1] This resolve had been passed by Congress on May 21, 1776. *JCC,* 4:372. The
board was prompted to write this letter by an August 5 resolve instructing it "to
furnish the Committee of Treasury with the names of the British officers and
other prisoners, who are entitled to the allowance made by Congress of two
dollars per week, with the times of their captivity and the places where they are
quartered." *JCC,* 5:632.

Abraham Clark to Elias Dayton

My Dear Friend,   Phila. Augst 6th. 1776.
     Your favour of the 25 July & Mr Caldwells of the 26 from the
German Flatts, I recd. A few days ago, which I Answered in a Letter
to Mr Caldwell, having the day before wrote to you [1] by a Doctor
going through Albany to the Army at Ticonderoga. Yours of the
20th of July from Fort Stanwix I recd yesterday. I have frequently
informed you of the Situation of Our Army in the Jerseys Watching
that under Genll. Howe on Staten Island. Could I believe my Letters would come Safe to you, my Pleasure in Writing would be
Equal to that you express in receiving them. The Kings Army remain on the Island fortifying every Pass, their Numbers unknown,
but we with reason believe they are daily receiving reinforcements.
40 Vessels great & small arrived a few days ago. The Numr. of our
Forces in Jersey I am not able to inform you of; they are to consist
of at least 16 Thousand when Compleated. The greater part of the
Militia of Pennsylva. were either there or going, who are to stay till
the Army is Compleated. They form a Chain from Amboy to Eliza.
Town Point where strong works are erected at an Amazing expence
of labour Chiefly effected by our Militia before the Pennsylvanians
arrived to their Assistance. The Jersey Militia upon the Arrival of
other Forces returned home to get in their harvest, since which they
are again taking the field. What works are thrown up at Amboy,
blazing Star &c I am not able to say. I know nothing of any design
to Attack the Kings Forces on the Island, it rather seems An Attack
from them is waited for, and it is said such an Attack is soon expected to be made above N. York near Kings Bridge to which place
the Ships that went up the River I hear are returned. Eliza. Town
was in great Consternation upon Genl. Howes taking possn. of the
Island, but at present I believe they are very easy. I frequently in-

formed you Mrs. Dayton had sent the Chief of her goods to Springfield. Many that moved away from E. Town have since returned.

You no doubt have been informed by the Papers of the Flags sent
by Lord How to Genll. Washington with Letters he refused to receive as they were only directed to George Washington &c. You have
also I suppose seen the Printed Narative of what passed in Conversation between Genl. Washington & Colo Patterson who came with
a flag from Lord Howe.[2] We lately sent a flag to his Lordship to
settle An Exchange of Prisoners. He received the Officer with great
Politeness, manifested a deep concern that he had not Arrived before Independency was declared, professed a great regard for America especially the Massachusets Bay that had so Signally honoured
his family. He gave Genll. Washington the Title of Genll. and
called us *the United States.* He consented to the exchange of
Prisoners, proposed immediately to Set all his prisoners at liberty
relying upon the honour of the American States to return him An
equal Number when in their Power. By a Flag to Genll. Howe an
Exchange of Prisoners was also Agreed upon so far as fell within his
department, Canada being he said out of it.

An Indian War hath broke out to the Southward. The Over Hill
Cherokees have commenced Hostilities in the back part of Carolina,
killed 30 or 40 in one Settlement and had about 120 beseiged in a
Fortress which it was thought must Surrender before Succours could
Arrive. Forces were Marching against the Indians. Genll. Clintons
Fleet and Army remain inactive below Charles Town since his de-
feat, his Forces Sickly. No News from Lord Dunmore since he left
Guins Island and went up Potomack River.

Last Saturday our Gondolas Attacked the Kings Ships Near
Doobs Ferry. They fought About 1 1/2 hours, hulled the Man of
War several Times, and fared in the same manner themselves; they
lost but few Men, several wounded, and I believe came of[f] the
second best, tho' the Commander Writes that he hopes soon to give
the Kings Ships *Another drubbing.*[3] This days Post since I began
this Letter brings Accounts of more of the Enemy Arriving in the
Narrows—an Addition to what I have mentioned of at least 20
Transports. And by the last Accounts bro't this day I find our Force
in the Jerseys were by no means Equal to what I Supposed from
former information, as above mentioned.

I Spoke to our President for the Commissions you desire may be
sent, he tells me you must Apply to Genll. Schuyler who hath got
Spare Commissions and can Supply your Regt.

I dare Say you have a good Regiment, and hear their Commenda-
tion with pleasure, but had you seen a Regiment that went near two
Weeks ago to New York raised in Maryland, and Another Paraded
this day in the Statehouse Yard from the Deleware Government,

you would have Altered your Opinion, these were all Stout Men Mostly of an Age and Size. The two battalions above mentioned were the finest I ever saw.

I lately mentioned to you a Ship belonging to Congress Arrived at this Town from France with 1,000 Stand of Arms, 10 Tons of Powder & Blankets, since which I find she brought 30 or 40 Tons of Lead or more, Salt Petre &c &c. Several Valuable Prizes, this days post Advises, were lately brought into the Eastward. We are also informed that the Portugees have declared War Against us by Seizing Our Vessels in their Ports.[4]

Our Election for Council & Assembly, Sheriff &c come on next Tuesday in all the Counties of New Jersey. I now feel the want of you in Eliza. Town. I sat down to consider to whom I might Venture to Write on Politicks, and have none that I dare speak plainly to. Had you or my much Esteemed Friend Mr. Caldwell been there I should have been at no loss. I have none like minded. I have friends it is true but none there now that I dare Speak with freedom to. I have wrote to Several, and desire they will not keep my Letters Secret, so that I hope I shall not be Charged with Secret Practices.

As to my Title, I know not yet whether it will be honourable or dishonourable, the issue of the War must Settle it. Perhaps our Congress will be Exalted on a high Gallows. We were truly brought to the Case of the three Lepers. If we continued in the State we were in, it was evident we must Perish—if we declared Independance, we might be saved, we could but perish. I assure you Sir I see, I feel the danger we are in, I am far from exalting in our immaginary happiness. Nothing short of the Almighty Power of God can Save us—it is not in our Numbers, our Union, or our Valour that I dare trust. I think an Interposing providence hath been evident in all the events that Necessarily led us to what we are. I mean *Independant states* but for what purpose, whether to make us a great Empire, or to make our Ruin more compleat, the issue only can determine.

You & Mr. Caldwell it seems diverted yourselves with the Power given in his Commission. I find it was useful however, for in his last he informs me of his Commanding a Garrison.

Genll. Schuyler makes the same Complaint as you do for want of Cash. His Letter came to Congress the same day with yours & Mr. Caldwells from the German Flatts. 200,000 Dollars was immediately sent to the Pay Master General, being part of 500,000 just before Ordered to be sent.[5] The Congress, or rather some of the members tells me that if your Regimt. is near three months in arrear of Pay, it is not a Neglect of Congress, but a Neglect somewhere Else, as they have sent Seasonable Supplies.

I am glad to hear a person so high in my Esteem as Mr. Barber so honourably spoke of by you. I never doubted but he would do honour to his Appointment—he is young and in the bloom of Life and a large field for Promotion is open before him, and I can't help but look upon him [as] designed in Providence for some important Station. I most gratfully Accept your Congratulation on Acct. of my Appointment. Believe me my Dear friend I am not in a place of my own Chusing. I had much rather took an Active part in our own State, I think I could have been more useful to my Country there where I had a Sufficient Share of Influence, and where I could have Served my friends much better than here. Besides, I have found my health much interrupted, Pent up in a Close Town, deprived of Air and Exercise, and excessive hot from the Reflection of the Sun on the Buildings & Pavement.

Excepting my health I am as Agreably Situated as I could expect. Doctor Witherspoon, Mr Hart & my Self quarter together, and endeavour to make our Lives as agreable as Possible.

What you say respecting your Regimts. returning in the fall, will be Attended to in a proper Time.

Remember Sir, what I frequently mention that when I write to you or Mr. Caldwell I mean always to Address you both, but with regard to your familys I can say no more than that I have not heard of their being unwell. I am my Dear friend, Your Sincere Friend, & Huml. Servt.   Abra. Clark

P.S. You'l please to Accept this on Plain Paper, our dignity don't afford Gilt, and our pay scarcely Any. Ric[har]d Lawrence on Staten Island is Colo. of a Regimt. under the Crown & commands the Tories there Joined with some Regulars.

RC (PHi). Addressed: "To Elias Dayton Esqr., Colonel of a Jersey battalion at Fort Stanwix."

¹ Not found.

² On this point, see *JCC*, 5:612; and Washington, *Writings* (Fitzpatrick), 5:297n.55, 321. The "Printed Narative" may be found in Washington, *Writings* (Fitzpatrick), 5:321n.37.

³ For an account of this action, which was transmitted to Congress by Washington in his August 5 letter to Hancock, see Clark, *Naval Documents*, 6:37–38.

⁴ Rhode Island governor Nicholas Cooke had informed Washington of the seizure of American vessels in Portuguese ports in a July 29 letter that Washington had forwarded with his August 5 letter to Hancock. *Am. Archives*, 4th ser. 4:659–60; and Washington, *Writings* (Fitzpatrick), 5:371. Portuguese ports had been declared closed to American shipping in an edict issued by the king of Portugal on July 4. *Am. Archives*, 4th ser. 6:1255.

⁵ See Clark to James Caldwell, August 1, 1776, note 3.

John Hancock to John Haslet

Sir,   Philadelphia 6 Augst. 1776

The Congress having Instructed their Committee immediately to deliver as many Arms as are necessary for your Battalion, Robert Morris Esqr. will give the orders for the Delivery. And I have it in Charge from Congress to Direct that as soon as the Arms are Rec'd, you do without loss of time March your Battalion to Amboy in New Jersey, & Acquaint Genl. Washington of your Arrival there, and follow such orders as you shall Receive from him.[1]

I am Sir, Your very hum sert,   J H Pt.

LB (DNA: PCC, item 12A). Addressed: "To The officer Commandg. the Battalion of Continental Troops at the Barracks, Philada. Col. Haslet's Battalion."
[1] See *JCC*, 5:631.

William Hooper to Jonathan Trumbull, Jr.

Dear Sir   Philadelphia August 6. 1776

Col Williams obligingley gave me a sight of a letter from you. I am sorry to find you so much in the plaintive strain and that you have such just occasion for it. You mention that you had wrote me. Be assured that I have not received a line from you, or I should have used my small abilities to lessen the difficulties with which your department is go grievously embarrassed. Congress is not well informed of the state of the Northern Army. The distance of that Station, the variety of Impediments which Sickness, Climate, the failure of duty in officers and men have thrown in the way have been insurmountable even to the most spirited and well meant intentions of this Congress. Unless some measures are immediately taken to strengthen your post I augur that Burgoygn will soon set foot in Albany. The Stars in their courses seem to fight against our attempts in your Quarter. And What the enemy and desertion have spared seem to be reserved only for the horrid depredations of Sickness. Heaven watch over the remains of what from its numbers was once formidable.

I flatter myself that I shall hear from you frequently. You never can want a subject, whatever concerns the publick or you privately or officially will be interesting and important to me as a publick officer and as your friend.

I wish to know very minutely the state of the Army in your quarter, and should there be any part of information which you mean to trust only to my own private ear, I shall most faithfully obey your Injunctions in this respect. A large body of Troops Regular Militia are on their way from this to New York. I wish they may arrive seasonally.

A Capt Weeks has taken 3 prizes valued at 45,000 and sent them here; they have already arrived.

No other Intelligence worth Scribbling, which can be an excuse

for trespassing longer upon your patience than to subscribe myself
with Truth and regard, Your Friend and Obedt Servant,

Will Hooper

Tr (DLC). Addressed: "Jonathan Trumbull esqr, Paymaster etc, etc, Albany."

Marine Committee to John Bradford

Sir,   In Marine Committee, Philada. August 6th. 1776
    The Government of Great Britian during their Tyrannic sway
thought proper to mark the Port of Boston for Vengeance &
descending still more minutely they prohibited any business being
transacted at our Worthy President's wharfe.[1] In order to shew
one mark of our Contempt for their Authority We hereby desire
you will order all the Continental Prizes that arrive in your Port
to that wharfe & transact the whole of their business there or so
much of it as can conveniently be Confined to that place.
    We are sir, Your Obedt hble servts.

Robt Morris	Geo Walton
Joseph Hewes	Frans Lewis
Geo. Read	Fras Hopkinson
Benja Harrison	Arthur Middleton
	Wm. Whipple

Tr (MHi).
[1] Bradford was the Continental prize agent in Massachusetts.

Marine Committee to John Paul Jones

Sir   In Marine Committee, Philada. August 6th. 1776
    We have ordered the Provisions & Stores you requested, to be
sent onboard the Sloop Providence which you Command under
Authority of the United States of America, so that the said Sloop
being now ready for Sea You are to proceed immediately on a
Cruize against our Enemies & we think in & about the Lattitude of
Bermuda may prove the most favourable ground for your purpose.
    Herewith we deliver you an extract from the Journals of Congress
respecting the Navy Prizes &c by which you will know with precision what Vessells can be made Prizes & which not.[1] You have
also herewith a list of the Continental agents in each State & to
some of them your Prizes must be addressed according to the Port
they arrive in.[2] Your Cruize may be for Six Weeks, two or three

Months just as Provisions, Water & other Circumstances point out
to be best. If you gain any material Intelligence You must put into
the nearest port of the Continent & dispatch an Express to us with
the same. You must by all opportunitys transmit us an Account of
your proceedings & of such Occurrances as you meet with. You are
to be particularly attentive to protect, aid & assist all Vessells &
property belonging to these States or the Subjects thereof. It is
equally your duty to Seize, take, Sink, Burn or destroy that of our
Enemys. Be carefull of the Sloop, her Stores and Materials, use your
People well thereby recommending the American Naval service to
all who engage in it, and we also recommend Humane kind Treatment of your Prisoners. These things duely observed will recommend You to the attention & regard of this Committee.

We are, sir, Your hble servants,

John Hancock	Geo Walton
Robt Morris	Arthur Middleton
Joseph Hewes	Fras. Lewis
Geo. Read	Fras. Hopkinson
	Wm. Whipple

RC (DNA: PCC, item 58). Written by Morris and signed by Morris, Hancock,
Hewes, Hopkinson, Lewis, Middleton, Read, Walton, and Whipple. Addressed:
"To John Paul Jones Esqr, Commander of the Sloop Providence."
   [1] See JCC, 4:253–54.
   [2] See JCC, 4:300–301.

North Carolina Delegates to
the North Carolina Council of Safety

Gentlemen   Philadelphia August 6, 1776
   We have this morning obtained an order upon the Continental
Magazine for half a Ton of Gun powder for the use of the back
Inhabitants of North Carolina.[1] A Mr McDonald an Inhabitant of
the County of Rowan being on his way home with a Waggon has
engaged to take in that quantity & proceed immediately to Salisbury
with it. We shall direct him to deliver it to General Ruthufurd, in
his Absence to Mr Matthew Lock, in case of both being absent to
Mr Hugh Montgomery. We induced to this measure from information which we have obtained that the Indians have fallen upon
the frontiers of the Colony & that our people are in the most
distressed and defenceless situation from the want of Ammunition.

We doubt not we shall meet your hearty approbation of this measure & beg leave to subscribe ourselves, with Great Respect, Gentlemen, Your most Obed. Humble Servants,

> Wm Hooper
>
> Joseph Hewes
>
> John Penn

RC (Nc–Ar). Written by Hooper and signed by Hooper, Hewes, and Penn.
[1] See *JCC*, 5:633.

Samuel Chase to Benedict Arnold

My dear Sir.   Philadelphia. Augst. 7th. 1776
I wrote you immediately on my Return to this city (abot 18th July) and acknowledged the Receipt of your Letter dated from Montreal the 11th June. In that Letter You admit the Receipt of my Letters of 31st of May & the 3rd of June. The last post brought Me your favor of the 12th of July from Crown Point. I have received no other Letters from you than the above. As You do not inform Me of the Receipt of my long Letter from Saratoga of 6th June I presume it miscarried.[1]
There are in all about 120 Sail of our Enemies fleet arrived at Staten Island. Our Army at N York consists of about 18,000 Men, of which 3,600 are sick; our Flying Camp in the Jerseys of about 5,000. Seven Battalions from Boston, and two from Virginia are ordered to N. York. A Battalion from the Delaware States passed thro this City yesterday, and the Militia are coming in every Hour. Our Vessells are very successful in taking prizes.
I beg you will from Time to Time communicate with your usual Candor and without any Reserve the Numbers and Condition of our Army, & such observations as you think will explain the Subject to Me, both of Men & Measures. No more will [be] disclosed than you desire.
I am distressed to hear so many Reports injurious to your Character about the Goods seized at Montreal. I cannot but request all persons to suspend their opinion, & to give You an opportunity of being heard. Your best Friends are not your Countrymen.
Mr Carroll requests his Compliments to you. Make Me remembered to Gen. Gates. Tell him I saw his Letter to Mr. J. Adams, that I cannot understand his Message to Me, & shall, if I can get the Letter, write to him.[2] If not I wish he wod. explain fully & explicitly what he means. I take his Letter unkind & think he ought to have wrote to Me, or at least have wrote so as to be understood by Mr.

Adams or Myself, which is not the Case—he knows my Esteem & Friendship for him. Adieu. Your affectionate & obedt. Servt.

Saml. Chase

[*P.S.*] In what State is our Navy on the Lakes?

RC (NHi). RC damaged; recipient and missing words taken from *Am. Archives,* 5th ser. 1:810–11.
  [1] None of Chase's letters to Arnold mentioned in this paragraph have been found.
  [2] See Samuel Chase to Horatio Gates, August 9, 1776.

Abraham Clark to James Caldwell

My Dear Friend,   Phila. Augt 7th. 1776
    Your favour of the 26 July from the German Flats I recd and the next day after wrote you by Post, at the same Time recd. a letter from Colo. Dayton of the 25th & since that I recd. one the Colo. Wrote the 20th from fort Stanwix, to which I wrote a Long answer Yesterday Which I have yet by me, as the President will Write this day to Genll. Schuyler and hath engaged to send it in his Packet, in which I purpose to get this a place. If this Should find you at the German Flats, and the Colo. is at Fort Stanwix, I hereby Authorize you to Open & read his Letter & then forward it to him, as I Expect my Letters to Either of you will be considered as intended for both. We have no News to day. This morning one of our Large Frigates was Launched,[1] two others of 24 & 26 Guns were some Time ago Launched & are Rigging. I regret my being moved to this Congress. I think I could have been of more Service in our own Province than here. I remember what Cesar Said in passing the Alps, "That he had rather be the first in a Small Village in the Alps, than the Second in Rome." This will not exactly apply to myself, as I did not Esteem myself the first in the Jersey Convention, and I am sure I am far below the Second here. It is however in some degree Applicable.
    In your Letter you tell me of our feasting here. Indeed we have plenty, but I dare say you have the best feast. My want of health will not suffer me to relish delicacies.
    News as far as my present Station will permit I have given in the Letter to the Colo. More I might in confidence Say were either of you Present, but I dare not Risk more in a Letter. I think I informed you in my last that Money to pay your Regiment was sent forward—and the matter relative to your Regiments returning to the Jerseys in the fall was not proper to mention yet, from

the uncertain issue of the War to the Northward. I am Dear Sir, most Affectionately Yours,

Abra. Clark

P.S. I don't recollect the Death of any of your hearers since you left us but Thos. Williams who died two Weeks ago or something more.

RC (MeHi).
[1] Robert Treat Paine's diary entry for this date reads: "Very hott, Sultry. The Frigate Washington launched." MHi.

Committee of Secret Correspondence to Silas Deane

Dear sir   Philadelphia August 7th 1776
The above is a Copy of our last, which went by the Dispatch, Captain Parker.[1]

The Congress have since taken into consideration the heads of a Treaty to be proposed to France, but as they are not yet concluded upon we cannot say more of them per this conveyance.

You will see by the News papers which accompany this, that the expidition against South Carolina is foiled by the gallant resistance made there. The Enemy, much diminished by Sickness, it is thought will attempt nothing farther in those Parts. The People of North Carolina, who at first had taken up their Bridges, and broken the Roads to prevent the Enemys penetrating their Country, have since, being ready to receive him, repaired the Roads and Bridges, and wish him to attempt making use of them.

Gen. Howe is posted now on Staten Island near New York with the Troops he carried to Halifax when he was driven out of Boston. Lord Howe is also arrived there with some reinforcements, and more are expected, as the great push seems intended to be made in that Province. Gen. Washington's Army is in possession of the Town, about which Many entrenchments are thrown up, so as to give an opportunity of disputing the possession with G. Howe, if he should attempt it, and of making it cost him something, but it is not so regularly fortified as to Stand a Siege. We have also a flying Camp in the Jerseys, to harrass the Enemy if he should attempt to penetrate through that Province to Philada.

In the different Colonies we have now near 80,000 Men in the pay of the Congress. The Declaration of Independence Meets with universal approbation, and the people every where Seem more animated by it in defence of their Country. Most of our Frigates are

Launched in the different Provinces and are fitting for Sea with all the expedition in our power. They are fine ships and will be capable of good service. Our small Privateers and Continental arm'd Vessells have already had great success as the papers will shew you; and by abstaining from Trade ourselves while we distress that of our enemys, we expect to make their Men of war weary of their unprofitable and hopeless Cruisses, and their Merchants Sick of a Contest in which so much is risk'd and nothing gained. The forming a Navy is a very capital object with us, and the Marine Committee is ordered to bring in a plan for increasing it very considerably. The Armed Boats for the defence of our Rivers and Bays grow more and more in repute. They venture to attack large Men of war, and are very troublesome to them. The papers will give you Several instances of their success.

We hope that by this time you are at Paris, and that Mr Morris has joined you,[2] whom we recommend to you warmly, and desire you may mutually co-operate in the public service.

With great esteem we are, Dear sir, Your very hble Servants,

B Franklin

Benj Harrison

Robt Morris

RC (MeHi). In a clerical hand and signed by Franklin, Harrison, and Morris.

[1] See the July 8 letter of the Committee of Secret Correspondence to Silas Deane printed above. In his November 28 letter to the Committee of Secret Correspondence, Deane acknowledged receipt of "Your favor of the 7th August last, covering a copy of yours of the 8th of July." Wharton, *Diplomatic Correspondence*, 2:196. The original was undoubtedly thrown overboard when Capt. Parker and the *Dispatch* were captured on July 22, 1776.

[2] Thomas Morris, Robert Morris' half-brother, who had recently been appointed as agent for Congress at Nantes. See Robert Morris to Deane, August 11, 1776. For an account of his appointment and subsequent fall from favor because of his incompetence and dissolute behavior, see Wharton, *Diplomatic Correspondence*, 2:460–63; and *NYHS Collections* 20 (1887): 145–56. See also Adams, *Diary* (Butterfield), 2:368n.2.

William Williams to Joseph Trumbull

Dear Sir   Philadelphia Augt. 7th 1776

I gratefully acknowledge your favors of 30th ult. & 4 Inst the first inclosing the well grounded Complaints of our Bror. Jonathan of his & the Northern Army's unjust & strange Treatment. A Letter came to Congress at the same Time from Genl Schuyler, containing 2 or 3 sheets justification of the plan of Deserting Crown Point, & possessing the east of Ti[condero]ga which to my apprehention & by my own personal Knowledge I judge insufficient. It also expresses in pretty strong Terms the want of money. That & many other Letters were comitted to the board of War.

I communicated yours & the inclosed to many Members whom I cod trust who all seem to feel keenly, but also seem utterly at a loss how to redress the grievances radically. I pressed some of that Board on the Subject, & lent them the Letter in Consequence of which they brot in the enclosed Resolutions, which were passd some days since, almost unanimously contrary to Expectation, as the original of the Design is to find out what Schuyler has done with his Money.[1] It extends also further &c. I endeavoured immediately to get a Copy to send you, but the Secretary under pretence of Hurry &c put me off, which I did not like very much, & finally obtained the original from the Board of War & put off writing, till I cod get them, as I had nothing material. Tho I am sensible the Presidt. has sent Copys to Each as due they are not attested but true Copys. I fear our Galleys second best is very ill. By the Generals Acct they cant attack again 'till a good deal repaired. By being so confoundedly raked I shod think they drew up in Line of Battle, along side the Ships, which I suppose is not Galley mode of fighting. What is to come next, God only knows. Things look very dark on our side. I shant much wonder if Burgoyne & Howe shod effect a Junction of their Forces. Congress seem to me infatuated, in seeking after a thousand Reasons of the miscarriages in Canada by a Committee of that purpose &c while the Fault is in themselves, in neglecting & abandoning that Army to inevitable Destruction, & then severely censure officers & Soldiers for their ill Conduct in not making Bricks without Straw or even Stubble. Poor Wooster a faithful officer is treated most inhumanly by Mr.———[2] & sundry men in Congress tho they cant support any thing against him, by any Proof but the most confident assertions of their own. Many of us grieve & lament the Fate of that unhappy Army, but as yet see not how nor what to do. G. Schuyler how good soever he might be if present &c will be their Ruin to Comand & guide the affairs at a 100 or two miles off, but I dont see at present that it wod be possible to remove him, if the utter ruin of the Continent was to be the known Consequence of his Continuance in office. Endeavors will not be wanting however to save them but I believe they will be too late, for I dont not expect Eyes will be opened till Burgoyne gets to Albany, & then, but I will forbear.

The dayly Business of Congress after dispatching a constant series of Business contained in Letters, receiving Reports, attending to Motions &c is by a Committee of the whole House to indeavor to settle Articles of Confederation, which are drawn up & printed for the use of the Members only. We make slow Progress in them as every speck of ground is disputed, & very jarring Claims & Interests are to be adjusted among us, & then all to be agreed to by the sevl Legislatures, so that between both, I almost despair of seeing it accomplished. I have not heard a word of your affairs. Congress have been, & in some things, are now very lavish of money & in others very close. There seems to be Spirit in some of the southern agst. the nothern Colonies & all their officers and affairs, so that you wod stand a worse Chance for belonging to them.

You will see the Resolves are calculated to keep you all honest. They were occasioned by yr Bror's Letter & had a primary Reference to a Nothern Gent.

If you think it convenient you will furnish our Bror Jonathan with a Copy of the whole to whom also make my kind Compliments, & to Colo. Huntington from whom I never expect to hear another word. Shod be glad to hear frequently from you, & will not be in your Debt if I can find any thing worth writing.

Your most affectionate Friend & Brother,

Wm Williams

P.S. I was sorry to forget asking you at N Y & I had again forgot to ask you where is Bushnel, & why dont he attempt something.[3] When will or can be a more proper Time than is or has been &c. I was knowing to his coming &c & that you were acquainted with the Plan &c.

RC (Ct).
    [1] These resolves of August 2, amending regulations adopted on June 5, 1776, required paymaster, quartermaster, and commissary officials to transmit weekly accounts to Congress. See JCC, 5:418, 627–28.
    [2] Undoubtedly Samuel Chase.
    [3] David Bushnell (1742–1824), inventor of the submarine Turtle. See Benjamin Franklin to George Washington, July 22, 1776, note.

John Hancock to Charles Lee

Sir,   Philada. August 8th 1776

The Congress having this Day received a Letter from Genl. Washington containing very important Information,[1] I do myself the Honor to enclose you a Copy of the same. You will there perceive the Genl. Clinton with the Troops under his Command, has joined Genl. Howe at Statin Island, having left South-Carolina soon after the defeat he and Commodore Parker sustained at Sullivan's Island.

In Consequence of this Intelligence the Congress are convinced that the Enemy, by collecting their whole Force into a Point, are determined to make a most vigorous Exertion at New York; and in Order to ensure Success in that Quarter, are disposed for the present, to overlook every other Object. The getting Possession of that City, and the Junction of the two Armies under Generals Howe & Burgoyne, seem to be the grand objects they have in View, to the Attainment of which they give up every inferior Consideration.

In this Situation of our Affairs, the Congress being of Opinion your Services in the Middle Department will be necessary, I have it in Command to direct, that you repair as soon as possible to the City of Philadelphia, there to receive such Orders as they may think proper to give you.[2]

The Attack at New York being hourly expected, and the Event of it uncertain, I am to request, you will use the greatest Expedition on the Way.

With the best Wishes for your Health & Prosperity, I have the Honour to be, with the utmost Respect, Sir, your most obed. & very hble Sert.   J. H. Prest.

LB (DNA: PCC, item 12A). Addressed: "Genl. Lee, South Carolina."
[1] Washington's second letter to Hancock of August 7, containing intelligence about the recent arrival in New York of "General Clinton . . . and the whole Southern Army." Washington, *Writings* (Fitzpatrick), 5:382–83.
[2] See *JCC*, 5:638.

John Hancock to George Washington

Sir   Philadelphia Aug. 8. 1776

Your letters of the 7 with the papers enclosed are received and now under consideration of Congress.[1]

Enclosed I send you a resolution passed respecting lieutenant Josiah. He was first lieutenant of captain Nicholas Biddle & was taken in a ship capt Biddle had made prize of, by the Cerberus frigate.

By a letter which he found means to convey he informs that "he is used worse than he ever thought one Englishman could use another—that he was sent before the mast with the rest, but upon refusing to do duty was given under the charge of three boatswains mates & expects the gangway soon as he is daily threatened." [2]

An Order is this moment pass'd for calling general Lee from the Southward, & to morrow is appointed for electing a number of major generals & brigr. generals.

I am, Sir, your very huml Servt,

John Hancock Presit

[P.S.] You will please to mention the matter of Lieut. Josiah as real information, but not discover that it was by Letter, as it may prove injurious, in case he is not exchang'd.

RC (DLC). In the hand of Charles Thomson, with signature and postscript by Hancock.

1. These letters are in PCC, item 152, 2:343–46, 359–62, and Washington, *Writings* (Fitzpatrick), 5:379–83.

2 See *JCC*, 5:635–36. Further information about British mistreatment of Lt. James Josiah of the Continental brig *Andrew Doria* may be found in Clark, *Naval Documents*, 5:1270–71. For correspondence between Washington and Admiral Howe relating to the exchange of Josiah, see ibid., 6:235; and Washington, *Writings* (Fitzpatrick), 5:447–48.

North Carolina Delegates to the North Carolina Council of Safety

Gentlemen   Philadelphia August 7 [*i.e.* 8] 1776 1

We wrote you lately by the Post informing you that we had sent half a Ton of Gunpowder to the Western Inhabitants of North Carolina that they might not want, as far as it was in our power to prevent it, the means of defence against the Indians. The Waggoners have been detained here by some private business of their own till now, but this day they propose to set off. You will be the best Judge whether to order a guard for them thro Guildford or any other part of our Province, as their Route is by the upper Road which Mr Sharp & Alexander are well acquainted with.

We send you inclosed a Copy of a letter which this day came to Congress from General Washington.2 We thot it interesting to you as it tends to free the Southern Colonies from the Apprehensions of immediate injury & will from Clintons removal give them an opportunity to provide for their defence in case of a Winter Campaign against them. We must most earnestly importune you to compleat the Continental Battalions. You will now have leisure to recruit them, and in our next to you we hope in behalf of Congress to hold forth such Encouragement as will make that Task very easy. The Circumstance of being comfortably cloathed for which we are making all the provision we can will no doubt weigh much with men to enlist tho' you will remember the Value of the Cloathing is to be deducted from their pay.

The secure state of your Sea Coast at present gives your Board an Opportunity to direct all your Attention against your Enemy Indians. The gross infernal breach of faith which they have been guilty of shuts them out from every pretension to mercy, and it is surely the policy of the Southern Colonies (and justice to our fellow whites on our Frontiers not only will vindicate but loudly demands such a Conduct) to carry fire and Sword into the very bowels of their Country & sink them so low that they may never be able again to rise and disturb the peace of their Neighbours. To extinguish the very race of them and scarce to leave enough of Existence to be a vestige in proof that a Cherokee Nation once was, would perhaps be no more than the blood of our Slaughtered Countrymen might call for. But Christianity the dear Religion of peace & Mercy should hold our conquering hands & while we feel the resentment of Men We ought not to forget the duties of the Christian. Women and Children are not a Conquest worthy the American Arms—their weakness disarms rage. May their blood never sully our triumphs. But Mercy to their Warriors is cruelty to ourselves. We mean not to sport with their pains or to exercise wanton acts of Cruelty upon them if the Chance of War should throw them into our hands, but to exercise that manly and generous method of pursuing them to destruction which our own Customs & the Law of nations will vindicate. We have been large upon this Subject, as we have it much at heart to quiet the Apprehensions of our Frontiers, that we may be able to oppose our whole Strength to Clinton in the Winter who will then most certainly pay us a visit.

We are Gentlemen, With great Respect, Your most Obedt Humble Servants,   Wm Hooper

Joseph Hewes

John Penn

RC (Nc–Ar). Written by Hooper and signed by Hooper, Hewes, and Penn.

[1] This letter was almost certainly written on August 8, the day Congress received the letter from Washington mentioned in the second paragraph. Since Washington's letter was written early in the afternoon of August 7, it is unlikely that it reached Philadelphia the same day.

[2] Washington's second letter to Hancock of August 7. Washington, *Writings* (Fitzpatrick), 5:382–83.

Caesar Rodney to Thomas Rodney

Sir,   Philada. August 8th 1776

As I have Recd no Letter from you by the last Post, and have little or no Intelligence Except What you'l find in the papers, am at a Loss what to write you.

The Delaware Battalion is under Marching order for Amboy Subject to General Washingtons further orders.[2] They are Compleatly Armed, as fine Guns as you Could wish to See.

Haveing a few Idle Minutes I have inclosed you a paper Containing a few Queries and Submit to you whether that, or Something like it taken or Copied in an unknown hand and Secretly distributed so as to become public at this time might not be of Use, by drawing the serious Attention of the people at this important Crisis.

But as I know but verry little, or rather nothing of the present Politics or the disposition of the people at this time, Wholely Submit the matter to you and wish the people may Consider their True Interest.

Mr. McKean is yet in the Jerseys, and not likely soon to return.[2] The Terms of Confederation now before the Congress, and our Colony not represented without Read and me Both, therefore Cannot Expect to see you in Kent verry soon.

I am yrs.   Caesar Rodney

RC (InU).
[1] See John Hancock to John Haslet, August 6, 1776.
[2] Thomas McKean was colonel and commander of the Fourth Battalion of Philadelphia Associators, which had left Philadelphia the week of July 15. His July 26 letter to his wife describing the unit's recent engagement with the British is in John M. Coleman, *Thomas McKean, Forgotten Leader of the Revolution* (Rockaway, N.J.: American Faculty Press, 1975), pp. 184–85.

Secret Committee Minutes of Proceedings

Augt. 8. 1776.

Come. met. Present Morris, Hewes, Lewis, Bartlett, Livingston. Letter to J. P. Merckle Esqr. respectg. the borrowg. money in Holland on the credit of the U. S. was signd by the Come. Letter from Mr. A. Gillon[1] covering his draft on Floriar [Florine] Charles Mey of Charles-town South Carolina for 11,147 4/5 dlls. likewise directing Mr. Morris[2] to pay the balance due to him by Messrs. Willing, Morris & Co. to this Come. was read. Orderd that Mr. Morris report the balance due Mr. Gillon by Messrs. Willing & Morris & apply the same to the credit of the Acct. wch. this Come. has with that House, & that he transmit the draft on Mr. Mey to Charlestown with orders, that if produce can be purchasd & shippd from that State without any great risque to invest the amount therein on the public Acct. If this cant be done then the money to be pd. to the Govr. of S. Carolina towards paying the wages of the troops in that departmt.

MS (MH).
[1] For additional information pertaining to Gillon's contract, see Secret Committee Minutes of Proceedings, October 25, 1775, and July 18, 1776.
[2] A footnote in the copyist's hand keyed at this point reads: "It appears by Mr. Gillons letters to Rob. Morris that Rob. Morris was his Partner in the Contract, in wch. the profits were very high. See his Letters in the Papers of the Sect. Committee." For other comments on Robert Morris' commercial transactions, which were similarly added to this copy of the Journal of the Secret Committee when it was transcribed sometime after October 5, 1778, see Secret Committee Minutes of Proceedings, September 27 and December 14, 1775, and October 18, 1776.

Samuel Chase to Horatio Gates

Dear Sir.   Philadelphia Augst. 9th. 1776

Mr. J. Adams shewed Me your Letter to him from Tyonderoga, of the 17th of July,[1] Wherein You write "I desire if Chase is returned to Congress, he may know how much I have been *deceived* & *disappointed* in being removed from a Place where I might have done the public Service & fix'd in a Situation where it is exceeding doubtful if it will be in my Power to be more than the wretched Spectator of a ruined Army." "Mr. Chase passed too speedily through this Country, he saw superficially, & like a sanguine Man, drew Conclusions from the Consequence, and not the Cause. Tell him, if he and I meet, he must expect to be called to a serious Account, upon this Matter. I know he is my sincere Friend, but I also know he has *deceived himself and his friend.* I am not angry. I am only vexed with him." After this Recital of so unkind, so unfriendly, so injurious a Letter, permit Me to ask you a few serious Questions. Why not write to Me if You conceived yourself injured or deceived? How have you been *deceived* and *disappointed* by your Removal from N York to the Command in Canada, in what particulars and by whom? Did I ever make a Profession, or communicate an opinion or relate a fact in which I was not sincere & faithful? When did I pass too speedily through the Country in going or returning from Canada, and to what does this Relate? What Things did I see *superficially?* Deal in the particulars & point out where I was mistaken, as to Men, Things & Circumstances. I admit that I am constitutionally warm & sanguine, but be pleased to Name the Instances in which I drew *Conclusions* from the *Consequence* and not the *Cause?* If ever You & I should meet, I will with Candor & Integrity & as a Friend, answer you in all your Inquiries, or I will with pleasure by Letter give you full Satisfaction. I will now only ask you one more Question. In what Instance have I deceived Myself or You?

I will not be angry with you, but I am not only vexed, but mortified, chagrined & exceedingly hurt by your Suspicious and very unfriendly Expressions. You have held up your Friend as a Man who had deceived and disappointed you, as a superficial observer & of so warm & weak a Constitution as to draw Conclusions from the Consequence and not the Cause. An Imputation on my Understanding I can forgive, A charge that I have disappointed & deceived You, from want of Knowledge & without Design, I can forget. I will add no more, but that I always was, and still am, with Sincerity, Your affectionate and Obedt. Servant,   Saml. Chase

RC (NHi).

[1] For Gates' letter of July 17 to John Adams, see Bernhard Knollenberg, ed.,

"The Correspondence of John Adams and Horatio Gates," *Proceedings of the Massachusetts Historical Society* 67 (March 1942): 147–48. See also John Adams to Horatio Gates, August 13, 1776.

Samuel Chase to Philip Schuyler

My dear Sir   Philadelphia Augst. 9th. 1776

Be pleased to accept my Thanks for your truly polite and affectionate Letter of the 1st Inst. which I received by yesterdays Post. I am to leave this City in an Hour to return to my Home. I hope Heaven has heard my prayers, & your friendly wishes. I expect to find one of the best of women & of wifes in a much better State of Health, than when I was compelled to leave her.

I have great Reason to believe that France would readily listen to an Application from the *united States* of America, but when we shall be confederated States, I know not. I am afraid the Day is far distant. Three great Difficulties occur—the Mode of Voting, whether by Colonies, or by an equal Representation, the Rule by which each Colony is to pay its Quota, and the Claim of several Colonies to extend to the South Seas. A considerable Diversity of opinion prevails on each Head. The Confederacy is to be transmitted to each State for their Concurrence.

It is probable France will not enter into an alliance with Us before We have confederated. If ever We do, it will take a considerable Time to effect it, and the opportunity may be lost of striking some great & decisive blow.

The paper enclosed contains all the News here. Our day of Trial approaches, God grant Us Success, or our Country is undone.

I can add no more, only to assure You of my unalterable esteem & Friendship. Believe Me in every Vicissitude to be, with Sincerity, Your assured Friend, and affectionate Servant,

                                                            Saml. Chase

[*P.S.*] I expect to return to Congress in a Month; in the interim be pleased to write to Me at Annapolis Maryland.

RC (NN).

Thomas Jefferson to Francis Eppes

Dear Sir   Philadelphia, Aug. 9th, 1776.

As Col. Harrison was about to have some things packed, I set out upon the execution of your glass commission, and was surprised to find that the whole glass stores of the city could not make out anything like what you desired. I therefore did what I thought would be best, imagining you wanted the number you mentioned at any event, and that not being able to get them of that form, you would take them of any other. I therefore got 4 pint cans, 10s.; 2 quart do. 8s.; and 6 half-pint tumblers, 6s., all of double flint. So that there still remains in my hands £4 16s., Pennsylva. currency.

Your heckle is not yet come. It seems the man who had promised to sell it to the gentleman I employed to get it, now raises some difficulties either to get off others which he calls the set, or to enhance the price. However, the gentleman still expects it, and I am after him every day for it. Our galleys at New York have had a smart engagement with the men-of-war which went up the river; it is believed the enemy suffered a good deal.[1] The galleys are much injured, though we lost but two men. The commander writes us word he retired, that he might go and give them another drubbing, which in plain English meant, I suppose, that he was obliged to retire. Gen. Washington commends the behavior of the men much. They lay pretty close to the enemy, and two of the galleys were exposed to the broadside of their ships almost the whole time. The damage done them proves they were in a warm situation. Madison (of the college) and one Johnson, of Augusta, were coming passengers in the New York packet; they were attacked by one of our armed vessels, and nothing but the intervention of night prevented the packet being taken. She is arrived at New York, and they permitted to come home. In a letter by them, we have intelligence that the French ministry is changed, the pacific men turned out, and those who are for war, with the Duke de Choiseul at their head, are taken in.[2] We have also the king's speech on the prorogation of parliament, declaring he will see it out with us to the bitter end.

The South Carolina army with Clinton Sr., arrived at Staten Island last week, one of their transports, with 5 companies of Highlanders, having first fallen into General Lee's hands. They now make Lord Howe 12,000 strong. With this force he is preparing to attack. He is embarking his cannon; has launched 8 galleys, and formed his men-of-war into line of battle. From these circumstances, it is believed the attack of New York will be within three or four days. They expect with the utmost confidence to carry it, as they consider our army but as a rude undisciplined rabble. I hope they will find it a Bunker's Hill rabble. Notwithstanding these appearances of attack, there are some who believe, and with appearance of reason, that these measures are taken by the enemy to secure themselves and not to attack us. A little time will shew. General Arnold (a fine sailor) has undertaken to command our fleet on the lakes. The enemy are fortifying Oswego, and I believe our army there, when recovered from their sickness, will find they have lost a good campaign, though they have had no battle of moment.

My love to Mrs. Eppes. I hope my letter by last post got there time enough to stay Patty with her awhile longer. Adieu.

Th. Jefferson

MS not found; reprinted from Jefferson, *Papers* (Boyd), 1:487–88. Addressed: "Francis Eppes, Esq., At the Forest, By favor of Col. Harrison."

[1] Washington's August 5 letter enclosing Col. Benjamin Tupper's account of an engagement between the galleys under his command and the British ships of war in the Hudson River is in PCC, item 152, 2:329–32, 337, and *Am. Archives*, 5th ser. 1:762–64, 766–67. For other accounts of this August 3 engagement, see Clark, *Naval Documents*, 6:38–39, 49, 121.

[2] The rumor that the former foreign minister duc de Choiseul, a known anglophobe, had returned to favor was false, but there had been a recent shift in French policy toward America. The French Council of State's acceptance of Vergennes' proposals to aid America had resulted in the resignation in May of the pacific finance minister Turgot, whose program of budgetary retrenchment would be thus curtailed by increased royal expenditures. Turgot's departure left the council dominated by men who favored greater intervention in the American war. For a discussion of France's initial involvement in the American war effort, see Jonathan R. Dull, *The French Navy and American Independence* (Princeton: Princeton University Press, 1975), pp. 30–49.

John Adams to Abigail Adams

Aug. 10. 76

Yours of 30 and 31 July was brought me, to day, by Captain Cazneau. I am happy to think that you, and my oldest son, are well through the distemper, and have sufficient Receipts. Nabby, I believe is also through. The Inflammation in her Arm, and the single Eruption, are nearly as much Evidence, as I had to shew—and I have seen Small Pox enough since I had it, to have infected 100 Armies. Tommy, I shall hear by next Post, is happily recoverd of it, I think. Charley, my dear Charley! I am sorry, that it is still pretty clear, that you have not taken it. But never fear, you will have it.

This Suspence and Uncertainty must be very irksome to you. But Patience and Perseverance will overcome this, as well as all other Difficulties. Dont think of Time, nor Expence. 1000 Guineas is not worth so much as security to a Wife, a good one I mean, and four Children, good ones I mean, against the small Pox. It is an important Event in a Mans Life, to go thro that distemper. It is a very great Thing, for a whole Family, to get well over it.

At the same Time that I am in a State of suspence, Uncertainty and Anxiety about my best, dearest, worthyest, wisest Friend, in this World, and all my Children, I am in a State of equal Suspence, Uncertainty, and Anxiety about our Army at N. York and Ticonderoga, and consequently about our Country and Posterity. The Lives of Thousands, and the Liberties of Millions are as much in Suspence, as the Health of my family. But I submit to the Governance of infinite Wisdom.

Had my Advice been followed, in Season, We should now have been in Safety, Liberty and Peace, or at least We should have had a clear and indisputable Superiority of Power. But my Advice was not regarded. It never was, and never will be, in this World. Had N.Y., N.J. and Pensilvania, only been in compleat Possession of the Powers of Government only 3 Months sooner, We should have had an Army, at N.Y. and Amboy, able to cope with double the Number of our Enemies. But now We trust to Chance: to the Chapter of Accidents: a long Chapter it is, as long as the 119 Psalm: and well it is for us that it is so. If We trusted to Providence, I should be easy, but We do not.

I have now come to a Resolution, upon another Subject, which has kept me in suspence for some Time. I must request of you, to interceed with your Father to procure for me, two Horses, and send them to Philadelphia, with a servant, as soon as possible. I shall wait for their Arrival, let it be sooner or later. The sooner they come, the more agreable to my Wishes, and the better for my Health. I can live no longer, without Riding. If Bass is willing to take one more Ride with his old Friend, let him come, if he declines, send somebody else. I shall wait for Horses.[1] If the Congress should adjourn, I shall attend the Board of War, untill they come. The General Court, I think might do something. Whether they have ever thought of granting me, a farthing, for my Time, I know not. Mr. A.[2] had an Horse and a fine Chaise, furnished him, by the Committee of Supplies. Perhaps they might furnish me with a Pair of Horses too. Pray mention this to Coll. Warren or Coll. Palmer. If nothing can be done by them, if I have Credit enough left, to hire two Horses and a servant, let it be employed. The Loss of my fine Mare, has disconcerted me. The General Court will send some Gentleman here to take my Place. But if my Horses come I shall not wait for that.

RC (MHi). Adams, *Family Correspondence* (Butterfield), 2:83–84.

[1] Joseph Bass arrived in Philadelphia with Adams' horses on September 5. See Adams to Abigail Adams, September 5, 1776.

[2] Samuel Adams.

William Floyd to Unknown

Sr,[1]   Philadelphia August 10 1776

The Situation of our provence, or State, is truly alarming; and it gives me Concern that I cannot hear more particularly what its true State and Circumstances are; I beg you would favour Me with a few lines on that Subject, as often as your time will permit. Be pleased to let me know what you hear of the Situation of our friends on the Eastward part of Long Island, what is become of General Woodhull, Mr Hobart, Tredwell, Mr. Smith and others. Have you heard any thing from my family, has any of our friends Got off the Island with their families, or what must they Submit too; Despotism or Destruction I fear is their fate. We have nothing new here; all Important News is with you. Is our Convention Siting, are they forming Goverment, where are the two armies, what are their probable Intentions, is New York to be Evacuated as well as Long Island with out fighting, or will our army like the Romans of old Consider the Invaluable prize for which they are Contending and with their fortitude attack the Enemy where Ever they can find them; knowing that Death is Rather to be Chosen than life upon the terms our Enemies will Suffer us to hold it.

If our Convention is not Sitting please to Inform me who I can Draw upon for money to pay my Expences, And youl very much oblige, Sr., your very humble Servt,   Wm Floyd

RC (WHi).
   [1] Floyd probably wrote this letter to a member of the New York Convention, but the recipient has not been identified.

John Hancock to George Washington

Sir,   Philadelphia August 10th. 1776.
   Conceiving it highly necessary you should be informed as soon as possible of the Promotions the Congress were yesterday pleased to make in the Army of the American States, I do myself the Honour to enclose you a List of the same by Express.[1]

The Continental Battalion, commanded by Colonel Haslet, will begin their March this Day for the Jerseys; where, on their Arrival at Amboy, the Colonel has Orders to acquaint you of the same.[2]

I have the Honour to be, with the greatest Esteem & Respect, Sir, your most hble Serv.   John Hancock Presidt

[P.S.] The Inclos'd Letters please to order to be Deliver'd.[3] The Commiss[ion]s [are] Inclos'd in each.

RC (DLC). In the hand of Jacob Rush, with signature and postscript by Hancock.
   [1] See JCC, 5:641, 644.
   [2] See Hancock to John Haslet, August 6, 1776.
   [3] These were Hancock's letters of this date to William Heath, Joseph Spencer, John Sullivan, and Nathanael Greene, informing them of their promotions to the rank of major general; to James Read, John Nixon, Arthur St. Clair, Alexander McDougall, Samuel Holden Parsons, and James Clinton, apprising them of their promotions to the rank of brigadier general; and to William Tudor, telling him of his promotion to the rank of lieutenant colonel. PCC, item 12A; and Am.

Archives, 5th ser. 1:883. See also *JCC*, 5:641, 644–45; and Washington, *Writings* (Fitzpatrick), 5:372, 379–81.

John Hancock to George Washington

Sir,   Philada. August 10th. 1776.
                                                            6 o Clock P. M.

I am this Minute honoured with your Favour of the 8th and 9th inst. per Post.[1] Having sent off an Express this Morning, at which Time, I forwarded Commissions for the General officers appointed yesterday by Congress, I shall not detain the Post to send the Commissions ordered by the enclosed Resolve.[2] In the mean Time, you will please to direct the Persons to do such Duty as you shall think proper. Their Commissions shall be transmitted by the first opportunity.

I will lay your Letter before Congress on Monday Morning, and immediately inform you of the Result.

I have the Honour to be, with every Sentiment of Respect, Sir, your most obed. & very hble Sert.   John Hancock Presidt

RC (DLC). In the hand of Jacob Rush and signed by Hancock.
  [1] This letter is in PCC, item 152, 2:363–70, and Washington, *Writings* (Fitzpatrick), 5:402–6.
  [2] See *JCC*, 5:644.

North Carolina Delegates to the North Carolina Council of Safety

Gentlemen   Philadelphia Aug. 10 1776

We wrote you yesterday [1] by express to General Lee with dispatches requesting his immediate return to the Eastern Colonies. We then mentioned to you that Congress in order to encourage the completion of the Continental Regiments had offered a considerable bounty to all non commissioned officers & Soldiers who would enlist for the space of three years. Congress are deeply impressed with the necessity of making inlistments if possible *during the War* but at any rate for the space of three years; as frequent enlistments prevent Soldiers ever becoming expert in discipline and often put it in their power to quit their Station at a time when their Services are most necessary for the publick safety. We recollect that our State hath given a bounty of 40s to every man who has engaged in the Continental Regts raised in No Carolina. By way of œconomy & to save that Bounty to the Colony in part by making it a continental charge We would propose that 5 dollars more be given to every non commissioned Officer and Soldier already enlisted who will engage for the space of the War & if that cannot be effected, *for a limited time*; We wish a longer at any rate than three years, tho that will come within the intention of Congress. In increasing the Regts begun to their proper number the new Recruits will be entitled to the 10 dollars bounty in case of the proposed extension of time in the enlistment. We imagine that this will operate to produce a very happy alteration in the state of our Carolina Army especially as the Soldiers will in a short time receive decent & comfortable Cloathing.

We are Gentlemen, With great Respect, Your obedt Humble Servants,   Wm Hooper

Joseph Hewes

John Penn

RC (Nc–Ar). Written by Hooper and signed by Hooper, Hewes, and Penn. *N.C. Colonial Records,* 10:740–41. RC damaged; missing words supplied from Tr.

¹ On August 9 the North Carolina delegates wrote this brief note to the council of safety: "The Above Resolves being interesting to our Province We have thought it our duty to send Copies of them duely authenticated." Signers Collection, InU; and *N.C. Colonial Records,* 10:740. The resolves enclosed in this letter were a June 5 resolve increasing the salaries of regimental surgeons, a June 26 resolve offering a $10 bounty to "every non-commissioned officer and soldier" who enlisted for a term of three years, and a July 5 resolve dealing with the appointment of regimental chaplains. *JCC,* 5:419, 483, 522.

William Williams to Joseph Trumbull

Dear Sir   Philadelphia Augt. 10th. 1776

On the repeated Request of Genll Washington for an additional number of Major & Brigadier Generals, & representing the necessity of them to assist in Command in a day of Action, which He is daily expecting, Congress yesterday took up the matter, & have appointed a number of each sufficiently large viz Maj Generals Heath, Spencer, Sullivan & Green, & Brigadier Generals Reed of N. H., Nixon of Mass., St Clair of Pena., McDougall, Parsons, whom you Know & Clinton, N. Y.¹ Poor Wooster a worthy Officer is neglected, boundless Efforts have been used to blast his Character in Congress by one of the Canada Comissioners.² He has been represented by him as a most worthless contemptible Felon & the most liberal abuse thrown out against him in Congress, such as I think totally inconsistent with their Honor & Justice to suffer, but so it is. Nor has the author escaped severe Remarks by the Friends of Wooster but the former undauntedly persisted in his Reflections, & has fixed a deep Prejudice against him in a majority; tho not a single Charge can be supported against him, & He has been honorably accquitted by a Committee, whose Report by address &c, has been yet kept of[f] & recomitted.[3] However on the Tryal for Maj Gs. he carried six votes twice agst the same No. per Heath, & one for Sullivan with much opposition. A 3d ballot was had & Heath carried it by 7 vs 6. The other Majr Genlls were all unanimously chosen. There was no intention to make more than three, but as it was thot necessary to take them in succession, Green was so worthy & high in Esteem, that on motion He was added with an eager unanimity. Reed carried 10 votes, Nixon 8, St Clair 8, McDougal 7, Parsons 11 & Clinton 7. Thus a Door is opened, a fine parcel of Promotions. I know not whether any thing will be done about them at present. Nothing yet moved. I hope in God, they & all will acquit themselves like Men & be strong in the Day of approaching Conflict, & may the Lord of Hosts be on our Side & vindicate our rightious Cause agt our most unjust & more than Savage Foes.

I am Dear Sir your affecte Friend & Brother,

W Williams

[P.S.] Genl Gates has wrote a more favorable Acco of our Nothern Army.[4] It is talked out of Doors of adjourning to the Jerseys.

Please to let me know Cap. Dyers best arguments for a majority, his present Rank &c. I wod gladly serve him.[5]

RC (Ct).
[1] See *JCC*, 5:641.
[2] For further criticism of Samuel Chase's handling of Canadian affairs, see John Adams to Horatio Gates, August 13, 1776, note 2.
[3] On August 17 Congress approved the report of this committee, which found "nothing censurable or blameworthy" in Gen. David Wooster's conduct. *JCC*, 5:664–65.
[4] Gen. Gates' July 29 letter to John Hancock, which was read in Congress on August 8, is in PCC, item 154, 1:19–21, and *Am. Archives*, 5th ser. 1:649.
[5] See Williams to Joseph Trumbull, August 20, 1776.

James Wilson to Jasper Yeates and John Montgomery

Dear Gentlemen   Philada 10th Augt 1776

In my Letter to you and the other Commissioners I have inclosed a Resolution of Congress mentioning a Matter to be enquired into by you and them.[1] I enclose to you Major Blaine's Proposals upon the Subject.[2] You know, as well as I do, his peculiar Activity and Fitness for an Employment of this Kind. He is now at the Camp in New Jersey, where I expect to be in a few Days.

The Recollection of my own Feelings about a Year ago tells me how anxious you are about News and Politics. I will embrace a small Interval of Leisure to gratify you a little. Our Convention has been sitting a considerable Time; but I believe they are not yet nearly arrived at an End of their Business. Our Friends Ross and Smith seem sometimes pretty well pleased with what is going on; but, at other Times, not entirely so. The legislative Power, I am told, will be vested only in one Body, to be annually elected. A Rotation in this Body is suggested as a Check upon it and upon its Members. A septennial or Decennial Convention, with Powers to correct and amend the Errors discovered in the Constitution or Administration, is proposed. Such a Convention, to support its own Importance, will, in my Opinion, either *find* or *make* Mischief. To make it salutary, the Constitution should be a bad one. Perhaps, however, such a Convention, to meet at very considerable Distances of Time, such as 50 Years, might be of Service. By that Time, some of the Wheels of the Machine, tho' well made and properly put in Motion at first, may be out of Repair. A Governour and Council are proposed as the executive Power. I have heard very little concerning the Judges.

I would not close this Letter before the Post came from New York. I have been with the President, and have seen his Letters from General Washington. The Intelligence contained in them is very interesting, and gives Reason to look out for something in a short Time that will be still more so. You have heard, I presume, that the British Troops to the Number of eight Thousand under General Howe landed some Weeks ago on Staten Island. They have been since joined by the Forces under General Clinton and Lord Cornwallis, who have been drove from South-Carolina; by Part of the Hessians and of General Fraser's Regiment. Their Number, by this Time, probably amounts to fifteen thousand. More are every Day expected by the Enemy. Our Force at New-York and its Neighbourhood is 17,000, but many of them are sickly; and from the Nature of the Country are much detached from one another. The Militia now in New-Jersey under the Command of General Mercer may, I presume, be about eight thousand. Their Numbers are hourly increasing. The Evening before last an hundred Boats were discovered carrying Troops from Staten-Island on Board the Ships that lie near it. Some of those Ships were falling down towards Sandy Hook. All Appearances indicated a general Embarkation; and the Design of that Measure, in all Probability, is a general Attack. General Washington writes that the Spirits of our Men are by no Means depressed at this Prospect. The Crisis is approaching. God grant that it may be fortunate. I think all Things considered, we have no Reason to despair. The Enemy, after having allowed our Troops so much Time to fortify themselves, must make the Attack under every Disadvantage.

Our northern Army is now in a much better Situation than it has been in for some Time past. We are augmenting, with much Rapidity, our naval Force upon Lake Champlain. Part of General Burgoyne's Army is at St John's, and is likewise busied in making naval Preparations. Colonel St Clair was yesterday made a General Officer. His Character stands deservedly high.

It will give me Pleasure to hear from you. I am, Dear Gentlemen, Your very humble Servant, James Wilson

RC (PHC).

[1] For Congress' resolution of August 6 inquiring of the commissioners whether "the garrisons on the Ohio and its waters, should be supplied with provisions by contract or by a commissary," see *JCC*, 5:634. Wilson's brief letter of transmittal, dated August 10 and addressed to the "Commissioners for Indian Affairs in the Middle Department," is at MH.

[2] Not found.

John Adams to Samuel H. Parsons

Dear sir   Philadelphia August 11. 1776.

Last Evening I recd yours of 7 July. It should have been August I suppose.[1]

I am perfectly of your opinion of the Policy, and the Necessity of offering Land to inlist Soldiers. There is a difficulty attends it. Some Colonies have no Lands to give. However this might be got over, if the General would recommend the Measure—but it seems to me it never will be done, untill he does.

Congress has already ordered a Paymaster to every Regiment.[2] Whether these officers have been appointed or not I cant say—if proper Persons were recommended to Congress, they would be appointed at once.

I can now inform you that We have made a great Number of Promotions, and give me Leave to assure you that none ever gave me more Pleasure than yours.[3] I had the Pleasure of doing Justice to your Character upon the occasion, at least as far as my Voice and Testimony would go, from an acquaintance of about 24 years. Tyler is Coll of your Regiment and Prentice Lt Coll, Durkee Coll of the twentyeth and Knowlton Lt Coll.[4] Whether the Promotions We have made of General officers, will allay the Discontents you speak of, or increase them I know not. Let the Rank of officers be as delicate a Point as it will, the Rank of Colonies is equally delicate and of more Importance. The Massachusetts Bay has not its Proportion of General officers. And the Mass. Colls I expect will be discontented. I cant help it. They are brave Men I doubt not. But whether they are Gentlemen of liberal Education, of any Knowledge of the World, of any Spirit of Command, of any Extent of Capacity, I know not, never having had the Pleasure of any Acquaintance with any of them save Porter, Sergeant, and Ward. Of Porter and Ward I have a very good opinion, but they Stand low in the list. Knox and Porter must be promoted eer long.

I am grieved to my inmost Soul, for a Province, which I love and revere above all Things in this World, excepting that whole of which it is the most powerfull Part, I mean America. Winslow, Ruggles, Saltonstall, Barker, and many others of our ablest officers, were abandoned Tories. Prebble and Pomeroy were incapacitated with Infirmities of Age. Warren and Thomas are fallen. Ward, Fry and Whitcomb have resigned. So has Leonard. Heath unfortunately has not a Reputation, equal to his Merit. If this is owing to Slander I wish to God he would prove it to be a Slander. Nixon is brave, but has not a large Mind that I can learn. In this State of Things that Province which ought to have an indisputable Superiority to every other upon the Continent, has now in the List of General officers an undisputed Inferiority. I never will bear this long, let it occasion what discontents it will among the Collonells. Altho I have hitherto been as steady an advocate for Promotions in succession, generally as any Man, I will nevertheless, totally disregard the Succession, and exert my Utmost Endeavours to promote young Fellows whose Genius, Learning, Sentiment, Authority, and Spirit I can answer for, over the Heads of old ones, who will leave it disputable whether they have either or not.

I am out of all Patience at the Dishonour and Disgrace brought upon my Native Province. There are young Gentlemen, who have every Qualification necessary, Osgood, Ward, Austin, Tudor. I wish they all had Regiments. I have serious Thoughts of moving to have our Major General Warren, Lincoln or Orne, made a Continental Major General. I know there would be a Vote for it here. Let me beg of you in Confidence to give me the Characters of our best Massachusetts Field officers. I want to know if there are men fit for Generals. If not it is high Time to make some new ones.

If there is a Partiality against the Field officers of that Province, and they are not recommended in Proportion to their Merit, I wish to know that, because such a Partiality may be rectified. If their Merit is inferiour I wish to know that, that better officers may be introduced in their Stead. Excuse this freedom, which I have indulged in Confidence, that no ill use will be made of it. I am with Respect, and Esteem, your Affectionate Servant.

LB (MHi).
[1] Parsons' letter to Adams, dated July 7, 1776, is in the Adams Papers, MHi.
[2] For Congress' June 25 resolve on appointment of paymasters, see JCC, 5:479.
[3] Parsons had been promoted to brigadier general on August 9, 1776. JCC, 5:641.
[4] See JCC, 5:644.

Josiah Bartlett to John Langdon

Dear Sir,   August 11th 1776

Yours of the 28th ulto is come to hand and I congratulate you on your late appointment.[1] Col Whipple sets off to morrow morning for Portsmouth and takes with him your commission as Continental Agent and will be able to inform you every thing relative to it. He will be likely to make a little stop at New York and will go by the way of Providence and if possible procure the guns for your ship &c which stops may prevent his being with you as soon as this may reach you, but will no doubt in a few days after.[2] He takes with him sixty thousand dollars for the account of New Hampshire.[3]

By the public prints you will see there is a new emission of Brigadier Generals and four of the former Brigadiers promoted to Major Generals. We find some difficulty to give satisfaction in the appointment of officers and on the whole it was thought the appointing the first Continental Colonel in the respective States to the rank of Brigadiers was the least liable to objections.

You have no doubt heard that Clinton and Cornwallis since their defeat at South Carolina have joined General Howe. Governor Dunmore and his ragamuffins it is said have left Virginia and are supposed to be going to join General Howe. I think we may expect that some important event will soon take place at or near New York. God grant it may be favorable to the United American States.

August 13th. Col Whipple left us for New Hampshire yesterday 2 o'clock. I am your most obedient,   Josiah Bartlett

Tr (DLC).

[1] An extract of Langdon's July 28 letter to Bartlett expressing concern over his duties as naval agent is in Clark, *Naval Documents*, 5:1258–59.

[2] In a letter dated August 20, 1776, and signed by Robert Morris pursuant to a Secret Committee order of August 10, Thomas Mumford of Groton, Connecticut, was requested "to deliver unto Colonel William Whipple Four Tons of Gun powder (Cannon powder if you have it) for the Use of the Continental Frigate *Raleigh* built in New Hampshire—if he should apply for the same." See Journal of the Secret Committee, fol. 91, MH; and Clark, *Naval Documents*, 6:244.

[3] See *JCC*, 5:637.

Robert Morris to Silas Deane

Dear Sir,   Philada August 11th. 1776

I have been so exceedingly harrassed with Public business of various kinds that it has not been in my power to be so good a Correspondent to you as I always intended, but as you know my situa-

tion you'l make allowances & excuse it. I am much Concerned that
we have been so unfortunate in our remittances to you. One ship
whose Cargo Cost £6000 Curry and upwards has been taken sometime since. This Cargo was intended for Cadiz to address of Messrs.
Duff & Welsh with orders to hold the Net proceeds at your disposal
but as they will never receive it you need not write to them on the
Subject. Since that a Brigt Charming Polly (first Capt Mr Falk),
Capt Lacey, has been taken in this Port with a Cargo of near £3000
Curry that was bound for Bourdeaux Cons[igne]d to Messrs. Delap
with orders to account with you for the Net proceeds. Besides these
Genl. Washington has unloaded either two or three Vessells that
were loaded on purpose to make Remittances to you and their
Voyages by this means are broke up. Other Cargoes are & have been
necessarily detained by the Men of Warr on our Coasts and in our
Bays &c. Hitherto you will think your self unlucky in these untoward circumstances and you have really been so, but this must not
dispirit us for you may depend on it, I will persevere in making you
the necessary Remittances with all possible Expedition, and you
will in the end be fully Convinced of my attention to you. By this
Conveyance I remit Sundry bills to Messrs. Saml. & J.H. Delap
amounting to £2000.0.9 Sterlg with orders to hold the same at your
disposal, this amount being towards the Indian Contract and you
will apply it accordingly. By other Conveyances I shall remit more
bills as fast as I can get them. In the mean time I hope you will appear in such a respectable Character as to be able to obtain all the
Indian Goods on Credit untill the remittances get safely to hand.
These Goods will be exceedingly wanted and I most sincerely wish
you may not have lost one Moment in obtaining & sending them
out. I have lately recd. a letter from my Brother Tom dated at
Marseilles the 8th June giving much usefull & important intelligence. By that letter I find he will meet you in France and I flatter
myself he will prove a valuable & useful acquisition to you, as you'l
find him Master of the Language, tractable, Capable & quick of apprehension. He has been a wild youth heretofore but if he is now
sensible of former Follys he may be the more valuable Man for it. I
beg leave to recommend him to your Friendship & Patronage. Keep
him with you, advise him for his own sake to attend most constantly & steadily to the transactions you have in hand as I shall
procure him proper appointments provided he shews himself Capable of serving his Country. Of this you'l be able to Judge & from
you I shall expect impartial accounts of his Conduct. I wish him to
become a good Historian, to understand the Politicks of most
Countrys in Europe as they regard one another as well as the particular Police of each Kingdom or State; in short it is my advice that
instead of passing his time in pleasurable pursuits he shou'd make
use of his present opportunity and advantage & lay the foundation

of a Character that may become respectable & Conspicuous in the World. The present troubles will afford him opportunitys of applying all his knowledge & abilitys be they more or less. He possesses a good deal of Mercantile knowledge & is acquainted personally and by Fame with many of the first Houses in Europe. Therefore it seems to me the present opportunity of Improving our Fortunes ought not to be lost especially as the very means of doing it will Contribute to the Service of our Country at the same time.

I have in a former letter told you the whole Continent wou'd be in want of Woolen Goods the ensuing Winter and you may depend that sufficient supplys cannot be sent out in time. We have lately got in a most Noble Crop of Flax and every body that understand cleaning & manufacturing of it are employed. This will furnish large quantitys of Coarse Linens, but Linens of about 2/ to 3/ stg per yard, good sheeting Linens, Table linen, Ravens or other Duck fit for Tents, Sail Cloth of all sorts, Cambricks, downs, muslines, &c will all continue to be much wanted, all sorts of Cutlary Ware, Copper, Tin & Lead & every kind of Goods fit for Winter Wear must bring any price. I therefore propose that Tom & you shou'd try your and our Credit jointly and propose to some of the most wealthy Houses in France to ship out quantitys of suitable Goods to Martinico & Cape Francois to be reshipped from thence hither. I dont care how much Value you send the more the better especially if you can get Insurance made on the Value from the West Indies here against all Risques. We will employ good Vessells in transporting them hither and it will very often be in my power to obtain Convoy as our Frigates will frequently be cruizing in the West Indies. I wou'd propose that you shou'd immediately send off as large a Value as you can in Winter Goods & an assortment every Month afterwards suitable for the Season at which they may be expected to arrive.

These Goods may if you please come out 2/3ds on Account of Willing, Morris & Compy and 1/3d on your Acct. You must fix with those that ship them the length of the Credit and the Interest to be paid for their advances as well as their Commissions &c. Youl observe that British Manufactures were before the present Contest shipped from England in the greatest abundance for 2 1/2 per Cent Com[mission]s on 12 months Credit after which 5 per Cent Interest to Commence if the payments were not then made; I am very sensible we cannot expect that Confidence from France & other Foreign Merchants now, that we formerly enjoyed with the Merchants in England, but I know that all Trading People do & must run Risques & that they are content to do so, when paid an equivalent. Now when it is Considered that from our late Non-Exportation agreement, and from other interruptions to Commerce, it is not possible we can remit bills previously or have proper

Funds in Europe, it will not be thought strange that we shou'd under such circumstances seek for Credit, and if our Cause is Crowned with success (which I think must be the case sooner or later) there is little danger in trusting us or indeed none at all, & that on the Contrary if we shou'd be unsuccessfull the Goods may be stopped in the West Indies for you may be sure we will not order them from thence unless we see perfect security in so doing. I say when these things are attended to, not half the danger will appear that may at first be immagined. Now if the Goods arrive safe we can sell them instantly for ready Money at very high prices and wou'd immediately Invest the Money in the purchase of Tobacco, Indigo, Flour, Wheat & such other produce as may suit the French Market. If Insurance can be made on these Products against all Risques the Remittances will thereby be rendered Certain & the payment for the Goods Speedy. I hope therefore you will exert yourselves to the utmost to Effect this plan and if any French or Dutch Houses choose to join you in it they may be a third, you a third & we a third or in any other proportion you like better. At Martinico Wm Bingham, Esqr. & Mr. Richd Harrison will receive & forward the Goods, at Cape Francois Mr. Stephen Ceronio or in his absence Mr. Jno. Gaignard. Tom knows Ceronio & indeed so do you. He is capable & faithful to the last degree but if any better Method occurs to you, do therein as you think best. If any Character of our House is wanted to gain the necessary Credit Tom knows where to apply for it. You may depend that the pursuit of this plan deserves your utmost exertion & attention so farr as your Mind is engaged in the making of Money for there never was so fair an opportunity of making a large Fortune since I have been Conversant in the World and You may assure yourself and all Concerned in this matter that I will manage whatever comes here to the utmost advantage and make the most immediate returns for the Value, therefore I hope you will execute something Considerable without delay.

I am sorry to tell you that Coll Harrison is now left out of Congress & set off for Virginia Yesterday. Mr Dickenson is also out & at present none of the Committee here but Dr. Franklin & myself. We must move for an addition to this Committee as Mr. Jay stays in New York & Mr. Johnston in Maryland. There are many changes in Congress since you left us some for the better & some Worse. Our Frigates are really fine ships and the Marine Committee have it in charge to report ways & means for increasing it and this can be done with great facility & dispatch, so that you may expect these States to become very formidable on the Seas next Summer or sooner. However I must referr you to the Public papers for News as I have sent a good many to Messrs. Delap & wrote to Jno. Bradford Esqr. at Boston to send more from thence.

They will deliver or forward them to you, and with sincere Esteem, I remain, Dear Sir, your affectionate Friend & mos. hble servt.

Robt Morris

RC (CtHi).

John Adams to Abigail Adams

Aug. 12. 76

Mr. A[dams] setts off, to day, if the Rain should not prevent him, with Coll. Whipple of Portsmouth: a Brother of the celebrated Miss Hannah Whipple, a sensible and worthy Man. By him I have sent you two Bundles of Letters, which I hope you will be carefull of. I thought I should not be likely to find a safer opportunity. By them, you will see that my private Correspondence alone, is Business enough for a lazy Man. I think I have answered all but a few of those large Bundles.

A French Vessell, a pretty large Brigantine, deeply loaden, arrived here yesterday from Martinique. She had 50 Barrells of Limes, which are all sold already, at such Prices, that the Amount of them will be sufficient to load the Brig with Flour. A Trade We see, even now, in the midst of summer is not totally interrupted, by all the Efforts of our Enemies. Prizes are taken in no small Numbers. A Gentleman told me a few days ago that he had summed up the sugar, which has been taken, and it amounted to 3000 Hdds. since which two other ships have been taken and carried into Maryland.

Thousands of schemes for Privateering are afloat in American Imaginations. Some are for taking the Hull ships, with Woolens for Amsterdam and Rotterdam—some are for the Tin ships—some for the Irish Linnen ships—some for outward Bound and others for Inward Bound India Men—some for the Hudsons Bay ships— and many for West India sugar ships. Out of these Speculations many fruitless and some profitable Projects will grow.

We have no News from New York. All is quiet there as yet. Our Expectations are raised—the Eyes of the World are upon Washington and How, and their Armies. The Wishes and Prayers of the virtuous Part of it, I hope, will be answered. If not, yet Virtues grow out of Affliction.

I repeat my request, that you would ask some of the Members of the G[eneral] Court if they can send me Horses, and if they cannot that you would send them. I can live no longer without a servant, and a Horse.

RC (MHi). Adams, *Family Correspondence* (Butterfield), 2:88–89.

John Adams to Abigail Adams

Aug. 12 76

Mr. A. and Coll. Whipple, are at length gone. Coll. Tudor went off with them. They went away, about Three o Clock this afternoon. I wrote by A and Coll. Whipple too. By the latter I sent two large Bundles, which he promised to deliver to you.

These middle States begin to taste the Sweets of War. Ten Thousand Difficulties and wants occur, which they had no Conception of before. Their Militia are as clamorous, and impatient of Discipline, and mutinous as ours, and more so. There has been seldom less than four Thousand Men in this City at a Time, for a fortnight past, on their March to New Jersey. Here they wait untill We grow very angry, about them, for Canteens, Camp Kettles, Blanketts, Tents, Shoes, Hose, Arms, Flints, and other Dittoes while We are under a very critical Solicitude for our Army at New York on Account of the Insufficiency of Men.

I want to be informed of the State of Things with you. Whether there is a Scarcity of Provisions of any Kind, of West India Articles, of Cloathing. Whether any Trade is carried on, any Fishery. Whether any Vessells arrive from abroad, or whether any go to sea, upon foreign Voyages.

I wish to know likewise, what Posture of Defence you are in. What Fortifications are at Nantaskett, at Long Island, Petticks Island &c. and what Men and Officers there are to garrison them. We hear nothing from the Massachusetts, lately, in Comparason of what We did, when the Army was before Boston.

I must not conclude without repeating my Request, that you would ask some of the Members of the General Court to send me Horses—and if they cannot, to send them yourself.

RC (MHi). Adams, *Family Correspondence* (Butterfield), 2:89–90.

Thomas Jefferson's Notes on the Inquiry into Esek Hopkins' Conduct

Aug. 12. 1783 [*i.e.* 1776][1]

I

The Commodore'[s] excuse for not going to Southern colonies agreeable to orders.[2]

Before he left capes of Delaware, he heard the Liverpool was joined to Ld. Dunmore, which made enemy an overmatch, & many of his men sea sick.

Commodore Esek Hopkins

He did not go to N. Carolina because [he] received intelligence the enemy's force had gone from there & from S. Cara. to Georgia. (His men recovered as he got to the Southward).

He did not go to S. Carolina for the same reason & because [he] had no pilots.

He did not go to Georgia because enemy's ships as he heard were all there & too strong.

He app[ointe]d Abaco as a rendezvous, & to wait there 15 days for each other; he chose that place because nearer to Georgia than to S. Carolina.

He got there with all his fleet except the Fly & Hornet, & as he was to wait 15 days for them he thought he might as well form [an] expedition somewhere. He heard from (a whaler I believe) that there was 200 barrels of powder cannon &c. at [New] Providence belonging to king. He therefore went there. But the night he arrived the Governor removed the powder. He took the cannon.

He did not go to Savanna because while at Providence he heard all the enemy's fleet had assembled there & were too strong for him.

On his return Northwardly he took a bomb brig for which [he] received thanks of Congress.

He carried [the] cannon to Rhode Isld. rather than to the Carolinas because [they were] not wanting in the Carolinas, & he thot he could get more safely into Rhode Isld.

He did not deliver them to Govr of Connecticut as ordered by Congress, because he had them as ballast, and found he could not get ballast at N London without sending to N. York, a delay which he could not admit, as Gen. Washington wrote him he apprehended the enemy would attempt to block him up in N. London.

He delivered them to Govr. Cook of Rh. Isld. because he offered him pig iron as ballast in lieu of them, & Govr. Cook undertook to deliver them to order of Congress.

After he returned from Providence he was not at liberty to go to the Carolinas because his instructions directed him to go to Rh. Isld.

Had not pilots to carry him into inlets of N. Carolina or over Charles town bar.

Commodore did not send vessel for intelligence into Southern colonies because both Fly & Hornet parted with him within 2 days after sailed, in bad weather & the Hornet never joined him, the Fly not till he got to Providence.

A clause in his instructions authorized him to depart from his instructions if in his discretion he thought it for the public good. If he was mistaken then it was no crime.

Instructions are never given positively & it is right they should not be, because of change of circumstances.

II.

The Commodore had a premeditated design not to go to the Southern colonies but to Providence

Because he did not send into Chesapeak for certain intelligence.

Because he did not send his vessel of intelligence into N. Carolina, but only sais he heard enemy had left that place whereas in truth the Cruiser remained there alone & had above 50 prizes with her.

Because he did not send into So Carolina for intelligence.

He had better gone there for rendezvous than to Abaco because Gadsden had promised him on seeing signals to send out Pilot boats.

because he might have crossed the bar

because it was nearer to Georgia than Abaco was.

Because 2 days before he got to Abaco he told Major Nicholas he was to go to Providence, whereas he sais in his defence he did not intend to go there till he reached Abaco, (the rendezvous appointed) & then finding the Fly & Hornet separated he thought he might as well employ the time of 15 days which was agreed on to wait there, in some expedition.

The not meeting the Fly & Hornet could not prevent him from going to Savannah because they were mere vessels of intelligence, not of force. They only carried, one of them swivels, the other 3. or 4 lbers.

There was no cannon in N. Carolina, so were much wanting there.

He was furnished with 2 vessels on purpose to procure sure intelligence to direct his motions, particularly the Fly a very swift vessel was bought & fitted out on purpose.

After the expedition to Providence why did not he then go to Carolinas or Southern colonies, that being not only the main object of his expedition, but in truth the object of equipping the Navy.

His management of engagement with Glasgow shews he wanted skill & activity.

Cannon not wanting for ballast because two of his officers say she had still ballast with which she had gone to Providence & returned.

He ought to have obeyed Congress in delivering cannon. Tho' he was come out of the harbor of New London with the cannon on board, he ought to have returned with them.

Objection that he had no pilots to carry him into inlets of N. Carolina and bar of Charles town not good, because he knew that (if true) when he set out: why did not he inform Naval Committee before he went that it might have been provided for, or delegates taken proper measures. Besides as to Charlestown, Gadsden had agreed with him.

From Chas. town to Georgia 1 day's sail, from Abaco to Georgia 2 days sail.

Fort Johnston had more King's cannon than Providence; if cannon had been his object [he] might have gone & taken them.

At the time he returned from Providence there was the Cruiser & a tender with Govr. Martin waiting to join highlanders & 16 mi. below them were a number of transports with Clinton's army.

He had the Wasp with him a small vessel proper to send in for intelligence

From Ch[arles] to[wn] bar to Savanna bar 70 miles. From Abaco is 3 times as far.

Besides it was in Winter season when Northerly winds prevail which prevent his coming from Abaco to Savanna & facilitate it from Charles town

The objection is [not] that he did not exercise an honest discretion in departing from his instructions but that he never did intend to obey them.

True all instructions have discretionary clause. This proves they have some positive intention, otherwise there was never a positive instruction & never a disobedience of orders, which is not true.

Since return from Providence the fleet has merely acted in defence of trade of Eastern colonies.

MS (DLC). In the hand of Thomas Jefferson. Jefferson, *Papers* (Boyd), 15:578–81. The document consists of a single sheet (now restored after having long been treated as two separate sheets), containing Jefferson's notes in parallel columns on both recto and verso. The left-hand column (here designated part I) consists of statements Hopkins made in his defense during an inquiry into his conduct; the right (part II), of arguments obviously used to rebut Hopkins' claims.

¹ Jefferson apparently affixed this date to the MS in 1783 in the midst of examining and rearranging his papers when collecting and copying documents for James Madison relating to Congress' activities in 1776. See ibid., 6:273–74, 15:582n.1.

² On June 13 Congress had directed the Marine Committee to order Commodore Esek Hopkins to Philadelphia to answer complaints that he had disregarded orders, for which see Naval Committee to Esek Hopkins, January 5, 1776. On August 12 Congress heard the report of the Marine Committee on its examination of Hopkins' conduct, listened to Hopkins' testimony in his defense, and then debated the issue. After further consideration of Hopkins' conduct on the 15th, Congress adopted a resolution criticizing the commodore and declaring that his reasons for failing to pay "due regard" to his instructions were "by no means satisfactory." On the following day they adopted a formal resolution of censure against him but on August 19 ordered him to resume his command. See *JCC*, 5:439, 648, 658–59, 661–62, 667. See also John Hancock to Esek Hopkins, June 14, 1776. For some fragmentary notes on Hopkins' testimony in his defense and John Adams' retrospective comments on the inquiry and debates, see Clark, *Naval Documents*, 6:157n.2; and Adams, *Diary* (Butterfield), 3:405–6.

William Williams to Jabez Huntington

Hond. & dear Sir   Philadelphia Augt. 12, 1776

I had the pleasure of receiving your Favor of the 31st last for which I thank you, have beside, recd. only one Letter viz from the Govr. of the 26th, from my dear Colony since I left it, it gives me great pleasure to hear of the welfare of my Friends.[1] I arrived here the 28th after the most tiresome, sultry and fatigueing journey that ever I went thro & was immediately attacked with a severe Touch of the quick Step (according to Army Phrase) but am thro Divine Mercy recovered. Whether this climate or the summer or by means of the suffocated air of the City it is hotter than I ever experienced by much, I believe it is attributable to all these Causes. It is by far more desirable to be at home than here especially at this Season. Have no news of importance, if I had it wod be impossible you shod receive it first from me. You will see in the Papers that a late member of Congress is arrived in France. You will be at a loss but it must be Mr. Deane. About a week before Mr. Morris, one of Secret Comtee. read a Letter in the House from his Friend in Marseilles, mentioning that Mr.   was arrived there. No name was men[tione]d, but we had no Doubt who was meant. The acco contained of the Disposition of the French Court was not as favorable as wod be wished, it rather seemed as if they did not intend to meddle. You will also see what was printed here yesterday, that the Pacific Ministry of the Court are changed & Choisieul etc in. A Gent of Congress told me yesterday or before, he had a letter from France dated 9 June, a fortnight or more later than the other, mentioning no such thing & that the acco. is undoubtedly false.[2] I fear it is not to be relyd on. I doubt not King Geo. and his Ministry wod sacrifice half the Blood & Treasure of his Kingdom to keep the French still. I believe we have nothing but the justice of our Cause & the infinite Mercy of God to rely on for Safety; without Help of Foreigners, it is probable Mr.   Credentials will not intitle him to any Audience of the Powers of that Court, but [. . .] It is pretty certain we shall get nothing by the bargain unless it may be a Letter once in a while, & I cant say but the Secret Comtee may have one, tho no Body knows it but themselves if they have. The standing Dish of Congress (when time will admit) is the Confederation, which is attended with difficulty here & I fear will be with more at Home. If imminent Danger did not enforce the Necessity of it, we shod differ yet more. I am not at Liberty to mention particulars, but soon as it shall be finished if ever, I shall immediately send copys, if here. I wrote His Honor the 10th of the Cargo of Genll officers appointed for the N. York Markett.[3] Your sons Rank cod. not admit of his being one tho I doubt not his merit wod otherwise entitle him. Great confusion wod take place if the order shod be much broke, the Genll. guard against it his Letters [. . . .] Since the above appointments Lt. Cols Durkee & Tyler are added to the List of Cols. in Arnold & Parsons room & Majs Prentice & Knowlton are Lt. Cols.[4] The Majors places not yet filled. The Declaration of Independence seems to have given great satisfaction to all the Colonies this way & has been everywhere proclaimed by order of the Conventions or Assemblys with the great Ecclat of the People. S. Carolina, Virginia & Jersey have established their forms of Government. The first have chose Jno. Rutledge, Govr., the second, Patrick Henry. Col. Harrison leaves Congress the day being superseded & chosen privy Councillor. Jersey threaten Judge Stockton for Governor; some talk of Dr. Witherspoon, both are members of Congress. Mr. Alsop a member from York was much offended at the Declaration of Independence & expressed it very freely to his Convention & desired to resign. They spiritedly told him in answer that they most cheerfully accepted his Resignation. He is chaffed & gone a journey to Maryland. The Declaration had the vote of every Colony & almost every member. The Convention of this State are sitting, & framing a Constitution. Dr. Franklin will probably be their Governor. I hope our Colony will judge as I do, that it is impossible for us to get a better on the whole than our Fathers chose for Us & we have long practised upon with great Peace & Happiness, & that any alterations or Innovations wo'd be attended with dangerous Consequences.

I want to hear of every transaction etc in your Congress etc. Connecticut has been a perfect   or non Entity since I left it.

I am Sir with much Esteem & Regard, your cordial Friend & most Obed. H. Servt,   Wm. Williams

Tr (CtNhHi).
  ˙ Governor Trumbull's July 26 letter is in *Am. Archives*, 5th ser. 1:606–8.
  [2] See Thomas Jefferson to Francis Eppes, August 9, 1776, note 2.
  [3] Not found.
  [4] See *JCC*, 5:644.

William Williams to Oliver Wolcott

Hond. & dear Sir   Philadela. Augt 12th. 1776
The Governor & council of Safety of our Colony, hearing that you was much unwell & obliged therefore to return home, & thinking that our Representation was too small at most, & at this critical Time especially were very unwilling to have less than three attending, unanimously advised & insisted that Mr Hosmer or I shod attend

in your Place. It was very disagreable to me & wod by no means
have undertaken it, cod Mr Hosmer have been persuaded, but the
small Pox was an immoveable Objection in his Way & the Lot
fell upon Me & with great Reluctance I set out for this place &
reached it near the last of July, after the most Sultry & fatigueing
journey that I ever performed, by much. The City has been since
I came & yet is the most uncomfortable Place that I ever saw. It
is many Times almost impossible to get air enough to breathe.
There is some satisfaction in being accquainted more with the
World, in learning the Temper & Genius of America & much in
attempting to serve & promote its grand & most important interest,
else a Residence here wod be intollerable. I had & shod ever have,
on every other Acco. much more pleasure & Satisfaction at Home
& cod heartily wish there had been no call for my Attendance at
such a Season especially. But since I have been driven out to endure
this long the burning Heat, to forceably shake off my Domestic
Concerns, & hope for better weather abt the last of this month &c
for the sake of learning more thoroughly the Genius of Congress
&c, I shod endeavor to make my Self Content till the latter End of
Septembr., unless your Health will permit, & your Circumstances
&c. inclines you to relieve me sooner, which I willingly refer intirely
to your Inclination & shall govern my Self accordingly & beg the
favor that you wod let me know as soon as possible, when you will
set out & I shall probably meet you on the Road.

I cannot give you any acceptable News. Congress are yet busie at
all Intervals of crouding Business, in Setling a Confederation, it
Seem to labour hard & I fear a permanent one will never be
settled; tho the most material Articles are I think got thro, so as
to give great offence to some, but to my Satisfaction, the bold &
sonorous Chase (& some or all his colleagues) solemnly protest
against the Taxation Article &c & declare that they consider Maryland as having no further Concern in it, & that his Colony never will
nor never shall agree to it. They are all gone home, except Mr Stone,
to attend (they say) their Convention which sits this Day. Most of
the southern Colonies are as uneasie as they, but dont scold quite
so hard.

What will be the event of Things God only knows. If We were
to view only the rage & Strength of our Enemies, our Divisions &
the Wickedness of the People, We might well despair but They are
wicked also. Their Cause is certainly most unjust. The Judge of all
the Earth will do right, He has done great things for Us. He will
not yet forsake Us I believe, tho most of Us have forsaken him, I
trust many, many, thousands have not bowed the knee to Baal.

You will know eer this reaches You & perhaps sooner than We,
the Event of an important Scene opening at N York. The Movements indicate a Blow perhaps Decisive. I feel concern'd but not

at all discouraged. Let our Trust & Hope be in the Lord Jehovah & with Him is everlasting Strength.

I am Sir with sincere Respect & Esteem, your most obedt & very humb. Servant,   Wm Williams

RC (CtHi).

John Adams to Abigail Adams

Philadelphia Aug 13. 1776

Geography is a Branch of Knowledge, not only very usefull, but absolutely necessary, to every Person of public Character whether in civil or military Life. Nay it is equally necessary for Merchants.

America is our Country, and therefore a minute Knowledge of its Geography, is most important to Us and our Children.

The Board of War are making a Collection of all the Maps of America, and of every Part of it, which are extant, to be hung up in the War Office. As soon as the Collection is compleated, I will send you a List of it. In the mean Time take an Account of a few already collected and framed and hung up in the Room.[1]

A Chart of North and South America, including the Atlantic and Pacific Oceans, with the nearest Coasts of Europe, Africa, and Asia.

A Map of the British and French Dominions in North America with the Roads, Distances, Limits and Extent of the Settlements, humbly inscribed to the right Honourable the Earl of Hallifax and the other Right Honorable the Lords Commissioners for Trade and Plantations, by their Lordships most obliged and very humble servant John Mitchell.

A Map of the most inhabited Part of New England, containing the Provinces of Massachusetts Bay, and New Hampshire, with the Colonies of Konektikut and Rhode Island, divided into Counties and Townships: The whole composed from actual Surveys and its Situation adjusted by Astronomical Observations.

A new and accurate Map of North America, drawn from the famous Mr. D'Anville with Improvement from the best English Maps, and engraved by R.W. Seale: Also the new Divisions according to the late Treaty of Peace, by Peter Bell Geog[raphe]r— printed for Carington Bowles, Map and Printseller No. 69 in St. Pauls Church Yard, London, published 1. Jany. 1771.

To the Honourable Thomas Penn and Richard Penn Esquires, true and absolute Proprietaries and Governors of the Province of Pensilvania, and the Territories thereunto belonging, and to the Honourable John Penn Esqr., Lieutenant Governor of the same,

This Map of the Province of Pensilvania, is humbly dedicated by their most obedient humble servant W. Scull.

A General Map of the Middle British Colonies, in America, vizt. Virginia, Maryland, Delaware, Pensilvania, New Jersey, New York, Connecticutt and Rhode Island, of Aquanishuonigy the Country of the Confederate Indians, comprehending Aquanishuonigy proper, their Place of Residence: Ohio and Tïiuxsoxruntie their Deer Hunting Countries, Couxsaxrage and Skaniadarade their Beaver Hunting Countries: of the Lakes Erie, Ontario, and Champlain, and of Part of New France, wherein is also shewn the ancient and present Seats of the Indian Nations. By Lewis Evans 1755. Dedicated to T. Pownal Esqr. whom Evans calls the best Judge of it in America.

To the Honourable Thomas Penn and Richard Penn Esqrs. true and absolute Proprietaries and Governors of the Province of Pensilvania and Counties of New Castle, Kent and Sussex on Delaware. This Map of the improved Part of the Province of Pensilvania is humbly dedicated by Nicholas Scull.[2]

You will ask me why I trouble you with all these dry Titles, and Dedications of Maps. I answer, that I may turn the Attention of the Family to the subject of American Geography. Really, there ought not to be a State, a City, a Promontory, a River, an Harbour, an Inlett, or a Mountain in all America, but what should be intimately known to every Youth, who has any Pretensions to liberal Education. I am.

N.B. Popples Map is not mentioned here, which was dedicated to Queen Ann, and is recommended by Dr. Hawley. It is the largest I ever saw, and the most distinct. Not very accurate. It is Eight foot square. There is one in the Pensilvania State House.

RC (MHi). LB (MHi). Adams, *Family Correspondence* (Butterfield), 2:90–92.

[1] For references to contemporary sources of the maps Adams had collected, see Adams, *Family Correspondence* (Butterfield), 2:92n.1–9.

[2] The last two paragraphs of this letter were omitted in the RC and are printed here from the LB.

John Adams to Horatio Gates

Dear Sir   Philadelphia August 13. 1776

Your Favours of 24 June, and 17 July, are before me.[1] I wish with all my heart that you were Dictator at Ticonderoga, as much as it was intended you should be in Canada—not for the sake of promoting Mr Rice nor any other particular Person, but for the good of the Service in general.

I shewed your last Letter to Mr. Chase, who begged it to write you an answer. I have exactly the same Idea of him, which you express. He had the good of the Service at Heart, but was too Sanguine, and had too little Experience in such Scenes, and too little Penetration into the Characters of Men.[2]

I lament the wretched State of your Army: but am happy to find by your last Letter to Congress, that Things are getting into a better Train. The Small Pox must be cleansed out of the Army, or it will be undone. A Circular Letter went, Sent to you or to General Schuyler, for a compleat Return of every Thing in your Department to the War Office. We have as yet recd no answer. Let me beg of you to transmit it as soon as possible. The Want of regular Returns has ruined our affairs in Canada, and without them from every Department, We shall ever be in Confusion.

Since the Receipt of your Letter, I have procured Resolutions to be past that regular Returns shall be made at least once a Month, by the Commanding officer, the Pay master, the Quarter Master, Muster Master, and Commissary,[3] and if these Returns are not now made, I think there will Inquiries [be?] made, into the Cause of the [Neglect?], which will not be very pleasant to the Negligent. We shall know who is General, who Qu[arte]r M[aste]r, who Paymaster, who Commissary and who Muster Master, important secrets in Canada, which all our Penetration was never able to discover.

We are very anxious, for you and your Army, as well as for the General and his at New York. We expect some bold strokes from the Enemy, but I dont believe that How and Burgoigne will unite their Forces this year.

Aug. 14. Since the above was written We recd your Return. It is the most Systematical that I have seen. Your letter gives us great Joy.[4]

LB (MHi).

[1] These letters are in Bernhard Knollenberg, ed., "The Correspondence of John Adams and Horatio Gates," *Proceedings of the Massachusetts Historical Society* 67 (March 1942): 145–48. For Samuel Chase's angry response to Gates' July 17 letter, which was critical of Chase, see Samuel Chase to Horatio Gates, August 9, 1776.

[2] According to Benjamin Rush's later recollection, Adams once sharply attacked Chase "in a debate in which Mr. C—— insinuated the New England troops, as the principal cause of the failure of the expedition into Canada." Although Rush's account contains no information on precisely when this caustic exchange took place, it seems likely that it was during July or August 1776 when the report of the committee "to enquire into the cause of the miscarriages in Canada" was discussed in Congress. Adams, Rush wrote, replied that "the cause of the failure of that expedition was chiefly to be ascribed to the impudence of the gentleman from Maryland who has fomented jealousies and quarrels between the troops from the New England and Southern States in his visit to Canada, and (said Mr. Adams) if he were now penetrated, as he ought to be, with a sense of his improper and

wicked conduct, he would fall down upon his knees upon this floor, and ask our forgiveness. He would afterwards retire with shame, and spend the remainder of his life in sackcloth and ashes, deploring the mischief he has done his country." Benjamin Rush, *The Autobiography of Benjamin Rush*, ed. George W. Corner (Princeton: Published for the American Philosophical Society by Princeton University Press, 1948), pp. 140–41.

[3] These resolves were adopted August 2, 1776. *JCC,* 5:627–28.

[4] Gates' August 5 letter to Hancock, which was read in Congress on August 15 and contained "a general return of this army," is in PCC, item 154, 1:27–43. The "general return" has not been found, but Gates' letter has been printed under the date August 6, in *Am. Archives,* 5th ser. 1:795–97.

John Adams to Henry Knox

Dear sir   Philadelphia August 13. 1776

Yours of July 29, I duely received—But had not the Pleasure of Seeing Mr Byers the Cannon Founder. Mr. Paine who is upon the Cannon Committee, I suppose has attended to him.[1] He informs me that the Committee of which he is one are taking Measures to procure Copper as well as sulphur to be made in New Jersey.

I have obtained from a Gentleman here, very particular Directions concerning Fire ships and Rafts, and Receipts for all the Compositions. They are long and will be some trouble to transcribe. But if this Business lies within your Department, and you have any Curiosity to see it, I will send it you.

I am very much chagrined that the Massachusetts has not its Proportion of General officers. I wish I was better acquainted with the Persons and Characters of the Colonells from that State. It will never do, for the Massachusetts to furnish so many Men, and have so few Generals while so many other States furnish so few Men and have so many Generals.

I am, sir, your humble servant,   John Adams

RC (MHi).

[1] For additional information on James Byers' activities, see Robert Treat Paine to Henry Knox, July 27 and August 22, 1776.

Thomas Jefferson to Edmund Pendleton

Dear Sir   Philadelphia Aug. 13. 1776.

Yours of Aug. 3 came to hand yesterday.[1] Having had no moment to spare since, I am obliged to sit down to answer it at a Committee table while the Committee is collecting. My thoughts therefore on the subject you propose will be merely extempore. The opinion that our lands were allodial possessions is one which I have very long held, and had in my eye during a pretty consider-

able part of my law reading which I found alwais strengthened it.
It was mentioned in a very hasty production, intended to have
been put under a course of severe correction, but produced
afterwards to the world in a way with which you are acquainted.[2]
This opinion I have thought and still think to prove if ever I
should have time to look into books again. But this is only meant
with respect to the English law as transplanted here. How far our
acts of assembly or acceptance of grants may have converted lands
which were allodial into feuds I have never considered. This matter is now become a mere speculative point; and we have it in our
power to make it what it ought to be for the public good. It may be
considered in two points of view 1st. As bringing a revenue into the
public treasury. 2. As a tenure. I have only time to suggest hints on
each of these heads. 1. Is it consistent with good policy or free
government to establish a perpetual revenue? Is it not against the
practice of our wise British ancestors? Have not instances in which
we have departed from this in Virginia been constantly condemned
by the universal voice of our country? Is it safe to make the governing power when once seated in office, independent in it's revenue?
Should we not have in contemplation and prepare for an event
(however deprecated) which may happen in the possibility of
things; I mean a re-acknolegement of the British tyrant as our
king, and previously strip him of every prejudicial possession?
Remember how universally the people run into the idea of recalling Charles the 2d after living many years under a republican
government. As to the second was not the separation of the property
from the perpetual use of lands a mere fiction? Is not it's history
well known, and the purposes for which it was introduced, to wit,
the establishment of a military system of defence? Was it not
afterwards made an engine of immense oppression? Is it wanting
with us for the purpose of military defence? May not it's other
legal effects (such of them at least as are valuable) be performed
in other more simple ways? Has it not been the practice of all other
nations to hold their lands as their personal estate in absolute dominion? Are we not the better for what we have hitherto abolished of
the feudal system? Has not every restitution of the antient Saxon
laws had happy effects? Is it not better now that we return at once
into that happy system of our ancestors, the wisest and most perfect
ever yet devised by the wit of man, as it stood before the 8th century?
The idea of Congress selling [our?] unlocated lands has been
sometimes dropped, but we have alwais met the hint with such
determined opposition that I believe it will never be proposed. I
am against selling the lands at all. The people who will migrate to
the Westward whether they form part of the old, or of a new colony
will be subject to their proportion of the Continental debt then unpaid. They ought not to be subject to more. They will be a people

little able to pay taxes. There is no equity in fixing upon them the whole burthen of this war, or any other proportion than we bear ourselves. By selling the lands to them, you will disgust them, and cause an avulsion of them from the common union. They will settle the lands in spite of every body. I am at the same time clear that they should be appropriated in small quantities. It is said wealthy foreigners will come in great numbers, and they ought to pay for the liberty we shall have provided for them. True, but make them pay in settlers. A foreigner who brings a settler for every 100, or 200 acres of land to be granted him pays a better price than if he had put into the public treasury 5/ or 5£. That settler will be worth to the public 20 times as much every year, as on our old plan he would have paid in one paiment only. I have thrown these loose thoughts together only in obedience to your letter. There is not an atom of them which would not have occurred to you on a moment's contemplation of the subject. Charge yourself therefore with the trouble of reading two pages of such undigested stuff.

By Saturday's post the General wrote us that Ld. Howe had got (I think 100) flat bottomed boats along side, and 30 of them were then loaded with men; by which it was concluded he was preparing to attack.[3] Yet this is Tuesday and we hear nothing further. The General has by his last return, 17000 some odd men, of whom near 4000 are sick and near 3000 at our posts in Long Island &c. So you may say he has but 10000 effective men to defend the works of New York. His works, however are good and his men in spirits, which I hope will be equal to an addition of many thousands. He had called for 2000 men from the flying camp which were then embarking to him and would certainly be with him in time even if the attack was immediate. The enemy have (since Clinton and his army joined them) 15,000 men of whom not many are sick. Every influence of Congress has been exerted in vain to double the General's force. It was impossible to prevail on the people to leave their harvest. That is now in, and great numbers are in motion, but they have no chance to be there in time. Should however any disaster befall us at New York they will form a great army on the spot to stop the progress of the enemy. I think there cannot be less than 6 or 8000 men in this city and between it and the flying camp. Our council complain of our calling away two of the Virginia battalions.[4] But is this reasonable. They have no British enemy, and if human reason is of any use to conjecture future events, they will not have one. Their Indian enemy is not to be opposed by their regular battalions. Other colonies of not more than half their military strength have 20 battalions in the feild. Think of these things and endeavor to reconcile them not only to this, but to yield greater assistance to the common cause if wanted. I wish every battalion we have was now in New York. We yesterday received dispatches from the Commissioners at Fort Pitt. I have not read them, but a gentleman who has, tells me they are favorable. The Shawanese and Delawares are disposed to peace. I believe it, for this reason. We had by different advices information from the Shawanese that they should strike us, that this was against their will, but that they must do what the Senecas bid them. At that time we knew the Senecas meditated war. We directed a declaration to be made to the six nations in general that if they did not take the most decisive measures for the preservation of neutrality we would never cease waging war with them while one was to be found on the face of the earth. They immediately changed their conduct and I doubt not have given corresponding information to the Shawanese and Delawares. I hope the Cherokees will now be driven beyond the Missisipi and that this in future will be declared to the Indians the invariable consequence of their beginning a war. Our contest with Britain is too serious and too great to permit any possibility of avocation from the Indians. This then is the season for driving them off, and our Southern colonies are happily rid of every other enemy and may exert their whole force in that quarter. I hope to leave this place some time this month. I am Dr. Sir Your affectionate friend,   Th: Jefferson

P.S. Mr. Madison of the college and Mr. Johnson of Fredsbgh. are arrived in New York. They say nothing material had happened in England. The French ministry was changed.

RC (MeHi). Jefferson, *Papers* (Boyd), 1:491–94.

[1] For Pendleton's August 3 letter, as well as his August 26 response to this Jefferson letter, see Jefferson, *Papers* (Boyd), 1:484–85, 507–8.

[2] In Jefferson's draft instructions for Virginia's delegates to the First Continental Congress, published as *A Summary View of the Rights of British America*, he had argued that "our Saxon ancestors held their lands, as they did their personal property, in absolute dominion, disencumbered with any superior." Ibid., p. 132.

[3] Washington's August 8 letter to Hancock, which was read in Congress on the 12th, is in PCC, item 152, 2:363–67, and Washington, *Writings* (Fitzpatrick), 5:402–6.

[4] See the Virginia Council's August 3 letter, which was read in Congress on the 12th, in *Am. Archives*, 5th ser. 1:736. See also John Hancock to Andrew Lewis, July 22, 1776.

Francis Lewis to Elizabeth Gates

Dear Madam [1]   Phila. 13 Augt. 1776

I was favoured with your letter of the 6th Instant, wch. gave me the greater pleasure as it was delivered me by your son. He set of[f] this morning for PrinceTown in order to settle some matters with Mr. Wetherspoon. In my conversation with Bob upon the present state of the Colege I found his inclination was to return home. I advised him to the Contrary, but that he should consult Docr. Wetherspoon & be governed by his advice and as I expect the Doctor in Town this day shall advise with him. I am under no apprehention of any personaly danger at PrinceTown, at present I think it safer than in this City.

I perceive by your letter that you are alarmed at my son Morgans comming down Express to Congress. He brought nothing material more than the then state of the Army at Ticonderoga much reduced by the Small Pox and other disorders but since their removal from Isle au Noix they were recovering daily and reinforcemts arriving so that when he left Ticonderoga they were thought Sufficient to oppose G[enera]l Bourgoine on that Quarter who is on his part fortifying St. Johns & building boats &c in order to Cross the lake. The principal reason for Morgans comming down was briefly this. Genl. Gates, when appointed to the Command of the Army in Cannada, was impowered to appoint such officers as He thought proper. In consequence thereof he nominated Morgan Depy. Qt. Mast. Genl. When Genl. Gates got to Albany, the Troops under Sulivan had evacuated Cannada. Therefore Genl Schuyler claimed the Command of that Army whilest in the Colony of Nw York as Senior Officer, & of course Genl. Gates's appointments for Cannada were Null. This brot. Morgan down to sollissit redress from the Congress, as he had been put to a considerable expence in equiping himself for the appointment. General Sulivan was also disgusted at G[enera]l Gates's being appointed to that Command. He requested to resigne, however that he has withdrawn.[2]

At present our greatest anxiety is for the fate of New York which I greatly fear is devoted to distruction. The Ministeral Army on Staten Island are said to be 13,000 strong with a considerable Naval Force, and we hourly expect to hear the City is attacked. If so there is in my opinion little probability of it's being saved.

I can assure you that Genl. Gates and the Army under his Command were by their last letters in high Spirits, and under no apprehention of danger from that Quarter this Campaigne.[3] Whatever material may happen I shall duly advise you. I am, Dear Madam (Sincerely), Your very Humble Servt,   Frans Lewis

RC (NHi).

[1] Elizabeth Phillips Gates (d. 1783) was married to Gen. Horatio Gates. Lewis and the Gateses had been friends since the French and Indian War. Samuel White Patterson, *Horatio Gates: Defender of American Liberties* (New York: Columbia University Press, 1941), pp. 7–8, 13, 347.

[2] For Sullivan's threatened resignation, see John Hancock to Washington, July 26, note 3, and July 31, 1776. Congress elected Morgan Lewis "deputy quarter master general" of the northern army on September 12, 1776. *JCC*, 5:573.

[3] See Gates' July 16 and 29 letters to Hancock. PCC, item 154, 1:15–17, 19–22; and *Am. Archives*, 5th ser. 1:375–76, 649.

Thomas Nelson to John Page

My Dear Page   Philadelphia Aug. 13th 1776

I wish I could, by this Letter, confirm the report that prevail'd some weeks ago, of thousands of Men going into N. York daily, but alas! that like most others was not above half true. We receiv'd a Letter from the General yesterday, by which we find that he has not above 12000 effective Men, largely upwards of three thousand being sick & unfit for duty. God knows what will be the event. They have made good use of the pickaxe & Spade, excellent weapons for raw Troops in my opinion. To increase our misfortunes, the Militia that went from this province, I believe chiefly from this City, are deserting by Companies from Statten Island, in spight of all that be done to retain them.[1] They cannot bear the thoughts of those who are left behind, reaping all the benefit from the very extravagant price that Goods are sold at, without their coming for a share. So much for the Patriotic Citizens of Philadelphia. Notwithstanding these disadvantages I think we shall maintain our ground.

The Tidings from Fincastle are most acceptable to us. There is no other way of dealing with the Savages but by carrying the War into their own Country; & since they have reviv'd the old quarrel, I woud give them no quarter, but drive them into the South Sea if it were possible.[2]

Why are you so alarm'd at only two Battalions being drawn from you?[3] You have no Enemy now in the Southern Colonies but the Indians, & the back people will manage them. Clinton it is certain, is at Statten Island & we are told that Dunmore is there also, but whether that be true we know not certainly.

I was not very fond of the two Regiments being order'd from Virginia, because I did not think they would arrive in time to be of service at N. Y. but when we consider'd that you had no great probability of an attack being made upon you & that to oppose a proposition of that kind would savour strongly of Self we agreed to it. I wish to God they were at the Camp at this Instant. The two first Regiments being the best arm'd & disciplin'd ought by all means to march, if they can be prevaild on to reenlist, but without that there time is so short, that it would not be worthwhile sending them.

There is no occasion at this time for the Frigate; to that however I gave you a full answer by the last post.

The Committee of Safety some time ago sent the Accounts of the Colony against the Continent. Their Letter was immediately answer'd with a request that they would send the vouchers up, as the Congress had not in any instance pass'd accots without.[4] To this no reply has been given. The Accounts are now in my possession & there they will remain untill the Vouchers are produced. It will be attended with no expence to the Colony to send them up, as the cost of it will be defray'd by the Continent. Do my dear sir attend to this matter, for it is extremely disagreable to me, to be entrusted with business & not give it that dispatch which is expected & which the Notice of Affairs requires. There were 200,000 Dollars sent to the paymaster a fortnight ago, which I hope he has receivd before this. We will endeavor to get an advance of part of the money upon Account & advise you with our Success, but the Vouchers must be sent to us.

Adieu.   Thos Nelson jr.

RC (MH).
[1] Letters from Gen. Hugh Mercer and Col. John Dickinson, reporting the desertion of Pennsylvania Associators serving with Dickinson at Elizabethtown, N.J., were read in Congress on August 12 and referred to the Pennsylvania Convention. See JCC, 5:647; and Mercer's letters to Washington of August 10 and 11 and to Dickinson of August 11, 1776, in Am. Archives, 5th ser. 1:885, 894–95.
[2] See Thomas Jefferson to John Page, August 5, 1776, note 1.
[3] See John Hancock to Andrew Lewis, July 22, 1776, note 3.
[4] The Virginia delegates' letter requesting vouchers has not been found. Virginia's accounts were mentioned in the journals on September 16, but commissioners to audit them were not appointed until November 6, 1776. JCC, 5:761, 6:930.

Thomas Stone to the Maryland Council of Safety

Gent.   Phila. Aug. 13. 1776.
    I am very glad to be informed that Ld. Dunmore and his fleet have quitted the Bay and am hopefull this Circumstance will induce your Militia to lend Assistance to the Neighbours with more Alacrity than could be expected while an Enimy was hovering on their Coast.[1] You may be assured they are much wanted in the Jerseys and at N. York where an Attack is daily expected and at both which places our Strength is by no Means sufficient to oppose the Enimy with that Certainty of Success which every Man who considers the Importance of the Event must wish. Capt. Thomas is arrived with his Company. I shall rejoice to see Col Griffith with his Troops and shall with pleasure afford him and all other officers and Troops from Maryland any assistance in my power. I shall shew particular Attention to Col Griffith, Your recommendation entitling him to peculiar Notice.
    The Difficulties you have experienced in raising your Quota of the flying Camp I am convinced have been distressing, but I hope they are now pretty well over. You may have any Money you want from Congress upon Application. The Enimys Strength at Staten Island is 15,000 Men. The Hessians are daily expected. By the last Accounts, they were shiping their Men & making all necessary preparations for an Attack. Genl Washington is not so strong as we could wish.

Upon these movements of the Enimy he ordered a Reinforcement of 2000 from Jersey to York. The Maryld. Batt. was immediately sent to him but I beleive the Camp in Jersey were too weak to spare any more. I observe Many of the Militia of this State in Motion, but many are leaving the Camp and are not to be kept there by threats or Persuasions. I intend to leave this City, on this Day week, till which I shall be ready to execute your Orders, being Gent, Your most Obt. Sert,   T. Stone

RC (MdAA).
  [1] This intelligence had been reported by the council in its letter of August 9 to the Maryland delegates. See *Md. Archives,* 12:190–91.

John Adams to Abigail Adams

Philadelphia 14. August 1776

This is the Anniversary of a memorable day, in the History of America: a day when the Principle of American Resistance and Independence, was first asserted, and carried into Action.[1] The Stamp Office fell before the rising Spirit of our Countrymen. It is not impossible that the two *gratefull* Brothers may make their grand Attack this very day: if they should, it is possible it may be more glorious for this Country, than ever: it is certain it will become more memorable.

Your Favours of August 1 and 5 came by Yesterdays Post. I congratulate you all upon your agreable Prospects. Even my pathetic little Hero Charles, I hope will have the Distemper finely. It is very odd that the Dr. cant put Infection enough into his Veigns, nay it is unaccountable to me that he has not taken it, in the natural Way before now. I am under little Apprehension, prepared as he is, if he should. I am concerned about you, much more. So many Persons about you, sick. The Children troublesome—your Mind perplexed— yourself weak and relaxed. The Situation must be disagreable. The Country Air, and Exercise however, will refresh you.

I am put upon a committee to prepare a Device for a Golden Medal to commemorate the Surrender of Boston to the American Arms, and upon another to prepare Devices for a Great Seal for the confederated States.[2] There is a Gentleman here of French Extraction, whose Name is Du simitiere, a Painter by Profession whose Designs are very ingenious, and his Drawings well executed. He has been applied to for his Advice. I waited on him yesterday, and saw his Sketches. For the Medal he proposes Liberty with her Spear and Pileus, leaning on General Washington. The British Fleet in Boston Harbour, with all their Sterns towards the Town, the American Troops, marching in. For the Seal he proposes. The Arms of the several Nations from whence America has been peopled, as English, Scotch, Irish, Dutch, German &c. each in a Shield. On one side of them Liberty, with her Pileus, on the other a Rifler, in his Uniform, with his Rifled Gun in one Hand, and his Tomahauk, in the other. This Dress and these Troops with this Kind of Armour, being peculiar to America—unless the Dress was known to the Romans. Dr. F[ranklin] shewed me, yesterday, a Book, containing an Account of the Dresses of all the Roman Soldiers, one of which, appeared exactly like it.

This Mr. Du simitiere is a very curious Man. He has begun a Collection of Materials for an History of this Revolution. He begins with the first Advices of the Tea Ships. He cutts out of the Newspapers, every Scrap of Intelligence, and every Piece of Speculation, and pastes it upon clean Paper, arranging them under the Head of the State to which they belong and intends to bind them up in Volumes. He has a List of every Speculation and Pamphlet concerning Independence, and another of those concerning Forms of Government.

Dr. F. proposes a Device for a Seal. Moses lifting up his Wand, and dividing the Red Sea, and Pharaoh, in his Chariot overwhelmed with the Waters. This Motto. Rebellion to Tyrants is Obedience to God.

Mr. Jefferson proposed. The Children of Israel in the Wilderness, led by a Cloud by day, and a Pillar of Fire by night, and on the other Side Hengist and Horsa, the Saxon Chiefs, from whom We claim the Honour of being descended and whose Political Principles and Form of Government We have assumed.

I proposed the Choice of Hercules, as engraved by Gribeline in some Editions of Lord Shaftsburys Works. The Hero resting on his Clubb. Virtue pointing to her rugged Mountain, on one Hand, and perswading him to ascend. Sloth, glancing at her flowery Paths of Pleasure, wantonly reclining on the Ground, displaying the Charms both of her Eloquence and Person, to seduce him into Vice. But this is too complicated a Group for a Seal or Medal, and it is not original.

I shall conclude by repeating my Request for Horses and a servant. Let the Horses be good ones. I cant ride a bad Horse, so many hundred Miles. If our Affairs had not been in so critical a state at N. York, I should have run away before now. But I am determined now to stay, untill some Gentleman is sent here in my Room, and untill my Horses come. But the Time will be very tedious.

The whole Force is arrived at Staten Island.

RC (MHi). Adams, *Family Correspondence* (Butterfield), 2:95–97.

¹ On August 14, 1765, a Boston mob hanged stamp collector Andrew Oliver in effigy and destroyed the stamp agents' headquarters in Boston. Adams, *Diary* (Butterfield), 1:259–61.

² For Adams' role in the designing of a commemorative medal for General

Washington and the great seal of the United States, see John Adams to George Washington, April 1, 1776; Adams, *Diary* (Butterfield), 3:375–76; and Adams, *Family Correspondence* (Butterfield), 2:97–98n.2 and n.4.

John Adams to William Tudor

Dear sir   Philadelphia August 14. 1776

By a Return from the Adjutant General of the 10 instant, I see a new Brigade makes its appearance, under the Title of General Fellows's Brigade, composed of Coll Holman's, Coll Smith's, and Coll Carys Regiments, making in the whole 1544 Men. These I conclude are from the Massachusetts.

Neither the Council, nor the House, nor any Individual, of our Province, have ever mentioned one Word, in any of their Letters of these Troops or any one of their officers, an omission, like a thousand others, which have given me much Uneasiness.

I must therefore make use of my Friends at New York to gain a little Information, which the Province, from Regard to its own Interest and Honour, if they had no Regard to me, and their other Delegates here, ought to have given, of Course, without giving Us the Trouble of Writing Letters to Obtain.

Let me beg of you, Sir, to make the earliest Enquiry concerning these officers, their Characters, the Parts of the Province from whence they come, and the Kind of Troops under their Command, and as I see the Regiments are not full, whether any more Recruits are expected to fill them. I have a Suspicion that Coll Smith may be my Brother, but have never had the least Intimation of it, from any of my Friends.

We have nothing new, but the arrival of a large ship from Harve de Grace, with a very valuable Cargo of Duck, Powder, Lead, and dry Goods. This is all which has happened here to distinguish the anniversary of the 14 August, the Birth day of American Independance.[1]

Pray let me know if Major Austin is at New York, and if the new Promotions of General Officers is relished in the army.

I am, your Friend & servant,   John Adams

RC (MHi).
[1] See Adams to Abigail Adams, this date, note 1.

Thomas Nelson to Philip Schuyler

Treasury Office, Philadelphia, 14 August 1776. "Desires that the $22,000 lately despatched for the use of the army in Canada, which by its retreat is no longer absolutely necessary there, may be paid in part of the considerable balance due to Messrs. Price and Haywood of Canada." [1]

Tr (NN). This entry consists merely of the description made of Nelson's letter when it was calendared in the early 19th century before disappearing from the Schuyler Papers.

[1] Nelson wrote a similar letter this day to an unknown recipient relative to monies placed in Canada for the use of the army, "in case the specie be in your hands, that you will retain it until called for by the Order of Congress." *Parke-Bernet Galleries Catalog*, no. 2569 (May 16, 1967), item 42. Nelson undoubtedly wrote both letters on behalf of the Treasury Board, which had been directed on August 13 to send orders to Generals Schuyler and Gates "to pay all the specie that they may have in their hands, belonging to the United States, to Messrs. Price and Haywood." The board had been further directed to procure specie to discharge the remaining debt owed these gentlemen. See *JCC*, 5:643–44, 650.

Caesar Rodney to Thomas Rodney

Sir: Philadelphia, August 14, 1776.

I sent by Mr. *Robinson* (without having time to write) the thread you committed to my charge, converted into stockings; but whether the weaver has discovered as much care and ingenuity as the spinner, on that occasion, I cannot say, as I had but little time to inspect them. I wrote to you by young Mr. *Loockerman*, who promised you should have the letter as soon as he got home, but I do not recollect when he left home, but imagined you ought to have received it before you wrote to me, and yet do not find it mentioned.

Agreeable to promise, I sent some time ago to Mr. *Killon*, by *Matthew Henry's* vessel, in the care of *Richard Lockwood*, Esq., a quire of post paper. I have not heard yet whether it got safe to hand, and had not when I sent it time to write to him about it.

By your letter, I stand informed as to the names of your antagonists in the ensuing election; and am pleased to find you hope to succeed. But are you not too sanguine in your expectation?[1] I wish your ticket may be supported by the freemen of the County, because I believe those men wish to have the great work in which we are now engaged finished in such a manner as to afford to the community at large that personal safety, security of property, free enjoyment of religious persuasion, and that equal and easy distribution of justice, which they have a right to expect, and without which they cannot be happy.

I did not expect to be carried in the other ticket, because I see some names there who I believe are too far gone in personal prejudice and private emolument to do justice to merit, or to consider the rights and privileges of the people at large *their* interest.

But if the people can not or will not see these things, though glaring, they must and will suffer.

The time is now big with importance, as to Continental as well as Governmental matters. The armies at *New-York* are like to come to blows in a few days. One hundred and some odd transports, with *Hessians,* arrived at the *Hook* the day before yesterday. The *English* Army is supposed to be upwards of twenty thousand strong; ours better than thirty thousand, in high spirits, and eager for action, &c. I shall be able perhaps to write you more on that head in a few days.

I am, with much love to all friends, yours,

Caesar Rodney.

MS not found; reprinted from *Am. Archives,* 5th ser. 1:944–45.

[1] For more information on the defeat of Thomas' slate of candidates, see Thomas Rodney to Caesar Rodney, August 19, in Rodney, *Letters* (Ryden), pp. 103–4. See also Caesar Rodney to Thomas Rodney, August 21, 1776.

Secret Committee to George Washington

Sir   Philada. August 14th. 1776

You have annexed an extract of a letter we have just recd from Messrs. Clark & Nightingale Merchts in Providence Rhode Island.[1] This letter was laid before Congress who ordered this Committee to inform your Excellency of the Powder therein mentioned & to desire you woud take possession of it granting a Receipt for the same to those who have it in keeping in order that we may Account hereafter for the value of such part as may be adjudged to the Privateer that retook it.

By order & on behalf of the Secret Committee, I have the honor to be, Your Excellencys Most Obed Servant,

Robt Morris, Chair Man

RC (DLC). Written and signed by Robert Morris.

[1] An extract of the Clarke & Nightingale letter, containing an account of the cargo of the sloop *Nancy* remaining after it was retaken by the privateer *Schuyler,* is in *Am. Archives,* 5th ser. 1:943.

John Adams to Thomas McKean

Dear Sir,   Philadelphia Aug. 15. 1776

I recd your Favour of the 9th instant,[1] two days ago, and was exceedingly obliged to you for it, as We have had very little Intelligence from Perth Amboy.

Mr. Secretary Peters, upon my reading your Letter to him, immediately inclosed all the Barons Papers,[2] to General Washington, the Board of War not being inclined from any thing they could learn of the Baron to give him the Rank and Pay to which he aspires. It is impossible for me to know whether all the Barons Letters and Papers are sent, as my Friend Mr S. Adams, before I recd your Letter, was gone to Boston. Mr Peters has inclosed all that were in his Custody.

I am much obliged to you for the few Anecdotes, of Intelligence, in your Letter and should be very happy in a Continuance of your Correspondence. We have nothing new but the arrival of a Ship from Havre with a fine Cargo of Powder, Lead, Duck and dry Goods.

From N. York We are happy to hear that the Army is increased and that three Regiments have arrived there from Massachusetts, of Militia. The Enemies whole Force is now collected. Great and glorious will be the Fame of our Arms if we can give them their deserts. God grant it, and that you, my dear Sir, may have a large share of the Crop of Laurells. I am &c

LB (MHi).
[1] McKean's August 9 letter is in the Adams Papers, MHi.
[2] Undoubtedly the baron de Calbiac. See ibid; Baron de Calbiac to Richard Peters, August 13, in *Am. Archives*, 5th ser. 1:934; and Washington's letters to de Calbiac of July 23 and to Thomas McKean of August 6, 1776, in Washington, *Writings* (Fitzpatrick), 5:328–29, 375.

John Adams to Thomas Mifflin

Dear Sir,   Philadelphia August 15. 1776

I recd yours of the 5th instant by Tuesdays Post,[1] and laid it before the Board of War, who recommended Monsr. Weibert to Congress for the Rank and Pay of a Lieutenant Coll, and the office of an assistant Engineer, to which he was appointed without opposition and the President I suppose will transmit his Commission by the first opportunity.[2]

I am happy to learn that his Conduct, Skill, and Services have been so acceptable to you.

We are waiting with anxious Expectation, for Intelligence of an Attack. A Great Event it will be. The Thought of it, is enough to arrouse a Sleepier Soul than mine. I almost envy your situation. What Glory will accrue to our Arms, what Laurells will be reaped by our officers, if We should give the Enemy an overthrow. But if even the worst should happen, which is possible, Dulce et decorum est.

We have been making a fresh Emission of Generals. I wish to know how it Setts upon certain Stomacks. One Thing gives me much concern. The Massachusetts, which furnishes so many Men, has only two Generals, When other Colonies, which furnish very few Troops, have many more Generals. This I much fear will give disgust and discontent both to the People of the Colony and to the officers and Soldiers from that State. That Province never did and never will desire more than its just Proportion of the good Things of this Life, but I am vastly deceived in its Character if it can bear to have less. Will you drop me a Line now and then?

There is a Person who has been in some Place under you, whose Honesty, Diligence and Capacity for Business, intitle him to some thing much better than he has ever had. He has the Additional Claim of Suffering to a large amount, having been robbed in Boston of his all which was something handsome too. His Name is Nathaniel Cranch. If any Thing could be given him, better than what he has, it could not be more honestly bestowed.[3] I am

LB (MHi).
   [1] Thomas Mifflin's August 5 letter is in the Adams Papers, MHi.
   [2] See *JCC*, 5:656; and John Hancock to George Washington, July 1, 1776, note 1.
   [3] See John Adams to Richard Cranch, August 2, 1776.

Philip Livingston to Robert R. Livingston

Dr. Sir   Phila. 15th Augt. 1776.
   I recd. yours of the 11th Inst. this Day in Congress. The Post was gone before the house broake up, which put it out of My power to return you an Answer by him as you requestd. The N. York representation at Congress is reduced to three which renders the Constant Attendance of Every one here necessary. The Question, whether I would Accept of the Office of Govr. If the Convention Shd. Chuse me, is Important. I will give you my Ansr. with the uttmost Candour. I would much rather the Convention would not make Choice of me, for this only reason, that I am Concious of my unfitness for that Important office wch. will undoubtedly require a person of more Activity in business than I fear I should be. I trust you Know me too well to Suppose that this is a Sort of *Nolo Episcopari*. I have no Clerical Hypocricy abt. me, at Least I believe not. I Shall not however refuse to Accept, If the Convention Shd. think it for the Public Interest to Appoint me, Least my refusal Shd. be Construed by Some As A desertg the righteous Cause in which this Country is So deeply Engaged, at a Most dangerous Crisis, when the Enemy are, with a powerfull fleet & Army, Stareing us in the face, ready to devour us & Consequently the Most Strenuous Efforts & the utmost Exertions of Every Membr. of the Community are become Absolutely & Immediately Necessary. At so

Critical a moment it might have a bad Effect to have it Even supposed that any one who has had an Early part to Act in this Contest
Shd. not remain Ready to Step forward when Called upon by the
Public. I shall therefore think it my duty to Acquiece in Whatever
the Convention Shall determine, but Most heartily & Sincerely wish
that this Matter Might Appear to them in Such a Light, that they
might See it More for the Public Interest to appoint some Other
person.[1]

I shall to Morrow with the Other deligates write to the Convention which Ought to have been done Some time Ago, but our Apology is a True One, We have really been Exceeding busy.

Your Most Obedt servant,   Phil. Livingston

RC (N).
[1] George Clinton was elected the first governor of New York under the new
state constitution in July 1777.

Secret Committee Minutes of Proceedings

Augt. 15. 1776.

Come. met. Present Messrs. Morris, Lewis, Bartlett, Hewes &
Livingston. Ordered that Captains Read & Falconer be requested to
measure the bales of Canvass imported in the ship Morris from
Havre de Gras in order that the freight may be ascertaind, wch. by
contract is to be pd. in proportion to 10s sterlg. for a barrel of powder.[1] The Come. considerg. the favorable opportunity that now
presents for shipping off produce from this port, & other places to
the Southward, the Enemy's men of war being gone, Agreed that
the sum of 80,000 dlls be advancd Mr. Morris to be by Him laid out
in produce & exported on continental acct. Accordingly an order
was drawn on the Treasurer in his favor for that Sum.

The Committee have agreed with G. Meade & Co. Owners of the
Brigantine Two Friends, Capt. Vickorey, to charter sd. vessel, for a
voyage to Hispaniola & back, at the rate of 7s 6d Currency per bar.
of flour outward, 10s cury. per bar. powder inward. The vessel to be
insurd by Come. valued £1200.

Issued order on the Treasurer in favor of G. Meade & Co. for
619 73/90 dollars being the amount of their Acct. for sundry charges
& one month's freight of the Brigne Friendship. Order on the Treasurer in favor of Robt. Briges for 340 being for freight of G. powder
from St. Eustachia. Do. in favor Messrs Willing, Morris & Co. for
4442 66/90 in full of a ballance due to them as per Acct. dated 14
Inst. Order on the Treasurer for 4266 2/3 dlls in favor of Bayard,
Jackson & Co. being value of the Snow Dickenson charterd & insurd
by the Come., carried into Bristol on her passage to Nantes by the

Seamen; where She was seizd & condemnd.[2] Do. in favor of Isaac
Ruckless for 792 dlls being the amount of 1080 wt. powdr. at 5s per
lb & 6 stand Arms at 90s per Stand purchasd from him this date.

MS (MH).
    [1] For additional information on the ship *Morris*, which apparently made this
voyage pursuant to a February 5, 1776, contract of the Secret Committee with her
owners, Willing, Morris & Co., see Secret Committee Minutes of Proceedings,
February 5, 1776; and Clark, *Naval Documents*, 4:581, 6:387. See also Secret Committee Minutes of Proceedings, September 5, 1776.
    [2] For further information regarding this contract and the ill-fated voyage of
the *Dickenson*, see Secret Committee Minutes of Proceedings, December 26, 1775;
and Clark, *Naval Documents*, 4:1023–25, 1027–29.

James Smith to Eleanor Smith

My dear Elinor,   Philada. Augt 15th. [1776]
    I received your Letter two days since which gives me much plea-
usure to find your Thumb was got well. I blame myself for not
writing oftener but if you knew how much I am hurried between
Attending the Congress, Convention [1] & Assisting the Militia in
getting Necessaries here, for 'tis expected from the Militia of York
County & Cumberland that I should Assist them. If this excuse
wont pass I Cant frame a better. I am glad however I did not write
yesterday morning as I intended being then in a bad humour, having lost a New Cane at a Turtle Feast with Mr Hancock & the
Delegates last Week, & my new Hat & 37 Dollars in Paper money all
which I got safe yesterday. I got my Cane at the New Tavern, Genl
Worster had taken my hat in a Mistake & the Negro woman found
the money in my bed room amongst some old Papers. I have prevailed on my Land Lord to rent Littles New House, next Door to
the Tavern where I have an genteel bed room & 2 Closets with locks
& keys & a small Parlour below to do business in, so that I am quite
out of the hurry of the Tavern. I have got a touch of the Rheuma-
tism in my Shoulder by Sleeping with my Windows open. Mr
Adams says I very well deserve it, for being so Careless. I told him as
Mr Duchee prays for us every Day I thought there was no need to
take Care of ourselves. He told me God helps them who help themselves. Mr Hancock is a better Doctor, as he has something of the
Gout himself & has promised me some Pine buds to make Tea, however I have shut my Windows these 2 Nights & the Pain is almost
gone off, it never hurt my eating & Drinking.
    I dont like your Notion of Coming here. The Horse trots rough,
& the Mare is skittish, & all your Male friends are at Camp & all your
female ones in the Country. Besides as you Can't bring the Children
with you it woud distress them to be left behind. [Howev]er if you

Cant reason down your inclination I woud rather you woud go to your brother Billys & send Caezar up, & I would leave to go that far. But woud rather you wou'd send Caezar with the Horses to Philada. next week, & I will get leave to go home for some time—the week after.

Excuse all this stuff, & believe me to be your most affecte husband,

Jas Smith

[*P.S.*] Give Peggy & Betsy & Geo & John each a buss for me.

RC (InU). Addressed: "To Mrs. Elinor Smith, York Town, Pensylva. Favoured by Mr Gettys."

[1] Smith had also been elected a delegate for York County to the Pennsylvania Convention which sat in Philadelphia from July 15 to September 28, 1776. Because the convention also met in the State House, it was easy for Smith to alternate his time between Congress and the convention, which on the evidence of this letter he appears to have done. Although the earliest mention of Smith in the journals of Congress is his appointment to a committee on September 30 and Burnett conjectured that it "was probably his first day of attendance," this communication to his wife confirms his much earlier appearance. See *JCC*, 5:835; and Burnett, *Letters*, 2:1xv.

William Williams to Joseph Trumbull

Dear Sir   Philadelpa Aug 15 1776

Yours of the 12th I have recd. My avocations this Morng. are so many, I can write but very little if I had any thing worth writing about. I cant get my Bretheren to join in a Motion for Cap Dyer, tho they profess a hearty willingness to serve him.[1] They say Congress will expect a Recommend[atio]n from the Genl. & tis not safe to venture without. I dont know but it is necessary & I wish one cod be obtained, & I am certain it can be carried. If from some others it may serve. If Col Dyer is there He will certainly get it if possible & I shod think he may. I wrote him by the same Post I wrote you, but know nothing of his being at N York, perhaps it went on. If there yet give him my Complimts (& Mr Law) & desire him to write let me know his Errant & how matters go on in our Congress &c &c.[2]

I inclose Bro Jona's Letter, & one to Him, nothing worth reading, but have nothing agst your reading it, please to Seal & forward.[3] We have nothing new or material, all our Thoughts are exercised about the important impending Conflict at N. York. I want to hear every Hour. To God omniponent & all gracious I commit the Cause & all my Friends & Countrymen. I believe We need not greatly fear the Issue, our Army is strong & will not shrink I trust. Our Cause is just & will be defended, tho it pains me at the Start to think that many must probably fall.

I am yr most Affect Friend & Bror,   Wm Williams

In the utmost Haste.

RC (CtHi).
[1] See Williams to Joseph Trumbull, August 20, 1776.

[2] Williams' letter to Eliphalet Dyer has not been found. Dyer and Richard Law, members of the Connecticut Council of Safety, had been sent to New York to confer with Washington on defense matters. See Jonathan Trumbull to Washington, August 5, 1776, *Am. Archives*, 5th ser. 1:776.

[3] Williams' letter to Jonathan Trumbull, Jr., has not been found.

INDEX

In this index descriptive subentries are arranged chronologically and in ascending order of the initial page reference. They may be preceded, however, by the subentry "identified" and by document subentries arranged alphabetically—diary entries, letters, notes, resolutions, and speeches. An ornament (☆) separates the subentry "'identified" and document subentries from descriptive subentries. Inclusive page references are supplied for descriptive subentries; for a document, only the page on which it begins is given. Eighteenth-century printed works are indexed both by author and by short title. Other printed works are indexed when they have been cited to document a substantive point discussed in the notes, but not when cited merely as the location of a document mentioned. Delegates who attended Congress during the period covered by this volume appear in **boldface type.**

Accommodation; *see* Reconciliation

Accounts: miscellaneous, 77; secret committee, 78–79, 207–8, 271, 412, 437, 485, 642, 685–86; delegate, 91, 207, 322–23, 373, 399, 580; colony, 133, 676–77; military, 215, 534, 616, 637, 670; marine committee, 524; Massachusetts prize agent, 542; brig *Dispatch*, 580–81

Adams, Mr., 221

Adams, Abigail Smith (Mrs. John): letters to, 17, 60, 79, 121, 226, 323, 373, 400, 422, 434, 456, 465, 491, 521, 549, 556, 610, 624, 646, 659, 660, 668, 678; ☆ praised, 79; inoculated for smallpox, 375, 491–93, 521, 549–50; mentioned, 97, 116, 220

Adams, Charles, 678

Adams, Elizabeth Wells (Mrs. Samuel), 344

Adams, John: letters from, 3, 14, 17, 31, 40, 60, 72, 79, 95, 101, 112, 115, 121, 122, 134, 135, 175, 177, 179, 195, 196, 198, 209, 219, 226, 228, 261, 278, 279, 287, 290, 291, 294, 296, 297, 298, 303, 305, 323, 339, 345, 347, 368, 373, 375, 389, 390, 400, 402, 404, 414, 422, 423, 424, 425, 434, 456, 457, 465, 477, 481, 491, 492, 504, 521, 532, 540, 546, 549, 550, 556, 569, 604, 610, 611, 613, 615, 620, 624, 646, 653, 659, 660, 668, 669, 671, 678, 680, 682, 683; letters to, 45, 224, 375, 415, 506, 569; notes, 538, 545, 568, 592, 603; ☆ elected to Congress, xvii; attends Congress, xvii; on assuming government, 3–4, 17–18, 79–80, 135–36; requests assignment of Gens. Gates and Mifflin to Boston, 14–15, 121, 179; on independence, 17–18, 40–42, 278, 290–91, 298–99, 375–76, 423; on peace commissioners, 32; on Pennsylvania politics, 40–41, 423; confers with Gens. Washington, Gates, and Mifflin, 61; committee on letters concerning Canada, 66–67; on voting qualifications, 73–75, 96; praises wife's abilities, 79; on framing governments, 96–97, 134–35, 178, 197, 199; on serving as delegate, 97, 226, 551; on fortifying Boston Harbor, 101, 198; committee on foreign mercenaries, 111; committee on fortifying ports, 113; on establishing military academies, 115; on military affairs, 121, 287–92, 424–25, 611–14, 620–21, 683–84; on elections, 122; praises Patrick Henry, 122; debates declaring independence, 161–63, 346; committee to draft declaration of inde-

689

Dean, Benjamin, 460

Deane, Silas: letters to, 146, 154, 405, 635, 655; ☆ recommends outfitting privateers in Bermuda, 149; ordered to distribute Declaration of Independence in Europe, 405; remittances to delayed, 655–56; asked to advise Thomas Morris, 656; commercial transactions, 657–58; arrival in France, 665; mentioned, 127, 128, 129, 356, 357, 426, 427, 429, 573, 575

Deards, William, 523, 553

DeBerdt, Dennis, Jr.: identified, 489; mentioned, 513

Declaration of Independence: draft, 360; ☆ committee to draft appointed by Congress, 163, 192, 194, 260, 286, 297; drafted by Jefferson, 164; reported to Congress, 164, 345; Jefferson requests Franklin's comments on draft, 286; committee draft praised by Bartlett, 351; considered by Congress, 359–65, 378, 388, 391–92; revised by Congress, 359–64, 412; approved by Congress, 359–60, 381–82, 386, 388, 390–92, 399, 417, 420–21, 458; congressional attendance on July Fourth discussed, 364–65; signing discussed, 364–65; order of events in Congress on July Fourth discussed, 381–82; printed, 388, 390; distributed, 389–90, 391–94, 396–97, 405–7, 410, 412, 417, 420; considered foundation for government, 392–93, 396, 433; proclaimed in Philadelphia, 406, 413–14, 430; signed, 414, 509, 580; opposed by Robert Morris, 511; consequences of, 527–28, 582, 635; unanimously approved by colonies, 666; mentioned, xxv, 14, 165, 261, 281, 347, 374, 384, 402, 411, 413, 414, 432, 453, 459, 466, 473, 490, 498, 506, 520, 552, 555, 565, 604, 622, 624; *see also* Independence

Defense, coastal: Massachusetts, 3–4, 60, 101, 112–13, 169, 221, 295, 297, 345; Virginia, 37, 40, 43–44; committee on fortifying ports, 113, 149; militia engaged for, 124–25, 136–37; plan for militia reinforcement criticized by Oliver Wolcott, 143–44; removal of stock and grain, 156, 487; suggestions by John Adams, 198–99; Delaware, 265, 331; British transports captured, 307, 322, 332–33, 342, 351, 366, 368–69, 373, 389; recognition signals reportedly discovered, 342; New Hampshire, 350; Connecticut, 367–68; North Carolina, 409–10; submarines, 514–15, 638; Maryland, 583; *see also* New Jersey; New York City

De Haas, John, 77, 82, 83, 202

De Hart, John: elected to Congress, xviii; attends Congress, xviii

De Hart, Samuel, 451

De Haven, Mr., 418, 419

Delap, John H.: letters to, 426, 575; mentioned, 127, 134, 154, 428, 572, 573, 656, 658

Delap, Samuel: letters to, 426, 575; mentioned, 127, 134, 154, 428, 572, 573, 656, 658

Delaware: possible secession discussed, 160, 163; militia called, 173, 383; loyalists assemble in Sussex County, 204–6, 208; aided by Pennsylvania militia, 204–6; coastal defense, 265, 331; Continental troops, 265, 619–20, 627, 633, 641; militia mobilizing, 383, 397, 430, 434, 451, 456; Kent County loyalists' involvement in Sussex County, 432–33, 618–19; internal affairs discussed by Caesar Rodney, 432–33, 617–19, 681–82; elections for convention, 617–19, 681–82; militia officers appointed, 618; map listed, 669

Delaware (Continental frigate), launched, 449, 455–56, 477

Delaware Assembly: letters to, 136, 383; ☆ instructs delegates on independence, 210, 264

Delaware delegates: instructed on independence, 210, 264; divide on declaring independence in committee of whole, 359, 388; vote for independence in Congress, 359, 388

Delaware Indians, believed peaceful, 673–74

Delaware River, fortifications, 325, 331

Delegates: residences in Philadelphia, 14; alignment on preamble to resolution on assuming government, 20–21; instructions on independence, 40–41, 69–70, 93–94, 140, 158, 160–62, 164, 166, 168, 171, 182, 192–95, 210, 213, 264, 273, 275–76, 304, 316, 347, 372, 417, 419–21; support assumption of government in Pennsylvania, 92; remuneration, 207, 214, 322–23, 373, 399, 529; selection under draft articles

Advisory Committee

Library of Congress American Revolution Bicentennial Program

John R. Alden
James B. Duke Professor of History Emeritus, Duke University

Julian P. Boyd
Editor of The Papers of Thomas Jefferson, *Princeton University*

Lyman H. Butterfield
Editor in Chief Emeritus of The Adams Papers, *Massachusetts Historical Society*

Jack P. Greene
Andrew W. Mellon Professor in the Humanities, The Johns Hopkins University

Merrill Jensen
Editor of The Documentary History of the Ratification of the Constitution, *University of Wisconsin*

Cecelia M. Kenyon
Charles N. Clark Professor of Government, Smith College

Aubrey C. Land
University Research Professor, University of Georgia

Edmund S. Morgan
Sterling Professor of History, Yale University

Richard B. Morris
Gouverneur Morris Professor of History Emeritus, Columbia University

George C. Rogers, Jr.
Yates Snowden Professor of American History, University of South Carolina

DATE DUE

GAYLORD | | | PRINTED IN U.S.A.